Public Access to Government Information

SECOND EDITION

Information Management, Policy, and Services

Charles R. McClure and Peter Hernon

Editors

Curriculum Initiative: An Agenda and Strategy for Library Media Programs
Michael B. Eisenberg and Robert E. Berkowitz

Microcomputer Software for Performing Statistical Analysis: A Handbook for
Supporting Library Decision Making
Peter Hernon and John V. Richardson (Editors)

Public Access to Government Information, Second Edition
Peter Hernon and Charles R. McClure

Resource Companion to Curriculum Initiative: An Agenda and Strategy for
Library Media Programs
Michael B. Eisenberg and Robert E. Berkowitz

In preparation

Power, Politics, and Personality: The State Library Agency as a Policy Actor
June Engle

Managing Information for Competitive Positioning in Economic
Development
Keith Harman

U.S. Government Information Policies: Frameworks for Assessing Issues
and Options
Charles R. McClure, Peter Hernon and Harold C. Relyea

Microcomputer Graphics as a Library Resource
Bradford S. Miller

Investigation of Human Responses to Knowledge Representations
Mark E. Rorvig

Perspectives on U.S. Government Scientific and Techological Information
Charles R. McClure and Peter Hernon

Public Access to Government Information:
Issues, Trends, and Strategies

SECOND EDITION

PETER HERNON
Simmons College

CHARLES R. McCLURE
Syracuse University

ABLEX PUBLISHING CORPORATION
NORWOOD, NEW JERSEY 07648

Printed in the United States of America.

Library of Congress Cataloging-in-Publication Data

Hernon, Peter.
  Public access to government information.

  (Information management policy and services)
  Bibliography: p.
  Includes index.
    1. Libraries—Special collections—Government
  publications. 2. Libraries, Depository—United States.
  3. Freedom of information—United States.
  4. Government information—United States. 5. United
  States—Government publications—Bibliography
  —Methodology. I. McClure, Charles R. II. Title.
  III. Series: Information management policy and
  services series.
  Z688.G6H469 1988   026'.011'530973   88-19249
  ISBN 0-89391-522-X
  ISBN 0-89391-523-8 (pbk.)

Ablex Publishing Corporation
355 Chestnut Street
Norwood, New Jersey 07648

Contents

LIST OF TABLES xvi

LIST OF FIGURES xvii

ACKNOWLEDGMENTS xvix

PREFACE xx

1. PUBLIC ACCESS TO GOVERNMENT
    PUBLICATIONS/INFORMATION HELD IN
    DEPOSITORY COLLECTIONS   1

    Definition of Government Publications, Documents, and
        Information   3

        Government Publications and Documents   3

        Government Information   5

    "Access" to Depository Collections   8

    Assumptions Related to Public Access   11

    Goals and Objectives   12

    Bibliographic Control   13

    Bibliographic Access   15

    Collection Development   16

    Reference Services   17

    Technology   19

    Re-Evaluating Assumptions   20

2. **FEDERAL INFORMATION POLICIES** **25**

The Landscape of Federal Information Policies **28**

A Typology for Government Information That
Incorporates Significant Policy Issues **30**

Federal Organization for Information Policies **32**

Relationship between the Federal Government and
Other Stakeholders in the Information Sector **34**

Information Technology **35**

The Economics of Government Information **37**

Public Access and Availability to Government
Information **38**

Freedom of Information and Privacy **40**

Secrecy and Protection of Federal Information **41**

Examples of Two Key Policy Areas **43**

Distribution/Dissemination of Federal Information in
Electronic Form **43**

Electronic Information Technology **44**

What's at Stake **44**

Agency Responsibilities **47**

Managing Federal Scientific & Technical Information .. **48**

The Existing Context **48**

Improving the STI Policy System **49**

The Need for Action **52**

3. **IMPACT OF FEDERAL INFORMATION POLICIES ON
PUBLIC ACCESS TO GOVERMENT
INFORMATION** **54**

Public Access **55**

Overview **55**

GPO Sales Program **59**

Reagan Administration's Policy on Government
Publications **63**

Information Resources Management 70

Freedom of Information Act 71

Revision of Title 44, *United States Code*, Covering the
GPO 72

Toward a National Information Policy 74

4. **GOVERNMENT PUBLICATIONS AS A SIGNIFICANT
INFORMATION RESOURCE** 78

Producers and Distributors of Government
Publications/Information 79

Functions of Government Publications 82

Types of Government Publications 83

Administrative Reports 84

Committee and Commission Reports 84

Research Reports 85

Statistics 86

General Information Pamphlets and Fact Sheets 86

Periodicals 86

Press Releases and Other Ephemera 87

Directories 87

Handbooks, Manuals, and Digests 87

Bibliographies, Lists, Guides, and Catalogs 88

Decisions and Opinions 88

Rules, Regulations, Directives, and Circulars 88

Maps, Charts, and Photographs 89

Audiovisual Resources 89

Bills and Resolutions 90

Hearings 90

Journals and Proceedings 91

Laws and Statutes 91

Treaty Sources   91

Technical Report Literature   92

Patents   92

Technical Documentation   93

Formats of Government Information   93

The Elusive Nature of Government Publications As An
    Information Resource   97

5. BIBLIOGRAPHIC CONTROL OF U.S. GOVERNMENT
    PUBLICATIONS   99

Identification of Information   101

Description and Organization of Information Content   103

    Overview   103

    Indexing   104

    Sudoc Classification Scheme   109

Physical Accessibility   110

Changing Focus   112

6. DEVELOPING COLLECTIONS OF U.S.
    GOVERNMENT PUBLICATIONS   114

Collection Development   115

    The Concept   115

    Selection   117

    Retention Decision   120

    Use   121

    Self-Assessment of Documents Collections   123

Integrated Collection Development   124

Myths Hindering Integrated Collection Development . . .   129

Moving toward Integration   134

7. EXPLOITING TECHNOLOGY FOR GOVERNMENT
    INFORMATION COLLECTIONS 137

    Existing Technological Access to Documents Collections   139

        OCLC 140

        Online Bibliographic Database Searching 142

        Automated Systems 143

    Exploiting Other Technologies 145

        Microcomputers 145

        Video Technology 146

        Numeric Databases 147

        Microformatted Government Publications Online 149

        Facsimile 150

    Summary 150

    Strategies for Exploiting Technology 151

        Obtain Training 152

        Minimize Costs 152

        Set Priorities and Reduce Workload 154

        Increased Priority for Government Information
            Resources 155

        Obtain Technology Utilization Information 158

        Overcoming Resistance to Technological Innovation ... 158

    Exploiting the Technological Future 159

    Appendix. Selected Writings on Technological
        Applications for Depository Collections and Services
        162

8. IMPROVED REFERENCE AND REFERRAL SERVICES
    THROUGH INCREASED MARKETING AND
    AWARENESS OF GOVERNMENT INFORMATION
    RESOURCES 165

    Information Gathering Patterns 166

    Unobtrusive Testing 168

Reference Service 168

Referral Services 170

"Outreach" and Marketing Activities for Documents 172

Marketing of Depository Collections and Services 175

Role of the Government Printing Office 179

Improving Reference and Referral Services 181

9. **MICROFORMS AND ACCESS TO GOVERNMENT PUBLICATIONS** 186

Historical Overview 187

Microform Bibliographic Control 194

Microforms Collection Development ...., . 196

Overview 196

Reasons for Collecting Microforms 197

Potential Areas for Collecting Microforms 198

Use Patterns 199

Indexing 201

Collection Space and Facilities 202

Increasing Microform Competencies 203

Managing Microfiche Distribution and Library Collections
.... 204

10. **TECHNICAL REPORT LITERATURE (By Gary R. Purcell)** 207

Public Access to Technical Report Literature 207

The Nature and History of Technical Report Literature 210

Attributes of Report Literature 211

Publication, Distribution, and Bibliographic Control of Technical Report Literature 216

Organizing and Accessing the Technical Report Collection
.... 223

Key Issues—Technical Reports 224

11. **ADMINISTRATIVE CONSIDERATIONS FOR
INCREASED ACCESS TO GOVERNMENT
PUBLICATIONS/INFORMATION** 229

The Administrative Environment 231

Factors Affecting the Current Status of
Documents 231

Administrative Assumptions 234

Decision Making 235

Budgeting and Resource Allocation 237

Personnel Development 244

Decision Support Systems 246

Establishing a Research Basis for Documents
Administration 251

12. **INTEGRATING GOVERNMENT INFORMATION
RESOURCES INTO LIBRARY SERVICES** 255

The Concept of Integration 256

Analyzing Documents Integration 258

Increasing Documents Integration 261

Administrative Organization 261

Physical Location 264

Planning and Evaluation of Services 266

Professional Development and Staff Training 267

Involvement in Decision Making 268

Marketing 269

Coordinating Services and Activities 271

Increased Integration 274

13. **PHYSICAL FACILITIES AND SPACE MANAGEMENT**   276

   Assessment of Current Situation 278

   Identification of Equipment and Support
      Facilities 279

   Physical Arrangement 281

   Traffic and Use Patterns 283

   Additional Issues Affecting Adequate Physical
      Facilities 286

   Space Planning 286

   Renovation and Rearrangement 287

   Automation Considerations 287

   Physical Facilities for Microcomputers 288

   Physical Facilities for Microformatted
      Government Publications 289

   Location 289

   Space Requirements 290

   Physical Arrangement 292

   Equipment and Storage 294

   Additional Considerations 297

   Designs for the Future 302

14. **PROCESSING DEPOSITORY PUBLICATIONS** 305

   Background 306

   Online Bibliographic Services 310

   Additional Automated Processing Strategies 313

   Issues and Prospects 315

   To Catalog or Not to Catalog 315

   GPO Administrative Decisions and Activities 316

   Training and Retraining Documents Librarians 318

   Microforms 318

Vendor Applications 319

Shared Processing and Retrospective Conversion 320

Prospects 321

15. **PLANNING AND EVALUATION OF GOVERNMENT INFORMATION SERVICES** 323

Systems Concepts for Planning and Evaluation 325

Planning and Evaluation 328

Performance Measures 332

State Plans 339

GPO Inspection Program 341

Increasing Planning Effectiveness 343

16. **COOPERATION AND RESOURCE SHARING** 348

Overview 349

Present Day Examples of Resource Sharing for Government Publications 356

Networking, Cooperation, and Technology 357

Electronic Information Requires A New Framework 359

Role of Research 362

17. **RESTRUCTURING THE GPO'S DEPOSITORY LIBRARY PROGRAM** 365

GPO's Depository Program As Presently Constituted 366

Overview 366

Critical Assumptions 369

Importance of Performance Measures 371

Alternative Structures for A Depository Network 373

Specific Structures Suggested in the Literature 376

Types of Alternative Structures 379

Conceptual Basis for Depository Library Network 382

Caveats That Require Attention 382

Proposed Structure 383

Moving toward a Reassessment 388

18. **EXPLOITING STATE AND LOCAL INFORMATION RESOURCES** 391

Selected Major Writings 392

Types of Publications 396

Bibliographic Control 398

Collection Development 400

Technology 403

User/Use Patterns 405

Future Directions 408

19. **ACCESS TO INFORMATION FROM INTERNATIONAL GOVERNMENTAL ORGANIZATIONS (By Peter I. Hajnal)** 411

Documents and Publications of IGOs 412

Bibliographic Access 423

Collection Development 426

Policy Statements 426

Distribution Policies and Practices of IGOs 431

Acquisition Methods 434

Depository Libraries 435

Selection Tools 437

Future Challenges 439

Appendix 1. Checklist of Examples Cited in the Chapter   442

Appendix 2. Selected List of IGO Sales Catalogs 445

20. **EDUCATION OF THE GOVERNMENT INFORMATION PROFESSIONAL** 449

Formal Options 453

Course Work 453

Continuing Education 459

Internships 462

Informal Options 462

Prospects for Employment and Career Advancement 464

Encouraging Educational Change 466

21. **MAINSTREAMING GOVERNMENT
PUBLICATIONS/INFORMATION** 469

Encouraging the Change Process 471

Internal Change in the Organization 472

Affecting External Change 474

Skills for Change Agents 475

Issues for National Change 476

Importance of Documents 476

Planning and Evaluation 478

Developing Effective Collections 479

Minimize Attention Given to Bibliographic
Access 480

Exploiting Technology 480

Continuing Education 481

Individual Commitment and Dedication 481

Need for Leadership 482

Future Prospects for Change 483

BIBLIOGRAPHY 489

AUTHOR INDEX 509

SUBJECT INDEX 514

List of Tables

4–1 Number of Publications Distributed to Depository
     Libraries (per Fiscal Year) **95**

List of Figures

1–1   Summary of Questionable Assumptions Related to Public
    Access of U.S. Government Publications **21**

2–1   Overview of National Information Policy Issues Related to
    the Government's Provision of Federal Information ..   **29**

2–2   Summary of Significant Policy Issues **31**

2–3   Federal Organization for Information Policies **33**

2–4   Summary Recommendations for Federal STI Policy
    Mechanisms **51**

3–1   Selected OMB Pronouncements Affecting Access to
    Government Information **69**

4–1   Producers and Distributors of Government Publications/
    Information **81**

4–2   Branch of the Federal Government Producing Each Type
    of Government Publication **85**

4–3   Formats in Which Types of Government Information Are
    Distributed **94**

5–1   Depiction of Bibliographic Control for Government
    Information Sources **100**

6–1   An Example of a Preliminary Matching of Federal
    Agencies and Subject Areas **119**

6–2   Self Assessment Techniques **125**

6–3   Overview of Integrated Collection Development **127**

6–4   Worksheet for the Establishment of Government
    Publications Collection Development Objectives **128**

6–5	The Concept of Integration	130
7–1	Summary of Types of Software and Library Applications	147
7–2	Equipment/Training Requirements for Electronic Information Service Levels	153
7–3	Cost Considerations for Government Information Formats	156
8–1	Unobtrusive Studies of Documents Reference Service	169
8–2	Representative Products of the GPO Marketing Program	180
8–3	Potential Weaknesses to Effective Marketing of U.S. Government Publications	181
9–1	Conceptual Model for Interpreting the Reasons for Acquiring Microformatted Government Publications	198
9–2	Selected Agencies, Document Types, and Titles Available in Microformat, and Appropriate Finding Aids	201
10–1	Types and Formats of Technical Reports	216
10–2	Federal Technical Report Environment	219
10–3	Selected Policy Issues Concerned with Report Literature	227
11–1	Analyzing the Departmental Administrative Environment	233
11–2	The Decision Making Process	236
11–3	Analyzing Resource Allocations for Government Publications	241
11–4	Combined Program-Line Item Budget	243
11–5	Design Considerations for the Development of a System for Library Management Information	248
11–6	Classification Scheme for Recording and Reporting Information about Libraries	248
12–1	Potential Constraints Affecting Integration of Government Documents	259
12–2	Integration of Government Documents and Allocation of Resources	262
12–3	Marketing Contingencies	270
13–1	Inventory of Major Equipment and Support Facilities	280
13–2	Bubble Diagram of Government Publications Area	284
13–3	Microforms Physical Arrangement	293
13–4	Microviewing Area	294
13–5	Microforms Storage Area	296
13–6	Organization of a Microfiche File Drawer	297
13–7	Criteria for the Selection of Microfilm/fiche Readers and Printers	298
15–1	General Systems Model	327
15–2	The Planning Process for Government Publications Services	329
15–3	Outline of a Planning Document	330

15–4   Depository Evaluation Criteria from Open System
       Characteristics **334**
15–5   Criteria for Setting Measures **337**
15–6   Relating Effectiveness to Efficiency **338**
15–7   Analysis of a Section from "Inspection Visit Form" **344**
16–1   Depiction of Resource Sharing for Depository Libraries . .   **351**
16–2   Summary of Resource Sharing Issues **353**
16–3   Depository Cooperation **355**
17–1   Critical Assumptions Underlying the Depository System . .   **371**
17–2   Implications of Centralization and the Concept of
       Government Information Resources on Selected
       Criteria **372**
17–3   Conceptual Model for the Depository Library Network . . .   **384**
18–1   User Groups and the Types of State Documents Consulted
       . . . .   **407**
19–1   The United Nations System of Organizations **414**
19–2   United Nations Publications: Sales Categories **420**
20–1   Outline of a Course "United States Government
       Information Policies, Resources, and Services" **457**
20–2   Contingencies for Government Documents Continuing
       Education **461**
21–1   Analyzing the Change Situation **477**
21–2   Characteristics of an Effective Change Agent **478**

Preface

Practice dominates the documents field; more attention is devoted to analyzing source material and reviewing various procedures for the organization and servicing of collections than to issues, trends, research, modeling, and conceptualizations. The field of documents librarianship must be viewed as one comprised of theory and research as well as practice. Jesse H. Shera's view of librarianship has application to the documents field. He notes:

> that librarians are . . . developing a highly efficient technology, and that the proliferation of knowledge necessitates a revolution in that technology are scarcely debatable. But a technology is a means, not an end. Lacking theory to give it direction and purpose, it drifts aimlessly. If it reaches its goal it does so only by fortuitous circumstance (Rawski, 1973, p. 41).

Documents librarians have refined various methods of practice, but have neither examined underlying assumptions nor placed their activities in a broader context. Instead, they emphasize the unique or special aspects of government documents services and collections rather than those elements that have commonalty with other library collections and services. The charge of Pierce Butler that librarians "know very well how to do things" but "have only vague notions of why they do them" is as true today as when he wrote it over fifty years ago. An additional observation he made is also still relevant:

> Unlike his colleagues in other fields of social activity the librarian is strangely uninterested in the theoretical aspects of his profession. . . . The librarian apparently stands alone in the simplicity of his pragmatism; a rational-

ization of each immediate technical process by itself seems to satisfy his intellectual interest. Indeed any endeavor to generalize these rationalizations into a professional philosophy appears to him, not merely futile, but positively dangerous. He is vividly aware of the precious subjective values which are involved in every contact of an individual with the cultural achievements of humanity. He therefore appears to dread the coming of science because he fears its heartless objectivity (Butler, 1933, pp. xi-xii).

The aim of librarianship is to being to the point of maximum effectiveness the social utility of information resources. If librarians are to become effective mediators between society and its information resources, they must be more concerned with functions than with practical duties. They must learn to adjust to new situations and innovations so that they can fit into an ever-changing profession. Librarians must understand, therefore, the nature and role of knowledge in society, and be concerned with not only that which is known but also the state of knowing.

By focusing on issues of momentary importance, librarians overextend themselves, lose their perspective, and do not engage in necessary planning and analysis. There must be (Kaser, 1978, p. 195):

> . . . a new awareness of the differences between transient and perpetual issues. Our response to the former should differ from our response to the latter. Too often the profession dissipates its energies and resources attempting to react to every meaningless blip that turns up on its radar screen.

Some documents librarians lament that they lack the time to develop specialized document delivery systems, conduct community analyses, and implement various means of evaluation. They plead that understaffing, as well as the amount of staff time spent in processing new arrivals and in furthering bibliographic control, prevent them from offering various services and integrating government information resources with other library holdings.
Yet evaluation counteracts personal bias, and provides administrators with data upon which to access program and service effectiveness and to improve existing programs and services. A constant theme of this book is the importance of planning, evaluation, and research.

Philosophy and theory are interrelated concepts that enable the formulation of a general body of principles and truths. It may be no wonder that information science is often regarded as the theoretical side of librarianship, and appeals to many researchers. Fry (1982) suggests that documents librarianship has the potential for contributing a unique body of theory. However, theory derives from librarianship and not from a type of information resource. The purpose of research is to create a body of knowledge and to work toward the development of theoretical bases.

In the case of collection development, for example, the theoretical base derives from viewing government information resources within the structures of a subject literature (Baughman, 1977), thereby collection development can be seen as designing and implementing a planning model, and refining it through evaluation. The process, therefore, takes into account how people gather and use information, the role of libraries in mediating the information needs of their clientele, and selection from the universe of government information resources those most needed by specific client groups. Collection development for government information resources does not differ from developing collections of other genre; it is part of an organizational planning process by which library staff members, adhering to written guidelines, determine how many publications to acquire and in how many copies, how long to retain them, and how to manage those that are retained (Buckland, 1975, p. 3).

Instead of focusing on source material produced and distributed by the Federal, and other levels of, government, this book is issue-oriented. By showing that issues relating to topics such as access to government information resources, collection development, and administration are not unique to documents librarianship, this book places selected topics related to documents librarianship in a wider context of the published literature and research.

Thus, the book has been written to meet the following objectives, to:

- Identify and discuss critically important issues related to increasing access to government information resources
- Offer solutions and recommendations by which government information resources and services can be made more effective
- Encourage more assessments that examine issues across levels of government, looking for common themes
- Emphasize the importance and need for a research base related to government information resources and services
- Encourage a critical assessment of current practices and traditional assumptions related to government information resources
- Provide an overview and syntheses of the authors' ideas, research, and opinions from previous, but disparate, writings.

But, perhaps most importantly, the book is intended to assist librarians and other information professionals in improving access to government information resources and in reassessing traditional assumptions related to government publications.

An important questions is: "How does the second edition differ from the first?" Each chapter was updated and reorganized to reflect the published literature as of spring 1988. Greater attention has been given to the role of technology and the information policy context that affects public access to government information resources. In this regard, *Public Access to Government Information* serves as a companion to *Federal Information Policies in the 1980's* (Hernon and McClure, 1987a). The addition of Chapter 2, discussing Federal information policies, is evidence of the increased attention given to policy perspectives in the second edition.

The book addresses issues, trends, and strategies relating to public access to government information resources. Public access is viewed within the context of bibliographic control, collection development and resource sharing, the role of information handling technologies, reference and referral services, the administration of documents collections and services, the integration of government information resources with other library holdings, the planning process, and the amount and type of education and training that documents staff members have. The depository library program of the U.S. Government Printing Office (GPO) is a primary focus; however, the issues identified may apply to other depository library programs as well. This discussion of issues should aid in the re-conceptualization of the depository library program and suggest strategies by which the program can be made more effective.

The coverage of the book includes printing and publishing programs of the United States government, as well as of state and local governments and international organizations. In order to provide a broad representation of issues and trends, Gary R. Purcell examined scientific and technical report literature. Peter I. Hajnal has contributed a general overview and analysis of international organizations. The chapters on information resources of state and local governments, and of international organizations, clearly demonstrate that common problems and issues exist regardless of level of government.

It is our hope that *Public Access to Government Information* will appeal to various groups (practicing librarians, documents educators and library school students, government officials, especially those administering depository library programs, and anyone interested in government publishing and printing programs and the role of the library community). The book provides an overview of a wide range of topics, discusses key issues, encourages planning and change, and identifies ways that might enhance public access and increase the effectiveness of depository library programs.

Many documents librarians are being asked to provide evidence of accountability (cost-benefit and cost-effectiveness) for their collections and services; however, they may not be aware of how to proceed. The book addresses such matters in both theoretical and practical terms. In this regard, it should aid not only those unfamiliar with government documents collections and services, but also seasoned documents specialists needing to keep abreast of major issues, trends, and writings, while improving the quality of services provided.

Peter Hernon and Charles R. McClure
March, 1988

Acknowledgments

We wish to express our thanks and sincere gratitude to the students in our various documents, research methods, evaluation, and information policy classes, over the years, who have provided feedback to our ideas, positive criticism, and analysis of issues related to government information policies, resources, and services. Without this constant intellectual challenge and stimulation, our analysis and conceptualization of government information policies and issues would have been weaker.

We wish to thank Cythnia Bower of the University of Arizona and Jan Swanbeck of Texas A & M University for their critical examination of the chapters related to technology and bibliographic control. Mr. Walter J. Johnson, the publisher and president of Ablex Publishing Corporation, has given both editions of this monograph his full support. Without his encouragement, this edition might not have been done.

And once again, we wish to acknowledge the support and sacrifices of our families (Elinor, Alison, and Linsay Hernon; and Vicky and Wendy McClure). Their support and tolerance frequently provided the impetus for us to complete projects that might not have otherwise been done. These studies serve as the backbone to this monograph.

1

Public Access to Government Publications/ Information Held in Depository Collections

The depository program administered by the Government Printing Office (GPO) represents a cooperative effort between the Federal government and libraries volunteering to serve as depositories. In accepting the publications, these libraries (excluding those of the highest appellate court) make them available to their immediate constituencies and the general public for free use on the premises. Some libraries circulate and loan their depository publications as well. Depository librarians often regard public access and free use as the primary purposes for both the creation and the continuance of the depository program, despite a lack of consensus concerning what these key terms mean and how they can be accomplished within the depository library setting.

The basic purpose of the depository program is "to provide reference collections of official publications in the 435 congressional districts of the 50 states and in the outlying territories of the United States, where they will be accessible free of charge to the public" (44 *USC* 1911). The *Guidelines for the Depository Library System* (1977, p. 1), on the other hand, identifies the purpose as "to make U.S. Government publications easily accessible to the general public and to insure their continued availability in the future." According to *Government Depository Libraries* (1983), the depository library program is based upon certain "principles" predicated on the right of the public to know about government programs, policies, procedures, and publishing activities. Senate report 87–1587, on H.R. 8141 or the Depository Library Act of 1962, states that the depository program makes "publications . . . readily accessible to the American public" (Schwarzkopf, 1982, p. 31).

Despite these well intentioned phrases, considerable differences of opinion exist concerning the operational definitions of "accessible," "easily accessible," "readily accessible," and "availability." Differences among the terms—accessibility, availability, and public access—are either confused or ignored. In this book, accessibility means the degree to which:

- A government publication is accurately identified bibliographically in appropriate reference works
- Information contained in government publications is made known
- The public seeks government information and encounters problems in gaining access to depository collections and in retrieving needed information from these collections.

Public access therefore exists when all members of the general public, regardless of race, religion, age, sex, or personal beliefs, can obtain government publications/information.

Equality of *opportunity* does not apply; clearly, factors such as one's ability to pay and knowing the "right" people may affect public access. Under the Reagan administration, and as well as with movement of Federal agencies toward the adoption of electronic information management and retrieval systems, issues related to the economics of information become important concerns. The high cost of extracting specialized information to meet single requests, and the necessity of managing information resources in the most cost-effective manner (controlling costs under the guise of reducing the burden on taxpayers), present significant access barriers.

Availability to government publications contained in depository collections implies something quite different from accessibility in terms of information. Availability of Federal information suggests physically obtaining the information in an understandable format within a specified period of time. Thus, accessibility to Federal information is meaningless if the user cannot obtain an actual copy of the necessary information, if the information is contained in microfiche and the library does not provide reproduction equipment, if the necessary information can be located but cannot be brought into the library within a relatively short time period, or if the necessary information resource is lost, misplaced, or otherwise unobtainable.

Access and availability to government publications are not always the same as access and availability to government information. Numerous examples exist where the identification of and access to a specific government document did not uncover the necessary government information. Access and availability to government publications are a prerequisite for access and availability to government information. But the term "publication" or "document" implies the packaging of government information, and that packaging today includes traditional paper copy monographs, serials, and pamphlets; databases; microforms; audiovisual resources; maps and charts; videotapes and telefacsimile; and so forth. Although this book emphasizes access, availability, and the public use of government publications and publicly available government information, such is done with the full realization that the information contained in government publications deserves primary attention.

Within the context of the terms discussed above, this book focuses on public access to government publications and publicly available information resources, the degree to which public accessibility and availability to government information resources is provided by the GPO depository library program, and recommendations or proposals to increase public accessibility and availability. By reviewing the current status of access to government publications in the context of the various topics presented in this book, a clearer assessment can be made of (1) the assumptions under which public access to government publications currently is based, (2) the existing practices, procedures, techniques, and concepts utilized to provide access and availability to government publications, and (3) the strategies and opportunities that can be exploited to increase access and availability to government publications, regardless of the level of government producing them.

This book stresses a number of themes. First, the GPO depository library program, as a whole, is not currently providing the general public with adequate access and availability to government information. Second, although a base of research related to government publications has been initiated, numerous areas still require empirical investigation and study. Third, if increased access and availability to government publications is to be accomplished, changes in the (1) operation of the GPO depository library program, (2) the organization and bibliographic control of materials, (3) the assumptions under which libraries and information professionals make government publications accessible and available, and (4) the level and types of resources allocated in support of the GPO depository library program and the maintenance of individual depository collections, will have to be made.

Finally, the book stresses the importance of the individual depository library/information professional in assuming responsibility and taking a leadership role to increase access and availability to government publications and their information content. Ultimately, this book attempts to provide a framework by which the general public can adequately gain access to those government information resources useful in decision making related to personal, professional, or civic activities.

DEFINITION OF GOVERNMENT PUBLICATIONS, DOCUMENTS, AND INFORMATION

Government Publications and Documents

International organizations generally differentiate between *documents* and *publications*, although the distinction may be imprecise and subject to change. Documents, the official records of meetings and other material issued for internal use, may be of interest to outside users and reach a larger audience. Publications, on the other hand, are more widely distributed, address a goal or mission of the agency, and inform the public. Complicating the distinction is the fact that documents may later become publications.

When dealing with the United States government, distinctions between what constitutes a publication and document become very imprecise. Writers and others commonly use the terms "government publications," "government documents," "public documents," and "public information" interchangeably. One study (National Commission on Libraries and Information Science, 1982) differentiates between a publication and a document; a publication comprises:

> any portion of government information produced by a Government entity which is made available to the public through printing, electronic transfer, or any other form of reproduction at Government expense and which is offered for public sale/rental or for free distribution (p. 78).

In contrast, a document signifies:

> a specific identifiable segment of information produced by a Government entity which may be made available to the public upon request under law or by administrative discretion, but which is not usually considered of such broad public interest as to warrant general publication or distribution (Ibid.).

Both of these definitions are general and have limited practical application. They do, however, underscore the difficulties encountered in defining basic terms covering government information services, products, and policies.

One frequently quoted definition of "publication" is "informational matter which is published as an individual document at government expense, or as required by law" (44 USC 1901). This definition is presented in the context of the GPO and has a narrow application; it applies only to the one title in the *United States Code*. Compounding the limitation is a failure to clarify the meaning of "informational matter," "as an individual document," and "published." To some, the word "published" is synonymous with "printed" and does not take into account the full impact of technology on information production, distribution, and dissemination, and the variety of formats in which information appears (see Chapter 4). Of course, others, including the Joint Committee on Printing (JCP), support a more expansive definition of "published."

Garrett E. Brown, as General Counsel of the GPO, rendered an advisory opinion concerning the meaning and intent of the title 44 definition. He maintained that government information available for depository distribution must first be printed as a publication ("Recent Opinions of the GPO General Counsel," 1982):

> the Depository Library Act [of 1962] does not direct that [the] Superintendent of Documents make published documents available in all possible formats to the libraries. It was the intent of Congress that only printed publications would be made available to depositories.

Since his pronouncement, the JCP has proposed several different definitions of a government publication. In one instance, it defined a government publication as "any textual or graphic representation printed or otherwise reproduced, in whole or in part[,] with appropriated funds or as authorized by law, for distribution to departments or to the public" (McClure, 1984b).

For various reasons, the definition articulated in 44 USC 1901 has remained unchanged. At any rate, the JCP has drafted a new definition but has not introduced new legislation to replace the existing definition. Instead, the committee's chairman drafted letters to executive agencies in which he treated the new definition as official or the result of the statutory process. He stated that a government publication is "informational matter which is issued as an individual product at Government expense or as required by law" (McC. Mathias, Jr., 1986). This definition substitutes the word "issued" for "published," and "product" for "document," therein creating the impression that electronic information and machine-readable tapes fall under the purview of the JCP and the depository library program. However, there is still much debate over the correctness or general acceptance of these views.

Government Information

Information is the content of a message or communication that is conveyed and assimilated by the person receiving that message. Information has six characteristics (National Commission on Libraries and Information Science, 1982, pp. 16–17). These are:

- Information is an intangible that can be made available in any media
- Information is not consumed by use; it can be resold or given away with no diminution of its content
- The price of information bears little relationship to the costs of making copies available; the "first copy" cost is likely to represent most of those costs, with reproduction costs being relatively minor
- The value of information often is determined more by when it is available than by the costs for making it available or even by what the actual content of it is

- The value of information increases as the amount of data involved and the degree of analysis given those data increases
- Information has value in the marketplace and is perceived as a capital resource, an investment, an essential tool for decision making, and a means for better management of tangible resources.

"Knowledge derives from the process people use to understand and analyze information;" information is a "main ingredient of knowledge" (Becker, 1978, p. 14). Information content (not the physical form of the message or communication) usually leads to a decision, action, or behavioral change, or it may add to one's knowledge.

Government information is a broad term that encompasses both published and unpublished information that the Federal government either does or does not intend to make public. The government may compile, generate, and/or maintain the information. The term "government information" does not "differentiate among the several sources from which the information is derived." Some information is (National Commission on Libraries and Information Science, 1982, pp. 20–21):

- The direct result of government generated action (e.g., legislation, regulations, and reports of government actions)
- Generated by the government, not as a result of government action, but as a necessary component of meeting functional needs (e.g., cataloging data produced by the Library of Congress)
- Created by the government based on data obtained from the public (e.g., much of the statistical data falls into this category)
- Obtained for the government by contractors (e.g., the reports from government sponsored research and development projects included in the ERIC indexing and abstracting service)
- Derived by processing data from both public and private sources (e.g., indexes to current literature in specific subject fields)
- Taken essentially verbatim from private sources (e.g., data extracted from private database services, stored in government databases, and retrieved).

Government information implies ownership;

Aside from the question of the propriety of government ownership of information, there is the conflict with private property rights if private sector information has been included in [the definition of government] information. . . . The problem arises because of the view that government information has been paid for by taxpayer funds and therefore ought to be made readily, even 'freely' available; . . . private sector information included in it might then lose its proprietary value (Ibid., p. 21).

Given the problems of defining "government information," the term "governmentally distributable information" might be substituted. It refers to

information brought together for governmental purposes from information in the public domain or within the scope of "fair use," or owned by the government itself, or that the government has obtained rights to distribute, or that is distributable under the Freedom of Information Act, subject only to the statutory limitations (such as national security, personal privacy, etc.) (Ibid., p. 22).

"The phrase 'brought together' is interpreted as generating, compiling, processing, collecting, and analyzing" information (Ibid.).

Public information encompasses that which a government agency chooses to impart on its own or the courts force it to release. Yet much information that is collected or developed at government expense through Federal grants and contracts is exempt from the Freedom of Information Act (FOIA)—see discussion in Chapter 2—when the information is not contained in agency records. Furthermore, contractors and grantees may not release it under the FOIA, even if it is held in agency records, when release would damage the interests of the copyright holder.

In contrast, *private information* is intended solely for internal use within government and not for public consumption. It is held in confidence out of respect for a privacy right or a statutory obligation. Therefore, it will not be released under the FOIA or any other law.

Recognizing that definitions for the term "private information" are controversial, six category components of the term are identifiable:

- *Information "private to the government"* is intended for internal use and not for external distribution. This category encompasses internal memoranda, work "in progress," correspondence (personal in the sense of being addressed to an individual, but clearly in an official capacity), and perhaps other similar kinds of records. The fact that the intent is one of internal distribution, though, in no way by itself limits access through such means as the FOIA
- *Personal information relating to employees of the government* includes personnel files and correspondence, confidential letters of evaluation, and similar information
- *Personal information relating to persons not employees of the government* includes information collected by the government about persons. Some of this information (e.g., that of the Internal Reve-

nue Service) may be statutorily protected, while other personal information may not be so protected

- *National security information* (e.g., that which is military classified) is quite different from the previously listed categories, although there may be some overlap. This category includes data related to security clearances for persons. The range of persons to whom this kind of information may be made available is determined by a "need to know"
- *Private information,* in the colloquial sense, is information in the possession of private individuals. It might cover the time when their relatives worked for the government
- *Private information also refers to ownership.* To illustrate, there is nothing "private" about *Chemical Abstracts* data, in any of the prior senses, although it is privately owned—copyrighted.

For the purposes of this book, private information refers specifically to the last two categories.

The availability of information in a "gray" area between released (public) and protected (private) information would be determined through mechanisms such as the FOIA, the Privacy Act, or judicial review. There are numerous examples of information falling into this gray area. Federal agencies such as the Internal Revenue Service and the Securities and Exchange Commission collect information that is personal or proprietary. In the mid-1980s, terms such as "sensitive but not classified" and "classifiable" information also have been used to describe this "gray" area. In some instances, when the Federal government collects information intended for internal use, that information may later become public.

In summary, existing definitions of government publications or information fail to generate widespread support and contain numerous loopholes. Since this book does not address private information and since there is no adequate definition of "public information" in the literature, the term "government information" refers to information that is available for public examination and use.

"ACCESS" TO DEPOSITORY COLLECTIONS

The depository library program was formally established in the late 1850s, when responsibility for distribution of congressional publications was transferred from the Department of State to the Department of Interior. The Secretary of Interior, it was stipulated, could designate "colleges, public libraries, athenaeums, literary and scientific institutions, boards of trade, or public associations" for the free receipt of these publications (11 *Statutes at*

Large 253). Further legislation mandated that the selection of these institutions be based upon congressional designation.

The position of Superintendent of Public Documents was created in 1869, and this Office, located in the Department of Interior, was charged with the responsibility for maintaining the depository library program. The Printing Act of 1895, which consolidated the laws on printing, binding, and distribution of public documents, transferred the Office of the Superintendent of Public Documents to the Government Printing Office and renamed it the Superintendent of Documents. The Superintendent was authorized to prepare indexes and catalogs as well as to deliver "all government publications" "to designated depositories or other libraries for public use without charge." The Act, in effect, established a "systematic program for the bibliographic control of government documents."[1]

The Depository Library Act of 1962, which consolidated existing statutes, increased the potential number of depository libraries. The wording of the 1895 Act was modified so that depository collections should be "maintained so as to be accessible to the public." The 1962 Act also expanded the number of categories for publications available for depository distribution and authorized the creation of two regional libraries per state. The overwhelming majority of libraries became selective depositories (i.e., could determine the amount of material to be received) and able to discard material after a five-year retention period, if these libraries operated under the jurisdiction of a regional depository or if they were a Federal library. Federal libraries can dispose of unwanted publications after first offering them to the Library of Congress and the National Archives and Records Administration.

All government publications, including those labeled as non-GPO publications (printed at field printing plants by Federal agencies and not printed at the GPO) became eligible for depository distribution. The only exceptions to this generalization related to publications intended only for official use, required for strictly administrative or operational purposes, classified for reasons of national security, and having no public interest or educational value. However, neither then nor subsequently were these exceptions defined in detail, with corresponding guidelines developed.

The number of depository libraries has increased dramatically over the years. There were 419 depositories in 1895, 594 in 1962, 1,045 in 1971, 1,311 in 1979, and 1,373 in 1983 (Hernon, McClure, and Purcell, 1985, p. 3). By 1988, the number had expanded to 1,394. These statistics illustrate that almost 350 libraries have achieved depository status since 1971. Further congressional redistricting, the availability of additional depository designations in already existing congressional districts, and the ability of some li-

---

[1] For a more complete discussion of the historical background, see Hernon, McClure, and Purcell (1985), Chapter 1; and Miller (1980).

braries to receive depository status by law rather than congressional designation[2] may result in the creation of even more depository collections.

Since depository libraries receive selected item numbers free of charge, it might be assumed that the program represents an inexpensive means of distributing, processing, and storing government publications of potential use to the clientele of a library as well as the general public. Depository libraries, however, incur expenses relating to staffing, facilities, storage, and access to the collection; these costs underscore the fact that depository publications are not devoid of costs. However, from this, it should not be concluded that the depository program is a "costly anachronism" (Hernon and McClure, 1988).

The Federal government absorbs the costs of printing, distribution, and bibliographic control. The government views the depository program as an economical means by which information is made available to the public. As Senator Frank J. Lausche, of Ohio, pointed out in the hearings leading to the 1962 Act (Congress, 1962, p. 173),

> If the depository library system were not available, the Government would be required to expend additional millions of dollars each year to provide comparable facilities to make its documents available to the American people. Hence, the educational as well as the monetary value of the libraries' services to the country should not and cannot be minimized.

In 1984 and 1985, the annual budget of the GPO intended for the depository program was around $20 million. For 1986, the budget dropped to under $18 million.[3] Whether the amount decreases or remains constant, GPO staff must still provide the same level of services and prepare as many publications as possible for depository distribution.

Under such circumstances, microfiche naturally becomes the primary format for depository distribution. Microfiche makes more titles available and in a format economical for production and distribution. On the negative side, microfiche reinforces a perception of many government publications as highly specialized and having a limited appeal. Further, many library users prefer paper copy and obtain needed information from browsing library collections. They regard government publications as difficult enough to use

---

[2] Law depositories are those specifically designated by the various acts of Congress relating to this matter. Within this category are state libraries, land grant college libraries, the libraries of the highest state appellate court, accredited law school libraries, and Federal libraries. Congressional depositories are those that are designated by members of Congress.

[3] Salaries and expenses for the Superintendent of Documents cover the operation of the Statutory Distribution Program (congressional), the Reimbursable Distribution Program (Executive Branch agencies), the Depository Library Program, and the Cataloging and Indexing Program. The practice of the GPO is to earmark approximately 83% of these monies to the Depository Library Program. Therefore, librarians browsing the *Annual Report* of the GPO can locate the total revenue appropriated for the Salaries and Expenses of the Superintendent of Documents. Taking 83% of that total will approximate the annual budget for the depository program.

in paper copy without encountering another barrier—the microformat. Generally, whenever they need microformatted documents, they generate paper copy of relevant sections, or the entire document, and add them to their personal collections for later reference.

Until depository libraries take more effective steps to accommodate the existing information-gathering patterns of their present and potential clientele, the implications of developing massive collections of microformatted government publications that will not be utilized to their potential must be carefully reviewed. Expansive collections of depository microfiche may tend to decrease the use, accessibility, and availability of government publications.

ASSUMPTIONS RELATED TO PUBLIC ACCESS

Only recently has there been an empirical basis of research findings by which commonly held assumptions related to public access to government publications can be tested. McClure and Hernon (1983), Hernon, McClure, and Purcell (1985, Chapter 2), Hernon and McClure (1987a) summarize research and other writings related to public access of depository publications/information. A composite view of the findings of the literature suggests a set of *a priori* assumptions within the following general areas:

- Staffing and resource allocation in support of depository collections
- Perceived importance and/or value of government information
- Criteria to identify acceptable performance standards related to access and availability of government information
- Appropriateness of government information for various types of target audiences
- Competency, training, and appropriateness of those professionals who handle the collection and servicing of government information
- Comparison of the services that libraries provide for government information to those provided for other types of information
- Inclusion or exclusion of government information in traditional reference sources
- The development of policies and techniques for the acquisition, organization, and dissemination of government information
- The ability and role of the Federal government in identifying, controlling, and disseminating information effectively to the general public.

Other areas where assumptions must be identified and tested will be identified throughout this book. But the above list suggests a starting point by which access and availability to government publications can be examined.

The following sections of the chapter identify and discuss a number of specific areas where commonly held assumptions affect access and availability to government information. These areas include: goals and objectives of the GPO depository program, bibliographic control, bibliographic access, collection development, reference services, and technology. Although these areas will be more fully developed elsewhere in this book, they deserve brief comment here because of their significant impact on public access to government information.

GOALS AND OBJECTIVES

Section 1911, title 44, of the *United States Code* indicates that the depository program provides "reference collections of official publications" through the United States and its territories for the free use of the public. However, this section was intended as "one of the conditions that libraries must satisfy to retain their depository status, and not as a statement of the basic purpose of the program" (Schwarzkopf, 1982, p. 8).

In the 1970s, the Depository Library Council to the Public Printer approved the *Guidelines for the Depository Library System* (1977), which delineated the purpose of the program, its objectives, and the duties and obligations of member libraries. The Guidelines, the accompanying "Minimum Standards for the Depository Library System," and Chapter 19, title 44, of the *United States Code* provide the framework under which the GPO inspects depository libraries.

Both the Guidelines and the "Minimum Standards" are open to interpretation, are defective, and could not withstand a rigorous examination by those knowledgeable of measurement and evaluation. The Guidelines do not differentiate between goals and objectives. The three objectives actually comprise one goal—to make "U.S. government publications easily accessible to the general public and to insure their continued availability in the future." The other two statements support this long-term aspiration. The Guidelines then skip to specific points around which objectives could be developed. These points emphasize *resources* (inputs into the program) rather than *outputs* (services, issues of quality, and staff performance). Objectives (short-term, specific, and measurable statements that attempt to allow the organization to strive to achieve its goals) are absent.

The Guidelines advance a goal statement relating to public accessibility and a condition that libraries must meet—the availability of these publications for the future. However, the concept of "easily accessible" is not defined, and those highest appellate court libraries serving as depositories are exempted from the goal. Supporting information about the goal statement ignores this exemption; instead, one must locate it under 44 *USC* 1915.

The Guidelines and "Minimum Standards" do not define key terms (e.g., depository libraries will provide "sufficient staff" and "space"). To what extent do depository libraries answer reference questions and make referral to a source that will answer a question? How accurate are their responses? McClure and Hernon (1983) discovered that some libraries refused the general public access to their depository collection, that depository personnel could only answer a small percentage of test questions accurately, and that the majority of unanswered questions were not referred to another source—either internal or external to the library.

The Guidelines further assume that what is "good" for one depository is "good" for all the other libraries in the program. Yet the program consists of academic, public, state, and special libraries—each of which has different missions, goals, and objectives. Instead of defining public access and setting objectives by which the extent and type of such access can be measured, the Guidelines and "Minimum Standards" do not provide an adequate basis for determining and improving current practices and dealing with program weaknesses in an electronic and technological age.

Evaluation of the depository program through an inspection program or other mechanisms is not likely to be effective without the formulation of meaningful goals and objectives. Such pronouncements must recognize differences within depository library membership and challenge libraries to plan, improve, and engage in effective decision making.

BIBLIOGRAPHIC CONTROL

Bibliographic control encompasses those "activities directed to ensure the recording of descriptive, subject, and analytical information concerning a body of documentation and the organization of that information . . . with a view to efficient use" (Marulli, 1979, p. 13). Although bibliographic control is closely related to accessibility and availability, it is not the same. A government publication benefiting from bibliographic control may be neither accessible nor available. A commonly held assumption that increasing bibliographic control automatically leads to increased accessibility and availability must be re-examined. Further, the assumption that *all* government publications and information resources should be entered into a depository library program (or some system for centralized bibliographic control) also demands re-examination in light of recent research indicating the limited number of items typically selected by many libraries in the GPO depository program.

Much of the printing and publishing performed by the Federal government has not been identified or entered into the GPO depository program. Estimates are that the program includes somewhere between 40 and 60% of the universe of Federal publications. Many librarians maintain that the full extent of government printing and publishing (regardless of format) merits both identification and eligibility for depository distribution. The belief is that someone at some point in time will want or benefit from source material heretofore not identified or acquired by a particular library. Bibliographic control is a worthy but elusive goal; the primary question is, "Should all source material from the government be available for depository distribution?"

The bulk of the item numbers eligible for depository selection has limited appeal to the library community. Research examining patterns among the most frequently selected item numbers reveals that not all selective depositories even take the *Monthly Catalog of United States Government Publications* (Hernon and Purcell, 1982). A sizable percentage of depository libraries receive fewer than 25% of the available items. Further, the percentage has increased dramatically over the past decade (Hernon, McClure, and Purcell, 1985).

The identification of the universe of government information resources and their availability for depository distribution are not synonymous concepts. Further, it is important to recognize that there are three facets of bibliographic control (Simonton, 1962):

- Internal control—provided by the bibliographic information given on the information resource itself
- Institutional control—the measures employed in individual libraries to organize and catalog information resources
- External control—provided by reference sources, bibliographic databases, and other such services.

Only recently have there been significant efforts to improve the degree of internal bibliographic control over government publications. For many publications entering the depository library program or one of the clearinghouses in the Federal government (e.g., NTIS or ERIC), acceptable identification of the document in terms of standard bibliographic data can be gleaned. However, for the majority of nondepository publications, the vast printing of non-traditional information packages (such as microforms, computer tapes, and audiovisual resources), and numerous in-house publications of selected agencies, inadequate internal bibliographic control is the rule rather than the exception.

The degree of bibliographic control provided at the institutional level, for government information, is closely related to the degree of internal control given the source when it arrives. The vast majority of depository collections do not catalog their collections, preferring to organize materials by classification number. At the most, government publications might be placed under the Dewey or Library of Congress classification scheme and, hence, receive additional institutional bibliographic control.

External bibliographic control applied to government publications is still largely inadequate, but remains an area in which significant progress has been made in recent years. The increase in privately produced indexes and findings aids, since 1970, has compensated for the lack of internal and institutional bibliographic control, to some degree. More recently, the availability of bibliographic databases specializing in government publications has added overall to external bibliographic control.

BIBLIOGRAPHIC ACCESS

By emphasizing one aspect of bibliographic control, this section underscores the importance of certain factors to the identification and retrieval of needed government information resources. The *Monthly Catalog* selectively covers paper copy and microfiche government publications, indexes titles rather than content, and has a cumbersome arrangement. Thick issues and lengthy volumes may inhibit use. Consequently libraries purchase supplementary indexes and require additional means of providing access to government publications/information. Interestingly, increasing the number of depository staff does not guarantee greater descriptive or subject access to resources contained in the collection (Richardson, Frisch, and Hall, 1980). It might be noted that the typical depository:

> collection is not likely to have even one full-time librarian; more often than not, the librarian is assigned to the collection for one-third of his work time. This staffing pattern supports the conclusion that depository libraries view documents as not requiring or deserving high levels of professional attention. The same generalization holds for other levels of staffing. More libraries indicated that they had higher numbers of students . . . than any other category of nonprofessional staff. All of this suggests that most libraries think documents are not . . . as deserving of attention as books, and that they require no more than simple maintenance (i.e., shelving) (Ibid., p. 475).

Periodical indexes normally found in a general reference collection inadequately lead to government publications. Instead, the sources leading to government publications are more likely contained in separate documents collections. Obviously one must first associate government publishing with an information need and then devise effective search strategies to uncover the relevant source material. The underlying assumption is that government publications contain a substantial amount of unique and valuable information.

Various specialized indexes and bibliographies found in documents collections might lead to information not found elsewhere; however, special knowledge of the existence of such sources is required. Mistakenly,

> in many libraries the *Monthly Catalog* is seen as the basic index to government publications, all government publications. Although experienced document librarians recognize this fallacy, how many users are likely to be aware of the deficiency in coverage (McClure, 1978, p. 417)?

Libraries having one of the *Monthly Catalog* services offered by Brodart Library Automation Division (Williamsport, PA), Information Access Co. (Belmont, CA), LSSI (Germantown, MD), and Auto-Graphics Inc. (Pomona, CA) may unintentionally be perpetuating this misconception. Easy access to government publications from a stand-alone microfiche or optical disk reader encourages library users and some staff members to forget the source from which the database was constructed. They tend to assume that all government publications are included.

Given the wealth of specialized reference aids, combined with the cost of those commercially produced, it would seem that selective depositories, to a large extent, should only acquire those that provide access to the types of government publications most often required by their clientele (e.g., congressional hearings, statistical reports, and periodicals).

COLLECTION DEVELOPMENT

Collection development is a decision making process that determines specific materials that will be obtained in terms of subject content, format, and other criteria. Collection development becomes a framework by which all the various departments in the library work toward common collection goals and standards.

Depository libraries can meet a large percentage of the requests for the more frequently needed government publications by identifying and making available the few types of publications and the subset of titles that account for a large percentage of the demand on a depository collection. As Fry (1977, p. 115) notes,

> the accumulation of large numbers of little-used publications for prestige purposes only should be avoided. Such abuse has implications beyond the particular library situation inasmuch as printing, distribution, and library handling costs are also affected.

The more depository libraries try to acquire titles that meet single requests, the more publications they must obtain. The more acquired, the higher the cost for processing, storage, and service. Consequently libraries need to determine how many demands they want to meet internally and to rely on resource-sharing for lesser-used titles.

Given space limitations and the small number of staff typically servicing a documents collection, more libraries may be increasing their selection of depository microfiche, while decreasing their selection of paper copy. Selection, however, cannot be equated with use. In fact, many depository libraries may be selecting much more than is used (Hernon and Purcell, 1982). Depository microfiche collections, in some instances, are either going unused or only small segments of the collection receive use (Hernon, 1981). Viewing government publications available from the GPO as a free resource, combined with the view that libraries provide the public with access to government information, has contributed to a program based on potential or perceived need (the public or societal good) rather than actual use patterns.

As discussed in Chapter 6, the five-year retention policy mandated by the GPO for selective depositories should be relaxed so that these libraries have greater flexibility in developing selection and retention policies. Further, the acquisition of backfiles by individual libraries should be based on a needs assessment. For example, libraries may not need a complete set of the *Congressional Record* and its predecessors, the *Monthly Labor Review*, or *Problems of Communism*. Perhaps use patterns focus on selected years. In such cases, backfiles, including those in a microformat, need only concentrate on particular years. Selectivity is essential, given the high cost for many microform sets and variability in their potential appeal to client groups (Hernon, 1981, pp. 29–47, 59–66; Hernon and Shepherd, 1983).

To be effective, collection development within an institution requires a sophisticated delivery system for titles falling outside selection/retention profiles. At present, the GPO depository library program lacks this capability to provide lesser-needed titles on a uniform basis. This lack of capability may partially account for the over-selection of depository microfiche. There may be specific reasons for not always viewing individual depository collections in a larger perspective. Perhaps rural depository libraries place restrictions on expenditures for telephone calls, or certain regional depository libraries provide less than full service. Whatever the reasons, weaknesses in the program merit investigation and immediate attention if the depository library program is to function as an interlocking network and if selective depositories are to focus their collection building efforts on the more heavily needed source material.

REFERENCE SERVICES

Analyzing the historical record suggests that the concern for high quality reference service was, in large part, a rationale after the fact for the trend toward the establishment of separate collections (Hernon, 1978, pp. 31–50).

For years, government publications were a resource that libraries were unsure how to handle. Libraries were receiving an increasing volume of government publications, and often lacked sufficient time and staff to process them as fully as they did other materials. Given these factors, libraries moved toward the creation of separate collections and the labeling of government publications as unique information resources.

A commonly accepted advantage of the separate collection came to be that experienced library personnel provided "special" assistance needed by clientele. Some librarians suggested that "when documents are integrated with a general collection, a less specialized reference librarian handles inquiries concerning them and cannot gain the detailed experience necessary for full effective service" (Leavitt, 1961). By the 1930s, there was "a far greater number and variety of interesting government documents than ever before, and a much greater demand for such material; hence the need for some special consideration" (Saville, 1940). Government publications within separate collections became isolated from other library holdings and branded with a stigma.

Obviously, the quality of reference service was not a primary factor in the movement toward separate collections. Frequency of documents use in academic institutions is not related statistically to any of the following variables: organization of the collection, the classification scheme employed by the library, the percentage of depository items received, the percentage of government publications entered in the public catalog, the number of staff members servicing government publications, and whether the library circulated government publications (Hernon, 1979). More important considerations are the individual competencies of documents staff, the mission of the institution (research or teaching), and the perceived value of government publications in relation to other available information resources.

Two studies (McClure and Hernon, 1983; Hernon and McClure, 1987b) have found that the higher the degree offered by the academic institution, the larger the percentage of item numbers selected, the greater the number of volumes held, the larger the library budget, the greater the number of staff, and the likelihood that government publications are housed in separate collections serviced by experienced personnel did not result in more accurate service. Documents staff members, even those situated in separate collections, infrequently engaged in referral either internal or external to the institution, even when they admitted that they did not know the answer to a question. Apparently, documents staff members often view their collections as self-contained and leave information seekers to resolve their own information needs.

The general public has experienced problems in gaining physical access to depository collections located in private academic institutions and accredited law schools (McClure and Hernon, 1983; Armstrong and Russell,

1979). Further, "some Federal depositories are difficult to gain access to because they are located on military posts" (Watts, 1982, p. 60). It is conceivable that certain libraries view public access largely in terms of their own clientele (e.g., the military, faculty, staff, and students) and not the broader public, in contradiction to existing Federal statutes on the matter. Ongoing research on these topics is needed.

For many collections, members of the general public would have to know that the library was a depository and that one of the conditions of depository status is that they are permitted access to the depository collection. However, broad segments of the population are unaware of the depository library program and will not demand access to publications even though their tax dollars subsidized printing and distribution.

TECHNOLOGY

Overall, staff members servicing depository collections have limited familiarity with information handling technologies and appropriate applications of such technologies to increase public access to government publications/information. On the whole, they are little involved in online searching of government documents databases, have limited access to online terminals, and have received only minimal training in the use of online databases (McClure, 1982b; Hernon, McClure, and Purcell, 1985). They also frequently do no use computer technology to develop management information systems or decision support systems that would supply them with information necessary for making decisions regarding services and collections, on a rapid and regular basis (Morton and Cox, 1982).

But the inclusion of electronic information in the depository program is not the same as having adequate technology within the library to access and disseminate such information. For example, at an open forum on the provision of electronic information to depository libraries, sponsored by the Joint Committee on Printing, there was wide agreement among the librarians present that such information should be distributed throughout the depository library community (Congress. Joint Committee on Printing, 1985). However, the information handling technologies available in depository libraries and the electronic literacy of depository librarians required to make such government information available and accessible simply is not present in the depository library program as a whole. Further, it is unlikely that the institutions supporting depository libraries would be willing to supply the necessary information technologies so that depository libraries can exploit electronic information resources effectively and fully (McClure, 1986). Individual depository libraries and the program itself should embrace information handling technologies and, where feasible and necessary to meet significant information needs of clientele, increase the variety of information resources within their domain. To achieve this, the depository program may require additional resources. Depository staff should exploit technological applications for specific purposes, justify the purchase and use of various technologies for depository collections, and demonstrate specific benefits—collection development, public or technical service, or management— that can result from exploiting these technologies.

Depository staff, on the whole, will have to become more technologically literate, make broader use of technology, and obtain the necessary resources for handling non-print information resources. The GPO and the JCP have responsibilities as well. They must participate in a review and rewriting of statutory and administrative law, and work with stakeholders in the information sector to make the depository program into an interlocking system of libraries exploiting information handling technologies.

The need and importance for developing a program to make the information in selected government electronic and machine-readable data files (those not falling under the Privacy Act or other restrictions) accessible and available to the public is without question. One would like to believe that increased distribution of government information, in the form of data files, through depository libraries will, in fact, guarantee increased access and availability. But such may not be the case. If the depository program is to be the mechanism to gain access to government information contained in data files, significant improvements regarding the program's structure, performance, financial support, and overall management must occur *before* the program can serve effectively in such a capacity.[4]

Before the number of information resources entering the program and the public dissemination responsibilities of depository libraries dramatically increase, the JCP and the GPO should determine the degree to which depository libraries are currently able to meet existing responsibilities and provide the necessary services. Of course, depository libraries should be willing to receive data files. However, whatever they receive should be effectively integrated into the library and the depository program as a whole. Equally important, the government, with input from various segments of the information sector, should determine the most effective means by which selected data files can be made accessible and available to the public.

RE-EVALUATING ASSUMPTIONS

The effectiveness of the depository library program, in terms of its ability to resolve information needs and provide adequate public access to information

---

[4] Kadec (1985) offers a useful discussion of various concerns about the management of the depository library program.

Figure 1-1.
Summary of Questionable Assumptions Related to Public Access
of U.S. Government Publications

Public access is the goal of the depository library program.
Public access can be equated with the number of libraries in the program.
The identification of the universe of government publications/information, and depository
  distribution of government information, are synonymous concepts.
Availability of government publications in a microformat and expansive documents collec-
  tions enhance public access.
The concept of public access is well articulated in the legislative history of various statutes,
  the Guidelines, and other basic documentation.
Government publications comprise a unique library resource whose use does not conform to
  standard collection development principles.
Library staff members operating out of separate documents collections usually or always
  provide high quality reference and referral services.
The majority of depository libraries use technology to improve public access.

resources, is based largely on a set of questionable assumptions (see Figure
1–1). Public access is not the goal of the depository program; rather it is one
of the conditions by which libraries (other than those of the highest appellate
court) obtain depository status. Public access cannot be equated with the
number of libraries in the program; no number signifies the *quality* of a
collection or service. The availability of government publications on microfiche, or in machine-readable or electronic form, increases the range of
available government information. On the other hand, a library's holdings of
government information resources become impossible to browse, and clientele may not make that random find. Factors such as the absence of portable
viewing equipment and congestion in the collection directly impact on public access.

Traditionally, public access has been viewed in terms of:

- Improving bibliographic control (e.g., the full identification of government publishing and the improved indexing of the *Monthly
  Catalog*
- Improving the ability of libraries to process rapidly incoming
  depository publications
- Expanding and refining the categories for selection and making
  improvements in the Sudoc classification scheme
- Enhancing the ability of depository libraries to select those categories of value to their collections
- Expanding the number and types of depository libraries; depository
  designation has become permanent as along as minimal legal requirements are met or unless the library voluntarily relinquishes
  the designation
- Permitting "cost recovery" and "cost reduction" concerns to take
  precedent over concerns of usage, access, and availability.

All assumptions underlying public access merit identification and investigation. The effectiveness and efficiency of that access should be measured. "Adequate" public access should be clearly defined to ensure the public's receipt of:

- Understandable, complete, accurate, and current information
- Information at an affordable cost (balancing cost factors against the social good, if this is deemed desirable)
- Information in a convenient and readily usable format
- "Reasonably" priced information
- The acquisition of information with the least expenditure of physical effort.

Availability and accessibility are meaningless if the public does not perceive government information as a logical option for the resolution of an information need.

Access to government information and the concept of adequacy should also be viewed in relation to the following factors:

- *Political and organizational*: the views, values, assumptions, and objectives of a bureaucracy or politician about the government's role in the provision of Federal information. Another factor is the degree to which the management of government information enhances the accomplishment of political objectives
- *Information to be made available*: identification of the content or specific data elements that the Federal government might provide to the public
- *Bibliographic control*: the degree to which the information is identified, accurately described, indexed, and listed in appropriate reference sources
- *Dissemination methods*: the processes whereby information is made available to the public, e.g., depository library programs, clearinghouses, bookstores, and online database services
- *Publication formats*: the decision about whether to issue and use paper copy publications, microforms, a magnetic tape, etc.
- *User awareness*: knowledge that the information exists.

Effective public access presupposes that the Federal government encourages both accessibility of, and availability to, information. The government must fully recognize its responsibility to communicate with those whom it governs. Public access also places depository library collections and services in a larger context—the range of information providers that distribute and disseminate government information. This book focuses on access via depository libraries. Elsewhere, we have discussed a broader array of government information providers (Hernon and McClure, 1987a).

If the depository program is to fulfill its potential, techniques must be explored to link depository libraries electronically—for resource sharing, document delivery, and reference services. However, the accomplishment of the linkage is complicated by the fact that the program consists of 1,394 libraries, not all of which share mutual missions and goals, view the provision of government information—to either their clientele or the larger population—as an item of organizational priority, or provide high quality reference services. As Watts (1982, p. 61), then Classification Specialist for the Library Division of the GPO and former Depository Library Inspector, pointed out,

> . . .one-fifth of the depository libraries are either unwilling or unable to perform their responsibilities and should be evaluated more completely by the GPO. . . . Some libraries keep their depository status so they can get a handful of "freebies" from the government. They do not understand what the collection could do for their patrons.

A critical problem for documents librarianship is the need for research analyzing the costs and benefits of public access to depository materials and services. Unfortunately, the variables reported in existing studies (e.g., Faull, 1980; Bregent, 1979; "Godort Program," 1982), as well as the assumptions their authors make, frequently are based on personal opinion, individual case studies, and incomparable data collection, rather than on valid empirical research. Without the formulation of meaningful objectives for the depository library program, costs and benefits cannot be fully computed. Instead, individual libraries would have to develop their own method of determining costs and benefits, which in turn minimizes the ability to make comparisons among various or all depository libraries.

As marketing and promotional efforts attempt to generate awareness and use of government publications and depository collections, questions such as the following merit consideration:

- What is the current popular impression and perceived value of a government publication?
- Does awareness result in increased use of a product and of libraries?
- How do different target groups gather and use information, and will marketing strategies be geared toward each target group?
- Are target groups willing to visit libraries?
- What caliber of reference service will depository staff members provide in response to needs expressed by the various target groups should they visit the library?

- What, if any, are the implications of target groups discovering that the needed publication is available only in a library on microfiche?
- Will the public experience problems in gaining access (physical, bibliographic, or professional service) to depository collections?
- What is the evaluation component of the marketing program, and does it recognize the differences between marketing a commercial product (e.g., toothpaste and cereals) and information?

The potential answers to some of these questions, based on existing research, suggests that the GPO must be more forceful in improving the effectiveness and efficiency of the depository library program. The GPO, in conjunction with the library community, should develop specific goals and objectives for the program, as well as determine the effectiveness of member libraries in meeting stated objectives.

Finally, it should be remembered that the collective findings of the studies discussed in this chapter are "damning" to a policy of "continue as we are." Change is required if the program is to be cost-beneficial. Schwarzkopf (1982, p. 19) may well be correct when he asserts "that the depository library program is basically a library sponsored and initiated program for the benefit of libraries, and not a program of overriding concern to the federal government or to the general public." To his assessment might be added the observation that the program traditionally has been viewed as one that collects government publications as public records of government administrative or operational activities, and only incidentally as information resources. Now, the program must do more than this; it must become a mechanism to increase public access to U.S. government information resources, and to serve as an interlocking network that improves the availability and use of Federal information. At the same time, as other chapters illustrate, methods that link Federal information to the publishing programs of other levels of government must be initiated. This way, the information-gathering public can search for, and retrieve, desired information, regardless of the level of government collecting or producing it.

2

Federal Information Policies*

Federal information policies provide a context and explanation for the practices followed by the government. Many librarians have commented on "less access to less information" under the Reagan administration (see Chapter 3) but have not always placed these developments within the larger Federal information policy framework. In some instances, i.e., the Government Printing Office's (GPO) pricing policy for sales publications (see Chapter 3), the library community may not fully understand the legal context in which prices are set. Further, GPO pricing practices, in fact, have been revised with the intent of providing "more access to certain publications at a dramatically reduced price" (again see Chapter 3). It is becoming increasingly important for librarians and others to understand the policies that shape particular government practices and to work toward changing the basic information policy structure, not just practices.

Many officials of the U.S. government, in turn, naively assume that the public can gain access to government information effectively and efficiently. Although managing Federal information activities in an efficient manner comprises part of the social good, the social good has not been translated into a set of criteria whose impacts have been investigated and incorporated into policy decisions. In addition, existing administrative and statutory law for information policy is frequently contradictory, ambiguous, and confusing; the design of Federal automated information systems rarely includes factors that will enhance public access; the increased authority of the Office of

---

* Portions of this chapter have been drawn from Hernon and McClure (1987a).

Management and Budget (OMB) for the development and oversight of Federal information policies influences what information is collected and made available to the public; and users wanting access to government information encounter numerous barriers. These barriers may be significant and decrease the amount of information accessible and available to the public.

Information policy is "a set of interrelated laws and policies concerned with the creation, production, collection, management, distribution and retrieval of information." These policies "profoundly affect the manner in which an individual in a society, indeed a society itself, makes political, economic and social choices" (Mason, 1983, p. 93).

The development and administration of Federal information policies are hampered by the lack of a clear and all-encompassing definition of government information. The definition guiding the GPO and the Joint Committee on Printing (JCP) is contained in title 44, *United States Code*, but this definition applies only to that title and key elements of that definition are not explained (see Chapter 1). Executive agencies regard the existing definition as pertaining only to "traditional printing," while the JCP and the GPO prefer a more expansive interpretation that includes, for example, electronic information.

The public has a right to gain access to information produced by the government. However, the current emphasis on cost-cutting in government restricts the type and amount of information produced, distributed, and disseminated. What is produced may not be in an easily accessible format. Complicating matters ever more is that decisions supposedly based on efficiency, in fact, are political. Furthermore, access to government information requires a sophisticated information-gathering public, one that can pursue alternatives and knows the full range of search options.

Recently, key policy issues related to government information have revolved around two basic themes:

- The Federal government's responsibility for the provision of information
- Which information to disseminate to the public and how to disseminate it most effectively.

Other issues involve clarification of the roles performed by different stakeholders in the information sector, matching the creation and dissemination of government information to specific information needs, and a resolution of the extent to which government information is a societal good, a commodity to be bought or sold, or a capital investment for the overall increased productivity of society at large.

There is no single corpus of statutory or administrative law to coordinate information policies of Federal agencies, to eliminate ambiguities in Federal information policies, or to clarify the confusing and contradictory array of services that agencies provide. An excellent illustration of the current situation is that between 1977 and 1987, Congress passed some 279 laws that, broadly construed, fall into the area of information policy. These laws cover (Chartrand, 1987):

- Telecommunications, broadcasting, and satellite transmissions
- International communications and information policy
- Library and archives policies
- Information disclosure, confidentiality, and the right of privacy
- Computer security, regulation, and crime
- Intellectual property
- Information technology for education, innovation, and competitiveness
- Federal information resources management
- Government information systems, clearinghouses, and dissemination.

This expanse of public laws is related, in piecemeal fashion, to a wide variety of areas ranging from education to homeless youth, radioactive materials, and library and information science.

Some issues still to be resolved involve the degree to which the development, implementation, and enforcement of information policies is to be centralized or decentralized; the need to clarify the relationships, legal bases, and myriad practices by which the GPO, various clearinghouses, and Federal agencies price information; whether the government should "profit" from the sale of government information; the enactment of safeguards that will ensure that privatized Federal information is, in fact, accessible and available to users regardless of the format in which that information appears; and the establishment of both inter-agency coordination and intra-agency integration of information policies.

Examples of other policy issues requiring attention include: (1) the effectiveness of the Federal government as a provider of timely and accurate information, (2) the role and responsibilities of various stakeholders in the provision of government information, (3) the degree to which government information available through information technologies enhances or detracts from user groups' access to that information, and (4) a determination of the government's responsibilities for training and assisting users to exploit information technologies that offer government information.[1]

---

[1] National Commission on Libraries and Information Science (1983) provides an excellent introduction to information issues and policies. This 74 page, annotated bibliography covers national information policy, the Privacy and Freedom of Information Acts, information resources management, data privacy and data security management, information technology, the Paperwork Reduction Act, and international issues and policies.

Because various information policies are interrelated, differences between or among them can be difficult to resolve. For example, by supporting a limited definition of government information, some government agencies can more easily circumvent the provisions of title 44, chapters 1–19, *United States Code*. Indeed, the Reagan administration's concern for efficiency and cost reduction provides an ideal opportunity for the Federal government to curtail the size and scope of its printing and publishing programs and to offer increased production, distribution, and dissemination opportunities to other stakeholders.

THE LANDSCAPE OF FEDERAL INFORMATION POLICIES

Since publication of the Porat study (1977, vol. 1, pp. 214–239), there has been little progress in developing detailed typologies of policy issues, using sophisticated methods to organize and relate issues or producing better methods of clarifying the issues and their interrelationships. One is left with the sense that every policy issue is (1) part of both a larger and smaller issue, and (2) resolution of any one policy issue is dependent on resolution of another.

Drawing upon the general, social science literature, Figure 2–1 offers a conceptual overview for representative (not comprehensive) policy issues and suggests nine principal themes. An analysis of a wide range of issues suggests that (Hernon and McClure, 1987a, Appendix H):

- The published literature is repetitive in the broad themes of the policy issues that it addresses
- Surprisingly little duplication exists among specific policy issues; each issue tends to emphasize specific and unique aspects of the broader themes
- The literature devotes little attention to issues related to (1) the role of libraries in the provision of government information, and (2) the information needs and gathering behaviors of user segments
- The issues become more "technologically," than user or "humanistic," driven with the passing of time
- Policy issues can be isolated in terms of their impact on other policy issues.

The issues shown in Figure 2–1 suggest the breadth of topics that are covered and affected by Federal information policies. Further, the issues have great impact on the specific practices of government agencies in their provision of government information. Perhaps of equal importance is the impact such policy issues have on the manner in which librarians and other

Figure 2-1.
Overview of National Information Policy Issues Related to the Government's Provision of
Federal Information*

NATIONAL INFORMATION POLICY (Excluding International Issues)

A. Interaction between government and technology
    1. Promotion of research related to information technologies
    2. Ownership of new advancements in information technology if funded by the government
    3. Selection of information technolgies for use by the government

B. Interaction between government and other stakeholders
    1. Competition between government and other stakeholders
    2. Responsibility for providing value-added enhancements
    3. Responsibility for collecting, organizing, and disseminating which types of government information to which user segments

C. Government collection, transfer, and dissemination of government information
    1. Intra-governmental transfer of Federal information
    2. Types of information to be collected, organized, and disseminated
    3. Contractor/submittor responsibilities for electronic data files
    4. Transfer of Federal science and technological information for innovation and commercialization

D. Structure and organization of the government
    1. Locus of authority for coordinating and regulating information policies
    2. Coordination with state and local governments
    3. Centralized versus decentralized information policy development
    4. Executive versus legislative controls

E. Pricing of government provided information
    1. Value of information as a commodity
    2. Definitions of "cost recovery"
    3. Use of government subsidies and incentives
    4. Impact of fees on access

F. Standards and compatibility of government information services and products
    1. Deciding what specific areas are to be covered by standards
    2. Responsibility for the development of standards
    3. Bibliographic control issues

G. Role of the GPO and its depository library program
    1. Revision of chapters 1–19, title 44, *United States Code*
    2. Role of the GPO as a printer or distributor
    3. Role of the JCP in an information environment
    4. Enforcement responsibilities
    5. Relationships with other depository programs
    6. Types of information and formats included

(Continued)

Figure 2-1. *Continued*

H. The public's information needs and information-gathering behaviors
1. Value of information as a "social" or "public" good
2. Government's responsibility to increase awareness and do marketing
3. Availability versus access
4. Role of libraries
5. Determining the information needs of specific user segments and the specific types and formats of government information needed
6. Responsibility for the provision of government information to user segments that are "disenfranchised"

I. Privacy, security, and copyright of government information
1. Responsibility for disclosure systems
2. Criteria for anonyminity of data and users
3. Ownership of types of government information at various stages of service or product enhancement
4. Guaranteeing First Amendment protection
5. Maintenance of accurate and reliable data
6. Control over who gets access to what types of government information and under what situations and conditions

*Reprinted from Hernon and McClure (1987a), p. 262.

information professionals acquire, organize, and disseminate information. Recognizing the importance and complexity of these issues can assist information providers—such as librarians—in developing strategies that affect the Federal information policy system and better meet the information needs of government information users.

A TYPOLOGY FOR GOVERNMENT INFORMATION THAT INCORPORATES SIGNIFICANT POLICY ISSUES

Figure 2–2 identifies 17 issues that have significant impact on the effectiveness with which the Federal government provides information. These policy issues are grouped under a typology generated by an extensive review of the social sciences literature. The broad categories of this typology for organizing information policy issues include:

- *Federal Organization for Information Policies*: the structure of the government regarding the provision of Federal information
- *Relationship between the Federal Government and Other Stakeholders in the Information Sector*: responsibilities and roles of

Figure 2-2.
Summary of Significant Policy Issues

Federal Organization for Information Policies
1. Should the Federal government have centralized or decentralized information policies?
2. Should formal mechanisms be established that encourage continuing dialogue about Federal information policy among the various stakeholders in the information sector?
3. What is the role of the Office of Management and Budget in the development and management of information policies?

Relationship between the Federal Government and Other Stakeholders in the Information Sector
4. What responsibilities does the Federal government have for legislating and regulating access to government information?
5. How can adequate bibliographic control be maintained over government provided Federal information?
6. Should Federal information activities be administered as a "business" or as a public service?

Information Technology
7. Should the Federal government use various information technologies for the collection, organization, and dissemination of government information?
8. What criteria should the government follow in selecting information technologies for the provision of Federal information?
9. To what degree is the Federal government responsible for providing training or increasing the competency of user segments and government information intermediaries (such as information brokers and libraries) to access adequately government information available through various information technologies?

The Economics of Government Information
10. To what extent should federally provided government information be considered as a commodity or as a societal good?
11. How should the Federal government price government information?

Public Access and Availability to Government Information
12. What Federal information does the government have a responsibility to make accessible and available to the public?
13. Should Congress reconsider a revision of chapters 1–19, title 44, *United States Code*, or proceed on a "piecemeal" basis with the development of Federal policy governing publication, distribution, and dissemination of government information?
14. What is the role of depository library programs in the government's provision of Federal information?

Freedom of Information and Privacy
15. Do the Privacy and Freedom of Information Acts adequately protect the public's right to know?

Secrecy and Protection of Federal Information
16. Do laws relating to secrecy and classification define the only types of protected information?
17. Does a unified policy framework cover protected information?

agencies and organizations engaged in the production, distribution, and dissemination of government information

- *Information Technology*: applications of information technology and their effect on the government's provision of Federal information
- *The Economics of Government Information*: costs and benefits of government provision of Federal information
- *Public Access and Availability to Government Information*: the rights of the public and the responsibilities of the government to make Federal information accessible and available
- *Freedom of Information and Privacy*: the rights of the public to gain access to government agency records, while at the same time protecting information that should not be released
- *Secrecy and Protection*: the rights of the government to withhold information for the common protection of the public and national security.

Although these categories are not mutually exclusive, they offer a means for the organization of various policy issues and a realization that some of the issues have a broader impact than others.

Federal Organization for Information Policies

Issue 1. Should the Federal government have centralized or decentralized information policies? Under a centralized approach, one agency has primary responsibility for the design and enforcement of Federal information policy. The Office of Management and Budget (OMB), for example, may design and enforce information policy, but Federal agencies implement that policy. A decision to centralize the development of Federal information policy would require a clear understanding of the philosophy of the Federal government regarding the creation, organization, distribution, and dissemination of government information, as well as provision for access to that information. "Vertically oriented agencies by definition cannot take broad horizontal views" of the effects of information technology on national information policies (Porat, 1977, vol. 1, p. 241). Because of the lack of such horizontal integration, each agency has established "fiefdoms" of information policies that are frequently disjointed and contradictory.

Issues related to centralization or decentralization encourage discussions about whether the Executive or Legislative Branch will dominant the development of information policies. Three structural arrangements are possible between the two branches:

- Executive dominant
- Coordinated executive and legislative
- Legislative dominant (see Figure 2–3)

Figure 2-3.
Federal Organization for Information Policies*

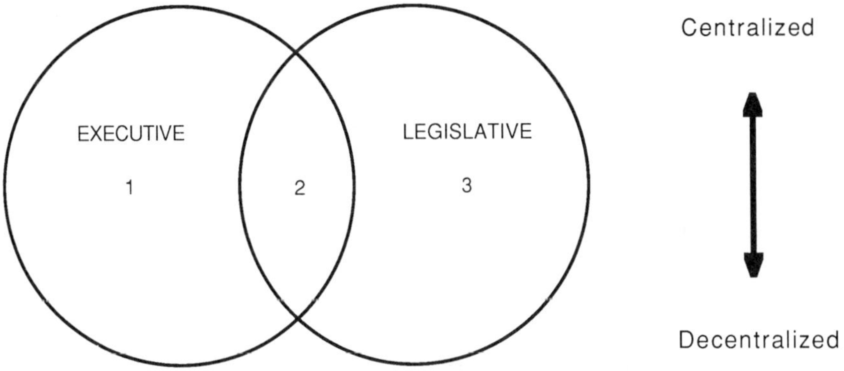

*The Judicial Branch is not considered in this model; however, it could easily be incorporated. Several options would then be considered in terms of centralized or decentralized administrative structures.

Because policy development is either centralized or decentralized in each arrangement, six administrative frameworks for the organization of the development of information policy are possible.

Structural re-organization for better information policy design and development (regardless of whether it is centralized or decentralized) requires extensive coordination and cooperation between the two branches. Currently the JCP and the GPO have limited power to enforce or execute the printing regulations on independent, regulatory agencies and executive offices, since title 44, *United States Code* provides an ambiguous legal base.

Issue 2. Should formal mechanisms be established that encourage continuing dialogue about Federal information policy among the various stakeholders in the information sector? A number of studies (e.g., Levitan, 1981a, b) have lamented the lack of formal methods by which the various stakeholders maintain an ongoing and active dialogue about policy issues and procedures related to the government's provision of Federal information and the effects of technology on that provision.

Because Federal information policies are decentralized, numerous agencies may repeatedly address the same or similar issues, concerns, and problems relating to the production, distribution, and dissemination of government information. Such a situation may create a sense of despondency on the part of stakeholders and does not encourage confrontation, discussion, and the speedy resolution of policy issues.

Issue 3. What is the role of the Office of Management and Budget in the development and management of information policies? The role of OMB has substantially increased in recent years. Some analysts perceive the agency as removed from direct interaction with the public and as dominated by matters of economy and cost-cutting in government and the political concerns of the Office of the President. This perspective provides philosophical commonalties with some for-profit stakeholders such as members of the Information Industry Association (IIA).

Based primarily on the enactment of the Paperwork Reduction Act (P.L. 96–511), and various policy circulars such as A-130, the "Management of Federal Information Resources" (December 12, 1985), OMB has moved toward the centralization of information policy within the Executive Branch and broadening its authority outside that Branch (Sprehe, 1984). However, its authority for the design and development of government-wide information policy is a matter of some debate.

Relationship between the Federal Government and Other Stakeholders in the Information Sector

Issue 4. **What responsibilities does the Federal government have for legislating and regulating access to government information?** Government responsibilities for legislation and regulation depend, in part, on the views one holds about the ownership of government information. At one end of a continuum, it can be argued that the public owns the information collected, created, and/or organized by the Federal government and that the government must guarantee public access to this information. On the other end, the argument can be made that the "marketplace," when allowed to operate, adequately regulates the collection, creation, and organization of government information.

Little evidence exists to support either argument to the exclusion of the other. First, Federal legislation and regulations, in some instances, systematically stifle creativity and innovation, establish an artificial pricing for services/products, and, at times, are complicated and contradictory. However, "marketplace" solutions ignore access to services and products by those who are disenfranchised, and limit the production of services and products to those perceived as "profitable." Disruptions of services may result due to delivery or production problems.

Issue 5. **How can adequate bibliographic control be maintained over government provided Federal information?** The degree of bibliographic control over all types and formats of government information is problematical. Since there is little agreement about what specific types of information are "public," an assessment of the degree to which bibliographic control exists also produces little agreement. Yet any discussion of the government's provision of information must address issues related to the bibliographic control of that information.

Bibliographic control is a shared responsibility among a number of stakeholders. The government may provide certain tools, e.g., the *Monthly Catalog of United States Government Publications*, but for-profit organizations such as the Congressional Information Service also produce basic indexes and other reference tools as well.

In many instances, the government supplied the initial capital investment for the development of bibliographic control devices, e.g., the National Library of Medicine's MEDLARS. Although for-profit organizations have provided value-added enhancements that improved bibliographic control over government information, numerous bibliographic "gaps" still remain.

Issue 6. Should Federal information activities be administered as a "business" or as a public service? Two opposing viewpoints about how Federal information activities should be organized prevail. The first holds that these activities should be organized as a business, i.e., based on recovering costs associated with providing an information service or product. Both user training (as in the case of the Bureau of the Census) and aggressive marketing strategies (as the GPO did when it established a major marketing effort in 1982) are essential. The other view suggests that cost recovery or profit-making on Federal information activities constitute "double payment" by the public. *All user segments* of the public, this view maintains, should have access to government information, without having to encounter additional cost and other barriers.

The term "business-like" suggests the efficient use of resources or the economic administration of those resources; thus, one is business-like if one is efficient. Another view is that "business-like" implies administering organizations as though they were market and profit-oriented. Spokespersons for OMB have written that Federal agencies ought to not only distribute and disseminate information at no cost to the government, but also, if possible, "recover some of the costs, and . . . [even] make a profit" (Sprehe, 1984, p. 359). Others would contend that while administering activities efficiently, is, in fact, a primary and appropriate role for the government, making a profit on information distribution is not. Perhaps some type of profit is legitimate for those who enhance government information through value-added services and products.

Information Technology

Issue 7. Should the Federal government use various information technologies for the collection, organization, and dissemination of government information? The Federal government has answered this question in the affirmative. However, there has been little formal attempt to assess the *specific impacts* of increased Federal dependence on information technologies for the provision of government information to specific markets. Information technologies and the advancements in various electronic formats—used by the National Technical Information Service (NTIS) and other Federal agencies—have significantly outpaced the policy structure for how best to manage these technologies (Congress, 1986). The assumption that electronic information *automatically* improves access must be reconsidered in terms of specific user segments of the public.

Applications of information technology for the provision of government information affect different segments of the public differently. Although the government can better collect, organize, and process information through the use of various information technologies such as machine-readable data files, this does not, automatically, guarantee access to that information. The current cost-driven basis for the government's use of information technology must be considered in terms of trade-off relationships with public access.

Issue 8. What criteria should the government follow in selecting information technologies for the provision of government information? Cost factors dominate the development of those criteria currently used in selecting specific information technologies for the provision of government information. Individual agencies apparently are encouraged to create information services and products that are cost-effective in meeting their mission. As long as the agencies themselves decide about contracting information services to non-Federal vendors and the type of information technologies that will convey government information (Congress, 1986), information systems may not be comparable and interchangeable across agencies.

The selection of information technologies has a direct relationship on the standards used in the creation and use of those technologies. For example, selection of 5 1/4–inch floppy diskettes as a carrier of government information assumes that all diskettes have a degree of compatibility. Existing standards of the American National Standards Institute (ANSI) and Federal Information Processing Standards (FIPS) assist in the selection of information technologies, their format and content, only if they are considered in the context of user information needs and available hardware and software.

Issue 9. To what degree is the Federal government responsible for providing training or increasing the competency of user segments and government information intermediaries (such as information brokers and libraries) to access adequately government information available through various information technologies? Responsibility for increasing users' technological literacy and other information handling skills is a critical factor in whether a particular information technology does or does not increase access to government information. Despite the trend to place government information in various technological delivery systems, little overall effort has been made to explain: (1) what the available types of government information are, (2) how the end user can effectively exploit the information or learn to manipulate the data within that information system, or (3) how organizations can manage Federal information resources for use in their particular setting.

Once again, decentralized information policies have produced inconsistencies across agencies. For example, the Data User Services Division of the Bureau of the Census offers numerous seminars and other training services either "free," i.e., federally subsidized, or at low cost to the public. Other agencies with significant responsibilities for the distribution or dissemination of government information, such as the GPO and the Department of Energy, have devoted significantly fewer resources to support such activities. For-profit stakeholders, such as DIALOG, provide excellent ongoing training seminars to ensure that users or intermediaries of their system increase their skills in extracting information from the system. Increasing awareness and developing specific skills related to using Federal information services and products may assist in making government information available to users, and not merely "accessible."

The Economics of Government Information

Issue 10. To what extent should federally provided government information be considered as a commodity or as a societal good?   A key philosophical issue is the degree to which government information is a commodity or a societal resource. For-profit organizations regard such information as a commodity to be bought and sold in the marketplace. As such, the marketplace should make the final determination of the value and cost of information. In addition, value-added information processes (Taylor, 1986) attached to government information should be passed along to the users.

The view that government information is a societal good holds that all user segments of the public supported the collection and organization of the information, either through direct participation or paying taxes. Therefore, the entire public should have access to and use of the information. This view assumes that any restriction on the public's ability to identify, access, and use this information reduces overall societal "progress" and productivity.

Both positions make assumptions about the:

- Importance of government information for national progress
- Potential for selling the information
- Profitability of the information
- Rights of the public regarding the information
- Responsibility of the government to encourage the maintenance of an informed electorate and citizenry.

Clearly, information production, organization, and delivery practices that result from each position differ. However, the notion that information is a "capital resource," i.e., providing for the future investment of both the market and the societal good can provide some common ground between the two positions. Resolution of this issue may be necessary before attention is directed to a number of other policy considerations.

Issue 11. How should the Federal government price government information? OMB and other Federal agencies have developed policy guidelines that encourage the pricing of information services and products. However, some confusion persists about *types or categories* of information services and products and whether the information service or product is intended for public distribution and dissemination. Further, there is confusion about pricing and a lack of differentiation among information products, value-added processes, and services for product support and development. Given these factors, pricing policies must be established, prior to (not after) the development of the various information services and products.

Terminologies that different Federal agencies use for pricing include "cost recovery," "self-sufficiency," "free," "cost-plus," etc. Cost structures vary widely within the government: a publication that is for sale from the GPO might be obtained free directly from the issuing agency or at a different price; microfiche purchases among the GPO, ERIC, and NTIS are calculated differently; and methods for computing the cost for the duplication and sale of a machine-readable data file vary widely.

There is general agreement that the Federal government should avoid pricing structures that encourage unfair competition with other stakeholders. However, "unfair competition" is rarely defined or considered in the context of specific market segments of the public. In short, Federal pricing of a machine-readable data file for the business community may be "unfair competition" but appropriate for scholars and researchers. Thus, a complicating issue becomes: "Can pricing policy differentiate among user information needs without the government privatizing the information or developing artificial price structures?"

Public Access and Availability to Government Information

Issue 12. What Federal information does the government have a responsibility to make accessible and available to the public? Instances where certain types of information are available from one Federal agency but not another, and perhaps at a different cost, occur on a regular basis. Philosophically, one can say that all public information should be available. Realistically, the public may not need all Federal information, and inadequate resources might be available to make such information available and accessible. Further, some stakeholders will not disseminate information that has minimal profit potential.

The government should not decide by itself what information to make publicly available, how that information will be made available, and who will have access to it. If the government controls these issues, more information will become private and only selectively available. Federal officials may be more likely to "reward" their supporters and "punish" their adversaries, by controlling access to such information.

Issue 13. Should Congress reconsider a revision of chapters 1–19, title 44, *United States Code*, or proceed on a "piecemeal" basis with the development of Federal policy governing publication, distribution, and dissemination of government information? Chapters 1–19, to a large extent, are based on the Printing Act of 1895. The proposed revision of title 44 in the late 1970s illustrates the problems in trying to revise this legislation without a firm overall Federal philosophy regarding information policy. In addition, reactions to the attempted revision demonstrated that various stakeholders have diverse interests.

During 1986–1987, for example, the piecemeal approach continued to be the preferred method for treating information policy issues, as exemplified by the introduction, or passage, of such policies as:

- An Government Information Agency (H.R. 1615, 100th Congress)
- The National Technical Information Corporation, which would be a wholly-owned government corporation (H.R. 2159, 100th Congress)
- *The Federal Technology Transfer Act of 1986* (PL 96–517) and the resulting Executive Order 13414, *Facilitating Access to Science and Technology.*

Yet none of these initiatives were carefully reviewed in the context of their impact on title 44, chapters 1–19, *United States Code.* Passage of individual policy mechanisms rather than a comprehensive treatment of Federal policy issues encourages a decentralized, ambiguous, and, at time, confusing and contradictory Federal information policy system.

Piecemeal consideration of Federal information policy also encourages vertical policy development but minimal horizontal coordination across Federal agencies. Effective revision of chapters 1–19 or a coordinated, decentralized approach requires greater consideration of philosophical issues and less focus on the political agendas of individual agencies and for-profit stakeholders.

Issue 14. What is the role of depository library programs in the government's provision of Federal information? The Federal government currently operates a number of depository programs including that of the GPO, the Patent Office, Geological Survey and National Oceanic and Atmospheric Administration (maps and charts), the Department of Energy, etc. There is minimal coordination among these programs, in terms of types of information distributed, and the specific missions, goals, and objectives guiding the provision of information.

Although the Depository Library Act of 1962 expanded membership in the GPO's depository library program, that program relies primarily on the Printing Act of 1895 for much of its statutory basis. Despite efforts to move into the distribution of electronic files, the program is not up-to-date with either advancements in information technology or meeting the information needs of the public: "the Library Program Services is a stepchild within GPO, and it is woefully behind the state of the art in applying technology to its own internal processes and to facilitating the delivery of and access to the information it processes" (Kadec, 1984, p. 416).

Many Federal agencies ignore the GPO's depository program and do not distribute their publications through it. Various waiver provision in sections 501 and 504 of title 44 help to justify minimal cooperation. Legal counsel for the GPO has written that "it was the intent of Congress that only printed publications [and not electronic information] would be made available to the depositories" (Congress. Joint Committee on Printing, 1984, p. 113). In addition, interpretations resulting from INS v. Chadha (1983) have intensified the difficulties of basing information policy on chapters 1– 19, title 44.

Depository programs such as the one administered by the GPO are beset with problems affecting their efficiency and effectiveness, as well as the extent to which the public is aware of and uses them. When Federal officials discuss the role of such programs, they typically focus on an "ideal," i.e., what these programs can do in theory, as opposed to "reality," i.e., what they are currently doing (effectiveness) and how well they disseminate information (efficiency). Until Federal officials examine depository library programs in terms of meeting information needs and clear measures of performance, these programs are not likely to be effective disseminators of government information.

Freedom of Information and Privacy

Issue 15. Do the Privacy and Freedom of Information Acts adequately protect the public's right to know? The Freedom of Information Act (FOIA) (5 USC 552) sets standards by which government *records*—not information—must be either made available to the public or withheld from disclosure. In addition, it details procedures to be followed in the request of government records from the Executive Branch. The Privacy Act of 1974 (5 USC 552a) is a companion piece of legislation in that it allows individuals to seek access to Federal agency records about themselves.

Amendments passed to the FOIA in 1986 may have the impact of restricting the public's use of this Act. At issue is determining a balance between the public's right to know and the government's right—and ability—to provide access to such information. Access to such information, whether requested under the FOIA or the Privacy Act costs both time and money. Ultimately, the government has more of both than does the average citizen.

With the increased reliance on electronic databases by government agencies to maintain and organize Federal information, both the FOIA and the Privacy Act are likely to be further tested. In the case of the Privacy Act, increased attention to maintaining security over Federal computerized information systems may result in a lessened ability for an individual to determine the degree to which personal records are, in fact, included in any particular system (Congress. Office of Technology Assessment, 1986).

Indeed, the key issue is the degree to which the FOIA and the Privacy Act can serve as two of this country's "safety nets" in guaranteeing public access to government information and records in an electronic age. Further, the role of information professionals, particularly librarians, in knowing how to use these laws and understand what they can and cannot be expected to accomplish has yet to be adequately addressed. Concern over the privacy and control of information about oneself is likely to increase in importance during the 1990s because of the government's increased reliance on electronic information systems and the ability of these systems to share data among themselves.

Secrecy and Protection of Federal Information

Issue 16. **Do laws relating to secrecy and classification define the only types of protected information?**   Protection encompasses both information regulation and classification. *Regulation* may mean that information is never disclosed (e.g., in the case of atomic energy information) or that it may eventually be released (e.g., congressional records, patents, trade secrets, and census data). *Classification*, a related concept, is synonymous with official secrecy and the Executive Branch's protection of information concerning national security and intelligence programs and operations. Secrecy permits qualified internal access (access within government on a "need to know" basis) to information, but under specific functional restrictions.

Classification policy concerns the management of that agency information determined to require secrecy protection in accordance with specified laws, directives, and court decisions. The policy articulates the purposes for withholding information from scrutiny, the type(s) of information resource(s) covered, who is eligible to classify information, the correctness of that person's decision, etc.

Protected information may encompass national defense or foreign policy, the third exemption to the FOIA (information resources protected by other statutes), trade secrets and confidential commercial or financial records, etc. Practically speaking, the term applies to atomic energy information as well as records of the Secret Service concerning presidential security (closed for 50 years), census data (depending on the nature of the file, closed for either 50 or 72 years), records of the House of Representatives (closed for 50 years) and the Senate (closed for 20 years), etc. As is evident from this brief discussion, numerous agency and congressional records pertaining to areas other than national security are protected and subject to specific agency regulations governing their release. Although the depository library program administered by the GPO offers numerous publications, these represent a small fraction of the information gathered, held, and possibly released by Federal agencies, the courts, and Congress.

Clearly, access to government information may require that information professionals be able to negotiate a complex maze of diverse practices and laws. At the same time, they need to protect their right (and that of the public) to gain access to government information. They must monitor government interpretations of "sensitive and classifiable" information and attempts to reclassify information or to restrict access to certain government information held in publicly available databases. The National Security Decision Directives issued by President Reagan, and his predecessors, in many cases, comprise secret law. These laws and policies are created in secret and their provisions are largely unknown to Congress and the American people. A danger is that "the national security state and its penchant for secrecy" impinges on personal freedoms and legitimate rights to know (Relyea, 1988).

Issue 17. Does a unified policy framework cover protected information? The United States government develops, and generally adheres to, general rules for determining when (or if) information becomes publicly available. Nonetheless, there is no single, unified, national policy governing which information will be protected or withheld from the public. Numerous policies exist (for example, see Chartrand, 1987); these cover various types of information subject to protection. At times, these policies are related. More typically, fragmentation occurs and the puzzle can be difficult to piece together.

Information subject to protection falls within the scope of the policies set by executive agencies, Congress, and the courts. The role of Congress and the courts in overseeing the development and implementation of public policy for protecting government information is obviously limited. Given the amount of information subject to protection and the number of policy interpretations that agency officials must make each year, an important concern is that neither Congress nor the courts can monitor the full use of classification and regulation authority in a comprehensive manner. Together with the

Executive Branch, Congress, however, sets statutory law; it shapes protection policy through the criminal code, the FOIA, and various other statutes. The courts may exercise their powers to accept, modify, or invalidate agency practices and the provisions of a statute.

Clearly, a general policy framework must address the value of increasing the degree of coordination among co-equal branches of government. Such a framework must also recognize the legitimate needs of each branch. The existing policy framework therefore is (and is likely to remain) decentralized. No one agency has primary responsibility for the design and enforcement of Federal policy for information protection. Inevitably, individual agencies might become overtly zealous in protecting information and controlling public access.

Congress, the courts, and the Executive Branch must balance both secrecy and openness. It is equally as important to ensure that information no longer subject to protection is reviewed and, when deemed appropriate, preserved according to the highest archival standards. Such information must also be placed under complete bibliographic control. Furthermore, the public must be informed of the existence of such information, and physical access to this information must be treated as a right—not a privilege.

EXAMPLES OF TWO KEY POLICY AREAS

Distribution/Dissemination of Federal Information in Electronic Form*

Federal government information policy is shaped in part by the First Amendment to the Constitution, by the FOIA, and by the provision in the Copyright Act that (generally) prevents the government from copyrighting information. The Privacy Act and the Paperwork Reduction Act also establish general rules governing collection and use of information by Federal agencies.

A principal goal of government information policy is the maintenance of general public availability of information in the possession of the government except where confidentiality is appropriate in order to protect a legitimate governmental or private interest.

Policies regulating the electronic collection and dissemination of information by a Federal agency must reflect the existing statutory obligation of agencies to make information available to the public. A Federal agency's responsibility to provide for public use of agency records should not be

---

* This section is an edited reprinting of part of Congress (1986). For supplementary information, see *Government Information Quarterly*, 5 No. 3 (1988).

considered to be fixed or fully satisfied at any point in time. Public access is a dynamic concept. If an agency has developed the ability to manipulate data electronically, it is unfair to restrict the public to paper documents. An agency cannot justify denying the public the benefits of new technology by preserving, without improvement, the same type of access that was provided in the past.

Electronic Information Technology

Increasing amounts of information—both private and public—are being maintained in electronic databases. This trend will continue and will accelerate. The electronic collection, maintenance, and dissemination of information by a Federal agency can undermine the practical limitations and legal structures that have prevented the agency from controlling public access to and use of the information that the government collects, creates, and disseminates.

Electronic information systems offer the opportunity to make more government information readily available to more public users. The technology also permits government information to be used in ways that are not possible when the information is stored on paper records.

Electronic information technology does not alter existing requirements that a Federal agency maintain and disclose information. Public information maintained by a Federal agency should remain freely accessible and easily reproducible, whether the data are maintained in paper or electronic form.

The Federal government must understand the consequences of electronic information systems and must recognize the need for new policies that will prevent these systems from being used in unintended ways. However, there is little communication among Federal agencies about electronic information activities; and little central administrative guidance.

What's at Stake

Computerized data systems can be expensive. Who will pay the cost? Will data users outside an agency be asked to pay high prices for public data that are now available for free or at minimal cost? What type of user fees are appropriate? Will submitters of data be required to share in the cost of the systems?

Other difficult questions also arise. Will electronic data be distributed in an equitable way that permits easy redissemination by all interested parties? Could dissemination arrangements give an agency or a private company monopoly control over public information? Will the government offer products and services in competition with private companies? Will access rights under the FOIA and other laws be fully preserved?

At a practical level, the dissemination problems presented by electronic data systems are significantly different from the problems presented by the distribution of government information in paper or other hardcopy formats. That difference arises in large part from the relative ease by which paper documents can be reproduced and used, and the relative difficulty of supporting the reproduction and use of electronic databases.

The redistribution of government information that is only available on paper continues to be a common practice. Since government information (generally) cannot be copyrighted, the information is in the public domain and anyone is free to reproduce the data or the document on which it appears. Because copying machines and printing presses have become commonplace and relatively inexpensive to operate, anyone can readily redistribute government data. Thus, no Federal agency is in a position to control the use or the redisclosure of public domain data that it generates during the course of its business.

It is entirely appropriate that Federal agencies are unable to regulate the use of government information. This inability prevents the government from maintaining an information monopoly, from exercising political control over data, and from limiting or discouraging others from using the data. It helps to assure a diversity of voices. Free flow of government information also encourages widespread use of a valuable resource that has been created with public funds.

The distribution of government information through electronic information system has a potential to allow Federal agencies to maintain a monopoly or near-monopoly over information. This potential arises because of the size, technical requirements, and expense of these systems.

A feature of an electronic data system is that the conversion of data into electronic formats can be expensive. The cost discourages the re-creation of a database from paper records and can be prohibitive unless the database can be copied electronically.

If copies of agency databases were routinely made available in machine-readable format, the possibility of agency control over the data would be lessened. However, Federal agencies are now asserting the right to deny requests for electronic copies of records. Agencies argue that their disclosure obligations are fully met by releasing printed copies of electronic databases. By refusing to provide an electronic copy of a computerized database, an agency may also be strengthening its monopoly over the most useful version of that database.

The practical difficulties of re-creating and redistributing electronic data mean that agencies can have a greater ability to control the way in which government data—which is in the public domain—can be obtained, used, and redistributed by those outside government. This is a significant potential danger with electronic data systems.

An agency might exploit control over government data for a variety of purposes. It might be used to create a constituency of data users who are dependent on the agency; to pressure government contractors into providing free services; or to sell public domain data for a high price and generate revenues outside of the appropriations process. Information control can also be used for overtly political purposes.

A hypothetical example can illustrate the potential of electronic data systems for affecting an agency's control over public information. Suppose that a statutory responsibility of Agency XYZ is the creation of a catalog of abstracts of government reports and publications. The purpose of this catalog is to make information about government data products widely available and to assure that the benefits of those products can be shared by all.

Issued in paper, such a catalog would be relatively inexpensive. Because the abstracts are in the public domain, anyone would be able to reproduce the catalog in whole or in part. Private publishers or individuals might reproduce selected portions of the catalog to meet the special needs of selected communities of users.

When Agency XYZ converts the catalog into an electronic database, the abstracts become more useful. For example, an electronic database can be updated daily. More important is the ability to create indexes of the data on demand. Each user can create individualized subsets of abstracts on subjects of interest.

This ability to create new subsets of data makes an electronic database very powerful and much more valuable than a paper catalog. Searches of the database become easier, faster, cheaper, and more thorough. This ability is so valuable that those unable to employ an electronic search system suffer from a significant disadvantage.

Agency XYZ was unable to control the use or reproduction of the publication when it appeared in paper. Suppose, however, that the agency is legally able to refuse disclosure of the computer tape containing the abstracts. Because of the great expense of duplicating the electronic database from the printed catalog, the agency would likely have the only copy of the electronic database for the catalog.

Concerns over monopolistic control of data are not necessarily avoided even if Agency XYZ should allow public users to search its electronic database. Without any competition for the computerized search services, the agency would have a captive audience of users. The agency would only have to offer services of its choice rather than services that might be demanded by users. The agency might provide free or low-cost service to favored users. It might charge high prices to some and use the profits to subsidize other users or pay for other agency activities.

If demand for services exceeded the supply, Agency XYZ might ration services and deny some people access to the database, perhaps even using political criteria. The agency might also impose substantive limits on computer searches for political purposes. The agency could even employ the system for surveillance purposes by keeping track of who is using the system and by monitoring the nature of requests.

By controlling access to the computerized search system, Agency XYZ would have a type of monopoly over data that were compiled at public expense for a public purpose. There would be no competition for electronic services. Diversity of distribution would, as a practical matter, be severely restricted. The open marketplace in information generated by the government would be diminished. The specter of government control of public data for political purposes would be raised.

This example is not entirely hypothetical. The details are an amalgam of real-life data systems now in place or under development. Some of the monopoly issues have already been the subject of litigation.

In summary, electronic information systems can produce unintended results. At this early stage in the implementation of these systems by the Federal government, it is important to understand what is at stake and what type of policies are needed to prevent undesirable consequences. It is likely that there will be a proliferation of these systems throughout the government in the next decade, and suitable policies must be developed *now*.

The new technology of electronic data distribution can undermine the practical limitations and legal structures that have prevented Federal agencies from exploiting the ability to control access to and distribution of the information that the government collects, creates, and disseminates. The Federal government must understand the consequences of electronic information systems and must recognize the need for new policies that will prevent these systems from being used in unintended ways.

Agency Responsibilities

In carrying out a statutory mandate to make government information publicly available, a Federal agency should use modern technology to improve the range and the quality of public access to agency records. As technology permits an agency to upgrade its own ability to access, copy, and manipulate data, an agency should make reasonable attempts to allow public users of agency information to share the benefits of automation.

To the greatest extent practicable, a Federal agency should support a diversity of information distribution mechanisms. Not all public users are willing or able to use computerized record systems. At a minimum, an agency must retain the ability to provide promptly paper copies of public records maintained electronically whenever those records are requested under the FOIA.

A Federal agency planning an electronic information system should actively consult with all parties who will be affected by or interested in the automation. This includes submitters of information, users, resellers, and potential information system contractors. Consultation will help to assure that any automated system sponsored by an agency will not only meet its own needs but also the needs of others.

Managing Federal Scientific & Technical Information

Issues related to Federal STI policies and their impacts on the overall growth and competitiveness of the United States have evolved into one of the most important policy areas that must be resolved. At congressional hearings held, in July, 1987, on a number of topics related to Federal STI, Doug Walgren, Chair of the House Science, Space and Technology Committee, stated that Federal policy governing STI was in disarray (Congress. House Committee on Science, Space, and Technology, 1987 [news release, p. 1]):

> Information with potential commercial value languishes inside [the] Federal Government because agencies do not aggressively seek a broader audience for its application. The Office of Science and Technology Policy, given a mandate by Congress to overcome these problems, has chosen not to exercise its authority . . . The Federal Government has a unique role in the collection and dissemination of the best scientific and technical information from around the world, and our economy can ill afford further abdication of that responsibility.

The concerns raised in this statement represent only a portion of the problems and issues contributing to the vacuum in U.S. STI policy.

The Existing Context

It is *not* that STI policies, since World War II, have received inadequate attention. In an analysis of the period 1958–1982, Woorster (1987) identified over 30 key reports and studies that have assessed U.S. STI policies. He concludes that recommendations from these reports have not changed substantially over the 24 year time period, perhaps, because there were few reassessments of the conceptual bases for Federal STI policies. Nonetheless, Woorster (Ibid., p. 321) concludes that "the U.S. scientific and technical information system . . . built in the Sixties and Seventies has been carefully, if not lovingly dismantled."

Unfortunately, the legal basis for the management of and access to Federal STI is a confusing patchwork of (at times) ambiguous and contradictory legislation. But while recommendations to improve or modify Federal STI policies have been both vociferous and consistent, the actual policies and information transfer mechanisms that manage and provide access to

Federal STI are becoming increasingly inadequate and ineffective. The Office of Management and Budget (OMB) circulars and other regulatory guidelines and legislation underscore that little consensus exists on either the objectives or the justification for government-wide STI policies. "In the absence of a national consensus of the goals of [and role of the Federal government in] the new information age, economics and technology are now shaping the future" (Dizard, 1985, p. 144).

The importance of STI policy issues is enormous. In terms of investment, the National Science Foundation estimates that $118.6 billion was spent on research and development (R&D) in 1986 and that 47% of this amount came from the Federal government (Congress. House Committee on Science. Space, and Technology, 1987). The result of this Federal investment is a broad range of STI. The term *Federal STI* is meant to include the immediate or "first-step" products of federally-sponsored R&D activities. Technical reports are a typical product; however, other products may include journal articles or conference proceedings. STI may be produced by Federal agencies (e.g., Federal laboratories) or researchers in the private or academic sectors conducting projects supported wholly or in part by a Federal agency. Thus, "Federal STI" may include STI produced either in the Federal, private, or academic sectors.

The vacuum of Federal STI policy is due, in part, to the lack of attention given to a number of key issues. The inability to deal with these issues in a broad conceptual framework has contributed to both the vacuum as well as the ambiguity and contradictions that exist in the policy system. An overriding problem relates to making a determination of where STI policy fits into the larger Federal policy system.

Federal STI policies are rarely considered as a distinct and separate entity in the Federal policy system. In fact, a fair assessment might be that STI policies have evolved as happenstance from more clearly defined areas of government information policy and science/technology policies. While it can be argued that STI policies must include— or at least be consistent with—government information policies and science/technology policies, such is clearly not the case.

Improving the STI Policy System

Existing Federal information transfer mechanisms may not meet R&D information needs because of a number of barriers to that transfer process. Federal policies related to STI transfer are based largely on models for the provision of public information and a societal context much different from that of today. Many of the assumptions underlying these policies are no longer appropriate and they fail to consider a drastically changed information technology environment for R&D information users (McClure, 1987).

Federal information policies also fail to recognize that scientists and innovators have different needs for different types of STI during the research/innovation process, e.g., recognition of opportunity, idea formulation, problem solving, prototype solution, commercial development, and technology utilization/diffusion. During the different stages of research, the scientist/researcher requires different types of information (White, 1975, p. 351):

> . . . information gathering behavior during a research project changes as (the researcher) progresses through the project and . . . certain behavioral patterns can be associated with each . . . research . . . [stage]. Behavior is affected directly or indirectly by the type of task being performed . . . .

Federal information transfer mechanisms address STI needs requiring subject disciplines and print-based overviews rather than the "processed" information that cuts across disciplines and are problem or issue-oriented. Yet "processed" information that includes interpersonal STI links many scientific disciplines and addresses *specific* information needs that are critical in the R&D setting.

The need for processed Federal STI in the innovation and technology development process appears to be injured by the manner in which Federal technical report literature is managed and disseminated (McClure, 1988). This literature may constitute the single most important storehouse of R&D results in the world. Some 65,000 items are added annually to just the NTIS database[2] (see Chapter 10). But if Federal STI is to be better utilized and have a *direct* impact on innovation and technology transfer, a coordinated and user-oriented STI policy system is needed. This policy system should ensure adequate access to and dissemination of technical report literature.

In short, a number of issues need to be addressed regarding Federal STI policy. Figure 2–4 summarizes the recommendations intended to improve Federal STI policy. These recommendations are not intended to be a comprehensive cure-all for Federal STI policies. Rather, they suggest basic factors and research areas that should be addressed in the development of a comprehensive U.S. STI policy system.

At a macro level, there is a growing recognition that the Federal government must better organize and orchestrate the management and provision of STI, if the United States is to increase its international competitiveness and regain its economic position. Such may require direct con-

---

[2] Interestingly, as this book is being written, the government's attention to STI is focused on the context of privatization of NTIS (efficiency of government) rather than on the development of STI policy instruments to increase access to and dissemination of Federal STI (effectiveness or impact of STI).

Figure 2-4.
Summary Recommendations for Federal STI Policy Mechanisms

1. Treat STI policies as a separate policy area—coordinated with but not subsumed under government information policies, science and technology policies, R&D policies, etc.
2. Provide guidelines for determining the status of Federal STI as public or private information.
3. Clarify the range of Federal information that constitutes STI, do not treat STI as part of "all government information," and recognize that there is no generic type of government information.
4. Develop guidelines for what constitutes adequate access to Federal STI.
5. Recognize the roles of different types of Federal STI in research and the scientific and technical communication process.
6. Promote the development and use of information transfer mechanisms that are interactive, operate in real time, and offer STI for specific decision stituations rather than broad subject areas.
7. Recognize that the agency's selection of an STI transfer mechanism affects the degree to which STI is accessed and used.
8. Consider how specific value-added processes can enhance access to STI for specific user groups in the R&D community.
9. Emphasize the use of interpersonal STI transfer mechanisms as a means for encouraging the access to and use of Federal STI—especially in the innovation process.
10. Recognize that the acquisition and storage of STI is not, in itself, assurance that STI will be accessed and used.
11. Review, coordinate, and clarify agency missions regarding the acquisition, organization, and dissemination of technical report literature.
12. Ensure adequate bibliographic control, awareness, and physical availability to Federal STI.
13. Establish policies and procedures that encourage users to access Federal STI rather than establishing barriers to that information.
14. Assist the R&D community to improve its information gathering, as well as management and IRM, skills for Federal STI.
15. Develop STI policy instruments from a basis of policy research rather than "informed opinion" and agency expediency.

gressional involvement and the development of a coherent set of laws and information policy guidelines. Somewhat paradoxically, at a micro level, there is also recognition that "the process of making use of science and technology in the public sector is too complicated to lend itself to a single policy, program format, or procedure (Congress, House Committee on Science, Space, and Technology, 1976, p. 43). Developing Federal roles that recognize the importance of both "macro" information policies and flexible alternative "micro" procedures for STI transfer at an agency level are essential.

The transfer of Federal STI can be considered from the perspective of the government's provision of STI or the user community's access to that

STI. Both perspectives are important and must be considered in a complex government and organizational environment when attempting to improve the provision of access to Federal STI. But, overall, both Federal STI transfer mechanisms and the information gathering/management behaviors of users of STI require change if Federal STI transfer is to be improved.

From the point of view of R&D firms and librarians, access to much of the Federal STI is inhibited by a broad range of potential barriers. Some of these barriers may be within the firm itself, while others may be related to the skills of the individual R&D user, the manner in which the Federal information transfer system operates, and the policies that affect the provision of and access to Federal STI.

Government policy makers must recognize the importance of developing a coherent STI policy system and work to eliminate the existing ambiguous and, at times, contradictory patchwork of U.S. STI policy statements. Such policies increase the R&D community's reliance on its own services to gain access to Federal STI. But, unfortunately, the STI gathering/management skills in many organizations are inadequate. Development of a comprehensive Federal STI policy system is essential if the United States is to increase its competitiveness and maintain a position of world leadership in science and technology.

THE NEED FOR ACTION

The longer that the development and enforcement of Federal information policy drifts or is dominated by stakeholders preoccupied with efficiency in government, the more difficult it will be to modify or abandon existing practices and policies. Myriad issues and problems plague the distribution and dissemination of "print" publications, and public access to the rich information resources available from government. Instead of solving these problems and ensuring an effective "safety net" for the provision of government information to the public, attention is now focusing on information in an electronic form and developing a patchwork of information resources management, bibliographic control, public access, etc. If the government and the public are to gain effective control over information policy, now is the time for action.

There is a genuine and present threat that the public's right to know, and its right to gain access to a broad range of government information sources, might be severely restricted given the present application of Federal information resources management (see next chapter). Currently, there is a:

- Lack of government-wide information policies that guarantee both equal opportunity and equal access to government information by the citizens of the United States

- Need to ensure an active government information dissemination stance.

Bipartisan leadership is required to address issues such as those identified in this chapter. An overhaul of Federal information policies is desperately needed, and the existing structure of piecemeal, decentralized, and uncoordinated guidelines and procedures should not continue to serve as a framework for national policy.

Broad segments of the American public cannot afford to be "information poor" as they enter the information age. But in the absence of government-wide information policies, and with increased demands for greater cost containment in government programs and services, there may be an erosion in the extent to which the public can gain access to government information, in an effective and efficient manner. Such an erosion could have a negative impact on the public's right to know and gain access to government information.

Government officials, private sector business people, individual citizens, librarians, and other stakeholders must recognize the importance of ensuring broadly based and effective access to government information. The public's interest will be better served and its right to government information preserved and enhanced by the development and implementation of Federal information policies that have, as their primary objective, a user perspective guaranteeing effective access to, and dissemination of, government information. These policies should not rely largely on "market forces" and an agency by agency approach to policy formulation.

Indeed, it is essential that librarians and other information professionals increase their awareness of Federal information policy issues. They must understand the impact and importance of the information policy system as it affects their particular situation and the degree to which they can effectively gain access to government information. Direct involvement in the policy making process will be the primary means by which information professionals can affect this policy system.

3

Impact of Federal Information Policies on Public Access to Government Information

To many people, United States government publications are synonymous with a general pamphlet describing a particular government program, service, or benefit; an investigative report (e.g., the 1987 *Report of the President's Special Review Board* commonly called the "Tower report"); or a report that endorses a particular viewpoint (e.g., the administration's view of arms control or the potential threat from another country). Indeed, the public, as well as the press, may criticize the expenditure of taxpayers' dollars for the publication of such pamphlets and reports. However, they may be unaware of the existence of other document types, the relationship of these publications to the more traditional serial and monograph, and policy decisions that affect the types of government information that is produced.

In fact, students enrolled in documents classes at library schools are often amazed at the number and quality of government information resources. They may remark that they only wish that they had known about the information content of government publications earlier in their college education. By the conclusion of the course, they have a perspective different from that of the average person and the typical library school graduate. They understand the impact of policy decisions on public access to government information and better recognize the value of government publications in meeting a diverse range of information needs.

If anything, government publications are becoming a more specialized resource, most likely consulted by members of the academic community, government officials, and persons employed by businesses and organizations doing consulting and research for government agencies. Many other people will settle for information more readily acquired and more popularly written.

Perhaps many government publications, other than the general information pamphlet, require a more sophisticated reading comprehension than the average person possesses. Further, government publications are often not as well-packaged as other information resources; they may reflect a narrow range of printing techniques and frequently are less appealing to read.

In sharp contrast to the private sector, the Federal government has frequently been restrictive in its selection and use of typeface styles to convey its messages to the public. This is part of the reason why government publications sometimes remain visually dull and uninteresting. Greater reliance on microfiche distribution argues against experimentation with, and adoption of, a wider range of typefaces. Further, the use of additional typefaces might increase production costs, a factor that mitigates against change. Too often, the government only functions as an advertiser when it produces flashy, eye-catching posters and publications.

When people decide to consult government publications, they may not fully understand how to gain access to them. Libraries do not comprise a primary institutional provider that the average person consults to resolve information needs (Chen and Hernon, 1982). Instead, this individual may consult Federal agencies or a GPO bookstore; she/he may even assume that one of these bookstores includes, or has access to, all government publications, that the bookstore staff answers reference questions, and that the holdings of the bookstores comprise more a reference library than a sales collection. As is evident, numerous misunderstandings can arise about government publications and Federal information policy.

Against this background, this chapter overviews public access and government publications in terms of the policy set by the Reagan administration and Congress. Concerned about waste in government, cost-effectiveness, and improved management over resources, both the executive and legislative branches of government are monitoring publishing programs and seeking to identify and eliminate needless and duplicative publishing. They are also attempting to more sharply define and limit the role of the government as a printer and disseminator. After analyzing administrative policy and its implications, the discussion of national information policy sets the stage for a consideration of alternatives to the depository library program as it is currently structured (see Chapter 17).

PUBLIC ACCESS

Overview

The theme of this book revolves around public access, which can be defined as any legitimate method that the public uses to examine, reproduce, or otherwise gain access to government information. Information can be made available to the public in different ways and for different reasons. Further, the government produces information that is not always intended for public use; in some cases, the public may have to take action to attempt to secure the release of such information. As shown in this chapter (and in other writings), four types of challenges threaten public access. These are the government's view of information resources management, fiscal constraints, impact of technologies, and national security restrictions. Under the Reagan administration, there has been a vast reduction of the regulatory functions of the government. Government is, either as a matter of economic policy or political ideology, shrinking in regard to its regulatory activities. In addition, functions once performed by the government have been turned over to private enterprise.

Some policies and practices of the Reagan administration may be contrary to maintaining an informed electorate, and may impede the public in conducting private business. The public is placed at a disadvantage in attempting to evaluate the costs and benefits of information policies and hold the administration accountable (Karp, 1985, p. 61). The administration appears to favor access to information on demand or upon request, but the public must know what is available before they can request it. In addition, they may have to pay for access to timely information. Access "on demand" is not the same as the regular dissemination of government information.

Currently, the government is questioning its responsibility to provide information to the public free of charge. Horton (1987, p. 81) postulates that:

> charging for the distribution of information raises the consciousness and aware-
> ness of users about the real value of the information and gives providers a
> better basis for making rational information pricing decisions. More precise
> knowledge about the cost of information might enable government providers
> to be more accountable to their superiors for benefits—cost determinations.

Horton and others view benefit within a narrow context—a subset of cost.

In some major instances, the government has attempted to control or decide who will have access to information either that it holds or that resides in private databases that have national security implications. For example, in 1982 and 1985, approximately 17% of the papers prepared by Photo-Optical Instrumentation Engineers for presentation at the society's conference had to be withdrawn because the Department of Defense maintained that the papers contained scientific and technical information restricted under the export control laws. Some scientific associations have barred individuals who are not U.S. citizens from attendance at their conferences because they suspect that, unless they did this, the Department of Defense might censor the papers. At the same time, agents of the FBI and National Security Agency have visited libraries and attempted to monitor library use by foreign nationals ("FBI Visits to Libraries," 1987, p. 4).

The 1984 Omnibus Defense Authorization Act allows the Secretary of Defense to withhold, from public disclosure, certain types of technical data having military or space application that could not be released to a foreigner without that person having obtained an export license. This provision eliminated a loophole that had allowed anyone who filed a request under the Freedom of Information Act to obtain such information. Karp (1985, p. 64) maintains that the provision infringes on the American public's right to know; a less informed public might lack the basis to challenge effectively administration policy and to hold the government accountable.

Neither the Reagan administration nor members of Congress single out publishing and information activities for scrutiny and management. Rather, they view these activities in the context of a political, economic, and social philosophy that covers the relationship between the Federal government and state and local governments, and government's role in society and the economy. This chapter examines the actions resulting from that philosophy.

The budget reduction efforts of the Reagan administration and Congress have had a profound impact on agencies and their provision of information to the public. The General Services Administration (GSA), for example, operates a series of Federal Information Centers (FICs), which place the public in contact with the appropriate Federal agency and answer general information queries. In 1982, the GSA reviewed the program with the intent of making it more efficient and reducing operating costs. As a result, FIC services were consolidated into twenty centers serving extended geographic areas via toll-free telephone systems. In locations where "the cost-customer-use ratio is insupportably high," toll-free service was discontinued. The GSA claims that "in no case where a toll-free line has been discontinued, does the cost for a three-minute commercial phone call exceed one dollar" (Knenlein, 1983).[1]

Cost reduction has also resulted in the curtailment of budgets and the number of staff for many public affairs, consumer affairs, inter-governmental affairs, and congressional affairs offices. The government is also letting more contracts with other providers in the information sector for the production and dissemination of information. Federal agencies are initiating or increasing user fees for access to government information, reducing the amount of information collected and published, releasing more information in machine-readable files and microform, attempting to have more information withheld from public scrutiny, privatizing information, and having the private sector "kick back" services/products with costs added on.

---

[1] Clearly, research should present unobtrusive test questions to Federal Information Centers. Such investigations should examine both the rate of accuracy as well as the amount of time that it takes to provide the service. The one dollar estimation is probably an exceedingly low estimate.

Katherine K. Wallman, executive director of the Council of Professional Associations on Federal Statistics, observed that (Randolph, 1987, p. 13):

> Tight funding levels for statistical programs in recent years have required agencies to alter the scope of ongoing activities by collecting information less frequently; reducing sample sizes, the content, and/or the geographic coverage of particular surveys; extending the time between data collection and publication; and eliminating or reducing the frequency, scope, and distribution of publications and other products. Moreover, the statistical agencies have found it increasingly difficult to introduce methodological and technological changes needed to keep ongoing programs current, to perform the research necessary to improve the nation's statistical sources, and to attract and retain high caliber staff.

State and local government officials, researchers, and the public find that Federal cuts have substantially reduced Federal services, such as the collection and reporting of statistical data. As Robinson and Stone (1987, p. 446) maintain,

> given the importance of Federal statistical services, further reductions in these services are likely to have a dramatic effect on the ability of state agencies to provide information useful for making a variety of decisions by state and area government[s] and business leaders.

Massive Federal cuts "substantially penalize state agencies as Federal agencies preserve national statistics immediately related to the agency mission and delete statistical services at the subnational level, especially those at the state level" (Ibid., p. 447). States wanting certain statistics, therefore, will have to subsidize data collection, analysis, and presentation.

In March 1986, the Joint Committee on Printing (JCP) announced that because of the 4.3% cut that the Gramm-Rudman-Hollings Act (P.L. 99–177, 1985) mandated for congressional printing and binding, the public would have to purchase congressional documents and could not receive them free from the House and Senate Documents Rooms. As a result of the public outcry, the JCP amended its policy. As of that June, members of the public may obtain one free copy of a congressional report or bill; additional copies may be purchased. Congressional committee hearings and prints are still free, although the number of copies printed for free distribution has been sharply reduced.

As noted by Fry (1978, p. 88), the scope and importance of publishing activities by the private sector underscores the fact that "governments at all levels have concentrated on the printing and distribution of documents with insufficient attention given to facilitating public access to their contents." Only in June 1982, did the GPO establish a marketing department and staff it with professionals. With the *Monthly Catalog of United States Government Publications*, the GPO concentrates on access to titles, not information content. Further, the titles marketed through the sales program typically appeal to general or selected audiences, and do not comprise the committee prints and hearings, research studies, or unique publications needed by special audiences.

GPO Sales Program

Publications may enter sales programs operated by official clearinghouses/distributors/disseminators. For example, the Superintendent of Documents (Sudocs), a part of the GPO, monitors printing requests issued to the GPO by the publishing agencies and selects those titles having sales potential for inclusion in the sales program.[2] Currently, the Sudocs sells print publications (paper copy and selected microfiche) and some electronic information on either an individual or subscription basis.

Sudocs has both a general and a special sales program. The general one is self-sustaining and pricing is based upon the "cost as determined by the Public Printer plus 50 percent" (44 *United States Code* 1708); revenues, therefore, are to exceed costs. The special program is subsidized and the Public Printer does not control prices; either external constraints or provisions specified in the *United States Code (USC)* dictate pricing policy.[3] The cost of the *Congressional Record* and the *Federal Register*, for example, has increased dramatically in recent years; however, the GPO does not set pricing policy for these titles. Clearly, the government is attempting to recoup more of the costs and to reduce the extent to which a title is subsidized.

In addition, the GPO has a consigned agent sales program. More than 60 consigned agents in other government agencies sell certain publications on behalf of the GPO. Pricing of publications through consigned agents may have some variability; their price may be higher than the GPO itself would charge. It merits mention that the GPO's sales program must be self-supporting at the title level, while the National Technical Information Service (NTIS) is self-supporting at the program level.

---

[2] Approximately 8% of what the GPO prints enters the sales program.

[3] The total annual budget of the GPO is more than $800 million. Congress appropriates very little of this amount. Under 44 USC 309, the GPO operates under a revolving fund. Expenses related to printing, binding operations, and the Superintendent of Documents sales operations are paid out of this revolving fund. The revolving fund is reimbursed with payment that customer agencies make for printing and binding or other services that the GPO provides or the receipts from the sales program. GPO's "Annual Corporations Bill" contains the authorization to use the revolving fund. In addition to the revolving fund, the GPO maintains programs that are directly funded by appropriations. For these programs the GPO has to go through the entire budget justification process. For a more complete discussion of funding see "Transcript of Depository Library Council Meeting" (1986).

Danford L. Sawyer, Jr., the Reagan administration's first Public Printer, believed that the GPO was inefficient and faced escalating costs and financial loss within the Office of Sudocs. He, therefore, created a marketing department, launched a high profile marketing program, issued a catalog of sales publications, raised the prices of sales publications, and sold a number of back titles as waste paper.

In 1982, he directed the Documents Pricing Task Force, comprised of agency officials, to develop a new pricing formula and to make recommendations "which would make government publications available to the public by the most efficient and least costly means possible under existing law." He also directed the Sudocs to reduce the number of titles in the sales program. The criterion for inclusion of a title in the sales program became its sales potential—"cut out the losers and accentuate the winners."

Since Sawyer's departure as Public Printer in 1983, the policy that a title must have a sales potential of at least $1,000 has been relaxed. The GPO works with Federal agencies to obtain copies of those publications that the agencies believe should be in the sales program but may not have significant sales potential. Since 1978, the sales program is required to be self-sustaining; the *Congressional Record*, certain publications from the Office of the Federal Register (e.g., the *Federal Register*), and publications for which an agency acts as a consigned agent comprise the exceptions to the self-sustaining mandate. It might be noted that for fiscal years 1979 through 1981, the sales program lost $20,000. This loss technically constitutes a violation of title 44, *United States Code*. Obviously, the Superintendent of Documents closely monitors the sales program so as not to have another loss.

The Documents Pricing Task Force completed its review and offered specific recommendations that were adopted in the fall of 1983. In essence, the pricing policy had taken averages of total anticipated sales volumes and total anticipated program costs and applied a proportion of these costs to publication and subscription services. A problem with this approach was that smaller publications were not priced commensurate with size. This practice created the perception among publishers and consumers that the prices of the smaller than average publications were too high. The Documents Pricing Task Force specifically addressed this issue by recommending that the GPO establish "a separate mechanism for selling small publications at a price commensurate with their size." To implement this recommendation, the GPO revised its pricing formula to incorporate a graduated handling scale based on the number of pages. The GPO also moved approximately 60 publications of consumer interest to the low priced publication program at the Consumer Information Center in Pueblo, Colorado.

Though it represented a substantial improvement, the graduated scale did not completely resolve the problem of perceived value because it did not fully consider trim size differences among publications with the same number of pages. Therefore, in 1985, Sudocs began pricing publications with standardized scales incorporating handling charges calculated on the basis of square inch per page. These scales attempt to keep a publication's price in line with the size of the publication. On March 26, 1986, Donald E. Fossedal, as Superintendent of Documents, applied similar broad scale charges to subscription pricing, with the affect that sales prices for less frequently issued periodicals were reduced. In fact, he has maintained that 80% of the serial prices are coming down in price.

As a result of these actions and application of a series of cost-control measures, the prices for a number of publications in the sales inventory decreased (or at least reversed the trend toward price escalation). In summary, it is important to remember that:

- Title 44 (USC) requires the GPO to apply the cost-plus 50% formula uniformly in assigning prices
- The General Accounting Office and the Documents Pricing Task Force requested that the GPO improve the allocation of its costs in developing prices. Apparently, the Sudocs has developed formulae based on actual operating data that more accurately assign costs to individual titles
- Smaller publications now carry lower prices and larger publications have higher prices.

The Office of Sudocs maintains that the cost of sales publications is still less than what the private sector charges for its publications. Such arguments, however, ignore the function of the government to communicate with those governed and provide a mechanism to hold official policies, practices, services, and actions accountable.

Many of the writings in the published literature such as "Less Access to Less Information by and about the U.S. Government" (American Library Association, 1988), a series of *fact sheets* distributed by the Washington Office of the American Library Association, condemn Sudocs's pricing policies. Yet such writings fail to differentiate between the general and subsidized sales programs and to address the above mentioned modification in pricing policy. Research studies need to investigate Sudocs's pricing policy and determine the *reasonableness* of the policy within two frameworks—one for cost-benefit and the other for the existing legal structure under which pricing policies are set.

On June 17, 1987, the Joint Committee on Printing (JCP) directed the GPO to sell publications that it has available in electronic format. The GPO therefore sells magnetic tapes that require special processing or cumulation, and regular tapes that do not require any special processing. Some of the titles offered include *Public Bills, Resolutions, and Amendments* ($18,750 per year); the *Congressional Record* ($29,300 per year); the *Federal Register* ($37,500 per year); and the *FCC Record* ($2,480 per year). In addition, the GPO sells tapes for the *Code of Federal Regulations*, the *U.S. Government Manual*, the *Official Congressional Directory*, *Statistical Abstract of the United States*, *Compilation of Presidential Documents*, and *the Monthly Catalog*.

Beginning in 1984, both the JCP and the GPO explored the possibility of initiating a series of pilot projects to test the feasibility of depository distribution and servicing of government information in electronic format. On April 9, 1987, the JCP passed a resolution urging the GPO to take appropriate steps to implement the pilot studies. The Public Printer responded to the JCP's request by asking the appropriations committees of Congress for $800,000 to establish a pilot project office and to begin the testing. The appropriations committees denied the funding for fiscal year 1988.

In a letter to the JCP chairman, Frank Annunzio, dated December 10, 1987, the Public Printer announced that he intended to enlist the cooperation of nongovernment information service providers to deliver online information services to selected depository libraries, at little or not cost to the government. Instead of requesting $800,000 from Congress, the Public Printer expressed his willingness "to use existing resources to comply with the JCP's desire to test electronic formats in depository libraries" ("GPO Gives Testing Electronic Formats to Private Sector," 1988). The GPO would supply an

> information service provider with government publication data tapes, at no charge, for loading onto its computers. The information would be retrievable online from terminals in a test group of depository libraries, where information searches would be conducted for citizens without charge" (Ibid.).

As a first step in setting up the test, the GPO proposed a presolicitation conference of nongovernment information service providers to discuss the issues involved (see *Commerce Business Daily*, December 22, 1987). However, in January 1988, the JCP, believing that a presolicitation conference was inappropriate at that time, postponed it indefinitely.

Nonetheless, the JCP asked the Superintendent of Documents "to develop a plan for electronic dissemination projects that would be 'appropriate within existing funds'." Staff from the GPO and JCP reviewed different projects and are now considering the dissemination of "Census data files not available in printed format, an EPA database scheduled for release . . . [in 1989], *Commerce Business Daily*, a gateway for access to DOE databases, and the bound *Congressional Record*" ("Information Technology Program Update," 1988, p. 13). On February 3, 1988, the GPO submitted a preliminary plan relating to these possible projects to the JCP and is "awaiting further guidance from [the] JCP before proceeding with development of the plan" (Ibid., p. 14).

Clearly, the JCP and the GPO acknowledge that depository libraries can play a role in the disseminator of electronic government information. The GPO has established a new Electronic Publishing Section that will meet (Ibid., p. 14):

> with other Federal agencies to discuss their needs for electronic publishing services. One of their top priorities is to explore the demand for CD-ROM services in the Federal Government and [the] role that [the] GPO could play in meeting those needs. This could someday pave the way for [the] GPO to "ride" agencies' requisitions for CD-ROM products, much like the way we order printed publications now.

The GPO is acting as if title 44 permits such distribution and is exploring alternative strategies to permit depository distribution of electronic information. Any plan for the deposit and servicing of electronic information requires extensive analysis and the incorporation of the views and concerns of various stakeholders in the information sector. Both the Association of Research Libraries and the Government Documents Round Table are engaged in such planning (See Chapters 7 and 16). However, neither the GPO nor the JCP are participating in program-wide planning that involves different types of depository libraries.

REAGAN ADMINISTRATION'S POLICY ON GOVERNMENT PUBLICATIONS

The extent and cost of government publishing programs, as well as the amount of duplicate and needless publications that are produced, are matters of concern to both the executive and legislative branches of government. The Executive Branch places its oversight function in the Office of Management and Budget (OMB), an agency concerned with cost considerations and perceived as less interested in public access to government information. Congress is also adopting fiscal constraints by re-examining programs, reducing budgets, and trying to control unnecessary publication.

The Paperwork Reduction Act of 1980 (Public Law 96–511), which became effective on April 1, 1981, directed the OMB to develop Federal information policies and standards. Further, the Act specified that OMB would reduce the information collection and record keeping requirements that the Federal government imposes on the private sector. The Act also included provisions for the management of information resources and the auditing of all major government information systems; each agency was required to designate a senior official charged with information management to report directly to the agency head. As a consequence, OMB (and the administration) views government information as a commodity—an economic resource that should be managed; the costs to both the public and government must be scrutinized and compared.

On April 20, 1981, President Ronald Reagan imposed a moratorium on the issuance of new periodicals, pamphlets, and audiovisual products, in the belief that the government spent too much on "public relations, publicity and advertising" and that "much of this waste consists of unnecessary and expensive films, magazines, and pamphlets." Issued the next day, OMB Bulletin No. 81–16 expanded upon the President's statement and directed the Executive Branch to "conduct a comprehensive review of all existing periodicals, pamphlets, and audiovisual products and those planned for fiscal years 1981 and 1982." Agencies were to identify and eliminate duplicative and wasteful resources.

In June, OMB issued a model plan for agencies to use in the development of new and improved control systems to implement the policies and guidelines specified in Bulletin No. 81–16. The same month, OMB released Bulletin 81–21, which required each agency to submit a plan for reviewing its information activities by September 1 of that year and to designate a single official who would be responsible for information resources management. OMB Bulletin No. 81–23, dated July 24, 1981, offered instructions for the reduction or elimination of recurring Executive Branch reports to Congress. As a result, the number of such reports entering the Serial Set has diminished.

In a related directive, Memorandum 81–14 of September 11, 1981, OMB directed Federal agencies to re-evaluate their information centers (e.g., clearinghouses, information analysis centers, and resource centers) to ensure that no unnecessary overlap existed, that these centers did not duplicate information services available from the private sector, or that the cost of the information services was not so low-priced that the government engaged in unfair competition with other stakeholders and impeded their ability to develop similar services.

On October 9, 1982, OMB issued Bulletin 81–16, Supplement No. 1, which furnished "additional procedures and guidelines for eliminating unnecessary Federal spending on the development, printing, and distribution of periodicals and recurring pamphlets." Agencies were directed to further scrutinize their publishing programs and to submit to OMB a list of periodicals and recurring pamphlets proposed for continuation after March 31, 1982. OMB "strongly discouraged" the initiation of any new publication.

The popular press, on the whole, supported efforts to control needless publication and reduce the Federal budget, but has discovered instances where agencies have discontinued valuable publications—some of which challenge administration policies and philosophical beliefs. For example, the *New York Times* reported that over nine hundred periodicals and recurring pamphlets had been discontinued; some of these were "dated, irrelevant or redundant," while others provided useful information ("Over 900 Federal Publications Halted," 1981).

During this time, in an effort to recover costs, Federal agencies increased the costs of a number of existing publications, curtailed free distribution, and cooperated in the production and distribution of individual titles. They cut back on consumer guides and envisioned a larger role for the private sector in the republishing of these titles for mass consumption. They also relied more heavily on microfiche distribution. Further, Federal agencies, such as the Bureau of the Census and the Bureau of Labor Statistics, curtailed their data collection and tabulation activities because OMB wanted to curtail expenditures and because the administration wanted to show the private sector that less red tape was being imposed on it.

The efforts to improve on the management of government information while reducing costs became known as "Reform 88." On October 8, 1982, OMB issued "Review of Federal Publications— Reform 88," which summarized the findings of its review of Federal periodicals and pamphlets. This report noted that 16% of all government periodicals and pamphlets identified would be discontinued or consolidated, that some agencies were not doing enough to eliminate unnecessary and low priority publications, that the costs of many publications (one out of every three government publications) could be reduced, and that agencies should continue their review of periodicals, in part to determine if higher user fees could be levied. According to the report, activities resulting in the elimination, consolidation, and cost reduction (e.g., lowering the production cost by reducing the number of copies printed and the frequency of issuance, or switching to publication in a microformat) of periodicals have saved the agencies some $20 million.

Federal agencies, it was reported, had identified over 12,000 periodicals and pamphlets in their inventories; the departments of Agriculture, Defense, Health and Human Services (HHS), and Treasury accounted for approximately three-fifths of the cost of all publications identified (Office of Management and Budget, 1983, p. 3):

> The average cost to produce each title is more than $11,000 and ranges from less than $3,400 in Interior to more than $22,000 in HHS. The per-copy cost varies among agencies from about 10 cents to about 50 cents per copy.

Although lifting the publication ban, OMB pledged to continue its monitoring of costs and content. Agencies still had to review their present inventory of government publications and to reduce it whenever possible. A list of titles slated for elimination and consolidation would be forwarded to the private sector so that publishers could decide which, if any, publishing activities they might want to assume.

A factor complicating the review process has been the definition of the term "periodical." As noted in the report, the definition contained in the *United States Code* is "complex and indefinite. Some agencies may have interpreted this definition so as to exclude most of their periodicals" from the scrutiny of OMB (Ibid., p. 6). Consequently OMB continued to monitor agency publishing programs and to look for periodicals subject to its directives. The purpose was to eliminate those not essential to the mandate of a particular agency.

OMB Circular A-114 was revised to govern the management of Federal audiovisual activities. According to OMB, between 1981 and 1985, some 3,848 publications were eliminated or consolidated—amounting to 150 million individual publications or about 25% of the total Federal inventory (*Management of the United States Government: Fiscal Year 1986*, 1985).

According to Joseph R. Wright, Jr., Deputy Director of OMB, the cutback in the size of agency publishing programs "will not affect needed and necessary printed materials that should be available to the public." He further opined that "use, not abuse, is the key phrase of the program [Reform 88] as we evaluate the importance and use of each publication" (Office of Management and Budget, 1983). The criteria related to "use," however, were not defined; the net effect of the budget cutting cycle was to reduce the size of publishing programs and to make government publications (and by extension, government information) less accessible and more expensive to the information-gathering public. The initiation of user and service fees, as well as publication in a microform, reinforce the image of government publications as comprising either a highly specialized information resource, one that should not be used except under special circumstances, or as a very general resource, one fulfilling a propaganda function.

For each title produced, agencies had to provide specific information to OMB on factors such as cost, volume, frequency of issuance, and revenue, if any, generated from subscription, mail order, and bookstore sales. The compilation of this information was difficult and time-consuming, since much of the information had not been previously collected or was not readily available in agency files. Upon completing this inventory, each agency reviewed its publications and made further eliminations, consolidations, and reductions. The agency then submitted a second inventory to OMB. The information collected from each agency was transferred to a computer file, reproduced in a printed format, and returned to the agency for verification and the correction of errors or omissions. The process was slow and complicated.

Under pressure to limit the number of titles published, government agencies sought alternative ways to distribute information—ways that might require minimal expenditures of human and monetary resources. For example, the Internal Revenue Service prepared taped messages on particular subjects and made these available to anyone willing to place a telephone call. Anyone outside the local area might have to assume the cost of the call, especially in those cases where toll-free numbers were unavailable. Yet agencies often do not effectively disseminate information about these services and the telephone number (these numbers may periodically change as well). An additional problem might be that if agencies do not revise their messages on a regular basis, callers might not receive the most up-to-date information.

In November 1984, OMB issued Bulletin No. 84–17, Supplement No. 1, which identifies the reduction targets necessary for Federal agencies to achieve the savings specified in the Deficit Reduction Act of the same year. Each agency covered by the supplement had a pro-rata reduction target of 25.6% for publishing, printing, reproduction, and audiovisual activities.

On May 2, 1985, OMB issued a revised Circular A-3, "Government Publications," and Bulletin No. 85–14, "Annual Report on Government Publications." These regulations expanded the authority of OMB under 44 *United ed States Code* 1108, which stipulates that OMB must approve the use of agency funds for the printing of periodicals. The circular instituted an annual review of Federal periodicals (defined as "any publication issued by a Federal agency annually or more often with a format, content, and purpose consistent in nature") and established guidelines and procedures for a coordinated and uniform method of agency reporting and OMB approval. As part of the detailed annual review (Bulletin 85–14), agencies must:

- List all current and proposed periodicals
- Identify actual and projected spending for both periodicals and nonrecurring (issued on a one-edition basis) publications
- Indicate the amount collected through the GPO sales program
- Justify the need for any new periodicals—either the "specific statutory authorization for its publication" or why the periodical "is necessary" in transcribing the public business that the agency is required by law to undertake
- Prepare and disseminate publications in the most cost-effective manner
- "Certify that the reported periodicals are necessary in the transaction of the public business required by law . . . and that mailing lists have been updated."

Within 45 days, OMB was to approve or disapprove each agency's annual report or any supplementary request for a publication.

During the fall of 1985, the JCP issued a memorandum to agency heads, similar to OMB's Bulletin 85–14, demanding that agencies prepare an annual report on government publications and submit it to the JCP. Although this report represents a duplication of effort, it illustrates that the JCP is attempting to regain its position as a primary stakeholder in Federal information policy. The Executive Branch seems to regard it as a secondary stakeholder.

On March 15, 1985, OMB published a draft circular, the purpose of which was to set a general framework for the management of Federal information resources. On December 12, 1985, OMB issued the actual circular (No. A-130) that provides the general policy framework for the management of Federal information resources (see Hernon and McClure, 1987a). The circular "seems to indicate that information is not a free good, and users shall be generally charged for government information, except where citizens may be financially or otherwise disadvantaged" (Horton, 1987, p. 81).

On June 8, 1987, OMB issued Bulletin 87–14, "Reporting and Inventory of Government Information Dissemination Products and Services." Agencies were reminded that:

> To achieve adequate management of the information dissemination function, . . . [they] need to maintain inventories of all their information products and services, to subject these products and services to systematic management controls, and to develop and implement internal policies and procedures for management of the products and services (p. 1).

The Bulletin applied to periodicals and non-recurring publications (defined in Circular No. A-3) and "machine-readable data files, software files, online database services, and electronic bulletin boards, issued or *disseminated by agencies to the general public*" (p. 2).

On August 7, 1987, OMB solicited public comment in the development of policy guidance concerning the electronic collection of information (see *Federal Register*, August 7, pp. 29454–29457). The proposed policy requires Federal agencies to certify that they have considered use of electronic information collection techniques as a means to reduce the burden on respondents and costs to the government. The purpose of the policy guidance is to force agencies to address systematically potential management efficiencies derivable from electronic information collection and to ensure that agencies consider the major legal and policy issues that arise in connection with the information collection. The revised policy will be issued as a supplement to Circular A-130. Therefore, A-130 will have broad policy significance and apply to both print and nonprint information resources. Clearly, under the guise of information resources management, OMB is attempting to manage the life cycle of government information products.

Figure 3-1.
Selected OMB Pronouncements Affecting Access to Government Information

DATE	PRONOUNCEMENT	TOPIC COVERED
1981	Bulletin No. 81-16	Directed the Executive Branch to review periodicals, pamphlets, and audiovisual products
1981	Bulletin No. 81-21	Agencies must submit a plan for reviewing their information activities and designate an official to be responsible for information resources management
1981	Bulletin No. 81-23	Ordered the reduction of recurring Executive Branch reports to Congress
1981	Memorandum 81-14	Ordered the re-evaluation of information centers
1982	Bulletin No. 81-16, Supplement No. 1	Supplied additional procedures for eliminating unnecessary spending on periodicals and pamphlets
1982	Reform 88	The name of the process for bringing government publications under more effective and efficient control
1983	Revised Circular A-76	Covered the performance of commercial activities by Federal agencies
1984	Circular A-114	Covered the management of Federal audiovisual activities
1984	Bulletin No. 84-17, Supplement No. 1	Identifed the reduction targets that Federal agencies must achieve
1985	Draft Circular	Covered the establishment of a general framework for the management of Federal information resources
1985	Circular A-3	Covered government publications
1985	Bulletin No. 85-14	Instituted an annual review of Federal periodicals and established guidelines and procedures for a coordinated and uniform method of agency reporting and OMB approval
1985	Circular A-130	Provided the general policy framework for the management of Federal information resources
1987	Bulletin 87-14	Linked the reporting and inventory of government information dissemination products and services to management and exerted "management controls over information products and services"

OMB is making information policy decisions based on the criterion of cost-effectiveness, as authorized in the Paperwork Reduction Act. Further, its policy directives have far-reaching implications (see Sprehe, 1984). Figure 3–1 summarizes the OMB policy directives discussed in this chapter. These directives instruct agencies to confine their dissemination activities to that information necessary for the transaction of public business as covered in existing statutory law.

The initial identification of needless and duplicative audiovisual resources, periodicals, and pamphlets has resulted in the demise of some key sources, and restrictions on the collection and tabulation of data, and the dissemination of information to the public. The amount of publishing still performed by the government masks this situation.

Information Resources Management

The Commission on Federal Paperwork was created in 1974 to investigate Federal statutory and administrative law, policies, and practices related to the collection, processing, and dissemination of government information, and to the management of information activities. One of the Commission's reports advanced the concept of "information resources management" and observed that "for data and information resources, no central, cohesive body of doctrine exists today; there is not even good information, advice or guidance to offer top management" (Commission on Federal Paperwork, 1977, p. 13).

Section 3504 of the Paperwork Reduction Act gives the director of OMB certain "authority and functions" related to the management of information resources. Through Circular A-130 and other guidelines or directives, OMB equates information resources management with reducing the volume of paperwork that Federal agencies create and collect, while, at the same time, enhancing the efficiency of those information resources under Federal control. More precisely, Federal information resources management is based on the following five principles (Reeder, 1986, p. 11):

- "Information is an economic resource . . . with value and a cost of production, and . . . must be managed like other scarce resources"
- Information has a life cycle, with each phase of that cycle affecting other segments
- For reasons of "economics and efficiencies" agencies should use technology to process information
- "The size and diversity of Federal operations mean that accountability for and management of information resources must be decentralized"
- The role of central management is to develop, implement, and continue a central policy framework under which agencies can function
- Information management presents "special responsibilities with respect to confidentiality, privacy, preservation of historic records, and public access.

OMB creates the impression that the first three principles are the most important.

The Office of Personnel Management is also supporting information resources management and attempting to privatize as many government functions as possible. It has attempted to reclassify and downgrade Federal librarians (see Hernon and McClure, 1987a, p. 126). Government officials in managerial positions are being urged to streamline, make their organization "much smaller and smarter," and focus "on quality in terms of service, work product, and people." They should "think about how to manage change" ("Managing Budget Cutbacks," 1987, p. 4). They are also expected to seek "cheaper ways of doing things, more efficient ways of doing things" (Ibid., p. 5). Clearly, the emphasis is on cost containment and increased productivity. As a result, greater attention within government is focusing on technology and its ability to enhance information resources management.

Privatization is also related to information resources management. OMB encourages agencies to review their programs and services, and determine which of these the private sector might legitimately assume. Clearly, privatization involves complex issues. On September 2, 1987, President Reagan established a Commission on Privatization. According to the President, the Commission would help him "to end unfair government competition and return government programs and assets to the American people" ("Privatization Commission," 1987, p. 7).[4]

FREEDOM OF INFORMATION ACT

In 1966, the Freedom of Information Act (FOIA) was enacted as public law. Amended in 1974 and 1976, it provides for the reconsideration of records withheld in government files. The Act recognizes the public's right to information so that they can be informed about what the government is doing and why. By implication, the government can be held accountable for its actions and policies.[5]

On April 6, 1982, President Reagan issued Executive Order 12356 (see

[4] According to "Privatization Commission," "the bipartisan Commission will study all activities of the Federal Government and report back to me [President Reagan] on which government programs, enterprises, and activities are more appropriately part of the private sector. In addition, the Commission is expected to review scholarly work on privatization and examine the accomplishments of other countries and State and local governments. Based on its findings, the Commission will propose how we can return appropriate Federal activities to the private sector through the sale of government operations and assets, the use of private enterprise to provide services for government agencies, or the use of vouchers to provide services to the public through the private sector. It will recommend legislative and administrative action that can be taken to accomplish privatization initiatives." [The Commission's report was published in spring 1988.]

[5] Hernon and McClure (1987a, Chapter 3) provides a detailed analysis of the Freedom of Information Act and the relationship of that Act to the Privacy Act. No direct amendments to the FOIA have been enacted since 1976, although various laws containing information protection provisions have been legislated during the past several years. In 1984, one of these "back door" amendments to the FOIA concerning the operational files of the Central Intelligence Agency was quite controversial.

Federal Register, pp. 14874–14884), which substantially increased the amount of information classified and withheld from public scrutiny. It increases agency discretion in imposing classification, allows for reclassification of previously released materials, and eliminates automatic declassification arrangements. By increasing the duration of official secrecy, the order lessens public access to agency records under the FOIA.

As a result of the Freedom of Information Reform Act of 1986 (P. L. 99–570), new fee schedules for requesting government records under the FOIA have been developed. These fee schedules, appearing in the March 27, 1987 issue of the *Federal Register* (pp. 10012–10020) may have the effect of further limiting access to government information, due to the limited fee waiver provisions. Thus, the impact of the Reagan administration's rules may be to limit use of the FOIA ("Washington Hotline," 1987).

As is evident, the Reagan administration and Congress are currently redefining and restricting public access to government information. Although depository libraries can potentially select a wide range of titles, these represent only a small portion of the information resources supported and provided by government agencies.

Much of the information generated through the FOIA never enters a depository collection. However, some agencies regard the National Technical Information Service as an outlet for the distribution of FOIA material. Libraries therefore can purchase such material. The sale of this material, however, may be contrary to the FOIA itself.

Depository librarians must recognize that the Act exists and produces information that complements their collections, that it provides access to unpublished information, and that the *Federal Register* and other reference aids alert readers to some of the types of information withheld and the procedures for invoking the Act.[6]

Stories and accounts based on information derived from invoking the FOIA are likely to appear in newspaper and periodical articles, as well as in monographs; most of these writings, however, are indexed in reference works found in the general, rather than the documents, collection. As this example illustrates, there is a complementary relationship between the documents and reference collections.

REVISION OF TITLE 44, *UNITED STATES CODE,* COVERING THE GPO

A discussion of national information policy and public access must take into account title 44 of the *United States Code* and the requirements it specifies. One problem is definitional; what constitutes a government publication? The

---

[6] *A Citizen's Guide on Using the Freedom of Information Act and the Privacy Act of 1974 to Request Government Records* (1987) is a useful guide that explains how to invoke the FOIA.

definition contained in the *Code* is general and does not adequately reflect the impact of technology upon government publishing, the various formats in which information appears, and the methods that agencies use to distribute their documents. Taking all of these factors into account produces a definition reflecting a "bewildering maze of terms and exemptions" (Morehead, 1983, p. 26). Further, definitions change over time as a consequence of technological, political, and social factors. For libraries, a definition has implications for bibliographic control, classification, collection development, depository distribution, and reference and referral service.

Ironically, documents librarians prefer an expansive definition exempting as little as possible, while the government generally favors a more restrictive definition. An important question becomes, "Would documents librarians select more information resources if they had an opportunity?" Existing research suggests an answer of "no" (Hernon and Purcell, 1982; Hernon, McClure, and Purcell, 1985).

Much of title 44 that pertains to the GPO is based on dated legislation, in particular the 1895 Printing Act. This fact was underscored in the late 1970s when the JCP began to re-examine parts of the title for possible revision. The JCP established the Ad Hoc Advisory Committee on Revision of Title 44, to identify the major issues and policy questions involved in revision. In 1979, H.R. 4572, which provided for improved administration of public printing services and the distribution of government publications, and the companion Senate bill (1436) were introduced into Congress. The legislation proposed a reorganization of the GPO into an independent agency governed by a board of directors, with the Public Printer and the Superintendent of Documents elevated to equal status. The bills also recommended the abolition of the JCP.

Before the mark-up of both bills, an amended bill (H.R. 5424) was introduced. This new bill expanded the GPO into an independent agency, changed the titles of the Superintendent of Documents and the Public Printer, and requested additional support for depository libraries. The exact framework proposed for the depository library program was vague and subject to interpretation, apparently because the framers did not have a specific plan or organization in mind and because they wanted a general bill so that they could legislate later by regulation. The legislation also recommended the abolition of regional depositories and assumed that a comprehensive index to government publications was both desirable and possible. Other weaknesses to the legislation included the hurried nature in which it was written, its drafting by a few, and the focus on detail rather than on the broad structure presented and the rationale behind the proposed structure.

The bill encountered extensive opposition and ultimately died in the 96th Congress. More recently, H.R. 1615, "The Government Information Agency Act," was introduced in 1987. This proposed legislation would centralize government printing and selected dissemination/sales programs.

However, there appears to be little support to pass this bill, for many of the same reasons the 1979 revision of title 44 failed.

Prior to the proposal of another depository structure or massive modification of the present one, greater efforts should be made to understand and critique the present structure. At present, there is an insufficient research base to do this. Also prior to the formulation of a new structure, goals and objectives should be formulated, reviewed, and revised as necessary. As well, alternate depository structures should be identified and analyzed as needed. Any structure should explore national information policy, one that incorporates information resources regardless of level of government.

TOWARD A NATIONAL INFORMATION POLICY

A national information policy recognizes that information is not solely (Kaser et al, 1978, p. 545)

> . . . a commodity to be bargained for in the marketplace; it is, rather, a vital life fluid coursing throughout the body politic, essential to its continuing renewal and growth. It is thus incumbent upon the nation to provide the requisite arterial system, as well as the free and equitable flow of all non-proprietary, nonconfidential information to each individual, regardless of location, level of comprehension, economic status, or other circumstance.

Further, information intended for the public should be available to all; restricted access to it impinges upon one's right to know and be informed. Government information resources present unique problems for the creation of a national information policy. First, not all information is publicly available; available information may not be easily accessible and understandable. Those able to manipulate the political environment and to pay for services have greater access to information. Second, government publishing takes more forms than simply a printed publication; this highlights the specialized nature of a considerable proportion of government publishing, and the limited appeal of much of this information. Third, libraries comprise but one provider of government information; they collect government information resources selectively. There is great variation in the extent to which the public consults libraries and their government resources. A truly national information policy must address all providers, regardless of level of government, and explore ways for them to coordinate and cooperate. And, lastly, libraries treat government publications differently—in a number of cases they comprise a second-class resource separated physically, administratively, and intellectually from other resources and services. As a result, library staff members and library clientele may experience problems in bringing all the available information resources held by the library to play in resolving an information need.

Reform 88 and OMB's various directives represent a restricted view of national information policy, one in which the interests of the private sector receive special attention, and public and library access to information is substantially reduced. As Levin (1983, p. 135) notes,

> The irony of this situation, especially given the philosophy behind it, is that the change involves a violation of American tradition. This tradition has always viewed information as having a public value and asserted the public interest inherent in a free flow of information. Thus, the government's historic failure to formulate a comprehensive national information policy has presented corporate special interests with an excellent opportunity to develop their own policy with full executive-branch cooperation.

Public access to government is indeed a cornerstone of our heritage and dates back to the Constitutional Convention and the Articles of Confederation. The Bill of Rights forges a clear American principle of open government. Efficient government requires both secrecy and openness, but the balance between the two is naturally delicate.

During the 1960 and 1970s, this balance tipped in favor of openness. These times witnessed a reaction to Vietnam and Watergate, and the enactment of certain legislation to increase public awareness and access to government information. The FOIA required Executive Branch agencies to release more information that they had gathered. The Family Educational Rights and Privacy Act of 1974 (the Buckley Amendment) and the Privacy Act of the same year (5 USC 552a) permitted the public to seek information that government agencies held on them. The Federal Advisory Committee Act of 1972 and The Government in the Sunshine Act of 1976 opened the meetings of advisory groups and selected government bodies. And both houses of Congress adopted resolutions opening most congressional meetings to public observation.

With the 1980s, and the actions and philosophy held by members of the Reagan administration and various members of Congress, the balance is shifting away from the open government movement to less public access to government information. This shift impedes the concept of a broad-based national information policy and defines the information life cycle and public access in terms of cost-benefit and cost-effectiveness for the government, with effectiveness being equated with cost and benefit viewed as a subset of cost (benefit becomes saving money for taxpayers). Information resources management examines efficiency, cost reduction, savings to taxpayers, and cost-recovery (see Sprehe, 1984).

Before a truly national information policy— one incorporating government information with other information resources—can emerge, the government must recognize the importance of public access and be willing to encourage it. As suggested in Chapter 2, a wide variety of issues and factors merit attention. Appendix H of Hernon and McClure (1987a, pp. 422–445) identifies other policy issues.

The interests of both the public and private sectors must be balanced with those of society. The answers to policy issues should not be based on supposition, opinion, and political clout, but rather on the collection and testing of empirically derived information. Various chapters in this book, as well as in *Federal Information Policies in the 1980s* (Hernon and McClure, 1987a), present our views and the findings of the existing research base on many of the policy issues related to the depository library program. The formation of a national information policy, one adequately addressing the needs of the public, will not be accomplished quickly. It must look to the past, present, and future for direction.

Ironically, the number of writings in the literature of documents librarianship that views government information resources in terms of a national information policy is minimal. Fry (1978) represents one of the major attempts to look at broad policy issues across levels of government and to identify a depository library structure that better meets the public's information needs. Surprisingly, the impact of his report was short-lived, and the report did not result in a further exploration of the *best* depository library structure for furthering public access to government information.

A national information policy must address the present and future formats in which information appears, and the types of products that must be produced. For example, an abundance of Federal information is available at the national level through databases and commercial vendors (Congress. Joint Committee on Printing, 1984). Now, there is a growing opportunity for more local retrieval of information, as information contained in these national systems is captured on optical disk. The full text of government publications (e.g., the *Congressional Record*, the *Code of Federal Regulations*, the *Federal Register*, or other serial titles) could be compressed onto laser disk. Further, numeric databases of a current and historical nature (historical commodity prices and economic time series), as well as the data files of a bibliographic utility, are also adaptable to this format.

Information technology serves as a catalyst for change. Technology has vastly expanded the options for the collection, maintenance, distribution, and dissemination of government information (Tyckoson, 1987). With the availability of government information in electronic form, the private sector can bid on contracts for setting up information retrieval and dissemination systems for Federal agencies. The private sector can also take electronic information and generate information products tailored to the needs of its customers, including the library community. At the same time, the private sector is concerned that the government might become a competitor and undercut some of the information services provided commercially.[7]

Depository libraries must keep pace with advances in information handling technologies and further develop their document delivery capabilities. Efforts should continue to link depository libraries electronically (Congress. Joint Committee on Printing, 1984), and to realize the ideal of national information policy. A strong national information policy that balances the various demands placed on access to Federal information is needed. Without such a policy, documents librarians and other information professionals are unable to plan information services, predict the actions of the Federal government related to access and dissemination of information, or cooperate with other information providers effectively. Further, documents librarians have a special and important role to play in the development of such policy. They must make their positions known and work effectively in the political milieu to ensure that the public has acceptable access to government information resources. Establishment of a national information policy that encourages access to information is both necessary and essential for the continuation of a democratic form of government.

---

[7] See Hernon and McClure (1987a) for examples of government and private ventures using information technology. This work examines assorted policy issues.

4

Government Publications as a Significant Information Resource*

The Federal government publishes information of value to almost anyone, including the person needing guidance on how to receive a pension benefit or to take care of household appliances or a garden, the state or local government official or businessperson needing access to government reports or statistical data, or an academician preparing a research paper for publication or seeking a Federal grant or contract. Many humanists might benefit from the diversity of publications issued by the Library of Congress and the Smithsonian Institution, as well as those contained in the Serial Set—a collection of congressional publications (Birdsall, 1976).

Lawyers will be interested in the content of public laws and congressional reports because these publications provide insights into legislative intent. Social scientists and members of the general public—especially around election time—may be interested in legislative histories, the process of tracing a bill from its inception into Congress to its passage as public law. They may want to see how a particular member of Congress voted on a bill or to examine a copy of a public law or a congressional hearing in which expert witnesses testified on various aspects of a particular subject. Committee staff members or other government experts, perhaps those in the Congressional Research Service, Library of Congress, prepare studies for committees to use in conducting their business; these committee *prints* provide excellent background information on a wide variety of topics.

The government publishes information on a surprisingly large number

---

* Portions of this chapter are derived from Hernon and McClure (1987a).

of subjects.[1] A difficulty, however, is that one cannot always anticipate the subjects on which a particular agency might publish. For example, the Bureau of Land Management, Department of Interior—not the Judicial Branch or the Department of Justice—issued *Finding the Law: A Workbook on Legal Research for Laypersons* (Washington, D.C.: GPO, 1982). This excellent guide identifies, and shows illustrations of, sources useful in monitoring administrative and case law, as well as selected titles for tracing legislative histories or statutory law.

The purpose of this chapter is to provide a brief overview of government information providers, identify the functions of government publishing, and highlight representative types and formats of government publications/information. For illustrative purposes, specific mention will be made of the branch of government issuing each type. The resulting discussion should correct a common misconception that government publications consist largely of ephemera and pamphlets and that these publications are a "secondary class" of information resource. Government publications are a primary resource for addressing a broad range of diverse needs. They convey information, much of which might not be available elsewhere. This discussion therefore provides a necessary background to the next chapter and its coverage of bibliographic control.

PRODUCERS AND DISTRIBUTORS OF GOVERNMENT PUBLICATIONS/INFORMATION

Producers and distributors include the three branches of government, independent and regulatory agencies, government advisory organizations, the private sector, and other stakeholders in the information sector. Figure 4–1 is a general depiction of the environment under which the general public and specialized constituent groups must gain access to needed government publications/information.

A clearinghouse (as defined by the Public Health Service and the Department of Health and Human Services) is a program that:

- has a specific focus or subject areas
- acquires information
- organizes and indexes the collection

---

[1] Given the importance of publications printed by the Government Printing Office as historical, research, and policy records, librarians and others are urging the agency to switch all printing to non-acid paper. The alkaline process, that is being promoted as the alternative, is cheaper and probably has a longer shelf life than acid paper. The *U.S. Reports*, for example, is already available to libraries, from reprint companies, in acid-free form.

- accepts inquiries
- responds to inquiries in a standardized and customized manner
- conducts and provides systematic searches of its information collection
- engages in outreach and dissemination for users.

Clearinghouses usually serve as the national focal point for a particular subject area or type of information resource. They identify information resources and may provide a referral service (Lunin and Caponio, 1987). Both the National Diabetics Information Clearinghouse and the Arthritis Information Clearinghouse provide reliable and objective information. Both the National Technical Information Service (NTIS) and the Educational Resources Information Clearinghouse (ERIC) offer access to a type of information resource—technical or educational report literature.

Information analysis centers generally select, acquire, archive, evaluate, analyze, and provide access to information in a specialized area. They differ from clearinghouses in that they selectively acquire information and evaluate the contribution that the information makes to knowledge and their audience. For a discussion of these centers see Rothschild (1987) and Carroll and Maskewitz (1980).

Quoting from *Marketing Moves*, the GPO's marketing bulletin,

The Consumer Information Center (CIC) was established in 1970 within the General Services Administration to assist Federal agencies in developing consumer booklets and promoting their availability. Since 1973, orders for publications have been filled from GPO's Public Documents Distribution Center in Pueblo, Colorado.

CIC lists three types of booklets in its quarterly *Consumer Information Catalog*: Free, special low-priced, and regular GPO sales publications. The free booklets, which make up about 45 percent of *Catalog* listings, are printed by Government agencies and given to CIC for distribution, with agencies covering the postage and handling costs. Current costs are about 35 cents a publication. CIC distributes about 70,000 copies of the average free booklet in a year.

The low-priced booklets are available to the public for 50 cents. This low price is possible because the publishing agencies are able to share in some of the costs usually paid by GPO. These booklets might not be appropriate for the GPO sales program either because of their small size or because the agency wants to reach a larger audience but is unable to cover the postage and handling costs. The agencies provide the booklets and the public pays 50 cents each to cover the costs of postage and handling. Around 20 percent of the booklets in the *Catalog* are in this category . . . . There are about 15,000 requests for the average low-priced booklet over the course of a year.

The remainder of the booklets are regular GPO sales publications. The average Pueblo distribution for a sales publication is 3,000 copies annually ("But I Want Everybody to Have a Copy!," 1987).

Figure 4-1.
Producers and Distributors of Government Publications/Information

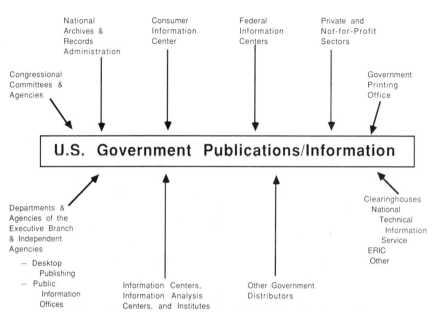

The General Services Administration also operates a series of Federal Information Centers (FICs), which place the public in contact with the appropriate Federal agency and answer general information queries (see Hernon and McClure, 1987a, p. 227).

Federal agencies receiving permission from the Joint Committee on Printing (JCP), U.S. Congress, may contract publishing to regional printing plants, contractors, and others (see 44 *USC* 501, 502, & 504). However, instead of contracting services, these agencies might establish their own printing plants. Further complicating matters, the Government Printing Office (GPO) contracts out about 73% of its work to more than 8,000 private sector firms (Struck, 1984).

The increased availability of microcomputers and desktop publishing enables any Federal office to become a producer and distributor of government publications. Following the Supreme Court's 1983 decision in *INS v. Chadha*, invalidating the legislative veto, the Executive Branch further questioned the assumption that Congress, through the JCP, could control public printing throughout the government. In 1987, the Department of Defense, the General Services Administration, and the National Aeronautics and Space Administration (NASA) announced their intention to no longer seek prior JCP approval for the acquisition of printing as specified in 4 *CFR* 8.800–8.02.

Such a shift in policy provides a clear reminder of the highly decentralized, Federal information environment. That environment lacks coordination and does not eliminate duplication of efforts. Further, retrieval of needed government publications/information requires awareness of this complex information environment and an ability to negotiate among an array of producers and distributors.

FUNCTIONS OF GOVERNMENT PUBLICATIONS

Merritt (1943), who examined information in the context of a printed publication, identified the major functions, purposes, or uses of these publications as follows:

- *Legislative*: congressional publications (e.g., bills, committee hearings and reports, and public laws) advance the legislative process
- *Administrative*: these publications (e.g., the *Federal Register*, the *Code of Federal Regulations*, and the *Calendars of the United States House of Representatives and History of Legislation*) serve as resources in the process of public administration
- *Reportorial*: these publications (e.g., annual reports of government agencies, decisions rendered by the courts, and briefs and opinions of the Attorney General) report a completed task or activity, or progress on the completion of an ongoing action
- *Service*: these publications are concerned with the public's quality of life, activities, and welfare. Much of the data collection by the Bureau of Labor Statistics, the Bureau of the Census, and other other statistical gathering agencies goes in this category.
- *Research*: these publications present research conducted or supported by a government agency
- *Informational*: these publications (e.g., pamphlets on welfare, social security, and health care) inform the public about the nature and activities of government agencies. They are educational and provide information useful for decision making.

Merritt analyzed publications reported in the *Monthly Catalog of United States Government Publications* (Washington, D.C.: GPO, 1895–) according to the purpose for which they were issued. Richardson (1982) extended Merritt's analysis to more recent years.

Using the *Monthly Catalog* for 1980, he combined reportorial, information, and service functions into one category. By doing this, he discovered that the enlarged category accounted for 82.2% of publications that the GPO identified and indexed. In addition, by making comparisons to the Merritt study, he demonstrated that the research function, as reported in this one index, has "grown significantly in the last 40 years" (p. 227).

Any overview attempting to categorize the information printed by the GPO can be misleading given the expanse of publications issued through this agency. For example, in 1987 testimony, Ralph Kennickell, the Public Printer, stated (Congress. House. Committee on Science, Space, and Technology, 1987, p. 174):

> about 65% of the approximately 14,000 titles in our sales program are scientific or technical in nature. The percentage is even higher for the Depository Library Program.

Such statements may be misleading since it is unclear what constitutes "scientific and technical" information. However, there does appear to be a *relative* increase in the amount of research and technical matter that the GPO has distributed during the second term of the Reagan administration.

Merritt's six broad groupings suggest numerous types of government information resources. However, some types are more important than others and result in substantially more publication. Due to policy decisions made by the Reagan administration, the number of *informational* publications that the government produces and distributes has been sharply curtailed.

TYPES OF GOVERNMENT PUBLICATIONS

The three branches of government generate unpublished records that complement published sources and document the administrative, political, economic, and other roles that the government exercises. These records (e.g., internal agency memoranda, letters, and working papers) comprise a specialized type of government information and will not be highlighted here.

Rips (1965) identified seventeen basic types of government publications that enable the Federal government to accomplish the functions that Merritt identified. In the 1984 edition of *Public Access to Government Information*, we expanded upon her typology and discussed eighteen types. The analysis reported here represents an extension of our earlier work and presents the following twenty-two types:

- Administrative reports
- Committee and commission reports

- Research reports and developmental studies
- Statistics
- General information pamphlets and fact sheets
- Periodicals
- Press releases and other ephemera
- Directories
- Handbooks, manuals, and digests
- Bibliographies, lists, guides, and catalogs
- Decisions and opinions
- Rules, regulations, directives, and circulars
- Maps, charts, and photographs
- Audiovisual resources
- Bills and resolutions
- Hearings
- Journals and proceedings
- Laws and statutes
- Treaty sources
- Technical report literature
- Patents
- Printed technical documentation (codebooks and other documentation that accompany machine-readable data files).

Figure 4–2 suggests the branches of government primarily responsible for issuing each type of publication. The Judicial Branch produces the fewest number of publication types. Except for patents, technical documentation, and bills and resolutions, a type of publication is not confined only to one branch of government.

Administrative Reports

Most government agencies issue an annual or other periodic report covering their accomplishments during the past year and their proposed budget and activities for the upcoming year. These reports frequently contain organization charts, list the services provided by the body, and summarize major agency activities. If a particular agency does not issue an administrative report, an agency higher in the organizational structure undoubtedly does so. At times, these reports are printed in the Serial Set.

Committee and Commission Reports

Both Congress and the President establish special committees and commissions to examine a significant economic, political, or social concern, a condition, or a foreign policy issue. These committees and commissions issue reports, many of which are available for public scrutiny.

Figure 4-2.
Branch of the Federal Government Producing Each Type of Government Publication

EXECUTIVE	LEGISLATIVE	JUDICIAL
Administrative Reports	Administrative Reports (by agencies falling under Y3 of Sudocs classification system)	Administrative Reports
Committee and Commission Reports	Committee and Commission Reports	
Research Reports and Development Studies	Research Reports and Development Studies	
Statistical Data	Statistical Data	Statistical Data
General Information Pamphlets and Fact Sheets	General Information Pamphlets and Fact Sheets	General Information Pamphlets and Facts Sheets
Periodicals	Periodicals	Periodicals
Press Releases and Ephemera	Press Releases and Ephemera	
Directories	Directories	Directories
Handbooks, Manuals, and Digests	Handbooks, Manuals, and Digests	
Bibliographies, Lists, Guides, and Catalogs	Bibliographies, Lists, Guides, and Catalogs	
Decisions and Opinions	Decisions and Opinions	Decisions and Opinions
Rules, Regulations, Circulars, and Directives	Rules, Regulations, Circulars, and Directives	Rules, Regulations, Circulars, and Directives
Maps, Charts, and Photographs	Maps, Charts, and Photographs	
Audiovisual Resources	Audiovisual Resources	
	Bills and Resolutions	
Hearings	Hearings	
Journals and Proceedings	Journals and Proceedings	
Laws and Statutes	Laws and Statutes	
Treaty Sources	Treaty Sources	
Technical Reports	Technical Reports	
Patents		
Technical Documentation		

Research Reports

In 1986, the Federal government spent some $50 billion to conduct research on a broad array of topics affecting American life. Research may be conducted on a myriad list of topics including health sciences, nuclear energy, space technology, agriculture, acid rain, and human psychology—to name a few. Formal reports may be disseminated by the GPO, the National Technical Information Service (NTIS), an ERIC clearinghouse, the private sector, or another provider in the information sector.

Statistics

The Federal government collects, tabulates, and publishes statistical data; in fact, it is the largest publisher of such data in the world. Active in this area are agencies such as the Bureau of the Census, the Bureau of Labor Statistics, the National Center for Health Statistics, the Economics and Statistics Service, and the Statistical Reporting Service (Department of Agriculture). The Bureau of the Census collects information on demographics and economic factors (retail and wholesale trade, service industries, manufacturing, construction industries, and transportation), and conducts censuses of agriculture and government. *Government Information Quarterly* has published a symposium analyzing the Bureau's decennial census (volume 2, number 4, 1985) and another covering the economic censuses (volume 4, number 3, 1987). The Bureau of Labor Statistics collects data on labor economics (e.g., employment, unemployment, productivity measures, prices, wages, industrial relations, and occupational and health statistics).

The importance of statistical data produced by the Federal government is evident from the existence of reference sources such as the *Statistical Abstract of the United States, Historical Statistics of the United States from Colonial Times to 1970*, and the *American Statistics Index*, a commercial index that highlights the statistical output of the Federal government. It might be noted that *Reflections of America* (1980), a work commemorating the *Statistical Abstract's* centennial anniversary, documents the impact of statistics on various facets of everyday life. Further, social scientists frequently consult government publications for their statistical content (Hernon, 1979). Only small amounts of statistical data appear in paper format; larger amounts are often available only on microfiche or in machine-readable form.

General Information Pamphlets and Fact Sheets

Many people associate government publications with this type. These publications offer suggestions, ideas, and techniques for people to lead a better, or at least more comfortable or enjoyable, life. Topics include how to purchase a home or repair a car, successful gardening techniques, methods to improve nutritional content of food, and explanations of laws and regulations.

Periodicals

The Federal government is a major producer of periodicals. Varying in content, appearance, value, and purpose, they range from those aimed at a narrow audience to titles having a broad appeal. A wide gamut of periodical types is published; these include research journals, newsletters from individual agencies, popular periodicals on specific topics, scenic or travel periodicals, etc.

Examples of widely known and used periodicals include the *Department of State Bulletin*, the *Monthly Labor Review*, and *Prologue*. Government periodicals are only selectively covered in indexes normally found in a library's general reference collection (McClure, 1978a). The *Index to U.S. Government Periodicals* and the *American Statistics Index* therefore become vital reference aids. The *Periodical Supplement to the Monthly Catalog* and its predecessor, the *Serials Supplement*, provide selective coverage of government periodicals. These last two sources only index titles, not content, and are limited to GPO publications.

Press Releases and Other Ephemera

These publications provide current information and identify agency activities, source material, publicly held meetings, proposed rules and regulations, and speeches delivered by important officials within an agency. Some agencies issue press releases in the form of a newsletter.

As agencies curtail their publication costs, they might reduce the number of press releases that they prepare and distribute, and offer more press releases on a subscription basis or through electronic bulletin boards. At the same time, they might limit coverage of proposed rules and regulations in the *Federal Register*, due to the high page charge cost for inclusion in this title. Clearly, access to press releases, as well as proposed and newly enacted rules and regulations may be fragmented, time consuming, and costly. Librarians need to become familiar with the policies and practices of those agencies whose activities match the information needs of their clientele.

Directories

These publications list officials of government agencies, agency resources, government bodies, places, and organizations. Examples of directories include the *Congressional Directory*, agency telephone directories, and the *U.S. Government Manual*. Larson (1981, 1985) offers an extensive listing of directories published from 1970 to 1984. Government directories are essential for the provision of fast, accurate, and current answers to "quick fact" reference questions and for referrals.

Handbooks, Manuals, and Digests

This type provides synopses, descriptions, or analyses of significant developments and issues. These publications may describe something and offer instructions for its repair. Some handbooks represent a compilation of factual information. The Department of Defense, for example, issues technical manuals identifying component parts of equipment and procedures for the replacement of individual parts. The Department also makes available the Area Handbook series, written through the Foreign Area Studies program of The American University, and providing an overview of different countries.

Bibliographies, Lists, Guides, and Catalogs

Both executive agencies and congressional committees issue lists of their publications. Sometimes, these lists are incorporated into press releases and newsletters. Zink (1988) is a useful compendium of government catalogs.

The GPO is a major producer of bibliographies, lists, guides, and catalogs. For example, it issues the *Monthly Catalog*, the *Publications Reference File*, subject bibliographies, and catalogs of sales publications. NTIS offers *Government Reports Announcements and Index* and various abstract newsletters that highlight new publications by subject.

Agency catalogs complement general indexes and provide users with access to information sources, not all of which are listed elsewhere. The Bureau of the Census, for example, prepares a monthly list of new products, an annual compilation of resources that it has prepared and distributed, and a major listing of census publications dating back to 1789.

Decisions and Opinions

The courts, regulatory agencies (e.g., the Interstate Commerce Commission and the Nuclear Regulatory Agency), the military, the Comptroller General (General Accounting Office), and the Attorney-General produce official decisions and opinions. Such renderings articulate the legal precedence for interpreting public laws and regulations, and offer a basis upon which to challenge statutory and administrative law. Publications containing decisions and opinions are of primary importance to any library interested in legal matters.

Rules, Regulations, Directives, and Circulars

Rules and regulations, commonly referred to as administrative law, represent the efforts of an agency within the Executive or Legislative Branch of government to establish the procedures by which statutory law is administered. For example, the President and Congress enacted the Food Stamp Program and placed it under the jurisdiction of the Department of Agriculture. The Department then developed the administrative rulings to implement the statutory law and to guide daily operations and decision making. Some departments and agencies issue regulations to guide the public in their dealings with the Federal government. The *Congressional Record* lists legislative regulations, while the *Federal Register* and the *Code of Federal Regulations* contain those for the Executive Branch.

Article I, Section 5, of the Constitution authorizes each House of Congress to determine the rules that will govern its proceedings. Standing rules continue from one Congress to another but are subject to change. Precedents encompass a broader concept; the precedents of the Senate comprise procedural law under which that House conducts its business. This type of law consists of standing rules, ad hoc orders, unanimous consent agreements of the Senate, and relevant statutory and constitutional provisions.

Maps, Charts, and Photographs

The major mapping agencies in the Federal government "annually produce over 53,000 new maps and charts and distribute over 160,000,000 copies" (North, 1983, p. 345). Examples of these mapping agencies are:

- Social Conservation Service and Forest Service (Department of Agriculture)
- National Ocean Service and Bureau of the Census (Department of Commerce)
- Defense Mapping Agency and Corps of Engineers (Department of Defense)
- Federal Insurance Administration (Department of Housing and Urban Development)
- Geological Survey, Bureau of Land Management, and National Park Service (Department of Interior)
- Federal Highway Administration (Department of Transportation)
- Central Intelligence Agency
- Tennessee Valley Authority.

Federal maps and charts include weather maps, soil maps, nautical charts, aerial photographic maps, geological maps, maps of countries and their major cities, topographic maps, etc. Special maps also display serial and space imagery and map data in digital form. NASA is an important producer of photographs taken from its various probes of outer space. *Government Publications Review*, 10, number 4 (July-August 1983), provides a useful overview of "Government Mapping."

Audiovisual Resources

The Federal government spends approximately $100 million per year on "the production, duplication, distribution, and off-the-shelf purchases of motion pictures, videotapes, slides and audio recordings" (*President's Private*

Sector Survey on Cost Control, 1983, p. 67). Due to the April 1981 directive of President Reagan and the subsequent directives from the Office of Management and Budget (OMB), "government spending on audiovisual activity decreased 13 percent from FY 1981 to FY 1982, the greatest decrease in five years. Furthermore, in-house production of motion pictures reached an all-time low in FY 1982" (Ibid., p. 69).

In February 1982, the floor proceedings of the House of Representatives began to be telecast on a cable system. Telecasting of the Senate's floor proceedings followed in June 1986. The National Audiovisual Center (NAC), General Services Administration, was created in 1969 to serve as a clearinghouse for Federal audiovisual material and to make these resources available for public use. NAC holdings are far from comprehensive but include slides, audio tapes, educational movies, etc. (See Huls, 1987).

Bills and Resolutions

Bills and resolutions are the form in which legislation is proposed in Congress. Written by members of Congress, their staff, special interest groups, or the administration, they comprise the basis of congressional law. As such, they are primary source material, critical for original research and investigation. Depository libraries receive this document type on microfiche, along with an accompanying paper index. Zwirn (1983) details the various types of bills and resolutions, their role in the legislative process, and methods for gaining access to them.

Hearings

Hearings may be publicly held or in closed session. They enable members of Congress to determine whether a particular action is necessary, to see whether legislation is warranted, or to draw public attention to an issue. They afford an opportunity to collect information from informed sources, to present a variety of viewpoints, to educate the public about an issue, or to call attention to the consequences of an action. Congressional hearings are either for an *oversight* (review existing laws on the basis of policy priorities, program effectiveness, or administrative discretion) or a *legislative* (focus on bills before Congress or a subject on which legislation is contemplated) purpose (Zwirn, 1983).

Executive agencies also hold hearings. For example, the Bureau of Indian Affairs interacts with Indian reservations. However, these hearings are infrequently published and may remain in transcript form in the offices of the agency or the National Archives, where they may be available for public inspection (Tate, 1983). The point is that a number of executive agencies hold hearings on topics of broad interest, and may make these publications available in transcript form. However, these hearings are neither published nor disseminated; they are not available in depository library collections or commercially produced indexes.

Journals and Proceedings

These serve as the records of each session of Congress. The journals are the minutes or summary of the actions and activities of both houses (e.g., the *House Journal* and *Senate Journal*), while the proceedings (e.g., the *Congressional Record*) contain the debates and speeches delivered on the floor as well as assorted other material. Both House and Senate proceedings appear on a cable network. Garay (1984) provides an excellent analysis of the relationship between broadcasting and the government. As he indicates, the printed *Congressional Record* is subject to congressional revision, while videorecordings are retained for only two months before being erased and used again. On the other hand, since audiorecordings "would be retained indefinitely in the Library of Congress" (p. 117), they become the archival copy. However, much of the decision making process occurs behind the scenes (e.g., in personal and telephone conversations with the president or congressional leadership, or in committees) rather than on the Senate or House floor.

Another type of proceedings, found in both the executive and legislative branches is that which reports on a special conference, seminar, or workshop. The purpose of these proceedings is to inform members of the government or special target groups, or to report on the exchange of ideas.

Laws and Statutes

This document type represents the culmination of the legislative history process. The first publication of a public law is a slip law, or pamphlet containing that law. At the end of a congressional session, slip laws are bound into the *Statutes at Large*, which is a chronological reprinting of the laws enacted each session. Effective topical access to the laws in force is through the codification of the law. The *United States Code* codifies Federal statutes and is received on deposit.

Treaty Sources

Treaties represent the result of foreign policy negotiation between the Executive Branch and another country. Congress enters into the process; it conveys its concerns and points of view to the administration, especially when the Senate must consider ratification of a treaty. Treaty sources include the text of the treaty, publicly available statements indicating negotiation strategies and sensitive issues, and reports indicating treaty benefits and liabilities. Useful information may be found in congressional hearings, reports and documents, and floor proceedings (the *Congressional Record*) as well as presidential messages, proclamations, and executive orders.

Technical Report Literature

Technical reports frequently result from government sponsored research and development activities, but are not confined to these. They are usually directed toward the specifications of a contract but also may be written to meet the information needs of a broader audience. As Purcell shows (see Chapter 10), the term "technical report literature" is broad and describes various types of publications. The final report for a government contract or grant is probably the most valuable of the types.

The responsibility for the announcement and distribution of technical report literature is fragmented among various clearinghouses, institutes, and the originating agencies. NTIS, ERIC, NASA, the Defense Technical Information Center (DTIC), and the Office of Scientific and Technical Information within the Department of Energy are examples of Federal agencies that have the announcement and distribution of technical reports as a primary function.

Patents

A patent for an invention is a grant by the Federal government to an inventor. Awarded by the Patent and Trademark Office, the patent right extends to the entire United States and its territories and possessions, for a period of seventeen years. Patents cover "new and useful processes, machines, manufacturers, or compositions of matter, new and distinct varieties of plants or organisms or new designs for articles of manufacture." They may be grouped into four categories: "utility patents, the largest category; plant patents; design patents; and reissue patents, which show corrections for patents previously issued" (Aluri and Robinson, 1983, p. 89).

For a discussion of "Patent Basics: History, Background, and Searching Fundamentals," see Brown (1986). As she observes,

> the U.S. patent system and the body of issued patents are key elements in meeting information needs related to technology and innovation. Most librarians . . . have little understanding of the value of patents as sources of technological information—and less knowledge about how to help users tap what has been called "the largest and most comprehensive body of technological literature in the world" (p. 381).

Technical Documentation

The proliferation of machine-readable data files and the creation of computer software to facilitate their use has led to a special type of government information resource—technical documentation. The availability of numerous software programs emphasizes the need for codebooks and other documentation explaining the layout, specifications, reliability of data, etc. Sometimes documentation is printed as a separate publication, while, in other instances, it is available in machine-readable form. A number of these types of informational matter are available through NTIS. However, others may have to be requested directly from the individual agencies.

FORMATS OF GOVERNMENT INFORMATION

The twenty-two types appear in six identifiable formats. These are:

- Paper
- Microform (microfiche and microfilm)
- Audiovisual (slides, filmstrips, sound recordings, motion pictures, videotape, etc.)
- Machine-readable (bibliographic, statistical and numeric, textual, properties, and full-text data files)
- Optical disk
- Electronic (videotex, viewdata, etc.).

As shown in Figure 4–3, the greatest number of types of government information sources is available in either paper copy or microform. Paper copy reaches the widest range of the general public, while microfiche (see Table 4–1) has become the preferred format by which the GPO distributes government publications to its depository libraries.

Since the table only covers the GPO's distribution to depository libraries, it does not represent the full extent of government printing or publication. Clearly, the government is a major producer of publications/information. However, both the figure and table examine publication output in terms of quantity; neither suggests quality. It might be noted that the totals for 1987 are significantly smaller than the GPO had anticipated. The reason is that the agency experienced problems with its microfiche contractor. With the contractor defaulting, the GPO had a sizeable backlog of titles awaiting filming and distribution. With the granting of new contracts, the backlog will shrink and totals for 1988 should reflect a dramatic increase in the number of microfiche titles distributed to depository libraries.

Figure 4-3.
Formats in Which Types of Government Information Are Distributed

Type	Paper	Microform	Audio & Visual	Machine-Readable	Electronic
Administrative Reports	X	X		X	X
Committee and Commission Reports	X	X			
Research Reports & Development Studies	X	X			X
Statistics	X	X		X	X
General Information Pamphlets	X	X			
Periodicals	X	X			X
Press Releases & Other Ephemera	X	X		X	X
Directories	X	X		X	X
Handbooks, Manuals, & Digests	X	X		X	X
Bibliographies, Lists, Guides, & Catalogs	X	X		X	X
Decisions & Opinions	X	X			
Rules, Regulations, Directives, & Circulars	X	X		X	X
Maps, Charts, & Photographs	X	X		X	X
Audiovisual Resources			X		
Bills & Resolutions	X	X		X	X
Hearings	X	X			
Journals & Proceedings	X	X			
Laws & Statutes	X				X
Treaty Sources	X				
Technical Report Literature	X	X		X	X
Patents	X	X			X
Technical Documentation	X			X	X

The full impact of the Paperwork Reduction Act, the Deficit Reduction Act of 1984, and various directives and guidelines issued by OMB on agency publication programs and information resources management remains to be determined. The number of paper titles distributed to depository libraries is substantial (over 98,000 titles from 1982 through 1986—see Table 4-1) and exceeds that produced by the entire American book publishing trade (Hernon, McClure, and Purcell, 1985). Nevertheless, paper copy distribution is yielding to other formats—ones more economical to produce and distribute and from which it is more efficient to derive information useful for management and decision making purposes. Desktop publishing will also affect the number of titles going through the GPO and its printing program.

Table 4-1.
Number of Publications Distributed to Depository Libraries (per Fiscal Year)*

	PAPER COPY		MICROFICHE		TOTAL**,***	
Year	titles	copies	titles	copies	titles	copies
1978	32,142	12,928,901	4,045	1,544,755	36,187	14,473,656
1979	69,878	19,580,302	16,553	7,473,049	86,431	27,053,351
1980	34,234	9,395,283	24,438	10,651,385	58,672	20,046,668
1981	37,385	11,923,321	27,993	12,820,265	65,378	24,743,586
1982	15,849	7,023,392	27,974	13,686,010	43,823	20,709,402
1983	18,292	8,553,839	43,850	21,748,730	62,142	30,302,569
1984	23,957	10,613,750	33,243	14,826,380	36,200	25,440,130
1985	24,247	10,306,385	30,794	13,318,687	55,041	23,625,072
1986	17,835	8,340,000	21,655	11,140,000	39,490	19,480,000
1987	19,359	7,651,000	21,907	10,832,000	41,266	18,483,000
TOTAL	293,178	106,316,173	252,452	118,041,261	524,630	224,357,434

*The data for 1978–1983 are derived from *Administrative Notes* (Washington, D.C.: GPO), number 16 (October 1983): 3. Mr. Mark Scully of the GPO supplied the more recent data in telephone conversations, March 3, 1986, November 9, 1987, and February 12, 1988.

**In some instances, the same work may be available in a dual format. Therefore, the totals represent an inflated estimation of the number of unique titles produced and distributed.

***The data presented in this table represent those titles and copies distributed through the Library Program Services, GPO. The table excludes those titles automatically distributed from other areas of the GPO (covering the *Congressional Record, the Federal Register*, and the *Official Gazettes*), as well as the Geological Survey and DMA maps coming from Denver, Colorado, and the microfiche of the Department of Energy, Oak Ridge.

A number of specific options exist for each format. For example, microfiche is available at different reduction ratios, including 19x, 22x, 48x, and 98x, and microfilm is generally issued at 16 and 32 mm. Given the diversity of options, there is a clear need for the adoption of, and adherence to, standards, such as the ANSI Standard for Information on Microfiche Headers (Z39.33), for microform creation, production, and distribution/dissemination.

Audiovisual resources can be classified as both a type and format. For a society that meets many of its information needs through interpersonal communication and is so closely tied to visual communication, audiovisual resources   comprise an important format for informing, educating, and entertaining the public. However, of the formats discussed here, the fewest number of types of government publications is associated with this format.

"Machine-readable files" is an umbrella term that encompasses a diversity of options. These files provide factual information or bibliographic citations and perhaps abstracts of the sources listed. They may also permit searching of patent files or the gathering and manipulation of statistical data. Some government files are "textual-numeric," which signifies that the records contain fields of both numeric and textual data. "Properties" databases convey dictionary or handbook type of data, and "full-text" databases offer both bibliographic references and the complete text of the source.

Data files that duplicate paper sources permit data to be displayed, manipulated, and compared. Other files either contain more data than are available in a published report or do not have paper equivalents. Chen and Hernon (1984) offer numerous examples of numeric data files and the Federal agencies that produce or distribute them. For instance, the Geological Survey provides information systems for geographic, geologic, hydrologic, and cartographic data in a variety of formats: tapes, computer output microfilm, or special computer queries of a database. The National Mapping Program offers digital, cartographic, and geographic data.

A number of government databases can be assessed from the agency itself, agency contractors or clearinghouses, commercial vendors, or libraries. Individuals with home computers linked to telephone lines can gain direct access to Federal databases such as those related to alternative fuels and the climate. The use of some databases does not involve a charge, while for others the cost covers only the search time, or the search time plus additional charges.

Videotex is the display of textual information, both words and numbers, on a video screen. Typically it implies a two-way system whereby viewers request information from a potentially larger collection of data. Other technologies come under the generic heading of "viewdata," the transmission of electronic pages and graphics over telephone lines, cable television lines, or broadcast television to either microcomputers or modified television receivers. The State Department, the Internal Revenue Service, the Department of Agriculture, and the National Oceanic and Atmospheric Administration (among others) have been, or are, involved in teletext and/or videotex projects (Schweizer, 1983).

As more information is produced in electronic and machine-readable form, it is logical to assume that distribution and dissemination efforts will build from this foundation. With the increasing use of microcomputers, Federal agencies can produce information on diskette, revise documentation without having to generate paper copies, and distribute diskettes rather than paper or microform copies. At present, users of government information can purchase data disks from NTIS, the Bureau of the Census, and other agencies. The Library of Congress is exploring optical disk storage for preservation and catalog card distribution (Hahn, 1983). The Patent and Trademark Office, the Securities and Exchange Commission, the Department of Agriculture, the Bureau of the Census, and the Bureau of Labor Statistics operate electronic information systems. Seekers of government information can also engage in online ordering of source material from the GPO, NTIS, and a host of clearinghouses.

Information technology may lead to the demise, or decreased importance, of some formats and have a profound impact on the government's willingness and capability to distribute/disseminate information. If the government provides information only in an electronic format, and if other stakeholders in the information sector determine that there is a need for printed information (and that it is profitable), then these other stakeholders may fill the void. The public will have to decide how much it is willing or able to pay for information that is potentially useful for informed decision making and knowledge about government actions, policies, programs, and services.

THE ELUSIVE NATURE OF GOVERNMENT PUBLICATIONS AS AN INFORMATION RESOURCE

Government touches all aspects of our daily lives, but the public is frequently unaware of the publications issued by their own government. These publications represent an effort to convey information, or to inform or persuade the public. They therefore comprise a means of communication between the government and those governed.

Few government publications are highlighted in trade journals and newspapers. Further, only a few commercial bookstores sell government publications, primarily because the GPO, by law, can only extend a 25% discount, not the 40% to which bookstores are accustomed. Many book jobbers only include a small portion of government publications among their offerings; those jobbers providing a number of government publications, to a large extent, emphasize items from the GPO sales program. Since the GPO now has its own standing order service, this lessens the need for many libraries to rely on a commercial jobber for gaining access to government publications. The inclusion of government publications in a general standing order service, however, serves as a reminder that government publications may contain useful, even vital, information. Government publications, indeed, complement more traditional information resources.

Many of the publications available from the U.S. government are unique sources of information covering a broad range of topics. Simply stated, librarians who ignore government publications or who do not treat them as important in either collection development and reference service bypass a resource that may not be duplicated elsewhere. Government publications provide original or scholarly information often times not published by the private sector. These publications convey official information and are useful for holding the government accountable or for understanding government actions or programs. Furthermore, government publications comprise a type of "primary source" material so essential in academic, scholarly, and research environments. In short, government publications must be recognized as a significant and integral part of any library collection. Their access and servicing must be integrated with other library collections.

The tasks of selecting, acquiring, processing, retrieving, and utilizing government information becomes more difficult and expensive as the number of titles produced annually remains so large, as government information appears in diverse formats, and as the production and distribution of government information occurs in a highly decentralized and competitive environment. The wide diversity of practice in the printing, distribution, and announcement of government publications constitutes a special challenge to libraries in the selection, acquisition, and servicing of collections. Basic to a solution of these problems is consideration of the long-range role of government information as essential to libraries in meeting a wide assortment of general and specialized information needs.

5

Bibliographic Control of U.S. Government Publications

Bibliographic control has been defined in various ways. Basically, it encompasses those "activities directed to ensure the recording of descriptive, subject, and analytical information concerning a body of documentation and the organization of that information . . . with a view to efficient use" (Marulli, 1979, p. 13). Its definition should also provide for:

- The identification of information
- Organization and description of information content
- Physical access.

Comprehensive bibliographic control of all government information resources regardless of format is an elusive objective, one that will probably never be fully achieved; to do so would require a substantial increase in resource allocation (e.g., human and financial) on behalf of governments, as well as total compliance on the part of government bureaucracies (see Figure 5–1).

The identification of Federal information resources is a worthy objective, but its actual achievement should be more of concern to government agencies functioning as printers, distributors, and disseminators (e.g., clearinghouses), and to the publishing industry, than to the library community. Librarians ought to be supportive of attempts to identify source material, but their primary purpose should be to provide better access to the major resources needed by their clientele and to improve document delivery capabilities through inter-institutional cooperation. Even government agencies such as the Government Printing Office (GPO) might place greater

Figure 5-1.
Depiction of Bibliographic Control for Government Information Sources

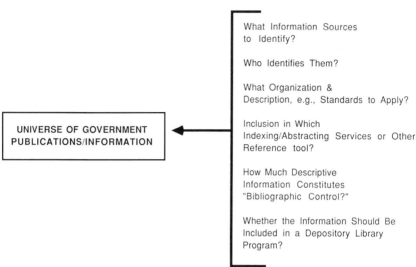

emphasis on organization (e.g., establishment of commonly accepted standards and improved indexing and abstracting services) and physical access (e.g., the initiation of current awareness and selective dissemination of information services), and less attention on comprehensive identification, especially for ephemeral, superseded, or outdated information.

The cost and the amount of time expended in the process of comprehensive identification is likely to outweigh the potential utility of the information provided. Traditional means of achieving comprehensive identification largely ignore the information-gathering patterns of people and the types of information they most frequently use. There are other priorities under the broad rubric of bibliographic control, even for such government agencies as the GPO. Other groups, including those in the private sector, can address lapses in identification efforts by these official agencies. For example, the Congressional Information Service offers a diverse range of historical indexing and source material.

Perhaps the overriding objection to the expense of identifying all government information is the concern that library users at some point in time will want or benefit from a publication heretofore not identified or acquired by a particular library. In times of financial retrenchment, limited space, and a small number of staff assigned to the maintenance and servicing of documents collections, such factors as quality of information, potential benefit, and frequency and type of use must be considered when developing information collections and services.

As will be noted in the next chapter, maintenance of high use collections must be supported by inter-institutional cooperation and a satisfactory document delivery system operated at the national level. Many libraries are now having to either curtail or scrutinize documents holdings and selections, without recourse to an adequate support system for materials needed but not owned within the institution. Both collection development and inter-institutional cooperation are complementary concepts; resource sharing enables libraries to obtain source material that falls outside their collection development policies.

By concentrating their efforts on collecting the types of information most essential to their clientele and the mission of their institution, by improving resource sharing capabilities, and by suggesting priorities in the identification of government information and in the physical description of material added to the *Monthly Catalog* database, librarians can become more effective and efficient information managers. They will be managing their limited resources (e.g., space, financial, facilities, and personnel) to address a large percentage of the information needs of their clientele. Adherence to the viewpoint outlined thus far is important, in part, because historically source material housed in documents collections has not been utilized to its potential, and because libraries have traditionally taken advantage of free depository distribution and selected more than was needed. Another reason for limited use or nonuse of government publications has been that the amount of time expended in the search is often totally out of proportion to the value of the information found (Hernon, 1979). Variations in quality of government information undoubtedly present a barrier to use.

Against this background, the remainder of this chapter examines the components of bibliographic control: identification of information, organization and description of information content, and physical access. The role of the library community in these processes receives special emphasis. Examples illustrate the difficulties of bringing government information resources under effective and comprehensive bibliographic control.

IDENTIFICATION OF INFORMATION

A number of government agencies, publishers, professional societies, organizations, and individuals are concerned with bibliographic control and with making government information more widely accessible. The diversity of practices among government units and agencies in the printing, distribution, and announcement of government publications has contributed to the demand for coordination and integration of bibliographic activities. Due to the Reagan administration's curtailing of government expenditures for government information, and the size of publishing programs, agencies are cooperating more in the bibliographic control and distribution of government publications.

Traditionally, Federal agencies have issued *thousands* of publications each year for which there is no bibliographic control. Many of these publications, printed outside GPO's control, have not been included in the *Monthly Catalog* as required by title 44, *United States Code*. Estimates suggest that only 40–60% of all government publications become eligible for depository distribution.

Many Federal publications may merit identification but perhaps not inclusion in the depository library program. Agencies such as the GPO and the National Technical Information Service (NTIS) do not distribute publications that are (Depository Library Council, 1978, p. 65):

- Considered of limited general interest
- "Printed in-house because they are needed quickly"
- "Additions to a series, new revisions or updates, which are not announced"
- Published by private publishers
- Issued by agencies' regional offices
- Originally intended only for in-house distribution
- Promotional or other ephemeral material.

Field offices, overseas plants, military bases, and government agencies using their own equipment prepare publications. Publications issued by regional offices of Federal agencies present awareness problems, especially if the agencies use a duplicating process that does not involve a printing press, issue publications in small enough quantity that they can circumvent the GPO, or engage in desktop publishing.

Numerous works produced by Federal contractors escape the bibliographic control efforts of the GPO and government clearinghouses. With knowledge and tacit approval of Federal agencies, the authors of these studies frequently copyright their works and turn them over to the private sector for publication (Rosenfield, 1986). Government agencies such as the Central Intelligence Agency and the United States Information Agency have secretly funded the private publication of books (Schnapper, 1985).

Over the years, the Joint Committee on Printing (JCP) has been generous in granting waivers that permit agencies to bypass having the GPO do their printing (44 *USC* 501, 504). There has not been effective control or complete monitoring over these printing operations. Fiscal constraints of the 1980s have afforded an opportunity for agencies to reassess their publishing programs, but only from a cost containment perspective. Other problems include the fact that agencies and field office staff are not always aware of the reporting requirement specified in title 44, and that agencies are shifting attention from print publishing programs to the electronic collection and distribution of information.

Nonprint source material also presents problems concerning identification and announcement. For example, there is no central producer or clearinghouse for machine-readable data files; files are highly fragmented and vary greatly as to quality and completeness of supporting documentation (e.g., codebooks) (Heim, 1983).

To say that fiscal constraints and reduced publication programs have encouraged more Federal agencies to rely on either the GPO or NTIS for general distribution of titles is a gross oversimplification of the Federal information/publication environment. That environment is exceedingly complex and undoubtedly will remain so. The Office of Superintendent of Documents has created an Acquisitions Unit that works with other units within the GPO to ensure that sufficient quantities for depository distribution are provided as part of an agency's initial print order. When librarians or others alert the Unit of a title that has evaded inclusion in the *Monthly Catalog* and depository distribution, GPO staff contact the responsible agency. If the title is not forthcoming and is not exempted from distribution by statute, the matter is referred to the JCP (see "Fugitive Publication," 1985). The Acquisitions Unit is generally passive; its staff do not visit agencies, but rather monitor printing within the GPO and follow up when another party observes a gap in depository distribution.

The efforts of different groups result in the disclosure of previously unknown publications, many of which are not brought to the attention of the GPO and its Acquisitions Unit. When the GPO discovers a title that has previously evaded bibliographic control and a decision has been made to offer that title to depository libraries on microfiche, the GPO will determine how many libraries have selected that category of publication and will procure the corresponding number of microfiche. Claims for copies selected but not received are fulfilled by duplicating GPO's master microfiche copy.

DESCRIPTION AND ORGANIZATION OF INFORMATION CONTENT

Overview

Description and organization of information content goes beyond the responsibility and capabilities of the library community. Government agencies and the private sector realize that they must be active in this area. In March 1976, the GPO began cataloging government publications according to the Anglo-American Cataloging Rules and the Library of Congress MARC format. The GPO also joined OCLC, a cooperative, online, shared cataloging network. In April 1977, the Library of Congress began distribution of the *Monthly Catalog* tape records in MARC II format so that libraries with access to computer facilities could reorganize the data for their own purposes.

In January 1981, the GPO assumed national authority for the cataloging of U.S. publications, and the Library of Congress (LC) stopped cataloging its publications. Now, if LC wants a document cataloged, it sends a request to the GPO.[1] The GPO also participates with LC in the name authority cooperative project. Consequently, whenever the GPO assigns a new AACR-2 name, that name is added to LC's authority file. Further, the GPO follows the cataloging service guidelines set by LC to produce a description consistent with the one created by LC. This collaboration between the GPO and LC has been beneficial to both agencies and the library community. For example, there are now *tracings* for all Federal agencies responsible for a publication, and the GPO provides a record of all series statements.

In spite of shared-cataloging experiments, technical report literature networks, and numerous individual indexing systems, there is duplication among the offerings of the various distributors of official publications. In effect, there is ". . . the 'overkill' of duplicate cataloging, on the one hand, and documents 'lost' through the holes of bibliographic control on the other" (Depository Library Council, 1978, p. 64).

One encouraging trend on the part of the GPO is the attempt to standardize practices for the cataloging and classification of U.S. government publications. Standardized procedures can improve significantly the ability of documents librarians to maintain bibliographic control over government publications, develop local online systems, and participate in cooperative networks. As an aid to depository libraries, the GPO has issued *A Practical Guide to the Superintendent of Documents Classification System* (1986).

Indexing

Undoubtedly better bibliographic control has resulted from the requirement that agencies forward copies of their publications to the GPO for cataloging. Further, the *Monthly Catalog* provides full cataloging information for many microfiche and other items in series. In a parallel trend, many librarians are now renewing their call for indexes that comprehensively cover the publishing output of the Federal government and provide complete bibliographic data. These librarians endorse either expanded coverage of the *Monthly Catalog*, with the inclusion of more source material (print and nonprint) and

---

[1] According to Kadec (1985, p. 285), "the Library of Congress has transferred responsibility for cataloging of government documents from itself to the LPS at GPO (without transferring accompanying resources) ostensibly to 'avoid duplication,' but also to conserve its own cataloging resources. However, the Library of Congress still insists on review of catalog copy and control of decision making in the realm of cataloging. The retention of such territorial imperative adds considerably to document processing time and inevitably detracts from the utility of the *Monthly Catalog* . . . ."

more extensive bibliographic information, or the creation of an online database that includes all government information resources.

Providing more complete coverage makes a print index more cumbersome for librarians to use as a selection tool and for researchers seeking citations pertinent to their information needs. Alternative ways to present information become important when physical appearance and the size of an index begin to inhibit use. Herein was the advantage of developing a machine- readable database for *Monthly Catalog* records that provides an alternative to conducting a manual search. The availability of the *Monthly Catalog* and *Government Reports Announcements & Index (GRA&I)* on CD-ROM sharply reduces search time. In addition, a number of indexing services are available online. Undoubtedly, users will find it more convenient to sift through quantity in an online environment; quality, however, is a separate issue.

Problems that users might experience when they consult the printed *Monthly Catalog* or even its equivalent on CD-ROM or rollfiche can be easily demonstrated! Assume that an individual wants to select sixty titles, related to a common theme, from an index, and make the citations conform to the specifications of a recognized style manual. The person would experience great difficulty in doing this. First, style manuals do not adequately cover government publications or provide sufficient examples (Basefsky, 1979).[2] Second, the *Monthly Catalog* appears to place entries under personal author, when, in fact, they conform to the Sudoc classification scheme; entries are arranged according to issuing agency. Third, the form of the issuing agency name displayed in the body of the entry may differ from that in the section heading, because the GPO may be slow in changing the headers on its tapes when an agency changes its name. Fourth, the *Monthly Catalog* provides descriptive information for paper copy publications even if the publication was distributed as microfiche; thus, bibliographic information for government publications in microform is difficult to ascertain. And, finally, entries in the *Monthly Catalog* may contain incomplete or erroneous information. In efforts to resolve some of the problems, the Government Documents Round Table (GODORT) of the American Library Association and the Depository Library Council to the Public Printer have provided input on the quality of cataloging records for government publications and made recommendations to assist libraries that use the *Monthly Catalog* tapes (Myers, 1985)[3]

---

[2] *The Complete Guide to Citing Government Documents* (1984), of course, provides numerous examples. However, this manual has not displaced other style manuals or become the final arbiter for making stylistic decisions.

[3] In cooperation with Marcive Inc., the libraries of Rice University, Texas A&M University, and Louisiana State University are attempting to "clean up" the GPO tapes. The corrected tapes would have great utility for libraries wanting to include GPO distributed publications in their online catalogs. The tape clean-

The *Monthly Catalog* includes records for publications distributed through the depository library program, marks these with a black dot, and assigns an item number to them so that depository libraries may decide which publications to select. A number of publications indexed, however, are identified as ineligible for depository distribution; typically, these are produced in regional printing facilities or by private contractors for a government agency. To gain access to these nondepository publications, a number of libraries subscribe to the Readex Non-Depository Microprint Collection (begun in 1953) and/or LC's Documents Expediting Project (a service specializing in the acquisition and distribution of nondepository publications to its clientele).

Apparently, depository libraries have received a significant proportion of nondepository publications through the depository program, without being aware of the fact (Zink, 1983). Further, "the placement of the item number and black dot elements in the *Monthly Catalog* entries was far from complete" (Ibid., 1983, p. 179). These errors lessen the *Monthly Catalog's* value as a guide to locally held resources. They also result in needless duplication of efforts, since library staff members may be purchasing titles that they do not realize are already in the collection.

Due to the emergence of the GPO as a micropublisher, one can question why the *Monthly Catalog* lists so many publications not available for depository distribution. According to one writer, "the basis for the traditional listing of non-depository publications was that only a single copy of each title, required for cataloging and classifying, was received by the Government Printing Office and thus distribution was impossible" (Ibid., p. 180). The GPO, however, now routinely procures microfiche copies of many titles received for cataloging and inclusion in the *Monthly Catalog*. This fact underscores the need to explain criteria by which titles become eligible for depository distribution, to analyze the types of source material that depository libraries select, to refine resource sharing capabilities, and to determine the cost-benefit and cost-effectiveness of the depository library program.

---

up program is intended "to accomplish the following goals" ("GPO Tape Clean-Up," 1987):

- "Make corrections and changes noted in the *Monthly Catalog*
- Code missing control numbers (Sudocs Stem, OCLC, and Technical Report numbers) into the appropriate fields
- Change or delete duplicate and availability records, including serials, supplementary titles, infrequent serials, and monographs in parts
- Correct inaccurate fixed fields and indicators
- Correct spelling and index listing errors
- Provide a means for inserting a holding library code and/or location code for materials distributed in microfiche
- Automatically process all records against the Library of Congress subject and name authorities files."

It should be noted that Marcive expects to accomplish these goals while this book is in press.

It should be emphasized that the Library Programs Service of the GPO retains a second-generation microfiche copy from which claims for microformatted publications can be filled. However, this service only benefits those libraries that have already selected the appropriate item number. Libraries not selecting that item but needing access to a particular microfiche publication must turn elsewhere in their search for a copy.

Since government publishing is decentralized and government agencies are still extensive producers of publications, there is (and never was) no single index to U.S. government publications. Typically, government produced indexes are selective and/or cover the publishing program of one producer or distributor. *GRA&I*, for example, includes publications that NTIS distributes; not all of these publications technically comprise government publications. Librarians and others who want to obtain bibliographic access to NTIS publications must rely on this index and the NTIS database. Simply stated, the belief that the *Monthly Catalog* or the OCLC database provides a substitute for *GRA&I* or the NTIS database is incorrect:

- The *Monthly Catalog* and OCLC list few NTIS publications
- *GRA&I* lists publications faster than does the *Monthly Catalog*.

Indeed, subject searching for a particular NTIS publication in the *Monthly Catalog* may be an exercise in futility (McClure, Hernon, and Purcell, 1986, pp. 113–127).

The ERIC clearinghouses and their *Resources in Education (RIE)* include much more than government funded and sponsored research. The *Publications Reference File (PRF)*, also produced by the GPO, lists publications currently in the sales program of the Superintendent of Documents and often includes titles more current than those found in the *Monthly Catalog*. In addition, government agencies and the private sector issue indexes, bibliographies, and catalogs that supplement the *Monthly Catalog*, *GRA&I*, and *RIE*.

The fragmented nature of government publishing, the assortment of available indexes and bibliographies, and the idiosyncrasies of available indexes, confuse library users and often require them to depend on assistance from the documents staff in negotiating the maze of government publishing. It is no wonder that users may prefer to browse and to avoid print indexes whenever possible. Research should be conducted to determine the extent to which access to the *Monthly Catalog* or another service for government publications on CD-ROM or rollfiche will change information-gathering behavior.

Periodical bibliographic control is the identification of appropriate periodical titles and the indexing of specific information contained in the periodical, as well as the provision of descriptive bibliographic information about the title, date, volume, and pagination that enables the individual to locate the particular issue in which the information is contained. Bibliographic control of government periodicals can be described by the following levels of indexing, listed from general to specific:

- Listing of periodical title only
- Indexing of articles by author and title
- Indexing of articles by author, title, and subject
- Indexing of articles, reports, announcements, and other features in the periodical by author, title, and subject
- Indexing of specific information contained in articles, reports, announcements, and other features
- Indexing by nontraditional categories (other than author, title, and subject).

Because all indexes generally provide equal bibliographic identification of periodicals in terms of volume number, date, pagination, etc., specificity of indexing (e.g., the number and type of index terms assigned to each item to be indexed) is a better measure of bibliographic control for periodicals than it is for other document types.

Although bibliographic control of government periodicals is improving, it is still not adequate. A conservative estimate is that half of the titles listed in the *Periodicals Supplement to the Monthly Catalog* (which does not include all government periodicals) are indexed in any source. The *Monthly Catalog* does not provide access to the information contained in government periodicals. Bibliographic control is limited largely to the first level—the listing of the periodical title. With the increased inclusion of government titles on MARC tapes, bibliographic control at this level will continue to increase. Bibliographic control of the *information contained* in the various government periodical titles is still inadequate and likely to remain so for some time to come.

For purposes of access and collection development, a strong case can (and perhaps should) be made to acquire only those serial titles that are indexed.[4] Since the *Monthly Catalog* does not provide analytics for periodical articles, access to information content in such periodicals requires the use of privately published indexes. Consequently, many depository libraries are simply storage centers for publications that are unlikely to be accessed except by serendipity. Clearly, indexing strategies for U.S. government peri-

---

[4] It might be noted that *Reader's Guide* has only indexed six government periodicals since 1978. Gilligan and Hajdas (1986) provide a checklist of 200 government periodicals that indicates over 50 services that index these periodicals. This list is an excellent beginning point for the review of periodical titles held and access points to their content. Clearly, *American Statistics Index* and the *Index to U.S. Government Periodicals* provide the broadest coverage.

odicals must be reconsidered, and a number of periodical publications should be either indexed or discontinued.

It is essential that library staff evaluate indexes and publications on the basis of library goals and objectives, user needs, collection development policies and practices, scope of indexes, index costs, the specificity of indexing needed, index organization, and the currency of titles needed and indexed. Index scope relates to the specific topical areas covered and the number of titles indexed. The specificity of indexing has to do with the number and types of index terms used to describe the contents of government publications. The organization of the index includes arrangement, ease of use, and readability. Especially important for nonhistorical indexes is currency. Currency suggests three dimensions: (1) prompt indexing of the publication immediately upon its appearance; (2) limited time lag between indexing, publication of the index, and receipt of that index for library/personal use; and (3) prompt availability of the material indexed, or provision for document delivery service.

Documents librarians can improve user access to government publications, and resolve some of the deficiencies associated with indexes such as the *Monthly Catalog,* by exposing their clientele to online bibliographic database searching. The advantages of online searching relate to the access to current publications, the availability of additional items or fields that are searchable, the ability to combine search terms (introducing more specificity to the retrieval process and allowing librarians to search under more than affixed subject headings), reducing the time spent in the identification of relevant government publications, and, if necessary, the ordering of titles online (Murphy, 1985).

Government publication indexes are rarely available in other locations in the library. This fact underscores the view that general reference sources contain relatively few document citations, and that the identification of document source material is increased by availability to specialized indexes and other reference aids. By sending someone to most general reference indexes, librarians have, by default, excluded the likelihood that the person will utilize government publications.

Sudoc Classification Scheme

Successful retrieval of government publications from the shelves or microfiche drawers may require the assistance of specially trained staff. Yet even these individuals may not be able to utilize the collection to maximum advantage (McClure and Hernon, 1983). Under a specialized classification scheme such as the Sudocs, which does not organize material by subject, effective browsing of the collection becomes difficult. In many cases, users must be aware of not only the issuing agency and format, but also the type of material (e.g., Serial Set) and the date when the source was published.[5] If searching for post-1983 Serial Set publications, users must check one area of the documents collection (assuming the library has a separate collection housing all government publications), while for pre-1983 Serial Set publications a different search procedure is necessary.[6]

PHYSICAL ACCESSIBILITY

To be effective, bibliographic control must take into account the speed of delivery and the quality of information content, as well as the format in which government information appears. Format should not create a barrier to the retrieval of needed information. Creating a better awareness of the information content of government publications may assist efforts to "mainstream" government publications with other information resources, therefore resulting in more use of depository resources. Indexing and abstracting services need to highlight information content, while at the same time informing users and library staff members of variations in format.

Librarians must improve bibliographic control over those resources most frequently needed and used by their clientele, regardless of format, while at the same time enhancing resource sharing capabilities. They should be supportive of the GPO's efforts to make its automated list of item numbers into a union list of depository library holdings. The GPO could produce the list of items selected by libraries in a given geographical area. Such lists, however, can only serve as general indicators; they do not specify the date when a library began to receive publications under an item number or the completeness of subsequent holdings.

In cases where depository resources are distributed to assorted branch libraries on a university campus, documents librarians should be able to anticipate the holdings of a given branch library and investigate the extent to which the public has access to depository holdings. A problem, in some cases, is that libraries may receive depository publications from a central processing unit on campus, as well as purchase some publications and receive others gratis or on exchange. Those that are depository publications may not have been so designated, or the staff may assume that a requested

---

[5] For example, a 1978 publication date does not mean that the GPO automatically picked up that title and included it in the *Monthly Catalog.* The GPO may have cataloged the title any time between 1978 and the present. Herein is the advantage of conducting an online search or using a special *Monthly Catalog* service such as that offered by Auto-Graphics, Inc.

[6] Beginning in 1981 all Serial Set publications (House or Senate documents or reports) have been assigned a Y1 class number instead of the numeric sequencing dating back to 1789. The search for Serial Set publications may necessitate examination of shelves for paper copy holdings and cabinets for microfiche holdings. That search might be in the Y1 or numerical sequencing areas.

publication was not received through depository distribution. Consequently, the public might be denied access to depository publications.

Physical availability also extends to the ability of library staff and users to locate desired publications on the shelves or in microfiche cabinets. Misshelving (or misfiling), as well as crowded shelves and cabinets, impose retrieval problems. Physical availability can be further affected by the arrangement of collections and the extent to which depository publications are kept in a separate collection. It is possible that basic finding aids (e.g., the *Monthly Catalog* and the *Publications Reference File*) are located in the office of the documents librarian and are therefore inaccessible when a staff member is not on duty.

Barriers to physical access to government publications are numerous and must be eliminated if overall use and integration of government publications is to be accomplished. Open stacks encourage browsing and increase access to government publications. Prompt and easy access to microfiche/microfilm viewers and copiers is essential to "physically access" the information contained in such formats. The orderly arrangement of materials on the shelves is a prerequisite for physical access, and weeding of outdated or irrelevant publications can improve physical access. In addition, extended hours of operation, or at least hours of operation for the documents area that are similar to those for the library as a whole, increase physical access. Other less tangible yet equally important factors such as clear labeling of materials, good direction and signage systems, and knowledgeable staff significantly affect physical access to government publications.

The physical accessibility of documents collections is one area largely under the direct control of individual libraries. Depository libraries can increase significantly physical access to government publications simply by addressing some of the issues raised above and by increasing their awareness of problems related to physical access.[7]

---

[7] The Legislative Committee, American Library Association, prepared a draft memorandum that presumably "reflects the legislative goals of the membership and the overall goals and objectives of the Association" (Vernon, 1987). The document specifies that:

- ". . . comprehensive bibliographic control of all government publications be provided through nationally recognized databases and library networks
- . . . all government publications and government produced information be disseminated in whatever format is most appropriate for the information, most cost effective, and most [beneficial] for government agencies, libraries, and the general public
- . . . depository libraries be recognized and funded to operate as Federal information centers for public access.

The Association endorses a comprehensive and coordinated sales program for government information which offers on a cost-recovery basis all government publications in whatever format, without pricing basic documents beyond the reach of nonprofit libraries and information centers responsible for providing public access" (p. 4).

No supporting documentation specifies how these general and sweeping recommendations will be

Individual depository libraries should investigate their own situations and ensure that the public can locate needed publications in a timely manner. The perceived value of government publications/information declines when users experience problems in "tracking down" potentially useful material. It merits note that some faculty members from baccalaureate institutions will not request online searching of bibliographic databases because the search would most likely identify source material not locally held. Instead, they want better access to the resources already contained in their institution's depository collection (Hernon, 1979). The importance of physical availability cannot be ignored; it is as important as the other facets of bibliographic control.

CHANGING FOCUS

Some significant bibliographic control-related issues currently facing the documents field include the development of document delivery systems, inter-institutional cooperation, collection development (planning for the controlled growth of documents collections), and stimulating awareness and use of documents collections. Bibliographic control, a topic that has perhaps received an overabundance of attention in the literature of documents librarianship, is a means to aid librarians in the selection and retrieval of information needed by their clientele; it is not an end unto itself. As has already been indicated, attention should be focused on the acquisition and accessibility of materials most potentially useful and most heavily used. For many libraries, lesser-needed materials should be acquired and retained on a highly selective basis.

Bibliographic control contains four major elements: (1) the location, (2) acquisition, and (3) recording of publications, as well as (4) the provision of subject access. Each of these elements has aspects that may be viewed as internal and external to individual libraries. In relation to the external aspects, librarians advise on national bibliographic control policy and make recommendations on such matters as the establishment of standards, authority lists, and improved distribution, cataloging, and indexing systems. They offer guidance in the preparation of guidelines for the minimal servicing of documents collections, while encouraging government agencies and the private sector to improve mechanisms by which new publications are announced.

---

implemented. The discussion in this chapter of the book questions the practicality and feasibility of the recommendations. Comprehensive identification is an impossible goal to realize. Further, the recommendations ignore the competitive (e.g., political, and economic) environment in which information policies are formulated and implemented. Stakeholders do not necessarily share the same goals. And, finally, change must be built from existing laws and practices. There cannot be a radical departure from the present.

In relation to the internal aspects, librarians acquire, and facilitate access to, those information resources needed by their clientele. In the process of improving bibliographic control over their own collections, some of them are investigating the feasibility of developing and joining database systems. In brief, this chapter has suggested that librarians should be involved primarily in those aspects of bibliographic control that have the greatest implications for increasing access to government publications.

Bibliographic control issues must be resolved at a number of different levels before increased access to government publications can be realized. First, greater coordination among various government agencies (at the local, national, and international levels) must be accomplished to identify publications appropriate for complete bibliographic control and to standardize the format and content of bibliographic information for government publications. Second, increased use of various information handling technologies, such as online catalogs and automated shelflists, is needed—by both government agencies and individual libraries. Third, recognition that all government publications are not necessarily worthy of bibliographic control, or that the activities related to providing such control are not cost-effective, is necessary. Finally, government documents librarians must look to issues of bibliographic control in the larger context of providing increased access to government information, improved collection development, as well as better use and increased integration of government publications as information resources. Bibliographic control should be considered only as a means toward a larger end, i.e., increased access to (and use of) government publications.

6

Developing Collections of U.S. Government Publications

A collection development policy sets the parameters of the documents collection including the levels of government collected, a determination of how comprehensive or selective the collection should be, and criteria for selection and retention. It also demonstrates that collection development is an ongoing decision making process by which staff members guide all the library collections to meet predetermined goals and objectives. Any subset of the whole collection, such as the documents holdings, must adhere to the overall library and institutional mission and goals. Documents, including those housed in separate collections or published in nonprint formats, should not be treated as a specialized or unique resource isolated intellectually from other library holdings. Further, documents, even those received "gratis" through the depository program, are not a free or inexpensive resource. Their costs relate to processing, storage, use, staffing, and the need for adequate finding aids (e.g., the purchase of commercially produced indexes).

In the belief that libraries must control all parts of their collections, this chapter presents an overview of collection development as applied to government publications, and identifies major research findings. The chapter, however, does not explain the steps involved in conducting collection development; works such as Evans (1987) and Hernon and Purcell (1982) discuss different aspects of "how to do collection development." The chapter, though, does suggest that depository libraries, other than regionals, should be very selective in the acquisition and retention of government publications, concentrating on those most likely to be used. In short, a formal,

114

written, collection development policy statement is essential for effective access to government publications.[1]

The ultimate purpose of collection development, in terms of service, is to make information resources accessible to the library's community. Clearly, collection development is a critical determinant of the user's ability to gain access to government publications. However, the degree to which collection development for government publications is integrated into overall library collection development is likely to affect the bibliographic accessibility, physical availability, professional service, and status of government publications. These four criteria combine to provide the basis for administrative integration of government publications.

Collection development is a preliminary prerequisite to the administrative integration of government publications/ information into a library's collection. Thus, this chapter also presents an administrative overview of the relationship between collection development and integration of government publications, and identifies myths regarding collection development for government publications. The chapter contains a worksheet that librarians can use to manipulate the collection development process and integrate government publications more fully into the library collection. In its conclusion, chapter offers suggestions for implementing the integration process.

COLLECTION DEVELOPMENT

The Concept

Collection development deserves the constant attention of all professional staff members. However, in many cases, collection development for government publications is assumed to be a self-directed activity—one that operates almost by default. The acquisition of materials and their appearance on

---

[1] The GPO expects each depository library to "formulate and implement a written depository collection development policy which articulates the library's strategy for identifying and meeting the government information needs of the local area. This policy should be formulated using the same criteria discussed in Section 2 of the *Federal Depository Library Manual.*"

"The depository collection development policy should also address procedures for obtaining documents requested by patrons but not selected by the library: inter-depository coordination of selections; resources available locally; and inter-library loan services."

"Any change in the *quantity* of documents selected should not negatively affect the *quality* of the documents collection or the library's ability to meet the government information needs of the local area. At a minimum, depositories should seriously consider selecting the items listed in the most relevant of the *Federal Depository Library Manual's* 'core collections.' GPO's *Subject Bibliographies* and the *Publications Reference File* (PRF) should also be reviewed in order to make informed collection development decisions" ("Guidelines for the Depository Library System," 1987).

the shelves is assumed to be evidence of collection development, whereas there is actually more to the process.

In practice, the development of documents collection should conform to the same practices as those applied to other library materials; therefore, it should address factors such as determining how much and what material to acquire (by subject, content, format, etc.), the number of copies, how long to retain the material, and how to manage what is kept. Some documents librarians may not view collection development in its full dimensions and they may place a higher priority on processing and bibliographic control.

Collection development is a planning process encompassing decision making regarding the selection and retention of material, as well as the initiation of an evaluation component. Through evaluation, libraries can determine the extent to which their holdings provide for and meet the information needs of their user groups. Libraries can also gauge such factors as the types of resources needed and make the most effective allocation of financial resources. Further, they can then set priorities among competing resource needs, better cope with limited spatial environments dictating the controlled growth of collections, and improve access to the major resources needed by client groups. The objectives of collection development are to:

- Provide for the information needs of the library's community
- Increase the quality of information resources available to the library's community
- Allocate available financial resources for the efficient purchase of information resources
- Develop procedures by which the effectiveness of the collection vis-a-vis the information needs of the community, are regularly evaluated.

The more libraries try to acquire sources to meet single and infrequent requests, the more publications they must acquire. The more acquired, the higher the cost for processing, storage, and service. In addition, excessive acquisition of materials creates congestion on the shelves, which itself constitutes a reason for limited use of documents collections (Hernon, 1979).

Libraries that want to develop collections that emphasize the most frequently needed source material must be able to draw upon inter-institutional cooperation for lesser-needed material. Thus, collection development techniques require attention in two areas: (1) collection development activities within the institution, and (2) the development of a system for the prompt and reliable delivery of requested source material among depository libraries. The lack of effective resource sharing and document delivery systems serves as a major deterrent to libraries that want to limit documents collection building to a carefully selected body of materials.

Government publications collection development in libraries should reflect institutional goals and objectives, and include source material that is of current and potential interest to the clientele. Libraries must decide how widely to collect and how much to collect in each subject, discipline, topic, or area of study (Baughman et al, 1980, p. 94). They can do this by addressing factors such as curriculum, subject literature, institutional mission, format, date of publication, publication quality, intended audience, and cost.

The concept of collection development could extend to the referral process, that is, situations in which libraries serve as a clearinghouse for the referral of user requests to other information providers. Under such circumstances, the identification of appropriate "outside" sources of information is a logical extension of the collection development function of a library. Where this is the case, it should be remembered that government information appears in a variety of formats and that libraries are but one mediator of the universe of publicly available government information.

Selection

Selective depositories do not choose all the titles that the GPO and the Depository Library Council to the Public Printer believe should be common to all depository collections. In fact, not all depository libraries select basic titles such as the *Monthly Catalog, Statistical Abstract of the United States*, and the *Congressional Directory* (Hernon and Purcell, 1982).

Since a high percentage of item numbers have limited value to most libraries, perhaps even including regional depositories, one can question whether it is necessary to make them all available for depository distribution. It might be time for re-examination of distribution decision making and practices. Identification of the universe of government publications, and the inclusion of these titles in depository distribution, need not be thought of necessarily as synonymous concepts. At the request of the Depository Library Council, the GPO has encouraged "depository libraries, either solely or in conjunction with neighboring depositories . . . [to] make demonstrable efforts to identify and meet the Government information needs of the local area." "'Local area' is determined by the library size, its distance from any other depositories, and/or the U.S. Congressional district" ("Guidelines for the Depository Library System," 1987).

The intent of this policy statement is to:

> shift the focus of . . . collection development . . . away from a required minimum item number selection and towards a collection development strategy aimed at more directly meeting the government information needs of the local area (Ibid.).

If depository libraries, indeed, attempt to meet the information needs of those situated in the "local area," they will have to spend substantially more time reviewing item selections and evaluating the existing collection. They will have to know their enlarged community and apply these insights to collection development and the marketing of depository services.

The identification of U.S. government publications from the item list does not constitute "selection." Numerous non-GPO publications never enter the depository library program for distribution. Thus, the selection process should probably include an awareness of non-GPO publications and concentrate attention on specific Federal agencies that are known to produce publications of interest to the clientele of the local library. However, the selection of non-GPO publications should be based on a clear set of collection development goals and objectives, as well as specific selection criteria.

Newly established depositories must decide which item numbers to select, while existing depositories should review and update their selection profile. The problem is that both types of libraries receive a list of item numbers devoid of any reference to subject areas in which agencies frequently publish. To assist libraries and their collection development decision making, the library of the University of California, Riverside, has captured information about depository item numbers in machine-readable form (dBASE III for use on an IBM PC, or compatible hardware, with hard disk capability). The database includes all active item numbers available for selection since September 1984. The staff are "assigning broad subject or discipline concepts to each record to further enhance the utility of the database as a collection development and management tool" (Mooney, 1986, p. 3).

The collection development staff at Ball State University is also reviewing the GPO item number list and attempting to impose a general subject classification upon it (see Figure 6–1 for an example). The purpose is to identify which government bodies issue source material of value to each academic department. Such information will be included in the written collection development policy statement and guide the library in the level of intensity that it collects from each government body.[2]

The approach taken at Ball State University is more useful than the type of core list of basic titles displayed in the *Federal Depository Library Manual* (1985). The *Manual* provides a core list for law, small/medium sized public, and small academic libraries, but does not place suggestions within a subject context. Further, the recommendations are based upon complier preferences as opposed to research into use patterns. Unless a list is cast in subject terms, it does not provide libraries with options and opportunities to

---

[2] The strength of a collection and the intensity of collecting may be characterized in terms of levels (*Guidelines for Collection Development*, 1979): minimal, basic, study, research, and comprehensive. Hajnal (1981, pp. 93–98) defines the five levels and discusses their application to documents librarianship.

Figure 6-1.
An Example of a Preliminary Matching of Federal Agencies and Subject Areas*

SUBJECT AREA	FEDERAL AGENCY
Architecture	Energy Department, E
	Federal Energy Regulatory Commission, E2.
	Energy Information Administration, E3.
	Housing & Urban Development Department, HH
	National Park Service, I29.
	Heritage Conservation & Recreation Service, I70.
	National Capital Planning Commission, NC
	Architectural & Transportation Barriers Compliance Board, Y3.B27:
	Advisory Council on Historic Preservation, Y3.H62:
Art	Fine Arts Commission, FA
	Library of Congress, Prints & Photographs Division, LC25.
	National Endowment for the Arts, NF2.
	National Museum of American Art, SI6.
	Freer Gallery of Art, SI7.
	National Gallery of Art, SI8.
	National Portrait Gallery, SI11.
	Senate Art & Antiquities Commission, Y3.Ar7:
Geology	National Oceanic & Atmospheric Adm., C55
	National Environmental Satellite, Data, and Information Service, C55.200:
	Geological Survey, I19.
	Bureau of Reclamation, I27
	Bureau of Mines, I28
	Bureau of Land Management, I53
	Library of Congress, Science & Technology Division, LC33.
Gerontology	Older Americans Volunteer Programs, AA2.
	National Institute on Aging, HE20.3800:
	Aging Administration, HE23.3000:
	National Clearinghouse on Aging, HE23.3100:
	Advisory Council on Social Security, Y3.Ad9/3:
	Federal Council on Aging, Y3.F31/15:
	Senate Special Committee on Aging, Y4.Ag4:
	House Select Committee on Aging, Y4.Ag4/2

*Stanley P. Hodge, Director of Collection Development, Ball State University Library, developed this classification.

address different missions, goals, and objectives. The availability of a core list does not replace the selection function of collection development. Collection needs change over time, as do government publishing programs. Therefore, collection development must be viewed as an active, ongoing process that involves dynamic decision making.

Retention Decision

With few exceptions, the GPO mandates that selective depositories retain government publications for a minimum of five years. Studies of academic social scientists (Hernon, 1979; Hernon and Purcell, 1982) and users of public libraries (Purcell, 1980) have shown that these client groups often do not consult government publications over three years of age. Those deviating from this pattern supplement recently issued publications (issued within the last three years) with statistical data (time series). Historians, of course, rely on older source material, but often those within a few recognizable types (e.g., the Serial Set, congressional hearings and debates, and statistical data).

Research into the half-life[3] of selected serial titles suggests that a five, or even a three, year retention policy should not be applied uniformly across levels of government and documents types and titles. For example, the lifespan of the *Federal Register* and the *Monthly Labor Review* is relatively short (less than five years), while *Federal Probation* has a much longer lifespan (Hernon and Shepherd, 1983). Nonetheless, even for these titles, it is questionable whether selective depository libraries need to collect or retain complete files beginning with a journal's inception. These libraries should be able to identify the number of current years most likely to receive use and to concentrate their holdings within those years.

Clearly, the GPO should re-examine its five-year retention policy and provide libraries with guidance concerning retention decision making. At the same time, documents librarians must become familiar with concepts such as Bradford's law of scattering[4] and the portrait of collection development given in this chapter. The principles of collection development (e.g., for retention decision making) are similar to those for developing collections of other library resources. Undoubtedly, general investigations into book and periodical availability, which were intended as an aid for determining the extent to which library collections are used and the cost of that use, have value to the documents field.[5]

---

[3] Half-life is the number of journal publication years counting back from the base year (e.g., the year of the index or other source used as the basis for determining citation patterns) where the articles have accounted for 50% of the total identifiable citations.

[4] Bradford (1948) discusses the law of scattering.

[5] For examples of such studies see Lancaster (1977) and Buckland (1975).

In some instances, libraries have not weeded their depository collections for years. Faced with severe and immediate space shortages, they must cope with a significant amount of congestion in the collection. They must quickly develop strategies for reviewing source material that might be discarded or sent to another depository. An academic library, for example, might consider whether the material supports the mission and curriculum of the institution, the level of use that material has received, proximity to other depositories, availability of paper copy publications on microform, and extent to which the information content is outdated or duplicated in other source material. Obviously staff will begin the reviewing process in those areas of the collection where they suspect that they can immediately dispose of numerous titles.

Actually, decision making regarding retention should not be a one-time or irregular process. Staff members should engage in a collection review on a regular basis and review the collection objectives and the information needs of clientele. Unless they do so, retention decision making becomes associated with crisis management.

Use

Documents use patterns for academic social scientists, in particular economists, have received the major emphasis in the research literature (Hernon, 1979; Hernon, 1982; Hernon and Purcell, 1982). These faculty members most often consult government publications conveying statistical data. They also make frequent use of serials, annual reports, reports of investigation and research, and committee and commission reports. Economists, for example, are most likely to rely on a few document serials (e.g., the *Economic Report of the President*) and publications of selected government bodies (e.g., the Bureau of the Census and the Bureau of Labor Statistics). Given the importance of statistical data, the *American Statistics Index*, produced by the Congressional Information Service, takes on added importance. With this index, and perhaps access to the accompanying microfiche package, libraries can improve access to statistical data needed by their client group. Thus, depository libraries ought to promote the strengths of the depository collection actively and aggressively, and show how it supplements library holdings in other formats.

A relatively defined group of government bodies and documents types may account for a large percentage of the most heavily used source material (Hernon and Purcell, 1982). Attempts to develop comprehensive or extensive collections will add titles at an exponential rate; perhaps a basic concentration of government bodies and documents types comprises part of the nucleus, or core, of all fields. In other words, there may not be as many different core bodies and documents types as there are special fields. Core resources, as have been found to exist with journal literatures, appeal to a variety of fields. For example, the *Monthly Labor Review*, which is a periodical covering labor and public policy, appeals largely to faculty members in fields such as business and economics, demography, history, law, public administration, and sociology (Hernon and Shepherd, 1983).

Library retention of more government publications than client groups require presents problems in gaining access to needed source material. Shelves overcrowded with publications of varying quality, and drawers of compacted microfiche not arranged in proper sequence, undoubtedly have a negative impact on users in their search for pertinent source material. The problems involved in making documents available when needed by library users may be different by an order of magnitude from those associated with providing other library materials for users. The factors that create greater problems in providing documents are the high rate of obsolescence for many documents, the ephemeral nature of a substantial proportion of the materials, the extensive number of separate titles, and the marginal quality of many bibliographic access resources. For these reasons, documents librarians must keep use patterns in mind when making selection and retention decisions.

Existing research indicates that academic social scientists rely upon their subject literature and interpersonal sources (e.g., colleagues) for awareness of source material. They do not make extensive use of indexing and abstracting services and bibliographies housed in libraries (Hernon, 1979; Hernon and Purcell, 1982). In fact, libraries may not comprise a major resource in the information-gathering of these social scientists. Further, these researchers and teachers may be satisfied with their present information-gathering strategies and believe that awareness of additional source material may overburden them with information. Consequently, they may question the value and quality of information for which they must undertake a sustained search.

Faculty members having to teach a number of different courses at baccalaureate institutions may be generalists, who seek capsulized information rather than the detail contained in government publications. Faculty members at other academic institutions may have access to the small body of heavily used government publications from other channels. In addition, over time, academic social scientists become familiar with the publishing programs of the agencies with which they deal. These individuals may not always seek ways to gain access to a wider range of source material. Consulting bibliographic aids and library collections may not be an effective means of gaining access to either government publications or government information retained in machine-readable form. The exception would be numeric data files that various commercial services offer.

If government publications housed in depository collections are not utilized to their potential, what are the implications, then, of an acquisition policy that encourages the selection of a vast number of government publications, many of which will not be heavily used? Libraries should carefully select the levels of government, government bodies, and documents types and titles needed, regardless of the format in which source material appears. The relationship of the source material to current and potential user needs, and the institutional mission and library goals, is the overriding consideration.

Self-Assessment of Documents Collections

Since many libraries enter only a small portion of their depository collection into card or online catalogs, and rely upon bibliographic tools for access to the collection, they should ascertain the extent to which they have acquired appropriate finding aids. To ensure that they are meeting the information needs of client groups effectively and efficiently, they should determine whether their clientele have to go elsewhere in their search for potentially high use publications. For relevant insights into these matters, documents librarians could monitor circulation records (if documents do indeed circulate), the types of reference questions asked, and interlibrary loan records. In addition, they could interact with client groups through outreach programs and formal use surveys. All of the information gathered could be useful, within the context of specific goals and objectives, to make selection and retention decisions, as well as to evaluate the collection.

Figure 6–2 suggests a form by which both depository and nondepository librarians can inventory their collections and reference needs. First, they can list those reference works held (sections A and B of the form) and match these to the information needs of their clientele. By monitoring the currentness of publication dates, they can determine if the sources owned are indeed the most up-to-date or if another title might be more beneficial. In this regard, it becomes important to not only list the reference works held, but also assess their frequency of use. Second, librarians can analyze circulation records and any patterns in the requested source material (section C). The purpose is to ensure that resource sharing does not extend to high interest documents types and titles. Third, they can monitor which databases are searched online (section D) and the interrelationship between manual and online searching. Since DIALOG now makes available numeric data collected by the Bureaus of the Census and Labor Statistics, librarians might also determine if online searching is used more for access to bibliographic citations or numeric data (e.g., occupational characteristics and unemployment figures).

As the figure illustrates, data useful for collection development can be gathered without directly contacting clientele. For insights into the physical accessibility of resources contained in the collection, documents librarians might identify selected topics of general interest to their clientele and take fifty or more citations from basic indexes (e.g., the *Monthly Catalog*, the *Publications Reference File*, and the *American Statistics Index*) on these topics. They could then search their shelflist and the collection to see how many of the titles can be retrieved. The exercise would disclose problems that clientele might experience in their search for government publications, and provide a measure of collection effectiveness. At the same time, librarians could look into referral options for source material not locally held.

Both the inventory and analysis of document delivery capabilities have value to both depository and nondepository libraries. Nondepository public libraries, for example, might discover that the *Monthly Catalog*, their card catalog, and their vertical file do not provide sufficient access to their documents holdings. Two central questions become: "Is the *Monthly Catalog* an appropriate index for documents retrieval purposes?, and "Do patrons need to be aware of publications not locally held?" Perhaps these libraries should discontinue their subscription to the *Monthly Catalog* and identify appropriate subject bibliographies issued by the GPO. They could then select government publications from the active files of the GPO, and distribute topical bibliographies that alert clientele to locally held resources. In this way, government publications become a more important information resource to the library; both reference staff and client groups have more effective and efficient access to potentially useful government publications.[6]

The two methods described in this section represent examples of ways to evaluate documents collections in both depository and nondepository libraries. Using these methods, library staff can determine whether the collection matches user needs and meets the objectives of both the collection and library. Evaluation should be conducted on a continuous basis, while every effort should be made to guarantee that the collection addresses local needs, current and potential (Robinson, 1981).

INTEGRATED COLLECTION DEVELOPMENT

The broad picture that relates collection development to integration cannot be overlooked or ignored. Thus, it is important that the concept of integration of government publications be clarified. Chapter 12 discusses the concept in greater detail and notes that the concept does *not* imply physical integration.

---

[6] Purcell (1981b) discusses collection development for nondepository public libraries.

Figure 6-2.
Self Assessment Techniques

A. *INVENTORY OF GOVERNMENT DOCUMENT REFERENCE SOURCES*

Count	Title	Publisher	Call Number	Publication Date

B. *INVENTORY OF GOVERNMENT DOCUMENT INDEXES AND CATALOGS*

Count	Title	Publisher	Call Number	Publication Date

C. *ANALYSIS OF INTERLIBRARY LOANS FOR GOVERNMENT DOCUMENTS*

Count	Title of Publication	Author/Agency	Publication Date	Requestor/ Department	S/M	Other Information

D. *ONLINE SEARCHING OF GOVERNMENT DOCUMENT RELATED DATA BASES*

Count	Data Base(s) Used	Vendor	Search Time	Requestor/ Department	Cost	Cities	Other Information

Four primary criteria can be suggested to assess integration of government publications. These are:

- *Bibliographic accessibility*, the degree to which a patron has equal access to reference sources related to government publications as to information sources of a more traditional nature
- *Physical availability*, the degree to which a patron can physically obtain a copy of a government publication compared to other more traditional types of publications held in the library
- *Professional service*, obtaining the same level of reference and referral competencies from the library staff for government publications as for other types of information resources
- *Status*, the degree to which government publications receive similar resource support (both tangible and intangible) compared to other types of library materials.

Accomplishment of integration, based on the above criteria, is essential for meaningful collection development and access to government publications.

The model depicted in Figure 6–3 attempts to relate overall library collection development to integration of government publications. The assumption is that an active collection development procedure for government publications will result in better integration of the documents holdings into the library collection as a whole. Further, the model stresses the importance of having clearly identified objectives for the documents collection. Boxes 1 and 2 suggest the primary inputs to the model. In short, two items, community requirements and analysis of existing collection, reflect the needs assessment aspect of the model. For developing any library collection (including that for government publications), the nature of the community (both users and nonusers) must be known. Librarians must be able to differentiate between the needs of their community for information resources and those of the collection as determined by the librarians themselves. While collection development must fulfill the information needs of the community, librarians have ultimate responsibility for the contents of the collection. The role of the library staff must include more than simply responding to the community; they must also direct, plan, and guide the collection toward certain predetermined goals.

Regardless of whether a library collection development policy exists, documents librarians must work with those individuals responsible for the selection and acquisition of materials. In terms of integrating the collection development policy for government publications into the overall library policy or activities, documents librarians may choose one of two basic approaches: a separate or subject policy.

The separate approach simply is a collection development policy that

Figure 6-3.
Overview of Integrated Collection Development

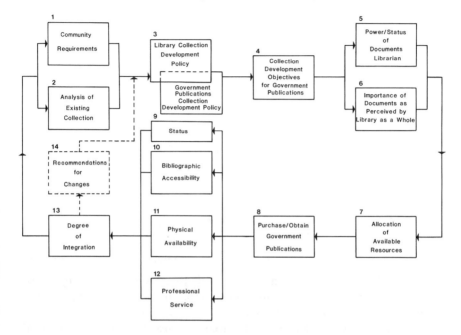

pertains only to government publications, although it reinforces basic premises set forth in the library policy. This approach preserves the integrity of government publications as a bibliographic unit, and the documents department retains primary control over the development of the collection. However, the documents department is more likely to "do its own thing" rather than support the overall collection development policies of the library.

The second approach is to employ a subject-oriented collection development policy for government documents vis-a-vis all the major subject collections/disciplines in the library. Proponents of this approach maintain that subject relationships comprise the basis by which core collections and in-depth research collections can be built (Baughman, 1977). Under such an approach, policies explaining the relationship between government publications and specific subject areas would be detailed. The effect of such an approach is to link government publications closely to the major subject areas in which the library collects. However, implementation of this approach demands considerable time and conceptualization, as well as an extensive research base. At this time, relevant research in the documents field is only now emerging (see Figure 6–1).

As indicated by the overlapping boxes in Figure 6–3 (box 3), the collection policy for government publications is developed as part of the

Figure 6-4.
Worksheet for the Establishment of Government Publications Collection Development Objectives

| I.   COMMUNITY REQUIREMENTS | | | |
Factors	Objectives	Completion Date	Evaluation Criteria
1. Significant increase in number of Graduate students in Scientific/ Technical departments	1. Develop departmental profiles by which NTIS microfiche can be purchased	one year	1. Establish profiles for eight engineering departments:
2.	2.		2.
3.	3.		3.
4.	4.		4.
II. COLLECTION ANALYSIS			
Factors	Objectives	Completion Date	Performance Criteria
1. Inadequate government reports/ documents related to energy	1. Review list of items selected to insure all material related to energy as being received via depository status	one month	1. Examination of items being selected and ordering items related to energy not currently being received
2.	2.		2.
3.	3.		3.
4.	4.		4.

overall collection policy for the library. Whether a separate or subject approach is taken, the process must include input from other members of the library. Part of this input can be obtained during the needs assessment phase (boxes 1 and 2), when documents librarians discuss the wants and needs of other library areas for government publications.

Regardless of the approach taken, the next step is to state objectives for developing the documents collection. Figure 6–4 comprises a worksheet that may be of assistance to documents librarians devising such objectives. Based on the analysis of two variables, community requirements and collection analysis, "factors" can be identified. A factor is any significant characteristic resulting from the analysis of the collection or of the community. In short, factors are conclusions derived from the needs assessment.

Once these factors are identified, objectives that respond to them are stated; these objectives should be explicit, measurable, and ambitious. Further, they must reinforce the collection development goals of the library as a whole. In the example provided in Figure 6–4, each factor has one objective. In reality, a number of different objectives may be required to respond adequately to a given factor. For each objective, librarians should also provide evaluation criteria in order that they (as well as the administration) will know if the objective has been accomplished. These objectives should be made known publicly to the individual responsible for overall library collection development, as well as to other librarians.

Returning to Figure 6–3, because of the unique nature of government publications, a critical aspect affecting an integrated collection development process is the power/status of documents librarians and the importance of documents as perceived by the library as a whole (boxes 5 and 6). Although both of these aspects are intangible, they cannot be overlooked. Power may be defined as the ability of an individual to modify others' behavior toward predetermined objectives. Further, political power depends on the person's formal status, charisma, and authority to enforce sanctions on other organizational members (McClure, 1980). This variable is likely to be related to the effectiveness with which the individual has successfully educated other librarians about the value of government publications as an information resource. Although no data exist on the point, the two intangible variables are likely to be related directly to the allocation of resources necessary for documents librarians to accomplish collection objectives.

After the available resources have been allocated and appropriate government publications and support materials (trade publications) purchased, the four criteria of integration must be examined, and the performance indicators formulated. Documents librarians will then be able to provide fresh input into the collection development policies for the documents collection and the library as a whole.

Addressing the final two stages, the degree of integration and making appropriate recommendations for changes (see Figure 6– 5), provides for an ongoing review of existing collection development policies. Without continuous input resulting from these two stages, as well as an analysis of the existing collection and community requirements, the integration of government publications into the overall library collection development will be limited. Evans (1987) details a number of the procedures presented in Figure 6–3, but in the context of library collections in general. However, much of that discussion can be applied in a depository setting.

MYTHS HINDERING INTEGRATED COLLECTION DEVELOPMENT

Administrative myths regarding collection development for government publications appear to hinder the integrated approach. These myths are identified in the form of assumptions that are usually *not* explicitly stated, but can have a significant impact on the documents collection. The first category of myths, which relates to collection development in general, has an effect on the accessibility of all types of materials in the library—including government publications. They are specifically identified because they must be confronted directly if documents librarians are to be successful in integrating government publications throughout the library. However, unless they are addressed, and disposed of, at the organizational level, they will have a debilitating effect on collection development.

Figure 6-5.
The Concept of Integration

CRITERIA	INDICATORS
1. Bibliographic Accessibility	Do patrons have the same probability of determining the existence of a certain government publication as they do of determining the existence of another information source?
	Do patrons have equal access to indexes and reference tools related to government publications as to those related to other information sources in the library?
	Do patrons have the same probability of obtaining specific information with government publications as they do with another information source?
2. Physical Availability	Do patrons have the same probability of locating and obtaining a specific government document (once its existence within the library is verified) as any other type of material in the library?
	Do patrons have the same opportunity to borrow government publications as they would another information resources?
3. Professional Service	Do patrons have the same awareness of the information sources available in government publications as for other areas of the library collection?
	Do patrons have the same opportunity to be referred to any appropriate government publication as to other information sources in the library?
	Do patrons deal with librarians who are competent, trained, and knowledgeable about government publications/information as they would with librarians who have other responsibilities?
4. Status	Do government documents receive similar resource support (staff, materials, equipment, etc.) as do other areas of the library?
	Do documents librarians participate in library administrative matters to the same extent as other librarians?
	Do the director and librarians perceive government publications to be as valuable an information resource as other library holdings?

One assumption, which occurs by default and not as a planned policy, is that available financial resources dictate collection development objectives. If available resources shape collection policies, librarians will be forever responding to constraints rather than manipulating them. First, the specific objectives for collection development should be established, then prioritized given the financial constraints. This strategy forces librarians to re-examine the needs of the collection, the information needs of their community, and the priorities between these two forces. Only after the needs have been established will available money be assigned to accomplish specific objectives related to these needs.

This myth is especially harmful to collection development for government publications in those cases where documents librarians have little status in the library. In such cases, money is allocated regardless of objectives and based, rather, on power of the individual area head; or documents librarians may have been simply "left out" of the allocation process. Either way, documents are viewed as less important than traditional materials. If documents librarians cannot (or will not) make a strong case for their utility, government publications end up at the bottom of the priority list. Documents librarians must be assertive and make known the needs, priorities, and objectives of documents collection development.

Integrated collection development must be based on an analysis of: (1) the library's community of users and nonusers, (2) the information needs of the community, (3) existing strengths and weaknesses of the collection, and (4) the attitudes held by the librarians regarding the appropriateness of government publications as an information resource. Community analysis implies a study of actual and potential client groups served by the library. It is difficult to understand how successful collection development can occur without access to information obtained about the characteristics and information needs of these client groups. Basing a collection policy on supposition or fragmentary experience is misleading and inadequately represents the information needs of the entire user community.

Libraries must collect information about the actual and potential users of the library, as well as identify their information needs and information-gathering behavior. In this way, they can determine the potential role of the institutional library as an information provider. Knowledge of the information needs of the user population serves as a base point against which the major provisions of a collection development policy can be judged and priorities established, and against which individual selection decisions can be made. In addition, the holdings of other information resources within the institution or the geographical area should be identified. The purpose is to reduce costs by avoiding unnecessary duplication and to increase the speed of access to requested materials.

A number of sources are available to assist libraries in devising and refining collection development policies for their documents holdings. Libraries wanting to undertake a community analysis might consult *Use of Government Publications by Social Scientists* and Appendix D, the faculty questionnaire of that book (Hernon, 1979). This questionnaire, with approval of the author, can be modified to meet local needs. Hernon and Purcell (1982) discuss the elements essential in formulating a collection policy and reprint collection policies is use at seven academic institutions. They also reprint a use survey that, also with authors' permission, could be modified to meet local needs. Libraries may even want to survey client groups about the information formats they consult (e.g., paper copy and microform), willingness to use government publications appearing in a microformat or government information in machine-readable or electronic format, and the types of government publications/information they would use in a non-paper format. Such information would be useful in making selection and retention decisions.

Documents librarians do not have to investigate the information needs of all client groups simultaneously and to the same depth. It is important, however, that community analyses be undertaken and that they be conducted on a regular basis. Documents use patterns can be considered in a large context—use of the library and its resources. If this is done, documents staff members can work with librarians in other departments to integrate administratively various library genre.

The second set of myths pertains specifically to the attitudes and assumptions that may be held by librarians and supported by library administrators regarding government publications. Foremost in this category is the "some in, some out" syndrome of documents for libraries with seemingly separate documents departments. In other words, reference librarians in different departments have their "favorite" documents that they want in their area, while the remaining publications reside in the documents department. Typical candidates include high visibility periodicals, census material, special reference sources, or "unique" information resources. An example of this assumption formalized in an acquisitions policy is:

> All substantial monographs and serials will be fully catalogued and incorporated into the general collection. Ephemeral materials and publications which do not lend themselves easily to cataloging, and those which can be serviced better by the documents librarians will be housed in the government documents departments (Futas, 1977, p. 183).

Ostensibly innocent, this policy allows for some "in" (the less important ones) and some "out" (the better ones). The net effect is to increase the function of the documents department as a warehouse by removing its most important information resources.

Another myth states that duplicate reference sources for government publications are to be avoided. This strategy can work to a disadvantage for government documents at two different levels. First, such an assumption means that basic documents reference sources (e.g., the *Statistical Abstract of the United States*) will be maintained in the general reference area. Numerous excellent government reference sources are thus removed from the documents area, because duplicates are not obtained. At a second level, trade reference works typically are not duplicated. Thus, depending on their physical location, basic indexes such as the *American Statistics Index* are not available to either the general reference department or specialized reference departments (e.g., that for business and economics).

Key reference works related to government documents must be

bought in duplicate when separate collections exist. Otherwise, many patrons are automatically excluded from the possibility of gaining access to government publications, because traditional indexes cover government publications so selectively. Libraries must escape the volume/title count mentality of obtaining more material that is less accessible. The purchase of duplicate key reference sources will increase access to existing government publications—many of which are typically inaccessible in many libraries. Without a collection development policy that allows—indeed, encourages—duplicate purchase of key government publications, integration will be hindered. Criteria can, and must, be established to determine when the purchase of duplicates is appropriate.

A sure tip-off to the lack of integration of government publications in the collection comes from a collection development policy statement in which government publications are considered as "other." The term itself implies treatment different from "regular" information resources and an attitude of second-class citizenship. Because "other" is a vague term or refers to miscellaneous sources, "other" materials either become hard to deal with or are relatively unimportant to the library. In brief, librarians should not allow government publications to be treated as "other."

A myth that is more than a problem of semantics states that because government publications are cheap, they cannot be very valuable. First, documents are "cheap" only for depository libraries, and then only in terms of the receipt of those item numbers selected. "Cheap" suggests less cost compared to similar materials available from private publishers. "Valuable" suggests that the information source has a potential to resolve the information needs of a current or potential user. If nondocuments librarians are not familiar with the value of government publications, documents librarians must inform (educate) them. Clearly, librarians and administrators who are ignorant about government publications cannot be expected to see them as valuable.

Another myth holds that government publications are self-contained materials and, therefore, do not require separate budgets for the purchase of additional reference resources, typically those from nongovernment sources. Such an assumption forces a dependence on government produced reference sources, and ignores the fact that the major (and often the best) reference tools to government publications/information are published by the private sector. To obtain access to government publications, resources must be allocated for the purchase of commercially produced reference sources, and documents librarians must obtain budgetary control over the collection development process for government publications. Independent budgets under the control of the documents department are essential in order that the organizational recognition of documents is encouraged and that documents receive a fair share of the total budget allocation.

Although depository status prescribes parameters for the selection of materials, the myth that collection development is a given due to depository status is incorrect. Selection of item numbers and their regular review, in light of specified goals and objectives and user needs, is a significant portion of collection development for government publications. Further, depository status does not mean that the library receives all U.S. government publications. Careful analysis and selection are required to determine which non-depository materials (including information resources from other levels of government) are appropriate to the collection.

These myths all work to limit the degree to which government publications are integrated into overall library collection development policies. Documents librarians must address these myths and educate their colleagues concerning the realities of documents collection development. Removing these myths will assist documents librarians in implementing an integrated collection development process.

MOVING TOWARD INTEGRATION

Collection development should become a planning process whereby a collection policy, reflecting user needs, is formulated, tested, and refined. The policy, therefore, is not an end in itself; it represents the commitment of a library to make selection, acquisition, and retention decisions based upon an evaluation component. Libraries need to determine how many demands they want to meet internally, and to rely on resource sharing for lesser-used titles.

It should be recognized that the accumulation of large numbers of publications that are never or infrequently used has implications far beyond individual libraries, in that printing, distribution, and library handling costs are all affected. Depository as well as nondepository libraries need to carry out active weeding programs, to acquire government publications selectively, and to review and revise selection criteria on a regular basis. Elimination of ephemeral, trivial, superseded, and duplicative publications from documents collections will better serve user needs.

Integrated government publications in terms of bibliographic accessibility, physical availability, professional service, and status is necessary, if library clientele are to receive the full benefits of government publications as an information resource. Without an integrated stance between library and documents collection development, the concept of integration is doomed.

Specific benefits are associated with integration: the avoidance of the purchase of materials duplicating the content of many government publications; provision of a wider visibility and utilization of government publications; an increase in staff awareness of the value and importance of government publications as an information resource; improvement in bibliographic access, physical availability, professional service, and status of government publications; and encouragement of the use of government publications in support of other subject areas/disciplines in the collection.

A number of strategies can be suggested to assist in developing an integrated approach and making documents librarians an integral part of the collection development team. Depending on specific library situations, some or all of these strategies may be appropriate. On a preliminary basis, documents librarians must be effective spokespersons for government publications, and demand equal treatment for documents as compared to other library materials. They have a responsibility to educate their colleagues concerning the myths previously identified and to demonstrate the value and importance of documents on a daily basis as a means of resolving a broad range of information needs. Further, they should inform the library's community about the potential of government publications to solve their information needs. They should also work closely with other librarians and administrators to make known the needs and requirements of the documents department/collection.

Regardless of the library environment, documents librarians can develop a collection policy statement. The contents of such statements have been described in detail elsewhere (Hernon and Purcell, 1982). Documents librarians can indeed initiate the development of such a statement. Once the statement has been drafted, it can be used as a vehicle to discuss the role of government publications/information in overall library collection development, to coordinate overall library collection development activities, and to better integrate government information resources into the mainstream of library collections and services.

Methods to initiate this discussion depend on the situation in the particular library; however, three basic approaches are likely. First, a draft collection development statement for government information resources can be submitted to the individual with overall responsibility for collection development, for comment. Second, the policy statement can be given to an already existing committee in the library for comment. Or, the director could establish a committee to review the draft statement. The last approach offers documents librarians an opportunity to educate their colleagues concerning the importance and role of government publications/information.

The draft policy statement should be based upon an assessment of the community served and an analysis of the existing documents collection. Data from such a study are essential to identify the cross section of information needs of client groups and to specify collection development objectives for government information resources. Without such data, the collection development process becomes a subjective maze of untested assumptions and biases that may or may not have any relationship to reality. By stating specific objectives and making them known to the rest of the library staff, personnel in other areas will become more knowledgeable about government publications/information and their role in overall library collection development.

The key component for integrated collection development of government publications is the provision of information services to library users. Collection development is not performed in a vacuum. A collection development process that neither addresses the information needs of the library's community nor responds to identified weaknesses in the collection itself is dyfunctional. Indeed (Evans, 1987, p. xv),

> collection development is an exciting and challenging area in which to work and selecting the right materials for the library's community is as intellectually demanding an activity as a librarian will encounter.

But, the overriding purpose of an integrated approach to collection development for government publications/information is to ensure equal bibliographic accessibility, physical availability, professional service, and status in comparison to other library resources.

Libraries that receive government publications have a responsibility and obligation to make effective use of these resources rich in information content. Libraries cannot afford to operate one (or no) collection development policy for government publications, and another for the rest of the library holdings. In times such as these, when budgets are limited and reflect declining purchasing power, available information resources—including government publications/information—must be exploited to their potential. Such exploitation requires a policy of administrative integration of government publications and an integrated approach to collection development.

7

Exploiting Technology
for Government
Information Collections

The information technology environment that affects the degree to which documents librarians can increase access to government information is changing on a daily basis. As the Lacy report concluded (American Library Association, 1986, p. 31),

> the new technology not only gives potential users quicker and more convenient access to wider bodies of information, including instantly current information, than can be provided by print alone; it also gives the user a new kind of ability to search through and manipulate the information and in effect to create new information by the selection, combination, and arrangement of data.

One implication of this statement is that if depository libraries do not exploit technology for increased access to government information, the user community, either directly or by use of other delivery mechanisms, will simply ignore depository libraries as the primary means for accessing government information.

Government information resources cannot be seen in isolation from either the library or the larger information environment. Indeed, documents librarians must broaden their perspective and realize that (1) recent changes in the development of new information technologies offer new opportunities to increase access to government information; (2) increasing amounts of government information are being collected, organized, and distributed via these new information technologies; and (3) documents librarians can exploit technology to facilitate greater physical access to individual documents.

Technological access necessitates an ability to access information resources at a number of different levels. At the first level, automated information systems identify the existence of a particular document, provide a complete bibliographic citation, and, perhaps, give a location where the item can be obtained. At a second level, technological access implies automated information systems that store and retrieve specific documents. And, finally, at a more sophisticated level, technological access can include the actual transmission of information requested; a specific report might even be received via telecommunications. For the vast majority of documents collections, only the first level has been implemented or is under consideration. In short, there is limited technological access to many government information collections.

In recent years, libraries have become accustomed to such phrases as the "information society," "computer revolution," "automated information systems," and other similar terms. These phrases all assume a fundamental and significant change in the creation, dissemination, and organization of information from that usually considered as "typical" for today's libraries and information centers. The underlying assumption is that the application of information handling technologies can (and will) improve the librarian's ability to acquire, organize, and disseminate information.

The word "technology" itself becomes ambiguous given the breadth of the definitions ascribed to it: applied science, science of mechanical and industrial arts, practices or techniques that improve the human condition, and so forth. But the sense of the word when considered in the context of libraries and information processing suggests less than a global view: the application of mechanical tools, or concepts that rely on mechanical tools, for improved access, organization, and dissemination of information. Such a definition stresses the importance of technology to the service goals of libraries and the information needs of their users.

Technological applications to government information collections have not been widely discussed, evaluated, or even identified. Without such assessment, one can easily slip into the traditional dichotomy of viewpoints related to technology; technology as a panacea versus technology as the doomsayer for society. Either view ignores the realities confronting documents librarians attempting to make the transition from a traditional mode of library operation to one that exploits those aspects of technology that are best suited for a particular library environment.

Numerous reasons can be advanced to justify increased technological access in depository collections. Arguments such as reduced costs of performing routine chores, better bibliographic control of individual documents, improved user services, and increased cooperation and resource sharing are typically mentioned. And, while these and other arguments are likely to be true, the primary justification for exploiting technology specifically for depository collections is that it will better integrate the depository collection into the library collection as a whole, improve the efficiency of library operations, and enhance overall access to government information resources.

Documents librarians have yet to maximize various information handling technologies as a means to increase integration of, and access to, government information resources. Also, available information handling technologies have not, as yet, been analyzed concerning their specific impacts, costs, and benefits for the typical depository collection. One conclusion, however, is clear. Most documents librarians generally have failed to integrate technological access to documents successfully, and to exploit available technologies to increase user access to government information.

This chapter will not review the broad topic of information handling technological applications for libraries. Such information can be obtained by reviewing the *Annual Review of Information Science and Technology*, appropriate sections of *Library Technology Reports* (American Library Association, bimonthly), and journals such as *Information Technology and Libraries*, *Advanced Technology/Libraries*, and *Microcomputers for Information Management*. In addition, Hernon and McClure (1986, pp. 288–289) list newsletters, periodicals, reference works, and monographs covering applications of microcomputers in a library setting.

This chapter, instead, provides a brief overview of the current use of selected library technologies in documents collections. (See Appendix at the end of the chapter for a selected list of writings pertaining to technology and documents collections). The chapter also offers suggestions on how increased technological access to government information resources can be obtained. After a review of recent research findings related to use of technology in documents collections, potential applications are discussed. The chapter concludes with an analysis of possible strategies that will increase technological access to government information resources held in library collections.

EXISTING TECHNOLOGICAL ACCESS TO DOCUMENTS COLLECTIONS

Before discussing the impact of technology on documents collections, it might be useful to identify current areas of technological utilization. The next section of the chapter discusses the use of OCLC, online database searching, and the development of in-house automated systems. The emphasis here is on recent uses made of these technologies in depository collections.

Contrary to the impression created in *Provision of Federal Government Publications in Electronic Format to Depository Libraries* (Congress. Joint Committee on Printing, 1984), depository staff may not have immediate access to a microcomputer to conduct online database and OCLC search-ing. The microcomputer might be located in technical services or another area of the library. However, when the staff do engage in the use of a tech-nology, it is most likely to be a search of OCLC. Only a few libraries use another bibliographic utility, purchase GPO tapes for local use, use micro computers to produce keyword indexing or to create a documents holding file, engage in other uses of technology (Hernon, McClure, and Purcell, 1985).

OCLC

The inclusion of bibliographic records from the *Monthly Catalog of United States Government Publications* in OCLC, which began in 1976, represents a milestone in improving bibliographic control over publications distributed by the GPO. Bibliographic utilities, database vendors, and some libraries use the GPO tapes of catalog records that are available through the MARC tape distribution service at the Library of Congress. A bibliographic utility may engage in cataloging and provide current and retrospective conversion for the archival tapes resulting from cataloging in OCLC. It may also engage in interlibrary loan, reference and bibliographic verification, and the pro-cessing of GPO tapes for inclusion in local circulation and online catalog systems.

Walbridge (1986) discusses OCLC and its uses for shared cataloging and resource sharing. OCLC offers improved control of serials through a Serials Control Subsystem, which can create union lists of holdings. The OCLC 086 search field (Sudocs number) for depository publications offers "system users shelflist search possibilities—specific items and families of materials can be searched and located" (Ibid., p. 332).

OCLC records in which "GPO" appears in any position in the 040 field are GPO cataloging records. When "GPO" appears at the beginning of the 040 field, the GPO was the original source of cataloging. When "GPO" appears after another agency's code, the GPO changed the other agency's cataloging to meet GPO standards. Since October 1980, the GPO has cataloged in the "master mode," which means that it can change the database record when another source has done the original cataloging. All cataloging done under GPO contract is verified as meeting GPO standards before it is entered into OCLC.[1]

GPO serial records that were previously available only to OCLC users are now available through the Library of Congress. This distribution means that GPO serial records are available to other networks, including the Wash-ington Library Network (WLN) and the Research Libraries Information Network (RLIN). Serial records in the *Monthly Catalog* tapes contain issue-

---

[1] It might be germane to point out the 074 field. It is an indicator of regional depository holdings.

specific bibliographic information, while the OCLC cataloging record describes a serial in its entirety.[2] Non-OCLC users can obtain "pure" GPO serial records through the Library of Congress as well.

OCLC could add holdings symbols to the records of items distributed through the depository program. These symbols would identify depository libraries receiving these items, encourage resource sharing, and increase interlibrary loan. However, the holdings symbols would not indicate when that library began receiving an item or if a publication was missing from the collection. As of this time (spring 1988), the inclusion of these symbols in the database is still under discussion.

Some libraries have entered their *Monthly Catalog* holdings in their own online catalogs (see chapter Appendix). Other depository libraries have relied on the services of a commercial vendor for the preparation of catalog card sets, obtaining computer-readable tapes for loading into their online catalogs, or developing COM (computer output microfilm) catalogs for their holdings of GPO publications. Marcive, Inc. (San Antonio, Texas), for example, matches item numbers against the GPO tapes and produces card sets, COM, and/or tape records for subscribers. The same company is currently cooperating with three libraries to correct the GPO tapes and to make them more adaptable for inclusion and manipulation in online catalogs (see note 3 of Chapter 5).

Library staff members interested in the placement of records for GPO publications in online catalogs should review Bowerman and Cady (1984). They constructed a cost-effectiveness model for obtaining bibliographic records, comparing costs and quality of cataloging, and evaluating choices among the alternatives.

Powell, Johnston, and Conrad (1987) explored the use of the OCLC database for cataloging the documents collection of The College of Wooster Library, a selective depository. They examined the availability and quality of records for current U.S. government publications on OCLC; the time lag between the date of the receipt of a document and the appearance of its OCLC record; the time necessary to search the data, attach holdings, or catalog the publications on OCLC; procedures such as the mechanics of follow-up searching; staff needs; and the costs of implementing such a project. They tested the feasibility of attaching library holdings to only slightly modified records in the OCLC database. Their aim was to devise a cost-effective method for including the records of depository publications in an online public access catalog for the library as a whole. Such a system, they suspected, would result in increased circulation of depository holdings.

Libraries acquiring additional Federal publications, those not contained in OCLC, would have to explore methods for including these other

---

[2] See Bower (1984) for examples of each type of entry.

records in their online catalog. Unless they do so, the online system is not comprehensive; however, users and general reference staff might presume comprehensiveness. Depositories might also consider a cooperative project aimed at adding records to the OCLC database for pre-1976 documents.

Online Bibliographic Database Searching

Access to online bibliographic databases containing primarily government publications has increased significantly. Online searching of government documents databases can provide increased access to specific types of government information resources not indexed elsewhere, reduce the time lag between availability of the document and its bibliographic access, reduce library expenditures by eliminating the need for printed indexes that may be only infrequently used, reduce time needed for actual searching, improve search strategies and effectiveness of searches because of Boolean and proximity operators (among other techniques), increase access to documents because they have been tagged by search fields unique to government information resources, and reduce search problems. Further, online searching can assist collection management by utilizing information in various search fields such as publication year, format, and issuing agency, and by showing the titles in demand.

However, difficulties regarding staff training, access to appropriate computer equipment, the possibility that the library may not own many of the titles identified (Hernon, 1979), and online search costs can limit the application of this technology to government information collections.

As Murphy (1985, p. 169) indicates,

documents librarians must consider the advantages and disadvantages of online searching. Do online bibliographic databases duplicate the citations found in printed index equivalents or do these two mediums complement each other? Is one method of searching less labor intensive than the other? Which format is more cost effective?

Furthermore (p. 178),

As access to computerized bibliographic retrieval systems at library reference desks increases, it may become easier to search online without considering the specific needs of the information seeker. Certainly, online bibliographic databases are a useful resource for reference librarians. However, it is important to remember that an online search cannot substitute for a manual search and vice-versa; the two search methods complement each other.

Yet many depository personnel infrequently engage in database searching of any kind. Further, they may lack formal training in searching protocol.

Regional depositories in the GPO program do not conduct more database searching, or make greater use of technology, than do selective depositories (Hernon, McClure, and Purcell, 1985).

Four companies (Auto-Graphics, Inc.; Brodart Library Automation Division; Information Access Co.; and LSSI) produce cumulative, self-contained versions of the *Monthly Catalog*. These services offer records in microform or compact or optical disk. Brodart, for example, offers "*LePac*: Government Documents Option" on compact disc. *LePac* provides keyword searching and quick access by author, title, subject, and Sudocs number. Because updating is bi-monthly, subscribing libraries may have to search OCLC for recently published items.

The availability of one of the *Monthly Catalog* services in a prominent location in either a general reference or depository collection may significantly increase use of those government documents included in this one index and available through the depository program. The relationship of such services to online searching remains to be determined. Clearly, library staff and users are becoming dependent on such services (Hernon and Mc-Clure, 1987b). An increasing percentage of library users may not need to engage in online searching for quick determination of a pool of potentially relevant titles. On the other hand, reliance on stand-alone services may encourage more users to explore other library services such as online searching and CD-ROM products for statistical data (see subsequent section of this chapter).

Stand-alone services do not displace other library resources. Rather, they comprise one step in the process of information gathering and may only duplicate coverage of the printed *Monthly Catalog*. Both *PAIS Bulletin* and *Government Reports Announcements & Index*, for example, supplement the *Monthly Catalog* and are available on CD-ROM. If anything, the cost to libraries of providing library users with access to government information will increase. As an alternative, depository staff might have to reassess priorities and move money from one budget category to another.

Automated Systems

For purposes of this chapter, an automated system is computer based; accomplishes specific goals related to the access, organization, or dissemination of information in a documents collection; and/or provides management information that assists librarians in making decisions related to the collection. Typical information in an automated system can include bibliographic information, textual information, circulation data, acquisitions information, user information, and a host of management information including budgets, personnel, inventories, and more. A number of useful sources can introduce documents librarians to automated systems and online services (Matthews, 1980, 1982; Saffady, 1983; and Corbin, 1985).

Automated systems for government information collections can be developed under any of the following approaches (Corbin, 1981, pp. 15–18):

- *Purchase or lease a turn-key system.* A turn-key system is one that is ready to be installed as a complete package by a vendor or contractor. Usually, it is intended to address a specific function or area of functions, such as acquisitions, circulation, and serials control
- *Share an automated system with another library via a network or through a formal cooperative agreement.* Such approaches rely on an online time sharing mode of operation, in which the libraries either share a basic system and apply it to meet their own purposes, or actually input and manipulate the same primary database and supporting system software
- *Modify a system from another library.* The library purchases programs and appropriate hardware and adapts the programs to meet the specific needs and objectives of the library. Typically, the modifications are done on the software of the system to be adapted
- *Piggy-back the system onto existing and available institutional hardware and software.* This approach assumes that the library has access to institutional computer services—either the computer services of the university or local government. The documents collection typically accepts some "constraints" in the software rather than making significant changes
- *Develop the system locally.* Here the documents staff, perhaps with the assistance of a library systems analyst, designs, programs, tests, de-bugs, and implements the system. Although this approach allows for greater control over the system and ensures its appropriateness for the local library, it assumes the availability of expert staff, significant time commitments, and knowledge of sophisticated issues related to both equipment and programming.

Although these approaches are presented individually for purposes of illustration, in practice they are often combined and used in conjunction with each other as a means of developing the final product.

Writings by Morton (see chapter Appendix) offer an excellent example of a local system that has been "piggy-backed" on a commercial software package—in this case DATATRIEVE. He identifies the benefits of having an automated shelflist for documents but also indicates the need for having some in-house expertise related to the development of automated systems. Using such a system as the one developed at Carleton College (Morton and Cox, 1982), access to and control of the depository collection might increase significantly, and management information for collection development is readily available.

Despite such "success stories" regarding the development of automated systems for government information collections, most depository librarians have neither developed such systems nor utilized available computer technology to improve management, control, and availability of government information resources in their collection. Indeed, instances where such systems are developed result largely from the personal interest and dedication of one individual. Instances where a locally developed system has failed because the person responsible leaves the employment of the institution are not uncommon.

Stephenson and Purcell (1986) have discussed "the potential advantages that sophisticated automated records systems offer for both the control of government documents and the integration of the documents function into other automated library systems" (p. 191). In a 1985 article, they "identified the functional requirements for automating documents collections" (p. 57) and listed selected serials software control systems potentially useful in automating documents collections. Another significant opportunity for automated systems applications for government information resources is the use of existing institutional software packages. Many academic institutions and local governments use different software packages for various forms of records management. As the Carleton College Library demonstrated, impressive use of these software programs for the management of documents collections can be accomplished without having sophisticated programming skills (since the software is "canned") and without significant cost. The critical ingredient for success, it appears, is the desire and dedication of documents librarians who attempt to develop such systems.

EXPLOITING OTHER TECHNOLOGIES

The three traditional forms of technological applications previously discussed (OCLC, online bibliographic database searching, and automated information systems) are likely to be exploited first by most libraries as a means to increase access to depository collections. However, one should not lose sight of the fact that these types of technologies are only a beginning. A brief discussion of other technologies with possible applications for a documents collection opens a "world of potential" for exciting and challenging prospects.

Microcomputers

The proliferation of microcomputers, and their increased capabilities and reduced purchase price, has been nothing short of incredible. Microcomputers can be used to acquire, organize, control, and increase access to bibliographic and managerial information in many library settings (see Hernon and McClure, 1986). The implementation of in-house automated systems for serials control, circulation, indexing, statistics, reference service, and more is now possible with relatively little capital outlay.

As of spring 1988, an IBM compatible microcomputer with 80286 CPU turbol speed, 640 K Ram Expandable 1 MB, 2 hard/2 floppy controller, 1.2 hi-density drive, 20 MB seagate hard drive, Hercules graphics adapter, parallel print port, AT style key board, monitor, and real time clock (battery backup) costs $1,295. A 1200/300 modem costs another $75.00. A good quality printer and interface can be obtained for approximately $500.00. A variety of reasonably priced software is also available. Thus, an extremely powerful, sophisticated, and speedy microcomputer, with a variety of software packages, can be obtained for approximately $2,500.

For many separate documents collections, use of microcomputers for assistance in various bibliographic, organizational, and administrative chores is a perfect match between the needs of a unique collection and the power available from a microcomputer. Figure 7–1 summarizes types of software applications discussed in the literature identified in the chapter Appendix. The figure illustrates that different types of software perform different functions and that microcomputers lend themselves to a variety of depository applications.

Stephenson and Purcell (1984) discuss the benefits of using technology for making collection development, reference, cataloging, circulation, and managerial decisions. To assist library clientele in discovering the types of government resources appropriate to their information needs, Smith (1986) reports on the development of menu-driven microcomputer software that defines search questions through a series of sorting sequences. This precursor to an expert or knowledge-based system simulates actual steps of a reference or search query. Students and other library users may, therefore, be able to locate potentially useful source material without needing the intervention of staff.

Video Technology

Videotex is the display of textual information, both words and numbers, on a video screen. Typically, it implies a two-way system in which the viewer can request information from a potentially larger collection of data. Other related technologies come under the generic heading of "viewdata," the transmission of electronic pages and graphics over phone lines, cable TV lines, or broadcast TV to either personal computers or modified television receivers. Examples of government bodies that have used or are using teletext and/or videotex include the State Department, the Internal Revenue Service, and the National Oceanic and Atmospheric Administration (Schweizer, 1983).

Figure 7-1.
Summary of Types of Software and Library Applications

SOFTWARE	PURPOSE
Word Processing	Creating, editing, and printing reports, etc.
Writing Aids	Spelling checkers and analysis of writing style
Database Management	Organize, store, manipulate, and retrieve data
Financial Management	Perform calculations and formatting for tabular reports, e.g., budget forecasting
Project Managers	Produce time schedules for project completion
Graphics	Presentation of data through bar and pie charts, line graphs, etc.
Statistical Analysis	Process data and perform statistical analyses

CATEGORY	DEPOSITORY APPLICATION
Collection Managment	Maintain accounting and decision support systems, implement a series control file or documents check-in file, prepare reports, analyze in-house recordkeeping, and produce files of documents holdings
Current Awareness	Development of finding aids and mailing labels
Public Service	Online and COM catalogs; online searching of bibliographic, numeric, and full-text files, maintain expert systems; and provide reference sources and statistical data, e.g., the private sector's CD-ROM products

Green Thumb, an experimental videotex project funded by the Department of Agriculture and the National Weather Service, was tested in Kentucky from March 1980 to July 1981. Two hundred participants could connect electronically to county extension offices through their home television sets and telephone lines. Farmers most frequently requested marketing and weather information. Since many of them encountered technical problems with the use of the system, they still relied heavily on newspapers and radio broadcasts (Case, 1981).

Technology is currently available for depository collections to be linked together through a videotex system that allows, for instance, transmission of information, electronic mail, and conferencing. Clearly, such applications could significantly improve public access to government information and have profound implications for the future of reference services and the depository library program.

Numeric Databases

A growing trend in both the private and public sectors is to create databases that contain numerous files of original data. Numeric and other machine-readable data files (e.g., those produced by the Bureau of the Census or distributed by the National Technical Information Service) are proliferating at a significant rate. Thus, documents librarians are faced with the challenge of not only providing more statistical information to patrons, but also of being able to manipulate original data files, obtain the specific data necessary, and program the computer tapes as needed for unique outputs not originally provided by the supplier (Heim, 1983).

For illustrative purposes, it should be noted that the University of Florida Libraries, Gainesville, have provided data services since 1971, when the reference department and system group joined together to serve as a summary tape processing center for the 1970 Census of Population and Housing (Pope, 1984). As this example suggests, documents librarians, where feasible, can be integrally involved in promoting the use of numeric data files, since many of these files are government produced or convey government information.

There is no comprehensive finding aid to government produced machine-readable data files. Examples of such files can be found in various sources such as *A Directory of Computer Software* (NTIS, annual), *The Federal Software Exchange Catalog* (NTIS, annual), *Directory of Computerized Data Files* (NTIS, annual), and *The Federal Data Base Finder* (Information USA, 1987). But simply having lists of files does not ensure access for depository library clientele. Documents librarians cannot ignore this evolving form of Federal information in their collection development practices and reference and referral services. They should be aware of the activities of state data centers (see Redmond, 1986) and send clientele to such centers when appropriate for resolution of an information need. They should also take into account that the Bureau of the Census offers online access to Federal users of its international database (IDB). The IDB contains statistics on the demographic, social, and economic characteristics of all countries throughout the world. Users can access the database through computer terminals or microcomputers with dial-up capability.[3]

Through DIALOG Information Services, Inc., and The Glimpse Corp., the Bureau of the Census also offers CENDATA, an online file that provides selected summary data from all Bureau programs. It also includes Bureau news releases and the most current ordering information on Bureau products. Slater Hall Information Products (Washington D.C.) offers numerous statistical datasets on CD-ROM. For example, it provides "SHIP's County Statistics," which contains more than 1,200 items of statistical information about each U.S. county, state, and metropolitan area. The CD-ROM includes the data from the Bureau of the Census's COSTAT2 tape plus additional data on population, employment, and agriculture. The "SEARCHER" software enables users to create their own tables for screen

---

[3] The data contained in the database are collected from national statistics offices in various countries, international organizations, research centers and universities in different countries, and Federal agencies such as the Agency for International Development. For information on the database, contact: Center for International Research, Scuderi Building, Room 409, U.S. Bureau of the Census, Washington D.C. 20233.

display, immediate printing, or disk storage. Data extracts can be downloaded for use with spreadsheets.[4]

The Federal Home Loan Bank Board distributes data files through NTIS. The files contain financial data, for example, on Federal Savings and Loan Insurance Corporation-insured institutions. The three major data series involved are: *Thrift Financial Report, Quarterly Semiannual Financial Report*, and *Branch Office Deposit Report*.

Files such as these not only provide answers to factual questions (e.g., the number and rate of unemployed by occupation) but also permit the manipulation of data for statistical comparisons. Online searching for numeric data and the expansion of manual searching for statistical information offer depository libraries the opportunity to become a more important information provider indispensable to the resolution of more information needs. This online capability will probably appeal to faculty members and their students at those institutions willing to absorb the search costs. More than ever, research must focus on the information needs of client groups, how they gather and use information, and the role of libraries and database searching in this process.

Microformatted Government Publications Online

The marriage of online database searching with micrographics is especially important for documents librarians, because numerous databases of government information can supply microfiche for actual publications contained therein. Examples of such databases include those developed by the Congressional Information Service (CIS) and the National Technical Information Service (NTIS). Online searching of such databases provides increased bibliographic access to source material, and the possibility of online ordering directly through appropriate vendors offers increased physical access.

The benefits of access to online government documents in microform are numerous and include rapid ordering, efficient accounting procedures, and the ability to purchase only the individual document necessary rather than all documents within an item category. The acquisition process can be done from any physical location that has an online terminal, and physical access to a broader range of government publications than those from the Government Printing Office (GPO) is possible. On the other hand, it should be remembered that online ordering involves a special service charge and that library users often prefer to use paper copy publications. Yet microfiche

---

[4] Gene Essman & Associates (Wheat Ridge, Colorado) offer a package of almost 30 diskettes that reprints data from the Bureau of the Census's 1986 *State and Metropolitan Data Book* and the 1987 *Statistical Abstract of the United States*. For an extensive listing of government information resources available on CD-ROM, see Russell (1988).

comprises the primary format for depository distribution. Clientele must be made aware of this and every effort made to make microform use seem natural and convenient.

Facsimile

Facsimile transmission refers to a process whereby a printed paper document is encoded by one facsimile machine and transmitted, via telecommunications lines, to a second machine, where it is reproduced once more in print form (Lancaster, 1982, p. 36). The following benefits can be realized by libraries using this technology:

- Time is saved in forwarding the request for information to the information source node
- Time is saved in the delivery of the material to the requesting library for pickup by the user
- Costs for complete document transmission can be significantly reduced for short to medium sized documents
- Use of the technology is straightforward and requires little staff training.

For purposes of interlibrary loan and resource sharing, significant advantages can be realized. The same is true for inter-office communication.

For the depository library system, facsimile technology has great potential because a network structure for transmission has already been established between the GPO and depository libraries. (Under that structure, regionals serve as the nodes linking the GPO to other depositories). Use of facsimile could significantly enhance access to government information if regional and some selective depository libraries maintained facsimile equipment. Complete printed documents could be rapidly sent and received; because few copyright restrictions apply to government publications, a broad range of resources could be made available through this technique. As McKean (1981, p. 118) notes, "the prognosis for facsimile in libraries is good," but for depository collections as well as most libraries in general, it is an untapped resource.

SUMMARY

This brief discussion of microcomputers, optical discs, videotex, numeric databases, microformatted government documents online, and facsimile is offered more as a menu of possible technologies for use in the depository library system than as a comprehensive review of the current state of the art. Indeed, one should realize that many of these technologies are now being combined and transformed into newer and even more powerful technologies— possible applications of fiber optics, bubble memories for increased storage, and other technologies have yet to be fully explored by libraries.

One reason that many members of an academic community initially want to purchase, or gain access, to a microcomputer is that they would like to make use of the wordprocessing capability. Microcomputers are now readily available for other uses (see Figure 7–1). Government officials can distribute datasets on diskette, send wordprocessed reports, engage in desktop publishing, and participate in electronic mail. Technology is clearly impacting upon the production, distribution, and dissemination of government information.[5] Less (but still a lot) is becoming available in printed format; the depository program must embrace technology if it is to prosper and operate effectively in an information age.

As Lancaster (1982) has pointed out, libraries have been affected by computers and telecommunications in two ways. The first, and less important, has been the application of computers for record keeping and various forms of bibliographic control. Much more important and powerful is the use of computers and telecommunications to allow libraries to increase their access to outside databases and information resources. As he notes (p. 149),

> it is far-reaching because, besides greatly increasing a library's capabilities for literature searching and question answering, it completely changes the economics of access to information . . . [and] changes all previous notions of 'collection,' and 'libraries.'

Clearly, strategies to exploit the use of information handling technologies for government information resources are necessary.

STRATEGIES FOR EXPLOITING TECHNOLOGY

In order to exploit the various technologies discussed in this chapter, as well as other types of information handling technologies, a carefully developed program of increasing applications for technology utilization in depository collections is necessary. Since possible strategies in such a program are numerous, only a few will be suggested here; each can be modified to meet specific conditions and circumstances at an individual library. However, developing such strategies is essential if the depository library of the future is to provide effective access to government information resources.

---

[5] The House Committee on Government Operations produced *Hearings on Electronic Collection and Dissemination of Information by Federal Agencies* (Washington, D.C.: GPO, 1986) and *Electronic Collection and Dissemination of Information by Federal Agencies: A Policy Overview* (Washington, D.C.: GPO, 1986), which highlight agency activities and identify major policy issues of importance to librarians and others.

Obtain Training

Until documents librarians better understand potential applications for the documents collection, utilize appropriate technology, and upgrade competencies in this area, removal of other technology related constraints is not likely to occur. Yet, of all the strategies to be discussed, staff training is the easiest to implement and the one over which documents librarians have the greatest control.

Numerous strategies exist to obtain necessary training. With two-thirds of existing depository libraries situated in academic institutions (many of which encourage staff to take courses either by providing time-off or by payment of tuition), librarians have access to formal courses related to technological applications. Attending short courses or workshops also can be an efficient means to obtain an introduction to a specific topic. Many automation vendors offer training seminars at reasonable prices throughout the country. Another approach is to find a mentor in the technology area of specific interest. Self-initiated learning oftentimes is more effective than other more traditional forms of continuing education. Regardless of which approach is taken, documents librarians have many opportunities for training and should regard Figure 7–2 as a checklist of service levels, equipment, and training.

Minimize Costs

A first concern that documents librarians typically raise has to do with the perceived costs associated with utilization of such technology. Figure 7–3 identifies cost considerations for government information, regardless of format. In some instances, actual costs can be minimal. For example, a microcomputer with adequate disk storage, as was already noted, is reasonably priced. Costs can be reduced if they are shared throughout the library or with other agencies/departments within the institution. Second, the documents department might have access to existing technologies, *if the librarian were only to ask!*

In those instances in which such services are already provided for the benefit of the institution as a whole, depository librarians may be able to initiate information handling technologies without any capital outlay. What is required, primarily, is "piggy-backing" the technological use for the documents collection on existing services available in the local institution.

Depository librarians situated in university and college libraries might obtain access to the central computer system on campus, and its available software, simply by requesting a password from the appropriate channels. Depository collections in public and special libraries have the same potential for gaining access to the city council or organizational computer system.

Figure 7-2.
Equipment/Training Requirements for Electronic Information Service Levels

SERVICE LEVELS	EQUIPMENT	TRAINING
Bibliographic/Textual		
Basic	a-k,n,p,q	Basic subject search training through regularly conducted vendor courses, CE (university, school, or state sponsored training), self training, or user group
Intermediate	For compact disk storage, add j,m	Intermediate search training using all of the above sources
Full		Familiarity with subject, advanced database search training, using all of the above sources
Non Bibliographic		
Basic	a-k,m,n,p,q,r,s	a) Knowledge of file; b) Basic search strategy; c) Downloading and replicating skills (Training would be accomplished through manuals, on screen directions, and basic search strategies. Could be accomplished through on site training)
Intermediate	a-s	a-c (see above); e) Software training on R-Base and Lotus 1-2-3 (would require off site training)
Full	a-s Tape processing would require access to main frame	a-d (see above); e) Specific retrieval software training; f) advanced search strategy training; g) Subject skills for accessing content of the database (would require off site training)

DEFINITIONS

Basic Service.	Includes online search of library's holdings, selected database access, providing data on floppies to users without interpretation. Cost of equipment is moderate. Training costs are low.
Intermediate Service:	Includes bibliographic online searching involving a variety of databases, downloading of data, providing software for patrons and simple searches of raw data. Cost of equipment is moderate. Training costs are moderate.

Full Service: Includes comprehensive bibliographic searching on a wide range of databases, nonbibliographic extraction and manipulation of data files, full range of software. The cost of equipment is high. Training costs are high.

EQUIPMENT LIST			
a.	PC limited 286-12 AT or equipment	$2,695	
b.	Seagate 40 MB, 40ms access hard disk w/ automatic head parking at power down	819	
c.	AT multifunction card	200	
d.	w/ piggyback expandable Ram card	60	
e.	60 Mb tape backup	795	
f.	Enhance Graphics Adapter monitor	479	
h.	Near letter quality dot matrix printer	600	
i.	9600 baud modem card	995	
j.	2 Hitacji 2500s Cd-ROM drives + cables and card	1,600	
k.	Phone line @ $20/mo plus usage	350	
l.	R:Base System V dbms or equivalent	500	
m.	TMS/Alde CD-ROM full text retrieval software or equivalent	595	

n.	DOS or Xenix/unit operating system	$300	
o.	Lotus 1-2-3 or equivalent	300	
q.	Telecommunications software	200	
r.	Software maintenance (10%–12% of cost)		
s.	Supplies—paper, floppy disks, printer ribbons or cartridges, disk cleaner Storage—floppy disk tubs, tape racks, optical disk filing racks, printout binders and racks		

Source: "Government Information Technology and Information Dissemination: A Discussion Paper" (1987), pp. 6. 7. 11.

Outright purchase of most information handling technologies is not feasible for many documents collections. Therefore, their services must be better integrated through existing institutional programs.

Set Priorities and Reduce Workload

Numerous surveys indicate that the typical depository collection has a maximum of one full-time professional and one paraprofessional, with minimal student or volunteer assistance (Hernon, McClure, and Purcell, 1985). Thus, documents librarians who are conscientious in meeting the responsibilities of the profession, and who attempt to follow the *Guidelines for the Depository Library System* (1977), find that they constantly have too much work to accomplish and too little staff to get it all done.

Documents librarians must formulate written priorities and objectives for what is, and is not, to be accomplished. In stating such priorities, inclusion of objectives related to identifying and implementing technological applications are appropriate and necessary. After priorities have been set and discussed with various administrators in the library, some of the *less* important (not unimportant) activities can be put on the back burner (See Chapter 15 for a discussion of planning).

It is not likely, in the foreseeable future, that documents collections will receive an influx of staff and a reduction in duties. Thus, to eschew possible applications of technology in the documents collection on the basis of excessive workload and limited staff is tantamount to saying that such applications will never be implemented. Finally, it should be stressed that effective implementation of various forms of technology can reduce traditional work responsibilities. Indeed, after initial start-up commitments, many of the technological applications discussed in this chapter are, in themselves, the best strategy to remove constraints related to workload and staffing.

Increased Priority for Government Information Resources

A frequent comment made by librarians who manage separate documents collections is that their collections have low priority for technological applications, relative to other departments or areas in the library. Such a situation reflects a political constraint that can only be removed by documents librarians who demonstrate: (1) the overall importance of the documents collection and its need to be integrated (philosophically, administratively, and in terms of service) into the library as a whole; (2) a concrete plan of action demonstrating how appropriate technologies can be utilized effectively in the collection; and (3) a strategy of technology utilization that "piggy-backs" applications from other systems, or otherwise has limited cost.

Without such efforts, applications of new information technologies may bypass the documents area in the library. Low priority may be placed on utilization of technology in documents collections because of high start-up costs, inappropriateness of such technologies for documents, or perceived lack of benefits resulting from such technological application. The strategy in this case is for documents librarians to promote the appropriateness of technology utilization for the collection within the context of library-wide goals and objectives. Such a strategy implies obtaining political support from other library staff and demonstrating specific benefits that would result from technology utilization. Marketing the usefulness of various technological applications must come after documents librarians have achieved increased training and knowledge of those technologies appropriate for a documents collection.

Depository librarians might also volunteer their library as a test site for

Figure 7-3.
Cost Considerations for Government Information Formats

	TEXTUAL		ELECTRONIC			
	Paper	Microform	(Raw data on tape, disc, etc)	Disk, tape	Online	CD-ROM
Production of copies by publisher	Yes	Yes	Yes	Yes	N/A	Yes
Storage: Space	Cost/linear foot including shelving	Cost/linear foot including cabinets	Cost/linear foot including tape readers, disk readers	Cost/linear foot including tape readers, disk readers	Cost/linear foot N/A	Cost/linear foot storage cabinet
Environment	Some controls	Some controls	Strong controls	Strong controls	N/A	Strong controls
Distribution Costs	Postage/UPS Handling	Postage/UPS Handling	Special Mailers Mail/UPS	Special Mailers Mail/UPS	Telecommunications down loading	Special mailers mail/UPS
Access Charges (non-staff)	Indexes	Indexes	Tech. Documen. Retrieval software Analysis software	Tech. Documen. Retrieval software	Technical Documentation Retrieval software	Interface with terminal software
Equipment	Copying machine	Reader/Printer	Computer with peripherals terminals printer	Tape: Computer Disk: reader/print terminals printer	Terminals printer	CD, disk drive

Figure 7-3. *Continued*

Staff:						
Record keeping	Yes	Yes	Possibly	Possibly	N/A	Yes
Disposition (selectives only)	Yes	Yes	Yes	Yes	Yes	Yes
Reference serv.	Sampling days	Sampling days	Yes - Use log	Yes - Use log	Yes - Use log	Yes
Bibliographic control	Yes	Yes	Yes	Yes	Yes	Yes
Training	Yes	Yes	Yes	Yes	Yes	Yes
Preservation	Binding Deacidification	Air conditioning Acid free materials	Back-up copies Routine recopying Cleaning of media Maintenance of equipment	Back-up copies Routine recopying Cleaning of media Maintenance of equipment	Back-up copies Routine recopying Cleaning of media Maintenance of equipment	Back-up copies* Cleaning of media* Maintenance of equipment*
Ease of use* Patron training re-quired*	Yes - Time Log	Yes - Time Log	Yes - Time Log	Yes - Time Log	Yes - Time Log	Yes - Time Log
User satisfaction*	Patron evaluation form*	Patron evaluation form	Patron evaluation form	Patron evaluation form or on tape	Yes - Final display screen	Patron evaluation form

Source: "Government Information Technology and Information Dissemination: A Discussion Paper" (1987), p. 8.

reviewing new databases and CD-ROM products. Vendors often provide the required hardware in exchange for data gathering, which usually involves no more than having staff and patrons complete survey forms. In return, staff familiarize themselves with new services and obtain a basis for comparing one service to its competitors.

Finally, documents librarians must be constantly on the lookout for "piggy-backing" or otherwise involving the collection in technological applications intended primarily for other areas. For example, they can volunteer for online database training even though the terminals are in the reference department. It is better to have some search capability of government information databases by the documents librarians than none! Documents librarians can also investigate the use of existing technologies for application to the documents department/collection. Often times, a low institutional priority can be overcome by strategic planning, expanding the department's political power base, and adapting documents use of technological applications to existing systems either in the library or in the institution at large.

Obtain Technology Utilization Information

Obtaining written information about information handling technologies as applied to government information collections is a difficult task. As suggested in the first section of this chapter, the number of writings that describe specific applications of technology to documents collections is small but increasing. These writings tend to focus on specific applications and may not convey the most up-to-date information. It is probably more useful to contact librarians who are currently using different technologies and "pick their brains" for suggestions and current information.

Documents librarians should be knowledgeable about various information handling technologies. This means that they should read the current literature, attend workshops, and obtain demonstrations/information from the various vendors. In addition, documents librarians who have attempted various types of technological applications should submit written plans, reports, and studies to ERIC and professional journals for use by other documents librarians. Those librarians who have initiated technological applications for documents collections, but have not produced any written summaries of their projects, should do so and make the information available. Finally, professional organizations could assume responsibility for providing clearinghouse information regarding the application of information handling technologies to documents collections.

Overcoming Resistance to Technological Innovation

Successful application of information handling technologies requires an ability to overcome staff, and perhaps personal, resistance to such innovation.

Such feelings are not likely to be reduced by argument or reasoning, but may be related to whether people are involved in decision making. The single most important fear that people have about information handling technologies is not obsolescence, the breakdown of the system, or the costs, but ". . . that interpersonal relationships will suffer with the coming of more sophisticated technologies" (Fine, 1982, p. 213).

Other studies have pointed to the consideration that technological changes must be dealt with from the "attitudinal or psychological point of view" (Luguire, 1983, p. 344). Thus, the implications are that group dynamics, interpersonal skills, leadership, involvement in decision making, and understanding/empathy will be necessary to overcome "future shock" fears of the impacts of information handling technologies on libraries. Fine (1982) has suggested a number of psychological strategies to deal with such resistance, and documents librarians would be well advised to review these specific strategies. These librarians might also consult Hernon and McClure (1986, pp. 46–55) for additional suggestions relating to the implementation of new technologies. Regardless of the quality and appropriateness of the technological equipment, if staff refuse to use it or use it improperly because of psychological resistance, there is little reason to allocate the time and resources for technological support.

EXPLOITING THE TECHNOLOGICAL FUTURE

The overview presented in this chapter suggests some applications of information handling technologies in depository libraries related to OCLC, online database searching, automated systems, and management information systems. The following constraints can limit technological applications in documents collections: complacent document librarians, the amount and type of training required, the costs involved, excessive workload and limited staffing, low priority of documents, limited access to technology utilization information, and resistance to technological innovation. In each of these areas, documents librarians can develop strategies to minimize the impact of the constraints.

Training is easily available, and the costs of some applications are minimal—especially if they can be "piggy-backed" on other library or institutional applications. Excessive workload and limited staffing can be remedied by setting priorities and using the technology to be developed as a means of reducing workload. Further, clear demonstration of benefits resulting from technological applications will allow librarians to learn from one another. However, library staff must accept this responsibility and provide the initiative for utilizing various information handling technologies in the documents collection.

The side effects of the technological revolution have yet to be seen, but

DeGennaro (1983, p. 634) has commented that, as a result of automation, "libraries will get deeply involved in implementing office automation systems including word processing, financial, personnel, statistical, and other functions." Indeed, these functions can be easily performed by many of the current personal microcomputers currently on the market. One might argue that librarians' limited use of office automation equipment is years behind that of the business world, and contributes significantly to low library productivity and inefficient use of professional librarian time.

Looking into the future, a number of possible impacts can be identified as a result of applying information handling technologies to government information collections:

- *Greater time available for professional activities*— many of the routine and repetitive chores can be performed (and rightly so) through automated information processing
- *Increased reliance on external collections*— with technological access to a broad range of government information, "*comprehensive* collections" will be neither necessary nor affordable
- *Improved public services*—because many technical service activities can be automated or eliminated, professional librarians will be able to develop more and better programs for documents public services
- *More training and technology-related skills necessary*—documents librarians will have to be knowledgeable about the broad range of technologies discussed in this chapter, as well as how technologies interact and how they can be applied for increased organizational effectiveness
- *Increased integration*—depository collections can be better integrated into library information services and systems, thereby encouraging increased access to government information resources.

These and other impacts depend, of course, on the ability of documents librarians to exploit technological applications for specific purposes, to justify the purchase and use of various technologies for government information collections, and to demonstrate specific benefits that can result from exploiting new technologies.

A number of issues and important questions related to increased exploitation of information handling technologies for the depository collections have yet to be resolved. These include:

- *Bibliographic control*: will technology increase or decrease bibliographic control, and according to what specific criteria of bibliographic control can these changes be measured?

- *User access*: will technology become a barrier between the information source and the user, or will technology remove existing barriers between the user and the source?
- *Organization of materials*: does utilization of a specific information handling technology force a "rearrangement" of documents (such as microforms), and how does rearrangement of materials affect overall access to the collection?
- *Physical access versus bibliographic access*: increased reliance on the various online systems provides greater bibliographic access to documents without always increasing physical access; therefore, is knowing that a document exists helpful, if the document cannot be obtained without considerable cost or delay?
- *Collection development and management*: in what ways do information handling technologies assist in the decision making process for collection development, or do these technologies tend to replace the decision making process through "collection development by default?"
- *Staffing patterns*: what specific staff skills and competencies will be necessary to maintain the information handling technology; how can the depository collection obtain "start-up" staffing when developing the technology; and how will technology utilization in the depository collection affect library staffing considerations?
- *Space and physical resources*: will technology require the collection to commit greater space and physical resources to warehousing of materials and equipment, or will space be freed for other activities?
- *Integration*: will technology provide a basis for greater interaction and planning with other information services in the library, or will the depository collection continue to be "separated" as a unique operation with special access known only to depository staff?
- *Funding*: what funds will be used to pay for new technologies? Should materials money that has been traditionally used for the purchase of books and journals be used to purchase CD-ROM, pay online access costs, etc.?
- *Networking and cooperation*: can technology be generalized to depositories in other library environments; can it provide a basis for resource sharing, increased regional access to information, or improved interlibrary loan procedures?

Space does not permit a detailed discussion of each of these areas where impacts are likely to occur, nor should one consider the above to be a comprehensive list of the various issues related to information handling technologies. Given the nature of individual depository collections, other issues will certainly be identified.

With effective application of information handling technologies in depository libraries, the number of potential services and operations are limited only by one's imagination! Consider the depository collection that automatically provides each month computer generated, custom-tailored bibliographies to hundreds of faculty (or community members); or a distributed microcomputer system in which various departments or agencies have direct access to the holdings and can order copies of the documents directly from the depository; or COM catalogs with updated holdings and subject files that are produced and updated monthly for selected patrons; or automated systems that track the ordering, receipt, circulation, and deselection of titles by producing regular management information for the library. These and other applications are technically possible today in depository libraries.

A central theme of this chapter has been that depository librarians must learn how to exploit various information handling technologies, and must apply those technologies that can provide the best payoffs for their particular library environment. Clearly, all the information handling technologies discussed here will not be appropriate for each depository. However, greater utilization of existing technologies can enhance physical and bibliographic access to government information resources.

For now, however, the success of applying technology for increased access to depository collections will be determined primarily by the initiative and dedication of individual documents librarians. If documents librarianship is to escape from negative biases regarding traditional information services and the depository library program, documents librarians must set priorities concerning how information handling technologies can best be utilized to benefit both the library and the user. Once the priorities have been determined, depository librarians can then initiate a program to assess potential technological applications in their library, develop a plan to implement such technologies for increased access and organization, and increase overall dissemination and use of government information.

APPENDIX. SELECTED WRITINGS ON TECHNOLOGICAL APPLICATIONS FOR DEPOSITORY COLLECTIONS AND SERVICES

"Automatic Bibliographic Control of Government Documents: Current Developments," *Documents to the People*, 15 (December 1987): 224–246.

Beckman, Margaret et al. *The Guelph Document System . . . with a Manual of Procedure* (ERIC, ED 255 228).

Bortnick, Jane, ed. "Electronic Collection and Dissemination of Federal Government Information," *Government Information Quarterly*, 5, no. 3 (1988), entire issue.

Bower, Cynthia. "OCLC Records for Federal Depository Documents: A Preliminary Investigation," *Government Information Quarterly*, 1 (1984): 379–400.

Bowerman, Roseann and Susan A. Cady. "Government Publications in an Online Catalog: A Feasibility Study," *Information Technology and Libraries*, 3 (December 1984): 331–342.

Case, Donald and Kathleen Welden. "Distribution of Government Publications to Depository Libraries by Optical Disk: A Review of the Technology, Applications, and Issues," *Government Publications Review*, 13 (1986): 313–322.

Chrisman, Barbara. "PC-FILE Index for Federal Government Depository Items," *Administrative Notes*, 9 (February 1988): 6–7.

Congress, Joint Committee on Printing. *Provision of Federal Government Publications in Electronic Format to Depository Libraries*. Report of Ad Hoc Committee on Depository Library Access to Federal Automated Data Bases (Washington, D.C.: GPO, 1984).

Gillham, Virginia. "CODOC in the 1980s: Keeping Pace with Modern Technology," in *New Technology and Documents Librarianship*, edited by Peter Hernon (Westport, CT: Meckler Publishing, 1983), pp. 89–98.

———. "The CODOC System: An Update for the Mid-1980s," *Government Publications Review*, 14 (1987): 465–469.

Hickey, Thomas B. and David J. Rypka. "Derived Search Keys for Government Documents," *Information Processing and Management*, 15 (March–April 1979): 99–108.

Higdon, Mary Ann. "Federal Documents Processing with OCLC: The Texas Tech Experience—Planning, Utilization, and the Future," in *Government Documents and Microforms: Standards and Management Issues*. Proceedings of the Fourth Annual Government Documents and Information Conference and the Ninth Annual Microforms Conference, edited by Steven D. Zink and Nancy Jean Melin (Westport, CT: Meckler Publishing, 1984), pp. 89–97.

Jamison, Carolyn C. "Loading the GPO Tapes—What Does It Really Mean?," *Government Publications Review*, 13 (1986): 549–559.

———. "Planning for Documents Automation," *Documents to the People*, 15 (December 1987): 247–252.

Jones, Ray and Thomas Kinney. "Government Information in Machine- Readable Data Files: Implications for Libraries and Librarians," *Government Publications Review*, 15 (1988): 25–32.

Kadec, Sarah T. "The U.S. Government Printing Office's Library Programs Service and Automation: An Insider's Commentary," *Government Publications Review*, 12 (1985): 283–288.

Kinney, Thomas and Ray Jones. "Microcomputers, Government Information, and Libraries," *Government Publications Review*, 15 (March–April 1988): 147–154.

McClure, Charles R. "Online Government Documents Data Base Searching and the Use of Microfiche Documents Online by Academic and Public Depository Librarians," *Microform Review*, 10 (Fall 1981): 245–259.

———. "Provision of Federal Government Publications in Electronic Format to Depository Libraries . . .," *Government Information Quarterly*, 3 (1986): 113–116.

———. "Technology in Government Documents Collections: Current Status, Impacts, and Prospects," *Government Publications Review*, 9 (1982): 255–276.

——— and Peter Hernon. *Academic Library Use of NTIS: Suggestions for Services and Core Collection* (Springfield, VA: NTIS, 1986, PB86–228871).

Mooney, Margaret T. "Automating the U.S. Depository Item Numbers File," *Administrative Notes* [Office of the Superintendent of Documents], 7 (November 1986): 2–4

Morton, Bruce. "Attitudes, Resources, and Applications: The Government Documents Librarian and Computer Technology," in *New Technology and Documents Librarianship*, edited by Peter Hernon (Westport, CT: Meckler Publishing, 1983), pp. 43–59.

———. "Implementing an Automated Shelflist for a Selective Depository Collection," *Government Publications Review*, 9 (1982): 323–344.

———. "An Items Record Management System: First Step in the Automation of Collection

Development in Selective Depository Libraries," *Government Publications Review*, 8A (1981): 185–196.

———— and J. Randolph Cox. "Cooperative Development between Selective U.S. Depository Libraries," *Government Publications Review*, 9 (1982): 221–229.

Myers, Judy E. "The Government Printing Office Cataloging Records: Opportunities and Problems," *Government Information Quarterly*, 2 (1985): 27–56.

An Open Forum on the Provision of Electronic Federal Information to Depository Libraries (Washington, D.C.: GPO, 1985).

Plaunt, James R. "Cataloging Options for U.S. Government Printing Office Documents," *Government Publications Review*, 12 (1985): 449–456.

Pope, Nolan F. "Providing Machine-Readable Numeric Information in the University of Florida Libraries: A Case Study," in *Numeric Databases*, edited by Ching-chih Chen and Peter Hernon (Norwood, NJ: Ablex Pub. Corp., 1984), pp. 263–282.

Powell, Margaret S., Deborah Smith Johnston, and Ellen P. Conrad. "The Use of OCLC for Cataloging U.S. Government Publications: A Feasibility Study," *Government Publications Review*, 14 (1987): 62–73.

Scott, Jack William and Anne Marie Allison. "United States Documents in an On-line Catalog," *The Serials Librarian*, 1 (Summer 1977): 365–371.

Smith, Karen F. "Robot at the Reference Desk?," *College & Research Libraries*, 47 (September 1986): 486–490.

Stanfield, Karen. "Documents Online: Cataloging Federal Depository Materials at the University of Illinois," *Illinois Libraries*, 68 (May 1986): 325–329.

Stephenson, Mary Sue and Gary R. Purcell. "Application of Systems Analysis to Depository Library Decision Making regarding the Use of New Technology," *Government Information Quarterly*, 1 (1984): 285–307.

————. "The Automation of Government Publications: Functional Requirements and Selected Software Systems for Serials Control," *Government Information Quarterly*, 2 (1985): 57–76.

————. "Current and Future Direction of Automation Activities for U.S. Government Depository Collections," *Government Information Quarterly*, 3 (1986): 191–199.

Swanbeck, Jan. "Federal Documents in the Online Catalog: Problems, Options, and the Future," *Government Information Quarterly*, 2 (1985): 187–192.

Technology & U.S. Government Information Policies: Catalysts for New Partnerships (Washington, D.C.: Association of Research Libraries, 1987).

Tyckoson, David A. "Appropriate Technologies for Government Information," *RQ*, 27 (Fall 1987): 33–38.

Veatch, James R. "Automating Government Documents Orders with a Microcomputer," *Government Publications Review*, 12 (1985); 137–141.

Walbridge, Sharon. "OCLC and Government Documents Collections," *Government Publications Review*, 9 (1982): 277–287.

————. "OCLC and Improved Access to Government Documents," *Illinois Libraries*, 68 (May 1986): 329–332.

8

Improved Reference and Referral Services through Increased Marketing and Awareness of Government Information Resources

The published literature on documents reference and referral service is narrowly based; most typically, it focuses on the ability of specially trained staff located in separate documents collections to provide high quality reference and referral services. The literature tends to extol the reference value of government information resources, encourage greater use of their information content, and identify specific examples of "outreach" programs that attempt to make client groups more effective users of government information resources housed in library collections. The literature, which is largely descriptive, generally rehashes the same points that have been examined and re-examined for decades (Hernon, 1978).

The purpose of this chapter is to highlight reference and referral services, to reiterate that effectively designed and implemented services can result in greater use of documents collections (these services, however, must address how people gather and use information), and to reflect current research findings related to documents reference and referral services. The literature does not fully reflect the extent and types of reference services provided by documents staff. In fact, research has not identified and categorized the range of activities and responsibilities commonly assumed by documents personnel. Only with such research can priorities reflecting institutional goals and objectives be set and realized.

The research into documents reference and referral services, to date, should encourage managers to ask:

- What is the quality of reference service in our library? Is this level acceptable? Why do we believe the level is acceptable/unacceptable?

- What ongoing evaluation and educational programs do we employ to improve the quality of reference service? How successful are these programs?
- Does the library have a clear sense of the reference service objectives that the staff are trying to accomplish? How do these objectives relate to other library objectives?

Answers to these questions are critical especially since research has challenged the claim that documents staff members, even those situated in separate departments, regularly provide effective and efficient reference and referral services (Hernon and McClure, 1987b). It would seem that reference and referral services are often taken for granted and that staff (as well as members of the Government Printing Office and the Joint Committee on Printing) prefer to focus on issues other than quality of reference service.

If government publications/information housed in libraries are to be utilized to their potential, library client groups, both present and potential, must receive high quality, personal reference service that alerts them to the value of these information resources and provides them with ready access to needed source material. The extent of personal assistance offered to client groups depends, in part, on the number of staff, their commitment to provide reference service, and their ability to negotiate the complex maze of government printing/publishing programs. Thus, this chapter emphasizes two perspectives: (1) the role and obligation of depository libraries to provide reference and referral services, and (2) the responsibility of the Government Printing Office (GPO), and other government agencies administering depository library programs to encourage use of reference and referral services at the local depository.

INFORMATION GATHERING PATTERNS

Any person, group, institution, or mediated channel of communication might conceivably be drawn upon in an effort to resolve an information need. The array of information providers might be characterized as personal (e.g., friends, co-workers, and colleagues), institutional (e.g., formal agencies, libraries, and businesses), and mass media (print and electronic). As is evident, the library is only one of many information providers. In some situations involving an information need, libraries might not be consulted at all, while, in others, they might comprise an intermediary step in the search for information, or be the provider that effectively revolves the information need.

People often prefer to acquire information on an interpersonal basis—through interaction with a friend or colleague. They might also contact government officials for answers to specific questions and the receipt of relevant documentation. According to Soper (1976, p. 401),

> . . . a seeker of information, for whatever purpose, will go first to a source he perceives to be the most accessible to him. In spite of the possibility that the information he needs may exist in a more authoritative form elsewhere, even in a form more intellectually accessible to him than that closer to hand, he will tend to be satisfied with what he finds nearest and not search further. The cost to the user of going beyond his immediate environment may outweigh the cost of using sources that are judged inferior by other knowledgeable people.

Personal collections are perhaps "easier to use because they are smaller and not as complex as institutional libraries" (Ibid., p. 414).

In addition, technological advances may erode the position of libraries, and have an impact on information gathering patterns of certain segments of the public. Due to technological advances, people may not gather information in the future as they have in the past. They might turn more to microcomputers systems, or new innovations, as a means to obtain necessary information.

Currently, many people use libraries less for research purposes than for the selection of recreational reading, browsing of current periodicals and newspapers, and study-hall and reserve reading purposes. Readers frequently seek books and periodical articles, and may be unaware of other types of information resources. If government publications contain unique information, many people may not be so informed. Card catalogs in libraries housing separate documents collections seldom include a substantial listing of their documents holdings. Moreover, indexes and other bibliographic tools found in general reference collections often provide no more than limited access to government publications. Only when someone consults separate documents collections can the full range of specialized bibliographic tools be tapped.

There is evidence that some users of separate documents collections browse areas of the collection and only occasionally use specialized bibliographic tools. Perhaps users need to place greater reliance on library staff members for assistance, but do not want to disturb librarians preoccupied with other duties. To complicate matters, many documents collections are handled by a small number of staff members. Left on their own, many users will be unable to find all the needed information and may turn to other information providers out of desperation. The question becomes: What type of service do library users receive when they do, in fact, consult reference staff members? The answer to this question, especially if there are negative ramifications, has an impact on information gathering patterns of clientele, the GPO's and library administration of depository libraries, and the GPO's marketing program. Will people consult libraries and their depository collections if they receive less than adequate service? The next section of this chapter provides insights into these questions.

UNOBTRUSIVE TESTING

Reference Service

Reference service is multi-faceted; in the case of documents librarianship, the research literature tends to focus on one aspect of reference service, the accuracy with which staff members correctly answer factual and bibliographic questions. Unobtrusive testing, as the research methodology is known, explores the rate of accuracy provided by reference staff unaware that they are being tested. Recently, unobtrusive testing has received extensive treatment in the published literature (see, for example, the May and November, 1987, issues of the *Journal of Academic Librarianship*, and Hernon and McClure, 1987b).

Figure 8–1 identifies the unobtrusive investigations that have been conducted solely in the field of documents librarianship. When the findings from these studies are combined with the findings from other unobtrusive investigations—those covering general reference librarianship (see Hernon and McClure, 1987b, pp. 4–5 for a complete list of the studies), it is generally discovered that a surprisingly large number of reference staff members:

- Provide "half-right" answers to test questions
- Are unfamiliar with the contents of basic publications in their reference collections
- Spend minimal time in conducting reference interviews and in searching for answers. It is as if they have an internal clock that limits the amount of assistance they provide
- Conduct superficial reference interviews and may fail to identify the actual information need
- Are becoming overly dependent on technology (they may not realize that, for example, "*Le Pac*" has a paper equivalent, the *Monthly Catalog of United States Government Publications*
- Assume the GPO is the sole government printer and distributor of official publications
- Exclude *Government Reports Announcements & Index* or other non-GPO reference sources from their search process
- Are inadequately trained to cope with questions about NTIS and technical report literature.

Figure 8-1.
Unobtrusive Studies of Documents Reference Service

STUDY	GEOGRAPHICAL AREA COVERED	CORRECT ANSWER RATE(%)	TYPE OF LIBRARY INVESTIGATED
Hernon & McClure[a],[*]	Midwest, West, & South[*]	62	Academic & Public
Hernon & McClure[a],[*]	Unspecified	58	Unspecified
McClure & Hernon[b]	Northeast & Southwest	37	Academic
McClure, Hernon, and Purcell[c]	Midwest, South, & West	42	Academic & Public
Way[d]	Los Angeles Area	65	Law School

[*]Note: The Hernon and McClure work contains two, separate studies.

[a]Peter Hernon and Charles R. McClure. *Unobtrusive Testing and Library Reference Service* (Norwood, NJ: Ablex Publishing Corp., 1987).

[b]Charles R. McClure and Peter Hernon. *Improving the Quality of Reference Service for Government Publications* (Chicago, IL: American Library Association, 1983).

[c]Charles R. McClure, Peter Hernon, and Gary R. Purcell. *Linking the U.S. National Technical Information Service with Academic and Public Libraries* (Norwood, NJ: Ablex Publishing Corp., 1986).

[d]Kathy A. Way. "Quality Reference Service in Law School Depository Libraries: A Cause for Action," *Government Publications Review*, 14 (1987): 207–219.

In the case of the documents studies, the most frequent reason for an incorrect answer was that library staff gave wrong information. In a number of instances, staff responded with "don't know" and terminated the search without suggesting any referral; or they claimed that the library did not own a source that would answer the question (when, in fact, the source was on the shelf).

These findings apply to both academic and public libraries, regardless of department (general reference or government documents), size of the budget or collection, population of the community, geographical area, or staffing patterns. The level of degree offered at the academic institution does not alter these findings; staff at doctoral-granting institutions do not answer more questions correctly than do their counterparts at baccalaureate- and master's-granting institutions (Hernon and McClure, 1987b; McClure and Hernon, 1983).

The collective findings (from the 20 studies identified in Hernon and McClure, 1987, pp. 4–5) do not mean that every library in the United States or member of a public service staff conforms to the general profile sketched. Rather, the writings document a pattern of many libraries and their staff, that appears to be constant over time. Consistency among study findings supports the advancement of a general reference rule:

> Reference staff in academic and public libraries, regardless of department, provide correct answers to approximately 55% of the factual and bibliographic questions they receive.

This rule is based on staff responses to: (1) questions often considered easier than average to answer, and (2) requests primarily for paper copy material. The impact on the accuracy rate of "harder" questions or questions requiring alternative information formats (i.e., electronic) has not been investigated.

The collective findings underscore that library managers must accept responsibility for the development and implementation of an ongoing program of evaluation and improvement. No longer should they merely read the published results of unobtrusive evaluations and assume that their library performs at a higher rate of accuracy. Clearly, the body of published unobtrusive investigations suggests problems in providing effective and efficient service. The key issue is whether library managers will assess their local situation and take corrective actions, where necessary, or whether staff in a number of libraries will continue to conform to the 55% rule. For a discussion of managerial issues and corrective strategies, see Hernon and McClure (1987b), McClure and Hernon (1987), and McClure and Hernon (1983).

Referral Services

Given the complexities of government activities and publishing programs, referral service performs an important function. It leads library staff members and library clientele to a range of information resources, not all of which are available in printed form. Further, referral can result in access to timely and easily understandable information, and can demonstrate that libraries provide an essential link in the information environment. Libraries do not contain comprehensive collections, but their staff members can assist the public in negotiating various information providers for the prompt resolution of an information need.

Referral, as is evident, can be more than sending someone to the card catalog, a particular reference source, or member of the library staff. Referral can and does take place in a wider context than a particular library or, in the case of academic libraries, the immediate resources of the institution. An expanded concept of referral service views it as actively helping clientele to "make contact with an outside resource by making an appointment, or calling an agency" (Childers, 1979, pp. 2036–2037).

Depending on the knowledge of individual staff members, the type and availability of local resources, and the extent of local cooperation, numerous opportunities for referral could conceivably exist. On the one hand, referral could be "internal"—to another staff member or area of the library, or it could be directed to another depository library (selective or regional) or other information providers (e.g., GPO bookstores, Federal Information Centers, or specific government agencies, clearinghouses, or centers). The depository library program, in theory, encourages referral among depository libraries: libraries attempt to meet the information needs of their own clientele as well as extend assistance to other depository libraries. This assistance might be in the form of interlibrary loan or providing answers to specific questions. Variation, however, occurs in how depository libraries interpret their responsibility to fulfill these obligations (Schwarzkopf, 1975). A central question becomes: How frequently do documents and general reference staff in depository libraries engage in referral, either of an "internal" or "external" nature?

As part of the unobtrusive testing reported in McClure and Hernon, (1983), Hernon and McClure (1987b), and McClure, Hernon, and Purcell (1986, Chapter 5), referral activity was monitored in GPO academic and public libraries for both depository and NTIS distributed publications. The documents personnel tested infrequently engaged in referral activity. They tended to view their collections as self-contained, and to believe that they lacked the necessary resources to address specific questions. When referral was suggested, it was generally internal to the library. Instead of suggesting referral, staff members would admit that they did not know the answer, or speculate that the question might not be answerable. In effect, they left the information seeker to decide whether the question merited further searching and which information provider might be the most helpful. This finding is all the more amazing in that many patrons lack a clear understanding of government structure and the methods for searching out needed information. Staff members generally do not place the library in the context of the entire information environment and identify other search options.

General reference staff also tended to avoid referral, even to the depository collection in their own library. The exception to this generalization might be those instances in which they were busy and wanted to "move clientele along." It was easier to make referral than to work with another patron (Hernon and McClure, 1987b). General reference staff members tended to associate questions with the resources of a particular department. By limiting referral to specific collections, the entire resources of an institution, or a wider array of formal institutional providers, go untapped.

Documents staff members (as well as general reference personnel) must fully realize their role as disseminators of information and assume the responsibilities that professionalism demands. If they cannot disseminate specific information, including the provision of knowledgeable referral service, for what purpose do they provide reference service? Indeed, inadequate referral service will not make the 55% Rule a phenomenon of the past and improve the quality of reference service (and the accuracy) of referral service. Curiously, documents librarians want other information providers to be aware of, as well as to make referrals to, the depository library program. Yet documents librarians themselves infrequently provide referral services. Such a paradoxical perspective injures the ability of the patron to gain access to government information, and demands revision and improvement by documents librarians.

"OUTREACH" AND MARKETING ACTIVITIES FOR DOCUMENTS

"Outreach" activities fall under four goals: (1) increasing user awareness and access to government information; (2) acquainting or orienting users with library facilities; (3) instructing clientele in the use of libraries, commonly referred to as "bibliographic instruction;" and (4) expanding the delivery of government information to information-seekers outside the library. The first goal encompasses alerting people to the fact that libraries are primary sources of information and a principal means for meeting information needs. Through such activities, nonusers can become aware of library resources and realize that documents collections may contain information applicable to their needs. With the second goal, users are familiarized with library facilities and services, including physical layout, procedures, and staff. They become acquainted with the location of separate documents collections, documents staff members, the hours during which the documents reference service is provided, and circulation policies. The third goal, which is instructional, encompasses helping users to take maximum advantage of library resources in meeting their information needs. As a result of instruction, there should be improvement in library skills and less dependence on library staff members for finding information contained in the collection. Finally, the delivery of information outside of library facilities allows librarians to provide prompt resolution of a patron's information needs, with minimal inconvenience to that patron.

Since many depository library collections are operated by a small number of staff charged with developing and maintaining the collection, documents "outreach" programs are frequently available only on a small scale. Librarians can select, from among various approaches, those most beneficial to their particular situation (Reynolds, 1975). Some of these approaches can easily be accomplished, while others are more time-consuming. Regardless of which ones are tried, it is important to evaluate them on a regular basis, so that modifications can be made or approaches discarded in favor of new ones.

Librarians might devise their own current awareness and selective dissemination of information services, by which clientele not only become aware of new source material received by the library but also gain access to sources pertinent to their professional needs. Clientele might be encouraged to peruse new titles and to select the ones meriting duplication, in microfiche or paper copy, for personal collections. Library staff members might also advise faculty members and other clientele on the purchase of microform viewing equipment for departmental or home use.

In order to increase user awareness, librarians can experiment with such techniques as signs, articles for student and local newspapers, sections in library handbooks promoting documents use, and guides for depository collections. They could also meet with faculty members individually or at departmental meetings. Librarians can ascertain the research and teaching interests of new faculty members, and invite them to a library orientation in which they are exposed to library services and to sources of potential interest to their subject specializations. In individual discussions, librarians can expand upon the number and location of potentially useful sources, as well as inform faculty members that certain types of information needs will be addressed over the telephone. Acquaintance with library facilities can be accomplished through brochures, newsletters, student and new faculty orientations, and tours of the documents collection.

To address the orientation-related goal, librarians can develop handbooks, bibliographic guides for specific disciplines, and tours of the library and documents collection. The tours can be self-guided, and dependent on such visual aids as directional signs and wall diagrams that show the major features of the department. Orientation tours can be offered to interested groups. For example, elementary school students touring libraries can be introduced to depository collections by having them examine census block maps and pinpointing the location of their homes. They might also be shown maps and photographs taken from different probes of outer space. In addition, they might observe online searching or explore subject searching on a CD-ROM version of the *Monthly Catalog*.

An instructional role adds another dimension to documents reference service. Instruction in the use of documents collections and sources can be traced back to the early part of this century. However, many instructional programs have been implemented on a limited scale, and little research has been conducted in this area. Bibliographic instruction has been accomplished by class lectures, tours, term paper clinics, and reference rap sessions (at prearranged times, students receive extensive assistance with class papers and projects), cassette taped instruction outlining the steps for conducting legislative histories, special seminars and workshops, formal courses on library usage, and computer-assisted instruction that might suggest how to search specific indexes or to negotiate separate documents collections arranged by specialized classification schemes. Smith (1986) discusses microcomputer software that offers on-screen guidance to those needing government information but unsure of which source to consult.

College and university students constitute the primary target group for many of the instructional approaches. For example, instructional library lectures conducted through the classroom have been a popular method of library instruction as reflected in the literature of documents librarianship. These lectures are course related and generally chart library skills necessary to complete assignments. They are intended to familiarize students with library staff members, library policies and procedures, research literature, and search strategies. In some cases, after delivering the lecture, documents librarians leave the sources discussed on book carts in the documents department for students to peruse at their convenience.

A weakness to course related instruction is that it is often narrowly conceived. It focuses on library resources of potential and actual value to general or specific information needs. Students are introduced to the ways that librarians gather information and are encouraged to abandon or modify their existing information gathering strategies. They become acquainted with indexing and abstracting services, but often do not associate these tools with information needs arising outside of that class and that particular assignment. (To some extent, technology might be a change agent. Students will return to a service repeatedly, regardless of their information need). Further, libraries are portrayed as "the" information provider and not as mediators of the information environment.

Staff from various libraries in the same locality might participate in joint seminars and explain the differences among the collections. Such seminars would suggest the types of resources, print and nonprint, accessible through libraries in the immediate area, while at the same time providing library staff with a familiarity with each other's services, resources, and expertise. These seminars could be expanded to include representatives from other information providers. The resulting dialogue could be useful both for developing referral services and becoming aware of new source material.

These programs, however, frequently do not reach nonusers or those who have yet to be made aware of the value of government information resources. In such instances, programs and services that provide direct document delivery to information users is essential. Typically, such programs are linked to other more traditional programs previously discussed. But the benefit of such programs is the likelihood of reaching nonusers and demonstrating that specific government information resources can be identified and made available promptly and accurately. Further, such delivery programs can be targeted at specific library target audiences—such as health care professionals—who may not be aware of government information resources in their particular field. However, until it has been proven (by placing the actual publication in their hands) that such materials have value and resolve a particular information need, they may not be willing to exploit the range of resources held by libraries.

In summary, the list of programs presented in this section, although far from comprehensive, illustrates some of the possibilities at the disposal of librarians. *Academic Library Use of NTIS* (1986) offers additional program suggestions. Library staff members need to experiment with various options and find those most advantageous to their situation, but they should do so within the context of a marketing program. This program should take into account situations in which the number of library staff members assigned to "outreach" and reference programs is small, and in which the demand for a service may outpace the ability to supply it. There may be a point beyond which librarians may not be able, or motivated, to provide a service. In these cases, librarians may discourage overall demand for a service, or reduce the demand coming from certain segments of their constituency. It is necessary, therefore, to evaluate programs; to determine which ones yield the maximum return with the least expenditure of time, resources, and personnel; and to realize the scope of the word "marketing."

MARKETING OF DEPOSITORY COLLECTIONS AND SERVICES

Depository libraries must consider marketing strategies appropriate to the services they offer. As Kotler (1975, 1982) succinctly discusses, the basic steps for a marketing program include:

- Conceptualizing the market
- Analyzing the market
- Determining the market programs
- Administering the marketing programs.

These steps are interrelated; the last two are dependent upon the ability of the library to conceptualize and analyze its market fully and accurately.

Marketing problems facing libraries and their documents collections can be identified through the occurrence of any, or a combination of, problems such as too few users, decline in responsiveness to users' information needs, poor image, user dissatisfaction, and insufficient funding. Reflecting on the current situation faced by many libraries, it is evident that many (and perhaps all) of these problems exist, and that aggressive marketing may enable libraries to deal with these problems effectively. Information relevant to marketing can be gathered from a review of the information environment, that is, by conducting user/use studies (Hernon, 1979; Hernon and Purcell, 1982). Paraphrasing Kotler, such a review should address questions such as:

A. Depository Library Market
    1. Who are the major markets and publics to be served?
    2. What are the major market segments in each market?
B. Clientele
    3. How do the clientele feel about the library (what are their perceptions)?

    4. What are their information gathering patterns?

    5. What are the present and potential information needs that they believe the library can satisfy?

C. Competitors

    6. What are the other information providers, institutional and other, that compete for the same market?

    7. How successful are these competitors in satisfying information needs of the present and potential library users?

D. Macroenvironment

    8. How have the library's information services and programs been influenced or affected by social, economic, technological, governmental, and cultural developments?

After conceptualizing library markets, the next step is to analyze these markets. Such an analysis involves the identification of library marketing problems, and examination of library structure and library consumers. In all these areas, it is essential that a needs assessment study be undertaken.

As discussed earlier in the chapter, the public often does not associate libraries, let alone their documents collection, with their information needs. Further, libraries frequently do not comprise a major institutional provider that the public consults. Findings such as these underscore the marketing problems faced by libraries. Kotler (1975, pp. 82–85) has labeled these problems as:

- *Negative demand* ("the important segment of the potential market dislikes the product . . .")
- *No demand* ("all or important segments of a potential market are uninterested or indifferent to a particular offering")
- *Latent demand* ("a substantial number of people sharing a strong need for something which does not exist in the form of an actual product or service")
- *Faltering demand* ("a state in which the demand for a product or service is less than its former level and where further decline is expected in the absence of remedial efforts to revise the target market, offering, and/or marketing effort").

Each of these library marketing situations demands specific marketing tasks. In order to regulate the level, timing, and type of demand for library programs and services, in the context of their current goals and objectives, librarians need to analyze the library market structure and the needs of their clientele.

The library market is not homogeneous. Libraries must tailor their information programs and services to meet the needs of specific target markets. Thus, analyzing the needs of each library segment is a major component of market research.

After having analyzed the library markets, appropriate strategies can be utilized to focus on the following four areas (D'Elia, 1980–1981):

- *Market Penetration*: encouraging more use of existing services by present user groups
- *Information Services Development*: developing new services for present nonuser groups
- *User Group Expansion*: delivering existing services to new markets among present nonuser groups
- *Diversification*: developing new services for new markets among present nonuser groups.

Implicit in the last two strategies is the assumption that there exists within the population of nonusers a group of potential users who might, if available services fit their needs, be persuaded to use libraries and their documents collections. It appears, therefore, that the development of appropriate marketing strategies is dependent upon not only the library's ability to conduct marketing surveys among its user groups, but also its ability to identify and survey the potential users among the nonusers.

Librarians seeking to develop programs and services will have to depend on the information obtained through the analysis of library markets by determining the level of interest, the needs, desires, and aversions of those for whom the programs/services are intended. Then each library program initiated can be more easily justified, because answers to the following sample questions have been gathered:

- Do the clientele grasp how the library program is positioned in relation to competing programs, and what its distinct benefits are?
- Do users show a preference for this library program over competing offerings?
- Do enough people indicate an intention to participate?
- Do enough people believe the program meets their needs?
- How do clientele feel about the form, quality, and accessibility of the intended program?

Marketing can only be effective when it is aimed at target audiences and the improvement in library services, just as advertising is most persuasive when the project itself is worth buying. In short, the information gathering public should be viewed as consumers of a product or service offered by the library.

As should be evident, public relations, including advertising and publicity, only comprises a small part of marketing activities. Promoting library programs and services is an ongoing activity, one that provides data useful for all phases of marketing. It keeps the library in touch with the present and potential information needs of its clientele.

One problem traditionally associated with some of the "outreach" programs already discussed has been that often they have not attracted a large audience and that, frequently, those who attend are already heavy or moderate library users. Consequently, librarians may not be reaching the range of user groups desired; they may need to examine the literature of marketing and select target markets rather than make a quixotic attempt to win every market and to be all things to all people. Librarians should distinguish among possible market segments, concentrating initially on those segments with the highest potential response, and design programs to meet specific preferences.

Once it has been decided to proceed with a marketing program, librarians should inform the target audience about specific information services and products, and their benefits. At the same time, they should create genuine interest and a desire to participate. After all, the purpose of "outreach" programs is to stimulate, create, and/or develop user dependency on government information resources, in particular those held in libraries. However, it should be cautioned that, since people encounter a large volume of advertising daily, no advertisement has more than a fraction of a second to attract and capture attention. The packaging of the advertisement and its message must, therefore, be distinctive. The words used must communicate program benefits in terms that are meaningful to the target audience. The total advertisement must convey one clear theme, because rarely will attention be held for a sufficient time to register more than one or two ideas.

In effect, librarians should try to reach the target audience with a minimum of wasted coverage, deliver maximum exposure to the program, and demonstrate how the program addresses information needs. Therefore, librarians should consider using specially prepared materials, brightly colored directional signs, and pleasing graphics (see Chapter 8, Hernon and Richardson, 1988).

Whichever strategy is used, it is important to estimate the number of people encountering a particular advertisement and the number of times that the average person has been exposed during a given period. Such information suggests how successful library advertising has been and can be used in planning additional programs. Librarians will benefit from an examination of that portion of marketing research dealing with motivation and program effectiveness. They must, therefore, be concerned that the marketing program adheres to written goals and objectives, and has an evaluation component.

ROLE OF THE GOVERNMENT PRINTING OFFICE

The GPO has initiated current awareness sources, *U.S. Government Books* and *New Books*, that alert browsers to potentially high interest "book titles" in the sales program. These aids do not adequately lead researchers to the information content of specialized sources (e.g., research reports, committee and commission reports, committee prints, and congressional hearings) to which they are likely to have greater need. On the other hand, the *Monthly Catalog* is now too bulky to browse, on a regular basis, and to discover the full range of information content. Consequently there remains a major void in the awareness of, and access to, high quality, recently issued GPO information resources of potential value to specialized audiences (e.g., academic scientists and social scientists).

In addition to attacking this problem, the GPO might investigate the document delivery capability of the depository library program in order to determine its ability to supply needed source material in a timely manner. The GPO should ensure that the depository library inspection program takes into account the quality of reference service provided to client groups. The agency should work actively to improve the quality of depository reference and referral services (e.g., by sponsoring regional workshops and ensuring that a member of each depository staff participates).

Cherns (1979, p. 295), a former official of Her Majesty's Stationery Office in Great Britain, has hypothesized that the depository library program in the United States:

> absorbs too much of the attention, resources, and organization of the USGPO in relation to the ultimate use made of the material distributed—energies and resources which might be better applied to the servicing of the wider public requirement for official publications.

To the contrary, insufficient support is provided (Hernon and McClure, 1988). The GPO must re-evaluate its role and be willing to become a more active partner in improving public access and in requiring that a higher quality of reference service be extended.

In this context, it should be noted that, in June 1982, a separate marketing department within the GPO began operation. Figure 8–2 indicates areas in which the department has been active. The GPO identifies target audiences, selects titles from the sales program of potential appeal to these groups, and advertised these titles in journals likely to be read by members of the preselected target audiences. The GPO also conducts a special or mass mailing to target audiences. Generally, orders from 10% of the target population make the mailing successfully (incoming orders offset expenditures).

Figure 8-2.
Representative Products of the GPO Marketing Program

Advertisement in Trade Magazines

Assistance to GPO Bookstores (e.g., signage, brochures, and relocation)

Creation of Marketing Department

Development of:

    Depository Library Brochures

    Marketing Moves, irregular newsletter of GPO since 1982

    Posters

    Public Service Announcements (radio and television commercials)

Ensuring That Documents Orders Can Be Placed through DIALOG

Honoring New Depositories and "Outstanding" Existing Ones

Replacement of *Selected U.S. Government Publications* with *U.S. Government Books* (Fall, 1982, Vol. 1, Number 1), a quarterly, illustrated publication containing 64 pages and *New Books* (1982, Vol. 1, Number 1), a bimonthly list of new sales publications

In cooperation with depository librarians, the GPO has produced radio and television commercials calling attention to the depository library program. However, the success of such announcements cannot be determined; no evaluation component exists and is linked to formal objectives. Nonetheless, the impact of certain announcements may be minimal. Figure 8–3 lists potential weaknesses to the marketing program. The interrelationships between the various factors depicted in the figure must be explored.

A number of the radio and television announcements are aimed at school children and assume that their information needs are best met from government publications. Further assumptions are that general reference staff will automatically refer a question to a documents department/collection, and any inquiry addressed to the local public library will result in the name and location of the nearest depository library. Clearly, underlying assumptions to any marketing strategy merit review and correction, where necessary, if the impact of the intended announcement is to be realized.

Information needs and information gathering patterns comprise extremely complex areas of research. The complexity increases when researchers, government officials, and librarians attempt to alter existing information gathering behavior. These three groups must place the library in the context of the larger information environment and view the library as one potential information provider among many. Information needs must also be viewed as part of the person, situation, and prejudices with which information needs are associated in the user's mind. Without this context, those interested in depository library collections cannot adequately design pro-

Figure 8-3.
Potential Weaknesses to Effective Marketing of U.S. Government Publications

---

Awareness of new source material does not guarantee increased use (What programs, e.g., selective dissemination of information, have been initiated to make access to government publications easier?)

The GPO is attempting to market government publications as regular books, while downplaying their specialized information content

Many libraries equate marketing with publicity

The marketing program is aimed at certain segments of society

The marketing program neither fully addresses how people gather and use information nor the role of government information in comparison to other types of information (libraries and the GPO sales program comprise two, of many, information providers; people prefer to gather information from interpersonal rather than institutional providers; and the public often bypasses libraries in their search for information)

More documentation is available largely or solely in a nonprint format; people often have a bias against microforms

People may already have sufficient information on a topic; access to government publications produces an "overload" of information (consulting documents collections and reference tools can be a difficult, time-consuming process, one that leads to information not held by that library as well as to information of varying quality)

The pricing of government information resources affects the extent to which the public will purchase resources

The public is largely unaware of what a government publication is; they tend to equate it with a general information pamphlet

The public is largely unfamiliar with depository library collections, their purpose and types of resources included

---

grams to meet the wide range of information needs (Chen and Hernon, 1982).

IMPROVING REFERENCE AND REFERRAL SERVICES

Librarians need to capitalize on the demand for data relating to government activities, or else see researchers and others turn to alternative sources of information. When the public seeks alternative sources, libraries may well play only a marginal role in resolving their information needs. Librarians must engage in a dialogue with library users and nonusers, ascertain their research needs, and add to the reference collection accordingly. Librarians must constantly evaluate the role they can play in meeting the information needs of their clientele. Unless this is accomplished, reference and referral services will not be meeting the legitimate demands that should be placed on them.

Referral, which is an integral part of reference service, necessitates knowledgeable insights into which organizations, agencies, libraries, etc., can best respond to user needs. Clientele should be given the name of a person, agency, or library to contact if no other information is available in the library on a specific topic. Referral, as a result, becomes more personal, and users become aware that libraries, although not always having the information they need, may be centers for referral service to agencies actually holding the information.

Fielding reference queries from their clientele comprises but one activity performed by documents reference staff. However, existing studies do not fully identify the myriad of other activities performed or analyze the types of reference questions received. Studies from the general reference field have shown that a majority of questions are of a direction or ready reference nature, No comparative studies of documents reference service, however, have been reported.

Reference librarians are often dissatisfied with the traditional methods of gathering statistical information relating to use made of reference desk personnel, but are unsure of alternatives. However, numerous sources exist that provide suggestions in this area, e. g., Association of Research Libraries (1987). Reference questions have generally been recorded by entering marks on a sheet for each day of the month. Numbers are then tallied and comparisons in departmental reports, monthly and annual, are made as to the numbers and types of reference queries for past months and years.

As an alternative, data on reference queries could be collected, coded, and analyzed by a statistical analysis software package (see Hernon and Richardson, 1988). Administrators could use the data collected to schedule staff at the reference desk, observe patterns in the questions asked, and engage in collection development (search for source material to answer certain questions better and more fully). Documents librarians might also be able to use the data collected to demonstrate the number and complexity of questions received.

The gathering and analysis of reference questions does not indicate the accuracy of staff responses. In this regard, the unobtrusive studies previously mentioned assume added importance. Reference staff members must not limit themselves to monitoring and improving the service extended to those clientele who actually request reference desk assistance. They must also examine support services, ascertain the information needs and information gathering behavior of client groups, initiate and evaluate "outreach" programs, and view collection development as part of a decision making process.

Too often, the research conducted in the documents field is limited to case studies that probe a particular library and one of its services. The generalizability of such research is indeed limited. Future research should expand the population, examine interrelationships among programs and services, and address questions such as:

- Are library clientele hesitant to approach the documents desk to request assistance? Is the hesitancy influenced by librarians who appear preoccupied with their own work?
- Can clientele differentiate among documents librarians, clerical staff, and student assistants concerning roles and duties?
- If students have requested reference assistance once, are they likely to approach the same librarian again for further assistance on the same topic or use of a particular source?
- Does attendance in a library "outreach" program significantly affect student perceptions about the roles and duties of documents librarians, and affect student willingness to request assistance?
- Are users satisfied with the assistance and the information that documents librarians supply?
- If government publications are held in a separate collection and on a floor other than that of the main reference collection, what problems (if any) arise in referral service from reference to documents librarians?
- If users do not understand the librarian the first time they asked a question, or could not find the resource, does it bother them to ask the same librarian for further assistance?
- What are effective ways by which the quality of reference service can be improved?
- How effective is the GPO marketing program in inviting greater use of depository collections (do users follow through on the invitation, and what was their experience like)?
- What types of reference questions should depository libraries attempt to address:
  - Should they attempt to answer any question involving a request for government information?
  - Should they provide the same level of service for all questions asked?
  - Are they responsible for the accuracy and up-to-dateness of the information that they disseminate?
  - What degree of referral, if any, is to be provided, and to which information providers?
- What are the implications for the depository library program as an interlocking network when users experience divergent levels of service and are not referred to depositories better equipped to handle certain requests?

- Should documents staff members be required to participate in continuing education programs, and to receive advanced training?
- Is the depository library program cost-effective, or cost-beneficial (if it is not, should the GPO and Congress make a financial commitment toward improving the quality of reference service)?
- Can a national program to promote the collections and services of depository libraries be successful, if, upon consulting libraries, the public encounters undistinguished reference service?

At the same time, documents departments must develop reference policy manuals and set departmental goals and objectives within the parameters of those maintained by the larger organization.

Given current funding levels, some authors (e.g., Morton, 1987) are questioning how long depository libraries can continue to devote so much collection space and money for staff, facilities, and reference aids to support massive documents collections that have limited use and are poorly serviced? Documents librarians will be (and in some cases are being) asked to justify the need for expensive commercially produced bibliographic retrieval tools for accessing government publications. This is especially true in those instances where monies for documents collections must compete against the need for other library acquisitions. Funds cannot always be diverted from other budgetary categories to meet the alleged needs of depository collections, especially where documents receive limited use and reference services are less than adequate.

In demanding equal treatment for government publications in comparison to other library resources, documents librarians must demonstrate the value and importance of documents as a means of resolving a broad range of information needs. Further, they must work closely with other librarians and administrators to make known the needs and requirements of the depository collection. However, they cannot be effective spokespersons for government information resources if they have limited knowledge of larger Federal policy issues, government publishing/distribution/ dissemination programs, and provide unsatisfactory service to users of the depository collection.

Reference and referral services for government information resources should be of concern to documents librarians, library administrators, and government officials overseeing depository library programs. Until they all assume part of the responsibility, the quality of depository reference service is not likely to improve substantially. But short-term patchwork of depository programs will not solve the long-range problems of providing high quality access to government information resources. Improved management of depository collections, on-going educational programs for depository librarians, and greater support for depository libraries from the GPO are all needed. But, in addition, formal, funded, and valid studies into the effectiveness of depository library programs, and the extent of access to government information that participants in each program provide, are necessary immediately. It is vitally important that the research literature on documents reference and referral services grow substantially and assist in developing the potential role of depository reference personnel as effective mediators of the information environment.

9

Microforms and Access to Government Publications

As of 1988, Federal agencies have continued to increase their reliance on microforms for the dissemination of government information. Indeed, the association of microforms with government publications brings to mind the activities of the Government Printing Office (GPO), Educational Resources Information Center (ERIC), the National Technical Information Service (NTIS), Library of Congress, the National Archives and Records Administration, the Bureau of the Census, and other Federal agencies. In addition, some agencies produce microforms in-house for the purpose of archival storage and dissemination (e.g., through intergovernmental exchange programs).

A detailed analysis and comparison of agency microprinting (the reduction of an image to a smaller size, and its printing usually on film) and micropublishing (a broader concept implying the selection of materials for microfilming, microprinting, promotion, and dissemination) programs is beyond the scope of this chapter. Complete analysis of just the GPO's micropublishing program would have to address topics such as its goals and objectives, its relationship to other governmental micropublishing and microprinting programs, the relationship of GPO's sales and micropublishing programs to the depository library program, the burden of "information overload" on libraries already facing severe space shortages, the role of regional depository libraries in the provision of lesser-used resources, and any problems encountered by depository libraries in their everyday dealings with the GPO.

This chapter, instead, focuses on microforms collection development, improved user access to microforms, and the need to enhance bibliographic control over the resources needed by client groups. It does not provide a general introduction to micrographics or micrographic technology; Saffady (1985) provides an excellent introduction to these topics. More specifically, the chapter discusses the historical development of the GPO micropublishing program and the proliferation of microformatted government publications entering the depository library program; bibliographic control, collection development, and use patterns of microforms; core literatures and their indexing; and personnel development for managing microform collections. The chapter stresses the importance of obtaining and using government microforms to increase access to government publications.

HISTORICAL OVERVIEW

For years, various Federal agencies have been involved in microprinting. Government micropublishing, on the other hand, began with scientific and technical report literature but later "expanded to include the educational research materials produced in HEW's [Department of Health, Education, and Welfare] ERIC program, economic and business information in SEC's [Securities and Exchange Commission] Disclosure files, and similar publishing programs" (Powell, 1977, p. 3).

In 1970, A.N. Spence proposed to the Joint Committee on Printing (JCP) that the GPO enter the field of micropublishing and "offer filmed documents to customers either in addition to or in lieu of printing" (Depository Library Council, 1978). The Public Printer maintained that his responsibility was "to distribute Government funded and created documents as widely as possible to the taxpaying public at the lowest possible price" (Schwarzkopf, 1978, p. 163). He realized, though, that there was an ever-growing concern among librarians about the vast amount of government publications that they were receiving. He noted that microforms relieved space problems and that they could "be more speedily and economically retrieved than can hardcopy" ("Micropublishing and the Government Printing Office," 1974, p. 1).

With authorization from the JCP, Spence established a Micropublishing Advisory Committee, consisting of ten experts from government and industry. He also supported a survey of depository libraries to ascertain their reaction to a micropublishing program. After having received the results of GPO's technical studies and of a survey in which 75% of the respondents expressed interest in receiving some microform documents, as well as having encouragement from the Advisory Committee, he requested that the JCP authorize a micropublishing program.

Further development of the GPO micropublishing program was delayed due to criticism and confusion within the library community concerning factors such as the proposed reduction ratio, lack of standards, and the unsatisfactory nature of the *Monthly Catalog of United States Government Publications* as a tool for gaining access to government publications. The untimely death of Mr. Spence, in January 1972, was another delaying factor.

Thomas F. McCormick, the next Public Printer, proposed in 1973 that depository libraries be resurveyed about their interest in receiving publications on microform. He recommended that if there was sufficient interest, the JCP should permit a pilot project for the distribution of some microformatted publications. He also suggested that, if successful, the program could be expanded to include other depository categories.

In February 1974, the GPO surveyed depository libraries through Part II of the 1973 *Biennial Report of Depository Libraries*, and sought their preference for paper copy or microform distribution in those categories of publications that they were already receiving. The findings, which confirmed those of the earlier survey, suggested that 83% of the depository librarians wanted a microform format in at least one category of material. However,

> . . . many librarians responded [to the survey] in somewhat of a vacuum when composing their answers. For example, neither type nor quality of the microform to be distributed was known at the time either by librarians, or for that matter by the GPO itself. GPO was merely trying to determine whether or not there was an interest in microform distribution, and librarians responded accordingly. There was interest. Many librarians thought that the distribution of microform was inevitable and that their role was to indicate preferred categories. It would be difficult to interpret the survey as more (MacDonald and Sieger, 1978, p. 39).

In 1974, the Public Printer formally requested a pilot project for testing the feasibility of a micropublishing program. Approved in 1975 by the JCP, the project, which lasted from the latter part of that year until the middle of the next, tested the feasibility of micropublishing the *Code of Federal Regulations* (CFR). The project

> was based on a small sample of test libraries selected by the GPO. Many aspects of the project were not handled very well—the timing was poorly planned, there was very little time afforded the libraries for creating a reasonable test environment, and not all libraries used the *CFR* under documented conditions (Cline, 1979, pp. 23–24).

Further, the *CFR* did not receive extensive use, from library staff and users, in all of the test sites. Nevertheless, the GPO declared the project successful and, in July 1976, requested approval from the JCP to start microform distribution to depository libraries.

Many librarians supported GPO's plans for microfiche conversion, particularly of non-GPO titles. Some thought that microfiche distribution, especially of non-GPO titles, would enable them to maintain the same level of selection as that experienced before their encountering severe space limitations for paper copy collections. For others, microfiche comprised a means for expanding selection profiles. The feeling was that the availability of government information in a microformat improves public access to the universe of government publications having public interest or educational value.

Almost from the beginning of GPO's proposed entry into the micropublishing field, representatives from the Information Industry Association (IIA) voiced opposition. They did not want the GPO to enter arbitrarily those information dissemination fields that were already serviced effectively by the private sector. Further, they claimed that the sales of commercial companies would be severely damaged and that elimination of the private sector would reduce libraries and the public to a single source of access to government information—the Federal government.[1]

The GPO saw itself as not trying to compete with the private sector; rather it viewed microfiche conversion as a cost-effective alternative to the production, binding, and distribution of current publications (1976–) in paper copy. The private sector, actively collects and disseminates older material and publications not provided by the GPO. In addition, the private sector organizes and refines information into its most marketable form. Consequently, the GPO does not compete effectively with the indexing/abstracting services provided by the private sector.

Not all of the products and services related to microformatted government publications generate a profit. In such instances, private enterprise is less enthusiastic about entering the market, and typically the responsibility falls to the government. Thus, the government and private sector complement each other—for the benefit of the public. In part, Office of Management and Budget Circular A-76, "Performance of Commercial Activities," clarifies and defines the relationship. Yet that circular does not adequately maintain creative tension between the public and private sectors. Indeed, were it not for a degree of tension, libraries and the public would be the primary losers.

In March 1977, Senator Howard W. Cannon, chairperson of the JCP, wrote a letter to the Public Printer granting authorization for the GPO micropublishing program and for conversion to microfiche. The concept of a

---

[1] Some background information on the controversy between the private and public sectors may be in order. In November 1977, James Adler, then president of Congressional Information Service, wrote Paul Zurkowski, president of the Information Industry Association, concerning the GPO's intention to distribute selected depository publications on microfiche. For a discussion of Adler's letter, the letter of Zurkowski to the Public Printer, and the response of the Public Printer, see McClure (1978b).

microform sales program was expressly prohibited. At about the same time, the GPO Micropublishing Council, representing the depository library community and the private sector, was created. According to its charter, the advisory group provides:

> an understanding of the capabilities and limits of micropublishing technology; a broad overview of the requirements of the information users and intermediaries; careful balancing of the interests and capabilities of the public and private sectors; the clarification of relationships between the GPO and Federal agencies that generate and disseminate information; and understanding of total system economics which will permit the balancing of costs and benefits among organizations involved in order to achieve the optimal use of new technologies; and development of criteria for the selection of Federal Government publications for conversion to microforms ("Charter of the Public Printer's Council on Micropublishing," 1978, p. 1).

In April 1977, the Depository Library Council devised a list of titles and categories recommended for conversion to microfiche. It also recommended that regional depository libraries receive both silver halide and nonsilver sets of third generation microfiche. Throughout the rest of the year and for part of the next, there was discussion about whether libraries would receive silver halide or diazo microfiche. It was even questioned whether silver halide would be reserved for distribution to regional depository libraries— those libraries most likely to need permanent or archival copy.

At the October 1977 meeting of the Depository Library Council, the GPO supplied a list of titles or categories for which there would be cost reductions in depository distribution of microfiche. Agreement was reached on a list of titles recommended for conversion. Later, the GPO announced that converted titles could be selected in either their original paper copy format or microfiche.

In early November 1977, depository libraries received their first major shipment of GPO microfiche, which included some 355 General Accounting Office reports. In the same month, the results of a survey of depository libraries concerning the availability of microform equipment was reported. Anne Shaw, chairperson of the Microforms Task Force of GODORT (ALA), found that 13% of the responding libraries did not have a microfiche reader, that 38% lacked microfiche reader/printers, and that 91% did not have a fiche-to-fiche duplicator (Shaw, 1977). With the expanding GPO micropublishing program, as well as the diversity of offerings by the private sector, many libraries began to reconsider the number and types of microform equipment they needed to provide adequate access to microformatted government information.

In April 1978, Dr. Albert Materazzi, Manager of the Quality Control and Technical Department at the GPO, made available the findings of a study "The Archival Stability of Microfilm." His conclusions supporting depository distribution of diazo film, as opposed to a silver halide base, received widespread support.[2]

As a micropublisher, the GPO produces a silver halide master that serves as "archival copy." The agency, at some point in time, will turn that master over the to National Archives and Records Administration. Library Programs Service of the GPO obtains a second generation copy of the archival master. This copy can be used to produce paper copy or to generate microfiche copies for those libraries filing a claim that they had not received that title originally. GPO's sales program also uses the copy for its on-demand service.

At meetings held between April and September 1978, the Council on Micropublishing established cost criteria for GPO titles recommended for microform conversion, and a replacement policy for damaged, lost, or stolen microfiche. At the Depository Library Council meeting of October 1978, "discussions proved to be somewhat less theoretical than at previous meetings and attention was directed to specific practical issues." Further, "librarians were no longer debating whether or not they wanted to receive microfiche, but they were asking how to manage microfiche as a part of their libraries' resources" (Cline, 1980, pp. 21–22). At this meeting, it was reported that Congress was urging more extensive use of microforms in an effort to reduce printing costs, and that defective and deteriorating microfiche would be replaced. The GPO planned to distribute diazo film to depository libraries, while retaining silver halide film for archival and reproduction purposes. It was also announced that studies concerned with the aging of microforms would continue.

In 1978, Coopers and Lybrand, an independent consulting firm, studied GPO operations and estimated that the first year of the micropublishing program saved the GPO in excess of $1 million. In the opinion of the evaluators, the:

> GPO should be allowed to expand its use of microfilm technology and allow micropublishing to be offered as a general GPO service. There are many benefits to be gained by easing restrictions and allowing GPO to be more comprehensive in the use of micrographics (Congress. Joint Committee on Printing, *Analysis and Evaluation* . . ., 1979, p. 283).

In the same year, over 5,000 non-GPO publications were converted to over 2,000,000 microfiche and distributed to depository libraries.

Currently, the GPO micropublishing program thrives. In fact, in the years since 1978, the number of titles converted to microfiche has increased

---

[2] For a copy of the report see Hernon (1981).

dramatically. Microfiche is now the preferred format for distribution to depository libraries and will remain so especially in a time of fiscal restraint on the part of the government.

Severe pressures to better manage the Federal budget and curtail expenditures have encouraged Congress to reduce the GPO's budget, just as Congress has done to most other Federal agencies. However, the GPO's responsibility to maintain its programs and services has not been reduced. At the same time, Circular A-130, "The Management of Federal Information Resources, issued by the Office of Management and Budget in December 1985, directs executive agencies to honor the provisions of title 44 of the *United States Code* and distribute publications through the GPO. Facing a relatively constant flow of new titles eligible for inclusion in the depository program in a time of dwindling budgets, the GPO, from 1984 through 1986, made hard and controversial decisions. Agency officials intended to convert more publications to microfiche and to reduce the amount of paper copy distribution. Yet the JCP and its staff, with the support of the library community, opposed any substantial shift to microfiche distribution.

In January 1987, the JCP, in an oral directive, instructed the GPO to continue paper copy distribution of those item numbers that depository libraries preferred to receive in that format ("Dual Format Issue," 1987). The importance of dual format as a significant policy issue therefore ceased. It is not likely to re-emerge unless budgets tighten up and Congress issues a deep cut directive. Still, with significant cuts in the budget, the GPO might be able to continue distribution in dual format on a short-term basis. Nonetheless, the GPO has asked the Depository Library Council to determine which item numbers *must* remain in paper copy. It is the hope of the GPO that it does not have to use the recommendations. However, it is prudent planning to have such recommendations in case of an emergency.

In the mid-1980s, the GPO issued guidelines for determining the suitability of a publication for conversion to microfiche and for preparation of the microfiche. The GPO is trying to improve the quality of the microprinting done both by agencies and on a contractual basis. However, a congressional agency cannot hold executive agencies accountable for the quality of filming they do. The GPO may acquire microfiche prepared by an executive agency or its contractor. If the quality of the filming is inferior, the GPO may encourage the agency to have the document refilmed, redo the filming itself, or distribute the document in its present condition.[3]

---

[3] According to the policy statement issued by the Superintendent of Documents ("Format of Publications Distributed to Depository Libraries," 1987), "publications will be sent to depository libraries in either paper or microfiche format. Distribution will be made in microfiche rather than paper format, when appropriate, to minimize the cost of printing and binding and to help alleviate space problems in depository libraries. Some series and types of documents may be distributed in both formats, when it is cost effective for the

Federal government and beneficial to the library community. In such cases, selective depository libraries may choose to receive paper or microfiche format, but not both. Regional depositories will receive documents in hard copy and microfiche when both formats are distributed.

Documents published by Federal agencies in microfiche will be distributed to depository libraries in that format. Documents published in paper format will be reviewed for suitability for conversion to microfiche. Primary considerations will be the physical characteristics of a publication, the nature of its content, and its relationship to other publications. Consistency of format and optimum usability of depository collections will be continuing objectives.

The following guidelines will be applied to determine whether publications are suitable for distribution in microfiche format:

- Documents whose physical characteristics make them unsuitable for microfiche conversion will be distributed in paper, when possible, regardless of other considerations. These characteristics include: (1) height greater than 11″ or width greater than 14″, including publications that contain foldouts or are accompanied by other materials that exceed 11″ high or 14″ wide; (2) color or half-tone illustrations that are essential for use; (3) continuous tone photographs; (4) characters that are illegible or smaller than six point type; (5) updates and inserts required (e.g., loose-leaf services); and (6) paper other than white
- Popular and consumer oriented publications will not be distributed in microfiche. Two factors in determining whether a publication falls into this category are the topic and the intended audience. Nontechnical documents on subjects like gardening, child care, etc., will not be converted. Publications intended for the general public, high school students, the homeowner, the elderly, etc., also will not be converted. Most brochures and pamphlets fall into this category
- Documents whose primary purpose is to provide news or public awareness of Federal programs and activities will be distributed in paper format. In particular, this includes newsletters, bulletins, circulars, and periodicals in a magazine format
- Standard reference works will be distributed to depository libraries in paper format. Standard reference works are defined as documents that are of broad interest and designed by arrangement and treatment to be consulted for definite information, rather than continuous reading. Examples of such publications are dictionaries, directories, indexes, almanacs, bibliographies, handbooks, manuals and guides, telephone books, and publication catalogs
- Law reference publications, except bills, will be distributed in paper or both formats. Law reference publications include regulations, rules, instructions, orders, interpretations, opinions, decisions, laws, and bills. Bills will be distributed in microfiche format only
- Posters, maps, charts, and pictures will be distributed in paper format. Exceptions may be allowed for large map sets that are usable in microfiche format
- Documents less than 14 pages in length will not be converted to microfiche, because it is not cost effective. Exceptions to this are individual issues of series, single volumes, or transmittals, when the original document or series was distributed in microfiche format
- Documents classified as addresses (typically speeches) will be distributed in paper format
- Annual reports that describe the missions and activities of major Federal agencies, and other organizations of particular interest, will be distributed in paper format. Significant compilations of statistics issued as annual reports by government bodies at all levels also will be distributed in hard copy. Annual reports for most smaller or subordinate organizations and programs will be converted to microfiche format for distribution
- Proceedings and papers from symposia, conferences, or meetings will be converted to microfiche for distribution
- Scientific and technical publications will be distributed in microfiche format. This category includes publications intended for a specialized audience and that provide technical treatment of any subject or report research on scientific and technical subjects
- Documents that are primarily compilations of statistics compiled from surveys and on specialized topics will be distributed in microfiche format. Exceptions to this are major statistical compilations issued annually by Federal agencies, which are considered standard reference works
- Documents intended for use by or of particular interest to librarians (for example, documents published by the Library of Congress) will be distributed in the format in which they are originated

As is evident, as the decade of the 1990s approaches, problems and controversies surrounding the GPO's micropublishing program have decreased. The private sector is turning its attention to the electronic collection and distribution of government information. There are greater corporate opportunities and profits in this area. The GPO must now consider issues related to the distribution of electronic information. Clearly, microform issues are yielding to electronic issues.

MICROFORM BIBLIOGRAPHIC CONTROL

Bibliographic control has aspects that may be viewed as internal and external to a library. In relation to the external aspects, librarians advise on policies involving national bibliographic control and offer recommendations on matters such as depository programs and improved distribution mechanisms, and cataloging and indexing systems. They can also encourage the public and private sectors to improve the way in which they announce new microformatted publications and to adopt standards for microfiche produced by individual agencies.

- Corrections, errata, updates, etc., will be distributed in the same format as the original work
- Publications for the visually impaired will remain in paper format

Scope. This policy pertains to all U.S. government documents subject to distribution to depository libraries.

Application.

- This policy will be applied in the following manner, based on the way in which documents are issued:
  - *Serials.* Serials are publications issued in successive parts, usually bearing a numerical or chronological designation, and intended to be continued indefinitely. A decision to distribute a serial in microfiche format will apply to all future issues
    - *Monographic series.* These are groups of publications related to one another by the fact that each item bears, in addition to its own title, a collective title applying to the group as a whole. Series may be numbered or unnumbered. Earlier numbers of numbered serials will not usually be converted
    - *Periodicals.* These are dated publications issued three or more times a year. Conversion of a periodical will begin with the first issue of the volume or year
    - *Semiannual, annual, and biennial publications.* These are publications issued twice a year, once a year, and every two years, respectively
  - *Monographs.* Monographs are defined as publications complete in one part or a finite number of separate parts. An individual decision as to distribution format will be required for each monograph
- The Director, Library Programs Service, is responsible for (1) ensuring the publications are distributed to depository libraries in the appropriate format; (2) conversion of hard copy publications to microfiche format and production of depository copies; and (3) providing accurate counts for ordering publications to appropriate officials, including the GPO Customer Service Department, Regional Printing Procurement Offices, and other Federal agencies
- Exceptions to this policy must be authorized by the Director, Library Programs Service or his/her authorized designate."

Librarians calling for uniform standards for government microfiche want:

- Standard and accurate eye-readable data on the header conveying author, title, publisher, date of publication, edition, the number of microfiche containing that publication, reduction ratio, the Superintendent of Documents number or a space provided for the addition of a library classification or file control symbol
- Indexing of microform publications, many of which are parts of series consisting of unique bibliographic parts
- Accessibility of microforms through indexes and the identification of publications as available on microfiche
- Provision of abstracts for microforms listed in paper copy indexes
- Compilation of titles available to depository libraries on a microformat
- The marketing and advertising of microfiche through the GPO sales program
- Adoption of ANSI Standard for Information on Microfiche Headers (Z39.33) so that Federal agencies will use the standard on all of their future microfiche products.

Further, whatever standards and practices are adopted must be developed with new technology (e.g., videodiscs, satellite transmissions of information, and cablevision) in mind.

At the same time, GPO officials attempt to work with printing offices of different government agencies in planning of their microformatted products. The purpose is to

> assure high quality products that will be compatible with the GPO produced fiche. However, in present practice, when the fiche is initiated by the agency there is likely to be more variation in terms of headers, reduction ratios, format, and film quality since many of these microform publications are developed without consulting the GPO. In these cases the . . . [GPO] serves only as a distributor since it has no control over the production of these fiche (Cline, 1980, p. 23).

Sometimes, libraries have specified that they want to receive an item number in paper copy. However, an occasional publication may arrive on microfiche. The reason might be that the agency unexpectedly sent the GPO a microfiche, rather than paper, copy. Instead of blowing the copy back to paper form and distributing the required number, the GPO merely duplicates and distributes the microform, causing consternation among depository librarians.

In relation to the internal aspects of bibliographic control, librarians acquire, and ease user access to, those information resources needed by their clientele. In the process of improving bibliographic control over their own collections, many of them should develop decision support systems that improve decision making and their ability to make retention decisions. For example, from an automated system, they could identify those microfiche pamphlets received five years ago and review this pool of documents for retention or deselection from the collection (see Chapter 11). Clearly, librarians should be involved primarily in those aspects of bibliographic control that have the greatest implications for their daily activities.

MICROFORMS COLLECTION DEVELOPMENT

Overview

A small number of government bodies (e.g., departments, agencies, and congressional committees) accounts for the greatest amount of use (Hernon and Purcell, 1982). Holdings beyond what might be labeled as a functional collection enable libraries to satisfy client's immediate demands for various lesser-needed resources, but the maintenance of such large collections is a very costly option. Extensive selection and retention of government publications in paper copy format require more shelving space than many libraries have available. Expanding microform collections will at some point present major collection management problems, as well as require the acquisition of additional viewing and reproduction equipment, the hiring of staff knowledgeable about microforms, and the location of new storage facilities. Variations in quality and lifespan of publications create a difficult trade-off situation in which the value of a few sources must be weighted against the cost of staff and space to process and store a wide range of lesser-needed sources. Further, congestion in the collection presents retrieval problems such as those encountered in finding misshelved titles. When clients search indexes and collections for source material of potential value, they may discover sources of varying quality and have to spend more time in the search for information than they would prefer.

Libraries expanding their selection of microformatted government publications may not be managing the total library resources toward a common goal. Two opposing philosophies for the documents collection appear to prevail. The paper copy collection, on the one hand, might consist of the more heavily needed titles, while the microform collection represents an effort to build a research collection consisting of lesser-used materials and to minimize processing time. Such a philosophy seems to represent a desire to build a self-contained collection, one necessitating few requests for materials received through inter-institutional cooperation.

Although the development of written policy statements does not by itself constitute collection management, these statements provide the basis from which sound collection management principles can be applied. The following parts of this section examine the reasons for library selection of microformatted government publications, and provide a brief outline of the areas in which partial depositories might develop microformatted holdings.

Reasons for Collecting Microforms

Writings in library literature have identified numerous reasons for acquiring microformatted government publications, but have not placed them within the framework of a conceptual model encouraging libraries to collect and retain, to a large extent, only those government publications that receive the greatest amount of use within the institution (see Figure 9–1). Since frequency of need encompasses a wide range of responses, from no to high needs, libraries will have to settle on that amount that they can best handle internally and leave the rest to the province of inter-institutional cooperation. By viewing source material within the context of specific subjects, librarians can determine the importance of a type of publication (e.g., hearings or committee prints) or an individual title to the collection. It should be noted that quality indexing is a prerequisite for labeling a source as indispensable and part of a core.

The conceptual weakness to the model depicted in the figure is that it depicts the acquisition process as a choice of either paper copy or microform. Since source material is available in other formats, libraries must determine the one(s) most appropriate to their users, collections, and circumstances. *Format should not dictate selection.* Consequently, government publications should not be acquired in a microformat if the major reasons for so doing are merely to reduce processing time, save space, or reduce costs. Such reasons must be balanced against collection objectives and functions, as well as user needs, preferences, and user information-gathering behavior. The relationship of the source material to the functional collection should be the overriding consideration. By subjecting a microform package to the scrutiny of a needs assessment (e.g., through a user survey), as well as prioritizing collection needs, library staff members can determine the importance of microformatted source material to the total library collection and to client groups.

Libraries might need extensive backfiles only for selected titles (see Chapter 6). The acquisition of backfiles should be based on a needs assessment. For example, libraries may not need a complete set of the *Congressional Record* and its predecessors. Perhaps use patterns focus on selected

Figure 9-1.
Conceptual Model for Interpreting the Reasons for Acquiring Microformatted Government Publications

	SCOPE OF COLLECTION	
STATED REASONS IN LIBRARY LITERATURE	CORE HOLDINGS	LESSER NEEDED RESOURCES
to acquire needed research material		
to acquire out-of-print items		
to acquire rare and costly items		
to acquire reference publications		
to control theft and mutilation		
to duplicate heavy used materials		
to fill in gaps in the collection		
to reduce binding expenditures		
to reduce processing time		
to replace badly worn copies		
to save space		
other		

years. In that case, backfiles, including those in a microformat, need only concentrate on particular years. For this reason, the purchase of microforms from the private sector should frequently depend on the availability of purchase options. Selectivity is essential, given the high cost for many sets and variability in their potential appeal to client groups.

Potential Areas for Collecting Microforms

Discussion of collection development raises questions about what individual libraries should collect and retain in a microformat. A general essay can neither predict local circumstances nor address the needs of all types of libraries, depository and nondepository. Still, certain general observations are in order; subsequent sections of this chapter will expand upon these general observations.

Selection decisions depend on factors such as the type of library, institutional mission, degree programs, client needs, budget allocations, amount and type of available equipment, storage facilities, amount of space allocated to viewing equipment, availability of needed documents in a microformat, quality of the microform package and finding aids, and the extent to which bibliographic tools are held. Depository collections in academic and public libraries (partial depositories) might consist of paper copy functional collections supplemented with a microform collection of the more frequently needed source material. Sources of marginal importance should be weeded and eliminated from selection profiles.[4]

Financial constraints necessitate a careful review of those sets of microformatted government publications that an academic or public library depository might consider. At the Federal level of government, these libraries, as a general recommendation, might potentially draw upon source material represented in the *American Statistics Index*, perhaps that of a nondepository nature, and in the *CIS Index*. This way, these libraries would have additional current statistical data and congressional material. Supplementing these holdings might be selected ERIC and NTIS publications, backfiles (perhaps the *Congressional Record* and the *Federal Register*) based on a needs assessment, and GPO distributed microfiche (e.g., bills and resolutions, the *Publications Reference File*, and printed reports from the Bureau of the Census). For a research library, other specialized collections of current and retrospective publications might be appropriate. The CIS "Documents on Demand" service provides libraries and users with prompt access to current source material not contained in the local collection.

USE PATTERNS

Recognizable patterns exist for the use of GPO microform collections housed in depository libraries (Hernon, 1981; Hernon 1982). Perhaps the bulk of many microform collections go unused. When depository microfiche are consulted, use probably centers on publications of government bodies such as Congress, the Department of Energy, the Executive Office of the President (e.g., the Central Intelligence Agency), the Office of the Federal Register, and the General Accounting Office. Further, use probably extends to microformatted bills and resolutions, the *Congressional Record*, the Serial Set, and ERIC distributed publications.

As discovered in a survey of academic economists and political scientists (Hernon, 1982), nearly half of the documents users (46.4%) would alter their information-gathering patterns if microfiche became the only distribution format. Clearly, survey respondents preferred paper copy; however, some would be willing to adopt to the format change, but would do so

---

4 Chapter 6 of Hernon and Purcell (1982) contains a sample collection development policy statement.

"grudgingly" and would perhaps consult government publications less frequently than they did in the past. Common complaints about microfiche were that they are "difficult to use" and "less convenient," and that the format "discourages browsing." For some social scientists, there were already vast quantities of available source material in paper copy. The availability of even more material (as government publications, especially combined with a nonpaper format) produces an "information overload" and makes evaluation and selectivity all the more necessary.

It might be useful to review the major barriers that would have to be overcome if social scientists were to rely on microform. First, high quality viewing equipment must be available at a reasonable cost for home or office use, or libraries must circulate viewing equipment. Second, better reproduction equipment is necessary; paper copies should be "sharp and easily read." Third, consulting microforms can be "bothersome and time-consuming, as well as produce discomfort and eyestrain; it requires additional use of libraries and increases the personal costs involved in locating needed information." Fourth, the browsing capability of social scientists is sharply curtailed. If ease of searching diminishes, they will act upon few impulses. Explained another way, further development of microform collections "will all but eliminate the random find." Fifth, social scientists will be reluctant to place class readings from microformatted source material on reserve. And, finally, some social scientists find "machines intimidating." Perhaps once the present generation of high school students, who have grown up with microform technology, assumes professional positions, this last complaint will be reduced.

Librarians must be sensitive to the information needs and gathering strategies of their clientele. They must reduce the amount of time that their clientele spend in libraries searching for potentially relevant source material. To do this, they might develop current awareness programs and document delivery services that would offset the loss of browsing capability with microformatted government information. In addition, the acquisition of a *Monthly Catalog* service that provides the context of that index on optical disc will reduce the amount of time spent in the identification of a wide body of GPO distributed documents.

Unless Federal government officials and librarians take an active role in developing value-added services for microformatted government information, the expansion of microform holdings may result in declining use of government publications as an information resource. More libraries must give greater attention to developing collections emphasizing the selection and retention of the more heavily needed source material and leaving lesser-needed source material to the province of inter-institutional cooperation. Microforms can play a role in developing documents collections, but user needs and preference must be adequately addressed.

Figure 9-2.
Selected Agencies, Document Types, and Titles Available in Microformat, and Appropriate
Finding Aids

MAJOR AGENCIES	FINDING AIDS
Bureau of the Census	American Statistics Index, Census Catalog and Guide, Data User News, Monthly Catalog, Monthly Product Announcement, and Publications Reference File
Central Intelligence Agency	American Statistics Index, Government Reports Announcements & Index, Monthly Catalog, and Publications Reference File
Department of Energy*	American Statistics Index, Energy Research Abstracts, Energy Abstracts for Policy Analysis, Government Reports Announcements & Index, Monthly Catalog, Publications Reference File

DOCUMENT TYPES AND TITLES	FINDING AIDS
Appropriation Hearings	American Statistics Index, CIS Index, Monthly Catalog, and Publications Reference File
Bills and Resolutions	GPO's "Finding Aid: Bills and Resolution Paper Index to Microfiche," CIS Index, and Congressional Record
Congressional Record	Congressional Record Index, The Federal Index, and various online services
Federal Register	CIS's Index to the Federal Register and indexing produced by the Office of the Federal Register
Serial Set	American Statistics Index, CIS Index, Monthly Catalog, Numerical List, and Publications Reference File
Serials/Periodicals	American Statistics Index, Index to U.S. Government Periodicals, and Monthly Catalog

*For a discussion of the role of the Office of Scientific and Technical Information within the Department of Energy's research and development activities, see Coyne et al (1986).

INDEXING

Assuming that researchers and librarians can identify core collections, librarians will want to improve the bibliographic listing and physical access for those agencies and types of publications likely to receive the most use. Figure 9–2 lists the finding aids for potentially important depository microfiche and underscores the fact that the *Monthly Catalog* provides an abundance of information. Access to government information is indeed fragmented, and reference tools maintained by the the private sector perform a vital service.

The best efforts of the public and private sectors are needed if long-standing barriers to improved public availability and access are to be overcome. Fry (1978, pp. 91–92) has succinctly summarized the role of the private sector thusly:

> Government documents comprise a fertile area for the private sector, given the imperfect and somewhat primitive state of bibliographic control, growing public recognition of their importance as an information resource, and the fact that documents, being in the public domain, are not copyrighted as they are in most foreign countries. There is intense competition in the provision of commercial information services, and publishers search out programs in areas which competitors have not entered and for which there is potential demand. The case for commercial publishing of government-derived information should not be misread. In general, the private sector offers the public and libraries selectively what they need and cannot readily obtain through the government.

In brief, government produced indexes offer access to source material possibly comprising core collections, but not always as completely as that provided by the private sector and its indexing/abstracting services. Both the public and private sectors must be encouraged to produce bibliographic aids and current awareness services to core collections, and in a timely manner.

Online bibliographic databases tend to be more current than printed indexes. In the case of NTIS's bibliographic database, the online version is more comprehensive than the paper index, *Government Reports Announcement & Index* (McClure, Hernon, and Purcell, 1986). The conducting of a comprehensive literature search often requires examination of both print indexes and online databases (Murphy, 1985). Clearly, research studies need to focus on indexing, and compare different services. Only in this way can standards be developed, and users more easily employ similar search strategies among various bibliographic aids.

COLLECTION SPACE AND FACILITIES

A basic problem for depository libraries relates to a concern with the growing influx of microformatted material. Where will the material be stored, what facilities will be needed to encourage their use by patrons, and what equipment is likely to be required? It should be recognized that the commitment of the GPO to microfiche distribution requires a major policy shift on the part of many depository libraries to maintain this material. Any design of depository collection facilities for microformatted government publications must facilitate the use and availability of these publications to the clientele. Emphasis must be placed on a design that encourages users to help themselves, treats microforms as normal bibliographic material in a library environment, and integrates microformatted government publications into the mainstream of the library's collection. Within these parameters, Chapter 13 examines some basic issues relating to space and facility design for microformatted documents collections, and the physical location of these information resources within the library.

INCREASING MICROFORM COMPETENCIES

Documents librarians must have basic knowledge about both government publications and microforms (as well as new information handling technologies). Although they may have taken formal courses in these areas, three constraints typically are working against that likelihood. First, many librarians find themselves with responsibilities regarding microforms and documents by chance, not choice, and have not received formal training. Second, the course offerings on microforms and government documents are limited at most library schools. And, finally, the staff of a documents departments may consist, largely or entirely, of paraprofessionals with little or no formal training.

Librarians responsible for microform collections must have a broad range of technical skills in addition to their specialized knowledge base. In this sense, they should have practical experience operating, maintaining, and evaluating various types of equipment (including cameras, readers, and printers) and microforms (including microfiche, microfilm, aperture cards, and microprint). They must also be able to perform basic operations such as cleaning lenses, removing paper jams, and making minor adjustments on machines, while learning how to adapt different technologies to their work environment (including fiche to fiche duplicators and utilization of facsimile satellite transmissions).

Documents librarians handling microform collections must engage in planning and the establishment of goals and objectives, the development of procedures to accomplish objectives, and the evaluation of the extent to which the objectives have been accomplished. Priorities must be set concerning the specific activities to be accomplished. Further, they must see that adequate resources are available to complete the tasks and that written plans for accomplishing the tasks are provided. If careful planning is undertaken, documents librarians can make the most of scarce resources.

Because of the inherent difficulties with microforms and government publications, and because of their typical second-class treatment in many library situations, documents librarians must be political activists in the organization. These staff members must promote the use of microformatted publications, educate library personnel to the unique characteristics of these publications, and integrate microforms into the mainstream of reader services. Thus, documents librarians must maintain an ongoing campaign to educate other members of the library and impress them with the value of government publications/information, regardless of the format in which they appear.

Of course, documents librarians need to be involved in appropriate professional activities and participate in specialized organizations such as the Government Documents Round Table (GODORT) of the American Library Association and the National Micrographics Association—to name but two. Involvement in such organizations will assist them in maintaining or increasing their awareness of new issues, sources, and methods for identifying and resolving problems related to microforms. They should use every opportunity to review and improve local conditions and enhance the ability of library clientele to resolve their information needs fully and expeditiously.

Both tangible and intangible rewards should be made available to those participating in personnel development. Ultimately, both the organization and the individual benefit. Human resources are the most effective and least utilized resources available to many organizations. Increasing the effectiveness of the organization by personnel development—especially in areas such as microforms and government documents—must be the responsibility of both the individual library staff member and administration.

If the goal of integrating microformatted government documents in terms of bibliographic control, physical availability, and professional service is to be achieved there is no substitute for competency. Competency must be evident in areas of basic knowledge, technical skills, administrative ability, service orientation, ability to manipulate the political environment, and professional activity. Only when documents librarians commit themselves to an ongoing program of personnel development will microformatted publications become an integrated information resource in the library, patrons be able to gain access to these sources more effectively and efficiently, and documents librarians provide the quality assistance that is required.

MANAGING MICROFICHE DISTRIBUTION AND LIBRARY COLLECTIONS

The micropublishing program of the GPO represents an area of rapid change and illustrates the complexities of monitoring a government decision making process. The GPO must take into account the views and perspectives of diverse groups such as:

- The administration and different Executive Branch agencies
- Congress, including the JCP and appropriations subcommittees
- Depository librarians

- Library organizations and groups
- The Depository Library Council to the Public Printer
- Private and not-for-profit sectors.

Cost-effectiveness factors (actually cost containment) in the preparation, distribution, and handling of publications are the overriding concern of the Federal government. Depository libraries need to look at the information content of microformatted government publications in relation to collection and user needs, and institutional mission. Needless to say, the Information Industry Association and other representatives of the private sector, users of government information, and other groups approach the topic from other perspectives.

The Reagan administration, which regards information as a priced commodity, is trying to curtail government expenditures for non-defense related activities and the size of publishing programs. Congress is also re-examining programs, restricting budgetary expenditures, and trying to control unnecessary publication. With the obsession for cost-savings in government, agencies view both microfiche and electronic distribution/dissemination systems as viable alternatives to publishing in paper format. A microfiche program has both strengths and weaknesses. It makes more information available, and in a format economical for production and distribution. On the negative side, it reinforces a perception of many government publications as highly specialized and having a limited appeal. Further, many users, including social scientists, prefer paper copy. They regard government publications as difficult enough to use in paper copy without encountering another barrier—the microformat.

Increased utilization of microformatted government publications necessitates an awareness of such factors as the quality of personnel and their service attitude, the location of the microform collection in the physical setting, user reaction, quality of viewing and reproduction equipment, availability of viewing equipment for loan (home and office), quality of the microform itself, relationship of microformatted documents to holdings of government publications in paper copy as well as to the availability of the desired information in traditional monographic and periodical formats, the relationship of libraries to other institutional providers, and the extent of user preference for information gained from interpersonal sources and the mass media.

Libraries, in a number of cases, need to develop and maintain functional documents collections supplemented with effective and efficient referral and document delivery systems. Extensive holdings of infrequently requested source material raise questions of cost-effectiveness (and cost-benefit) and of how well taxpayers' monies are spent. Closer congressional scrutiny of Federal programs may raise major issues concerning depository library programs and the amount and type of use they receive, as well as the diversity of client groups served.

More public attention needs to focus on the management of Federal information, including its costs. Since the cost of information provision is rapidly escalating and many library budgets are reflecting no growth situations, librarians and government officials must shift from a preoccupation with the economics of microforms (savings in space and money) to more of a concern for and analysis of what is lost from a consumer's point of view when information becomes available only in a microformat. Certainly, libraries will select microformatted government publications when desired information is unavailable in another format. They should, however, not gather large numbers of little- and non-used publications in any format.

A final point is in order. Although microforms comprise the central format under which depository distribution now occurs, increasingly they are being associated with technologies of today or yesterday. Electronic and machine-readable information involve newer technologies and enable documents librarianship to keep pace with developments in information transfer mechanisms and other areas of library activity. Documents librarianship continues to focus more and more on government *information* as opposed to government publications, documents, or microforms.

10

Technical Report Literature*

The technical report is the primary publication type used for the dissemination of vast quantities of information derived from federally funded research and development projects. The report is also the primary publication type that major industrial firms use for the internal reporting of the results of proprietary research and development activities. Because technical reports have attributes that distinguish them from the majority of other government publications as well as items published by the private sector, they are accorded separate treatment here. This chapter deals with several facets of technical report literature, including public access; the nature and history of technical report literature; the publication, dissemination, and bibliographic control of report literature; and the organization and utilization of report literature collections. The chapter concludes with a discussion of selected policy issues related to the role of the Federal government in the dissemination of report literature.

PUBLIC ACCESS TO TECHNICAL REPORT LITERATURE

Report literature constitutes an information resource that covers a wide range of subject matter and is indispensable to the research needs, innovation, and product development of the scientific, technical, and business communities, of faculty at various colleges and universities, and to govern-

---

* Gary R. Purcell, University of Tennessee, wrote this chapter.

ment itself. Because of the value of report literature, intellectual and physical access to these publications should be accorded at the maximum level possible. Maximum level intellectual and physical access signifies that bibliographic records for technical reports should be easily located in indexing and abstracting services that are commonly available, Furthermore, copies of technical reports should be obtained readily from predictable suppliers. At the national level, certain problems prevent users of report literature from obtaining maximum intellectual or physical access.

Perhaps the foremost, current barrier to public access is the fragmentation of responsibility that exists among government agencies for the announcement and distribution of technical reports. Several major agencies share the responsibility for serving as clearinghouses that publish indexing and abstracting services and that distribute copies of report literature. Although there is an increasing degree of cooperation among Federal agencies that process and disseminate these documents (Smith, 1981, pp. 5–18), there are still problem areas where a lack of both standardization and cooperation result in duplication of effort (Henderson, 1981, pp. 19–26). In addition, an unknown but sizable quantity of government sponsored report literature is available only through the originating or publishing agency. Thus, further fragmentation of access to this information occurs. A second, major barrier to public access to Federal technical report literature is the lack of knowledge by some potential users of the range of subjects contained in this body of documents. Although the variety of topics addressed by Federal research and development activities is very broad, public perceptions of the subject content of technical report literature are likely to be limited to reports covering aspects of scientific and engineering research (McClure, Hernon, and Purcell, 1986, p. 136).

Yet another significant barrier to public access to Federal report literature is a widespread lack of knowledge of librarians regarding the use of basic bibliographic sources and the strategies useful for identifying and locating report literature. Related to this is the tendency for librarians, particularly in academic and public libraries, to associate Federal government publications with the Government Printing Office (GPO) rather than agencies such as the National Technical Information Service (NTIS) that disseminate technical report literature (Ibid., pp. 130–138).

The vast quantity of Federal technical reports produced and disseminated each year makes it impractical for any library to acquire more than a fraction of the Federal reports produced. Selectivity in acquisition decreases the likelihood that any individual or specific report will be included in any given library's collection. Because the users of technical reports typically want access to current and timely information, the lack of immediate physical availability often serves as a barrier to the use of report literature.

Another barrier to the use of report literature results from the publication type itself and the ways that a report is created. Wang and Alimena (1981) of the Bell Labs Technical Reports Service comment on some of the attributes intrinsic to the nature of report literature that create problems in the acquisition, control, and access to these publications. According to them (pp. 28–29),

- "The sheer volume of reports produced in the U.S. alone would inundate any collection, unless one selected reports carefully
- Countless organizations generate technical reports. As many as three types of institutions may be involved in the creation and distribution of one report: (1) institutions performing the research, (2) sponsoring agencies, and (3) distributing agencies. Both sponsoring and distributing agencies may control the distribution and accessibility of reports according to differing standards; the producing agency may also directly distribute reports. Thus, availability varies widely for each report, and from institution to institution
- Not only do many institutions produce reports irregularly, but often they do not index or even announce the availability of completed reports. It is sometimes not clear who sponsored a report, or when it originated
- Conventional abstracting and indexing publications, and other bibliographic services, frequently are of little aid in identifying technical reports
- The report number format varies according to the specifications of each sponsoring institution, usually having some internal significance. Not only the sponsoring institution, but also the producing and the distributing agencies (if different), may assign other report numbers to the same document. Adding to the confusion, a grant or contract number may also appear on the report
- Reports often go out of print shortly after publication."

Another factor that could result in the creation of a barrier to access to Federal report literature is an ongoing proposal to implement a program of privatization of the largest of the report literature clearinghouses—NTIS. Privatization will be discussed in a subsequent section of the chapter. Suffice to say here, privatization would enable the private sector to disseminate selected technical reports, while, presumably, the government (or a contractor) maintained an archival collection of lesser and no demand items.

Lastly, other problems hinder public access to report literature. Among these are the cost of reports, the proliferation of report series codes, and the lack of standardization in the use of subject terminology. Each of these problems will be discussed at greater length in this chapter.

THE NATURE AND HISTORY OF TECHNICAL REPORT LITERATURE

The technical report is a form of publication intended for the rapid dissemination of information. It is most commonly used to report progress on, and the final results of, scientific investigation. The report is usually published by government contractors in response to the reporting requirements of a Federal R&D contract. The *Glossary of Information Handling* (Department of Defense, 1964) defines the technical report as a form of publication. According to the definition,

> A report concerning the results of a scientific investigation or a technical development, text or evaluation, [that is] presented in a form suitable for dissemination to the technological community. The technical report is usually more detailed than an article or paper appearing in a journal or presented at a meeting. It will normally contain sufficient data to enable the qualified reader to evaluate the investigative process of the original research or development.

The quantity of government sponsored technical reports published each year in the United States is substantial. As early as 1963, it was estimated that the United States government and its contractors issued as many as 100,000 technical reports each year (The President's Science Advisory Committee, 1963, p. 19). Although no reliable data are available, estimates of the current production of report literature range well beyond this figure. NTIS alone adds in the range of 65,000 new reports to its holdings each year and has more than 1.2 million titles in its bibliographic database.

It is generally agreed that technical report literature, as we now know it, can be dated from the publication of a series of reports first published by the U.S. Geological Survey, in 1902, under the title *Professional Papers of the United States Geological Survey*. Eight years later, another technical report series, the *Technologic Papers of the National Bureau of Standards*, was initiated (Auger, 1975, p. 9).

As important to the development of report literature as these early series were, it was the information needs pursuant to World War II that brought about the most significant growth in the quantity of technical report literature. In 1941, a U.S. government agency, the Office of Scientific Research and Development (OSRD), was created with the mission to mobilize the nation's scientific and technical information resources in order to meet defense needs. Both this and other agencies authorized a substantial amount of defense related research by contract, and required contractors to submit progress reports and a final report on each of the contracts. As a result, government sponsored research, and the publication of technical report literature, increased dramatically and continued to do so.

At the end of World War II, the Federal government initiated another action that increased the quantity of technical report literature available for public and private use. Teams of specialists were sent to Germany and Japan with the assignment to capture and interview key scientists, and to confiscate enemy documents of a scientific or technical nature. More than 1,500 tons of such documents were acquired from Germany alone (Subrumanyam, 1980, p. 148). A cabinet level committee, known as the Publications Board (PB), was established in 1945 for the purpose of bringing (Boyd and Rips, 1949, pp. 364–365):

> to the attention of the Director of War Mobilization and Reconversion scientific and technical information obtained from foreign sources or through war-time research sponsored by the United States Government, and to advise him regarding its release for publication.

Within a short time, the Publications Board received more than 5,000 documents a month. This agency began to assign accession numbers to the reports and to announce them in a weekly publication, *Bibliography of Scientific and Industrial Reports* (Subrumanyam, 1980, pp. 148–149). The Publications Board was soon merged into the Office of Technical Services (OTS). This new agency continued to be responsible for identifying and declassifying technical reports captured at the close of World War II, to produce an index and abstracting service that would provide greater access to these publications, and to serve as a clearinghouse for the dissemination of the captured reports and those that were newly published (Purcell, 1981a, p. 72). This agency was the predecessor of NTIS.

In the years subsequent to World War II, government sponsored research and development activities have increased substantially. So too has the quantity and variety of technical report literature. Through this period, several major government initiatives (e.g., the space program, the program to clean up the environment, and the energy program) were undertaken. As a consequence, thousands of technical reports were created. In addition, the ongoing research and development activities of the U.S. military establishment have also contributed significantly to this body of documentation. The quantity of report literature has increased to the point that this type of publication constitutes the greatest number of new publications issued by the Federal government each year.

ATTRIBUTES OF REPORT LITERATURE

In order to make effective use of technical reports, it is necessary to understand some of their major characteristics or attributes. Some of these have an impact on their use and accessibility. As already noted, technical reports are usually produced by an organization that holds a contract or grant with a Federal department or agency. The terms of the contract require that the contractor submit periodic reports on the status and progress of the project, with a final report to be submitted at the conclusion of the project. Although these are not the only types of technical reports, they constitute the types most commonly published.

Technical reports of the types mentioned above are usually directed toward a primary audience, namely the contract officer, and their main objective is to meet the specifications of the contract. Secondarily, they are written to meet information interests and needs of a more general audience within the scientific community. Because of time limitations and the restricted nature of the primary audience, technical reports are not usually submitted for peer group review, as are journal articles or monographs. In some cases, this would not be possible anyway, because of security restrictions placed on the documents. However, the results of a limited or nonexistent peer group review has been to compromise the status of the technical report. The reason for this is that the absence of the rigorous peer group review to which books and journal articles are subjected confers less status on the author of a technical report than on the authors of other publication types. Although this is less evident in some disciplines than in others, the technical report does not yet, and probably never will, have the status of monographs or scholarly journal articles.

Regardless of the status conferred by the publication of technical reports, the use of this type of source material, as contrasted with monographs and journal articles, results in a dissemination process that is both rapid and efficient. The results of ongoing research are made available to interested parties during the time the research is in progress, and the final results become available shortly after the project is completed. In addition, because technical reports are not restricted in length, and not governed by the same economic considerations as journal and monograph publishing, the results of the research can be reported in considerable depth and with the extensive use of tables and figures that display data. Typically, if published in journal or monograph form through a commercial publisher, it would not be possible to include as much data as can be included in a technical report. These attributes confer on the technical report a value that, for some purposes, exceeds that of a publication that underwent peer review.

Despite the generally acknowledged value of technical report literature, most of the literature concerned with this type of information source has overlooked the use, and impact resulting from that use, on the scientific and scholarly community. McClure (1988) identifies major use studies, the uses that the R&D community has made of report literature, and the writings that discuss the value of this literature. However, he notes the absence of "impact" studies; authors often equate use or value with impact. McClure also articulates the need for additional research to explore this and other issues related to report literature.

One possible statement of the primary value (or possible impact) of report literature is the effect that it has on fostering innovation. Caponio and Bracken (1987) argue that the speed with which information is transmitted through technical reports fosters creative and innovative thinking, as well as hastens the pace of scientific and technological progress. Nevertheless, research should track the impact of the use of report literature in fostering innovation.

A valuable outcome of current methods of producing report literature is that reports can be maintained "in print" indefinitely, through the use of microforms and microform "blow-backs" to paper copy. Thus, once a report has been issued and made available through a government distribution agency, it can be acquired at any subsequent time.

Another attribute of technical report literature is the great variety of subject content covered. Reports now are no longer limited to scientific and technical topics, but include other topics such as:

- Education
- Management
- Operations research
- Health planning and services
- Information processing

- Agriculture
- Business and economics
- Transportation
- Local government problems
- Behavioral studies

Further, various types of information such as "literature reviews, bibliographies, compilations of statistical data, catalogs, directories, and conference papers and proceedings . . ." (Subrumanyam, 1980, p. 153) are presented in report form. The increase in both subject matter and the types of publications has occurred largely as a result of the growth in the variety of projects sponsored by government agency contracts. Whatever the cause, the effect has been to create a widely varied range of resources published as technical reports.

It is possible to categorize technical reports in terms other than the previously noted dichotomy between progress and final reports. One distinction that should be made is between those reports available to the general public and those with restricted distribution, otherwise known as "classified" documents. Another distinction is between technical reports on research funded by Federal grants and contracts, and reports of proprietary research conducted by private enterprise. Sometimes research in the latter category is conducted pursuant to competing for government grants or contracts, and ultimately the results of the research will be published in the open literature. This chapter will focus on unrestricted reports.

Yet another distinction is in the purpose that the report serves. In 1967, the Committee on Scientific and Technical Information (COSATI) examined the production and dissemination of scientific and technical information, and a subgroup called the Task Group on the Role of the Technical Report established a taxonomy of types of technical reports, and identified and described eight types. The eight identified by COSATI are listed below with a brief characterization of each.

The individual author's "preprints".   Prior to publication, an author will circulate a manuscript for review by colleagues. On occasion, these "preprint" documents are given a formal designation and might be cited and, on occasion, indexed. Sometimes these "preprints" are incorporated into clearinghouses or information centers, with the result that they are indexed and abstracted, and ultimately disseminated.

The corporate "proposal-type report".   These documents are seldom distributed outside of an organization that prepares them for submission to a government agency. However, some are circulated privately to be used as examples of acceptable proposals. Nevertheless, they are usually not disseminated on a systematic basis through clearinghouses, and are not covered by indexing or abstracting services.

Institutional reports.   Private organizations and government agencies issue periodic reports of their activities, directed toward the lay public. These reports often provide a characterization of the programs, resources, and progress of the organization or agency. Useful because of the synthesis that they provide, these reports are often indexed, abstracted, and disseminated through clearinghouses.

The contract "progress report".   Probably the most common type of technical report, this is typically directed toward the sponsoring agency by the contractor and has as its purpose reporting on the progress of the work under contract. Progress reports are issued quarterly, semi-annually, or at other intervals, usually for the life of the contract. Although the final report might include some of the information reported in the progress reports, some information appears uniquely in this type of report. Clearinghouses, information centers, and publishers of indexing and abstracting services select and filter from among the published progress reports, and usually try to include only those that are most significant.

The "final report" on a technical contract effort.   At the conclusion of a government contract or grant, the recipient is required to submit a final report that details the methods, accomplishments, and the public benefit of the project. These reports differ widely in the extent of editorial oversight applied, and thus the quality and the scope of the reports vary considerably. Nevertheless, this is probably the most valuable among the various types of technical reports listed here.

The "separate", topical technical report. Some reports are published separately from the "progress" or "final" report form, and closely resemble journal articles both in style and type. They are sometimes given the names: research memoranda, research notes, research documents, technical memoranda, etc. Often they are submitted for publication as journal articles. However, they are often covered by indexing and abstracting services, assigned technical report accession numbers, and incorporated into the holdings of clearinghouses. The result is sometimes confusion between the technical report form of the document and its subsequent forms of publication.

The "book" in report form. Publications contracted for by Federal agencies occasionally appear first in technical report form. These are sometimes published as draft documents in order to elicit a response from the field, and other times simply to provide advance publication. However, some are never published in another form; thus, the technical report serves as the final form. Included are reviews, state-of-the-art reports, surveys, handbooks, and even glossaries. These are incorporated into the holdings of clearinghouses and are covered by indexing and abstracting services.

Committee type reports. The interim and final reports of various types of government sponsored committees and commissions, as well as national and international scholarly organizations, might be produced as technical reports, These normally present conclusions and findings, and, on occasion, include supportive material such as research papers, statistics, and even the text of hearings. These are often incorporated into the holdings of clearinghouses and are covered by indexing and abstracting services.

Until recently, the COSATI taxonomy was widely accepted as representative of the major types of technical reports. However, an expanded list, developed by the Department of Energy (DOE), identifies a total of 36 types and formats in which DOE research results are reported (Matheny, 1988). The list, reproduced in Figure 10–1, provides a more precise calibration than the COSATI list of the types of information sources. The DOE list includes electronic, and machine-readable, and print formats. When the technical report is viewed in the context of both lists, it is immediately apparent that the concept of the single research or project report, in print or near-print form, produced in an inexpensive fashion and designed for rapid production, is an outdated concept. As McClure (1988) notes, "there is no generic technical report."

The categories used in the COSATI and DOE taxonomies make it clear that the term "technical report literature" is far broader than previously conceived. If, in fact, all of the formats and types listed by DOE can be considered as technical reports, the DOE taxonomy necessitates a revision in our conceptualization of technical report literature and the role that technical reports play in the transfer of information. Furthermore, the DOE

Figure 10-1.
Types and Formats of Technical Reports

Topical Reports	Data Compilations
Conference Presentations	Conference Proceedings
Trip Reports	Maps
Translations	Video Tapes
Magnetic Tapes	Floppy Discs
Patent Applications	Environmental Impact
Progress Reports	Statements
Final Report	Dockets
Bibliographies	Hearings
Design Reports	State-of-the-Art Reports
Incident Reports	Proposals
Annual Report (Lab or Division)	Statistical Reports
Programmatic Reports	Theses
Engineering Drawings	Book Chapters
Computer Codes	Back-up Reports
Research Summaries	Executive Summaries
Manuals	SBIR Reports
User Guides	Guidebooks
	Newsletters

Source: McClure (1988).

taxonomy raises questions about the adequacy and utility of the resources that provide bibliographic access to the gamut of report literature and that integrate this literature with other information resources.

PUBLICATION, DISTRIBUTION, AND BIBLIOGRAPHIC CONTROL OF TECHNICAL REPORT LITERATURE

The publication of conventional technical reports occurs as a result of a process that generally follows this sequence. At an interim stage, or upon completion of a project, the contractor is required to submit a progress or a final report. This requirement, in almost every instance, has a specified deadline for delivery of the report to the contract or grant officer of the funding agency. In most cases, the report will be prepared in typescript form, with a sufficient number of copies generated to fulfill the requirement of the contract. Additional copies might be made for primary distribution to a predetermined constituency, or retained by the contractor to meet requests from interested parties.

Long-term, secondary publication of a technical report occurs when the report is submitted to one of the Federal repository/clearinghouses responsible for announcing and disseminating report literature (these are identified and described later in this chapter). Secondary publication through these agencies is both in paper copy and microform. The publication in paper copy generally is limited to a small number of copies to meet immediate demands, with subsequent paper copies derived from xerographic reproduction made from a microform negative.

Microform positive copies are also made from a microform negative. From the early 1970s, the most common size for microform copies is the 105x48 mm microfiche card. This card employs a 98-image grid system with a reduction ratio of 24:1 (Auger, 1975, pp. 71–72). Publication of reports on microfiche negatives enables the clearinghouse to maintain the document "in print" indefinitely, and the report can be reproduced on demand.

The methods of report literature distribution create two options for the acquisition of reports by libraries and information centers. These options are: (1) automatic order acquisition, and (2) "on-demand" acquisition. Automatic acquisition occurs as a result of automatic dissemination programs operated by distribution agencies. An example of this is the "Selected Research in Microfiche" (SRIM) program of NTIS (National Technical Information Service, 1987, p. 18). The SRIM program allows users to acquire report literature on microfiche automatically, as a result of a match between a predetermined user profile and the subject content of the reports. The match is determined by computer, and the user is automatically sent copies of all reports that meet the stated subject profile.

The acquisition of technical reports on demand can be almost as easy as the automatic acquisition, but it can also be very difficult. The difficulty associated with this process is dependent on: (1) whether the report resides in one of the repositories/clearinghouses, and (2) whether the bibliographic information that uniquely identifies the report is complete and correct. If both of these specifications are met, it is possible to obtain reports that are publicly available without undue loss of time. However, if the document is not in one of the clearinghouses, considerable time can be required to locate a copy for purchase or use. It might be necessary to obtain it from either the agency that sponsored the work or the contractor. If not needed for permanent acquisition, an attempt can also be made to acquire it through interlibrary loan. If any length of time has elapsed since the publication of the report, the possibility of success on each of the three approaches is diminished. If basic bibliographic information is absent, the institution trying to locate the report will encounter additional difficulties.

One of the most essential bibliographic elements for obtaining positive identification of a technical report to aid in its acquisition is the report series code. Report series codes are numbers assigned to technical reports either as report/accession numbers or as contract/grant numbers. Report/accession numbers are assigned at the time of publication by the issuing organization or the contracting agency, or when the publication is added to the clearinghouse holdings. Contract/grant numbers are set when the contractual relationship is established. Both types of numbers can be used in different ways for the purpose of acquisition and the identification of report documents.

Report/accession numbers are designed to provide unique identification for each technical report, regardless of its type. The contract/grant numbers identify all reports that are generated as part of a particular contract or grant. These numbers tie together reports that pertain to the same project. However, there are thousands of report series codes, assigned by hundreds of organizations and agencies. The number of separate report series codes has complicated the identification of report series and individual technical reports. This problem is accentuated by the fact that some reports are assigned more than one number. Initially there is a contract/grant number, and later one or more report/accession numbers might be assigned. The latter can be assigned by the original contractor, the sponsoring agency, the clearinghouse that distributes the report, or all of these.

A major step forward in providing control of report series codes occurred with the publication of the *Dictionary of Report Series Codes* (1962, with an updated edition in 1973 and in 1986); the 1986 edition was published under a new title, *Report Series Codes Dictionary*. The 1973 edition, which provides an excellent description of the problem in identifying report series codes, should be referred to by anyone who uses technical report literature on a continuing basis. However, the problem created by report series code is the constant development of new report series. Thus, even the most current edition of the dictionary is outdated before its publication.

Report series codes usually consist of alphabetical designations followed by numbers. Often the alphabetical designations are mnemonic, thus providing some indication of the organization or agency that originates the report. For example, reports issued by Dugway Proving Grounds near Toole, Utah, begin with the alphabetical designation DPG. However, organizations and agencies change names, and sometimes the alphabetical designators do not change. Whether or not they change, a problem occurs. If the alphabetical designators change, then the series is split. If the designators do not change, the advantages of a mnemonic devise are lost. The *Report Series Codes Dictionary* is a valuable resource for the identification of codes, either when people seek the code itself or the name of the agency or organization.

The quality of bibliographic control for technical reports has improved substantially during the past twenty years. Reports are announced more promptly, the quality of bibliographic entries is better, and the quality of indexing has improved notably. In spite of these improvements, many reports are still not listed in the major indexing and abstracting services responsible for announcing government sponsored reports. To some extent, this situation exists because some agencies utilize their own announcement and distribution system and do not make use of centralized systems. The effect of this is to fragment the sources of access to bibliographic records

Figure 10-2.
Federal Technical Report Environment

National Technical Information Service
NTIS

Department of Energy,
Office of Science and
Technical Information
DEO-OSTI

National Aeronautics
and Space
Administration,
Scientific and Technical
Information Branch
NASA-STIB

FEDERAL TECHNICAL REPORT DISTRIBUTORS

Defense Technical
Information Center
DTIC

Government Printing Office
GPO

Educational Resources Information Center
ERIC

Other Federal Agencies,
Clearinghouses, Information
Centers, and Federal Laboratories

announcing technical report literature. Another problem is that reports are sometimes not listed in a timely fashion (Copeland, 1981, pp. 48–53).

A number of Federal agencies have the announcement and distribution of technical report literature as their primary function. These repositories/clearinghouses are described below, with their major abstracting and indexing services identified. Figure 10–2 defines the dissemination environment for technical reports. The GPO is discussed in this chapter because it announces and distributes technical reports. The order in which the repositories/clearinghouses are listed is a rough approximation of their importance as suppliers of unrestricted technical report literature.

National Technical Information Service (NTIS).   This agency is the direct successor of the original Publications Board established soon after World War II. The agency has been variously known as the Publications Board (PB), 1945–1946; the Office of Technical Services (OTS), 1946–1964; the Clearinghouse for Federal Scientific and Technical Information (CFSTI), 1964–1970; and NTIS, 1970–present (McClure, Hernon, and Purcell, 1986, p. 11). During its history, the agency has expanded its services and increased the number of technical reports acquired per year.[1] At present, it acquires

---

[1] McClure, Hernon, and Purcell (1986, pp. 1–40) provide a more extensive history of the agency and a characterization of NTIS's products and services. NTIS also produces an excellent annual guide to its products and services (see National Technical Information Service, 1987).

reports from more than 300 agencies, including Federal agencies, state and local government agencies, private organizations, and foreign agencies and organizations.

The range of NTIS products and services exceed the collection and dissemination of report literature. The agency operates the Center for the Utilization of Federal Technology (CUFT), which facilitates the private use of selected Federal technology. NTIS also facilitates the licensing of patents developed as a result of Federal R&D efforts that have commercial potential. The licensing effort has as its objective to encourage U.S. companies to take advantage of Federal R&D work for commercial advantage to the private sector. NTIS also maintains a database, Federal Research in Progress, which is an inventory of data files from more than 50 Federal agencies on magnetic tape or floppy diskette. Through the Federal Software Center, NTIS offers more than 1,000 diskettes for sale.

Although NTIS has an extensive, but far from complete, inventory of government sponsored reports. The other agencies listed here account for the location of the majority of reports not found in NTIS. However, it is not mandatory that Federal agencies submit their publications to NTIS, and some Federal agencies do not deposit their reports with NTIS or, in some cases, with another clearinghouse. Therefore, users of NTIS bibliographic sources cannot be certain that all reports from an agency are included. In the event that a report cannot be located through NTIS's bibliographic resources, the sponsoring agency should be contacted.

Through the years, NTIS and its predecessor agencies have published an indexing and abstracting service that provides bibliographic access to report literature. *Government Reports Announcements & Index (GRA&I)*, that service, is arranged by broad topics and subtopics.[2] *GRA&I* includes the machine-readable bibliographic records for *Energy Research Abstracts (ERA)*, published by the Department of Energy, and *Scientific and Technical Aerospace Reports (STAR)*, published by the National Aeronautics and Space Administration.

Copeland (1981, p. 48) found that 94.3% of the titles included in *STAR* had been published in *GRA&I*. The percentage of reports that originally appeared in *ERA* and were later picked up by *GRA&I* was 78.8. However, in spite of this overlap, there is often a time lag between coverage in *GRA&I* and the other two bibliographic tools.

All of the bibliographic records included in all of the index and abstracting services published by NTIS and its predecessor agencies are available online through Lockheed Information Systems DIALOG, System De-

---

[2] McClure, Hernon, and Purcell (1986, pp. 16–17) discusses the announcement and bibliographic access services of NTIS. They place *GRA&I* within its historical content. Boylan (1967) provides a detailed account of the earlier report indexes and how to use them.

velopment Corporation ORBIT, Bibliographic Retrieval Service (BRS), and Mead Data Central. In addition, DIALOG has produced and OCLC will offer CD-ROM versions of selected parts of the NTIS database. The OCLC version also will include titles not found in the NTIS database but represented in the OCLC database. It is possible to search the NTIS database directly through one of the vendor services or to have NTIS search the database for a user (at a nominal charge). NTIS has published the results of more than 3,000 searches of its database. These bibliographies, which cover a wide variety of topics, actually include items from other databases and are announced in *Published Searches Master Catalog*, an annual publication available from NTIS. A "Mini Catalog" supplements the *Master Catalog*.

Educational Resources Information Center (ERIC). The U.S. Office of Education established the Educational Resources Information Center in 1966. Maintained by the successor agency, the Department of Education, ERIC is a decentralized operation that consists of subject area clearinghouses, each of which is responsible for acquiring, abstracting, and indexing materials on specific topics related to education. Abstracts of the report literature appear in *Resources in Education (RIE)*, published monthly since 1966. The abstracts are arranged by clearinghouse, and then numerically by an accession number. In addition to *RIE*, ERIC also publishes an index to journal literature in education titled *Current Index to Journals in Education (CIJE)*. The combined holdings of these two index and abstracting services are available online through DIALOG, ORBIT, and BRS. In addition, DIALOG and OCLC have produced CD-ROM versions of the ERIC file. The OCLC version includes items found in the OCLC database but omitted from the ERIC file.

National Aeronautics and Space Administration (NASA). The National Aeronautics and Space Administration, established in 1958, was an outgrowth of an earlier agency first known as the Advisory Committee for Aeronautics and then as the National Advisory Committee for Aeronautics. A subagency of NASA, the Scientific and Technical Facility (STIF), is responsible for abstracting and indexing report literature concerned with aeronautics and space, and with publishing *STAR*.

Department of Energy (DOE). The Department of Energy was created in 1977 from the merger of the Energy Research and Development Administration (ERDA), the Federal Energy Administration (FEA), and the Federal Power Commission (FP). The Department of Energy's Office of Scientific and Technical Information (OSTI) manages and disseminates DOE research results, provides worldwide energy information, maintains information management and accountability systems, and offers information management consulting and specialized services (Coyne et al, 1986). OSTI issues 22 publications such as monthly updates that cover broad subject areas (e.g., solar energy); semi-monthly bulletins on acid rain, radioactive waste management, etc.; *Energy Research Abstracts* that conveys the results of

Department funded research and reports from other Federal agencies, foreign organizations, and state and local governments; and *Energy Abstracts for Policy Analysis*, a monthly journal that identifies literature of interest to policy makers. OSTI also contributes to *INIS Atomindex*, "the comprehensive worldwide abstract journal covering nuclear science and its peaceful applications, which is published by the International Atomic Energy Agency on behalf of member states" (Ibid., p. 378).

Defense Technical Information Center (DTIC).   The center dates back to 1941, when it was created as the Office of Scientific Research and Development (OSRD). In 1951, it was known as the Armed Services Technical Information Agency (ASTIA), and, in 1963, the name was changed to Defense Documentation Center (DDC). In 1980, the agency became DTIC.

The Defense Technical Information Center handles report literature relating to defense efforts. It converts documents to microfiche; produces a computerized database of bibliographic citations; makes the citations available to Department contractors through DROLS, an online database; announces recent accessions in a paper catalog; and produces bibliographies such as the biweekly *Current Awareness Bibliography*. DTIC processes and offers both classified and unclassified data, information, and reports. Each year, DTIC adds about 30,000 technical reports to its collection; the agency has over 1.5 million documents. Approximately half of the technical reports accessioned by DTIC, at some point, are provided to NTIS for distribution to the public (Molholm et al, 1988).

Together with NTIS, the Office of Scientific and Technical Information (Department of Energy), the National Library of Medicine (NLM), and the Scientific and Technical Information Office (NASA), DTIC participates in CENDI (Commerce, Energy, NASA, NLM, and Defense Information). This organization strives to "improve the productivity of Federal research through efficient and responsive information programs and improved management systems." "This cooperation is vital since 92% of Federal R&D information is generated within the five agencies of CENDI" (Ibid.).

Government Printing Office (GPO).   The Government Printing Office, the main printing arm of the U.S. government, serves as a type of contract printer for Congress, congressional agencies, Executive Branch agencies, and the Federal judiciary. Among the many thousands of titles printed each year are a number of technical reports. These reports originate with agencies that have traditionally used the GPO as their printer. Some of these reports are also distributed by NTIS or ERIC, but others are only available through the GPO. However, the extent of duplication is only about 10%, and where duplication exists, the *Monthly Catalog* tends to list items 5–7 months later than does *GRA&I* (McClure, Hernon, and Purcell, 1986, p. 116).

Originating agency.   Because it is not mandatory for Federal agencies or their contractors to submit report literature to one of the government clearinghouses, the user or librarian cannot be certain that all reports are available for distribution through one of these sources. Therefore, on occasion it is necessary to contact the agency responsible for the publication of the report or responsible for sponsoring the research. Some agencies continue to maintain their own distribution facilities for report literature and for other publications. Direct contact with these agencies is desirable.

ORGANIZING AND ACCESSING THE TECHNICAL REPORT COLLECTION

With the exception of technical reports printed by the GPO and distributed as depository items, it is not possible to merge report literature into Federal documents collections organized by the Sudocs system. Therefore, it is necessary to consider briefly the other options for organizing a report collection.

Common practice in libraries and information centers indicates that the following methods of organizing paper copy technical reports are possible. These are arrangement by (1) subject classification, (2) originating source, and (3) accession number (Gray, 1953, p. 109). Each is discussed below in terms of its application to paper copy reports. Microfiche copies are almost always arranged by report number.

The subject classification method of organizing the collection is the assignment of classification numbers to reports in the same fashion as monographs and other materials in the collection. Libraries that have small collections of technical reports often simply incorporate the reports into the existing subject collection of the library. University or special libraries that acquire NTIS documents selectively in paper copy catalog the reports as they would any monograph and shelve them under the appropriate classification number. This method is more commonly used in general libraries that have a limited collection of report literature and that do not attempt to develop a systematic collection of reports. The advantage of the system is that an entry is generated for the general catalog, and that subject, corporate author, and title access are created. The disadvantage is that publications distributed or sponsored by a single agency are scattered in various locations throughout the library.

The originating source method of arrangement is designed to bring together reports published by each originating agency, and then arrange the reports by report number. This system makes use of the report series codes of the originating source, but cannot allow for utilization of more than one report series code. The method has the advantage of bringing together reports issued by a single corporate entry. A user can then examine several reports created by a single research center or laboratory. However, in practice this is unlikely to be a real advantage, because the user cannot be certain that the library or information center has all of the reports issued by any corporate entity. Nonetheless, there is an economic advantage to this method in that it is possible to organize and arrange a collection of reports with a minimum amount of time using this arrangement.

The accession number method involves minimum effort in determining the arrangement of the report collection. The procedure is to assign each new report a sequential accession number. It is the method generally preferred for large collections of report literature, because it conserves space and requires a minimum of shifting of the collection as the number of reports increases. However, this method of organizing reports distributes them throughout the collection by subject and originating source. Thus, in order to enable users to find their way around the collection, the library or information center must engage in extensive subject and corporate author cataloging.

KEY ISSUES—TECHNICAL REPORTS

The wide variety of topics now covered by report literature practically guarantees that most libraries will have occasion to acquire and utilize some technical reports, and libraries that specialize in scientific or technical subject areas already make extensive use of reports. The growing demand and utilization of report literature indicates that librarians must know the patterns of distribution and means of access to these resources. To this end, this chapter has identified the major government report disseminators. The chapter has also identified those attributes of report literature that affect public access. Further, major barriers to public access have been noted. To meet user demands for report literature, librarians must be acquainted with these barriers and know how to work around them when possible. They must also gain greater knowledge and skill in providing access to technical reports.

The results of a study of the effectiveness of academic and public libraries in providing access to report literature indicate that the level of success is quite low (McClure, Hernon, and Purcell, 1986, pp. 77–88). Clearly, library education programs must place greater emphasis on technical report literature in order to enhance the preparation of librarians in collection development and in retrieving these resources in a more effective manner.

At this point, it might be useful to summarize the key issues yet to be resolved if public access to government report literature is to be improved. The major issue that must be resolved is the allocation of responsibility among Federal agencies for the announcement and distribution of report literature. The privatization of NTIS will only accentuate the problem.

Serious disagreements exist in the development of a rational and logical framework to guide the development and implementation of Federal information policies. According to McClure (1988), the "policies regarding STI are at best a patchwork of public laws, guidelines, and a lack of a coordinated and coherent philosophy." Ballard (1987, p. 197) concurs and urges the Federal government to "take an active approach to enhance the application and use of STI." There is the need for an unambiguous government information policy that recognizes the diversity of types of report literature as well as the similarities and differences between report literature and other types of government information. Federal agencies responsible for the sponsorship of research or other funded projects should deposit their publications and data tapes with the appropriate Federal clearinghouse or disseminator. The intent is to reduce the amount of funded research that eludes bibliographic control and that is copyrighted and privately published (Rosenfield, 1986). Fragmentation in the distribution and dissemination of report literature would also be reduced.

The cooperative efforts that now exist through CENDI are commendable, but do not go far enough. Needless duplication in both bibliographic description and dissemination should be eliminated, and cooperation should extend to the GPO and other stakeholders in the information sector.

Additional issues that impact on public access also must be addressed. One of the most troublesome is the lack of government agency initiatives to facilitate user access to report series codes. The responsibility for this has been left to libraries and users; the government has not addressed the issue. A comprehensive, online, and up-to-date version of the *Report Series Codes Dictionary* should be produced. The database should include report series codes applicable to reports distributed by all Federal clearinghouses and disseminators. Report series codes for foreign report literature could also be included. The lack of current and readily accessible information on report series codes is a major problem confronting librarians and users of report literature.

Another issue that has a direct impact on public access to government information is the cost of report literature. This issue merits more attention than government information policy currently accords it. At present, the practices of clearinghouses and disseminators of Federal report literature are contradictory. The costs of technical reports vary dramatically. For example, when the same report is available from two clearinghouses, there is often a substantial price difference. A consistent, noncontradictory pricing practice should be adopted. Government information produced by research and development contracts is intended for the public good and for public consumption. Consequently, it is in the public's interest that this information be distributed at a price that does not discriminate by ability to pay. To do otherwise results in a policy that works at cross-purposes with the original objective of government as the producer of the information that promotes the public good. The imposition of high costs for report literature determines who will have access to the information, and virtually eliminates public access.for those with limited resources. The availability of technical reports through some clearinghouses/disseminators seems to suggest that these reports have limited appeal—utility to those able and willing to pay for access to information.

One of the most significant issues relates to privatization of government information sources and services, and the respective roles of the public and private sectors. Central to this issue has been the repeated efforts of the Reagan administration to place NTIS under the jurisdiction of the private sector. Some of the elements of the issue are:

- Government funded R&D reports would be distributed (at a higher cost) by one or more private sector firms that were not responsible for bearing the cost of generating the information contained within the reports. These firms would be the recipients of a major subsidy at government expense
- Private vendors would probably discontinue many of the unprofitable publications currently available from NTIS, thus limiting access to information that could be significant to selected users
- Agencies that are producers of government information use various methods to distribute their report literature. One of these is the GPO depository program. The prospect of depository distribution of reports that are also available for sale through a private vendor poses a complex and seemingly contradictory policy issue.

Moody (1986, pp. 157–162) provides a brief summary of the issues, while additional coverage can be found in "NTIS Privatization Study Responses to April 28, 1986 *Federal Register* Notice . . ." (1986).[3] The privatization issue has not yet been resolved, but continues to pose troublesome policy alternatives for the conduct of Federal information policy.

The coverage of issues concerned with Federal technical report literature that are discussed above is not exhaustive. Other areas of concern are also significant and impact on Federal information policies. Far too little is known about some of these issues for sound policy decisions to be made. A

[3] Information regarding the Department of Commerce's plans to privatize NTIS under a Federal Employee Direct Corporate Stock Option Plan (FED CO-OP), as an alternative to an A-76 approach was announced in *Commerce Business Daily* (1988). For additional information, see *Government Information Quarterly*, 5 (1988), number 3.

Figure 10-3.
Selected Policy Issues Concerned with Report Literature

A. Impact of Federal technical report literature. Although numerous studies have
    addressed the use of technical report literature, there is an absence of studies that
    document the actual impact on the research and development process of the
    information conveyed in report literature. Without conclusive documentation of the
    impact of report literature, a valid question can be raised about the wisdom of
    expending substantial funds to produce and disseminate documents where the
    impact is not known (McClure, 1988)

B. Relationship of Federal technical report literature to innovation. Claims made about
    the seminal role of technical report literature in stimulating technological innovation
    suggest a need for research that identifies the relationship between information
    disseminated in a timely fashion through the medium of technical report literature and
    the creative process in science and technology. If a strong relationship is discovered,
    this finding would suggest an urgent need to enhance report dissemination systems
    to facilitate this relationship (Caponio and Bracken, 1987, p. 12)

C. Relaxation or elimination of Federal contractor's reporting requirements. The
    production and use of technical report literature are affected by Federal agency
    requirements for reporting the results of R&D contracts. The relaxation or total
    elimination of requirements for a strict accounting and reporting procedure raises the
    fundamental policy questions of the purpose of the R&D contracts and who benefits
    from the results of the completed work (McClure, 1988)

D. Increased use of security classification and further control over the dissemination of
    scientific and technical information. Increased concern about the accessibility of
    scientific and technical information to foreign countries, particularly the Soviet Union,
    has led to an increase in the number of documents given a security classification and
    has resulted in limitations placed on the availability of technical report literature to
    other countries. The restrictions that apply to other countries also limit accessibility
    within the United States (McClure, 1988)

E. Improving the ability of the United States to compete effectively in international
    markets, while enhancing citizens earning potential. In a recent congressional
    hearing, Congressman Sherwood L. Boehlert raised two basic questions (*The Role
    of Science and Technology in Competitiveness*, 1987, p. 2):
    • "How can we ensure that the government sponsors research that industry can
       use?
    • How can we ensure that industry does use that research?"
    Both questions might be expanded to include the needs of American universities,
    small businesses, and other groups.

prerequisite for knowledgeable policy decisions is research leading to better
comprehension of the issues. Figure 10–3 identifies examples of additional
issues that need to be addressed and for which further research is required.

Most of the issues noted above represent existing barriers to public
access to government information disseminated through report literature.
They also demonstrate the need for a coherent government information
policy. There is a need for more librarians to take a stand on these issues and
to make their concerns known to persons responsible for establishing public
policy. Hoduski (1983) makes a strong case for a more active role by docu-

ments librarians and others on issues such as these. In line with her suggestions for a more politically activist role by librarians, a concerted effort by the library profession to urge the development of Federal policies that encourage rather than discourage public access could be the factor that will make the difference.

11

Administrative Considerations for Increased Access to Government Publications/Information

Access to library housed government publications and information resources does not occur merely through the acquisition and organization process. Other processes (e.g., collection development, bibliographic control, reference services, and outreach programs) take place. All these processes involve numerous administrative considerations that must be analyzed and that result in decision making. These administrative considerations link the library system to the larger information environment and enable library clientele to meet their information needs.

In its simplest terms, administration involves the coordination of both human and material resources for the accomplishment of stated objectives (Kast and Rosenzweig, 1985, p. 6). Further, the process includes four primary elements: (1) meeting individual objectives and organizational goals, (2) obtaining the full productivity of each organizational member, (3) developing and implementing specific administrative strategies to fulfill goals and objectives, and (4) insuring that information services and resources meet and resolve the needs of library clientele. Library administration is not an end unto itself, but seeks to increase access to information resources and services.

Librarians working with government information today are administrators first and librarians second. Since the vast majority of depository collections have a maximum of one professional staff member (Hernon, McClure, and Purcell, 1985), that person is responsible for an entire range of administrative activities—decision making, planning, budgeting, collection development, personnel and staffing, and so forth. Further, that librarian is likely to be the only person in the library most knowledgeable about the requirements, characteristics, and needs related to government information. Thus, if the documents librarian does not assert administrative control over the government information collection and coordinate its activities with other library information services and resources, then such responsibilities are not likely to be filled anywhere else in the library.

Compared to other types of librarians, those overseeing government information resources have exceptionally broad responsibilities. Documents librarians operating in a depository setting typically work in both technical and public services. They are expected to provide in-depth reference and referral services and, at the same time, exploit bibliographic utilities for cataloging government publications (among other activities). They must administer a collection of significant size, have to obtain adequate resources to make that collection accessible, and schedule staff to assist in the operation of the collection. In addition, they participate in bibliographic instruction and other outreach programs, market programs and services, plan for new or improved services and activities, and integrate those services with other library activities.

Documents librarianship requires skills and competencies related to both librarianship and administration. Further, specific administrative strategies must be devised to accomplish organizational goals and improve access to government information resources. Administrative strategies, which are carefully developed actions intended to obtain maximum benefit from available resources, require careful planning and decision making. These resources can be both physical (e.g., books, space, or equipment) and human; typically, human resources are the most important organizational resources, since individuals allocate money, materials, and equipment to accomplish specific objectives. To increase the quality of government information resources and services, administrative strategies usually attempt to affect the allocation of resources and behavior of certain individuals in the organization.

This chapter discusses basic administrative considerations related to increasing access to government publications/ information resources. The chapter presents the government documents administrative environment and assumptions underlying the administrative process. The chapter also discusses a number of specific factors related to administrative effectiveness. First, an overview of the decision making process is followed by a discussion of budgetary factors and the importance of personnel and staff training for documents collections. Second, decision support systems for documents collections are highlighted. And, finally, the chapter discusses the importance of conducting and consuming research as a basis for implementing administrative strategies.

Government documents librarians must learn how to evaluate and research their administrative setting carefully. They must understand the basic components of decision making, budgeting, management information and decision support systems, and personnel. Furthermore, documents librarians must conduct and consume research related to these administrative activities, if they want to integrate government information resources successfully throughout the library and if library clientele are to gain effective and efficient access to these resources. The vast terrain of administration cannot be covered in this brief chapter; however, the specific administrative topics covered are critical for increasing access to government information resources. A number of excellent administration texts are available for more detailed information regarding library administration (e.g., Stueart and Moran, 1987; Kast and Rosenzweig, 1985; and Hitt, Middlemist, and Mathis, 1983). The administrative topics of planning and evaluation will be discussed in Chapter 15 and will not be repeated here.

THE ADMINISTRATIVE ENVIRONMENT

Factors Affecting the Current Status of Documents

Two primary factors affect local access to government information: the degree of bibliographic control to be provided for these information resources, and the extent of the library's commitment to provide government information services. If for no other reason that by default, the administrative environment for government information is shaped by the manner in which the library addresses these two factors. Thus, before developing specific administrative strategies, documents librarians should assess the current status of documents vis-a-vis these two factors.

As Figure 11-1 suggests, the first variable, the quality of public services offered to the patron, includes the accuracy of reference answers, the number and types of programs offered, quality and comprehensiveness of reference sources, the amount of time for which professional reference assistance is extended to patrons, responsiveness to community information needs, access to online databases, and ability to provide decentralized information services to individual patrons. Based on these criteria, the department can be "graded" as providing high quality, low quality, or some measure in between, of public service.

The second variable, the degree of internal bibliographic control over resources in the department, encompasses the availability of complete cataloging records for all holdings, the maintenance of shelflists, access to documents through centralized library records, the availability of bibliographic reference tools, (as much as possible) the organization of information resources regardless of format for easy retrieval, and utilization of classification schemes for both depository and nondepository government information resources. Based on these criteria, the department can be "graded" on the degree to which bibliographic control is maintained over the government information resources under its jurisdiction.

The model shown in Figure 11–1 recognizes that other factors, such as organizational goals, resources, structure, and attitudes toward documents shape the administrative environment. Indeed, organizational priorities in each of these categories may force the documents department into a specific quadrant, regardless of the librarian's assumptions about appropriate levels of public services and bibliographic control for documents. Nonetheless, the factors related to organizational goals, resources, structure, and attitude toward documents should be identified in terms of both constraints and opportunities.

Because these four factors can affect the administrative environment in the department, they must be identified and described as a first step toward their control. Librarians must:

- Know the organizational goals and be able to justify departmental activities within that context
- Be able to identify the formal and information power bases within the organizational structure, and exploit each when necessary
- Be knowledgeable about total resources available to the organization, so that they can compete successfully against other library areas for adequate resources
- Promote the importance and benefits of the area to other librarians, in order to receive political and moral support when required.

The reality of organizational political life is that documents librarians must justify their needs, clarify goals, and demonstrate accomplishments *better* than other librarians if access to government information resources is to be improved. Justification is necessary, in large part, because competition for resources can be fierce within the organization. In short, each of these four factors must be addressed administratively to develop the overall effectiveness of the department.

The administrative environment does not exist by chance or happenstance. The above factors, which determine the nature of the environment, are allowed or encouraged to occur either by administrative design or neglect. Further, the documents librarians' assumptions of what is an "appropriate" environment typically reinforce that administrative design or neglect. If there is to be any modification in these factors (and others to be discussed below), documents librarians must identify specific factors to be changed and develop administrative strategies to implement change.

Figure 11-1.
Analyzing the Departmental Administrative Environment

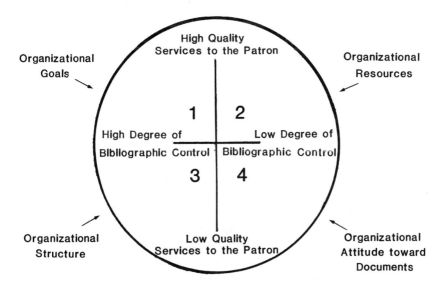

	DESCRIPTION OF QUADRANTS	
QUADRANT NUMBER	DESCRIPTION
1	High quality of public services with broad range of different services to patrons; excellent bibliographic control over all types of government publications including in-house automated information systems
2	High quality of public services with broad range of different services to patrons; minimal bibliographic control over government publications and complete reliance on hard-copy indexes
3	Low quality of public services with limited range of services to patrons and no outreach or marketing programs; excellent bibliographic control over all types of government publications including in-house automated information systems
4	Low quality of public services with limited range of services to patrons and no outreach or marketing programs; minimal bibliographic control over government publications and complete reliance on hard-copy indexes

Administrative Assumptions

The administrative philosophies of the director's office, as well as those of documents and other librarians, affect access to resources and the provision of services. Only rarely do librarians actually analyze the specific philosophies at work in the library. But to develop strategies one must know where the other organizational members are "coming from." Further, documents librarians must identify their administrative assumptions as well. Thus, a brief summary of the basic administrative philosophies typically found in the library environment will help to better understand "why decisions are made the way they are."

Since a number of textbooks and articles provide sophisticated descriptions of the various administrative philosophies, only a brief overview will be presented here (Koontz and O'Donnell, 1979, pp. 175–187). All the various administrative philosophies are based on assumptions—which are difficult to prove or disprove. But one's assumptions toward work and people affect the actual behaviors and administrative strategies that are used.

A first basic set of administrative assumptions, known as classical managerial assumptions (Wren, 1972), are task oriented; the most important aspect of the work environment is getting the work done. There is strict adherence to centralization of authority, and staff participation in library decision making is a privilege to be be jealously guarded. Control, rather than flexibility and innovation, is stressed, while strict lines of authority are maintained.

A second set of assumptions, from the human relations school of thought (Argyris, 1973, pp. 257–269), sees workers valued as individuals, and the group processes of decision making and participation are at least as important as the task itself. Indeed, the assumptions are that the individual will respond to rewards other than money, that the organization can best be studied based on social interactions, and that people will work more effectively if they "like" each other and have respect for each other. Other assumptions are that open and honest communication within the organization is necessary, that the process of getting work done must be seen in a context of personal values, and that each individual has a right to provide upward communication and feedback to superiors.

Both of these schools of thought are based largely on principles that are applied, in general, to all employees in most organizations. A relatively new school of administrative thought emphasizes the importance of environmental and situational factors rather than general principles (Luthans, 1976; Kast and Rosenzweig, 1985). Contingency management assumptions suggest that individuals are more likely to modify organizational behavior by manipulating environmental characteristics rather than direct threats and promises to individuals. It suggests that administrative strategies of an "if . . . then . . ."

variety will allow individuals to respond differently in different situations, yet still accomplish stated goals. Further, it develops specific administrative strategies to resolve situations based on individual characteristics of the people involved, the environment itself, and decentralized information access (Samuels and McClure, 1982, pp. 23–24).

The three philosophies of classical, human relations, and contingency are defined more easily in theory than in library practice. Typically, most libraries operate under basic classical management assumptions, with a pseudo-interest in human relations assumptions. In this context, one finds either "paternal despotism" or "laissez faire" administrative environments. Despite the specific environmental situation, documents librarians must be able to identify administrative assumptions and respond with contingency administrative strategies if there is to be any hope of shaping the administrative environment to benefit the documents department. Such strategies will be more effective if documents librarians are knowledgeable about the decision making process.

DECISION MAKING

Decision making, which is an administrative process of critical importance for increasing organizational effectiveness, usually involves three related topics: the decision making process, the decision maker, and the decision itself. Within each of these areas, decision making aims to influence value judgments held by other individuals. But, if one defines decision making as that process whereby information is converted into action, then decision making is largely concerned with the process of acquiring, analyzing, and reporting information to accomplish specific objectives. Because documents librarians have administrative responsibilities, they must be able to convert effectively a broad range of information resources and research findings into a coherent plan of action.

Figure 11–2, which provides a simplified view of decision making, suggests that:

- Effective decision making cannot occur without organizational goals and objectives
- Research is necessary to obtain and analyze appropriate information resources, as well as guide the evaluation process
- Environmental input and feedback should assist documents librarians in assessing the effectiveness of the decision made.

The decision making process is described here within an open systems perspective (see Chapter 15, which relates the process to the broader environment of the library).

Figure 11-2.
The Decision Making Process

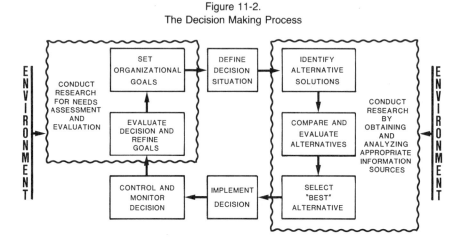

More specifically, this figure shows that the environment (defined as all organizational and societal factors) will affect library services and resources. Analyzing the environment is critical as a basis for setting organizational goals (Dougherty, Heinritz, and Kaske, 1982). Next, the decision situation is carefully defined and narrowed as much as possible, to provide a clear definition about what exactly is included in the decision situation, and what exactly is to be resolved. A key factor in the quality of the resulting decision is the degree to which alternatives are identified, compared, and selected.

The comparison and evaluation of alternative decisions enables administrators to consider a broad range of possible solutions, encourage creativity, and introduce a planning perspective on the decision making process. Of course, the decision must be implemented; that is, specific steps must be identified by the decision. Those steps or actions must be completed by the appropriate individuals at the appropriate time, and must meet previously agreed upon performance criteria. Based on the extent to which the decision results in the appropriate outcomes, as well as the consideration of additional or revised information from the environment, the decision outcomes should be evaluated against stated organizational goals and objectives; when necessary, goals should be revised. Underlying the entire decision making process is the need to collect, analyze, and integrate information through regularly conducted research.

The decision making process is sabotaged, and ineffective decisions are likely, without research taking place to identify, compare, evaluate, and select alternative decisions; to evaluate the success of the decision; or to determine the impact of the decision on the environment (Janis and Mann,

1977). Indeed, a typical (and usually ineffective) approach to decision making in some library settings is simply to define the situation in which a decision is necessary, and then implement the decision. This "two-step" process of decision making helps to explain why some government documents collections are unable to flourish in today's complex information environment and are, thus, becoming ineffective in providing adequate access to government information.

If, for example, the decision situation is "Should the government documents depository establish an in-house automated shelflist?" it appears foolhardy to purchase the equipment and necessary supplies, train the staff, and implement the automated shelflist without considering:

- What are the objectives of the automated shelflist?
- What is the cost to design and implement the system?
- Will the automated shelflist improve overall bibliographic control and reference services for government information resources?
- How will documents librarians be affected in terms of performing other responsibilities?
- How will online access to the shelflist impact the activities of other areas of the library?

These, of course, are but a few of the questions, regarding the decision situation, that might be raised. The point, however, is that each question requires evidence, at that particular library, to obtain accurate information to address that question.

Decision making for government information-related resources and services must be integrated into overall library decision making. Documents librarians must become politically active in the organization, participate in nondocuments related activities, and educate other library staff about the importance and problems of access to government information resources. Indeed, documents librarians must become involved in decision making and planning, if resource allocation and budgetary decisions are to take government information resources into consideration, and if the government information area(s) of the library is to receive an equitable allocation of those resources.

BUDGETING AND RESOURCE ALLOCATION

Documents librarians must have some direct control over the budget for their area of responsibility. Some administrators mistakenly believe that, because documents are "free," no additional budget is necessary. However, budget control over specific activities (e.g., for the purchase of nondepository publications, reference sources from the private sector, and equipment; as well as support for continuing education of staff) are critical factors that will affect the overall quality of the documents collection. Documents librarians are the persons best able to allocate limited resources and make decisions about the allocation of these resources in the documents area. Without a regular budget and some direct control over that budget, documents librarians are effectively hamstrung and must rely on "handouts" from the administrative offices or other departments for support.

Although documents librarians must have input and direct control over resource allocations related to government publications, they must also realize that the allocation of resources is a systems process—of which government publications is but one component. But documents librarians have to make an effective argument for a broader view of budgeting than simply the maintenance of library collections (Johnson, 1982, p. 31). Further, some library administrators are now recognizing the importance of input from middle management regarding resource allocations (Martin, 1982, p. 7). Thus, documents librarians must adopt an assertive stance to: (1) identify and define costs for government information resources and services, (2) make known and justify needs for improved services and access to resources, and (3) demonstrate specific benefits resulting from allocations made in support of government information resources.

In its simplest form, budgeting is the process of outlining library activities and services in terms of dollar amounts, obtaining adequate financial support for the library to accomplish its objectives, and allocating predetermined amounts of money to specific areas of library activities (Prentice, 1977, pp. 92–111). In addition, a budget, which is a formal and written document that outlines these expenditures, has impacts in the following areas:

- *Planning*: a budget expresses priorities for a specific planning cycle, usually a one year period, and suggests which library activities are to be funded at what levels of support during the forthcoming year
- *Control*: a budget attempts to ensure that specific amounts of resources are expended for only certain activities and services by indicating which activities, or which departments/agencies are to be allocated predetermined amounts of support, and clarifying who is responsible for those expenditures
- *Political relationships*: the budget expresses the relationships among the various departments/agencies funded by the institution, the degree to which department/agency heads can obtain support for their programs, and the perceived importance of those activities compared to other institutional activities

- *Basis for evaluation*: the budget also provides a basis by which the activities and services of the library can be evaluated in terms of *effectiveness* and *efficiency*.

Budgeting and resource allocation procedures at the department or area level (e.g., for government information resources) is as important as budgeting procedures at the larger institutional or organizational level. Indeed, in one study of large academic depository libraries, it was found that an average yearly direct cost of $151,000 could be identified for the operations of the government documents depository collection (Smith, 1982, p. 207).

The allocation of resources directly related to government publications/information resources must be identified and itemized. General categories to examine related to expenses include:

- Personnel costs
  -- Professional staff
  — Paraprofessional staff
- Information materials
  — Direct purchase of these resources
  — Purchase of reference tools produced by the private sector
- Supplies
- Equipment
  — Microform viewing and reproduction equipment
  — Microcomputer hardware and software
  — Storage and organization (for microforms, maps, posters, etc.)
- Contractual services
  — Copying machines
  — Purchase of online cataloging service for government publications
- Continuing education for staff
- Miscellaneous expenses.

These categories and descriptions, which are not intended to be comprehensive, suggest the general areas of expenses for operating government information collections, be they separated from or integrated with other library collections.

Once these basic expenditures for direct support of government information resources are itemized, documents librarians can produce an annual budget summarizing the expenditures. Furthermore, they can examine those expenditures in terms of specific objectives related to government information. Even though a formal budget will typically be prepared for the organization as a whole, and not specifically for government information resources, there is no reason why documents librarians cannot produce such a budget. The benefits from having an individual budget for government information resources are that the budget:

- Provides benchmark data concerning the total amount of resources and individual allocations related to government information resources and services
- Allows documents librarians to compare the extent to which the library provides resources for government information related materials and services, as opposed to other activities in the library
- Increases documents librarians' knowledge and control over expenditures
- Encourages documents librarians to relate identified expenditures to stated goals and objectives, and to modify either the expenditures or the objectives for greater operational effectiveness
- Provides a basis for maintaining long-term trend data to assess the relative growth, strengths, and changes in resource allocation for government information resources.

By developing an individual budget for government publications, by being able to specify individual costs for government publications-related programs and resources, and by documenting those costs and changes over time, documents librarians have a much stronger basis for making decisions and establishing plans. The limited use of such approaches probably helps to explain the wide discrepancies found in funding depository library collections (Cook, 1982).

Where the government documents collection is separated from other library collections, it might be useful to assess the degree to which other departments allocate resources for government information, in both print and nonprint formats. Figure 11–3 is a chart intended to provide a basis for such a comparison. The importance of utilizing an analysis similar to that suggested in the figure is to provide a basis for describing the treatment of government information resources compared to other departments, to assist in assessing the degree to which government information resources are integrated into overall financial planning at the institution, and to identify specific areas where attention (resource allocation) is required if adequate support for documents is to be obtained. Clearly, there is no "right" or "wrong" percentage of allocation for each of these categories; individual institutions will have to make that assessment in consideration of the goals and objectives set for government information resources and services.

A number of budgets have been suggested for use in library settings. But, in general, the budgets tend to be either line item (each type of expenditure is given an individual line on the budget) or program-oriented (the

Figure 11-3.
Analyzing Resource Allocations for Government Publications

RESOURCES	ALLOCATED TO THE LIBRARY AS A WHOLE	ALLOCATED TO GOVERNMENT PUBLICATIONS	PERCENTAGE

1. STAFF
  a. professional hours per week
  b. non-professional hours per week
  c. hours of public operation per week			

2. SPACE
  a. square feet of shelving-storage area
  b. square feet of office-work area
  c. number of reader stations			

3. EQUIPMENT
  a. identification and description of types
  b. current value of equipment
  c. cost of service contracts
  d. current yearly budget			

4. COLLECTION
  a. linear feet of available (books and periodicals) shelving
  b. linear feet of microform shelving (or drawers)
  c. volumes (or equivalents)
  d. circulation (or number of user contacts)			

5. BUDGET
  a. current annual budget
  b. purchase of reference tools and indexes
  c. non-reference acquisitions			

expenditures are linked to specific program goals and objectives). Line item budgets, which are easy and quick to produce, can specify individual expenditures clearly (Prentice, 1982, pp. 93–95). However, they tend to inhibit creativity, encourage the department/agency to use the same categories (items) year after year, and encourage revisions based on a certain percentage of expenditures for all items rather than looking at each item individually. A program budget, which is more difficult to produce, must include measurable program objectives. It fosters long-range planning, links expenditures directly to the accomplishment of objectives, and encourages evaluation of the program under consideration (Sarndal, 1979).

Figure 11–4 suggests a useful compromise between the two approaches. A program budget with line items is easier to complete than a straight program budget and simply incorporates the "items" or portion of items directly related to the program under consideration. In the example, the program "Documents Delivery Services" is described in terms of clearly identified objectives. The resources needed to accomplish the program objectives are specified with individual lines (items). Use of such a program budget by documents librarians has a number of benefits:

- Costs directly attributable to the accomplishment of a specific objective are itemized
- Performance measures are established for each objective and assist documents librarians in knowing the degree to which the program or activity is "successful"
- Programs that are not cost-effective can be identified and either modified or eliminated
- The ability of documents librarians to justify costs and request appropriate resources in light of program objectives is significantly strengthened.

However, an underlying assumption with such a budgeting approach is that the institution has stated goals and that the documents area can establish measurable objectives. Such an approach is essential if meaningful planning and the use of performance measures (see Chapter 15) are also to be accomplished.

The use of budgeting information is essential for the computation of cost-effectiveness ratios. Such ratios express the cost (which could include personnel, time, materials, equipment, overhead, etc.) per unit measure of a product. For instance, the cost-effectiveness ratio of shelving depository microfiche might be $1.50 per microfiche, if the professional staff are responsible for reshelving, whereas the ratio might be .63 cents if paraprofessional

Figure 11-4.
Combination Program-Line Item Budget

PROGRAM NAME: DOCUMENTS DELIVERY SERVICE

PROGRAM OBJECTIVES: 1. To deliver a requested government publication to faculty members within 45 minutes of the original request.

2. to increase the speed with which the government documents department can provide accurate delivery of requested materials

ITEM NAME	JUSTIFICATION	COST
1. Student Assist.	Student assistant during hours of operation is required in order that someone is always available to deliver actual documents	$700/mt
2. Copying	All documents/articles less than 45 pages or on microfiche will be copied for loan	45/mt
3. Portable Microfiche Readers	Purchase three portable microfiche readers to circulate with loaned microfiche	450
4.		
5.		
6.		
7.		
8.		
9.		
10.	START-UP	$450
COMMENTS: Student Assist. will be assigned additional responsibilities during the day	TOTAL COST	$745/mt

PROGRAM COMPLETION DATE AND BENCHMARKS: Program will be initiated September, 1989 and completed May, 1990; evaluation to be done December and May.

PERFORMANCE MEASURES FOR OBJECTIVE 1: Percentage of government documents delivered versus requested; a 70% fill rate will be considered successful.

PERFORMANCE MEASURES FOR OBJECTIVE 2: Average time per delivery of document; an average of 45 minutes or less will be considered successful.

staff reshelve microforms. Cost-effectiveness ratios can be improved only by one of two methods:

- Decrease the cost associated with the production of the item, and at the same time maintain the number of items produced
- Increase the number of items produced from the process, and at the same time maintain the level of costs associated with the process.

Few cost-effectiveness studies on government information resources and services have been reported in the literature. However, it is essential that documents librarians consider such ratios as a basis for decision making, planning, and the justification of resources and services.

Regardless of the budgeting approach taken at the institutional level, a budget for government information resources and services is essential for informed decision making and planning. Services and activities related to government information cannot be improved if documents librarians do not know current expenditures for existing services, specific costs for individual programs, the degree to which resources are useful in accomplishing stated objectives, or the likelihood that funds could be better expended on other activities. Documents librarians can neither afford to be ignorant of such financial factors nor can they allow themselves to be removed from the institutional budgeting process. Developing and submitting budgets is a critical factor for supporting services and resources necessary to increase access to government publications/information.

PERSONNEL DEVELOPMENT

Without adequately trained, knowledgeable, and forceful individuals serving as documents librarians, the value of government information, regardless of content, both within the library and for patrons, will be negligible. Documents personnel must be knowledgeable about specific areas of expertise, organizational goals, service philosophies for the user, and obtaining adequate resources from the organization in order to perform their duties. In this sense, documents personnel should develop their own resources and those of the organization as a means of improving the overall effectiveness of government information collections. Strategies for personnel development can help offset inherent difficulties with government information resources; this is especially true for those resources appearing in a nonprint format.

A program of personnel development can begin with a skills inventory, or the identification of specific areas in which personnel can become more effective during the performance of their duties (Mathis and Jackson, 1979, pp. 203–279). A skills inventory, however, should not be confused with a personnel evaluation process. Typically, personnel evaluation attempts to determine how well the employee has performed during the past year (or some given amount of time), and ranks that person in comparison to other organizational members. The results then can be translated into recommendations for salary increases or promotions (Kroll, 1983, p. 32). While both techniques can encourage skills development, a skills inventory should be a self-assessment process without direct pressure for evaluation.

A skills inventory, which comprises the first step in the process of personnel development, enables individuals to improve their knowledge, technical skills, attitudes, and overall effectiveness. In this sense, the emphasis is on the future, not the past, and providing strategies for improvement to occur. In a number of instances, the problems with many government publications collections are related to the skills/knowledge deficiencies of the documents librarians. On the one hand, many of them never received appropriate training before accepting the responsibilities of the position. On the other hand, those people who did receive some training may now find it inadequate or obsolete.

Yet final responsibility for personnel development rests with both the individual and the organization. Regardless of whether the individual is classified as a professional or paraprofessional, his/her development in terms of improved skills and knowledge is essential. The unique nature of documents librarianship demands special skills—and the application of rapidly changing technology to the field only adds to this demand. Ongoing training programs are essential if the quality of personnel is to be upgraded.

There must be formally developed training sessions for all personnel who begin work in a depository collection. Boss and Raikes (1982, pp. 147–170) reprint an excellent general outline for staff training, geared toward paraprofessionals. New staff members working with a documents collection should not be "dumped" there without considerable training with reference sources, the manner in which that collection is organized, the reference interview and search strategy techniques, philosophies of service, places and persons for referral, knowledge of how to operate various microform viewing and reproduction equipment, and a host of other topics. A program of staff training for all new employees, combined with a carefully planned program for continuing education, will greatly contribute to improved services for government information (see Chapter 20).

If the goal of integrating government information resources, in terms of bibliographic control, physical availability, professional service, and status is to be achieved, there is no substitute for competency. This competency must be evident in the basic knowledge, technical skills, administrative ability, service orientation, ability to manipulate the political environment, and professional activity of the staff. Only when documents librarians commit themselves to an ongoing program of personnel development will government information resources become fully integrated with other library holdings, patrons be able to gain access to these resources effectively, and depository staff provide high quality reference service.

DECISION SUPPORT SYSTEMS

The administrative environment in depository collections today is one that calls for accurate, timely, insightful, and effective decisions that facilitate the ability of documents librarians to accomplish predetermined goals and objectives. Because of a rapidly changing set of factors that affect the depository collection, the development and use of decision support systems (DSS) for the identification, organization, and use of data for decision making takes on increased importance. The complexitites of administering a medium to large academic or public depository library collection require (1) a conceptual approach by which the library identifies, collects, and presents information for library decision making; and (2) a practical approach by which procedures, techniques, and equipment are coordinated to provide librarians with information for improving the effectiveness and efficiency of library services and operations.

The term "DSS" has been defined in different ways. Some authors consider it as "a blending of computer information with decision-making analysis techniques from management science and operations research" (Heindel and Napier, 1981, pp. 319–320). Other writers label DSS as "a category of information systems used in organizations to assist managers in semi-structured decision processes" (Akoka, 1981, pp. 133–134) but not in the more routine and programmed decision processes. Finally, some authors see DSS as a natural progression from electronic data processing and management information systems, where information systems should conform to specific management styles and needs (Bommer and Chorba, 1982, p. 13).

Primary reasons for developing an information base useful for library decision making are to (McClure, 1984a, p. 7):

- *Reduce ambiguity by providing an empirical basis for decision making*: there is a need to reduce uncertainty by validating assumptions without replacing creativity and by searching for opportunities
- *Provide intelligence about the environment*: ignorance of the environment perpetuates ignorance of opportunities, isolates the library, reduces knowledge of competitors, and confuses the "proper" role of the library
- *Assess historical, current, and future states*: various scenarios must be considered to deal with the future effectiveness of the library; past and present performance can assist in developing those scenarios

- *Evaluate process and monitor progress*: the accomplishment of objectives cannot be determined, remedial action taken, resource allocations changed to meet different contingencies, or planning for the development of new goals and objectives cannot occur without evaluation.

The creation of a decision support system may increase the centralization over whatever information is collected and used, the costs associated with information collection and analysis, the percentage of librarian time spent in administrative activities, and the need for librarians to become more sophisticated users and consumers of statistical analyses.

Two levels of activities are necessary for the development of a DSS. First, there is a need for a conceptual basis from which such a system could be developed. Figure 11–5 suggests one possible approach. At a more practical level, some thought must be given to the specific data elements appropriate for inclusion in the decision support system (McClure, 1984a). Figure 11–6 identifies a method to assist documents librarians in identifying specific data elements. When used together, both figures may provide documents librarians with a point of departure for developing a DSS specifically for collections of government information resources.

There are two differing approaches by which management information can be obtained. The first, a functional approach, identifies a specific library service, activity, or operation, and defines it rather narrowly in terms of the likely data elements that can be collected to describe that activity; summary descriptive statistics are then produced. The second, a systems approach, coordinates the collection of management information from the perspective of describing the degree of success in accomplishing organizational goals and objectives. Although data elements specifically related to individual library activities are included, this approach also compares library activities and attempts to describe interrelationships among these activities.

Ideally, the systems approach has greater benefits for government information collections, since it would force integrated decision making related to documents services and materials. However, an initial beginning for developing management information for the documents collection will probably have to take a functional approach, due to the lack of actual decision support systems available for the library as a system. For many government information collections, such an approach can be utilized effectively by exploiting local institutional computer resources and canned software packages, or by using small microcomputer systems with preprogrammed statistical and spreadsheet software packages.

In those cases in which documents librarians lack adequate clerical staff, to say nothing of WATS telephone lines, microcomputers, word-processing and other software, and other automated office niceties, a DSS may seem to be nothing more than a pipe-dream. However, one might

Figure 11-5.
Design Considerations for the Development of a System for Library Management Information

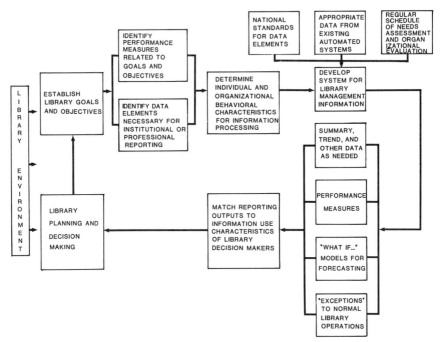

Source: Charles R. McClure, "Management Information for Library Decision Making," in *Advances in Librarianship,* vol. 12 (New York: Academic Press, 1983).

Figure 11-6.
Classification Scheme for Recording and Reporting Information about Libraries

Measures / Programmatic Functions	Financial Measures	Personnel Measures	Facility Measures	Activity Measures	User Measures	Outcome/ Performance Measures
Informational, Educational, Cultural and Recreational Services						
Resource Distribution Services						
Collection Development Serices						
Technical Serices						
Administrative and Support Services						

Source: *Library Data Collection Handbook.* (Chicago, IL: American Library Association, 1981), p. 19.

suggest that a significant reason for the lack of integration of, and access to, depository publications is the inability of documents librarians to make informed, accurate, and timely decisions based on empirical evidence rather than "best opinion."

Depending on the individual capabilities of the software selected, library staff could:

- Sort and search data by specific fields
- Monitor the receipt of orders and budget expenditures
- Transfer preliminary cataloging information from an order file to the online catalog upon arrival of a title
- Produce mailing labels, acquisitions lists, etc.

A DSS for managing government information resources could utilize some or all of the following fields:

- Level of government
- Issuing agency
- Type of publication (the 22 types discussed in Chapter 4)
- Format
- Distributor (GPO, NTIS, etc.)
- Individual title
- Series title
- Sudocs number
- LC or Dewey call number
- GPO item number
- Date surveyed (GPO)
- Date published
- Date selected/ordered
- Date received
- Received as depository or nondepository item
- Series holdings
- Subjects/descriptors
- Notes.

Libraries could enter such information for every government information resource received as of a certain date. Such a database enables staff and users to identify and retrieve resources regardless of level of government, format, and distribution source.

With such a database, libraries achieve administrative and intellectual integration for publications received from the GPO, National Technical Information Service (NTIS), and other Federal agencies; regional, state, local, and international bodies; and other countries. By expanding the database to include retrospective holdings, libraries increase their collection development and management capabilities. They begin to manage the *life cycle* of information resources within their domain. The *life cycle* begins with the selection and acquisition of a title. It also covers that title's receipt, processing, placement in the collection, and inclusion in an online catalog. The cycle concludes with ongoing evaluation of the title's *value* to collection goals and objectives. Software such as INMAGIC permits the integration of the various phases associated with the life cycle (see Hernon and McClure, 1986). Staff then quickly determine the status of a title at any time; is it on order, in processing, or on the shelf, in circulation, or missing?

The boolean operators ("and," "or," "not") available with programs such as INMAGIC enable staff to combine search fields and to further generate data and statistics useful for decision making. For example, staff could identify all microfiche pamphlets held for five or more years. They could then review these titles and make decisions about their retention (see Stephenson and Purcell, 1984).

With the inclusion of government information resources in online catalogs, staff and users would have to distinguish between government or nongovernment information. When they need information on a particular topic, they need not ascertain the level of government, type of source, format, etc. Rather, staff and users select from a menu of the entire resources of a library. They also see what is on order and currently in processing. At the same time, staff have a tool for collection evaluation and making retention decisions. They can also produce acquisitions lists and other current awareness tools.

Using dBASE III and an IBM PC with hard disk capability, the library of the University of California, Riverside, has captured information about depository item numbers in machine-readable form. The database, updated weekly, includes all active item numbers available for selection, those actually selected and those discontinued since September 1984. "Each record in the database represents a depository item number or, in cases, where a[n] item number has more than one Sudoc class assigned to it, a Sudoc class within a depository item number" (Mooney, 1986, p. 2). Each record gives item and Sudocs class numbers, name of the agency, title, format, survey number, type of document, date selected, location in collection, "and other local cataloging or processing practices" (Ibid.).

Staff at the University of California, Riverside, monitor the correction notices appearing on GPO *Shipping Lists* and edit database records as necessary. They have indexed the database to permit rapid retrieval of information by a predetermined field. They plan on "assigning broad subject or discipline concepts to each record to further enhance the utility of the database as a collection development and management tool" (Ibid., p. 3). Such an addition is critical and recognizes the importance of making collection development decisions within a subject context.

In various writings, Morton (e.g., 1982) has discussed an automated shelflist that links collection development decision making to planning and, by implication, a DSS for reviewing selection and retention decisions. This system represents a cooperative acquisition and retention program between two area libraries, Carleton College and St. Olaf College. A disadvantage, however, is the need for specialized software that is not widely available at the computing centers of many academic institutions.

The number of decision support systems currently used in library settings is small; thus, one would not be surprised to learn that there is even less chance of such systems being in operation at depository collections. Nonetheless, depository librarians must give attention to the development of systems that provide ongoing, accurate, and timely management information across a broad range of depository-related activities, if they are to increase integration of, and access to, government information resources. Indeed, support for such ongoing evaluation and assessment is essential for the maintenance of effective depository planning, operations, and services.

Librarians wanting to explore the use of decision support systems and microcomputers for decision making should review Hernon and McClure (1986). This work offers specific suggestions for using database management and spreadsheet software in support of library decision making. The opportunities and challenges are present for documents librarians to help themselves, assist their institution, and improve access to government information resources by exploiting microcomputers for the collection, analysis, and reporting of management information for decision support.

ESTABLISHING A RESEARCH BASIS FOR DOCUMENTS ADMINISTRATION

The four topics discussed in this chapter (decision making, budgeting, personnel, and decision support systems) have one important theme in common. They all depend on accurate and timely information, if administrative strategies are to be taken to increase the overall efficiency and effectiveness of government information collections. Obtaining adequate and timely information requires documents librarians to be knowledgeable about both *conducting* and *consuming* research. The complexity of operating government information collections requires greater knowledge about the research process, collecting and analyzing data, and awareness of how that process can impact and support library decision making and planning. The importance of the research process can only increase as greater opportunities and challenges, and increased flexibility for funding documents related services, becomes apparent.

Conducting and consuming research for the effective operation of government information collections can no longer be considered a luxury.

Rather, it is as important as having staff trained in reference or cataloging work. But, for the vast majority of documents librarians, it is very easy to rationalize the lack of exploiting research for administrative decisions because of demands on staff time, solving day-to-day problems, holdings a line against inflation, reduced budgets, rising costs, and limited knowledge about the research process.

Realistically, the successful incorporation of the research process for government information resources calls for a restating of priorities and perhaps recognizing that, although all activities are important, some might be more so than others. Those activities of greater importance are likely candidates for investigation and research. In short, as one documents librarian quipped, "If you think research is costly and time consuming . . . try ignorance!"

Documents librarians must assume greater responsibility for in-house research and investigation, for a number of reasons:

- The best place to conduct research is where the action takes place, i.e., at the local library. A continual criticism levied at many research studies is that they offer little applicability for a particular library. Realistically, librarians cannot expect a handful of library researchers to identify specific topics of interest to an individual library, to study the topic in such a narrow manner that it applies to a local library setting, or to make recommendations that are both feasible and appropriate for the local library
- Because most libraries do not have the resources to hire consultants to conduct research for them, local documents librarians will remain the focus for any research that is to be accomplished
- Basing administrative decisions on research is important because of the current need in the profession to examine traditional assumptions related to documents operations and services. In virtually everything done in a library, assumptions that may or may not be true are made
- Unless the library knows what it wants to do with its government information collection (has stated goals and objectives), can show that it does what it says it will do (is accountable), and can demonstrate, for instance, the reasons for allocating resources to one particular activity instead of another, limited support for government information services and operations is likely.

In short, conducting research to assist in the overall, decision making process is likely to take on increased importance because of the complexity of issues to be resolved and the limited resources available to resolve those issues.

The type of research needed in most library settings is *action research.* The primary difference between traditional and action research rests on the emphasis for improving the organizational effectiveness of a particular library/information center, as opposed to conducting research that is intended to have broad generalizability. Results from action research are intended to be *implemented*—to affect change in the library and, it is hoped, improve organizational effectiveness. Swisher and McClure (1984) describe the process of action research, while Hernon and Richardson (1988) detail specific methods for analyzing, interpreting, and utilizing statistical software programs in support of action research.

The research process (that is, identifying significant problems; developing objectives, hypotheses or questions to guide data collection; implementing a research design and methodology; analyzing data; and preparing statistical reports resulting from research) will lead to improved public access to government information. Ultimately, documents-related research is intended to improve the effectiveness of collections and services, increase the degree to which government information resources can resolve the information needs of the library's clientele, and prepare the collection for organizational change and continued adaptation to the environment.

Thus, the primary means to integrate research into library decision making and planning is to:

- Have clearly written statements of the goals and objectives for the library
- Be able to relate all research projects to a specific decision that is necessary or related to the library's goals and objectives
- Be able to demonstrate how the results from the research can assist the library in improving overall library effectiveness and efficiency.

Addressing these three points before any investigation is initiated is tantamount to asking "So what?" regarding the research to be conducted. If the answer to these questions is "It really doesn't matter and won't make an impact on library effectiveness," then other topics for research should be identified.

Intelligent answers to the above questions must come, indeed can only come, from documents librarians who have research knowledge, who can relate the research process to decision making and planning, and who understand the basic concepts of general systems theory as a means to describe and understand the operations of information services. Without such skills, documents librarians will be forced to accept traditional assumptions currently operating in the library. They will be unable to respond to the changing environments affecting the library and to demonstrate accountability and justify the existence of the collection if asked to do so. Further, the library staff may continue to do well (efficiently) activities that need not be done (ineffectiveness). By understanding basic research and statistical techniques, utilizing research to *support* decision making and planning, and encouraging research competencies in the professional staff, the documents staff will be better able to increase the effectiveness of the collection, respond to the information needs of current and potential clientele, and provide increased access to government information resources.

Librarians must move toward a more comprehensive view of managing human, physical, and information resources and of meeting identifiable goals and objectives. Information resources management (IRM) offers such an administrative perspective and is evolving into a management style that may be especially appropriate in library settings (Trauth, 1988). Librarians must accept responsibility for utilizing new management techniques and generally increasing their administrative skills. The challenge for documents librarians will be to increase the effectiveness of their collections and services with only minimal increases in available resources. Such can be accomplished primarily by increased administrative effectiveness.

12

Integrating Government Information Resources into Library Services

Public access, availability, and use of government publications/information can be increased by integrating these resources into the mainstream of library and information services. For too long, government publications have been seen as information resources that are "cheap" (thus, not valuable); pamphlet, ephemeral, and loose materials inappropriate for library collections; or "popular" materials that have limited utility for scholarly collections. Such beliefs simply misrepresent the value of the information content contained in government publications, and exacerbate the difficulty of integrating documents successfully into library and information services.

The term "integrate" suggests a combining of parts to form a whole. General systems theory, when applied to this concept, would add that the whole is more than the sum of its parts. Furthermore, each part has an interdependent effect on all other parts of the system as well as the total "essence" of the whole. If library and information services are seen as a system, and documents are a part of that system, then integration of government documents is best seen in a systems perspective. Indeed, the mainstay of successful integration is the fact that all the components of the system work toward the accomplishment of system goals (Kast and Rosenzweig, 1985, pp. 102–121).

Although the concept of integrating government documents is generally stressed at the organizational level (i.e., an individual library), additional consideration of the concept is necessary at other levels of analysis. Because individual libraries cannot maintain comprehensive collections that satisfy *all* information needs *all* the time, integration of documents also must occur within the context of local, regional, and national networks. Inclusion of documents in appropriate union lists, bibliographic databases, shared collection development activities among libraries, and the planning of information services is necessary. Furthermore, integration of the depository library program into government-wide information dissemination services and information services of the mass media are a third and fourth level of analysis yet to be adequately addressed.

The purpose of this chapter is to discuss the importance of the concept of integrating government publications/information into the mainstream of library and information services. After defining the concept of integration in greater detail and suggesting a method to analyze the degree of integration currently obtained for government information, a review of some current trends to increase integration will be presented. The chapter will conclude with a brief review of major issues yet to be resolved if successful integration of government information is to be accomplished. The underlying theme of the chapter is that integration of government information into library and information services is essential if public access, availability, and use of government information resources is to be increased.

THE CONCEPT OF INTEGRATION

Overall, integration suggests a contingency approach for comparing government publications/information to existing services and conditions provided to other types of resources. Contingency approaches are based on general systems thinking, which encourages an "if . . . then . . ." strategy of action based on individual situations and the unique environmental conditions affecting that particular situation (Luthans, 1976). This contingency approach, then, allows for unique conditions to be assessed to determine the level of excellence that the library clientele can reasonably expect vis-a-vis government publications/information. In short, the treatment of government documents collections and services should be at least at the same level extended to other types of library resources and services.

There are major criteria to consider regarding integration. The first, *bibliographic accessibility*, asks if clientele have the same probability of determining the existence of a government publication or information resource as any other type of material in the library. This criterion is critical because many patrons are automatically referred away from documents because these resources are discriminated against in traditional indexes, abstracts, and bibliographies. As an example, when a reference librarian sends a patron to use *Reader's Guide* or *Business Periodicals Index*, by definition, that librarian has said, "You probably do not need a government publication."

The problem of selective inclusion of government publications in general indexes is compounded by the fact that, in the vast majority of libraries maintaining separate government documents departments, the primary indexes to government publications (e.g., the *CIS/Index*, the *American Statistics Index*, the *Monthly Catalog*, the *Index to U.S. Government Periodicals*, the *Publications Reference File*, and *Government Reports Announcements & Index*) are removed from the general reference area. Bibliographic accessibility can be improved simply by duplicate purchases of key government reference tools or by placing such tools in a physical location where both general reference and documents reference staff can easily gain access to them.

The second criterion of integration, *physical availability*, asks if patrons have the same probability of locating a specific document on the shelf and checking it out, as they would any other type of material in the library. The implication is that government documents are logically organized on open stacks, that a knowledgeable patron can identify a specifically needed document and obtain it directly from the shelf, and, regardless of the format in which the information appears, that person has the opportunity to check it out for external library use. A number of documents collections have "closed stacks" in which patrons are not allowed to obtain directly (or browse) government publications. Guardians of collections in private institutions may prevent outsiders from entering the library to use depository publications until they have obtained special permission to do so. And, in a number of depository collections, publications are not checked out or depository microfiche are unavailable for circulation. These factors, which are easily remedied if the library wishes, can significantly increase physical availability to government publications.

The issues of open versus closed stacks, circulation versus noncirculation of documents, and access or the lack of it to collections through browsing affect the physical availability of government publications. Currently, little research has investigated the impact of these factors on access and user services. One study discovered that social scientists engaged in a significant amount of browsing when they attempt to locate government publications (Hernon, 1979, pp. 56–57). Additional study is required if documents librarians are to better organize and administer documents collections for increased user access and physical availability.

The third criterion, *professional service*, suggests that the patron should obtain the same level of professional service for government publications as for other types of library resources and services. Where the 55% Rule applies to reference service, the level of service should be reviewed and improved (Hernon and McClure, 1987b). The individual competencies of library staff working with government publications have a critical effect on the degree to which government publications are integrated successfully with other library services.

The fourth criterion, *status*, relates to attitudes, perceptions, and power relationships in the library. But, the impact of status on government documents collections and services is readily apparent. The documents librarian's vision and ability to articulate ways to obtain adequate resources are critical. One indicator of the status criterion is the degree to which the documents area has access to, and receives support for, the use of information handling technologies in comparison to other library departments. Yet documents areas frequently are excluded from participation in (and use of) automated information systems.

Furthermore, documents librarians may have less competency than other librarians regarding the use of automated information systems and online bibliographic database searching (McClure, 1982b; Hernon, McClure, and Purcell, 1985). Documents librarians believe that they receive less material resource support than other areas of the library (Cook, 1982). Equally important, documents librarians must be involved in decision making and be able to influence library policy. They must have at least equal status, resources, physical facilities, and impact on library policy, in comparison to other library staff, if they are to integrate government documents collections and services. The criterion of status is likely to require at least one full-time, specially trained, professional documents librarian, with administrative authority over the depository collection.

The concept of integration, which is holistic, suggests a combination or interaction of these criteria for establishing an organizational climate that encourages the overall effectiveness of services for government publications/information. A self-assessment centering on these criteria can identify specific areas where attention is needed. Relevant environmental factors must be considered and understood as a prerequisite for improving the overall quality of services for government publications and the degree to which these resources are integrated into other library and information services.

ANALYZING DOCUMENTS INTEGRATION

Because every documents collection has unique conditions and operates within situations different from others, it is important for library staff to assess the degree to which integration is occurring in their particular setting. The previous section identified four criteria that affect documents integration. Based on these criteria, constraints can be identified that limit the ability of library staff to increase integration of government publications/information. Once specific constraints, for an individual setting, are identified, strategies can be developed to minimize the impacts of the constraints.

A constraint, which may be defined as a factor or condition currently

Figure 12-1.
Potential Constraints Affecting Integration of Government Documents

INTEGRATION CRITERION	POTENTIAL CONSTRAINTS	TARGET FOR CONSTRAINT REMOVAL	DEGREE TO WHICH CONSTRAINT IS ACTIONABLE
Bibliographic Accessibility	—nonduplication of key government documents indexes and reference sources —exclusion of government documents from traditional indexes —exclusion of government documents from library catalogs and finding aids —. . .and so forth		
Physical Availability	—closed stacks for government documents, thus no browsing —no portable microfiche readers for lending —inability to circulate government documents —documents area hours of operation less than that of main library —. . .and so forth		
Professional Service	—too many responsibilities to attend continuing education opportunities —inadequate staff size for documents reference service —general reference librarians afraid of government documents —limited knowledge of specific document reference sources and indexes —. . .and so forth		
Status	—noninvolvement in library committees and decision making —need to obtain additional equipment or technology —librarians, administrators, patrons unaware of value of document sources —no budget control by documents librarian for equipment or collection —. . .and so forth		

affecting a specific service or operation, limits or reduces the likelihood that the goals or criteria suggested in Figure 12–1 can be accomplished. This figure, which suggests potential constraints within the context of each of four criteria for integration, seeks to determine the degree to which constraints are "actionable," that is, the degree to which the impact of a specific constraint can be limited. The potential constraints listed in the figure are selective; however, additional constraints within the various criteria will arise, given the individual setting for the documents collection in each library. The purpose of utilizing constraint analysis is to identify which specific areas that affect library services for government publications/information have the best chance of being modified or eliminated. The purpose is to assist librarians in concentrating on specific priorities rather than attempting to attack all issues simultaneously.

By determining the target for constraint removal and the degree to which the constraint is actionable, documents services can be assessed more methodologically. This process encourages a rational approach to determine which constraints have to be identified, who or what is responsible for the constraint, the likelihood that the constraint can be minimized, and, then, possible strategies to be used to minimize the effect of the constraint. Such an approach encourages the identification of priorities so that staff can concentrate their efforts on those areas where change is likely and services can best be improved.

Although the number of personnel typically assigned to government documents activities is small, and in many depositories the staff have an overwhelming amount of work to perform, depository librarians must examine their duties and routines critically. Setting priorities, recognizing that some tasks are less important (not unimportant) than others, and developing plans that will create change in areas that are actionable is necessary. Analysis of constraints can assist in setting priorities and increasing the degree to which documents are successfully integrated with other library and information services.

A second ingredient necessary for analyzing the degree of integration for government publications is to compare resource allocations for government documents collections to those for either the library as a whole or the reference department by itself. This approach is appropriate for those libraries maintaining a separate depository collection. Figure 12–2 suggests a framework by which such a comparison can be made. Until the documents staff identify the degree to which resources are allocated for "similar" services and activities, a meaningful basis for assessing information is difficult to obtain. Further, data from Figure 12–2, then, can be used as a means to justify changes that will increase integration of library and information services for government publications/information.

Four categories, as explained in Figure 12–2, provide a basis to compare resource allocations in the library as a whole, the reference department, and the documents department. Although these criteria suggest quantitative comparisons, a similar chart that stressed qualitative comparison could be developed. For instance, is the condition of the equipment worse, the same, or better than equipment in other areas of the library? Or, are the physical facilities similar for other types of library resources? The point, for both qualitative and quantitative comparison, is to assess the impact of resource allocation on integration.

The comparisons between the documents and reference departments are suggested only as a point of departure. A comparison with other departments within the library may be more appropriate. Further, no statement is being made that the same amount of resources is appropriate for both areas. However, resource allocations are overt statements of funding priorities, and such priorities affect the degree to which integration of government publications can be accomplished. Finally, it should be stressed that an appropriate percentage of resources to be allocated to a depository collection cannot be developed out of context of the organization's goals and objectives. The two preliminary assessment techniques described in this section can provide a basis to set priorities, minimize constraints, and develop techniques to increase overall integration of library and information services related to government publications/information. The documents staff, as well as other library personnel, must all recognize the current degree of integration of government documents and resource allocations before improvement can be made.

INCREASING DOCUMENTS INTEGRATION

Four broad areas must be stressed if the integration of government publications is to be improved:

- *First*, if government publications are to be integrated into the library as a whole, librarians must have a conceptual understanding of the relationship between government information and other library resources
- *Second*, both documents and other librarians must improve their knowledge, skills, and competencies related to the acquisition, organization, marketing, and dissemination of government information
- *Third*, administrative strategies must be employed to provide an organizational climate that encourages the exploitation of government information and assists in the overall internal integration of these important resources
- *Fourth*, external integration (i.e., that occurring outside the library) is necessary.

In this context, the general public, the mass media, and the business community must consider government information as a natural resource to resolve their information needs. The remainder of this section will discuss trends and strategies in those areas that can increase significantly the degree to which government information resources are integrated into library and information services.

Administrative Organization

Identification of where government publications/information resources are located organizationally in the library can be a telling factor that affects the degree of integration. Organizationally, the documents collection should be aligned with, or become part of, a department in the library that is both powerful and involved in decision making. Some possible organizational structures that may assist integration of government publications are:

- *Documents and reference are combined into the same department*; in this situation the head of the department has responsibility for both documents and general reference services
- *Documents as an individual section in the reference department*: in this situation the head of documents reports directly to the head of the reference department
- *Liaison for documents services*: in a nondepository collection, one individual is assigned staff responsibility (advises, coordinates, and

Figure 12-2.
Integration of Government Documents and Allocation of Resources

RESOURCES	ALLOCATED TO THE LIBRARY	ALLOCATED TO REFERENCE DEPT.	ALLOCATED TO GOVMT. DOCS.	PERCENTAGE OF ALLOCATION TO TOTAL LIBRARY REFERENCE	ALLOCATION GOVMT. DOCS.
1. STAFF • professional hours per week • non-professional hours per week • hours of public operation per week • dollar amount expended last fiscal year for professional development					
2. SPACE • square feet of shelving-storage areas • square feet of office-work areas • square feet for reader stations • total assignable square feet					

Figure 12-2. *Continued*

3. EQUIPMENT • current value of all equipment (microforms, major office equipment, automation, and computers) • cost of service contracts for all equipment • last three years of total equipment purchase costs					
4. COLLECTIONS • linear feet shelving and/or drawers • volumes (or equivalents) • circulation (or user contacts)					
5. BUDGET • current annual budget • purchase of reference tools and indexes • non-reference acquisitions • online data base searching					

makes recommendations for all library areas) to ensure effective use of government publications

- *Separate documents department*: this organizational structure is effective only when firm and significant commitments are made to the documents collection. The head of the documents department must have organizational power and be involved in library decision making.

Careful analysis of the organizational structure is important. Such an analysis can either encourage or discourage the degree to which one specific area participates effectively in the system (library) toward the accomplishment of organizational goals (Kast and Rosenzweig, 1985, pp. 233–261).

Under some organizational options, depository staff members report through either the director of public or technical services, or a department head (e.g., that for reference). Although it is difficult to predict where the depository can best be supported and best integrated, an organizational structure that closely relates the documents collection to the reference department is in order. These two areas must be closely coordinated for overall effective service, because staff and users should be able to draw upon the widest amount of available information. Typically such close coordination will occur at an assistant director level, given the broad range of responsibilities already present at that level.

Regardless of the specific organizational structure selected, the criterion for determining effectiveness is the degree to which that structure encourages bibliographic accessibility, physical availability, professional services, and high status of documents. Further, organizational structures may be changed when the goals of the institution or the environment change. If the documents area finds itself in an inappropriate organizational position—for whatever reason—attempts should be made to place it administratively with service-oriented and/or other "powerful departments" and not be "out of sight and out of mind."

Physical Location

Administrative organizational structure does not have to predict the physical location of documents within the library, although such is possible. In short, government publications can be physically located three floors distant from the reference department, yet both could have the same department head. Although physical location of documents will be determined, in large part, by whether documents are treated as a separate collection or are interfiled with other library resources, an attempt should be made to place documents physically in an attractive, central, and visible area within the library.

One temptation that must be avoided at all costs is to loose the integrity of a "separate" documents collection by removing microforms to the microforms departments, placing "high use" periodicals such as the *Monthly Labor Review* in a serials department, and locating the only copies of reference tools such as the *Statistical Abstract of the United States* in the reference department. Such an approach increases the effectiveness of another area of the library at the expense of the documents collection. The concept of the documents area as containing only "unimportant" or "less important" documents is reinforced. A false sense of security emerges; the assumption is that the "best" documents have increased access because they are bibliographically controlled elsewhere in the library. Furthermore, patrons must negotiate various areas of the library, and different staffs must exploit government information resources effectively. And, finally, the documents area may experience problems in relating numerous types and formats of government publications to one another.

The physical location of government publications in close proximity to the reference department appears to be the best means to encourage integration. Unless key reference sources for government publications/information are duplicated for placement at both the main reference desk and the documents area, patrons are not exposed to both types of resources. Further, general reference librarians forget or never develop skills related to documents, and documents librarians lose skills related to general reference, if the two areas do not closely coordinate their activities and services.

Although one might suggest that *interfiling* government publications physically with other types of library resources increases access, conclusive evidence has yet to be produced that a separate or integrated collection of documents is related to increased access, availability, and use. For documents collections that totally integrate all government publications into the general stacks, the physical problem of location is replaced by one of providing adequate bibliographic control.

However, the bibliographic control problem is a difficult one for government publications. First libraries tend to organize collections by publication format rather than information content. And, second, the usefulness of a card catalog for government publications in a library setting has not been adequately studied. Other catalog use studies indicate limited effectiveness of the card catalog, inability of patrons to understand the "rules" by which it is organized, and confusion among librarians concerning the catalog's primary purposes and goals (Lancaster, 1977, pp. 19–68). These difficulties are compounded by the complexities of applying the "main entry concept," especially with the application of Anglo-American Cataloging Rules (AACR-2) to government information resources.

Thus, physical integration and listing government publications in the card catalog *does not* replace the need to use effectively the various specialized reference tools produced by private publishers to gain access to government publications. The historical issue of integrating or separating documents collections from the rest of the library (Waldo, 1977) should not be confused with the issue of providing attractive, visible, and central access to government publications. Both factors affect the degree to which government publications are integrated successfully into library and information services.

Planning and Evaluation of Services

Successful integration of government publications into library and information services will not occur unless a formal written plan is first developed and implemented to accomplish integration. The planning process, which has been detailed elsewhere (McClure et al, 1987), encompasses a review of the institution's mission, the establishment of goals and objectives, the development of programs or activities that accomplish the objectives, and evaluation of the success of those programs vis-a-vis the stated objectives. The typical written plan has the following component parts (McClure, 1982c):

- Philosophy and library mission
- Goals and objectives
- Needs assessment
- Implementation and program development
- Administrative control of the planning process
- Evaluation
- Using study findings to affect change.

Goals and objectives related to improving bibliographic accessibility, physical availability, professional service, and status must be established if overall integration is to be improved, priorities set, and effectiveness increased.

Assuming an organization goal of "providing high quality reference and referral services to library clientele," some typical objectives (measurable and time limited) that might be established as a means to increase integration and respond to that goal are:

- To increase by 15% the number of hours that documents librarians provide public service at the main reference desk within the next year
- To demonstrate online bibliographic database searching techniques unique to government documents databases to 75% of the nondocuments reference librarians
- To purchase one of the *Monthly Catalog* services on CD-ROM for placement in the documents reference area, within this academic year. The strategic placement of this service would be very important. The intent is to obtain the maximum benefit.

These three examples illustrate possible objectives that can be set to increase the degree to which government publications are integrated into the library.

Once objectives are set and the programs initiated, evaluation can occur. Indeed, without stated goals and objectives, overall effectiveness cannot be assessed. Each of the stated objectives should be evaluated in terms of *effectiveness*, i.e., the degree to which they were, in fact, accomplished; and *efficiency*, i.e., the amount of resources (staff time, money, equipment, etc.) necessary to accomplish them. Formal use of the planning process provides a basis for justification and accountability of documents services, a means to assess the amount of change that has occurred. and the degree to which integration is increased. Further, planning and evaluation provide a means to keep "on track" and maintain priorities for what will be done as opposed to what could be done to improve integration (see Chapter 15).

Professional Development and Staff Training

Competent staff that are knowledgeable about government information resources, and have professional attitudes regarding the provision of information services for these resources, are essential if the overall quality of library information services is to be improved. At the professional level, a program of professional development for both documents and nondocuments librarians is necessary. For documents librarians, professional development may involve updating or improving existing skills (e.g., current awareness of new reference tools) or obtaining new skills (e.g., learning how to program a microcomputer to maintain an in-house shelflist of documents reference sources).

An assessment of the current level of knowledge and skills that nondocuments librarians possess must be made. Depending on the results of that assessment, professional development in any of the following areas might be appropriate:

* Increased knowledge about basic documents reference tools
* Advanced training on specific indexes, such as the *American Statistics Index*
* Search strategy techniques for documents
* Organization and bibliographic control of documents
* Review of search strategies for online bibliographic and numeric databases emphasizing government information
* Implementation of online catalog systems for government information
* The structure, organization, and referral services for the depository library program.

Clearly, this list is but a selection of possible topics. In many cases, documents librarians can conduct workshops and/or seminars in-house for other librarians, but, depending on the topic, a need for formal training, attending professional workshops, or classes may be appropriate.

Staff training for paraprofessionals is also essential. All paraprofessionals in the library who might be approached for reference or public services should be knowledgeable about what types of public service questions should be referred to the documents area. They should also know the location of basic parts of the collection, services, and reference sources within the library. Furthermore, they should be familiar with the operation of equipment and have basic interpersonal skills so that they will assist and not frustrate users. A formal program of staff training should be developed and implemented to ensure staff effectiveness (Boss and Raikes, 1982).

In short, both professionals and paraprofessionals must maintain adequate levels of understanding and skills related to government publications/information. In many cases, documents librarians must "educate" other library staff members, both formally and informally, about the mysteries of documents services. In other cases, formal classwork and other types of continuing education (Conroy, 1978) can be utilized to increase the competencies of library staff related to depository collections and services. Either way, an ongoing program of professional and staff development is critical for successful integration of government information resources.

Involvement in Decision Making

Government information resources, which are but one component of the library system, are both affected by and affect other components of that system. Thus, an intangible, yet critical, factor influencing the degree of integration is the extent of personal power and the ability of the documents staff to influence organizational decisions. Documents librarians must be active in the library power structures and affect decisions if they expect to obtain adequate resources for the support of government publications and to increase the awareness of other library staff regarding the importance of government information.

As an example, documents librarians must have some direct control over the budget (e.g., the purchase of reference sources and equipment). Some administrators mistakenly believe that, because government publications (at least in a depository collection) are a free or "cheap" resource, they require no additional budget. Documents librarians are in a position to assess the budgetary needs and requirements related to government publications/information. But to gain the resources necessary to meet these needs, they must have the support of other librarians and library administrators.

There are a number of subtle techniques by which documents librarians can become involved in the library as a whole and become a more effective part of the total library decision making process. First, they must become active on library committees, study groups, or task forces. By serving, for example, on a search committee for another librarian, documents librarians can help ensure that the new staff member has some basic knowledge or appreciation of government information and is willing to learn more about these resources; similar analogies can be made with other committees. Active promotion and communication skills are essential if the case for documents integration is to be made effectively to other library staff. But this promotion must be based on facts and logic if credibility is to be maintained.

Another approach is to *initiate* participation in policy development or long-range planning for the documents department and its relationship to the rest of the library. Documents librarians can request assistance from other librarians and administrators. They can also involve other library staff in program planning or policy development. An assertive stance is required to "get involved," make known the needs and challenges for government publications/information, and offer suggestions to better integrate government information into the library's collections and services. This strategy is especially useful when combined with demonstrating an interest and participation in issues and problems that affect the library as a whole or other library areas.

If successful integration is to occur, documents librarians must "tie-in" to the various mechanisms for decision making, offer suggestions and strategies to increase the importance of government publications, initiate specific recommendations by which these publications can be better integrated into other library services, and promote the importance and usefulness of documents as a resource that responds to the information needs of library clientele. Whatever actions are undertaken should be implemented within the context of organizational goals and objectives.

Marketing

Government publications/information must be marketed both within and outside the library if they are to be integrated successfully with other library and information services. Of special interest to this section is the marketing of government information resources within the library as a means of furthering integration. Simply providing publicity is not the same as developing a marketing approach. Marketing is a process that increases the delivery of library products and services to various target audiences. A target audience is a clearly defined group of individuals within a given market to whom a specific library product or service is intended for delivery and use. The key to successful marketing is knowing what products and services can be pro-

Figure 12-3.
Marketing Contingencies

		INFORMATION SERVICES	
		EXISTING SERVICES AND PRODUCTS	NEW SERVICES AND PRODUCTS
TARGET AUDIENCES	EXISTING TARGET AUDIENCES	1. MARKET PENETRATION	2. INFORMATION SERVICES DEVELOPMENT
	NEW TARGET AUDIENCES	3. TARGET AUDIENCE EXPANSION	4. DIVERSIFICATION

OVERVIEW OF CONTINGENICES:

1. *Market Penetration*: Increase the Percentage of the Existing Target Audience Using Existing Documents Services and Products

2. *Information Services Development*: Establishes New Documents Services and Products for the Existing Target Audiences That Better Address Their Information Needs

3. *Target Audience Expansion*: Increases Use of Existing Documents Services and Products by New Target Audiences for Whom Such Services and Products Are Appropriate

4. *Diversification*: The Library Develops New Information Services and Products for New Target Audiences

Adapted from: Philip Kotler, Marketing for Nonprofit Organizations (Englewood Cliffs, NJ: Prentice Hall, 1975), p. 167, with permission of Harvard Business Review, Inc. where an earlier version appeared by Igor Ansoff, *Harvard Business Review*, September, 1957.

moted effectively by the documents area, matching the awareness and desire to use those products and services, and effective delivery of the services and products (Kotler, 1982; Kotler and Fox, 1985).

An overview of the marketing process suggests two principal concerns that affect the degree to which successful marketing can be accomplished. The first is the identification of target audiences. The documents staff can either target existing audiences or identify (or create) new ones. The second concern relates to services and products. Either the documents staff promote existing products and services, or they must develop new information services and products. By comparing the relationship among these possible variables (see Figure 12–3), four possible marketing strategies are possible.

If the documents staff want to market existing services and products to existing target audiences, the strategy is *market penetration* (cell 1 on the figure). If new services and products are to be developed for existing target audiences, the strategy is *information services development* (cell 2). If existing services and products are to be marketed to new target audiences, the strategy is *target audience expansion* (cell 3). And, if both new target audiences and new services and products are to be developed, the marketing strategy is known as *diversification* (cell 4).

For most documents marketing efforts, the strategy of market penetration (e.g., promoting existing services for existing target audiences) is the norm, although some effort may be made in target audience expansion (e.g., promoting existing services to new target audiences). However, efforts should be made to exploit marketing strategies of information services development and diversification (cells 2 and 4). Documents products and services must be diversified and developed for new target audiences, because documents librarians cannot be content to provide the same products and services to the same target audiences over time.

To develop a marketing plan, specific marketing objectives should be established. In general, marketing objectives concentrate on positioning, costing distribution, and packaging library products. Such objectives focus on:

- The extent to which a product is delivered to a target audience
- The extent to which a product or service is visible to a target audience (e.g., awareness)
- Determining the appropriateness of the cost of the service or product (i.e., the amount of resources the target audience is willing to expend to obtain the product or service)
- The degree to which the product or service is packaged to facilitate ease of use
- The extent to which the product competes against other similar products from competitors.

Developing marketing strategies, with appropriate objectives that answer the issues listed above can help to ensure an effective marketing program for government publications/information.

Ideas and possible promotion strategies abound for government publications and are limited only by one's imagination. Edsall (1980) provides numerous suggestions for marketing library products and services that can be easily applied to government information resources. Another author (Reynolds, 1975) has developed a list of over forty techniques in such areas as document instruction, exhibits, handouts, and publicity. A combination of the practical ideas suggested in these two publications and the marketing concepts presented earlier in this section will provide an excellent basis to market government publications/information within the library and the institution, and to increase integration.

Coordinating Services and Activities

Whether government publications are physically interfiled or separated from the remainder of the collection, close coordination, shared planning/scheduling, and communication between the documents staff and other library staff is critical. In the area of public services, the following examples should be of joint interest to both documents and other librarians:

- Bibliographic instruction
- Programming and outreach services
- Reference and referral
- Online bibliographic database searching.

Broad activities within technical services also must be jointly coordinated:

- Collection development
- Bibliographic control
- Equipment purchases and maintenance
- Processing.

Other areas, of course, lend themselves to coordination, but emphasis should be placed on those areas where either (1) increased public access to government publications/information will result, or (2) increased physical availability to government information resources can be accomplished.

Perhaps the most exciting area for better integration of government publications/information with library services is through various automation projects and the development of online catalog systems that include government publications *and* other library material ("Automatic Bibliographic Control of Government Documents," 1987). Such coordination between government publications and other types of library resources can significantly increase integration, access, and bibliographic control over government publication. However, in a 1987 study of academic libraries with membership in the Association of Research Libraries, only 10% of the respondents indicated that the GPO cataloging tapes were being loaded into any type of automated system at that library (Turner and Latta, 1987). Thus, the prospects for integrating government publications into existing automated systems may be exciting but the reality is that few such efforts have been undertaken.

One important strategy to pursue as a means of increasing coordination for documents library and information services is to "piggy-back" such services with other library and/or institutional services already in place or being planned. The concept of piggy-backing government information resources suggests that documents services and operations are improved by exploiting operations not originally intended for documents but having potential application to government information.

Some examples of piggy-backing include the utilization of computer terminals and equipment outside the documents area—and perhaps outside the library—to perform online bibliographic database searching. The staff might also see that appropriate government information resources are included in outreach programs for senior citizen shut-ins. Furthermore, they might convince other librarians that a simplified cataloging record should be included in any new program for converting library holdings to an online catalog. And, finally, they might use a statistical analysis software program for the mainframe computer (e.g., SAS or SPSS), or a microcomputer (e.g., StatPac, StatView 512+, or SYSTAT), supported by the university or library departments, as a means to analyze the relationship between documents circulation and item-number selections.[1] In each of these instances, the underlying theme is for the documents area to utilize resources, supplies, equipment, and personnel primarily dedicated to the provision of nondocuments services.

The above examples have stressed the coordination and piggy-backing of documents largely within the library and parent institution. However, documents librarians must also take a broader view. They must realize that a number of activities at the state and Federal levels affect documents integration. For instance, how effective is the local state library association's government documents group in lobbying the state legislature and appropriate agencies for improved bibliographic control? And, on another front, how many documents librarians within a given region have shared resources, obtained joint funding, or otherwise cooperated to produce better public access and availability to government publications/information?

If better coordination and piggy-backing of government publications services is to occur, the documents staff must:

- Have flexible goals and objectives that prioritize activities but permit unique and innovative approaches for the accomplishment of stated objectives
- Identify the areas (both within and outside the library) where available resources can be coordinated and piggy-backed onto documents services
- Re-tool or re-educate themselves, if necessary, to exploit available institutional or area resources (e.g., learn statistical skills to tie into the university computer system and to use a statistical software package)
- Leave the confines of the documents area, work with a broad range of information professionals, and be assertive in proposing strategies for coordinating and piggy-backing documents services.

Because a significant proportion of resources for library and information services will not be allocated specifically for government information resources, the documents staff must learn to tap into available resources—

---

[1] See Hernon and Richardson (1988) for a discussion of statistical software. This work identifies and discusses over 50 packages for the microcomputer.

regardless of the source of funding and the location of government publications within the local information handling environment.

INCREASED INTEGRATION

The first step toward increased integration of government publications/information into library services is to recognize the value of these resources as important and able to resolve clientele information needs. Next, documents librarians and other information access professionals must understand the complexities related to increasing integration. As suggested earlier, criteria of integration include bibliographic and physical accessibility, professional service, and status. To increase integration of documents, all four of these criteria must be considered within a systems framework. Under that framework, each component is interdependent with other components, all components facilitate the accomplishment of overall integration, and the sum of their interactions (e.g., integration) is a result of more than simply each individual component; the sum includes the effects of their interactions.

The next step is to assess the existing degree of integration of documents in terms of constraints affecting the criteria outlined in Figure 12–1. When this type of a "constraint analysis" is accomplished, the documents staff will have an excellent idea of what specific constraints should be targeted for removal, and which ones have the best chance of being minimized. After analyzing existing library resources available for the documents area (see Figure 12–2), specific budget areas that affect successful integration of documents can be identified.

Based on these two analytic techniques, specific strategies for increasing the degree of documents integration throughout the library can be developed. Some of the most likely areas for targeting such strategies include:

- Administrative organization
- Physical location
- Planning and evaluation of services
- Professional development and staff training
- Involvement in decision making
- Marketing
- Coordinating services and activities.

Without question, government information resources can be better integrated into library and information services by implementing the suggestions given in this chapter. Further, numerous other strategies and areas also can be identified where significant payoffs for increased documents integration can be obtained.

The benefits from increased integration of government publications/information into library and information services are both wide-reaching and significant. First, the library's clientele will have greater access to a broader range of high quality information resources. Second, librarians and other information access professionals will become more knowledgeable about the importance, quality, and applications of government publications/information as reference resources. And, perhaps more importantly, successful integration of government information provides the basis by which the public more easily obtains information necessary for effective participation in an open and democratic society.

Such benefits from integration occur only when government information is considered to be as important and valuable as other information resources. As Fry (1978, p. 13) stated, "library administrators need to consider government document collections [as] an information resource on an equal basis with books and serials." To accomplish this goal calls for a strategy to increase the degree of integration of documents into library and information services. Only when documents librarians and other information access professionals adopt such a strategy will public access and availability to government publications/ information be increased, and these resources be exploited for their unique and important information content.

13

Physical Facilities and Space Management

For many documents librarians, the topic of physical facilities management and space planning translates into strategies to "get better facilities and find more space." The management of facilities and space has taken on increased importance in depository collections because many of these collections have inadequate space, continue to receive large quantities of government publications, and are unlikely to acquire additional space for collection expansion in the near future. In addition, libraries receive new information technologies and staff must decide where to place the hardware and how it should be integrated with other physical facilities for maximum effectiveness (Boss, 1987).

Access, use, and, to some extent, degree of patron satisfaction with library housed government information resources must be considered in light of the physical facilities and space provided for these materials. The psychological and physical atmosphere in which patrons attempt to use a collection affects library use. As Cohen (1980, p. 190) notes,

> Too many librarians have raised the collection and the tools of the trade to icons. . . . Although few realize it, the interiors, the furnishings, and equipment within a library modify the ability of the institution to adequately utilize and display its wares.

The "principle of least effort," as detailed by Zipf (1949), governs the use of many library collections. This factor is especially important and should be "carefully taken into account in the planning of library buildings and in the allocation of storage space" (Lancaster, 1977, p. 319).

276

The physical facilities for housing and servicing government information resources must be carefully planned and encourage access to materials rather than be a hindrance. Physical facilities include all equipment, furniture, storage materials, and user-service items in which either information resources are housed or from which information services are provided. In a budgetary sense, physical facilities are capital expenses, that is, expenses that are one-time and non-recurring. Stacks, reader stations, card catalog files, microform readers and printers, display cases, service desks, and so forth are illustrative of such considerations.

Space management is a process whereby the placement of physical facilities and services within a given area maximizes access to the information resources and encourages library staff to provide accurate and effective information services. Thus, the arrangement, organization, and relationship of physical facilities, as well as information services and sources, are primary areas for attention when considering space management for government information collections.

Other chapters have drawn attention to a number of factors affecting access to government information resources over which librarians have limited control, e.g., bibliographic control by Federal agencies, distribution procedures, and Federal information policy. But physical facilities and space management are one area where local librarians and library administration can *directly* affect the excellence of the collection, its organization and access to the information resources. Further, while some librarians might suggest that improved physical facilities and space management are a result only of financial considerations, this chapter stresses that strategies requiring limited budgetary increases can lead to significant improvements.

Government information collections that are separated from other library collections present unique problems and challenges related to physical facilities. Documents collections that are integrated into the main collection rely on physical facilities and space allocation in an entirely different context than do materials that are separated. Therefore, this chapter will discuss physical facilities and space management considerations in the context of separate government information collections, those that are typically depository collections.

The purpose of this chapter is to provide an overview and introduction to assessing and improving physical facilities and space management for government information collections. Procedures will be suggested by which documents librarians can assess the current status of physical facilities and space allocation in the documents area. Next, selected issues related to physical facilities and space management will be reviewed in terms of their effect on access to collections and services. After a discussion of specific concerns for facilities and space related to microformatted government publications, the chapter concludes by encouraging documents librarians to develop specific strategies for improving physical facilities and space management.

ASSESSMENT OF CURRENT SITUATION

Before the physical facilities and space allocation for government information collections can be improved, one must first examine the current situation. In general, space utilization can be described in terms of one of the following three areas:

- *Stacks area*: dedicated primarily to the storage and organization of government information resources
- *Public services area*: dedicated primarily to the provision of information services to patrons, including reader stations, information desks, catalogs, index tables, microform readers-printers, and copying machines
- *Staff work areas*: dedicated primarily to the processing and servicing of government information resources, including staff offices/work tables, processing/holding of sources in preparation for placement in stacks area, and production of bibliographic records.

Assessment of space and physical facilities in terms of these three areas enables documents librarians to better match the use of facilities and the allocation of resources to the purposes for which the facilities and space are dedicated.

The relationship between structure and function should also be kept in mind when assessing the current allocation of space and facilities to the documents collection (Cohen and Cohen, 1981, pp. 76–90). Structure comprises the arrangement, the relationship of physical facilities and space to other factors in the area as well as to the library in general, and the manner in which facilities are organized within the area. Function is simply the purpose for which something is intended, e.g., what is expected to be accomplished with this particular piece of equipment? Both factors must be considered together when assessing the overall strengths and weaknesses of the collection, since there is frequently a trade-off relationship between them.

Finally, the assessment of physical facilities and space cannot be made in isolation of the goals and objectives of the government information collection and the library as a whole. For example, a collection that includes all depository microfiche will require different physical facilities and space allocations than one in which the microfiche are organized and made available from a central microforms area. Although every collection may present unique characteristics that impact on structural and functional arrangements of space and facilities, a number of general assessment techniques can be suggested to review current facilities and space allocation.

Identification of Equipment and Support Facilities

Many institutions regularly inventory equipment and support facilities in order to:

- Assess the location of each item
- Evaluate its condition
- Maintain a central record of the item's status
- Review the appropriateness of the item staying in its current location, being removed or replaced.

Conducting a regular inventory of equipment and support facilities for the government information collection is essential for determining the appropriateness of the equipment for the services and objectives of the collection.

Figure 13–1, which outlines an inventory form to be used in a government information collection, identifies and describes the major pieces and condition of equipment and support facilities in the area. In general, such items fall into the categories specified. The first is stacks, and the objective here is to identify the total number of double-sided shelving sections or equivalents in the area, and the amount of linear shelf space that is available. Another objective is to describe any specific shelving areas in the collection.

The second part of the figure attempts to identify any cabinets that are used for storage and organization of information resources, such as vertical files, microform cabinets, or map cabinets. The inventory information needed for this category includes a description of the condition of the item, the purchase price and date, a description of the storage capacity (in terms of the number of items of linear feet of storage available in the cabinet), and an identification or inventory number if assigned. The third category inventories cabinets, filing cabinets, credenzas, lockers, and storage facilities.

The next category of materials, which includes microform equipment, covers all readers/viewers and printers, as well as any tables or furniture used expressly for microforms. For each item, the name and model should be identified, along with a description of its working condition, the purchase price and date, and any identification or inventory control number. The same descriptive information should also be provided for any computer-related equipment such as online terminals, microcomputers, or terminals for bibliographic utilities.

Finally, an inventory of major public service furniture, including study carrels, chairs, and tables should be made. It is especially important to

Figure 13-1.
Inventory of Major Equipment and Support Facilities

A. *STACKS*
   1. Total Number of Double-sided Shelving Sections: _____
   2. Total Linear Feet of Shelving: _____
   3. Display Shelving (Vertical) in Linear Feet: _____
   4. Shelving for Specific Areas, e.g., Reference:

Area	Linear Feet of Shelving

B. *STORAGE CABINETS* (For Information Sources)

	Description/ Condition	Purchase Price/Date	Storage Capacity	ID Number
Hardcopy Files				
Microforms				
1. Microfilm				
2. Microfiche				
3. Microcard				
Maps				

C. *OTHER STORAGE CABINETS* (SUPPLIES)

	Description	Condition	ID Number

D. *MICROFORM EQUIPMENT*

	Name/Model	Description/ Condition	Purchase Price/Date	ID Number
Readers				
Printers				
Tables				

E. *COMPUTER-RELATED EQUIPMENT*

	Name/Model	Description/ Condition	Purchase Price/Date	ID Number
Terminals				
Microcomputers				
Bibliographic Util- ities				

F. *PUBLIC SERVICES FURNITURE*

	Seating Capacity	Description/ Condition	ID Number
Study Carrels			
Chairs			
Tables			

G. *OTHER MAJOR EQUIPMENT SUPPORT FACILITIES*

	Description/ Condition	Purchase Price/Date	ID Number
Card Catalog			
Files			
Kardex			
Copiers			
. . . and so forth			

determine both seating capacity and the condition of the furniture. Other major pieces of equipment, such as card catalogs and a Kardex, should also be identified. Specific criteria for all the items described (e.g., appearance, working condition, ease of use, and age) can be listed and the condition of these items assessed.

Each library will want to add and delete types of equipment and support facilities as appropriate and as needed. Nonetheless, this type of an inventory is essential for documents librarians to gain a general sense of the amount, type, and condition of current equipment in the area. More specifically, with these data, librarians will have a factual basis to:

- Determine the overall dollar value of the equipment currently located in the documents collection
- Provide a general assessment of the working condition of equipment that patrons must use to gain access to the collection
- Assess the quality of the equipment in terms of its appearance and reliability
- Provide a basis for comparing the allocation of equipment and support facilities to the documents collection versus other areas of the library.

Of course, knowing what equipment is available to support the government information collection is not the same as knowing how well that equipment supports the objectives and activities of that collection.

Physical Arrangement

After completing an inventory of equipment and support facilities, a diagram or floor plan of the documents area should be made. The floor plan simply illustrates the actual available floor space in the documents area, and the location of the physical facilities within that area. One of the easiest approaches is to first make a skeletal outline of the area to be diagrammed, and only include the borders of the documents area, nonmovable walls, and other physical items that cannot be moved or re-arranged. In many cases, documents librarians can obtain the original floor plans or "bluelines" used to build the area in which the documents are currently housed and simply copy the skeletal outline from those plans. Regardless of which approach is taken, the floor plan should be drawn to scale—usually one-quarter or one-eighth inch to a foot. By developing such an outline floor plan, copies can be made that, at a later time, can be used as a basis for designing new arrangements without constantly having to redraw the skeletal configuration.

A floor plan should be developed for physical equipment, furniture, stacks, work areas, etc., as currently organized in the area. After this task has been completed, a number of basic questions related to physical arrangement can be answered:

- What is the total square footage allocated to the government information collection, and how is that square footage allocated among:
  - Stacks and storage of materials (including microforms)
  - Staff work and office area
  - Readers' services and study carrels?
- Are clear functional areas or activities organized together, or are various functions (storage, work, and service) intermingled throughout the collection?
- Is the storage and arrangement of materials logical and easy to follow? What provisions for control over materials and the offering of services have been made?
- Are the various service points in the area clearly identified and located in close proximity to materials or equipment for which they are responsible?
- Are public access and staff used computer stations in easily accessible locations that allow users to work effectively at the computers/terminals?
- Do patrons have study tables or carrels where they can use the materials without undue disturbance and interruptions?
- Do staff have work/office areas where they can perform duties effectively without disturbing patrons using the collection?

These, of course, are but a few of the questions that can be posed when assessing the current floor plan of a library area. Additional questions and issues to consider can be found in a number of works that deal specifically with space and physical facilities (Leighton and Weber, 1986; Cohen and Cohen, 1979; Lushington and Mills, 1979). The overriding concern, however, is, "Do the current space and physical facilities allow and encourage the documents staff to provide effective information services, adequate access to resources, and a comfortable environment that encourages use of resources both today and in the foreseeable future?

Special attention should be given to assessing the relationship among the activities (service objectives) to be accomplished and their physical organization and arrangement in the documents area. The collection should not constitute an "obstacle course," and efficiencies in design must be recognized (Strain, 1979). By use of a "bubble" diagram superimposed over the floor plan, documents librarians can easily see the:

- Relative position among functional areas of the collection and physical location
- Degree to which the functional activities are encouraged or hindered by their location and relationship to other functional areas
- Arrangement of user services vis-a-vis other functions
- Percentage of space that is allocated to the support of various functions.

Figure 13–2 is an example of a "bubble" diagram superimposed over the skeletal floor plan of a documents collection. This particular example shows clearly separated functional areas that are centralized and not dispersed throughout the entire collection. Further, the functional areas depicted in each of the bubbles flow together naturally and suggest a logic or organization that the patron can understand.

Floor plans and "bubble" diagrams are especially useful to obtain "the big picture" of how an area is organized, and the manner in which the available space is allocated. The technique is especially useful to assess the collection in terms of user services, reader stations, study carrels, and other area designations that affect the patron directly. A floor plan that is "chopped up" into many similar functional areas in different locations impedes access, confuses the user, and becomes difficult to service and organize effectively.

Traffic and Use Patterns

Another area for assessment is the manner in which users move through the documents area, and the frequency and type of use made of the various equipment and facilities. Knowledge of these factors can assist documents librarians in better understanding user needs, user preference(s) for specific types of services and facilities, and the appropriateness of the existing facilities for meeting such needs.

Figure 13-2.
Bubble Diagram of Government Publications Area

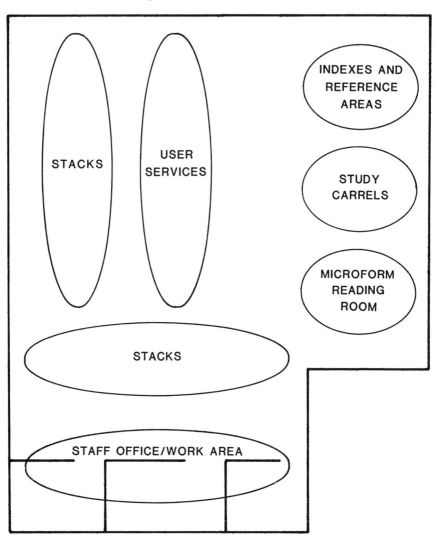

When considering the traffic and use patterns of the documents area, a number of general suggestions can be offered:

- Clustering of similar activities in the same general physical area should be encouraged

- Adequate provision for control and supervision over special materials and services (such as microforms) should be provided
- Reader stations and study areas should be removed from traffic flow and user-assistance areas
- Staff work areas should be removed, as much as possible, from reader stations and study areas
- Patrons should be able to locate indexes and key service areas such as reference and circulation immediately upon entering the area
- Appropriate noise reduction techniques, lighting, and access to equipment should encourage use of equipment without impinging upon activities in other areas
- Stacks should be logically arranged in one sequence that can be easily traced throughout the collection.

Further, a clear arrangement of physical facilities that encourages central traffic flows with secondary feeder routes can assist patrons in locating necessary resources and in using available services more effectively.

A number of techniques can be used to assess current traffic flows and use of existing equipment. First and foremost are those techniques that rely on direct observation of traffic flow and use. With the basic floor plan (discussed above), unobtrusive observation of the number of people using specific areas, equipment, and services can lead to a tally of use for various times of the day. Further, mapping of the primary traffic flows within the area can also be done on the floor plan. In short, a matrix can be produced. It shows how many people used (or were serviced at) specific areas/equipment in the library, at what times during the day, and for what specific duration. Hall (1978) and Roberts (1978) describe how such an analysis can be performed.

Another technique to assess equipment and facilities usage is to conduct a work sampling. Although intended primarily to determine the amount of time staff spend on performing various job-related activities, the methodology can also be applied to use of equipment and facilities (Goodell, 1975). For example, at randomly determined times during the day, a tally can be maintained of the number of people using the microfiche readers, the number waiting in queue to use the machines, and the percentage of time that such equipment is broken or otherwise unavailable for use. Similarly, a work sampling of the various services offered in the documents area, such as reference and online searching, can be conducted. In addition to having a better understanding of traffic and use, documents librarians can evaluate the scheduling of staff to specific responsibilities and the appropriateness of equipment to user needs. They can also compare the reliability of different types of equipment as a basis for future purchases.

Assessment of traffic and use patterns by both the staff and patrons can significantly improve physical access to materials as well as the utilization of space in the documents area. As with the other assessment techniques suggested, empirical data collection and analysis are essential if successful evaluation and improvements are to be accomplished.

ADDITIONAL ISSUES AFFECTING ADEQUATE PHYSICAL FACILITIES

The assessment techniques suggested above will assist documents librarians in identifying specific areas and topics to improve the physical facilities for, and arrangement of, government information resources. However, a number of issues related to improved facilities should be briefly discussed and considered. The following issues, although not comprehensive, are especially important for planning adequately for tomorrow's space, equipment, and facilities needs related to the government information collection.

Space Planning

Given the large number of government information resources available, documents librarians must *plan* for an orderly growth and control over the documents collection. Formulae have been suggested for the number of documents typically found in a linear foot. For instance, the number of pieces in the collection divided by total linear feet of shelving provides the average number of documents per linear foot. For most depository collections, this average is between 45 and 55 documents per linear foot (Reynolds, 1979, p. 99). Once such a figure is computed, the converse can be applied, i.e., knowing how many documents are received per year, or expected to be received in the next year, can yield an estimate of how many linear feet of shelving will be necessary. For microfiche, one inch of filing space contains 56 diazo microfiche in individual microfiche envelopes, with a weight of approximately one-half pound, or 43 microfiche envelopes with 86 microfiche packed two per envelope, with a weight of approximately three quarters of a pound (Hernon, 1981, p. 202).

Because it is unlikely that the majority of documents collections will be allocated additional space endlessly, appropriate strategies will be necessary to control needed space and to project the amount of space needed in forthcoming years (Daehn, 1982). Thus, the number of documents obtained, the need for weeding, carefully developed collection development policies, and effective space utilization of existing facilities become critical factors for documents collections. If strategies are not initiated to manage this influx of space requirements, documents collections will be increasingly consumed by a warehouse or storage function rather than the provision of user and information services.

Renovation and Rearrangement

Since the early 1970s, fewer resources have been made available for the construction of new library buildings or obtaining increased space. For many libraries, the best chance to increase space utilization for documents collections is to renovate and rearrange existing facilities. The first section of this chapter may assist documents librarians in assessing the strengths and weaknesses of existing physical facilities without having to hire building consultants or obtain enlarged and new quarters.

In many instances, physical facilities and space utilization can be improved simply by rearranging the layout, functions, and location of resources and services within the area already established for the documents collection. For a relatively small capital investment, collections can be moved or shifted easily (Amodeo, 1983) with significantly increased access to the collections, better organization of resources, and a more logical arrangement of resources and services vis-a-vis the physical constraints of the building. For example, running the order of resources in stacks in a snake-like arrangement up to a wall (instead of leaving an aisle against the wall) can add a significant amount of shelf space. Regardless of the specific technique, documents librarians, at least for the foreseeable future, are likely to have to rely on internal renovation and rearrangement techniques, with minimal capital outlays, to increase the effectiveness of existing physical facilities.

Automation Considerations

To obtain maximum access to documents collections, increased reliance on information handling technologies is necessary (see Chapter 7). Thus, libraries will have to consider space management of microcomputers, terminals, printers, and other such equipment, while looking at the impact of technology on employees and the work environment. Consideration of ergonomics, "the design of equipment for worker's health and comfort . . . the study of worker's relationships to their physical environment" (Cohen and Cohen, 1981, p. 63), will be essential if government information collections are to exploit information handling technologies.

Thus, an entirely new perspective on the organization of physical facilities will be necessary in the near future to accommodate the automated office and a vast array of information handling equipment. Indeed, the term "configuration" is used to discuss the manner in which microcomputers are physically organized and arranged for the most effective use of terminals, wordprocessing, electronic mail, telefacsimile, online database searching, and other technologies. Special equipment and furniture that support different technologies (to say nothing of electrical circuitry, heating, lighting, ventilation, and other factors) should be considered in developing automation related facilities. Any plans for renovation and rearrangement of physical facilities should carefully consider factors related to information handling technologies. Library staff should consult appropriate textbooks (see, for example, Cohen and Cohen, 1981) to make certain that the renovated facility of today meets the requirements of the automated facility of tomorrow.

PHYSICAL FACILITIES FOR MICROCOMPUTERS

Hernon and McClure (1986) provide an overview of decision making that merit attention in creating an environment more conducive for use of microcomputers. Boss (1987) expands upon their introduction and discusses automated office procedures. He also presents space requirements, layout considerations, and electrical and telecommunications requirements for automated library systems. Additional chapters address space requirements for optical media and telefacsimile, as well.

Ergonomics factors must be considered within the following broad areas that tend to interact with each other:

- *Microcomputer hardware*: including such factors as screen glare, adjustable height of video display terminal, color, and location of keys
- *Microcomputer software*: including factors such as ease of use, display, and level of competency needed to operate the program
- *Work environment*: including adjustable lighting, proper viewing distance, privacy, and surrounding noise levels
- *Employee comfort and safety*: including amount of continuous time at the microcomputer workstation, rest periods, and electrical hazards.

Recent research has demonstrated that appropriate ergonomic considerations related to the use of computerized systems produce significant increases in worker job performance and overall organizational productivity (Westin et al, 1985, pp. 9–4 to 9–7).

However, successful intervention strategies require:

- An awareness on the part of the library staff that ergonomic considerations must be addressed
- Recognition that organizational resources will have to be spent on the provision of ergonomically sound work environments
- A willingness to review periodically, as an ongoing process, the ergonomics of the microcomputer workstation environment.

Further, library administrators will have to recognize that different individuals may require different ergonomic conditions; an effective work environment for one may not be effective for another.

The introduction of significant technological change calls for restructured jobs. Specific techniques to assess the workflow and technologically based jobs have been described elsewhere (Kesner and Jones, 1984). Indeed, the microcomputer can reduce some of the tedious, repetitive work, free up time for more "professional activities," and allow staff members to have more direct control over what activities are to be performed.

Galitz (1984) presents criteria that should be considered when restructuring a job as a result of greater use of technology. Job design therefore becomes important; it increased job satisfaction and motivation, and provides for job enrichment. Further, job design is an important strategy to reduce work anxiety related to technostress. Clearly, attention to human and administrative factors related to successful microcomputer-based library decision making is essential if effectiveness, efficiency, and individual productivity are to be increased.

PHYSICAL FACILITIES FOR MICROFORMATTED GOVERNMENT PUBLICATIONS

A coherent plan for government information collections must cover the storage, organization, and equipment support necessary for accessing microformatted government publications. Although local constraints will vary from collection to collection, a plan for microform areas must consider trade-off relationships among costs, user services, and staff efficiencies (Roselle, 1982). Many of the general observations offered in the preceding section of this chapter apply to microform facilities; however, some unique factors can assist documents librarians in improving physical facilities for microformatted government publications.

Location

A basic consideration is finding a suitable location in the library for microformatted government publications. Typically, three primary alternatives are possible. Inevitably, however, location is based on the broader issue of centralizing/decentralizing microforms (Folcarelli et al, 1982, pp. 118–124). All microformatted government publications can be either housed in the documents area or centralized as part of a library microcollection outside the documents area. A third approach, a combination of the first two alternatives, provides a central microform area but allows certain "special" sources to be maintained in the documents area.

From the vantage point of documents librarians, the first alternative usually is the most attractive. This approach allows specialized staff to assist the patron in using resources that are frequently hard to find, loosely controlled, and organized in a complex fashion. However, since the patron may not recognize the difference between microformatted government documents and other types of microforms, some confusion may result. Furthermore, a number of series from agencies such as the GPO and the General Accounting Office are partially in one format or the other, necessitating that they be maintained together; and, of course, there is duplication with other areas in the library due to equipment purchase, staffing, etc.

The second approach may be promoted by the library administration, because it is often less costly to centralize all microforms in one place. But, a likely problem is that the microform area turns into a warehouse regarding government publications—there they remain because no one is immediately available to explain their use, refer to appropriate indexes, or suggest alternative avenues of search. Unless there is excellent cooperation between the documents and microforms areas, or unless the microform librarian is skilled with government publications, the patron is likely to be the loser when documents are placed in the microforms area.

The combined approach is a compromise that typically satisfies no one and creates more problems than it solves. It has most of the costs of the decentralized approach without all the advantages. The primary difficulty is determining which items go where—with some in microforms and some in documents. Excellent bibliographic finding aids are required, but patrons may feel more like pin-balls as they bounce back and forth between the two areas.[1]

The ideal location of microformatted government publications appears to be built around the first alternative: locate them in the documents area, or at least close enough for them to be serviced by documents personnel. Obviously, more total space will be needed to store and organize these sources. An enclosed room, or a "room" made out of microstorage cabinets, can be established. Emphasis must be placed on user services, and this approach encourages both use and service.

Space Requirements

A critical consideration of facilities design is, "How big an area must be dedicated to storage and use of microformatted government publications?" If the documents area is to establish a section devoted to microformatted pub-

---

[1] For example, the GPO distributes bills and resolutions on microfiche, with the accompanying finding aid in paper copy. Without careful planning, documents librarians and patrons may have to negotiate two areas of the library to find the desired bill or resolution.

lications, some reasonable estimates of (1) how many sources will be in the area, and (2) how many people are expected to use the area, must be made.

The first step requires a careful definition of what specific sources will go into this area. Some or all of the following may be included here:

- GPO microfiche
- Federal agency microforms (GAO, NASA, NTIS, ERIC, DOE, etc.)
- Private sector sets of microfilm, microfiche, and microprint (e.g., CIS and Readex)
- State/local government microforms
- National/informational government microforms.

Depending on how one defines "microformatted government publication," there could be a broad range of sources stored in this area.

The second step, then, requires an inventory of how many microformatted sources are currently held in the documents area, as well as throughout the library. The sources can be inventoried by recording the number of linear feet of micro-sources (including Readex microprint, microfilm, etc.). The total of these estimates can then be translated into the number of drawers for microfiche or microfilm, or linear feet of shelving. A cabinet ten drawers high measuring 23 in. long × 28 in. wide by 51 in. high will store 1,350 16mm rolls of microfilm, or 900 35mm rolls of microfilm. A cabinet with identical dimensions but eight drawers will store 41,600 4 in. × 6 in. or 3 in. × 5 in. microfiche cards (Youngren, 1976).

A third step is to estimate the next five years' potential growth of microformatted material. This can be done by looking at how many sources were added during the past two-three years and getting a rough idea of yearly growth. Single collection purchases anticipated over the next few years, estimates of linear feet of microfiche to be shipped from the GPO, and an additional safety factor of at least 25% should be included. Depending on the type of filing system and cabinet manufacturer, an estimate of the number of cabinets required and of their square footage can be made. Provision should also be made to include three to five square feet of access in front of each linear foot of cabinet drawers for physical access to open drawers. Storage requirements for current and future holdings can be estimated by adding all of this together.

A space estimate also must be made for the area needed to provide reader services. Possible items in this category include:

- Reader stations
- Desk-study stations
- Indexes and bibliographic aids area
- Copying services.

The principle items, of course, are viewing stations and writing areas. Two factors will determine space requirements here. The first is the number of patrons to accommodate at the same time, and second is the amount of micro-related equipment that will be available for use.

An estimate of 30–35 square feet for one reader station, that includes enough room to make notes while using a reader, is reasonable. By multiplying this figure by the number of people expected to be served, and/or by the number of equipment stations, an estimate of space requirements for reader services can be made (see Leighton and Weber, 1986).

The two totals (one for materials storage and the other for readers' services) will give a rough estimate of the number of square feet required for the microformatted documents area. This will be a bare bones estimate in that it assumes no space for reference assistance, staff work area, or circulation/control. These operations would be absorbed in the established areas of the documents department. The estimate of space requirements as described above is less than ideal, but more than expedient.

Physical Arrangement

The microformatted government publications area must be located within or adjacent to the documents department to provide high quality service. Ideally, a corner area could be enclosed by the use of office partition furniture. Use of such partitions allows the area to be easily remodeled, expanded, or otherwise changed. A number of librarians have preferred to have microform storage cabinets serve as "walls" for such an area. Unfortunately, this technique is less changeable and not as effective, as partitions, for noise reduction and light control.

Control and supervision of the area should be performed by the staff in the documents department. Therefore, a single entrance/exit to the area via the documents department is most effective. The area should also allow, or encourage, assistance from staff; to do so, the area should be located in close proximity to a service point such as a reference area. Although staff members will probably not have to remain within the microformatted area either to supervise or control access to sources, they should be immediately accessible for assistance.

In general, the layout of a microform area should be simple. A patron entering the area should be able to understand the basic arrangement and functions easily. Areas that should be easily identified include storage, viewing, copying, and librarian assistance (Boss and Raikes, 1981, p. 58; Boss, 1987). As previously suggested, the microformatted documents area is really composed of two separate areas. The first is a storage area for microforms; and the second is a viewing/use area. Because the purpose of the two areas

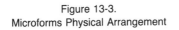

Figure 13-3.
Microforms Physical Arrangement

differs, so too do the arrangement and control of each. Figure 13–3 presents one approach to providing an orderly physical arrangement and layout that encourages use and access to microforms.

In addition to storage considerations, patrons who are viewing microforms should not be disturbed by noise, traffic, or other distractions associated with the finding of specific microforms. Nothing is more annoying than trying to concentrate on reading microforms while the librarian and another patron are rummaging around looking for a specific source. Furthermore, cabinets need at least 3 feet of front access space. This can easily infringe on space allocation for the reading area. Finally, persons studying/reading a microform should have as much privacy as possible.

Individual reader stations with separate study lights are preferred. The temptation to place long rows of tables in the reading area should be avoided; instead, space out the various viewers and leave table area for note-taking. Tables may be too high for comfortable note-taking; small tables placed perpendicular to the reader (on either the left or the right) are much more comfortable for writing; and table rows do not provide the same sense of privacy as individual carrels. Provision of "extras," such as portable tables

Figure 13-4.
Microviewing Area

with typewriters and other amenities, helps to overcome the inherent hesitancy patrons might have toward the use of microforms. Figure 13–4 provides an example of a well-organized and attractive area for microviewing.

The actual location of readers within the reading area can be improved by grouping similar machine types next to each other. Such a strategy allows patrons easily to determine which reader will provide them with the "best" image on a comparative basis. If possible, chairs that can be adjusted for height should be available, in order that taller and shorter individuals can be comfortable while viewing microforms. Finally, each machine should be numbered (for quick identification when one breaks down or needs repair) and described. The machines should include easy to understand operating instructions.

Equipment and Storage

Considerations regarding equipment for microformatted government publications fall into three basic categories. The first is equipment for storage; the second is equipment for processing, bibliographic control, and dissemination; and the third is equipment for reader viewing and use. The comments in this section are intended as basic considerations and are not a comprehensive account of required equipment.

Storage equipment will be the easiest category to identify. Myriad companies produce high quality storage equipment for microforms. In general, microfiche and microfilm cabinets and standard shelving units must be obtained. Manufacturers currently produce microfilm cabinets that stand on top of existing cabinets; they open in a vertical shelving arrangement and are excellent space savers, since they do not occupy additional floor space.

The storage area must be logically organized and established so that users can find, and gain access to, the desired source on their own. Typical arrangements of source material will depend on the method of bibliographic control practiced by the specific library. However, GPO microfiche can be arranged by Sudocs number, and other source material simply by accession number. These accession numbers can be either created by the library or incorporated from an agency number such as that used by ERIC or NTIS.

The organization and arrangement of cabinets can be frustrating, because the various manufacturers do not standardize height, width, and length. Because of this factor, one should carefully determine, when purchasing cabinets from different manufacturers: (1) how they will look next to each other, (2) if space above the cabinet can be utilized for vertical drawer cabinets, (3) if internal drawer arrangements are consistent among cabinets, and (4) the specific number of microformatted items that can be stored in the cabinet. Figure 13–5 shows an example of a well-organized and efficient storage area.

Care should be taken to ensure that the filing of the actual microforms is logical and consistent throughout all the storage facilities. Materials should be filed front to back, left to right, top to bottom, throughout. Drawers must be clearly labeled, with index cards scattered liberally throughout the contents of a drawer for the quick identification of specific sources. This procedure reduces the number of times that an individual microform has to be removed simply to identify its class or accession number, and, thus, reduces the probability that an item will be misfiled on its return. Figure 13–6 shows an example of a well-organized microfiche file drawer with, easy-to-read labels and easy access.

Necessary processing equipment includes spool-to-spool viewers for fast quality control or inspection of microfilm, hand viewers for quick viewing of microfiche, and a collection of low acid empty spools, microfiche jackets, splicing equipment, etc. Additional items to organize the collection (a Kardex, card catalog, and other finding aids) may be necessary (Saffady, 1985, pp. 64–83; Boss, 1987).

As a part of the processing equipment, librarians must consider the provision of printers—in a number of forms. Reader-printers for microfiche, microfilm, and microcards will be necessary in order that individuals may quickly obtain legible copies of anything they are viewing in a microformat. Furthermore, with the increased amount of items produced on microfiche and the number of individuals or organizations having microfiche readers, a

Figure 13-5.
Microforms Storage Area

fiche-to-fiche duplicator also is a necessity. Fiche-to-fiche duplicators are becoming affordable and make excellent copies. And, because many government publications do not carry copyright, they are legally reproducible in whole or in part.

Finally, a number of viewing machines will be necessary. Readers for microfilm, microfiche, and microcards must be easily available to users, and patrons should not have to "commute" around the library to use a reader. Readers should have various magnification lenses for proper viewing. Further, the availability of portable microfilm/microfiche readers is essential. Since many government publications are available only in a microformat, documents librarians must encourage their circulation and use by providing equipment that can be checked out. There is no reason why both microfiche and a portable reader cannot be loaned to patrons. For a discussion of reducing resistance to microforms and changing usage patters, see Boss (1987).

Figure 13–7 offers a summary of criteria for the selection and evaluation of microform readers and printers. Special analyses in *Library Technology Reports* (Chicago: American Library Association) contain additional criteria for evaluating micro-related equipment.

Figure 13-6.
Organization of a Microfiche File Drawer

Additional Considerations

Because of the unique nature of microformatted publications, the design of adequate facilities must take into account the electricity and lighting requirements of the area, the amount of weight centralized in the area, procedures to ensure climatological control for the microforms, and, finally, the attractiveness/comfort of the area for the user.

Considerations of lighting are essential due to the nature of microforms themselves. A viewing room should not have outside windows, and if a viewing area must be located in a space with windows, appropriate covers should be installed. Overhead lighting in a viewing room is necessary, but should be substantially reduced from normal operation levels. The use of dimmer switches is an excellent means of adjusting overhead lighting to reduced levels. Individual study/writing lamps next to the readers help reduce overhead lighting requirements, improve image viewing, and do not interfere with others using the room (Folcarelli et al, 1982, p. 127). Electricians must be consulted to ensure adequate circuitry for the number of viewers, printers, etc., to be placed in the room. Grounded strip outlets running along walls are best. Wires running across open areas to outlets should be avoided, and adequate outlets should be available.

Figure 13-7.
Criteria for the Selection of Microfilm/fiche Readers and Printers

A. READERS
    1. DIMENSIONS
        The size and weight of the reader will depend largely on the ability of the manufacturer to integrate in a compact fashion the design characterstics listed below.
    2. SCREEN
        a. Size
            Screen size should be at least 11 in. wide by 14 in. high. For reading newspapers on microfilm, it is desirable to have a screen at least 15 1/2 in. wide to accommodate a 1 : 1 blowback of a newspaper.
        b. Angle
            The reading angle on the screen should be variable to prevent fatigue caused by reading in a fixed position.
        c. Height
            Screen height above the table should be variable to enable reading ease for tall and short users.
        d. Illumination
            The screen should be evenly illuminated from the corners to the center.
        e. Brightness
            Brightness should be adjustable to accommodate (1) reading positive and negative microforms, and (2) various degrees of ambient lighting.
        f. Surface
            Screen surface should be nonglare to suppress reflections from the surrounding area.
    3. IMAGE QUALITY
        a. Type of Projection
            There should be internal projection to allow for use under conditions of ordinary lighting.
        b. Resolution
            The image should appear with sufficient definition as to compare favorably with the original from which the microform was produced. (The Library Technology Program's microform reader test program specifies resolution of 5.01/mm at the center and 4.01/mm at the edges and corners as good performance.)
        c. Focus
            The focus of the image should be consistent and should not be affected by vibrations caused by normal machine use of changes in film gate temperatures.
        d. Distortion
            The image should appear bright, clear, and sharp. Refocusing should not be required to read any portion of it.
    4. MAGNIFICATION
        The readers should provide a range of magnification from 15X to 48X. A single lens system, providing variable magnification and automatic focusing, is preferable to a series of interchangeable lenses that require careful storage, installation, and maintenance.
    5. IMAGE ROTATION
        Image rotation of 360 degrees should be provided.

6. FILM TRANSPORT ASSEMBLY

The glass flats that hold the film in place must be separable and easily removed for cleaning. The glass flats should automatically separate when the film advance knob is rotated. It should be impossible to advance the film if the flats are closed.

7. FILM ADVANCEMENT

It should be possible to advance and reverse the film at two speeds—at a rapid speed and a slower speed. If the film drive is motorized, it should be variable between high and low speed.

8. CONTROLS

All controls, e.g., film advancement, focusing, and scanning, should be easily accessible from a seated position. All controls should be clearly labeled.

a. Focusing

The focusing device should operate smoothly and easily. It should move the image to either side of the "in focus" position with a single turn of the hand. The device should be securely mounted so that no lateral shifting of the image occurs during focusing.

b. Scanning

A scanning device should be provided for both horizontal and vertical positioning.

c. Magnifying

A variable magnification knob should be provided to allow the user to determine (with a zoom lens or an autofocus lens and screen) the most legible size of the image.

9. HEATING, COOLING, AND NOISE

The film gate temperature must be within the acceptable limits specified in ANSI Standard Methods of Testing Printing and Projection Equipment, Z38.7.5. The Microfilm Reader Standards, PH5.1.A cooling system, should be met. Operation should be silent.

10. ELECTRICAL POWER REQUIREMENTS

The readers should be operated on standard 120 volts, 60 cycles.

11. SAFETY FACTORS

a. All surfaces, corners, and edges of the reader should be free from burrs and roughness, to prevent damage to film or hands. The reader should have a stable base to prevent its being knocked over. There should be no hazardous electrical current leakage.

b. All accessories should be attached to the machine. Parts should be easy to attach and accessible for cleaning and repair. The projection lamp should be of a type readily available from commercial sources and easy to change. Glass flats, mirror, screen, and lenses should be easy to clean.

12. OPERATION

Operation should be simple and clearly illustrated. A diagram for threading reels should be provided at each reading station. Simple, well illustrated, and attractive instructions should also be provided.

B. READER-PRINTER

1. PROCESS

Ideally, the printing process should yield positive paper copy from both negative and positive microtransparencies at the flick of a switch.

2. QUALITIES OF THE PAPER COPY
   a. Sharp, clear, and legible.
   b. Noncurling.
   c. Nonsmearing.
   d. Nonfading.
   e. Capable of being marked with pen, pencil, felt-tip, or typewriter.
   f. Permanent paper and image.
   g. Available in two sizes—8 1/2 in. × 11 in. × 14 in.—to allow compatibility with existing filing system.
3. CONTROLS
   a. Print button should be easily accessible from a seated position.
   b. Multiple copy feature is desirable.
   c. It should be possible to install a coin meter.
   d. Finished paper copy should be accessible from a seated position.
4. SPEED OF PRINT PROCESS
   Print processing should be completed within 30 to 45 seconds, and preferably less.
5. PRINT AREA
   There should be marks on or beside the screen to indicate the exact dimensions of the image that will be produced in paper copy.
6. WASTE
   Exposure control should be automatic and sufficiently accurate that trial exposures are not required. Wastage normally should not exceed 5%.
7. QUIET OPERATION
   The reader-printer should have a quiet operation, making it suitable for use in an open reading area.
8. MAINTENANCE
   If a process involving the use of solutions is employed, the solution trays should be easily accessible for filing and easily removable for cleaning with the least possible hazard of spillage. The rollers should be also be readily accessible for daily cleaning. Loading the paper supply should be an easy operation.

C. OTHER FACTORS
1. Consider "creature comforts" related to readers and printers that facilitate or detract from ease of use:
   a. Distance from user to machine.
   b. Lighting controls.
   c. Access to control knobs and easy explanation on each.
   d. Sharp or protruding points, safety hazards.
   e. Glare/viewing haze.
2. REPAIRABILITY
   The degree to which the operator or owner can repair minor problems without calling for service.
3. THE ULTIMATE TEST
   USE THE EQUIPMENT YOURSELF FOR A SIGNIFICANT PERIOD OF TIME!

Source: Adapted from Holmes (1970, pp. 33–37).

Whenever sources such as microforms and their supporting equipment are grouped together in a high density arrangement, a check on the amount of weight can quickly determine if the structure of the area is strong enough to support the substantial weight to be put there. Whenever possible, heavy cabinets or equipment should be placed against a wall or other support -- especially if the sources/equipment are not on the ground floor.

Climatological control is a consideration as well. Dust, light, tempera-ture, and humidity can cause substantial damage to microforms. ANSI Stan-dard PH1.43–1976 provides guidelines in these areas.[2] Basically, micro-forms should be stored in cool temperatures (65 degrees F), with low humidity (20–40%). Furthermore, equipment may be needed to remove dust or other pollutants from the air, depending on the location. Attention to these standards will prolong the life of the microforms and be cost-effective in the long run.

The GPO suggests that microfiche should be stored at temperatures under 80 degrees F, with 20–40% humidity (Hernon, 1981). The GPO only reproduces diazo microfiche for depository distribution; however, libraries are likely to receive microfiche documents in a vesicular and silver halide format as well. Additional storage requirements and techniques should be considered for maintaining the condition of these resources. Libraries should use acid free containers, reduce air pollution in the storage area, not wrap microfiche with rubber bands, and so forth.

Special attention should be given to making the user comfortable in the reading area. Because of eye fatigue and what some have referred to as the general "unpleasantness" of microform viewing, the following items should be considered. Cool temperatures should be maintained in the area; since many viewers radiate heat when used, a reading area can become warm very quickly. Comfortable seating and work areas should be provided; straight-back chairs with no padding are very tiresome to someone sitting at a micro-form viewing station after a number of hours. Noise distractions and traffic flow in the area should be reduced as much as possible. Finally, the environ-ment should have colors and be aesthetically pleasing—esthetic comfort may be as important as physical comfort (Draper and Brooks, 1979).

Space limitations are likely to force many documents collections to purchase/replace paper copy holdings with microforms. Large collections of the *Federal Register*, the Serial Set, congressional hearings, census publica-tions, etc., simply will have to be obtained in a microformat or perhaps not obtained at all. However, the holdings should concentrate on high use titles and minimize the collection and retention of low use titles (see Chapter 6 for

---

[2] The American National Standards Institute produces technical standards on a broad range of topics, including microforms. To obtain a publications catalog listing these standards, write the American National Standards Institute, Inc., 1430 Broadway, New York, NY 10018.

additional discussion of this point). Given the volume of publications distributed in a microformat, the planning and establishment of suitable physical facilities is essential.

DESIGNS FOR THE FUTURE

Physical facilities and space requirements for microforms and other resources/services must be carefully considered if government information resources are to be easily accessible by library clientele. But, for many documents collections, simply renovating existing facilities, redesigning the arrangement of resources and services, or increasing the quality and comfort of the furnishings in the collection is yet to be accomplished.

The importance of physical access cannot be overstated. Allen and Gerstberger (1968) found that the most important criterion for people in their selection of an information source is ease of access. Thus, an accessible source of low quality will be chosen before a less accessible source of higher quality. One implication of this finding is that simply improving the quality of the information services available from the documents collection will not, in itself, increase use of the source material is physically inaccessible.

Such research suggesting that "ease of use," "easy accessibility," and the "use of an information service is in indirect relationship to the effort required to access the service or source" has clear implications for documents collections. Indeed, it would seem that:

- All services should be clearly identified and located within the documents collection
- The various types of government information resources must be logically organized, easy to find, and open for browsing
- Physical facilities and space must facilitate the easy location and accessibility of resources and services
- Users must perceive access to resources and services as "easier" or "less troublesome" than doing without them.

Confused arrangements, split locations for various collections of government information resources, chaotic functional activities throughout the area, and limited signage to direct attention to sources and services must be minimized (Reynolds, 1975).

The services and resources provided by the staff of the government information collection should dictate the physical facilities, space management, traffic flows, and arrangement of resources—not the other way around. Unfortunately, many librarians view documents collections as "givens" and refuse to consider alternative arrangements. Thus, the self-assessment process suggested in the first section of this chapter is essential if documents librarians are to improve physical facilities and see the collection as it appears to patrons.

The physical facilities of the documents collection must be considered as an additional factor necessitating evaluation, planning, and strategies for improvement. For many collections, reliance on microforms and information handling technologies will be a necessity despite staff hesitancies. Many depository librarians simply will not have adequate room for necessary resources and services, unless, with their physical facilities, they incorporate a philosophy based on immediate physical access to "core" or high use resources, and a maximum of two day physical access to lesser-needed resources. Reliance on various forms of automated information processing will become a necessity, rather than a luxury, and physical facilities must be renovated to facilitate this change.

First, it was integration of micrformatted material and supporting equipment into the collection. Now, integration of automated information processing equipment into the collection's physical facilities is currently a key issue in facilities management and space planning. But documents librarians should note the increased likelihood that computer tapes and electronic files may soon appear regularly as part of depository library shipments ("Information Technology Program Update," 1988, p. 13).

In the future, it is likely that documents librarians will have to consider strategies for the organization of and access to computer tapes and other electronic forms of government information. New facilities will have to be established for the proper storage of these electronic files, and new equipment will be needed to make the information in these electronic files available to the user. Although the Joint Committee on Printing has encouraged both the GPO and depository libraries to move toward accepting distribution of electronic files, most depository librarians have yet to consider proper facilties and space management planning for such electronic information sources.

Existing standards and guidelines for physical facilities are of limited usefulness for depository collections. Neither the *Guidelines for the Depository Library System* (1977) nor the GPO's *U.S. Depository Library Inspection Visit Form* (n.d.) address the physical facilities necessary for supporting documents collections. Although the *Guidelines* and the inspection form contain a number of criteria related to space, the utility of both forms is limited. For instance, section V of the *Inspection Visit Form* asks questions such as:

- Is the space provided for depository public services
  _____ adequate?   _____ limited?   _____ inadequate?
- Is the space for processing new depository materials
  _____ adequate?   _____ limited?   _____ inadequate?

- Is space for housing the depository collection
  ____ adequate? ____ limited? ____ inadequate?
- Does the space in the library includes suitable private work areas for
  ____ the person responsible for the depository?
  ____ depository support staff?
  ____ no depository staff members?
- Are tables and/or carrels for in-house use of depository publications
  ____ adequate?
  ____ needed in the near future?
  ____ inadequate?

Such "evaluation criteria" have limited meaning, questionable application, and unclear definitions. After all, the sense of "adequate" space for depository public service, "adequate" space for tables, and "suitable" work areas is left to the discretion of the individual inspector and depository librarian. In short, there are no standards and inspection questions have little impact on improving physical facilities and space utilization in most documents collections.

Primary responsibility for assessing and improving physical facilities and space utilization in a depository collection rests directly with documents librarians. They must be knowledgeable about physical facilities and space requirements, able to demonstrate costs and benefits for renovated facilities, and able to justify the need for these facilities and space requirements to appropriate administrators. Further, they must recognize that even the best collection of government information resources will be unused and inaccessible without careful planning and evaluation that leads to high quality physical facilities and space utilization, and that encourages access to government information resources.

14

Processing Depository Publications

Despite the high quality of many government publications, their widespread dissemination through the GPO depository library program (and presumably other depository programs), and an emerging awareness in the library community regarding the value of these publications in meeting the information needs of clientele, government publications housed in libraries are frequently inaccessible and under-utilized. Such a pronouncement may, at first, seem harsh, but a review of major research studies suggests a need to increase access to and use of government publications.

Although a number of reasons might explain the limited exploitation of U.S. government publications in many libraries today, how these materials are processed has a considerable impact on access and usage by diverse client groups. Technical processing routines continue to exert significant influence on the overall utility of government information collections and the degree to which materials in these collections can be accessed.

For purposes of clarification, "technical processing" is defined as those activities conducted by a library to make a specific information resource ready for public and staff use. Typically, these activities include acquisition, cataloging and classification, and labeling. Indeed, technical processing is a *support* activity, i.e., a process that assists in making information resources bibliographically identifiable, logically organized, and physically accessible by the patron. In short, technical processes are not an end unto themselves— especially in terms of accessing and using government information resources.

This chapter examines technical processing of GPO publications in the context of libraries with separate depository collections. For nondepository libraries, technical processing of government publications is (1) typically accomplished in the same manner in which other materials are processed; (2) minimized by the use of check-in files only, avoidance of cataloging, or placement in a vertical file-type physical arrangement; or (3) unnecessary, since the library does not actively collect and make available government publications. Sachse (1981, pp. 32–66) provides a useful overview of processing techniques for government publications in nondepository libraries. By and large, however, primary responsibility for making U.S. government publications accessible and available for use falls on individual depository libraries.

This chapter does *not* discuss specific aspects of processing. Harleston and Stoffle (1974) wrote the classic description of processing and other technical services related to government publications. Much of the information and procedures suggested in their work remains useful today. The *Federal Depository Library Manual* (1985) also offers specific recommendations for technical processing and includes useful examples of day-to-day routines. Godden (1984) and Hahn (1987) have written practical textbooks for library technical services—much of which can be applied to a government documents context.

After a brief review of the historical development of technical processing for government publications, this chapter presents selected issues having significant impact on effective technical processing of government publications. The chapter concludes with a discussion of prospects and recommendations to improve technical processing. Underlying these discussions is the belief that greater attention must be given to developing effective technical processing procedures for government publications and integrating such processing with overall library technical services.

BACKGROUND

With the exception of a few local programs developed by innovative libraries (usually to satisfy a need peculiar to a given library), most technical service operations for documents, through the early decades of this century, centered simply on the basic function of acquiring and storing government publications. Few libraries attempted to provide original cataloging. Working with major bibliographic tools such as the *National Union Catalog, New Serial Titles*, and the *Monthly Catalog of United States Government Publications*, libraries acquired and processed publications in the same manner for many years. Typically, neither a card catalog nor a shelflist was produced, but in some instances, local needs necessitated the creation and maintenance of a serials list or other printed holdings list. The dependency on printed bibliographic sources and manual processing techniques forced a "3x5" mentality upon libraries and left technical service librarians reluctant to accept new approaches, especially the formidable process of bringing bibliographic control to a growing body of government publications.

Many of the early writings concerning processing concentrate on the "best" means to catalog and/or classify government publications, and, parenthetically, whether cataloging and classification were actually needed. Boyd (1941) discussed the processing of documents as a variable of use and argued for selection criteria, check-in files, and the creation of other in-house records. A *Notation for a Public Documents Classification* (Jackson, 1946) addressed the classification issue. This classic work called for a simplified cataloging format and a uniquely designed in-house classification scheme that could be used for *all* types of government publications. Since that time, the literature is replete with writings discussing the relative merits of:

- Cataloging government publications or providing a simplified non-AACR approach to cataloging, or not cataloging at all
- Relying on the Sudocs classification scheme or developing an in-house scheme for all types of government publications
- Integrating the cataloging and classification of government publications with the techniques used for other library resources (Myers and Britton, 1978).

Although a number of writers suggest that libraries with a selective collection of documents "will find that integrating government publications into the established areas of the library will promote use of the material" (Sachse, 1981, p. 53), no empirical evidence has yet to appear supporting either the separate or integrated view.

Over the years a plethora of writings have discussed in-house systems for cataloging and classifying government publications. Indeed, as Hernon (1978, p. 31) points out in his historical review of library reference services for government publications, much more attention has been given to technical service related topics than to use, reference services, and public access. The passing of time has produced few specific insights into costs, requirements, benefits, or degree of access resulting from one approach over another. Recently reported studies have concentrated on the cost of cataloging and the inclusion of government publications in online catalogs (see the writings specified in Figure 7–1).

Although a number of writings appeared in the 1960s and 1970s regarding classification and cataloging of government publications, little overall concern for analyzing processing methods and their impact on access was evident. Indeed, in the classic guide for documents, written by Schmeckebier and Eastin (1969), no mention is made of processing techniques or procedures to access and organize materials. If depositories wanted a complete catalog record, they were forced to order card sets from the Library of Congress (if the document had been cataloged), or to produce original cataloging based on available bibliographic information. Indeed, it was not until the early and mid-1970s that the GPO became actively involved in developing techniques to assist librarians in better cataloging and processing government publications (Morehead, 1978; 1983).

One of the more positive effects of early automation attempts was the availability of bibliographic tools and specialized collections on microform. Expanded holdings, old and worn out materials, and specialized holdings lists (union catalogs and serials lists) were all candidates for conversion to microfilm (Saffady, 1978; 1985). The use of microforms not only was a departure from traditional printed formats, but also made it possible for libraries to distribute their holdings broadly, and at a reasonable cost to other libraries. However, one of the major drawbacks to microformatted holdings was a library's reluctance or inability to maintain access. Microfilming was innovative and space saving, but it was also time consuming and, at times, costly.

Processing difficulties related to government publications were not limited to printed materials. Because of the difficulty of gaining access to all publications handled by the GPO, Readex Corporation introduced a microcard service that provided complete coverage of all depository and nondepository publications cited in the *Monthly Catalog*. Such "subscription services" served to increase the archival nature of the documents, since (1) microcards were frequently stored away from the rest of the documents collection; (2) there were no catalog records, analytics of contents, and only limited finding aids; and (3) there was no support for the production of paper copy from the microcard version of a document.

In the 1970s, libraries began to give serious consideration to automated systems; many libraries had adequate financial resources to develop their own systems or to contract for an outside system developed especially for libraries. Librarians wanted systems that required little software maintenance locally. Responding to this surge toward library automation was a growing number of commercial companies involved in developing automated library systems. Baker & Taylor and CLSI (to name but two) were advising librarians on hardware capabilities and developing software packages for complete automated circulation systems. The more innovative libraries employed qualified programmers/analysts, developed their own systems that covered a wide range of functions, and provided numerous computer-generated outputs.

Generally absent from these local developments, however, were efforts to bring better bibliographic control to government publications. This absence of effort was due in large part to a long-standing low priority placed on the bibliographic control of documents, and to the changing nature of the technical processes themselves. A notable exception to this situation was the Guelph Document System that the University of Guelph implemented in 1965. This in-house batch system, based on simplified coding procedures (not classification), provided both a catalog and subject, author, and title access to the local documents collection (Gillham, 1982).

In a typical library attempting automation, librarians are caught between continuing traditional methods and processes and adapting to the evolving technology of online systems. A consuming interest of libraries developing automated systems was the hiring of librarians trained in the nature and use of automation, and the retraining of librarians as the transition from manual processing to automated operations progressed. The most difficult aspect of retraining librarians was instilling in them the confidence that, after decades of doing things one way, the new, computer-assisted ways could be mastered.

Largely because government publications departments often had responsibility for their own technical processes—which typically were not integrated into overall library processing—training of documents librarians in automation did not occur. Further, documents librarians appeared to show only minimal interest in the possibility of automating various technical services. The combination of (1) not being integrated into overall library technical processing, (2) demonstrating minimal interest in possible applications, and (3) failing to obtain training in automation skills allowed many documents librarians to continue as if the automation of library technical services was neither happening nor affecting their area of library operation.

Until the late 1970s, general approaches to technical processing of government publications were limited. By and large, the vast majority of libraries with significant documents collections continued much as they had in the past: selecting item numbers from the GPO, receiving shipments of government publications, checking shipments against their "Daily Shipping Lists," affixing Sudocs numbers on the documents received, marking documents with an ownership and date received stamp, and placing documents on the shelves in Sudocs arrangement for public use.

Depository libraries engaged in minimal cataloging and perhaps produced card sets. The Sudocs classification number (although based on issuing agency) was seen as adequate "subject" description. In-house bibliographic control techniques were minimal, with perhaps possible use of a Kardex serials check-in system or, in some rare instances, a short-title shelflist. In general, however, the typical documents collection still does no cataloging, relies on Sudocs classification, has minimal in-house control procedures, and processes materials only to the point of transferring the Sudocs number onto the publication prior to shelving (Richardson et al, 1980).

For example, the 1985 *Biennial Survey* inquired about the percentage of documents cataloged by the library (including records adapted from

OCLC, WLN, or another source). According to "Biennial Survey Results" (1985, p. 2),

- Only 19% of the responding depositories cataloged 75% or more of the documents received
- Some 60% of the responding depositories cataloged 25% or fewer of the documents received.

Although respondents may have interpreted "cataloged" differently, it appears that most depository collections do not catalog the publications received.

With the availability of GPO cataloging tapes through the MARC tape distribution service at the Library of Congress (in 1976), libraries could produce (or have produced) catalog cards. As an alternative, they can include GPO publications in COM (computer output microform) catalogs or local online systems that are "either vendor supplied or locally developed" (Plaunt, 1985, p. 454). At some future time, as more libraries implement online systems, the typical arrangement might be for depository libraries "to fully integrate document cataloging into . . . principal cataloging system for maximum access by both patrons and library staff" (Ibid.).

ONLINE BIBLIOGRAPHIC SERVICES

The technical processing of library resources, especially the cataloging of books, took a quantum leap forward with the appearance of OCLC, the Research Libraries Information Network (RLIN), and the Washington Library Network (WLN). OCLC was established in 1967 to provide online services for colleges and universities in Ohio, but the system rapidly expanded to include other libraries and soon became available nationally.

Through much of the 1970s, the (Myers, 1985, p. 29):

GPO operated like most library cataloging departments. . ... GPO generally followed cataloging rules, conventions, and guidelines, but it also established new name and subject headings, and interpreted cataloging rules, independent from other cataloging agencies. The catalog records which GPO produced during this period are not always consistent with files based on LC rule interpretations and LC authorities for names and subjects, which serve as a national standard. If a name did not appear in LC's name authority file, GPO established the name for its own authority file. LC might later establish the name in a different form.

In July 1976, the GPO began to use OCLC for cataloging and generating magnetic tapes for preparation of the *Monthly Catalog*. In October 1977, the

GPO began to establish corporate name headings through the Name Authority Cooperative Project (NACO) administered by the Library of Congress. Personal name headings were added to the NACO project in 1979. Now whenever the GPO assigns a new AACR-2 name, that name is added to LC's name authority file.

One of the most significant enhancements to OCLC, in terms of gaining access to government publications, was the 1980 implementation of the "086" government documents search key. When a document is cataloged on OCLC, the Sudocs number appears in that field and is searchable.

Chapter 7 provides additional description of the OCLC database and its coverage of government publications. For example, it notes that OCLC is still considering a 1980 proposal by the GPO to implement an automated holdings system for GPO-cataloged items. Under one proposed arrangement, item number selections for all regional depositories would be loaded into the OCLC database, while another option advocated the loading of item selection profiles for selective depositories. Either way, the database would indicate holdings even for those depositories that do not catalog via the OCLC system. The utility of having holding depositories immediately listed for each document is apparent; however, maintenance of accurate holdings records would be a local responsibility, and may place added pressure on documents librarians to process claims, enter changes, and update records.

The possible applications of OCLC for government publications technical processing, which Walbridge (1982) has nicely summarized, include the following:

- *Cataloging subsystem*: produce complete sets of catalog cards for government publications included in the database
- *Serials control*: identify and produce bibliographic records of serials included in the database with potential applications for local "check-in" and recording of serials holdings
- *Public access*: availability of public access OCLC terminals can directly support bibliographic access and identification of government publications
- *Online access*: with use of the 086 search key, documents librarians can obtain bibliographic information regarding most documents classified under the Sudocs classification scheme and included in the database
- *Acquisitions*: ordering and accounting of materials (not government publications) that may be used in support of a documents collection.

The actual number of depositories exploiting such services for government publications, however, is unclear.

First, it should be pointed out that simply because the host library has

an OCLC terminal, use of the terminal for government publications technical processing does not necessarily follow. One study of the use of OCLC by
depository librarians indicated that fewer than 5% of responding depositories had an OCLC terminal in the documents area (if a separate collection),
that only 1% had any training on OCLC applications, and that the most
frequently mentioned applications used by the librarians were to obtain the
Sudocs number or bibliographic information about a publication, and not to
input records (McClure, 1982b).

The following concerns limit the utility of the cataloging component of
the system: multiple records in the OCLC database with conflicting bibliographic information, incomplete coverage of the various nondepository
publications, the ongoing disagreement about the use of AACR-2 for main
entries, and the limited use of subject added entries for GPO publications.
Nonetheless, the availability of those records within the database marks a
considerable step toward effective processing of GPO government publications. Unfortunately, there is virtually no research regarding actual use of
OCLC by depository collections, analysis of government publication records
within the database itself, or the degree to which local libraries use any of
the various subsystems for government publications in an *integrated approach* with other library technical processing.

The one exception to the above generalization relates to an examination of bibliographic access to publications distributed through the National
Technical Information Service (NTIS) and contained in OCLC. The OCLC
database provides bibliographic access to some NTIS distributed publications. However, neither the *Monthly Catalog* nor the database can serve as
a replacement for use of *Government Reports Announcements & Index*
(*GRA&I*). Overall, McClure, Hernon, and Purcell (1986, Chapter 7) discovered that approximately 10% of the sample *GRA&I* entries were duplicated
in the *Monthly Catalog* and 30% were duplicated in the OCLC database.
Further, the most effective search strategy for NTIS publications in both
OCLC and the *Monthly Catalog* is a title search. Apparently (p. 121),

> general policy governing the OCLC database . . . makes no distinction
> between the inclusion of GPO depository or non- depository NTIS publica-
> tions. The determination that a particular NTIS publication is, or is not, in-
> cluded in the OCLC database is likely to be a local library decision and not
> determined by OCLC since Federal agencies (such as the GPO) do not provide
> OCLC with cataloging tapes of NTIS publications. Thus, the NTIS publica-
> tions that are included in OCLC represent those NTIS publications that the
> local participating library deems "important" (however defined).

The appendix of *Academic Library Use of NTIS* (1986) explains procedures
for locating NTIS publications in the OCLC database. These instructions
inform readers about how to locate NTIS publications by title, personal and

corporate author, and about subject searching of the OCLC database available from BRS Information Technologies.

Additional Automated Processing Strategies

The Guelph Document System, developed in the 1960s at the University of Guelph, is an important bibliographic utility for government publications, regardless of the agency or level of government producing an information resource. A consortium of libraries in Toronto (Ontario, Canada) was eventually formed and became known as CODOC. The union file from this consortium is produced on microfiche for the contributors, and made available to other libraries on a fee basis. The CODOC system, which does not follow prescribed rules of AACR-2, has considerable flexibility. It can generate bibliographic records for government publications, holdings lists, and various union lists. Further, the coding system, which has been adapted for online use, draws together information resources, regardless of form, format, issuing agency, and level of government. Such a system has value to a number of Canadian and some United States libraries (see Gillham, 1982, 1987).

CODOC will probably never exert a major impact on depository libraries in the United States. However, the Canadian system serves as a reminder that libraries should integrate information resources, government with non-government. Further, users should have all the documents resources, regardless of level of government, issuing agency, or format brought to bear on the resolution of an information need. Libraries concentrating on the GPO tapes appear to be saying "we accord better bibliographic control to GPO distributed publications and are willing to grant second class status to the overwhelming majority of other government publications/information resources."

An excellent example of an in-house system that produces a simplified shelflist and other bibliographic products has been developed at Carleton College. Such a system complements the manipulation of GPO tapes and provides collection management analyses, standard bibliographic records, holdings lists, and shelflists. (Chapter 11 discusses an automated system in the context of a decision support system and offers an example of the management benefits that can be derived from such a system). Specific objectives of the system include the ability to retrieve a record by keying on (Morton, 1982):

- A single record component, e.g., Sudocs class, title, or even keyword in title
- Any combination of record characteristics, e.g., combinations of keywords in a title, the item number with year published, or date received with author.

Libraries should definitely investigate the development of such a system and abandon manual shelflists and other time-consuming record keeping procedures.

Although online database searching is only infrequently seen as a tool for assisting in the processing of government publications, it can be of value. The acquisition process for government publications can be significantly simplified by identifying and ordering government publications directly from the terminal. For instance, bibliographic records from the GPO can be identified and verified from the *Monthly Catalog* and the *Publications Reference File (PRF)*. After the correct item has been identified (assuming one uses the *PRF* file on DIALOG), that title can be ordered online from the GPO. This ordering process, done for either paper copy or microfiche publications, is likely to have special value for nondepository collections.

A similar process can be used for a number of non-GPO publications, as well as government publications made available through private firms. For instance, all publications listed in the *CIS Index* and the *American Statistics Index* can be ordered online; government publications in the NTIS, ERIC, and other databases can also be ordered online. For libraries wanting to simplify their acquisition of government publications, use of online bibliographic databases has a number of advantages:

- Reduces in-house record keeping and invoicing
- Exploits the use of deposit accounts, if the library so desires
- Reduces the time lag between the ordering and receipt of material
- Combines the process of bibliographic verification with the process of ordering
- Permits ordering to be done from any physical location at which a terminal is located.

This strategy may be largely ignored by many documents librarians because they do not conduct online database searches or they have minimal access to terminals. In addition, online ordering may be considered too expensive or may result in a significant increase in the number of microforms purchased.

Finally, note should be made of the potential applications of microcomputers for processing government publications. Microcomputers are appropriate for "self-contained" and separate depository collections. Following the lead from CODOC and the Carleton College system, simplified bibliographic information can be input into a data file or a number of data files for such activities as:

- Serials control
- Label production
- Title or Sudocs number file
- Specialized holdings list.

The availability of microcomputers with hard disk capability increases both storage space and the advantages of relying on microcomputer hardware and software for processing and management decision making.

With the growing number of publicly available databases of government information resources, more libraries may wish to catalog documents online, especially with OCLC. They might also access or load records from the GPO cataloging tapes themselves, or through the services of commercial cataloging firms, bibliographic utilities, or online database vendors. Swanbeck (1985) considers the use of a commercial cataloging service such as Marcive, Inc. as the most cost-effective.

The cataloging of documents in many libraries still lags far behind the processing of other resources. The disparity may no longer be due to the lack of cataloging resources or the degree of difficulty traditionally attributed to government information resources. With online access through multiple access points, libraries can no longer justify the relegation of government publications to the bottom of the processing list. Nor can it be asserted that documents require expertise beyond that held by the typical processing department.

ISSUES AND PROSPECTS

The preceding sections have provided a selective overview of the background and current status of technical processing for government publications in the context of the depository library. In general, technical processing for government publications has continued much as it has in the past, and has been relatively untouched by information handling technologies and innovative processing procedures. As noted in the first section of the chapter, the "3x5 catalog card mentality" appears to dominate technical processing for government publications—if technical processing is seriously considered for documents in the first place! This current state of affairs can be understood only in the context of a number of issues that remain unresolved, but must be addressed if a library is to develop an effective plan for technical processing of government publications.[1]

To Catalog or Not to Catalog

Perhaps the critical issue to address related to processing government publications is whether the library wants to catalog such resources. If that answer is "yes," it must then determine the degree of cataloging that will be

---

[1] The need for local changes to database records input by the GPO should be minimal, primarily limited to adding an LC or Dewey class and local holdings. However, some institutions are inherently incapable of accepting someone else's cataloging without modification.

required. Currently, most depository libraries do not catalog the majority of government publications, preferring to accession those received and put them on the shelves in Sudocs or agency/chronological order. The reasons offered for not cataloging government publications include:

- Too costly; requires additional staff
- Cataloging rules for government publications are inappropriate, and numerous changes for each government publication are necessary, regardless of the bibliographic record available in a given database
- The emphasis of the GPO on micropublishing complicates the cataloging process
- Adequate bibliographic access to government publications is achieved through standard paper copy indexes and online bibliographic databases
- Much of the cataloging detail for government publications is non-informative.

These reasons may or may not be valid for a particular depository setting. General card catalog use studies suggest a wide disparity of usefulness, effectiveness, and access due to cataloging (Lancaster, 1977, pp. 19–68). Other studies have found that social scientists prefer browsing and do not rely heavily on the card catalog for access to government publications (Hernon, 1979, pp. 55–57). Reasons for cataloging government publications usually revolve around the assumption that having complete card sets in the main card catalog, or records integrated into the library's online catalog, will improve access to and availability of government publications. Unfortunately, there is no evidence or empirical research that strongly supports one case or the other (Waldo, 1977).

But recent advances in technology have minimized the importance of the cataloging issue. Since bibliographic records are available in OCLC for publications listed in the *Monthly Catalog* since 1976, and with the increased availability of paper copy indexes for government publications, bibliographic access to GPO publications has improved. Further, with the availability of numerous government publications databases online, the importance of cataloging government publications is being replaced by the importance of having a logical means to classify and arrange the documents (such as Sudocs) on the shelves. Indeed, one might argue that access to and availability of government publications are severely impaired when classified in a non-Sudocs classification scheme!

GPO Administrative Decisions and Activities

Although the GPO has taken a greater interest in processing issues related to government publications since the mid-1970s, much is still required if libraries are to use these cataloging records for depository publications. Between 1976 and 1980, records produced by the GPO were done independently of the Library of Congress (LC) and may have been changed by the LC. Thus, the "correct" version of a government publication record for this time period needs to be determined. Beginning in 1981, the GPO assumed authority for cataloging Federal documents, taking over the responsibility from the LC.[2]

As Myers (1985, p. 36) points out, "the primary purpose of the *Monthly Catalog* is to list new documents, not to provide cataloging records." The index contains "true" cataloging records for (Ibid.):

- "Monographs in one part, and some multi-part monographs for which all of the parts are listed in the same issue of the *Monthly Catalog*
- Serials which are sold on subscription, or which are published three or more times a year and are not sold as separate issues. These records appear in the annual *Serials Supplement* [now called *Periodicals Supplement*] issue."

The rest of the records in the index are "availability records;" "their purpose is to announce the availability of the issue, not to provide a catalog record for a new bibliographic title" (Ibid.). Availability records appear for the following types of resources (Ibid.):

- "Publications such as errata slips and shipments of loose-leaf pages . . .
- Separate but related materials such as parts of a hearing, especially when the parts are listed in different issues of the *Monthly Catalog* . . .
- Single issues of publications such as the *Statistical Abstract* . . . which are serials not listed in the *Serials Supplement* issue of the *Monthly Catalog*.

"Many publications have records in the *Monthly Catalog* because they are available separately, not because they are new bibliographic titles. For most publications of this sort, there is no true catalog record on the GPO tapes" (Ibid.).

The GPO routinely updates records in the OCLC database and has done so for years. However, the GPO has no procedure for correcting "errors on cataloging tapes after the tape is distributed" (Myers, 1985, p. 40). Myers (1983, 1985) discusses this and other problems in greater detail.

Unless adequate attention is given to basic issues (such as adding item

---

[2] It is OCLC's administrative decision to have LC records for government documents override (or bump) GPO records from the database.

number designations to the records loaded in OCLC), documents and other librarians attempting to exploit automated access to government publications records, increased networking and resource sharing, and construction of in-house integrated catalogs will be stymied.

Training and Retraining Documents Librarians

Another issue that must be raised is the limited degree to which documents librarians have embraced information handling technologies related to technical processing for government publications. Apparently, many documents librarians are unfamiliar with the workings of OCLC, have limited knowledge of online bibliographic database searching, are unable to design and develop in-house automated processing systems, and have not been supported in their libraries in obtaining such training and increased competencies (McClure, 1982).

Due to the lack of exposure to automated technical processing innovations, as well as to myopic views on documents processing by library administrators, documents librarians have been largely excluded from the planning process for technical processing applications that are being developed in other areas of the library. Thus, the integration of library technical processing for government publications with other processing procedures is minimal, and in a number of cases treatment of government publications is left to the traditional "3x5 catalog card mentality." Once documents librarians become more conversant with technological applications through continuing education or other methods, they will still have to educate their colleagues about the importance of automated processing for government publications. In short, training related to government publications is likely to be needed throughout the library.

Microforms

The distribution of government information in a microformat by the GPO has grown significantly in the past decade, and now microfiche is the primary format for depository distribution. This change has a number of implications for the technical processing of government publications, including:

- Provision of adequate storage facilities under proper climate conditions
- Reduced ability to check for quality control of received microfiche, and verification that all microfiche on the "Daily Shipping List" were, in fact, received
- Obtaining adequate bibliographic information on microfiche headers that are eye readable

- Ensuring that microfiche relates to the functional needs of the clientele and other library collections
- Physical separation of microfiche from other government publications, and perhaps from other library resources
- Greater difficulty maintaining correct shelf order of microfiche.

Unless depository librarians carefully consider new management and collection development techniques for microform holdings, they will grow a massive, unweeded garden dominated by one crop—inaccessible microfiche.

The other side of the microforms question relates to the ability of documents librarians to exploit microform technology for increased effectiveness of processing and better access to information. A good example is the use of COM catalogs; Brown and Schlipf (1982) have reported on a process by which micrographic and computer indexing reduces file bulk, produces security copies, easily updates a COM catalog, and allows for rapid retrieval and distribution of a local documents collection. Such a perspective shows that microform technology, in this case COM technology, can be effectively exploited for the benefit of technical processing and user access. Documents librarians must devote additional attention to such strategies now and in the future.

Vendor Applications

While automated technical processing systems have been developed and are currently being expanded for "regular library resources," attention given to government documents systems is often more limited. If government publications are cataloged similarly to other library resources, if complete records are available, and if the bibliographic information fits the formats supplied by the vendor, then processing of documents may be included in a vendor supplied turn-key package. However, the more likely situation is that a library provides only minimal bibliographic records for U.S. government publications (and virtually none for international, other country, state, and local documents). A vendor may not be able to assist the library when it comes to processing government publications.

Stephenson and Purcell (1985) identify 14 commercially available serials control systems that are adaptable for processing government publications. INMAGIC, one of these packages, can be used for the development of a decision support system that traces titles from their ordering to their receipt, processing, and placement on the shelf. Clearly, documents librarians have options and opportunities. However, "before acquiring any serials system, a library should perform an in-depth systems analysis and design study" (Ibid., p. 70). Plaunt (1985) and Swanbeck (1985) also discuss the types of issues library staff should explore.

Shared Processing and Retrospective Conversion

Assuming the availability of terminals, sufficient staff, adequate training, and the financial resources to process government publications online, a library must next determine if processing will be inclusive or selective. It is a major undertaking to catalog all government publications that a depository library receives. Even if it were possible to catalog all currently received documents, very few libraries could seriously consider the retrospective cataloging of all previously received documents. At this point, it becomes obvious that sheer numbers and not necessarily the complexity of the material may constitute the major obstacle to the online processing of government information resources. Technology holds the answer to the problem, and that technology is currently available.

For many years, the Association of Research Libraries (ARL) has advocated shared cataloging as an equitable solution for the vast quantities of uncataloged microforms in libraries. Consortia of various sizes have also been formed to reap the benefits of shared cataloging. The CODOC system itself is a prime example of a cooperative effort in the processing of documents. Further, a number of states participate in regional networks to provide bibliographic input and access to state documents (Nakata and Kopec, 1980; Lane, 1987).

For both the participants in a bibliographic utility and other network members, online access to a growing number of documents records would greatly facilitate the retrospective conversion of government documents collections. Through the receipt of archival tapes, a library could easily generate paper, microfiche, or microfilm copies of a documents catalog or produce an integrated catalog, depending on the classification system used and the access points desired. For libraries with online catalogs and circulation systems, the simultaneous input of documents records or the loading of archival tapes into the system could result in online access to the documents collection with a variety of searchable fields or access points.

Even with the technology of today, which is rapidly evolving at both the local and network level to allow online management of many library functions, the body of governmen documents yet to be cataloged poses a formidable long-term project for one library to undertake. Shared cataloging or shared processing, to some degree, would seem to be a logical approach to the problem. Members of large networks could share the responsibility of documents cataloging based on a division of resources by item number, or by some other means suitable to the needs and capabilities of the participants.

It merits noting that the GPO investigates (1) any titles brought to its attention that had not entered the depository program and (2) any references in the *Monthly Catalog* to titles that had not been shipped to depository libraries.[3] The apparent slowness in depository distribution of such titles may be traced to the fact that the issuing agency cannot supply copies or that the GPO reprinting process takes a long time. If, by chance, librarians turned up a large cache of fugitive documents that had not been cataloged and had escaped bibliographic control, the GPO would probably consider these documents as outside its normal work flow.[4] Such a characterization would signify that the GPO might have to hire either temporary staff to process the titles or a contractor that would follow GPO procedures and standards, and have access to GPO files. Clearly, a cooperative relationship exists between the GPO and depository libraries. They work together to identify publications and to make them available to the public.

PROSPECTS

Traditionally, many libraries have relegated government publications to a low priority. Low priority of the documents collection is an historical condition that is not easily changed. In fact, it is characterized by an attitude in the library that presumes limited importance of government information resources. Removal of this constraint requires time and careful planning, political involvement on the part of documents librarians, and the development of a strategy of integrating government information resources into other areas of library operations and services. Until these information resources are better integrated, in terms of administration, services, and attitudes, increased technical processing will be dependent primarily on the personal interest and commitment of documents librarians.

Prospects for carefully reviewing the importance of, need for, and strategies for technical processing of government publications are continuing to improve as more librarians, especially library administrators, realize the value of government publications received through the depository library program. OCLC has provided enhancements that address the unique needs of government publications, but much remains to be done. The private sector is taking greater interest in government publications and offering

---

[3] For a few years, the GPO cataloged titles upon their receipt; physical processing occurred after completion of cataloging. Now physical processing occurs first. This way the GPO can be certain that it has received the required number of titles, can make arrangements from the issuing agency for receipt of the additional copies, and prepare "rain checks" that forewarn depository libraries of any shortage. The GPO can also be certain of the format in which the title will be distributed to depository libraries.

[4] Another example of "separable from the normal work flow" would be the GPO intention to receive data tapes from agencies and turn the tapes over to a non-government information provider (a contractor) for conversion of the information into a form that depository libraries could use. In effect, the government provides source data and the contractor makes the data available online.

packages that depository staff might consider for technical processing and management decision making. Offsetting these positive factors, however, are reduced library budgets, wayward priorities of the GPO, and the need to encourage documents librarians to become more active and knowledgeable about automated technical services.

The decision to process government information resources must be made locally, and documents librarians should have a major role in influencing that decision. Whether processing is done centrally or in the documents collection also must be a local decision. But with online access to a national network and database such as OCLC, processing should not be a task beyond the capability of a typical processing unit or documents staff trained in online techniques.

It remains to be seen whether libraries will take advantage of existing information handling technologies and cooperative efforts to improve bibliographic control for government information resources, or if there will be a continuation of a wait-and-see philosophy. Some libraries may find the Sudocs classification system adequate for their needs, and online processing of documents may not be necessary or advisable. For other libraries, the lack of adequate processing and bibliographic control may result in continued under-utilization and physical chaos. For libraries that want or need online capabilities to better serve their patrons, the framework for cooperative efforts exists. Participation in shared cataloging programs may offer the greatest potential for success in achieving efficient and cost-effective results.

15

Planning and Evaluation of Government Information Services

Access to library government information resources depends, in no small part, on the success with which the documents staff plan and evaluate the overall effectiveness of the various services and operations that they offer. Further, depository librarians today are faced with a broad range of challenges and opportunities to improve the effectiveness of their collections and services, to respond better to the information needs of the clientele, and to provide the necessary leadership to make government information resources an important component in the information environment. But the path to successful depository services and increased organizational effectiveness calls for skills and competencies beyond those of answering reference questions correctly, cataloging resources, or developing programs and services. The necessary prerequisite skills and competencies are also related to administrative skills in terms of the ability to conduct and understand research, make decisions concerning the allocation of scarce resources, and plan/achieve increased organizational effectiveness.

The development of skills in these areas has gained in importance for a number of reasons—all of which tend to increase the complexity of gaining access to government information resources effectively and providing appropriate information services. First, demands for more and higher quality services continue to increase. Documents librarians face increased expectations from both users and government agencies, especially since the depository program serves as a safety net providing the public with access to government publications and certain other information resources. Second, the costs for documents related services and resources have increased, while budgets have remained relatively static or have declined. Third, the advent of sophisticated information handling technologies has created opportunities for improving the effectiveness of documents related services. And, finally, documents librarians, regardless of library type, are beginning to realize that they cannot provide all the information services needed by their clientele. Instead of attempting to perform many services in a mediocre fashion, documents librarians need to set priorities and perhaps provide fewer services at higher levels of effectiveness. It is all the more essential that documents librarians minimize "common sense," or intuitive, decision making and improve their planning, research, and evaluation skills.

Such skills are essential if government information services are to be both effective and efficient. Effectiveness is the degree to which organizational goals and objectives are accomplished, while efficiency is the degree to which resource allocations (e.g., staff, materials, equipment, time, and space) can be minimized. Increased attention to effectiveness and efficiency is necessary, given the complexities of government information services, changing environmental impacts on the depository collection, and increased demands by administrators that government information collections and services be made accountable. Documents staff members must be able to demonstrate planning, evaluation, and action research skills if they want to increase organizational effectiveness and efficiency.

Action research skills can be defined as the ability to identify significant problems that do or might affect library operations, services, and collections; develop research questions related to the problems; collect and analyze empirical data that appropriately address those questions; make managerial decisions based on the accumulated data, and implement strategies to improve those operations. Documents staff need to ask questions such as:

- Do library patrons use some portions of the collection more than others, and if so, which ones, and why?
- Do bibliographic instruction programs improve the patron's willingness to request reference assistance and gain access to government information resources?
- How successful are general reference librarians and documents paraprofessional staff in answering reference questions and making appropriate referral?

Learning to ask such questions, and not to accept blindly the profession's long-held assumptions about government information services and activities, is critical if libraries are to improve services and increase access to resources.

The purpose of this chapter is to provide an introduction to planning and evaluation of government information services and operations in the context of general systems thinking. After introducing basic systems concepts, techniques of planning and evaluation will be presented. Readers will then be introduced to performance measures for government information services and depository collections. Next, the chapter will review the current progress on planning for government information services by examining the "state plans" that many states, with the encouragement of the Government Printing Office (GPO) and the Depository Library Council to the Public Printer, have developed to coordinate and improve services and public access to government publications. The chapter will conclude with suggestions by which staff working with government information resources can increase their planning and evaluation skills.

Although the chapter cannot provide a tutorial on "how to" plan and evaluate government information services, it can offer a basic introduction and stress the importance of these processes. Indeed, the need for such skills is not unique to documents librarians—all information professionals must have an understanding of these important concepts. Improved planning and evaluation skills, as well as the acquisition of basic research skills, can result in increased access to government information resources. Further, setting goals and objectives, establishing performance measures, and evaluating the various aspects of government information services and operations are *essential* for increased effectiveness and for making the documents department accountable for its operations.

SYSTEMS CONCEPTS FOR PLANNING AND EVALUATION

Due to its flexibility, emphasis on the environment, and recognition that an organization has interdependent parts, general systems thinking is an excellent tool to use for better understanding the relationships among factors that affect library operations. A system is a set of two or more interrelated elements, of any kind, that are coordinated for the accomplishment of certain goals. Further, the properties of each element affect each other and the behavior of the system as a whole; the manner in which they affect the whole depend on the behavior of at least one other component of the system, and the system is *more than* the sum of its parts. In short, the interaction among the various systems elements combine to produce an "essence" or attribute of the system that is not achievable by the individual parts alone (Marchant, 1976, pp. 13–28).

Figure 15–1 presents the basic model for an open system; it is referred to as an open system because it exchanges resources with the environment. The parts of the general systems model can be briefly described as follows:

- Input   The system functions by importing resources (e.g., information, resources, and money) from the larger environment

- Throughput   The system moves resources through itself and transforms a resources, through some kind of process, into a product
- Output   The system sends the transformed resources back to the environment in the form of products, services, or other kinds of results
- Feedback   The system obtains information from the environment that assist it in regulating the importation of resources and other system activities; feedback among various parts of a system can occur without direct intervention through the environment
- Outcome   The impact of the output on the environment (e.g., the output from a reference system might have been no answer to a specific reference question, but the outcome might then be that the student was unable to turn in a term paper prior to the deadline).

All government information-related activities can be described in terms of input, throughput, output, feedback, and outcome. The model serves as a general reminder that the analysis of library activities can lead to the formulation of problems requiring research, the evaluation of services and operations, and the development of plans that will ensure that changes are made and that government information services become more effective.

In addition to the elements of the general systems model, other characteristics describe open systems, i.e., systems such as government information services (Nadler and Tushman, 1980):

- Differentation   As a system grows, it tends to become more specialized, to add components, and to develop additional transformation processes and feedback loops
- Equifinality   The organization and processes of different systems may reproduce the same end result (e.g., two different staff members may achieve the same result by using different system resources and processes)
- Negative Entropy   Ultimate entropy represents the death of the system; thus, negative entropy is obtaining adequate resources for the system to accomplish goals, to adapt to changing environments, and to support system differentiation
- Equilibrium Seeking   The system tends to move toward a state where all elements are successfully contributing to the organization's accomplishment of goals and objectives. When changes that result in an imbalance

are made, different system components restore the balance both within the system and in terms of the system's relationship with the environment.

These four characteristics of an open system describe the typical library organization. For example, as it grows, a library tends to become more specialized (differentiation), which allows for more services and other end-products to be accomplished by different methods (equifinality). Further, the library imports enough energy to survive and grow (negative entropy), and maintains a balance between resource requirements and expenditures to ensure the accomplishment of goals and objectives (equilibrium seeking).

For documents librarians to utilize planning and evaluation and make improved decisions, they should first identify and describe current services/activities. Unless they do so, planning and evaluation will tend to be haphazard at best. The general systems model and open systems characteristics are *tools* that force librarians to consider:

- How the various parts of the library work (or are not working) together
- The impact of government information resources on other areas of the library
- The success with which library resources are transformed into products and services
- How well the collection responds to the information needs of the library's clientele.

Such considerations are essential if government information collections are to be improved and access increased.

Figure 15-1.
General Systems Model

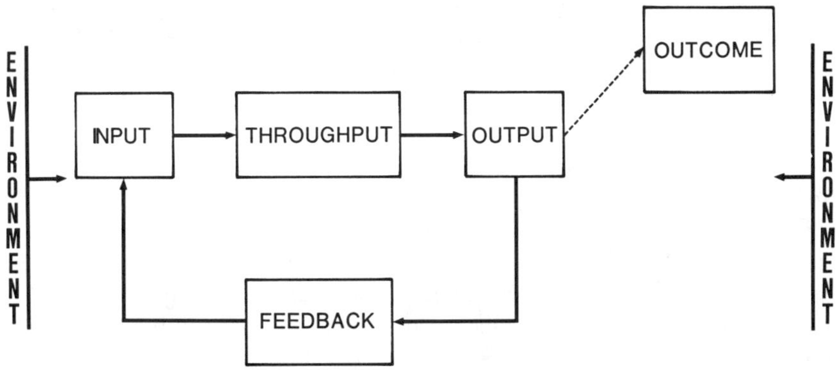

PLANNING AND EVALUATION

Space does not permit a detailed discussion of planning and evaluation processes or detailed approaches to implement them. However, various sources (e.g., McClure et al, 1987) provide additional insights into planning. As shown in Figure 15–2, a large part of planning deals with conducting research and:

- Determining appropriate goals for the library organization and objectives for system components
- Describing the current activities of the library, and the effectiveness of those activities
- Assessing the information needs of the library's clientele
- Deciding which library activities, services, and products should be provided, and which *best* facilitate the accomplishment of library goals
- Conducting formative (an ongoing and continuous process that generates information to be used to modify a system while it is in operation) and summative (at the conclusion of the program or operation; it is product oriented) evaluation.

The activities to be implemented at each of the above points may vary from one library to another, but each requires a process of asking appropriate questions, collecting and analyzing data related to the questions, and summarizing the findings to assist documents staff in making effective decisions.

Planning, a topic that has received much attention in recent years, is the process of setting goals and objectives, developing programs and activities to accomplish those objectives, and evaluating the effectiveness and efficiency of those programs when compared to the original goals and objectives. Goals (long-term directions for the library) and objectives (short-term, accomplishable, and measurable statements of action) must be established in writing before a library can engage in meaningful planning or undertake research successfully. The statement of goals and objectives provides direction for which research questions should be examined and for which problems in the library are top priority for decision making.

A planning document is a formal written statement that details goals and objectives, and delineates specific actions that will be taken within a certain period of time to accomplish objectives. It also suggests procedures to evaluate the extent to which objectives have been accomplished efficiently and effectively. The document provides the guidelines for "appropriate" activities that the various organizational members who are affected by government information resources have accepted. In the final analysis, the document is a statement of policies, priorities, and procedures.

Figure 15-2.
The Planning Process for Government Publications Services

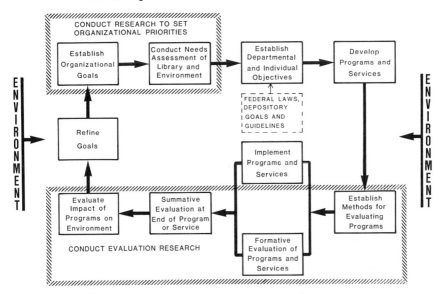

Figure 15–3 suggests an outline of major components for the planning document. The principal headings (Roman numerals) are appropriate for most government information collections. The subheadings can be modified, increased, or deleted dependent on the specific environment of the organization, and on its current procedures related to government information resources.

The evaluation component is essential for any system to modify goals and objectives, establish priorities, and allocate resources in such a manner that the various services and activities are accomplished effectively. Evaluation, which is the accountability aspect of planning, represents a measurement of effectiveness in reaching some predetermined goal (Suchman, 1972). Rossi and Freeman (1985) have written an excellent introduction to evaluation techniques. The techniques that they discuss can be applied to government information services and operations. Failure to include evaluation as part of the planning process is likely to result in the creation of a self-serving bureaucracy, increased distance between government information resources and the users, ineffective allocation of resources, poor credibility with governing bodies, and reinforcement of the status quo. More importantly, the library might continue programs, services, and operations that should have been ended because they no longer contribute to the accomplishment of goals and objectives.

Evaluation techniques may be of two kinds: *formative* and *summative*.

Figure 15-3.
Outline of a Planning Document

I.   Organizational Mission
     A. Philosophy of services, operations, and administration
     B. Assumptions under which the organization operates
     C. Brief historical development of the organization
II. Goals (Broad statements of purpose, long-term, and usually not accomplishable)
     A. For the organization
     B. For government information resources
III. Needs Assessment
     A. Data collection instruments to be used
     B. Community analysis
     C. Responsibilities for administration of data collection instruments and analysis of
         data
     D. Reporting needs assessment results
IV. Resources Available (Analysis of current operations related to government informa-
     tion resources)
     A. Space   D. Collection size/type
     B. Equipment   E. Collection budget
     C. Personnel
V.   Objectives (Specific statements of actions—short-term, measurable, and time
     limited)
     A. Public services
     B. Technical services
     C. Organizational or departmental matters (usually of an administration nature)
VI. Action Steps (Detailed set of procedures that, if followed, will accomplish the
     objectives)
     A. Time limits
     B. Resources to be allocated
     C. Individual responsibilities for specific tasks
     D. Development of performance measures
VII. Evaluation
     A. Effectiveness (were objectives actually accomplished?)
     B. Efficiency (how well—least cost or time—were objectives accomplished?)
     C. Analysis of operations and services in terms of stated performance measures
VIII. Summary and Reporting
     A. Written conclusions regarding the overall planning process for the previous
         year (or other specified time period)
     B. Maintenance of long term trend data as to performance
     C. Presentation of summary and recommendations to administration and others
         as appropriate

The purpose of summative evaluation is to *prove*, while formative evaluation seeks to improve. Both types of evaluation have a role in the planning process, and one is not intrinsically better than the other.

Evaluation of depository collections and services can be either internally originated (e.g., by the depository library itself) or externally oriented (e.g., by an outside agency such as the GPO). Judging from the professional literature and presentations at various professional meetings, in-house evaluation of government information services is minimal. The occasional inspection visits from the GPO account for the only formal evaluation accomplished at many depository libraries. However, the current inspection program is an unsatisfactory part of an evaluation process, for the following reasons:

- A limited number of GPO staff are available to implement the inspection program
- The stated goals for the depository program are inadequate
- The depository program lacks formal objectives
- The *Guidelines for the Depository Library System* (1977) do not actually apply uniformly across the myriad types of libraries inspected
- Sanctions are not enforced for those libraries failing to meet stated criteria
- Specific performance measures have not been formulated to assess actual quality of services and operations
- Evaluation has not been incorporated into the planning process at the local library.

These and other difficulties have been discussed elsewhere (McClure and Hernon, 1983, pp. 174–175). Without an adequate program of regular and valid evaluation, depository library collections are unlikely to provide effective and timely access to government information resources.

Watts (1982, p. 61), who served as an inspector for the GPO, suspected that "one-fifth of the depository libraries are either unwilling or unable to perform their responsibilities and should be evaluated more completely by [the] GPO." Undoubtedly, these libraries fall below the "standards" set by the *Guidelines for the Depository Library System* (1977) and fail to meet the institutional goal of providing access to government publications. Further, meeting depository "standards" may not, in itself, ensure effective access to resources and services.

Various professional associations have served as a rallying point for standards on types of services, collections, staffing, programming, and more. The most recent trend (at least in the public library setting) is to allow each individual library to develop criteria for "excellence" based on the unique needs of the community it serves as well as its particular organizational and administrative environment. Thus, the profession is in a state of flux as it moves from a rigid to an individualized philosophy of standards. Yet there remains the attitude that performance can be improved if only the profession would develop a set of standards that describe "excellence," "quality," or "the best approach" for a library service or operation.

Developing standards for government information collections is, and will be, a complicated business. On one hand, there is a need for various libraries to define activities, services, and programs consistently for purposes of comparability and compatibility. Further, government information collections need to report various descriptive statistics about activities to national or professional agencies/associations. Finally, researchers need to analyze data from the various libraries with some assurance that the data are reliable and valid. But, on the one hand, each collection may have local constraints and unique situations that will discourage the development of standards. Many documents librarians simply do not have the resources available to support the collection, analysis, and reporting of data to develop standards.

The utility of the "standards," as suggested in the *Guidelines for the Depository Library System* (1977), is questionable at best. In general, the *Guidelines* are a simplistic attempt to solve a rather complicated issue relating to the evaluation of government information collections and services. Further, they ignore the current national trend to integrate planning and evaluation at a local level, to meet local needs and information requirements, and to develop performance measures as replacements for "standards."

Until meaningful evaluation of depositories and specific government information services, and techniques of providing adequate access to government information resources, are accomplished through the use of performance measures, the overall effectiveness of both depository services and collections will be limited. Depository libraries, the GPO, and the Joint Committee on Printing must begin to realize the importance of performance measures, and to develop a body of administrative procedures tied to valid goals and objectives, if the depository program is to operate more effectively.

PERFORMANCE MEASURES

Performance measures focus organizational attention on specific areas of services and activities, and seek to determine their overall effectiveness and efficiency over time. A performance measure is a means of determining the degree to which goals and objectives are accomplished, services are provided, and resources are made available. Further, they assess the impact and interrelationship among the various components of information delivery and management with regard to effectiveness and efficiency.

In regard to efficiency, a performance measure examines, "How well are existing resources being used?" Efficiency-related performance measures for depository libraries might probe questions such as:

- What is the average use of the depository collection per staff member?

- How much of the budget goes for the purchase of materials as opposed to other types of expenditures?
- How many depository publications are actually used, how often are they used, and by what types of users?

In the area of effectiveness, performance measures look at, "How well are libraries doing what they say they are doing?" These types of performance measures would examines questions such as:

- How many documents that users seek can they find?
- What percentage of the depository collection meets institutional goals and user information needs?
- What degree of duplication and uniqueness can be identified between reference sources in the documents area and those in other areas of the library?

Clearly, performance measures can provide specific data for local planning and decision making. However, librarians should be aware of a number of key issues related to the use of performance measures (Hernon, 1987).

Two levels of performance measures are necessary for improved government information services/activities. At the first level, measures evaluating the depository library program are necessary. Performance measures can be established in all of the various areas specified in the *Guidelines* (once valid objectives are established), which would allow the depository program as a whole to be effectively evaluated.

As an example, statement 2–11 of the *Guidelines* states that the GPO will "provide assistance to libraries on problems of using the Sudocs system of classification." This statement fails to indicate what is meant by "assistance," what types of "problems" are acceptable for assistance, or what levels of response to a problem by the GPO are acceptable. Thus, for all intents and purposes, this idealistic statement indicates what one would hope "should be happening;" it allows for neither measurement nor a comparable means by which all depository libraries can assess the degree of success with which assistance is being provided for use of the Sudocs system.

At this first level, a conceptual framework is necessary to establish a basis for possible performance measures. Such a framework has already been introduced in this chapter in terms of general systems concepts. Figure 15–4 provides a brief description of nine open system characteristics; for each characteristic, performance measures might be identified. The areas depicted where performance measures would be developed are not comprehensive, but rather demonstrate the variety of methods and strategies available for establishing performance measures.

Returning to the example from the *Guidelines*, possible performance

Figure 15-4.
Depository Evaluation Criteria from Open System Characteristics*

CHARACTERISTIC	POSSIBLE AREAS FOR PERFORMANCE MEASURES
1. *Importation of energy*-a system functions by importing energy (information, products, materials, etc.) from the larger environment.	Resource Allocation Techniques Relationship between Resources and Goals
2. *Throughput*-systems move energy through them, largely in the form of transformation processes. These are often multiple processes (decisions, material manipulation, etc.).	Efficiency of Processes Decision Analysis Cost/Benefit of Alternatives
3. *Output*-systems send energy back to the larger environment in the form of products, services, and other kinds of outputs that may be intended or not.	Accomplishment of Objectives Impact of Outputs on Environment Appropriateness of Outputs
4. *Cycles of events over time*-systems function over time and thus are dynamic in nature. Events tend to occur in natural repetitive cycles of input, throughput, and output with events in sequence occurring repeatedly.	Trend Data of Outputs Flowcharting Degree of Programmed Decision Making
5. *Equilibrium seeking*-systems tend to move toward the state where all components are in equilibrium, where a steady state exists. When changes are made that result in an imbalance, different components of the system move to restore the balance.	Impact of One Component on System at Large Comparisons among System Components
6. *Feedback*-systems use information about their output to regulate their input and transformation processes. These informational connections also exist between system components, and thus changes in the functioning of one component lead to changes in other system components (second-order effects).	Mechanisms for Summative and Formative Evaluation System Change over Time Self-Assessment Methods
7. *Increasing differentiation*-as systems grow, they also tend to increase their differentiation; more components are added, with more feedback loops and more transformation processes. Thus as systems get larger, they also get more complex.	Political Relationships among System Components Cooperation/Coordination among System Components
8. *Equifinality*-different system configurations may lead to the same end point, or conversely, the same end state may be reached by a variety of different processes.	Ability to Match Individual Strength to System Requirements Comparisons with Depository Competitors
9. *System survival requirements*-because of the inherent tendency of systems to "run down" or dissipate their energy, certain functions must be performed (at least at minimal levels) over time. These requirements include: (a) goal achievement and (b) adaptation (the ability to maintain balanced successful transactions with the environment).	Interactions with Governing Board/Institutions Response to Environmental Demands Ability to Identify and Obtain New Resources

*From Edward Lawler, III, et. al, *Organizational Assessment* (New York: John Wiley, 1980), p. 267.

measures to assess the assistance given to depository libraries by the GPO on problems using the Sudocs system of classification might be:

- *Assistance Response Time*: in which the number of minutes for each direct response to a depository query for assistance is considered as a ratio over the number of times assistance is requested:

time between request for assistance and obtaining assistance

---

number of times assistance is requested

- *Assistance Usefulness*: in which the requesting depository would rank the GPO's assistance on a scale of 1–5 (1=very helpful and 5=not helpful), compute an average score on a monthly basis (or some other specific time period), and maintain records of these measures over time.

By setting performance measures such as these, by establishing specific data collection procedures to compute them, by defining carefully a "request for assistance" and "assistance," and by maintaining such data over time, a much more useful picture of the degree of success of the depository program in accomplishing this objective could be obtained. Until objectives and performance measures are established for the various statements in the *Guidelines*, as well as for the criteria given on GPO's *U.S. Depository Library Inspection Visit Form* (n.d.), meaningful evaluation of the depository program cannot be accomplished (see McClure and Hernon, 1983).

At a second level, performance measures appropriate to local depository libraries and documents-related services are necessary. Performance measures at this level typically fall into one of four possible categories:[1]

- *Community Penetration*: designed to measure the extent to which members of the community are aware of the library services available and to determine how often they use these services.
  EXAMPLE: Users as a percentage of the total community population served
- *User Services*: related to user behavior, these measures examine the requesting of material, the asking of questions, program attendance, and the circulation of resources.
  EXAMPLE: Title fill rate (by subject) (percentage of titles requested by patrons, by subject, that are available on the shelves)

---

[1] Other categories and types of performance measures are also possible. Hernon (1987) discusses these issues. He assesses the strengths, weaknesses, and utility of performance measures for decision making. Librarians considering the use of performance measures should review this article.

- *Resource Management*: designed to reflect internal management decisions about how funds are allocated, e.g., choices made regarding resources, facilities, and staff.

    EXAMPLE: Collection turnover rate (by subject) (percentage of total collection checked out per specific time period, by subject)

- *Administration and Finance*: reflect the decisions made by the library administrative staff. The administration, however, may not directly control some of these decisions.

    EXAMPLE: Depository funds as a percentage of organizational total.

Van House et al (1987) details a number of specific performance measures that libraries can apply to government documents collections and services, with some minor modifications.

Figure 15–5 lists criteria to assist libraries in selecting possible performance measures. By setting goals and stating specific performance measures that they wish to evaluate, libraries are stating areas in which additional planning and decision making will be necessary. For instance, by stating that they wish to increase title fill rate by 10% per year as an objective (the performance measure being title fill rate), the area for planning is related to collection development, especially if title fill rate is viewed within a subject context. Upon collection of pertinent data, library staff can initiate specific activities to increase the fill rate. Whatever performance measures a library uses, they should meet the criteria suggested in Figure 15–5. With the establishment of valid goals and objectives, and performance measures, for the depository library program as a whole (as well as for individual depository collections/services), librarians, government officials, and users could all make meaningful assessments of existing government information services as well as have a basis for improving such services.

Performance measures can be used for either formative (ongoing) or summative (at the end of an activity) evaluation. However, there may be trade-off relationships between specific performance measures. For instance, with regard to the two examples given earlier about assistance in the use of the Sudocs classification scheme, increasing the score on the measure "Assistance Usefulness" (ranking the quality of the assistance provided) might require additional preparation and response time for the measure "Assistance Response Time" (the number of minutes for the actual response). Thus, the score for "Assistance Response Time" would decrease.

Figure 15–6, which graphically represents the importance of this relationship, suggests that the relationship between efficiency and effectiveness may be one in which there is a "critical point," e.g., increasing the performance of either the effectiveness or the efficiency of a service diminishes the

Figure 15-5.
Criteria for Setting Measures*

Appropriateness: Will it do what I want?
   e.g., "Is it possible to compare the measure across depository libraries?"
Informativeness: Will it tell me what I need to know?
   e.g., "Will comparing depository libraries of similar size on circulation per capita show which libraries need assistance?"
Validity: Does it mean what I think it does?
   e.g., "Is the percentage of library budget allocated to the documents department a measure of library effectiveness or departmental effectiveness?"
Reproducibility: Would someone else get the same answer?
   e.g., "Would two depository librarians reporting on the same library come up with the same score for per capita use of depository resources?"
Comparability: Are we all measuring the same thing?
   e.g., "Do depository libraries in Nebraska use the same procedures and definitions to count circulaton as those in Florida?"
Practicality: Can we afford the time, money, and effort to gather data for this measure?
   e.g., "Is the information gained from the data worth the effort required to collect the data?"
Input for Decision Making: Will it provide data to assist decision makers?
   e.g., "Is the information likely to identify specific services or operations that can be improved and suggest strategies for their improvement?"

Adapted from Orr (1973).

performance on the other. This concept of a "critical point" is similar to the relationship between various performance measures. Because the performance measures are examining different components of the same system, they are interdependent; that is, changing one component of the system (such as retention policy) will affect another component of the system (such as collection turnover).

In addition to this trade-off relationship, a number of other factors must be remembered when using performance measures:

- Each performance measure emphasizes one facet of library activity only; measures are best used in conjunction with each other
- Conditions can be manipulated to improve the performance on a particular measure without always improving the quality of the service or operation, e.g., increase materials turnover rate simply by heavily weeding the collection
- There are no "right" or "wrong" scores on a performance measure; the scores are tied to specific library objectives and provide "benchmarks" to assess the effectiveness of library activities
- A primary use of a performance measure is to identify areas where change is desired, to determine if change has occurred, and to identify areas where additional research is required
- Performance measures should suggest not only what is happening in the library but also the quality of what is occurring.

Figure 15-6.
Relating Effectiveness to Efficiency*

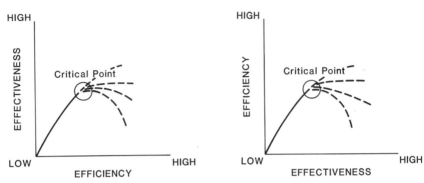

*At some "critical point" to increase significantly the effectiveness or efficiency of a library activity, a "trade-off" will occur and while one measure is increased, the other will begin to decrease.

Carefully selected, and intelligently used, performance measures enable librarians to ensure that goals and objectives are accomplished and to set priorities for resource allocation. Measures are also useful for justifying services and demonstrating accountability to outside funding agencies, and for identifying and setting priorities for areas of government documents services/activities that require formal planning. Use of performance measures requires the ongoing collection of selected data. For the depository library program, the primary set of data that describe depository libraries comes from the GPO's *Biennial Survey.* Unfortunately, the survey is unlikely to collect reliable and valid data from which meaningful performance measures can be developed (Hernon, McClure, and Purcell, 1985). For individual depository libraries it is unlikely that *any* regular data collection process occurs as a means to produce performance measures. For example, the performance measure "correct answer fill rate" requires a data collection process to describe (1) the number of reference questions asked, and (2) the number of reference questions answered correctly by staff.

Generally, neither the GPO nor individual depository librarians can describe the *quality* of services provided through the depository library program in terms of specific performance measures. Librarians and GPO officials have yet to indicate much interest in the maintenance of an ongoing process of data collection and analysis by which performance measures can be produced. Continued reliance on "input" data, e.g., the number of reference transactions, circulations, or materials added to the collection per year rather than "outputs," e.g., correct answer fill rate or title fill rate, provides little assistance in making decisions to better meet clientele information needs and increasing access to government information.

In summary, planning and evaluation of (1) the depository library program, (2) individual depository libraries, and (3) government information services/activities are a prerequisite for gaining effective access to government information resources. But planning is also necessary to coordinate services, reduce overall resource allocation, and increase access to resources not available locally. Ideally, a number of tiers of planning and coordination at the national, state, and local library level may be necessary if the overall purpose of the depository program and Federal statutes are to be accomplished. Some evidence is available to suggest that *planning* for government information services/activities at a state level is being loosely initiated with the establishment of "state plans" for depository publications and services. However, the purpose, contents, and implementation of such "plans" must be examined.

STATE PLANS

Recognizing the need for better coordination of the depository program in each state, the Depository Library Council to the Public Printer and the GPO have encouraged states to develop state plans. Ironically, the GPO is not requiring states to engage in planning. State planning has proceeded in spite of the fact that (1) the depository library program lacks formal objectives to which specific activities can be tied, and (2) many academic, and presumably other, depository libraries have not formulated written collection development policies covering their own institutions and resource sharing (Hernon and Purcell, 1982).

Faull (1985) analyzes the state plans completed as of July 1984 and points out major deficiencies in the planning process. As she observes,

> many librarians who first heard of state plans thought that they would afford an opportunity to improve services, create measurable objectives, and set target dates. Instead, the plans have merely reaffirmed the *Guidelines*. For example, one plan lists interlibrary loans as a service responsibility for regionals and describes those non- depository collections available in the state. The service responsibilities of selective depositories are listed as "to request those documents on interlibrary loan which their patrons do not have access to through the collection," and "to assist non-depository libraries in answering documents reference questions." However, the plan does not offer an evaluative component to suggest how well these points are being achieved. In reality, do selective depositories provide such service and if so, to what extent and how well? (p. 165)

"It is obvious that the documents community entered into the state plan concept without being adequately equipped or prepared for it" (Ibid.). Regrettably, state plans have not "lived up to their potential . . . for handling problems within the Federal depository program" (Ibid., p. 166). Where state plans have included goals and objectives, there is probably neither an evaluation component nor specific performance measures to assess the degree to which measurable objectives were accomplished.

As of the spring 1988, more than 30 states have completed state plans. Not every state, however, intends on developing a plan; thirteen of the plans are reprinted in *State Plans for Federal Depository Documents* (1984). There is no generic plan; rather, there are significant differences among various plans. Some plans merely reinforce the *Guidelines for the Depository Library System* (1977), while others are more ambitious. A plan may advocate the creation of a permanent body such as a state depository council to serve as a coordinating mechanism, to keep the "plan alive," and to provide regionals with an opportunity to exert a major role within the state. Examples of "model" plans might be the ones written for New York and Michigan.

The state depository council, or whatever the coordinating body might be called, might hold monthly or annual meetings that focus on local issues. Undoubtedly, emphasis on issues at the local level explains the reason for little coverage of state plans in the published literature for the past couple of years. Clearly, there is a need for a review of the operations of state plans within a planning and evaluation context. How much better off are the states as a result of the plan, and what objectives have been met?

Without greater consistency among state plans, activities within the various states cannot be compared and the effectiveness of the depository program determined and improved where necessary. A commitment to provide reference service, for example, should be linked to performance measures, the quality of service currently provided, and the extent to which the public has access to depository collections. Clearly, there is an underlying need for research, and the setting of measurable objectives, prior to implementation of the planning process.

One lesson that is clear for those who wish to embark upon the planning process is that the reasons why the organization intends to plan must be identified. The following is a partial list of possible reasons for planning:

- Establish library and system goals and objectives
- Serve political justifications of the larger institution
- Prove/disprove the value of the library or a specific program
- Provide a placebo for staff
- Improve library services
- Justify the performance of library staff members
- Evaluate the performance of library staff members.

Each of these has its own set of assumptions and its own procedures, and, perhaps most importantly, encourages a unique set of expectations from the library staff, administration, the government agencies overseeing the depository program, and the community, concerning the likely outcomes from the planning process.

As briefly sketched, planning must be regarded as a formalized and ongoing activity that recognizes the value of research and critically examines all underlying assumptions. Planning, which is an important and necessary activity in which libraries and the depository program must engage, should take into account differences that might emerge between the goals and objectives of the overall program and those of individual depositories. A final observation is in order; planning and evaluation must be recognized as a legitimate, essential activity associated with holding/retaining depository status.

GPO INSPECTION PROGRAM

In 1949, the GPO initiated the *Biennial Survey* as a mechanism to obtain an inexpensive, descriptive assessment of depository libraries. The survey represented the extent to which the GPO was willing, at that time, to collect data on depository libraries and to monitor their handling of depository publications (Hernon, McClure, and Purcell, 1985, pp. 11–12). The GPO, library community, and the Depository Library Council to the Public Printer recognized that, in addition to the survey, periodic, on-site evaluation was necessary. As a result, in 1975, the inspection program was created.

On a periodic basis, the GPO inspects depository libraries to ensure compliance with the *United States Code* and the *Instructions to Depository Libraries*. According to *Preparing for a Depository Inspection* (n.d., p. 2), "generally, libraries are inspected in chronological order by date of last inspection. Geography and climate are also a consideration when planning an inspection visit."

"The objective of the inspection is to accurately identify areas of strength and weakness" (p. 4). Furthermore, ". . . the evaluation of the library is based on the condition of the depository *on the day of the visit* (Ibid.). Quoting from *Preparing for a Depository Inspection,*

> During an inspection visit, the inspector performs two important functions. The primary responsibility is to report on the condition of the depository, using the Inspection Report form to evaluate the depository operation. In the Inspection Report narrative, they identify steps which must be taken to conform to the minimum standards for depository libraries as set forth in the *Inspections to Depository libraries* and the *Guidelines for the Depository Library System.*
>
> A second responsibility is to act as a consultant to aid the documents librarian in increasing the efficiency and effectiveness of the depository operation. Inspectors are interested in helping the Documents Librarian by offering

suggestions and support. The inspectors will ensure that the documents staff clearly recognizes the difference between a standard which must be met and a suggestion to enhance depository service.

During the visit, inspectors rate depositories in seven areas: depository collections (collection development), organization of the depository collections (initial processing and record-keeping), maintenance of the depository collection (discarding, binding, and replacement of documents), staffing (quality and quantity of depository staffing, and staff training), space (space and equipment needs of the depository), service to the general public (public service and promotion of the depository), and depository cooperation (interlibrary loan, referral, and cooperation with the regional library, the GPO, and other selective depositories). Regional depositories are rated in an eighth area—"regional depository."

Again quoting from the GPO pamphlet (p. 8),

> Each of these areas is covered by a category of the Inspection Report. In each of these categories, it is possible for a library to earn a total of 100 points. The point scores are divided into score ranges. It is the score range which is important in the inspection process, *not* the individual point score. There is no overall rating for the depository. The library is given a separate score for each area of depository activities.
>
> Score ranges are as follows: Excellent (100–90 points), Good (80–89 points), Satisfactory (70–79 points), Unsatisfactory (below 70 points). A score of "Excellent" means the depository has done an outstanding job in this category. There is little room for improvement. A score of "Good" means the library has consistently exceeded standards, but there is still room for improvement. "Satisfactory" denotes a library that has met minimum standards but could significantly improve in this area of depository activities. An "Unsatisfactory" score means the library has failed to meet minimum standards and must take immediate action to address deficiencies in this category.
>
> A library that fails three or more categories, fails the inspection and is placed on probationary status for at least six months. After this six months period has elapsed the depository is re-inspected. Both probationary status and scores of all excellents are extremely rare (less than three percent of all libraries inspected). Most libraries earn scores in the Good and Satisfactory score ranges.

Upon completion of the form, the inspector visits with the library director and summarizes inspection findings.

Library staff subsequently may submit questions to the inspector. "Approximately six weeks after the inspection visit, photocopies of the Inspection Report will arrive at the library. The Library Director, the Documents Librarian and the Regional librarian each receive a copy of the report" (p. 9).

The staff can then review the report and develop strategies for attacking areas of weakness.

Figure 15–7 critiques the section of the inspection form entitled "Service to the General Public" and raises both reliability and validity concerns. Both Chapters 13, "Physical Facilities and Space Management," and 16, "Cooperation and Resource Sharing," review other sections of the inspection form. Suffice to say here, the inspection process is linked to a program that treats all depositories (i.e., Federal, highest appellate court, academic, and public libraries) as the same and that lacks formal goals and objectives. Without goals and objectives, depository activities lack a context; neither program effectiveness nor program efficiency can be measured. Furthermore, the questions on the inspection form may be vague and not connected to a specific goal or objective. Instead of focusing on *standards*, the inspection program should incorporate performance measures.

However, much work remains if the inspection process is to be improved. Priority activities for the future should center on the development of program goals, objectives, and performance measures. All data collection efforts should relate to these goals, objectives, and performance measures. The purpose is to evaluate the depository program and its components, and to engage in planning—moving the program forward and making the necessary changes and adjustments. Development of state plans and the GPO inspection program do not substitute for a carefully crafted, ongoing process of planning and evaluation in the depository library setting.

INCREASING PLANNING EFFECTIVENESS

Planning and evaluation assume a philosophy of change and must be accompanied by a re-organization of attitudes regarding the importance of planning in an organization. As Taylor and Sparkes (1977, pp. 289–290) note, planning:

> is not so much a battery of techniques and systems as a style of management, and the main benefits from planning derive from a continuing dialogue about the future of the organization . . . .. But to start the dialogue involves a dramatic reorientation in management thinking—and a willingness to change.

Indeed, those documents librarians believing that change is unnecessary, or maintaining that formalized planning is inappropriate, will not successfully increase access to government information. Apparently, planning theory and techniques are well ahead of practice. Nonetheless, with the appearance of practical manuals such as *Strategic Planning for Library Managers* (Riggs, 1984), *Planning and Role Setting for Public Libraries* (McClure, et al, 1987),

Figure 15-7.
Analysis of a Section from "Inspection Visit Form"

VI.   SERVICE TO THE GENERAL PUBLIC

A.   Does the depository make available for free use/access in the library by the general public all Government publications?

_____ (1) yes._____ (2) no.

> **Observations and Analysis**
> How can we tell if the answer is indeed accurate?
> How is "free use/access" defined?
> The term "all Government publications" is too broad; it should refer only to the GPO deposit collection.
> The highest appellate court libraries are exempt from this requirement.

B.   For reference questions about Government publications, does the depository library maintain reference stations?

_____ (1) one of more_____ (2) more

> **Observations and Analysis**
> The question should specify only GPO deposit publications.
> A general question such as this should be followed up with indicators of quality; the number of stations should not be equated with quality.

C.   In the library at one or more points of inquiry, is it possible for a user to find:

_____ (1) resources in the Federal documents collection including specific titles?

_____ (2) location of wanted publications?

_____ (3) answers to reference questions or referral to a source or place where answers can be found?

_____ (4) guidance on the use of the collection, including the principal available reference sources/catalogs/abstracts/indexes/aids?

_____ (5) availability of additional resources in the region?

_____ (6) assistance in borrowing documents from a Regional or from other libraries?

_____ (7) user privileges extended to all patrons?

> **Observations and Analysis**
> Responses appear to be taken at face value.
> The question does not serve as a quality indicator.
> Differences among bibliographic identification, physical availability, borrowing, and copying (especially of microfiche) should be taken into account.

D.   Who determines circulation policy:

_____ (1) the depository staff?

_____ (2) the depository staff and administration?

_____ (3) the administration alone?

_____ (4) the professional staff as a whole?

_____ (5) the circulation department?

_____ (6) another department (_____)?

> Observations and Analysis
> What is the significance of this question?
> Are all types of depository materials available for circulation?

E. Does the library provide adequate facilities for:
    _____ (1) using depository documents?
    _____ (2) making copies from documents?
    _____ (3) reading microfiche?
    _____ (4) making paper copies from microfiche?
    _____ (5) making microfiche copies from microfiche?

> Observations and Analysis
> The question does not examine the number and quality of facilities.
> Are the facilities in working condition?
> What is the definition of "adequate" and "facilities"?
> The assumption is that the question examines only documents and microfiche received on GPO deposit.
> Does the question cover microfiche received from the private sector?

F. Is the depository collection publicized through:
    _____ (1) depository emblem on front door?
    _____ (2) announcements of titles/bibliographies/pamphlets?
    _____ (3) orientations/tours/classes?
    _____ (4) radio/television/other means/displays?

> Observations and Analysis
> "Other means" should not be grouped with radio, television, and displays.
> There is no opportunity to specify "other means"
> Why focus on these specific methods; are they presumed to be effective?
> The question should be tied to an objective and ongoing methods of evaluation.

G. Is reference assistance with regard to depository publications available to:
    _____ (1) all who request it during the same hours as general reference?
    _____ (2) all who request it but fewers hours than general reference?
    _____ (3) the institution's members only?

> Observations and Analysis
> Are both telephone and in-person questions accepted?
> Should both types of questions be accepted?
> Is service really offered to "all who request it"?
> The question does not get at the quality of the assistance. The question is not a good substitute for a performance measure such as correct answer fill rate.
> Is the answer to the question based on what documents librarians say, and if so, is this "valid"?

and *Output Measures for Public Libraries* (Van House, et al, 1987), documents librarians can implement planning and evaluation techniques.[2] In recent years, documents librarians have been subjected to pressures from their constituents to provide a broader range of services, from governing boards to justify their expenditures and demonstrate overall "value" to the library, from the GPO—which is evolving policies and procedures (such as its emphasis on micropublishing), and from administrators who frequently fail to see the importance or value of government information resources. Documents collections that will flourish in the next decade and effectively demonstrate their importance as providers of information services will be those that have identified the information needs of their clientele, developed goals and objectives, implemented programs to accomplish those objectives, and evaluated the success of those programs on an ongoing basis. In short, successful government information services/activities will be those that have developed an ongoing process for planning and evaluation.

Before a planning process can be implemented, the following conditions should prevail:

- The organization must be willing to change
- Existing management styles and assumptions must facilitate a planning process
- Adequate resources and staff must be available to support directly the planning process
- Both administrators and staff must have a basic understanding and competency about library planning and evaluation.

At the larger, philosophical level, additional factors such as the following should be met:

- Mechanisms that encourage open and effective communication among the officials of the depository library program, regional and selective depository libraries, and others providing government information services must be in place
- A willingness to assess the current operations and services related to government information resources openly and critically must be present.

These factors are likely to predict the degree of success with which planning and evaluation for government information services/activities will be accomplished.

---

[2] Although McClure et al (1987) and Van House et al (1987) were written in a public library context, the planning and evaluation techniques they describe can be adapted to other types of libraries. More specifically, the 12 output measures can be modified for use in a wide range of library settings, including depository collections.

The complexity and uniqueness of existing administrative techniques, local situations, and the resources available in a particular library preclude "cookbook" recipes for how to prepare an organization for the implementation of a formalized planning process. Library administrators and documents librarians must recognize existing conditions and constraints in the library, determine their knowledge and competency about planning and evaluation, and analyze the administrative assumptions under which libraries organize and service government publications. They should also assess the overall willingness of the organization to change. Recognizing and addressing these contingencies, librarians can develop administrative strategies to create an organizational climate that encourages the planning and evaluation of government information collections and services.

16

Cooperation and Resource Sharing

Until relatively recent times, very little of the information produced by and related to governments has been made available, other than in centrally located archives. Today, with the greater complexity of modern society and the role that a government plays in most areas of human activity, wide dissemination of large blocks of such information has become essential. Governments acquire and disseminate information in practically every field of endeavor, and providing for many of the information needs of those governed has become one of the expected services of government. For both retrospective and current study of government and its activities, libraries can play an important role. They collect publications through depository programs and enhance individual collections by engaging in resource sharing with other libraries, obtaining membership in the services of specialized centers (e.g., the Center for Research Libraries, Chicago), purchasing special microform sets, taking advantage of individual order plans available from the private sector, and so forth.

Only a few libraries purport to be libraries of record with comprehensive collections; even these libraries are not completely self-sufficient. Given the immensity and complexity of government printing and publishing programs, it is beyond the capacity of any one library (or of the library community) to acquire and maintain comprehensive collections of publications/information produced by the Federal government, or any other level for that matter.

Against this background, the purpose of this chapter is to provide an overview of the importance of cooperation for the depository library program, to identify some of the cooperative practices currently in use, and to chart new dimensions in resource sharing for the depository library program as an interlocking network. In effect, the following discussion serves as a background for the next chapter, which explores alternative structures to the depository program administered by the Government Printing Office (GPO).

OVERVIEW

At this time, many libraries are re-examining their reasons for cooperation and resource sharing. Large libraries, for example, may experience difficulties in assisting smaller libraries unable to reciprocate, while the number of smaller libraries wanting access to the holdings of large libraries is increasing. Tighter economics and ever-shrinking resources severely impact upon a willingness to share. Clearly, libraries are finding that informal working relationships are not enough and that contracts formalize responsibilities and expectations. Similarly, intrastate networks operated by state libraries must become cost-effective and cost-beneficial in order to attract scarce funding. Four types of network organizations have emerged most frequently. First, a network affiliates with the state library and serves libraries within the state. Second, a network serves the state but is government related and is not associated with the state library. Third, a network serves a state but is not government related. And, finally, a network may comprise a multi-state, nonprofit corporation. A characterization of networks can be viewed from another perspective—the impact of funding. Networks receiving funding, to aid libraries within a state in locating information from another library in the state, make use of Western Union TWX machines and other terminals linked together, computer output microform (COM) catalogs, and union lists of serials or special collections. Obviously, decreased funding under the Library Services and Construction Act (LSCA), and other official sources, has a dramatic impact on networking.

Cooperation, involving resource sharing, is an important bond that should unite the library community. Resource sharing relates to:

- Cooperative storage
- Access to little-used library material
- Cooperative selection, acquisition, and processing
- Document delivery
- Reference Service.

Interestingly, cooperative storage was more of an issue decades ago than it is now. From the 1930s through the 1950s, it was not uncommon for libraries in the same geographical area to establish cooperative storage for lesser-used materials. However, this type of storage typically did not encompass government publications. Access to lesser-used materials has always been a benefit of resource sharing. Ideally, libraries can concentrate on the selection and retention of high use publications, and turn to resource sharing for access to lesser-needed source material. The activities of OCLC and RLIN typify the benefits of cooperative processing and provide an example of major databases for cataloged records of government publications.

Unfortunately, participating member libraries enter only a small percentage of their government publications into either utility. And, although both utilities load the GPO tapes, "neither has offered special incentives or mechanisms for libraries to add specific holdings" (Turner and Latta, 1987, p. 38). Without holdings information, the "union catalog" aspect of both utilities for government publications is severely impaired. Thus, resource sharing for government publications via these utilities is limited, and those few libraries that have entered documents holdings for their collections may be "plagued" with an overload of interlibrary loan requests.

Document delivery naturally encompasses interlibrary loan and the physical receipt of source material needed by clientele and not locally held. Documents librarians assist each other in the answering of difficult reference questions and in the compilation of lists of locally held reference tools and microform sets. Undoubtedly, this aspect of cooperation depends more on personal relationships than on formal institutions/depository agreements.

The benefits of cooperation are:

- To become more familiar with other libraries, staff, and information providers
- To enable libraries to have more latitude in their selection and retention decisions
- To examine collection development with cost-benefit and cost-effectiveness in mind
- To further bibliographic control efforts
- To supplement locally available resources.

Figure 16–1 shows that formal cooperation can occur among libraries at various levels and can relate libraries to other information providers. The key is to remember that depository libraries (and libraries in general) comprise but one information provider. Resolution of information needs may require both formal and informal cooperation among different information providers.

The International Exchange Program provides the international focus represented in the figure. Under the 1886 Brussel convention (44 *USC* 1719), the Library of Congress (LC) administers the program and the GPO

Figure 16-1.
Depiction of Resource Sharing for Depository Libraries

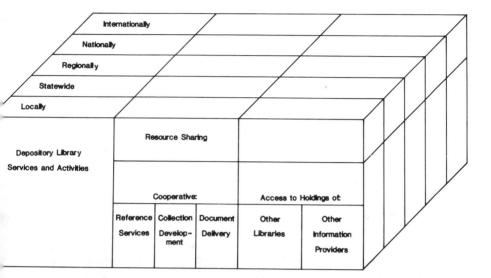

distributes the publications. Approximately 70 libraries, most often national libraries, receive U.S. government publications (primarily microfiche publications), but need not retain or make them available to the public. In return, each country forwards copies of its government publications to the LC.

Since the early to mid 1980s, there has been a growing interest on the part of librarians in establishing resource sharing activities at the state level. For example, a number of the state plans for government publications specifically mention objectives related to increased resource sharing and cooperation among state depository libraries to increase access to government publications. Interestingly, in the area of resource sharing, the plans have stressed bibliographic access among member libraries rather than various types of services or document delivery programs (Faull, 1985).

A number of states, such as Illinois have moved forward dramatically in such areas as *coordinated cooperative collection development*, defined as (Krueger, 1983, p. 3);

> the acquisition and maintenance by local libraries of collections of materials which meet the needs of the people they are intended to serve, enhanced by agreements between these libraries to cooperatively acquire and maintain materials which are not available at the local level and which are needed by their collective clientele.

Typically, such efforts are orchestrated by the state library or another key stakeholder in the state.

The process of *coordinated cooperative collection development* has great potential for depository libraries—especially if applied statewide. Indeed, the process could be used by regional depository libraries to assist selective depositories to provide increased access to government information. One key benefit from such an approach is that the process requires identification and resolution of a number of key issues related to resource sharing. Krueger (1986) provides an excellent overview of the process and has developed a list of key issues that participants must address if *coordinated cooperative collection development* is to be successful. Figure 16–2 reprints these issues; these issues could serve as an excellent discussion point for initiating such a strategy among the depository libraries on a statewide basis.

Point 4–5 of the *Guidelines for the Depository Library System* (1977), as revised in 1987, reads: "Depository libraries, either solely or in conjunction with neighboring depositories, should make demonstrable efforts to identify and meet the Government information needs of the local area." "*Local area* is determined by the library size, its distance from any other depositories, and/or the U.S. Congressional district. This 1987 revision of the *Guidelines* shifts attention from a required minimal level of item number selection and towards a collection development policy aimed at meeting the depository information needs of the local area. The GPO has urged depository libraries to "formulate and implement a written depository collection development policy which articulates the library's strategy for identifying and meeting the Government information needs of the local area" ("Guidelines for the Depository Library System," 1987). The policy (Ibid.):

> should also address procedures for obtaining documents requested by patrons but not selected by the library: inter-library depository coordination of selections; resources available locally; and inter-library loan services.

According to the *Guidelines for the Depository Library System* (1977), depository libraries comprise a network of selective, regional, and national libraries (point 11–1). All depository libraries should:

- ". . . Cooperate in reporting to the Superintendent of Documents new Federal documents not listed in the *Monthly Catalog*" (point 11–4)
- ". . . Cooperate in the development of tools for the identification and location of documents in other libraries" (point 11–5)
- ". . . Verify bibliographic information as completely as possible," when borrowing documents from other libraries (point 11–6)

Figure 16-2.
Summary of Resource Sharing Issues*

BIBLIOGRAPHIC ACCESS
- Should the holdings of small libraries be included in online bibliographic databases? Is the return worth the cost? To what degree will small libraries be able to contribute to the state-wide resource sharing effort? Are there enough unique holdings in small libraries to justify their inclusion on that basis alone?
- How will the various automated systems be interfaced? Can this be done at affordable costs? Since interfacing is a national concern, what can states do to encourage interfacing capabilities?
- How can standards for the quality of bibliographic records be developed and enforced?
- How should last copies be handled once identified in the database(s)?
- Should state (or Federal) monies support automated systems that are not based on MARC records?

INTERLIBRARY LOAN
- How to allow effective participation in the interlibrary loan network by libraries of all sizes and types (i.e., achieving a more equitable distribution of the workload)?
- Whether to reimburse net lenders?
- If costs are passed along, who should pay—the user, the borrowing library, the regional system, or the state library agency?
- Whether and how to achieve direct library-to-library interlibrary loan service rather than hierarchical service?
- How to transmit request rapidly?
- What mechanism to use to distinguish "urgency levels" of requests so that appropriate methods of transmittal and document delivery can be used?
- How to determine desired levels of performance? (Is 70% fill rate for a region or system good? What fill rate should be expected statewide?)
- Whether and how to hold system and state resource providers accountable for their response time performance?
- Is there a point at which the cost of interlibrary loan (including creating and maintaining bibliographic databases and supporting a document delivery program) becomes so expensive that the state must establish limitations? How can such costs be determined?

DOCUMENT DELIVERY
- How to incorporate new technologies, such as communication copiers and digital optical discs, in plans for improved document delivery?
- What performance criteria will be acceptable for document delivery and who will determine this?
- To what degree should libraries use commercial document delivery services instead of relying on each other and existing library networks?
- What level of delivery service is "affordable?"

RECIPROCAL BORROWING
- Whether to reimburse net lenders (some states and systems do, some do not)?
- If net lenders are reimbursed, should the state pay or should regional systems pay and on what basis will they be reimbursed?
- Whether to mandate reciprocal borrowing or wait for voluntary participation?
- How to develop guidelines, gain support for them, and see that they are widely distributed and understood. Guidelines such as whether materials can be returned anywhere in the system or state; how lost materials will be paid for; how fines will be charged and collected; methods for indicating fines were paid; and how delinquent patrons will be blocked from using other libraries.

- How to make the collection of all types of libraries, public and non-public, available on a walk-in basis without disrupting service to their primary clientele . . . .

COORDINATED COOPERATIVE COLLECTION DEVELOPMENT
- What will users "get out of" coordinated cooperative collection development? What might the goals of a statewide CCCD effort be?
- Can all sizes and types of libraries be involved or is CCCD only applicable for large research libraries?
- How can data be gathered that are not subjective and are comparable between all types and sizes of libraries?
- How can success be measured? What evidence will there be that CCCD activities accomplished what was hoped?

*Reprinted from Krueger (1986), pp. 165–166.

- ". . . Provide material on interlibrary loan at least for the regional depository" (point 11–7)
- ". . . Have a policy of providing photocopies of depository materials to other libraries no less liberal than for other library materials" (point 11–8).

A type of cooperative effort among depository libraries is the compilation of discard lists and the sharing of these lists with other regional and selective depositories. The purpose is to enable libraries to fill in gaps in their collections and to better meet the needs of their clientele for older publications.

Another issue that affects the cooperation and resource sharing capabilities throughout the depository library program is the role of the regional depositories. According to 44 *United States Code* 1912, libraries designated as regional depositories, "within the region served will provide interlibrary loan, reference service, and assistance for depository libraries in the disposal of unwanted Government publications." In short, the regionals have some responsibilities to encourage cooperation and resource sharing among the depository members within the region (except for Federal and highest appellate court libraries).

However, many of the regional depository libraries lack adequate staffing and other resources to carry on programs in support of such cooperation and resource sharing. Yet there is a belief that the regionals contribute to a nation-wide cooperative network and encourage successful resource sharing among the depository library members. The reality is that the depository library program does not, in itself, constitute a system of cooperation and resource sharing.

The *U.S. Depository Library Inspection Visit Form* (n.d.), especially in section "VII: Depository Cooperation," attempts to operationalize the points specified in the *Guidelines* covering cooperation into administrative law (see Figure 16–3). Section VIII of the same form specifies the respon-

Figure 16-3.
Depository Cooperation*

A. The depository library cooperates (ILL, referrals, etc.) directly, or through a system to which it belongs, with other depositories
    ____ (1) in the state?
    ____ (2) and with the Regional/s (unless lacking?)
    ____ (3) opportunity for cooperation does not exist.
    ____ (4) opportunity exists, but we do not cooperate.

B. The depository library cooperates with the Regional/s in building their comprehensive retrospective collection by offering discards/duplicates/gifts to them, and by redistributing weeded publications to depositories which can use them.
    ____ (1) yes, on a regular basis.   ____ (3) not as yet.
    ____ (2) yes, infrequently.   ____ (4) does not apply.

C. The depository cooperates in the development of tools, such as union lists, for the identification and location of documents in other libraries.
    ____ (1) yes actively   ____ (4) no projects of this kind are
    ____ (2) yes, but in a limited way.   being done.
    ____ (3) we tried, but could get no   ____ (5) projects exist, but we do
           cooperation from others.   not cooperate.

D. Does the depository provide original documents (or copies) on interlibrary loan, if so requested?
    ____ (1) yes, most (excluding   ____ (3) yes, but to Regionals only.
           reference/high demand/special   ____ (4) choose not to do so.
           collections).
    ____ (2) yes, some.

E. The depository library staff is familiar with the *Instructions to Depository Libraries* (latest edition):
    ____ (1) all of the staff?   ____ (4) none of the staff?
    ____ (2) most of the staff?
    ____ (3) supervisory staff?

F. Upon receipt of shipping lists, are necessary claims usually made within the amount of time specified?
    ____ (1) yes.   ____ (2) no.

G. Are sufficient statistics kept to complete the *Biennial Report of Depository Libraries*?
    ____ (1) Yes, and previous Report sent to GPO.
    ____ (2) Yes, but previous Report sent after the date requested by GPO.
    ____ (3) No, and previous Report not sent to GPO.

H. Are questionnaires and surveys received from the Superintendent of Documents promptly considered and returned (if necessary)?
    ____ (1) No later than the date requested by GPO.
    ____ (2) Occasionally after the date requested by GPO.
    ____ (3) Not at all.

---

*This figure was derived from section VII of the *U.S. Depository Library Inspection Visit Form* (n.d.).

sibilities of regional depository libraries. This section demonstrates that these libraries are overseers of the depository program in their jurisdiction and active participants in resource sharing at both the state and national levels. The depository library program is, indeed, built upon the premise that individual libraries, even ones holding regional status, cannot be totally self-sufficient, and that cooperation is essential. Research, however, has neither fully probed the extent to which libraries actually cooperate nor identified problems in cooperative efforts for depository publications.

The depository library program has not developed its own network structure; rather the program draws upon the regular services offered by a library. For example, where document delivery goes through the regular interlibrary loan service, loan requests must filter up and down the organization. Interlibrary loan is also subject to institutional scrutiny and the desire that the fulfillment of loan requests, or demands on the collection, do not exceed the institution's need for externally held resources. In some cases, libraries place restrictions on their willingness to fill loan requests. For reasons such as these, documents librarians often develop informal channels of communication whereby they can circumvent the formal structure. A study of depository collections, it would seem, is needed and should place the topic in a wider context—general institutional cooperation.

PRESENT DAY EXAMPLES OF RESOURCE SHARING FOR GOVERNMENT PUBLICATIONS

The advent of information handling technologies has furthered the opportunities for resource sharing. For example, individual institutions are relying on cooperative cataloging for the creation of union lists displaying the location of holdings. Once the GPO automated its list of item numbers, it was able to produce a union list reflecting which depository libraries selected particular item numbers. In addition, a union list could be produced for a given region, state, or locality, assuming the GPO was willing to do so. Chapter 7 discusses, in detail, these and other examples of technology derived resource sharing.

Individual libraries can engage in resource sharing and exploit the benefits of information handling technology. Carleton and St. Olaf College libraries provide an example of inter-institutional cooperation whereby areas of collection responsibility are defined. These two libraries practice cooperative collection development and provide prompt document delivery services between the two campuses (Morton and Cox, 1982). Together, both libraries minimize the selection and retention of nonessential and duplicative titles, while focusing on areas of collection strength and controlling the physical growth of the depository collection—focusing collection development on high need titles.

On a local or larger basis, libraries could produce an automated shelflist that collectively lists the items that they currently select. The shelflist could be produced in item number sequence and searched by fields such as item number, date added, survey number, Sudoc number, abbreviated title, the code of that library selecting a given item, publication type (e.g., pamphlet), format, and so forth. With this information, participating libraries could examine, on a regular basis, items within their collections. For example, they could carry out deselection by reviewing selections made five years previously. Comparing the date added field to format and publication type serves as a convenient method for collection evaluation and reviewing what should be retained jointly and/or individually, or discarded from both collections.

This type of information, readily available through an automated system (assuming standardization of practice and the use of similar hardware and software), is much more useful than a traditional card catalog, shelflist, or the recording of holdings in the *Monthly Catalog* or another index. As Morton and Cox (1982, p. 227) observed,

> Because of the implementation of cooperative collection development . . . the two institutions have substantially increased both the breadth and depth of their joint depository collections while cutting overhead in terms of stock, storage, and burgeoning demands on staff. The reality is that through cooperation the two depository collections have come to be viewed by local librarians as a single depository collection with two service points and two administrative chains to the Superintendent of Documents.

However, as they cautioned, cooperative collection development is made easier if participating institutions have formulated collection goals, objectives, and policy statements, as well as share a commitment to cooperate (Ibid., p. 228).

NETWORKING, COOPERATION, AND TECHNOLOGY

Networking presents libraries with opportunities to develop, expand, and refine services. According to Eisenberg and Williams (1986, p. 137), "networking can increase the availability and timeliness of information." Furthermore, networking supports "decisions regarding collections and services based on shared similarities in the information needs of library patrons and complementary aspects of collections rather than mere physical proximity" (Ibid.).[1] Networks may cover large geographic areas and provide for cooperative cataloging, interlibrary loans, serials control, reference service, circulation, and other services. Electronic mail may comprise a type of networking

---

[1] Hernon and McClure (1986) discuss microcomputer networking. Chapters present the experiences of one regional network and the opportunities that microcomputer based telecommunications offer.

and enable the constituency of a Federal agency to gain access to current information (See Hernon and McClure, 1987a).

The availability of information in electronic form may encourage different information providers to forge a partnership and develop a product that is mutually beneficial. For example, with the availability of the *Monthly Catalog* in machine-readable form, three libraries are now working with one commercial company to "clean up" the tapes and to ready them for loading into an online catalog (see Note 3, Chapter 5—pp. 105–106).

Individual libraries are also developing local services but offering them to other libraries either gratis or at cost. These libraries are encouraged to improve the product for mutual benefit. Clearly, microcomputers provide a means for libraries to develop and refine services as well as to benefit from applications developed at other institutions. Undoubtedly the literature of library and information science, in the foreseeable future, will report new examples of local services that have broad applications. The announcement of such services enables other libraries to learn about new developments and not to have to reinvent such services.

The future will see the development of new technologies and new applications from existing ones. Undoubtedly, there will be continued widespread growth of databases, machine-readable files, online software packages, programs of online searching, home access to information retrieval, and CD-ROM products that incorporate government publications/information. Without the planned and effective integration of technology and information in an electronic format throughout the depository library program, significant gaps will emerge among depository libraries. In effect, "haves" and "have-not" depository libraries and collections will emerge. In fact, there may be degrees of "haves" depending on budgetary and other factors. Clearly, the American public may experience difficulties in acquiring needed information. Further, more depository libraries will expect the "haves" known to hold the broadest range of government information to cooperate—make that information available to their users.[2]

---

[2] Viewing depository libraries in a "have" and "have not" context raises some significant considerations, especially as libraries plan for bibliographic control, collection development, and reference services for a wider range of nonprint resources. "How much it would cost a library to expand its role in the depository library program and how some of those costs might be recovered are key considerations. In addition to hardware expenses, the value added by any depository library, be it basic or sophisticated, could be significant"(*Technology & U.S. Government Information Policies*, 1987, p. 18).

Moreover, "examination of . . . various cost issues would occur for at least three stages: (1) set-up costs; (2) recurring/continuing costs; and (3) life cycle costs. Components will include costs related to equipment needs (including initial costs, maintenance, amortization and replacement, and so forth); telecommunications requirements; the added or different use of computing already in place in the library or the parent body; any necessary added space; physical plant renovation for electrical wiring or computer cabling; staff involvement in the integration of the new formats into collection development, bibliographic access, information mediation, library instruction, and collection preservation functions; the costs inherent in bringing together text databases, numerical databases, graphics databases, and bibliographic control databases in

As more libraries extend microcomputer services to their clientele and provide reference service for machine-readable data files, they will want to explore the type of service models offered by the University of Florida Libraries, Gainesville (Pope, 1984) and Texas A & M University library (Hall, 1986). At the first library, the reference department incorporates census and other machine-readable tapes into its regular service offerings. Access to such information blurs distinctions among forms and formats, while bringing more information resources to the resolution of an information need.

The second library has a Learning Resources Department open 94 hours per week and offers students, faculty, and staff access to assorted microcomputer hardware and software. Departmental personnel provide instruction in the use of microcomputers and actively engage in collection development for software. The Texas A & M University library works with technological advances to improve access to the types of information resources needed by its clientele.

According to the staff at OCLC, "as patrons accelerate into the future, libraries must as well. The alternative is irrelevance. And irrelevant institutions disappear ("Channel 2000 Viewdata Test Shows Promise for Libraries," 1981). This need to survive and prosper is the ultimate justification for the rapid and effective deployment of all applicable technology. The challenge for documents librarians is to see that their institution, the government publications collection, and the depository library program respond to change. As libraries and government agencies incorporate more technology and disseminate information in new formats, depository collections should not be regarded as mere storehouses for printed source material. Instead, documents librarians must explore ways to provide access to government information regardless of its format, and ensure that the structure of the depository library program looks to the future not the past.

ELECTRONIC INFORMATION REQUIRES A NEW FRAMEWORK

Technology & U.S. Government Information Policies (1987) is an important report of the Association of Research Libraries' Task Force on Government Information in Electronic Format. The report identifies certain issues related to depository distribution of electronic government information and

---

an expanded form of information delivery; the cost of new and more powerful information manipulation and delivery possibilities—i.e., the expanded user patterns which can result from electronic formats; and the relationship of all of these elements to the whole context of the information taxonomy and the practical and policy concerns implicit therein" (Ibid., p. 20).

emphasizes that document delivery systems and library resource sharing may undergo fundamental change. Electronic distribution may have an impact on the budgets of government agencies, libraries, and users, as well as the services offered by the public and private sectors. Equally as important, since libraries and the government incur costs, some form of cost recovery may be required. Cost recovery must be examined in the context of value-added enhancements provided to electronic government databases and files.[3]

As the report correctly notes (p. 16),

> Evolving patterns associated with electronic information will have a significant impact on the role of research libraries in the provision of national information services. Catalogs of research libraries could serve as regional or national gateways that contain references to information in electronic as well as printed formats whether held locally or elsewhere. This could lead in turn to an increased emphasis on linkages with state-wide and regional systems through advanced telecommunications networks. It is unlikely, however, since the use of electronic sources requires large capital and personnel investments, that sharing will necessarily lead to a reduction of current expenditures for any individual library.

Clearly, there is an urgent need to re-examine the depository program and its component parts prior to the introduction of electronic information, other than through bibliographic databases available from DIALOG and other vendors, on a large scale.

The needs for government information, regardless of format, will vary substantially among depository libraries. Therefore, a depository system such as that proposed in the next chapter, may be advantageous. Perhaps fewer libraries should be depositories; those remaining could function as intermediaries for the library community. However, prior to making structural changes in the program, there should be an extensive examination of inter-institutional cooperation and resource sharing from three cost-beneficial perspectives: that of the government, the library community, and the public. In addition, the legitimate interests of the private sector and other stakeholders merit recognition and addressing.

Change in the depository program "may lead to a redefinition of depository library service responsibilities in which government documents and gateways to government information will be focused along . . . [three] lines. . ." (p. 21). These are (p. 22):

- *"Basic services*: This level of depository library would serve as an information center in which there would exist a small government

---

[3] For a discussion of value-added enhancements, see Taylor (1986). Hernon and McClure (1987a) explores these enhancements in the context of government information.

document collection and a computerized gateway to electronic government information located elsewhere. The service might be focused more on self-help and on-demand levels. There would be a high cost per transaction but a small fixed cost

- *Intermediate Services*: This level of depository library would maintain a larger government document collection and some electronic information and gateways to other electronic information located elsewhere. This library might devise products which would work well through the gateways and might invest in developing value-added approached to the government information. The service would include more mediation and synthesis than the Basic level

- *Full services*: This level of depository library would contain research level government documents and a full range of electronic information and the most sophisticated gateways to other electronic information. The depository collection would be supplemented by related, locally available databases. The level of service would include the highest levels of value-added characteristics. There would be developed software packages and other approaches which would change wholesale government information into retail government information. The cost per transaction would be low and the fixed cost high.

The impact of electronic dissemination through the depository program would also have a profound effect on the role that government fulfilled. The report suggests five possible scenarios (pp. 11–12).

The supplying of government information in electronic format to libraries requires fundamental changes on the part of both government and libraries, in terms of cooperation and resource sharing. At the same time, change requires a reassessment of the legal framework under which the government operates. Information policies take on added significance because they shape the information environment, the format in which government information is produced, and whether the government even collects information. For the government to manage the life-cycle of government information suggests that greater attention will be given to cost-effectiveness, or more precisely cost curtailment and control over what is produced, distributed, and disseminated.

In such an environment, the amount of electronic information will expand and the number of print titles distributed will decline. Libraries are realizing a number of benefits to the incorporation of technology into reference and other departments. Now the depository program must be re-evaluated and better prepared for resource-sharing, cooperation, the electronic dissemination of government information, and functioning as an effective safety net for public access to government information.

ROLE OF RESEARCH

At present, the existing literature of librarianship does little to help us understand the implications or alternatives concerning library networking, though we can say with surety that networks can expand the effectiveness of libraries if properly designed and implemented. Beyond this, the literature is silent. What types of information needs do networks address most frequently? What categories of services are within the "national domain" of library networks? Who are the specific target clientele? These are all questions that can only be fully addressed by further research into library networks.

If little is known about library networks in general, even less is known about library networks for government information, in particular the effectiveness and efficiency of depository library programs. Studies have not delved into the GPO depository library program as a network for resource sharing. A few studies (some of which are over a decade old), however, have examined some aspects of networking but have not looked at the whole. It is known, for example, that regional depository libraries exercise some latitude in whether they extend interlibrary loan services to both other depository libraries and nondepository libraries in their jurisdiction. As noted by Schwarzkopf (1975, p. 97),

> Regional depositories do not believe that they are required by law to loan all the depository documents in their collection. They feel that first claim on the depository collection belongs to the clientele of the parent library and citizens in the local congressional district.

Before the type of network envisioned in the next chapter can be refined and implemented, much more needs to be known about the depository library program—its composition, effectiveness and efficiency, and the nature and extent of cooperation and resource sharing. Studies need to collect data over time and illustrate trends. The *Biennial Survey* conducted by the GPO does not provide a sufficient foundation for an understanding of the depository program over time (see Hernon, McClure, and Purcell, 1985).

Research should also test the document delivery capability of depository libraries. Such studies could see which libraries receive interlibrary loan requests; the number of, and reasons for the receipt of, these requests; the expenses and amount of time involved; and any problems discovered in the receipt of a requested publication (e.g., Do interlibrary loan staff at another institution persist in requiring a Sudoc number for a publication, in fact, contained in the Serial Set?).

Additional issues that merit investigation are (*Technology & U.S. Government Information Policies*, 1987, p. 21):

- "The opportunities now available for restructuring the program to take advantage of electronic information delivery
- Re-definitions of service responsibilities among all participants
- Geographic distribution of service points
- The burden of shared costs among Government agencies, libraries, and users"
- "The effectiveness of communication channels among all participants to encourage consultation in the development and implementation by the U.S. Government of public electronic information programs."

"What must be preserved is a program that provides equitable, no-fee access to basic public information for all citizens" (Ibid.). To this we might raise the question, "Should delivery systems such as depository programs be aimed at the citizenry or taxpayer, or should we substitute a more general word—public? *Public* refers to anyone residing in or visiting the United States and includes those individuals intending to become citizens.

When libraries are placed in proper context—as one information provider among many—they shrink in overall importance. Thus, by advocating studies and thinking that place libraries in a broader context, we echo the belief of Zweizig and Dervin (1977, p. 252):

> . . . the old model of user studies—the identification of who uses the library and how much—has been pushed as far as is helpful. In the context of . . . public librarianship, the demand is for designing new services, not continuing the old; for being accountable to diverse community groups, not simply retaining current users; for justifying even those continuing programs not currently threatened. . . . In order to design new programs, justify old ones, and meet expected demands, the public librarian must be able to speak to such issues as: What do people get from libraries that they can't get elsewhere? How did the library help the individual user? Once the question was, "How much use is made of the library?" Currently, the primary question is. "Who is the user of the library?" . . . The questions for the immediate future must be: "What uses are made of the library? What uses could be made of the library?"

Documents librarianship must also place itself in this broader context and shift its emphasis from matters of bibliographic control to public services and collection development (including resource sharing), examining the reasons for documents use and nonuse, and the effectiveness of libraries as information providers competing in a decentralized information environment. In the process, user studies must give way to investigations reflecting the uses to which libraries are put. "The important question then is not library use, not library users, but library *uses*. It is these 'uses,' these 'utilities' around which libraries can plan programs and can measure effectiveness" (Ibid., p. 251).

Unless the necessary research and development studies (model construction) are initiated, the depository library program will be crippled in its efforts to respond to future challenges. Furthermore, the program will be unable to take full advantage of new information handling technologies to move effectively to meet the information needs of the public. But the opportunities and challenges to depository librarians to exploit the new technologies through increased networking and resource sharing are great. By better use of such resources and techniques, access to government information can be significantly improved.

17

Restructuring the GPO's Depository Library Program

Many depository libraries, including regionals, are faced with congestion in the processing, servicing, and storage of government publications. They also have a limited number of staff and inadequate space for the expansion of documents holdings. The rapidly increasing number of government publications available for depository distribution each year complicates selection and retention decisions for the library staff, especially since a part of the publishing output is trivial, duplicative, and nonsubstantive. These and other difficulties related to the effectiveness of the depository library program are difficult to resolve, because of the program's structure, its placement within the larger organization of the Government Printing Office (GPO), and the limited flexibility that this structure offers local depository libraries.

GPO's depository library program, as presently structured, poorly supports the dissemination needs of government agencies nor does it adequately encourage increased access to government information resources. Research and development studies related to all phases of depository operations, including the need for goals and objectives, distribution practices, document delivery capabilities, costs and benefits of depository activities, the quality of reference and referral services, and user awareness and satisfaction are needed. To assist in the development of such research, this chapter builds upon the first chapter covering public access, analyzes the present structure of the depository program, finds it to be in need of restructuring, and recommends an alternative structure.

The comments and suggestions that will be made here are intended to improve depository operations and the expenditure of taxpayers' dollars as well as meet a wider range of present and future needs of the information-gathering public. Although the emphasis is on the structure (the organizational arrangement and relationship among system components) of the program, functional aspects (the purpose or activities of the system and its components) affecting that structure cannot be ignored. Thus, the emphasis will be placed on the depository structure, but, when necessary, functional factors will be considered.

Despite general agreement among documents librarians that the depository library program is a "good" one or that it is generally "successful," specific criteria for "good" or "successful" are not easily identified. Two broad categories of success that can be suggested are: (1) effectiveness or the accomplishment of goals and objectives, and (2) efficiency or the utilization of the least resources (time, staff, money, etc.) to accomplish those objectives. Without the establishment of goals and objectives, the effectiveness, strengths, and weaknesses of the depository program cannot be fully determined.

GPO'S DEPOSITORY PROGRAM AS PRESENTLY CONSTITUTED

Overview

A number of depository programs distribute government publications for use by the public. These programs exist for publications at the Federal level as well as state and local governments and international organizations. At the Federal level, depository programs have been established for the Government Printing Office (GPO), the Patent and Trademark Office, the Geological Survey, the Bureau of the Census, and so forth. The best known of these depository programs is the one administered by the GPO. Chapter 19, title 44, *United States Code*, provides the legal basis for the operation of this depository program.

A library may serve as a member of different depository programs. Therefore, it may have to meet the requirements and expectations of the United Nations, a state and city, U.S. Patent and Trademark Office, the GPO, and so forth.

A depository library program is one of cooperation between a government and libraries, in which each gives and receives something. The government provides free publications, in return for a commitment that these publications will be available to the general public. The libraries, in return, want many of these publications and realize that, without depository status, they would have to either purchase them or expend considerable time and money in monitoring new publications and publishing activities and in preparing and submitting requisitions. Depository libraries benefit from the arrangement; they receive publications free, automatically on standing order.

Based upon an analysis of 1,373 participants in the GPO depository program (not the present 1,394), one descriptive analysis (Hernon, McClure, and Purcell, 1985) found that over half of the libraries (56%) were academic and another 11% were law school libraries. Over two-thirds of the depository libraries, therefore, are academic. Another 20% are public libraries; incidentally, the percentage of public libraries has declined over the past decade. The remaining 13% comprises Federal, court of law, state agency, historical society, private membership, medical, and other libraries. Over 500 depositories select less than one-fourth of the available item numbers; that number has increased over the past decade as more publications have become available for depository distribution.

The depository program consists of two types of designations—congressional and law. Congressional designation requires the availability of government publications (those deemed of public interest or having educational value) "for the free use of the general public." The principle of law designation, which applies to certain types of libraries (e.g., Federal, land grant college, state appellate court, law school, and state agency) permits exceptions to use and retention practices.

Appellate court libraries need not make publications available to the public, and Federal libraries, which may discard publications at will by offering them to the Library of Congress and the National Archives and Records Administration, are not under the jurisdiction of regional libraries. Nonetheless, having two types of designations provides a mechanism for increasing the number of depositories within a congressional district. The assumption is that the creation of more depositories results in better public access to government publications.

Goals should serve as a basis for determining the effectiveness of a depository program. Unfortunately, since those formulated for the GPO program are poorly defined and inadequately stated, they cannot lead to a determination of program effectiveness (see Chapter 1). Another consideration important to evaluating or redesigning the structure of the depository program is to identify existing weaknesses with the program. The weaknesses related to individual depository libraries (both selective and regional) include:

- Lack of adequate support from the host institution in terms of personnel, physical facilities, and budget; in fact, many depository library collections are understaffed
- Poorly trained staff frequently service the depository collection

- Substantial variation exists in the quality of reference and referral services provided
- Lack of "programming techniques" to promote and integrate documents into the library/community
- Limited bibliographic control over publications
- Item selection is seen as collection development
- Ineffective use of technology for improved services
- Many libraries retain depository status primarily for the automatic, free distribution of source material that otherwise would be expensive to acquire.

Additional weaknesses in the depository library program that are related to the GPO include the following:

- Selection of "high quality" versus "low quality" documents is difficult because of item number grouping
- Lack of an effective inspection program based on measurable objectives
- Uneven distribution of depository library status between academic and other types of libraries (this creates an impression that the program is designed mainly to support higher education)
- Depository collections within private institutions (e.g., colleges and universities, or the Boston Athenaeum) cater to their own clientele and may discourage use by the general public
- Public libraries comprise too few of the member institutions
- Access to depository materials is primarily through academic and public libraries; other avenues of distribution are ignored
- Libraries wanting depository status, but situated in congressional districts already having the allotted number of depositories, might be able to provide better collection support and reference service than existing depositories (depository status is tied primarily to congressional districts)
- Geographic maldistribution (too many depositories in some congressional districts or geographic areas, and none, or not enough, in others)[1]
- The program consists of a diverse assortment of libraries (meeting

---

[1] Schwarzkopf (1972, ED 006177) has noted the problems with basing the depository library program on congressional districts. For example, congressional redistricting may result in the creation of more depositories than are theoretically permitted at present (some districts have more than the two depositories granted by representative designations). There is a wide disparity in population among congressional districts. Educational institutions and other significant library facilities are not uniformly spread throughout the district. Schwarzkopf believes that a number of depositories "do not deserve the designation; but there is a reluctance for them to voluntarily give, or be forced to give, it up."

different goals and varying substantially in selection patterns) rather than as a formal, interlocking network

- The role of the GPO as a congressional agency limits its effectiveness regarding Executive Branch agencies as well as individuals seeking information
- No unified bibliographic control or access exists to all government publications/information (there are major variations among agencies in their willingness to participate in depository distribution; broad types of documents are not fully distributed; and cooperation with clearinghouses such as the National Technical Information Service is inadequate)
- The program is identified with print publications and legally is restricted concerning the extent to which Federal agencies must make nonprint resources available for depository distribution
- Variations exist among regional libraries concerning the provision of interlibrary loan, reference service, and assistance to those depository libraries under their jurisdiction
- Member libraries exercise limited direction and control over the depository program.

The above mentioned weaknesses with the program can be traced, in large part, to the ambiguity of the program's goals and the specific roles that the GPO, the Joint Committee on Printing (JCP), the depositories, and other Federal information disseminators play in the distribution, bibliographic control, and access to government information (Richardson, Frisch, and Hall, 1980). Other weaknesses are attributable to the 1895 Printing Act and its outdated provisions. Although some of the above mentioned weaknesses comprise functional problems with the program, it is likely that structural considerations may address and resolve some of them. But, before a structural assessment can be meaningfully initiated, two critical assumptions under which the depository program operates must be identified and assessed.

Critical Assumptions

The first assumption relates to the definition of government information resources (see Figure 17–1). Depending on how one defines the term "government information resources," and the breadth of those resources that might enter the depository program, the structure of a network or a system will be affected.[2]

---

[2] *Networks* consist of two or more independent libraries or other information providing organizations joining together in a common pattern of information sharing. Since there must be both a regular sharing and a contractual agreement, networking represents a coordinated effort to solve common problems. A *system* may be defined as a set of independent components that have common goals, share similar resources, and interact with the environment.

The second assumption involves administrative control of the program. Administrative control ranges from highly centralized (where the government or some Federal agency retains the authority to direct and enforce the regulations regarding the operation of the network) to highly decentralized (where the individual depository library retains significant control over its specific activities, and responds to the environment without direction or interference from the government.

These assumptions are not "either-or" conditions; rather, they are scales between the poles of centralized versus decentralized and represent broad versus narrow concepts of government information. Depending on the designated purpose of a network, the depository program could fall into one of the four quadrants suggested in Figure 17–1. The depository program, as it now exists, falls into quadrant IV: centralized administrative control, with a rather narrow concept of government information resources. More importantly, however, the program falls into this quadrant by default, due to a lack of clear direction and objectives rather than some preconceived and developing perspective of the role of the depository program.

Identifying these assumptions, and determining the "appropriate" degree of centralization versus decentralization, as well as a broad versus narrow concept of government information resources, is critical. Figure 17–2 suggests the implications of the assumptions, in terms of the four basic quadrants they represent. Each quadrant that suggests an impact on the depository structure may or may not assist the accomplishment of specific system-wide objectives—assuming such objectives can and are stated.

A number of performance criteria can be suggested and are listed in the left column of Figure 17–2. A performance criterion is a specific result, activity, or expense that affects the overall effectiveness of a system. These performance criteria are ones that many documents librarians and government officials discuss in other contexts of depository library operations; however, these—as well as others—can be used to suggest how the various quadrants impact differently on them. In short, the decision about how the assumptions are defined will force the depository program into one of the four quadrants. Depending on the quadrant, the depository program then can be expected to be affected along the lines suggested in Figure 17–2.

For example, the performance criterion, public access to information, will have different measures of effectiveness based on whether the structure of the system is centralized/decentralized or government information resources are broadly/narrowly defined. Figure 17–2 suggests a subjective analysis of the impact of these quadrants on the performance criterion. As can be seen with the criterion "public access to information," the range of impacts—from very low to high access—is significant.

Obviously, it is important that the assumptions under which the program operates be clarified. As demonstrated in Figure 17– 2, each quadrant

Figure 17-1.
Critical Assumptions Underlying the Depository System

ADMINISTRATIVE CONTROL

	Decentralized	Centralized
Broad	I	III
Narrow	II	IV

CONCEPT OF GOVERNMENT INFORMATION RESOURCES

Centralization: The degree to which administrative control is retained by the highest hierarchical level in the system

Concept of Government Information Resources: The range of government agency publications that are entered into the system

represents a number of trade-offs when compared to other quadrants. This concept of trade-offs is most important when considering the structure of a depository library network. Furthermore, those individuals attempting to improve the effectiveness of the depository program may wish to determine the levels of acceptable performance on the criteria suggested in Figure 17–2 before they make an a priori decision concerning the best way to define the assumptions of centralization and the concept of government information resources.

Importance of Performance Measures

The two assumptions previously discussed underscore the importance of knowing, in advance, what is to be expected from the network. Until those expectations are generally agreed upon, the network will continue to be "all things to all people." And, although these assumptions affect both the structure and function of the depository program, no existing criteria have been developed to determine the effectiveness and efficiency of the depository program. Thus, any analysis of the existing depository program must address the need to develop clear criteria related to effectiveness and efficiency. Poorly constructed and nonmeasurable objectives only exacerbate the problem.

Performance measures are quantitative indicators of a system's ability

Figure 17-2.

Implications of Centralization and the Concept of Government Information Resources on Selected Criteria

QUADRANT / CRITERIA	I BROAD DECEN RALIZED	II NARROW DECENTRALIZED	III BROAD CENTRALIZED	IV. NARROW CENTRALI ED
Public Access to Information	HIGH	LOW	MODERATE	VERY LOW
Ability to Encourage Inter-Institution l Cooperation	VERY LOW	MODERATE	LOW	HIGH
System Personnel Requirements	VERY HIGH	MODERATE	MODERATE	VERY LOW
Local Control over Collections	HIGH	LOW	LOW	LOW
System Administrative Expenses	VERY HIGH	MODERATE	HIGH	LOW
Ability to Adapt Change	VERY LOW	LOW	MODERATE	HIGH
Degree of Bibliographic Control	VERY LOW	LOW	MODERAT	HIGH
Local Space, Personnel, Equipme it, Resources Req'd	VERY HIGH	HIGH	MODERATE	LOW

to accomplish objectives and respond to the needs of individuals using that system. Regardless of perceived difficulties related to establishing performance measures for the depository program, such measures are critically needed. Research into the development of performance measures for the depository library program is nonexistent. Despite this dearth of information about how to evaluate the program, there has been no shortage of suggestions that the program be changed or modified.

Systems concepts can be used to develop possible performance criteria for a depository library network (see Chapter 15 for additional discussion of this topic). Open systems characteristics are especially important when evaluating the depository library program, because they suggest not only possible areas for performance measures but also possible structures that will enable the network to better achieve specified objectives. Still, an evaluation of the depository program based on open systems characteristics contains certain assumptions (Churchman, 1979):

- The program is comprised of interdependent parts, each of which has an effect on the other parts
- The sum of the parts is more than the whole—there is an intangible "essence" to the system that results from the interaction of the various parts
- System components respond to the environment on a logical and orderly basis—although we may not know what that basis is.

Although systems thinking has been around for years, its use as a conceptual basis for the formal evaluation of the depository library program appears not to have been considered.

Until performance measures are developed, depository librarians will not know specific levels of performance that they are expected to fulfill, the GPO cannot set realistic regulations and guidelines, researchers cannot meaningfully evaluate the overall success of the network, and inspection of the depository libraries will not achieve its intended purpose—providing valid and reliable feedback to the GPO, depository libraries, and Congress.

ALTERNATIVE STRUCTURES FOR A DEPOSITORY NETWORK

The possible candidates for a depository library structure are limited only by one's imagination. Figure 17–2 depicts the constraints imposed by the government and the areas for priority activities. An inspection of the existing program and its functions suggests possible criteria to be considered in the development of an alternative depository structure. Research is required to determine the appropriateness of these criteria. Some possible criteria for the creation of an interlocking network (as opposed to a *program*) might include:

- Accommodate computerized information processing and other forms of information handling technologies
- Provide mechanisms for self-evaluation and demonstrate accountability to outside agencies
- Coordinate bibliographic control over a broader range of government publications that are "high demand" materials
- Provide physical and financial resources to assist member libraries/agencies in accomplishing program goals

- Provide formal programs of continuing education for depository librarians and certification that such education has occurred
- Encourage nonlibrary related institutions to serve as "depositories"
- Promote inter- and intra-institutional cooperation
- Minimize duplication of services provided by the private sector
- Increase access to government publications by a wider range of user groups
- Keep network costs at a minimum.

Various writers have criticized the existing depository library structure, called for the creation of more depositories (despite the previously mentioned program deficiencies), and requested subsidies from the Federal government for the purchase of bibliographic aids. However, such criticism has led to few detailed recommendations by which the program could be modified or replaced.

At the April 1980 meeting of the Depository Library Council to the Public Printer, another step in the structural hierarchy was proposed. Offered in an attempt to ease critical space and staff shortages faced by regional depositories, the proposal called for the maintenance of a backup collection that would relieve regionals of the requirement of accepting and retaining all items distributed through the depository program. There would be either "a national collection [within the GPO] or a system of super-regionals with federal support" (Depository Library Council, 1980, p. 6).

Another proposal for assisting regional libraries was presented at the Depository Library Council meeting of September 1980. It recommended that the GPO establish a network whereby regional libraries would no longer need to maintain comprehensive collections but would still support selective libraries within their jurisdiction. The GPO would be required to (based on a letter sent to regional libraries by Charles A. Seavey, then of the University of New Mexico):

- Provide a network coordinator
- Provide funding for a dedicated OCLC terminal for the documents department of each regional library (individual libraries would absorb all other costs)
- Have the holding symbols for regional libraries included in OCLC records at the time that the GPO inputs records
- Consider inputting retrospective holdings of regionals into OCLC.

Although this proposal does not resolve fundamental structural weaknesses within the depository program, it does provide another indication that serious problems exist and demand immediate attention, if libraries are to cope with the massive publishing output of the Federal government.

During the discussion surrounding the possible revision of part of title 44, *United States Code*, in the late 1970s, John J. Boyle, then the Public Printer, stated (*The National Publications Act*, 1979):

> . . . it may be worth considering separating the Superintendent of Documents Operation from the Government Printing Office, leaving the GPO where it is, and establishing Documents as a separate agency in the Executive Branch with a Commission to determine policy for broader dissemination of government information . . . . The cataloging and indexing function of the Documents department, albeit very important, could be located anywhere in government without destroying its effectiveness.

The proposed revision of title 44 also generated discussion on whether regional depositories should exist, but did not adequately explore alternative frameworks for the depository program.

Instead of embracing regional depositories on the basis of vested interests and current practice, librarians should explore different models and find the most viable way to further inter-institutional cooperation of lesser-needed titles. Whatever model is finally adopted must view the depository program as a formal network allowing member libraries to join together in a common pattern of information sharing. That network should also provide for:

- Bibliographic searching
- Cooperative acquisition
- Interlibrary loan and document delivery capabilities
- Reciprocal borrowing privileges
- Referral services
- Resource sharing
- Storage/preservation of little-used material.

Some of these operations can be supplied through such bibliographic services as OCLC, while others are in the domain of the GPO. Given the present and planned activities of the Federal government in regard the electronic distribution and dissemination of information, the depository program should be redesigned to take full advantage of appropriate information handling technologies and of a wider range of information appearing in nonprint formats. In this way, government information can be incorporated into a broader policy framework.

In summary, suggestions such as those presented in this section merit careful scrutiny. Alternative structures for a depository network must be analyzed and compared. GPO's program should not continue to operate largely on the assumptions on which it was created. Many of these assumptions are no longer valid given the changes in our society; the technological advances in information collection, storage, and processing; and the changing view of the role of the Federal government vis-a-vis the public.

SPECIFIC STRUCTURES SUGGESTED IN THE LITERATURE

Powell and Pullen (1958, p. 180) recommended a three-part depository system consisting of:

- *Regional depository libraries* housing comprehensive, permanent collections and providing interlibrary loan
- *Selective depository libraries* determining their own selection profiles
- *Information libraries* comprising small public and college libraries "whose funds for books and periodicals have averaged for 10 years or more, $20,000 or less per year." These libraries would receive 10% of the documents available for distribution, but need not retain them beyond the time of actual need.

In 1973 and 1974, an Ad Hoc Committee on the Depository Library System, of the Government Documents Round Table (GODORT), American Library Association, proposed a comprehensive network of local and regional depositories, under the direction of a National Depository Library. Morehead (1975, p. 46), who has summarized the recommendations of the Committee, notes that they "provide the library community with an outline for protracted discourse on a subject central to documents librarianship." He reported that major changes are needed, and, furthermore,

> There is a consensus that the current patchwork policies can only continue to vitiate that section of the law which states that "depository libraries shall make Government publications available for the free use of the general public."

Fry (1978, pp. 116–117), who also recommended change, maintained that it is urgently necessary to "determine whether a reformed and revitalized national depository system for government publications/information can cope with modern needs for prompt, equal and effective access by an information-dependent society."

Building upon the conceptual model suggested by Powell and Pullen, Fry recommended a five-tier organizational structure that makes documents from all levels of government accessible to the public. A National Center for Government Publications, a department within the Library of Congress, would provide central planning and cooperation for a "highly decentralized" service program. Other parts of the proposed structure include:

- *State library agencies*, perhaps in conjunction with another library, would fulfill the role of regional depositories
- *Resource centers* consisting of the major academic and research libraries would maintain comprehensive collections but without administrative responsibility for the depository system. In this way, they could concentrate on the information needs of their own clientele
- *Selective depository libraries* containing publications across levels of government would provide reference and document delivery services through the depository system
- *Government publications and information centers*, fulfilling a role similar to the information libraries proposed by Powell and Pullen, would enable educational facilities to obtain needed documents free of charge. This category, however, might contain "an amalgamation of a Federal Information Center (GSA) with a local public library" for "the provision of government information/publications services at all levels through inter-governmental cooperation" (Ibid., p. 126).

Fry (1980) later modified his original proposal and advocated a merger between the National Center for Government Publications and the National Archives and Records Service, on a separate but equal basis. "A long range planning and research component would be established to provide guidance for future program developments" (p. 116).

Hernon (1981) proposed the formation of a Federal Information Agency based on the merger of the GPO and National Archives and Records Service. His subordinate levels of the depository network were similar to those proposed by Fry. However, Hernon more fully developed the concept of information resource centers as a mechanism for providing public and school libraries with access to basic government publications.

Favoring a centralized agency for the control and distribution of *all* government publications, McClure (1982a) has detailed a structure that addresses the need for research and developmental studies. The structure that he outlined would attempt to ensure valid inspection and evaluation of the depository program, as well as encourage a system-wide recognition of the need for staff training. He envisioned a reduction of the number of regional libraries to eight, with expanded responsibilities and resource support from the government and an increased role for local public agencies as information resource centers.

The proposed National Publications Act of the late 1970s, which dealt with H.R. 5424 and revision of part of title 44, implied yet another structure; the exact framework, however, was vague and subject to interpretation. Apparently the framers did not have a specific plan or organization in mind, and they preferred a general bill so that they could later legislate by regulation. The Director of Distribution Services, within the National Publications Office, would be required to maintain a complete documents collection in cooperation with other government bodies. According to the legislative intent (*National Publications Act*, 1980, p. 41),

> such maintenance does not require the physical possession of copies of all Government documents, but merely directs that he have knowledge of all existing materials and that he have access to them for the purpose of making them available to depository libraries. The complete collection, and the Director's access to it, is intended to serve as a lending library of 'last resort' for the federal depository library system, providing a copy of, or access to, any Government publication requested by a member library of the depository system.

Due to the presence of this collection, libraries, it was suggested, could be selective in the acquisition of new source material. Perhaps a comprehensive collection was possible decades ago; its feasibility, now and in the future, is doubtful. The proposed legislation, which also recommended the abolition of regional depositories, further assumed that a comprehensive index to government publications was both desirable and possible.

In the first edition of this textbook, we developed a conceptual model (Figure 16–3, page 334 of that book) that proposed a Federal Information Agency as an independent government agency charged with the printing and binding of government publications. The Agency would also function as a clearinghouse for the availability of other types of information resources. A Council of Government Publication Officers, consisting of representatives from the three branches of government, would serve in an advisory capacity and ensure that the needs, requirements, and expectations of each branch were addressed.

A division of the Agency would administer the depository library program. The program would consist of regional and selective depositories, as well as information resource centers and research libraries. The research libraries would provide collection and service backup to depository libraries in return for the free receipt of government publications. These libraries could weed items from the collection as publications became useless or obsolete.

The conceptualization of the depository offered here differs from the earlier one. The model discussed later in this chapter requires a less radical reorganization of the existing program and rewriting of parts of title 44, *United States Code*.

TYPES OF ALTERNATIVE STRUCTURES

Any significant alteration to the present structure, especially if it is to accommodate computerization and perhaps even telecommunication, should be adopted only after extensive discussion and analysis within the library community, holding congressional hearings, and the completion of research and developmental studies. Discussions should explore what is theoretically the best as well as practically the most likely to gather widespread support.

The following presentation is offered *not* as a blueprint for change, but to revitalize discussion of (and to stimulate research into) alternative models and their feasibility for integrating government information more effectively into a national information policy. The result of national discussion and debate should be to blur distinctions concerning the level of government, issuing agency, individual depository program, and format in which information appears. At the same time, this discussion and debate should increase the value of government information resources to a wider range of libraries, many of which are currently known as nondepositories. In addition, more of the public's information needs should be addressed in a cost-effective and cost-beneficial manner.

The existing structure. The depository program operates on a clear hierarchy in which many local depositories report through regional depositories (with limited resources and authority) to the Superintendent of Documents. The Superintendent of Documents, which is but one part of the GPO, has additional responsibilities but limited powers of enforcement.

The centralized agency approach. This alternative structure combines all government printing activities into one central agency that has responsibility for the acquisition, organization, bibliographic control, printing, dissemination of the broad range of government publications, and coordination of existing publication activities among a host of agencies (e.g., NTIS, ERIC, and the Department of Energy). Given the centralization of publication activities, either the existing depository structure could be used or features from some of the alternative structures listed below could be combined.

Information resource center approach. This approach would encourage the establishment of collections with minimal item selection; the actual percentage received would probably not exceed 15. Since these information resource centers (IRC) would not comply with the same regulations as do regional and selective depository libraries, they could address unique information needs of specific clientele. They could be established in public, school, or special libraries. Such an approach would provide access to government publications to a wider audience, and assist libraries not wishing to obtain a larger percentage of item numbers. This approach has been discussed in greater detail elsewhere (Hernon, 1981).

Area regional depository approach. Much controversy exists concerning the role and effectiveness of the regional depository structure. An area regional approach would maintain the concept of regionals as an intermediary to assist local depositories or IRCs, but would reduce their number from the present fifty-one to a maximum of fourteen (the number of GPO regional printing plants). Having responsibility for a broader geographical area, these regionals would be subsidized in part by the central publication agency to perform specific activities, including instruction, inspection, collection development, networking and cooperation, and sales.

The voucher approach. Government publications would be sent only to those libraries or other public agencies submitting vouchers from the government for purchasing documents. Vouchers would be made available to appropriate information centers and libraries under specific guidelines. Such an approach would greatly reduce the costs of operating the existing program—one in which many depository items are not selected, and even many of those that are selected are never used. Local depositories and IRCs could, of course, purchase whatever they chose, or be given an allocation of vouchers to assist in overall collection development.

The commercial approach. A number of commercial vendors already have depository programs that are available on a "pay as you go" basis. Indeed, microformatted government publications of depository items, congressional materials, statistical data, and other types of information are commercially available. A structure could be established whereby all distribution of materials would be accomplished by a commercial vendor, either partially supported by the government or by local libraries and public agencies wishing to collect such materials. In short, the government would hire a commercial firm to provide depository services through any of the other structures suggested in this section.

Circular A-76 of the Office of Management and Budget lends credibility to this approach. In addition, discussions in the literature, since 1986, concerning the privatization of NTIS suggest that the Commercial Approach has powerful and articulate supporters (Caponio and Geffner, 1988).

The sales/depository approach. Instead of the existing system that separates sales and depository programs, the two could be combined. Each state might have a central sales office for public access and the purchase of materials, and be responsible for distributing depository materials to appropriate local agencies. Under this approach, local sales agencies might use a voucher system to obtain documents from the government, receive specific titles of publications on a depository basis, or simply purchase those items desired. This approach would place greater emphasis on marketing and selling government publications to the public rather than depositing them into what many believe to be archival storage in libraries.

The proposed *Government Information Act of 1987* (H.R. 1615) would have created a Government Information Agency by merging the collection, processing, and sales functions now carried on by numerous agencies. All Federal producers and collectors of information would be required to provide information to the Agency. The intent would be to make information available to the public from one source and to mandate uniformity in pricing. Creation of the Agency would demand the resolution of numerous problems, especially those related to the merger of functions now performed by the Legislative and Executive Branches of government. The relationship of the unified sales program to the depository program would have to be clarified. Nonetheless, this legislation underscores that myriad practices exist and confuse public access to government information.

The approval plan approach. Using the commercial vendors, once again, as a model, a structure could be established whereby local depositories and IRCs develop a profile of their information resource requirements with the government. The depositories and IRCs then receive regular shipments of government publications meeting those criteria. If materials, once examined in the local agency, do not meet expectations, these resources could be returned to the central agency for full credit. The structure for this approach could simplify existing depository arrangements with the Federal government by eliminating the role of regionals and reducing the number of staff required at the Office of the Superintendent of Documents. Such an approach, combined with the *Commercial Approach*, could take the government out of the publication/distribution business.

The state data center approach. One innovative approach to encourage the accessibility of census materials has been the establishment of State Data Centers. Using this approach as a model, each state could have a Documents Center that not only provided access to government publications but had specially trained staff to assist users in gaining access to government information. Under such a structure, the IRCs requiring the use of Federal publications might inspect publications prior to purchase, obtain expertise on how to utilize and gain access to the information, and provide referral service to the State Data Center. The major difference between the existing regional structure and the state data centers is the latter's emphasis on providing information services rather than having information storage as a major responsibility.

A comprehensive approach. Comprehensive in approach, this structure draws on existing Federal structures and incorporates a number of characteristics described in the various structures previously mentioned. The structures envisioned by Fry, Hernon, and McClure all build from this approach. Although these structures have variations, they share common characteristics.

With this in mind, the following discussion is offered in the hope that it might lead to further assessment of the depository program as an interlocking network for providing the public with access to government information and for attacking the deficiencies in the depository program described earlier in the chapter.

CONCEPTUAL BASIS FOR DEPOSITORY LIBRARY NETWORK

Caveats That Require Attention

The exploration of alternative depository structures will not yield profitable insights unless those offering a conceptualization address political and other realities. Only those structures that build from an existing base and require minimal rewriting of present statutes may be feasible. Feasibility centers around questions such as How do you practically and politically reorganize the program? How do you gain popular support for reorganization? What is the price tag, and what are the comparable strengths and weaknesses of the structure? Therefore, it is important to recognize and address the barriers that possibly inhibit the construction of the "ideal" model.

Section 1915, title 44, of the *United States Code*, identifies one barrier. Section 1911 directs depository libraries to make publications received through the GPO "available for the free use of the general public." The highest appellate court libraries serving in the depository program, however, are exempt from this provision. These libraries comprise a separate and unique class of depository.

According to section 1907, title 44, Federal depository libraries located within an area served by regional depositories do not report to (and are not held accountable by) regional depositories. Federal libraries "may dispose of unwanted Government publications after first offering them to the Library of Congress and the Archivist of the United States."

The intended purpose of the depository program is to provide the public with access to publications emanating from the government. In the case of the highest appellate court libraries serving as depositories, public access is narrowly defined. Surprisingly, one statement of purpose is intended to cover all areas of responsibility related to the government and participating libraries. Additional goals should extend to service, resource management, and administration (e.g., planning and inter-institutional cooperation).

Another caveat is that, conceptually, it may be more effective to centralize government information dissemination much as was suggested in the proposed *Government Information Act of 1987*. However, such efforts might best be seen as long-term goals. On a practical and political level, it appears that continued decentralized dissemination activities are likely to continue and that the various government information dissemination agencies, e.g., NTIS will continue to be treated individually.

Thus, the approach suggested in the next section, while it would encourage increased coordination among the various government information dissemination agencies, does *not* attempt to combine their missions under the GPO. Rather, the approach attempts to build on the existing structure and is concerned primarily with revising the depository library structure *within* the existing basic context of the GPO. Space does not permit a detailed review or the listing of recommendations by which the depository library program could become a government-wide depository network rather than a GPO-based network. However, such alternatives do deserve attention and consideration.

Proposed Structure

Figure 17–3 depicts the structure of the proposed depository library program. The program would remain in the GPO and one of its divisions, the Office of Superintendent of Documents. The current Library Programs Service would be restructured, with an expanded budget and number of staff, as the Office of Document Distribution Services. The Office would maintain microfiche holdings for all government publications distributed in that format and, upon revision of the title 44 definition of a government publication, provide backup services for nonprint government information resources distributed through the depository program. The Office would also give high priority to the depository library program, the development of goals and objectives to guide that program, the training of depository library staff, and inspection and evaluation.

The Office of Document Distribution Services should make use of advisory councils that are broadly based and represent a number of different groups, some of which might not be involved with documents work on a daily basis. One such group might comprise representatives from state and local governments.

The Acquisitions and Processing Units would be responsible for acquiring government information resources and processing them—providing bibliographic control. Processing includes the preparation of quality indexes, catalogs, and current awareness services. For example, the magnetic tapes used to generate the *Monthly Catalog* might provide the basis for a series of specialized indexes or catalogs arranged by subject or format of material (e.g., microfiche). With the *Monthly Catalog* becoming overwhelming in physical appearance and amount of information contained, less formidable and more quickly used sources are needed for both document selection and searching for source material (e.g., that comprising core collections).

Figure 17-3.
Conceptual Model for the Depository Library Network

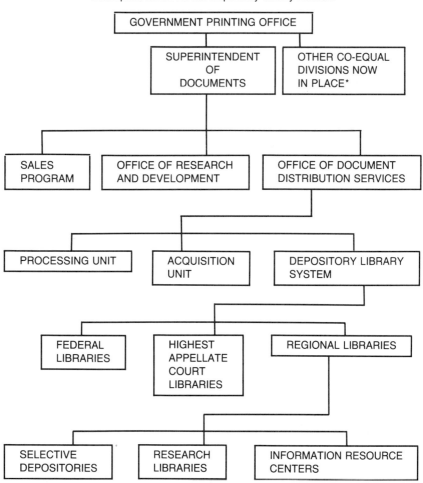

*This model does not examine the entire operations of the GPO and divisions other than the Superintendent of Documents.

The Office of Research and Development would assist both the sales program and Office of Document Distribution Services by participating in planning and marketing activities, promoting and announcing grants and contracts on a competitive basis, hiring consultants to review and revise basic documentation (e.g., depository program goals and objectives), and creating an environment recognizing the value of research to public policy issues.

The exact number of regional and selective depositories would be far less than at present; perhaps as many as half of the present member libraries need not retain depository status. Depositories would serve as a node in the transfer of information across levels of government since the regional libraries would collect and provide access to resources for the Federal, state, and local levels of government. The regionals would also serve as participants in all the depository programs operated at the Federal level. These libraries would serve as a central means for providing the public with access to Federal information.

The highest appellate court libraries would not be under the jurisdiction of the regionals. Still, they would cooperate with the regionals by serving as resources upon which regionals could draw. Of course, these libraries could also use the resources of a regional.

Each selective depository library would be supported by Federal grants and contain remote terminals, tied directly to regional libraries and the Office of Document Distribution Services, in order to take full advantage of the benefits of computerization. The initial capital investment, although large, would enable libraries, other institutional providers, and information consumers to exploit the network to full advantage. Perhaps clientele might have to assume some of the direct costs of using online services.

Regional libraries.   Regional depositories perform a useful function. In theory, they work closely with libraries in their geographical area, act as intermediary links between selective depositories and the GPO, and deal with the information needs of a region's client groups and libraries. In effect, they represent a larger geographical area and not just the clientele of one particular library. For reasons such as these, the authors do not recommend the elimination of regionals from the organizational scheme. They believe, however, that only fourteen of these libraries are needed; this number corresponds to the number of existing GPO regional printing plants.

Regional libraries would develop, as comprehensively as possible, collections pertaining to regional needs and interests. They would collect resources from other regions on a selective basis. Regionals would also develop cooperative relationships with other information providers (e.g., state data centers and the Federal Information Centers of the General Services Administration). The Office of Research and Development would provide financial support for the development and testing of appropriate models for determining the type of cooperative relationship.

Regional libraries would provide reference and interlibrary loan service, supervise the libraries under their jurisdiction, and serve as nodes in a national information network. The regional libraries would be eligible for Federal assistance so that they could better meet their own service obligations, the information needs of members of the public within their jurisdiction, and the resource requirements of selective depositories. Regional libraries would have at least one consultant librarian whose salary would be subsidized by the Federal government. The purpose of this position would be to work with other depository librarians to improve operations, services, and uses of technology throughout the region.

Regional libraries should also be funded to maintain an inventory of portable microfiche/film readers, as well as some reader/printers. At present, not all depositories have access to such equipment. These pieces can be loaned to various depositories on both a short- and long-term basis to increase availability and access to microformatted publications. In addition, Federal funding would ensure that regionals have a fiche-to-fiche duplicator. Without such equipment, they cannot carry out adequately their responsibilities for interlibrary loan and provision of replacement copies to area depositories.

Selective depositories, after submitting format grant proposals providing evidence of need, would be eligible for grants-in-aid to cover the purchase of equipment and essential bibliographic resources, or to develop services and programs that would enhance public access to Federal government information. The regional libraries, in conjunction with the Office of Document Distribution Services, would evaluate the importance and utility of individual requests.

Research libraries. Some major research libraries might not opt for the position of selective or regional libraries. The resulting financial, administrative, and collection responsibilities might be too great for them to assume. Instead, these libraries might prefer to maintain extensive collections within specialized fields in order to meet the information needs of their own clientele and to weed items from the collection as the items become obsolete or useless. Under the proposed structure, these libraries could request information from a depository library and, in return for the free receipt of government information resources, they would provide reference assistance or a loan service upon request from a regional library. These libraries, therefore, would constitute one channel by which depository libraries could borrow lesser-needed source material.

Selective libraries. A specified number of libraries could receive congressional designation, with the approval of regional libraries, as selective depositories. As selective depositories, they would be eligible for grant support and subsidies covering expenses incurred in filling requests from other libraries in the area. These libraries would collect high interest information resources of the Federal government. Retention decisions would be based on a flexible schedule determined from use studies conducted through support from the Office of Research and Development, rather than from an automatic five-year retention period, as is currently practiced.

Information resource centers. Many educational facilities (including some of the libraries currently holding depository status as well as school, small and medium sized public libraries, and small academic libraries) undoubtedly do not need a wide assortment of documents holdings. Based on the premise that a small and carefully selected collection would address a large percentage of the needs of the public that they serve, these libraries would receive core documents titles (identified by the Office of Research and Development and the Office of Document Distribution Services) on a gratis basis. These libraries could obtain other acquisitions at a discount. In addition, these libraries would have to report annual statistics to the Office of Research and Development on the use of the titles received gratis.

As Hernon, McClure, and Purcell (1985) demonstrate, a significant number of depository libraries take fewer than 25% of the available depository categories. Many of these libraries may take a maximum of 15%. The category of Information Resource Center, therefore, might appeal to libraries that are highly selective in the number of item numbers selected. These libraries could concentrate on the information needs of their own clientele without having to assume any obligations associated with depository status.

Summary assessment of proposed structure.

ADVANTAGES

- The structure realistically recognizes differences within depository membership. Federal and highest appellate court libraries would not be held accountable to regionals
- The structure encourages research and coordination with other institutional providers
- The depository program becomes an interlocking system that is future oriented and that uses information handling technologies
- A wider diversity of libraries have access to government publications but these libraries must provide indicators of use
- The depository program is encouraged to develop formal goals and objectives. The program is therefore subject to formal and meaningful evaluation. Accountability and cost-benefit become important considerations
- The proposed structure builds on the existing structure and, therefore, does not require a complete rewriting of Chapter 19, title 44
- Regional libraries serve as members of all depository programs in operation at the Federal level. There is coordination among the various programs

DISADVANTAGES

- The GPO and presumably the JCP remain at the center. The present depository program is generally perceived as a legislative program. The Executive Branch often does not want to deal with structural problems for a legislative program. The JCP has a printing orientation. The proposed structure offers the JCP an excellent opportunity to broaden printing to include the electronic dissemination of information. A number of people and groups (including some within Congress) will not favor increased oversight for a joint committee of Congress. Clearly, this disadvantage presents a significant problem

- The revised depository program requires increased government involvement and financial support. Congress may not be willing to subsidize the problem and provide it with technology

PROBLEMS

- Some perceive the depository program, as currently structured, as good. They question the wisdom of "tinkering" with the structure
- The cost-benefit of the existing program would have to be determined. There would have to be broad congressional and special interest group support for restructuring the program and revising Chapter 19, title 44. Attempted revision of title 44, in the late 1970s, is still remembered. It is recalled that the JCP was willing to abolish itself
- The structure requires an expanded role, staff, and budget for the GPO
- The amount of Federal support would be substantially higher than at present
- There would be a need to train many depository staff members as information access professionals

OPPORTUNITIES

- There is an opportunity to provide the public with access to more government information. At a time when Federal agencies are making increased use of technology, there would be opportunities to channel that information to the public in a useful form
- A greater diversity of the information needs of the public could be addressed
- Instead of focusing attention on just one aspect of the depository program (e.g., the current plight of regional depositories), the structure emphasizes how different parts fit together and how the entire network can accommodate future technologies.

MOVING TOWARD A REASSESSMENT

The depository library program needs to be viewed as a network capable of providing information across levels of government and geographic regions. More libraries, even those in the depository program, need to be highly selective in their acquisition and retention of government publications; lesser-needed publications should be obtained through inter-institutional cooperation. The structure detailed in this chapter views government publications/information within the context of a national information policy. That structure would require libraries holding membership in the network to provide cost-effective justification and evidence that performance measures are met. In return, these libraries would receive direct government support. Changes such as those proposed in this chapter would strengthen an often times weak and poorly supported depository program and provide a basis by which the general public can better obtain access to the myriad information resources produced by the government.

Regardless of the depository structure   whether it be the existing or an alternative one—the development of performance measures, as well as the articulation of what the depository system is expected to accomplish, is needed before alternative depository structures can be investigated. Any alternative structure will have strengths and weaknesses; trade-offs must be recognized. However, a rational approach can be used to determine which of the alternatives can best accomplish the objectives of the system and meet the expectations of system administrators and users. Although numerous structures and combinations can be suggested, each must be fully evaluated in terms of costs, benefits, impacts, and trade-offs.

Librarians, and others, should not focus their attention on just one aspect of the depository program (e.g., reference service); instead, they should examine how all the parts fit together and how the entire network can exploit technologies of the future. Congress, the GPO, and the library community desperately need descriptive research studies analyzing the present structure so that the extent of its effectiveness can be determined and any restructuring can be based on accurate, statistically significant data; these data should enable a better determination and comparison of costs and benefits for any proposed organizational scheme. Replacing or restructuring the existing depository structure without a research basis of information is ineffective decision making at best, and dangerous to the concept of public access to government information at worst. Research studies must replace opinion and untested assumptions.

The analysis of the depository structure presented in this chapter has identified a number of problems—many of which are conceptual and philosophical. But others are related to a lack of clear goals and objectives, and a paucity of performance measures that articulate expectations from the system. A research agenda regarding the depository structure would include the following:

- Analyze existing strengths and weaknesses based on quantifiable data

- Establish a short and long-term planning process between the government and local depositories
- Assess the extent to which alternative approaches support existing Federal information policies
- Identify alternative depository structures and the costs and benefits of each approach
- Establish performance measures for the various candidate depository structures
- Present a candidate list of goals and objectives to depository decision makers
- Develop a program for ongoing formal planning, review, and evaluation based on goals, objectives, and performance criteria.

With such information in hand, policy makers can make rational decisions for developing an effective depository system. In addition, we can all devise and review structures in order to find approaches that best meet the goals and objectives of the system. The American public's access to and knowledge of government information resources should increase as a result of such concerted efforts.[3]

---

[3] The Office of Technology Assessment, U.S. Congress is investigating "Technology, Public Policy, and the Changing Nature of Federal Information." The report, anticipated for publication in the fall, 1988, will explore alternative structures for the depository library program. The report, therefore, may revive national discussion of depository library structural arrangements.

18

Exploiting State and Local Information Resources

Publications of state and local governments contain useful, even vital, information for research purposes and decision making. Providing factual and interpretative information, they may comprise the most complete or only access to specific governmental activities, programs, or services. Their reference value relates primarily to the detailed, current statistical data they present; the reporting of agency functions, activities, and personnel; the listing of publications issued by specific agencies; the reporting of research findings; and a wealth of other published information. Dealing with publishing programs from these levels of government underscores the interrelationship among Federal, state, regional, and local (county and municipal) governments. In fact, Federal, state, and local governments frequently produce the best or only information on a locality.

Since state and local government publications appear in various formats, the term "publication or document" does not fully reflect the full range of available information. The term must yield to the broader term "information resources," which addresses both print and nonprint formats. A broader term, stressing informational matter, reflects the fact that governments communicate directly to the public through the creation and maintenance of toll-free telephone numbers, information centers, bookstores, data centers, and so forth , as well as through publications. These communication channels convey information by word-of-mouth as well as provide machine-readable data and printed publications to the public.

State and local governments clearly produce more information than that which is regularly made available to the public. Certain government information resources are collected and published primarily for administrative or operational purposes, but the large majority contain information of vital significance to the public. In most instances, only a small portion of those publications issued by state governments is acquired outside the state of origin. Furthermore, many libraries (including public libraries) neither widely collect nor service local publications—even those locally produced.

Against this background, the chapter identifies the major issues confronting the collection, retention, and servicing of state and local information resources. In particular, the chapter examines major writings in the field, types of publications, bibliographic control, collection development, technology, and user/use patterns. The chapter concludes with a discussion of areas benefiting from research and the need for improved access to state and local information resources. Indirectly, the chapter supports the development of decision support systems that blur distinctions among levels of government and encourage libraries to bring the full range of information resources in their collections to the resolution of their clientele's information needs.

SELECTED MAJOR WRITINGS

Generally, the major concerns discussed in the literature on state and local publications have been related to bibliographic control, acquisition, distribution, depository programs and legislation, union lists of holdings, exchange programs, reference value and uses, available microform packages, the identification of bibliographic aids, listings of particular types of publications (most typically state bluebooks and checklists), and potentially useful classification systems. Further, the literature frequently focuses on the publishing program of one state or local level of government, without exploring relationships to other levels. The writings commonly review the important information content of state and local government publications, and encourage libraries to expand their present collection activities.

The literature has discussed the selection and acquisition of state and local publications but not as these activities relate to other aspects of collection development—retention decisions or collection evaluation. Local publications have received disproportionately less emphasis in the literature than have state publications. Other characteristics of the literature include: infrequently reported research findings, emphasis on resources and types of publications rather than services, and publication in state and regional library journals or newsletters. Finally, the published literature suggests that municipal publications can be of two types: the unpublished archival type of record (e.g., staff memoranda or correspondence, and minutes of meetings) and published local documents (e.g., reports and newsletters). As Castonguay (1987, p. 186) observes, there appears to be a

> perception among librarians that local documents and local history materials are synonymous. In order to understand the courses of action needed to enhance the status of local documents, it may be necessary to link them with local history materials and to raise the interest of local librarians. Because local documents age into local history resources, perhaps it will be necessary to approach the two as opposite sides of the same coin, instead of separate entities.

The published literature is largely descriptive (explaining or identifying particular developments, or offering suggestions for collection development) rather than analytical (identifying problems and issues, analyzing them, and subjecting basic assumptions, practices, and beliefs to close scrutiny). Little of the purported research goes beyond a survey of current practices and beliefs.

Weech (1973) reported a major research study in the field of state publications. He analyzed the characteristics of publications appearing in the *Monthly Checklist of State Publications*, produced by the Library of Congress since 1910 and the best known general index to state publications, over seven time periods. The publications listed, he found, provided information useful to specific individuals or groups. Further, the number of publications of a service or research nature increased over time. Since the *Monthly Checklist of State Publications* represents a highly selective list of state publications, those sent to the Library of Congress by individual states, its value as a selection or current awareness tool is limited.

Two important articles are devoted to collection development. First, Weech (1981) discusses selection and acquisition process for state publications, as well as patterns of bibliographic control, state depository programs, and major collections (e.g., the Library of Congress, the New York Public Library, and the Center for Research Libraries). Next, Shannon (1981) provides a detailed analysis of collection development for local publications. He examines the nature and characteristics of local publishing programs, the problems of collecting these publications, the need for improved bibliographic control and resource sharing, municipal reference libraries, local depository programs, selection and acquisition, and major reference guides. He also notes relevant source material produced by the Federal government. In a separate work, both Weech and Shannon discuss the role of microforms in the development of state and local documents collections. They conclude that libraries can expand their holdings of state and local publications, while simultaneously exploring methods of resource sharing (Hernon, 1981).

A special issue of *Government Publications Review*, edited by Weech (1983b), is devoted to state information sources and provides extensive coverage of the topic. These descriptive articles examine bibliographic control, selected impacts of technology on the formats in which state governments disseminate information, and library collection development practices.

"The Documents on Documents Collection," organized by state, provides information into the laws and practices governing the administration of state depository programs. The collection, available on microfiche through the ERIC clearinghouse system (ED 247 940, ED 247 939, ED 263 923, and ED 263 922), provides sample contracts, forms, manuals, surveys, and promotional material. The microfiche reprint materials covering 1973 through 1983. More recent material is available on interlibrary loan from Public Affairs Service, University Research Library, University of California, Los Angeles.

Lane (1987), an excellent textbook, discusses "The Documents on Documents Collection" as well as other aspects of state documents librarianship. Her work, which complements *Public Access to Government Information*, draws comparisons among states and guides librarians in understanding state depository library programs and aspects of collection development, resource sharing, and bibliographic control.

Nakata and Kopec (1980) reviewed depository library programs for state and local government publications, and document the increased interest in microforms and the inputting of records into bibliographic databases. Their discussion, which focuses on distribution and bibliographic control, notes the efforts of individual states to support interstate networking.

Lewy (1974) points out specific problems related to access, availability, and bibliographic control of local documents:

- Local publications may not be listed in an index or acquisitions list
- Many publications are available in limited quantity
- Cities may not have a central depository or distributor for their publications
- Indexes listing local publications emphasize form rather than substance (bibliographic citations do not convey the full range of contents)
- The same publication might be issued in more than one series
- A given legislative or executive action might be discussed in more than one document and published in different forms (e.g., the budgetary process can result in the release of different documents and statistical data; user, therefore, might mistake one set of figures as the final set).

She reviews the types of publications produced and the value of their information content.

Castonguay (1984) identifies and analyzes different classification schemes that have been applied to local publications. His first chapter provides an excellent overview of current developments. Given the problems of bibliographic control and limited collection development practiced by many libraries, the quality of reference service becomes a critical factor in the retrieval of local government information.

Castonguay (1987) reports a national survey of academic and public library practices concerning the maintenance and management of local documents collections. He compares his findings to those of the major, previous surveys and reaffirmed that:

- "The percentage of local documents collections in public libraries is greater than in university libraries
- The Dewey Decimal Classification is the most commonly used classification by public libraries, and the Library of Congress Classification is the most commonly used in university libraries for local documents
- Cataloging practices are in the higher percentages for both public and university libraries
- Use of Library of Congress Subject Headings for subject cataloging of local documents is high for both public and academic libraries, although Sears List of Subject Headings would have a significant portion of adherents among public libraries
- At least 70% of both public and university libraries provide reference service for local documents; university libraries provide a fuller range of reference services than do public libraries
- Public libraries have more liberal circulation policies than university libraries for local documents
- Public libraries have larger, older archival collections of local documents" (p. 173).

Castonguay (1987, p. 177) also shows that:

a typical library collection of local government documents as consisting of less than 500 items, integrated into the general book, reference, or local history collections, with some maintained in a vertical file. . . . Most collections . . . are either 6–10 or 11–25 years old.

Durrance (1985) discusses "the local public policy information gap" and the need for libraries to "span" that gap. The library community can improve public access and "provide meaningful access to local government information." Durrance (1988) offers the first detailed analysis of the types of local government reference questions received by public libraries. Her analysis suggests that unobtrusive/obtrusive testing might produce useful insights into reference service and direct more attention to the local level of government. She observes that "the special problems associated with providing access to local government information have not yet been adequately addressed by the majority of public libraries." Definitely, ". . . the role of provider of local government information is not universally understood or even clearly articulated by librarians."

Ternberg (1982) discussed the publications of regional governmental organizations (generally voluntary in nature and containing representatives from local governments and perhaps from outside government altogether. They also serve more than one local jurisdiction and are typically involved with planning and not the direct delivery of public services). These organizations can be either general purpose (e.g., regional planning commissions or councils of government) or special purpose (e.g., plan or maintain a toll road, hospital system, or a service for a metropolitan area). General purpose organizations, however, are the more prolific producers of publications.

As this section has illustrated, some current and important writings have emerged for both state and local government publications. Comparatively less attention has focused on regional governmental organizations.

TYPES OF PUBLICATIONS

Executive branch agencies of state governments produce many of the same types of publications as issued by their counterpart at the Federal level. For example, both levels issue periodicals; press releases; annual, research, and statistical reports; informational handbooks and brochures; and maps. The other branches of state government usually do not generate as many publications as the executive branch and their counterparts at the Federal level.

There is substantial variation from state to state concerning the amount and types of legislative publications available. Those available usually focus on the process by which bills become public law; however, in many cases, hearings, committee reports, and proceedings are not published. The judicial branch of state government generates the least volume of printed publications. Some states produce official editions of the decisions and opinions rendered by state courts, while many states rely upon commercially produced sources such as those issued by West Publishing Company.

Assorted reference aids produced by the public and private sectors cover state government. Examples of the types of reference aids available include: bluebooks (conveying the structure, functions, and personnel of that state government, as well as statistical data); legislative handbooks, guides, and journals; statistical abstracts; industrial/manufacturing directories; checklists (official lists of state publications); and sources reproducing rules and regulations.

Three major reference guides to state publications are Parish's *State Government Reference Publications* (1981), Parish's *A Bibliography of State Bibliographies, 1970–1982* (1985), and Lane's *State Publications and Depository Libraries* (1981). In the first work, Parish has identified a variety of general reference sources that might appeal to various types of libraries. His listing may still be somewhat useful for collection development purposes. In the second work, he provides an annotated listing of more than 1,000 bibliographies produced by state governments. With Lane's work, knowledge about the establishment and operation of state depository programs, as well as the role of depository libraries in making public documents available to the general public, has greatly improved. She outlines the history of state efforts to improve bibliographic control over the vast outpouring of government publications, provides an overview of various depository programs in operation, makes reference to relevant legal citations, and offers synopses of key provision in depository legislation.

Local publications can take the form of (Lewy, 1974):

- *Annual reports and messages*—reports of operations for the past year and projections for the upcoming year
- *Bulletins*
- *Financial reports*, comptrollers' reports, budgets, and appropriation ordinances (the budgetary process)
- *News releases*
- *Ordinances and codes*—texts of laws (e.g., city charters and zoning and building codes)
- *Proceedings or minutes*—verbatim or revised records of meetings (these might contain annual reports, annual budgets, and statistical data)
- *Rules and regulations*
- *Statistical reports*.

Some municipalities might produce separate reference publications (e.g., checklists and bibliographies of official publications, manuals, handbooks, and directories), while others would provide similar information within one of the types identified by Lewy. For example, instead of issuing a separate directory of city officials and an organizational chart of city government, a municipality might insert such information into the proceedings or minutes of the city council.

Information about urban affairs appears in sources such as newspapers; publications of Federal, state, regional, and local government; special reports (e.g., those produced on a contractual basis); monographs; periodical and newsletter articles; and pamphlets produced by the private sector. Regional government organizations generate brochures, newsletters, annual reports, planning studies, factbooks, directories, and miscellaneous sources (e.g., maps and atlases, special research reports, and bibliographies) free of charge or for a nominal fee. Planning studies, however, are the most prelevant type; they "pull together a variety of information about the region being studied" (Ternberg, 1982, p. 496).

BIBLIOGRAPHIC CONTROL

Incomplete bibliographic control is not a problem unique to the Federal government and its publishing programs. In some respects, the situation at the state and local levels is more chaotic. Some states have bibliographic control and offer checklist coverage of their publications beginning with statehood or earlier. Such examples, however, are the exception rather than the rule. Almost every state prepares a checklist listing publications produced by state agencies; however, the quality, completeness, and frequency of issuance of checklists vary substantially from state to state, and gaps exist in the years covered by retrospective checklists. To complicate matters, the quantity of state publications is increasing, and, for states lacking comprehensive checklist coverage, numerous publications go unidentified.

To improve bibliographic control, the State and Local Documents Task Force, Government Documents Round Table (American Library Association) has developed *Guidelines for Minimum State Servicing of State Documents, for State Documents Checklists, for Inputting State Documents into Data Bases, for State Publications Depository Legislation*, and *for State Distribution Center Activities.*[1] The value of these guidelines, which convey broad statements about service activities, would be greatly improved by a detailing of specific performance measures for each of the statements given as a recommendation. The same criticism applies to these guidelines as to the documentation that the Government Printing Office (GPO) uses in operating its depository library program; the items are too general and vaguely worded.

Individual checklists of the states, the *Monthly Checklist of State Publications*, and the *Statistical Reference Index* provide an awareness of the publishing programs of individual states. The *Monthly Checklist of State Publications* lists the publications that individual states forward to the Library of Congress. Consequently, there is substantial variation from state to state concerning the comprehensiveness of coverage and types of publications included. *The Statistical Reference Index*, which the Congressional Information Service began in 1980, covers basic statistical publications of the states and major reports issued by state data centers. Emphasizing recently

---

[1] Lane (1981, pp. 193–198) reprints these guidelines.

published information, this selective index serves as a current awareness source and provides the type of information for which library clientele are most likely to consult state publications.

As an aid to libraries, a number of bibliographic guides have been developed. These draw together the basic reference publications of a state in an effort to assist libraries in further developing and updating their reference collections. However, since many libraries limit their collections to publications produced by their state government, such guides apparently are infrequently consulted. Libraries are more likely to rely on their state's checklist, depository distribution within the state, and state agency mailing lists. When they collect publications from other states, they are more likely to do so through exchange programs, purchasing commercial sources, or contacting specific government agencies, than they are to consult general indexes and checklists.

In an effort to improve the distribution and bibliographic control of state publications, many states have enacted depository programs. Considerable variation exists among these states concerning the number of publications available for depository distribution. In an effort to preserve documents or reduce the cost of printing and distribution, state agencies, in some cases, are turning to microform production and distribution.

Public access to municipal publications is, in many instances, limited; there is little bibliographic control over, and subject access to, municipal publishing. The quantity, type, and frequency of publication vary greatly among municipalities, and even within departments and agencies of the same municipality. Publications are often issued irregularly, printed in small quantities, and distributed on a limited basis. Although some municipalities issue checklists of their publications, such a practice is uncommon. Therefore, the publishing record for many cities is not preserved in a systematic manner. Even when the title of a particular publication is known, locating that work can present a problem. Furthermore, many libraries do not systematically collect municipal publications or widely publicize their holdings. As Nakata and Kopec (1980, p. 50) noted,

> The primary role of most local agencies is to govern. They may produce reports for their own internal use or as a requirement for their continued existence. Occasionally, as in the case of consumer agencies, they may publish documents for public consumption. However, most government publications are by-products of the agency's real business of governing and, as such, documents often appear irregularly and distribution is haphazard.

The *Index to Current Urban Documents* (Greenwood Press, 1972–) is the major, general bibliographic tool for the publications of many cities and counties in the United States and Canada. Many of the local documents represented here are microfilmed and sold. Given the purchase options, libraries can tailor their selections to meet specific collection development priorities.

Shannon (1981) offers an excellent discussion of municipal reference libraries, local depository arrangements, and exchange programs. Some municipalities have enacted depository arrangements or established municipal reference libraries. "Depository status may be voluntary, based on an oral agreement, or legislated" (Castonguay, 1984, p. 6). Existing legislation has frequently not resulted in the collection of *all* city documentation, because the ordinances were "loosely written, chiefly conveying an unenforceable intent" (Shannon, 1981, p. 70). Still, legislation serves a useful purpose; it calls attention to the need for deposit arrangements and for the preservation of local documentation. Several states (e.g., California, Nevada, and Texas) have developed state laws to ensure the collection of local documents. "The Nevada legislation could easily serve as a model for other states wishing to tighten bibliographic control of local documents, as well as improve access" (Castonguay, 1984, p. 7). Regardless of level of government, the identification of source material is a problem. Organization and description of information content, as well as physical access, also present significant obstacles to the awareness and use of state and local publications. No wonder many libraries do not collect, and many members of academic institutions do not use, publications from states and municipalities other than their own (Hernon, 1979). Researchers experience enough difficulties in acquiring information from their own state and locality, without broadening the search process to publishing programs of other states and municipalities. Thus, libraries must focus greater attention on collection development.

COLLECTION DEVELOPMENT

Libraries maintaining collections of state and local publications encounter problems associated with document acquisition, storage, and use. Although library holdings of these publications have increased dramatically over time, many ephemeral, superseded, seldom used, and never used publications remain in the collections. Because of this, libraries not wanting to preserve the historical record ought to identify the more frequently needed sources and to rely on resource sharing, or other means, for gaining access to lesser-needed materials. However, it should be cautioned that the identification of what is needed is *not* the same as always being able to acquire or purchase it, especially when the information source is produced in another state. Libraries, therefore, need to develop referral capabilities to government agencies, private organizations, and other library and information centers.

Libraries needing statistical information disseminated by state governments might rely on sources such as the *Statistical Reference Index* and the companion microform collection. Beyond the collection of needed statistical data, they should determine the types of information resources needed by their clientele. By conducting needs assessments and monitoring reference questions asked, libraries can determine those types likely to receive the greatest amount of use and explore ways to improve resource sharing for lesser-needed materials. They should also determine the type of general reference sources that would be useful in resolving the information needs of clientele. In this regard, libraries can select from among bluebooks, manuals and handbooks, current and retrospective checklists, state statistical abstracts, industrial/manufacturing directories, and guides produced by the public and private sectors.

Libraries have an alternative to the acquisition of expensive microform collections and the retention of low use publications. They can engage in resource sharing and develop document delivery systems for lesser-needed publications. The development of union lists of holdings, effective document delivery systems, and depository library programs can relieve individual libraries of the burden of collecting and retaining lesser-needed publications. Further, other opportunities for borrowing materials exist. For example, for a fee, a library can join the Center for Research Libraries (CRL), a nonprofit organization operated out of Chicago, for access to library materials of a research nature. These materials may be borrowed by a member library for research use. Since January 1952, the Center has collected, regularly and as comprehensively as possible, all state documents excluding session laws and compiled statutes; agricultural experiment station publications have been compiled selectively. There is also a selective collection of pre-1952 state documents. The advantage of this operation, to repeat, is the ability of libraries to maintain an in-house collection of documents for their own state, while borrowing lesser-used publications from the Center.[2]

Even for one's own state, librarians must decide how extensively to collect and retain official publications. Examining user needs will disclose patterns of use and provide a basic understanding from which libraries can identify those government bodies and types of publications to collect. Further, insights into the lifespan of serial titles can be gathered and will be useful in the formulation of a collection development policy, one designed to focus acquisition and retention decisions upon the more heavily need and used source material.

Collection development principles should also be applied to the selection and retention of local publications. Libraries should determine how extensively, and in what formats, they need to collect information resources for their own and other localities. They should decide if they want to serve as the center of record for their own municipality's publishing program, to

---

[2] Lane (1987) discusses other noted collections of state publications.

explore cooperative acquisition programs with nearby libraries, to collect publications from other cities selectively in paper copy, and/or to rely upon the resources of the *Index to Current Urban Documents* and its companion microform service.[3,4] Libraries should remember that much of a city's publishing program may be ephemeral in nature and that:

> Some documents are poorly printed, infrequently issued, on poor paper and poorly organized. Loose and unpaged documents often of a regulatory nature will disappear, and it has not been unheard of where boards of appeal cannot locate a complete file of their decisions (Shannon, 1981, p. 60).

Finally, library clientele rely on a few document types, and the serial titles that they consult frequently have short lifespans (Hernon, 1979).

Libraries should develop collection policy statements that cover all their resources, that integrate decision making regarding government publications with other information resources, and that address the scope of documents collecting, regardless of the level of government. This is especially critical for those libraries serving as depositories for more than GPO publications. Policy statements should not be created in a vacuum, but should be based on a detailed analysis of the information needs of client groups and the goals and objectives of the library. Libraries can identify the levels of government and types of publications most frequently needed, while exploring methods for the identification and availability of lesser-needed publications. Given the number of state and local governments in existence, the volume of publishing output, and problems related to bibliographic control, libraries must develop a rationale for what they include in, or exclude from, their collections.

Given the complexities of government activities and the nature of publishing programs, referral to other information providers (e.g., other libraries or government agencies) can serve a useful purpose. It can lead library staff members and library clientele to a range of information sources, not all of which are available in printed form. Further, referral can result in access to timely information. As is evident, librarians should develop contacts within government officials for not only the receipt of publications but

---

[3] According to Castonguay (1984, p. 15), "a library that acquires depository status may wish, at that time, to determine the retention period of documents to be collected, as well as any restrictions on the types of documents to be acquired. There are at least three archival retention options:
- The library becomes the central repository for all local documents
- If the municipality or town has a local archives, the library may turn over to the archivist any documents it has held for a specified length of time
- The library may enter into cooperative arrangements with nearby libraries, a local or regional archive, or an historical society. Such arrangements would designate length of retention, subject emphasis for each participant, disposing of duplicate documents, and whether the archives would be centrally located or dispersed among the members."

[4] Librarians setting up collection of local government publications should review Nakata et al (1979).

also the ability to refer clientele and their questions to the most appropriate source. By developing their referral capabilities, librarians can engage in collection development; they supplement present holdings and seek ways to better serve current and potential clientele. Referral can result in the acquisition of high interest titles, while improving the capability to acquire lesser-needed publications on an on-demand basis.

TECHNOLOGY

Technology is making a significant impact on the format in which information, especially from state governments, is available. Librarians may no longer be able to rely exclusively or largely upon published government publications and archival records to meet the information needs of their clientele. They must become aware that more state government information is computer stored and retrievable, available in computer output microform, and produced by wordprocessing (Weech, 1983a). Yet as Lane (1987, p. 52) cautions,

> databases and electronic bulletin boards are even more limited in their use than other formats for state information because communication hardware and appropriate software programs are necessary. Generally, state agencies have not established policies for making machine-readable information available outside the agency that created the database.

Nonetheless, state governments are exploring ways to permit direct public access to computer terminals and computer records, without public interference with an agency's essential operations or without releasing information that merits protection and withholding (*Report of the First National Conference on Issues concerning Computerized Public Records*, 1987).[5]

Telecommunications and video recording technology influence the packaging of state publications. For example, legislative hearings may be computer stored and retrievable; legislative hearings and floor debates are also preserved on audio or videotape, while public television networks selectively broadcast legislative hearings and deliberations. Further, the drafting, contents, and status of bills, as well as the recording of legislators' votes, will be less likely to appear in a print form in the future. Even though the bulk of activity focuses on legislatures, the judicial and executive branches are also using technologies. State courts have televised and videorecorded trials,

---

[5] According to *Report of the First National Conference on Issues concerning Computerized Public Records* (1987), the development of a variable definition of *public records* based on format in which the information is stored is not practical. Volume 2 of this work provides a state by state definition of public record.

while executive agencies are placing more data into computers but not generating printed publications.

State governments are taking advantage of technology and information resources management (IRM) techniques to improve their access to information and, ultimately, their decision making abilities (Kresslein and Marchand, 1987). Yet public information retained in computerized form presents access issues and problems, i.e., those related to cost recovery. A computer program produced by a government agency may be regarded as public property. Typically the information contained in the program should be subject to release under state freedom of information acts. State governments may limit the amount of personal data they collect and maintain as public records. In general, state governments do not view libraries and depository programs as part of the public access issue. Rather, access is equated with the development and maintenance of strong and viable freedom of information acts (*Report of the First National Conference on Issues concerning Computerized Public Records*, 1987).

Technology has been extended to the realm of library operations. First, there is the availability of microform sets covering state information sources. Second, a number of state library agencies have taken a leadership role in utilizing information technology for increased access to a wide range of state information resources (Owen, 1986). And, third, a number of states participate in regional networks (e.g., OCLC or the Washington Library Network) providing bibliographic input and access to state documents through computerization.

An advantage of placing state publications into national, or regional, online bibliographic networks is that states can generate their own checklists online.[6] With the inclusion of state publications, the holdings of member libraries are recorded and made eligible for sharing. However, many libraries either do not enter their state publications into the network or do so selectively. As a result, a true or complete union list for state publications has not been realized.

The application of technology also impacts local government publications. However, sufficient examples from which to generalize are difficult to document. It would seem, though, that the majority of uses relate to data collection and retrieval of computer stored information. The emphasis, therefore, is on executive agencies and the information they require for decision making. Much of what they collect is available only for use by local government officials. The same applies to state governments; for example,

---

[6] According to Lane (1987, pp. 11–12), "increasingly the state checklists are being produced from cataloging data, by mechanical reproduction of the card . . . or by manipulation of a database to produce the checklist . . . . Without doubt, more and more states will begin using cataloging data for checklist entries, and as economical programs become available will produce the state documents checklist directly from cataloging tapes."

access to the electronic information systems of state legislatures is generally restricted to legislators and their staffs.

The number and variety of microform sets at the local level is difficult to discover. Many of the standard sets cover newspapers, city directories, or census or genealogical records, rather than local publications. Given this situation, the *Index to Current Urban Documents* and its companion microform package fulfill a unique role—the availability of current city and county publications. Control Data Corporation, in cooperation with the National League of Cities, developed the Local Government Information Network (LOGIN). LOGIN offers a database of local government information, electronic bulletin boards and message system, and a news service. Some libraries offer searches of this online database for members of local government and the public.

The Urbana Municipal Documents Center is a joint undertaking of the city of Urbana, Illinois, and the Urbana Free Library. The Center has produced *The Urbana Municipal Documents Center Manual* (1987). Available on two diskettes, the *Manual* illustrates the organization of city publications and the preparation of detailed computer-assisted indexing. The *Manual* contains a 104 page thesaurus of subject headings and detailed instructions for organizing and indexing local documents. Since the Center serves as a co-publisher with the city, the *Manual* discusses the preparation of microfiche copies of source material. Both the *Manual* and the practices of the Center advance records management for local documents and provide a model for other municipalities wanting to improve bibliographic control over local source material and to develop a cooperative arrangement with city government.

Some cities are inputting local documents into OCLC. Certain libraries enter local publications in their online catalogs or have developed computer generated key-word in-context (KWIC) or out-of-context (KWOC) indexes for their holdings of local documents. Castonguay (1984) discusses computer indexing of local documents. However, most collections of local documents do not benefit from the use of information handling technologies.

USER/USE PATTERNS

To a large extent, library collections of state and local publications are small and limited to source material of the immediate state and municipality. Libraries might not even collect publications from their own municipality. Apparently many libraries either do not perceive a need or demand for publications of other states or municipalities, or view the obstacles to acquisition as exceeding the potential value of these publications.

Two different approaches to data collection have been used to ascertain user/use patterns for state publications. First, users have been queried directly about their use patterns. In this regard, social scientists from seventeen midwestern academic institutions responded to a mail questionnaire and selected in-person interviews (Hernon, 1979). In another study, staff from predominately academic and public libraries in the state of Tennessee distributed questionnaires to their users (Purcell, 1980). Third, librarians have been asked to characterize the users of their documents collections and the types of state publications consulted (Ford and Nakata, 1983; Purcell, 1983).

These studies suggest that academic economists, political scientists, and sociologists most likely become aware of state publications from citations in the monographic and periodical literature of their disciplines, and by contacting state agencies. Historians, on the other hand, rely upon their subject literature and assistance from library staff members. Indexes play a minor role in fulfilling the information needs of academic social scientists. The same faculty members surveyed indicated that they infrequently consulted municipal publications. When they did, they were most likely to rely on their subject literature and contacting municipal agencies, colleagues, and librarians for information about existing municipal publications (Hernon, 1979).

Similar to use patterns prevalent for Federal publications, social scientists often want to gain access to current information distributed by state governments, that is, information produced within the past three years. Those wanting access to current municipal information realize the problems related to the discovery and acquisitions of relevant source material, and are, therefore, willing to accept older source material produced by this one level of government. Durrance (1988) reports on the use of local government information in public library systems in northern Illinois. People combating community problems such as neighborhood nuisances, she found, were most likely to request local government information from a public library. These people were generally affiliated with citizen groups such as the League of Women Voters. Other investigations have found that "elected and appointed officials and leaders of citizen groups" were primary users of local government information (Ibid.). Yet use was often on an irregular basis. Clearly, little is known about heavy users of local government information housed in an academic or public library.

Probing use patterns in public and academic libraries Purcell (1980) found that clientele are often unaware of the types of information published by state governments. On the other hand, those using state publications do so for access to statutory and administrative law, court cases, historical information, statistical data, and business or commercial information. In seeking access to the information content of state publications, respondents often consulted card catalogs or browsed the shelves. It would seem that the heavy

Figure 18-1.
User Groups and the Types of State Documents Consulted*

USER GROUPS**

Public Libraries	Academic Libraries
Business People	Students
College Students	Faculty
Professional Persons	University/College Administrators
Local and State Government Officials	Local and State Government Officials
High School Students	Business People
Homemakers	Other Community Users
Farmers	

TYPES OF DOCUMENTS USED**

Public Libraries	Academic Libraries
Statistical Information	Statistical Information
Legislative Information	Legislative Information
Publications Reflecting Government Structure, Activities, and Personnel	Publications Reflecting Government Structure, Activities, and Personnel
Maps	Business or Commercial Information
Recreational Information	Research Reports
Business or Commercial Information	Judicial or Administrative Court Reports
Agricultural or Gardening Information	Maps
Administrative Rules and Regulations	Administrative or Regulatory Agency Reports
Research Reports	Administrative Rules and Regulations
Administrative or Regulatory Agency Reports	Recreational Information
Judicial or Administrative Court Reports	Agricultural or Gardening Information

*Taken from Ford and Nakata (1983) and Purcell (1983).
**The categories are listed in descending order of use, according to numerical averaging of survey responses.

use of browsing suggests a need to explore the role of browsing more fully among the users of state publications.

In separate studies, staff members from public and academic libraries were queried about the users of their state documents collections (Ford and Nakata, 1983; Purcell, 1983). Figure 18–1 summarizes the major user groups and the types of publications consulted by clientele using both types of libraries. In the case of some public libraries, local and state government officials made greater use of state publications than the figure suggests. Regardless of library type, statistical and legislative information were rated as the two most frequently used types of state publications. Some differences in ranking emerged for most of the remaining document types. For example, academic libraries rated judicial or administrative court reports a higher priority. Such findings have implications for collection development and suggest the categories of state publications likely to receive the most use and to be the most deserving of selection and retention. Many libraries need not collect lesser-needed types, even from their own state. Instead, if needed, these publications could be obtained through resource sharing.

Bibliographic databases, excluding OCLC, infrequently emphasize state and local documents. Thus, even if library staff members search a database, they would probably find few state and local documents. Still, it is worth noting that, when academic and public libraries use online services for providing access to state publications, they are naturally most likely to use OCLC. Few of the public depository libraries surveyed have ready access to computer terminals; those with terminals rarely placed them in public service areas. Further, public librarians admitted that they did not use non-bibliographic databases in their reference service, and that they would not refer clientele to a state data center (Purcell, 1983).

Purcell (1983) discovered that documents collections were not well staffed and that persons who were not specialists provided reference service. They did so without access to many reference resources. In Purcell's opinion, the prospects for improvement of the situation in the near future are not great. Public librarians still view the information needs of their clientele in terms of paper copy state publications held within the immediate collection and not in the broader sense of state information resources, be they in print or nonprint form contained internal or external to the library. He concluded that:

> The continuing growth in size and importance of state governments means that more individuals are likely to find state government information, both in print and machine-readable form, important to their needs. If this information is not provided by the public library, they will turn elsewhere and the public library will become less relevant to the information needs of a part of its population (p. 184).

Further, if public libraries carrying depository status provide limited services, what type of service do nondepositories extend? Clearly, public libraries should reassess the information needs of their clientele and determine if state information resources provide information not found elsewhere. In brief, they must reassess the value of state information resources in comparison to other information resources, government and nongovernment, and enable all library resources to be used effectively and efficiently in resolving the information needs of clientele. Whenever necessary, library staff members should be willing and able to make effective use of other information providers.

FUTURE DIRECTIONS

Many of the same problems and issues identified in other chapters are present for state and local levels of government. Libraries still must develop collections of high use publications, improve internal bibliographic control, increase the effectiveness and efficiency of resource sharing, and improve the quality of their reference service. The majority of the published literature in the documents field covers Federal publications; however, the literature covering state and local publications has grown over the past several years.

Because effective access to state and local information resources is dependent on librarians working closely with state and local governmental officials, strategies are necessary for both groups to work together more effectively. Despite tight state and local budgets, some direct support for libraries and user services supporting state and local collections is necessary. Further, simply developing depository laws and procedures at either the state or local level will not necessarily lead to better access and user services. Therefore, cooperation among government agencies, the state library agency, and other libraries in the state is essential if the public is to have increased awareness and access to state and local information resources.

Information resources of state and local governments represent enormous opportunities for research and publication. For example, research might explore the quality of reference service provided by state depository libraries. Additional research might identify user groups of state and local publications, ascertain their information needs, and develop core collections of high use publications for specific subject areas. Such studies would enable individual libraries to apply the methodologies and research findings to their particular situations, and to formulate sound collection development policies and performance measures.

Libraries, in conclusion, must view state and local publications in terms of information content and understand that the availability of documentation in nonprint formats impacts on the information needs and gathering strategies of their clientele. More than ever, government resources must be integrated with other library resources. In many instances, library clientele must associate government information with their information needs and then identify the appropriate level of government producing the desired information and the format in which the information is produced. All of these decisions complicate the search for appropriate information and may encourage library clientele to seek alternative information providers—one offering information more quickly.

With this in mind, libraries and state distribution agencies should develop current awareness and selective dissemination of information services. State agencies might also develop abstract newsletters highlighting recent publications by subject areas (and thereby lessen the need to consult general checklists) and provide a mechanism for the prompt receipt of requested information resources. Every effort should be made to target the more heavily needed source material to specific client groups, and to concentrate collection development efforts on such source material.

The document delivery capabilities of depository libraries merit investigation and, whenever necessary, improvement. For this reason, the future holds not only vast opportunities for research but also the development and testing of models. Greater attention must be given to the structure of state and local depository library programs and their ability to make use of existing and future technologies. The purpose should be to develop depository programs that collect and transmit information content across levels of government.

The challenge is for librarians to become more knowledgeable about state and local information resources; to work closely with state and local officials to improve the publication, dissemination, and bibliographic control of such resources; and to develop programs and services for local clientele that exploit the information content of these important resources. Increasing access to state and local information resources can have important and direct benefits for a library, since much of the information may pertain directly to the information needs of that library's clientele. However, librarians must create that awareness, and they respond accurately and effectively to present and potential information needs by exploiting state and local information resources.

19

Access to Information from International Governmental Organizations*

For the effective and efficient establishment, development, maintenance, and use of a collection of source material emanating from international governmental organizations (IGOs), it is essential to understand the nature, types, structure, and basic workings of IGOs, and the role of those organizations as originators of documents, publications, and databases. There is an organic relationship between the agencies and the material that they produce. Many documents and publications are issued by a given agency under a specific mandate. For example, the Security Council and other organs of the United Nations submit annual and special reports to the General Assembly in accordance with Article 15 of the UN *Charter*. Other documents, publications, and databases appear as a result of an agency's activities; examples include conference proceedings and statistical compilations. Still other documents, such as those of a program and budget nature, actually govern the operations of an agency.

The authoritative *Yearbook of International Organizations*** identifies three conventional categories of international organizations: intergovernmental organizations, international non-governmental and non-profit organizations, and multinational enterprises. The *Yearbook* (1987/1988, Appendix 5) defines international governmental organizations as bodies that are "based on a formal instrument of agreement between the governments of nation states; [include] three or more nation states as parties to the agreement; [and

---

* Peter I. Hajnal of the University of Toronto Library wrote this chapter.
** See chapter Appendix 1 for bibliographic citations to examples.

have] a permanent secretariat performing ongoing tasks." Archer (1983, p. 35) defines an international organization as "a formal, continuous structure established by agreement between members (governmental and/or non-governmental) from two or more sovereign states with the aim of pursuing the common interest of the membership."

Highlighting five characteristics of international organizations (inter-state basis, voluntaristic basis, a permanent system of organs, autonomy, and cooperative function), Virally (1981, p. 51) states that "an organization can be defined as an association of States, established by agreement among its members and possessing a permanent system or set of organs, whose task it is to pursue objectives of common interest by means of co-operation among its members." In terms of extent of membership, the usual distinction is between global (universal) and regional international organizations. The *Yearbook*'s main categories, however, are:

- *Universal-membership organizations*; for example, the World Health Organization (an IGO), and Amnesty International (an NGO)
- *Intercontinental-membership organizations*, whose membership exceeds a continental region but is less than universal; for example, the Organisation for Economic Co-operation and Development (OECD) and the Commonwealth Secretariat
- *Regional-membership organizations*; for example, the Organization of American States (OAS).

The *Yearbook* (1987/88) lists 4,546 "conventional" international organizations, of which 311 (6.8%) are IGOs, and 4,235 (93.2%), NGOs. When "non-conventional" entities—such as organizations emanating from other organizations, organizations of a special form, internationally-oriented national bodies, inactive or dissolved organizations, autonomous conference series, religious orders, multilateral treaties, and unconfirmed bodies—are also taken into consideration, the *Yearbook*'s total is 27,145 organizations, of which 3,897 are IGOs, and 23,248, NGOs.

This chapter will discuss documents, publications, and databases of IGOs, concentrating on problems of distinction between documents and publications, and questions of quantity, subject, and form of IGO material; publication, dissemination, and database-access policies and practices of IGOs; bibliographic access; and collection development.

DOCUMENTS AND PUBLICATIONS OF IGOs

Member organizations of the United Nations system (see Figure 19–1) set publications policies in accordance with the purposes of each particular organization. A report of the Joint Inspection Unit of the UN system (1984) identifies the following working criteria:

- Publications should bear a direct relationship to and promote projects and activities in the organization's approved program of work
- Publications should be directed to identifiable (target) readerships
- A distinction should be made between material of short-term value suitable for publication in a periodical and material of long-term value for publication in more lasting form (studies and monographs)
- Manuscripts should be written as simply and concisely as the subject matter permits
- Authors should write "with a more diversified readership in view than their immediate circle of specialists or professional contacts" [quoting the view of ILO]
- The estimated volume of demand and, in particular, the sales potential of manuscripts should be a major if not decisive factor in deciding whether to publish and in what numbers. The sales potential should normally, as a minimum, permit the recovery of reproduction costs (ILO)
- Publications should have quality, referring, as FAO puts it, "to the completeness and adequacy of the material presented and to the standard of writing which must be adapted to the audience"
- The quality and usefulness of contributions from substantive departments should be assessed on a comparative basis to arrive at a coherent and well-balanced program of publications (ILO).

The following related documents make it clear that these criteria are far from being universally accepted throughout the UN system: *Publications Policy and Practice in the United Nations System: Comments of the Secretary-General* and *Corrigendum*, and *Publications Policy and Practice in the United Nations System: Comments of the Administrative Committee on Co-ordination*. Nor are the criteria always followed in practice, as the Joint Inspection Unit itself points out. For an incisive analysis of IGO publishing policies and practices, see Cherns (1988).

IGOs distinguish between "documents" and "publications," although the distinction is often unclear and the division often fluid. The distinction is not merely theoretical but has implications for bibliographic control, collection development, and reference work. Many IGOs make their publications widely available but keep most of their documents internal. Some bibliographic tools cover both documents and publications (e.g., the *UNDOC: Current Index, United Nations Documents Index*, and the *Unesco List of Documents and Publications*), while others (e.g., the World Bank's *New Publications*) refer to publications only. Still others (e.g., the *Catalogue,*

Figure 19-1.
The United Nations System of Organizations

(A) 1. United Nations (UN). Established in 1945. Headquarters: New York, NY 10017, U.S.A.
(B) *Specialized Agencies*
2. Food and Agriculture Organization of the United Nations (FAO). Established in 1945. Headquarters: Via delle Terme di Caracalla, 00100 Rome, Italy
3. International Civil Aviation Organization (ICAO). Established in 1947. Headquarters: 1000 Sherbrooke Street West, Montreal, Quebec H3A 2R2, Canada
4. International Fund for Agricultural Development (IFAD). Established in 1977. Headquarters: Via del Serafico, 107, 00142 Rome, Italy
5. International Labour Organisation (ILO). Established in 1919; became a specialized agency in 1946. Headquarters: 4, Route des Morillons, CH-1211 Geneva 22, Switzerland
6. International Maritime Organization (IMO). Established in 1958 as Inter-Governmental Maritime Consultative Organization (IMCO). Headquarters: 4 Albert Embankment, London SE1 7SR, United Kingdom
7. International Monetary Fund (IMF). Established in 1945. Headquarters: 700 19th Street N.W., Washington, D.C. 20431, U.S.A.
8. International Refugee Organization (IRO). Established in 1948; ceased operations in 1952. Headquarters were in Geneva
9. International Telecommunication Union (ITU). Established in 1865 as International Telegraph Union; became a specialized agency in 1947. Headquarters: Place des Nations, CH-1211 Geneva 20, Switzerland
10. United Nations Educational, Scientific and Cultural Organization (Unesco). Established in 1946. Headquarters: 7, place de Fontenoy, 75007 Paris, France
11. United Nations Industrial Development Organization (UNIDO). Established in 1967; became a specialized agency in 1986. Headquarters: Vienna International Centre, A-1400 Vienna, Austria
12. Universal Postal Union (UPU). Established in 1875; became a specialized agency in 1948. Headquarters: Case Postale, CH-3000 Berne 15, Switzerland
World Bank Group:
13. International Bank for Reconstruction and Development (IBRD). Established in 1945
14. International Development Association (IDA). Established in 1960
The IBRD and the IDA are often referred to jointly as the World Bank
15. International Finance Corporation (IFC). Established in 1956
World Bank Group headquarters: 181 H Street N.W., Washington, D.C. 20433, U.S.A.
16. World Health Organization (WHO). Established in 1948. Headquarters: 20, Avenue Appia, CH-1211 Geneva 27, Switzerland
17. World Intellectual Property Organization (WIPO). Had its origins in the 1883 Paris Convention for the Protection of Industrial Property and the 1886 Berne Convention for the Protection of Literary and Artistic Works; established as WIPO in 1970; became a specialized agency in 1974. Headquarters: 34, Chemin des Colombettes, CH-1211 Geneva 20, Switzerland
18. World Meteorological Organization (WMO). Had its origin in the International Meterological Organization (which was established in 1878); established as WMO, a specialized agency, in 1950. Headquarters: 41, Avenue Giuseppe-Motta, CH-1211 Geneva 20, Switzerland

(C)   *Other Institutions in the United Nations System of Organizations*
  19.   General Agreement on Tariffs and Trade (GATT). In force since 1948;
        administered by a permanent secretariat. Headquarters: Centre William
        Rappard, 154, rue de Lausanne, CH-1211 Geneva 21, Switzerland
  20.   International Atomic Energy Agency (IAEA). Established in 1957.
        Headquarters: Vienna International Centre, A-1400 Vienna, Austria.

Part B: Documents of the Commission of the European Communities) cover documents only.

There are a number of definitions and characterizations (of varying adequacy) of the two categories of material. Marulli (1979, p. 187) offers one of the best:

- Publications are produced to fulfill the goal of the organization as a whole to "collect, analyze, interpret, and disseminate information," relating to its specific field of activity; they usually appear in printed form, in several languages, and are widely disseminated
- Documents are usually produced to support the work of specific organs of the organizations. As a rule, they appear in processed form and in several languages. Their dissemination may be restricted.

Even this definition does not address the subject in its full complexity. For example, it ignores the fact that many "documents" subsequently become "publications." Another definition of official publications, proposed by the International Federation of Library Associations and Institutions (IFLA), Official Publications Section, avoids making a distinction between "document" and "publication;" a postscript to that draft definition acknowledges the difficulty of making a clear distinction, and includes in the term "publication" "all items which achieve some circulation outside government" (Johansson, 1982, p. 395). As finally adopted by IFLA's Official Publications Section in August 1983, the definition states simply that "an official publication is any item produced by reprographic or any other method, issued by an organisation that is an official body, and available to an audience wider than that body" (International Federation of Library Associations and Institutions. Official Publications Section, 1983, p. 3).

Because they amplify IGO thinking about the two categories of material and the impact of that thinking and resultant decisions on the public, it is worth citing two more definitions. According to the UN (United Nations. Department of Conference Services, 1985, p. 7),

the term "document" is used to designate written material officially issued under a United Nations document symbol . . . regardless of the form of reproduction. In practice, the term is applied mainly to material offset from type-script and issued under a masthead . . .. Most documents are intended to serve as a basis for discussion at meetings of United Nations bodies.

Documents, understood in this sense, include reports, memoranda, notes, analyses, studies, surveys, replies to questionnaires, working documents, communications, addenda, corrigenda, and revisions (Ibid., pp. 7–11). In contrast (Ibid., p. 73),

> the term "United Nations publication" means any written material which is issued by or for the United Nations to the general public, normally under an authorization of the [UN] Publications Board. Such publications, which are usually offered for sale, include major studies, reports, statistical compilations and the proceedings of certain conferences, seminars and symposia, as well as such serial publications as yearbooks, *Official Records* of the principal organs of the United Nations, the United Nations *Treaty Series* and technical journals and bulletins . . . [and publications issued by] the Department of Public Information . . . designed to further public understanding of the work and purposes of the United Nations.

In the hope of further clarifying the distinction between the two categories, Hajnal (1988, p. 81) offers this definition:

> *Documents* are official records of meetings of IGOs and other material issued in the exercise of their functions, while *publications* are destined to inform the public about the particular organization and its activities. Documents are usually intended primarily or exclusively as working tools for internal use, although many documents are of interest to outside users and may reach a wider audience; publications are intended for wider distribution in the first place. Documents are often free of charge, while publications may be either free or priced. Documents are usually mimeographed, offset, or word-processed; publications are often printed. Documents may reappear as publications (unchanged or with modifications) if the issuing IGO does not consider them confidential and perceives a wider interest in them.

Several IGOs are prolific publishers. Notable among them are the UN and the major specialized agencies in the UN system— the United Nations Educational, Scientific and Cultural Organization (Unesco), the International Labour Organisation (ILO), the Food and Agriculture Organization of the United Nations (FAO), the World Bank, and, to a smaller extent, the World Health Organization (WHO) and the International Monetary Fund (IMF).* Outside the UN family of organizations, examples include the Organisation

---

* Figure 19–1 provides the names, acronyms, years of establishment, and location of headquarters of organizations in the UN system.

for Economic Co-operation and Development (OECD), the European Communities, and the Organization of American States (OAS). These and a few other IGOs are the major, international producers of documents, publications, and databases. Many other IGOs publish regularly, although on a more limited scale. Still others are "incidental, even if compulsive publishers" (Cherns, 1982, p. 24).

The major IGOs turn out a truly excessive number of documents and publications. In 1979 (the latest year for which comparative figures were available at the time of writing) the New York and Geneva offices of the UN produced 907,650 pages of material in the six official languages of the organization—English, French, Spanish, Russian, Chinese, and Arabic. (Most publications and documents appear in English, followed by French and Spanish; a much smaller number are produced in the other official languages of the UN.) The total number of page impressions for all copies of all UN editions was 930,734,945 (United Nations. Department of Conference Services, 1982, microfiche 3, p. 51). In 1981, the UN system of organizations produced 14,178,100 copies of 3,747 publications (the figures exclude documents) (Joint Inspection Unit . . ., 1984, p. 3). In 1985, the total number of page impressions for UN documents and publications was 812,061,203.[1]

Other large IGOs find themselves in a similar position. For example, in 1979, OECD produced some 100 monographs and twenty periodical titles, as well as approximately 14,000 documents, amounting to 62,300 pages of publications and 194,500 pages of documents (Organisation for Economic Co-operation and Development, 1982, microfiche 3A, p. 102). The total output of the European Communities was 793,000,000 page impressions in 1979 (European Communities. Court of Auditors, 1981). An inquiry about more recent statistics, while not yielding a comparable figure of total page impressions, resulted in the information that, in 1985, the institutions of the European Communities produced 171,310 proofread pages and 132,000 non-proofread pages.[2] Small wonder, then, that the IGOs themselves have been concerned with the enormous volume of their production of documents and publications. One of the more forceful statements on this subject was made in a report of the Joint Inspection Unit of the UN system of organizations (1980, p. 1):

> An excessive volume of documentation is a hindrance. It tends to obscure issues by diverting attention from essentials, and it complicates the work of intergovernmental and other meetings. At the same time, it greatly overburdens available staff resources and can cause serious delays in processing and

---

[1] Information from the UN Publications Board (undated and unpublished).

[2] Information from the Delegation of the Commission of the European Communities, Ottawa, Canada, July 1987 (unpublished).

delivery of documents. The efficiency and cost-effectiveness of the United Nations system would greatly improve if its volume of documents could be reduced, their quality were improved and they were issued on time.

The report adds that "intergovernmental bodies in almost all organizations have for decades called for a reduction of documentation, but with little effect" (Ibid., pp. 1–2).

Urquhart (1987, p. 109), a distinguished former senior official of the UN, puts the problem and one its main causes and consequences more succinctly:

> The UN has a seemingly limitless capacity to produce often lengthy documents in six languages and in immense quantities. Efforts to eliminate a document usually provoke a group of governments to demand its continued existence, and other governments will probably support them in case they wish to exert a similar privilege in the future. These reams of battleship-grey prose are a heavy burden.

Some savings have been achieved, but, while many cutbacks are salutary, others (e.g., the temporary suspension of the important summary records of subsidiary organs of the UN Economic and Social Council, or the suspension, in 1987, of the publication of the *United Nations News Digest*) seem to have been false economies. Will increased computerization achieve a substantial reduction of the volume of documents and publications? What publications will disappear because of funding limitations due to the United States withdrawal from Unesco or to the effects of the current financial crisis at the UN?

In connection with the financial crisis, the 1986 report of the UN "Group of 18"—formally called Group of High-level Intergovernmental Experts to Review the Efficiency of the Administrative and Financial Functioning of the United Nations—observes that "the volume of documentation, both in relation to conferences and meetings as well as in more general terms, has increased considerably and has, to some extent, surpassed the limit of what can be studied and constructively used by Member States" (United Nations. General Assembly, 1986b, p. 1). Notable among the Group's recommendations (Ibid., pp. 6, 8) are number 7, which is aimed at the curtailment of documentation, and number 8(3)(e) to reduce the number of reports and to avoid duplication of documentation. The "Group of 18" report and its recommendations were endorsed, with some qualifications, by the General Assembly in resolution A/RES/41/213 of December 19, 1986.

By curtailing its 1986 publications program, the UN saved some $1,500,000. Some of the economy measures that have been introduced are as follows (United Nations. General Assembly, 1986a):

- There is less external printing than before; for example, the UN itself will print *Report on the World Social Situation*
- Publication of some issues of certain periodicals (e.g., Volume 19, fourth quarter, 1986, of *World Cartography* and fifty of the eighty volumes of the *Treaty Series* projected for 1986) has been deferred
- The frequency of some periodicals has been reduced; for example, the *UN Chronicle* and the *UNDOC* will be published four, instead of eleven, times a year (United Nations. Budget Division, 1986)
- Distribution of the 1984 and subsequent annual cumulations of *UNDOC* on microfiche instead of paper copy
- Liquidation of rented warehouse space in New York for UN publications and documents, resulting in reduced storage space, print runs, and stocks of back titles
- Consolidation, deferral, or curtailment of the length of meetings of certain UN bodies, presumably resulting in reduced documentation
- Change of certain organs' entitlement from verbatim to summary meeting records, and the cessation of any meeting records for still other bodies.

Despite the curtailment of publication, IGO material, nonetheless, deals with a vast range of subjects. Figure 19–2 illustrates the subjects of concern to the UN. The following list of selected IGO periodical titles serves as further illustration:

- *Assignment Children* (UNICEF)
- *Atomic Energy Review* (International Atomic Energy Agency)
- *Bulletin on Narcotics* (UN Division of Narcotic Drugs)
- *Copyright* (World Intellectual Property Organization)
- *Cultures* (Unesco)
- *Direction of Trade* (International Monetary Fund)
- *Disarmament: A Periodic Review* (UN)
- *Economic and Social Survey of Asia and the Pacific* (UN Economic and Social Commission for Asia and the Pacific)
- *Finance and Development* (World Bank and International Monetary Fund)
- *Food and Nutrition* (Food and Agriculture Organization of the United Nations)
- *ICAO Bulletin* (International Civil Aviation Organization)
- *International Digest of Health Legislation* (World Health Organization)
- *International Labour Review* (International Labour Office)
- *International Social Science Journal* (Unesco)

- *OECD Economic Outlook* (Organisation for Economic Co-operation and Development)
- *Revista Interamericana de Bibliografía* (Organization of American States)
- *State of the Environment* (UN Environment Programme)
- *Telecommunication Journal* (International Telecommunication Union)
- *Weather Reporting* (World Meteorological Organization).

Figure 19-2.
United Nations Publications: Sales Categories

Sales numbers indicate: the language of the publication (e.g., "E/F/S"); the year when issuance was planned, not necessarily the actual year of publication (e.g., "83"); the sales category (e.g., "XIV"); and a final arabic number specific to the individual item. The numbering scheme varies slightly in Categories "O" and "XV".

O Geneva "O" sales numbers; publications of the Advisory Committee for the Co-ordination of Information Systems (ACCIS) and the United Nations Institute for Disarmament Research (UNIDIR); miscellaneous pamphlets of the Department of Public Information (DPI); and other unnumbered publications sold by the UN Sales Section.
   Examples:

GV.E.84.0.5	Directory of United Nations Databases and Information Systems, 1985 [ACCIS]
GV.E.82.0.2	Reptertory of Disarmament Research [UNIDIR]
GV.E.83.0.1.	International Register of Potentially Toxic Chemicals (IRPTC) Legal File [Geneva "O" publication]
DPI/678-80	The United Nations and Decolonization [DPA pamphlet without sales number]
[no number]	Lexique général anglais-français, avec suppléments espagnol-français et russe-français, 3e éd.

I General information and reference; DPI publications; indexes and bibliographies; publications on geography, cartography, disarmament, new sources of energy; basic reports; posters, kits and maps.
   Examples:

E.86.I.1	Yearbook of the United Nations, 1983
E.87.I.6	Index to Proceedings of the Security Council, 1986
E.85.I.23	World Cartography, Vol. 18 (1986)
E.81.I.11	Comprehensive Study on Nuclear Weapons
E.86.I.2	Space Activities of the United Nations and International Organizations

II.A. Business, economics, science and technology; includes monographs and serials prepared by the United Nations Centre on Transnational Corporations (CTC), Department of International Economic and Social Affairs (DIESA), and Centre for Science and Technology (CSTD).
   Examples:

E.87.II.A.4	Transnational Corporations and Technology Transfer: Effects and Policy Issues [CTC]

E.75.II.A.7	A New United Nations Structure for Global Economic Co-operation
E.85.II.A.18	ATAS Bulletin, No. 3: New Information Technologies and Development [CSTD]

II.B. Economic development: publications of the United Nations Industrial Development Organization (UNIDO) prior to January 1, 1987; as of that date, Category III.E. is used for UNIDO publications (*Catalogue of United Nations Publications*, 1988).
Examples:

ID/199	Information Sources on the Petrochemical Industry (UNIDO Guides to Information Sources, No. 29) [no sales number]
E.78.II.B.10	Industrialization and Rural Development

II.C. World economy.
Examples:

E.87.II.C.1	World Economic Survey, 1987
E.83.II.C.2	Overcoming Economic Disorder: International Action for Recovery and Development

II.D. Trade, finance and commerce: publications of the United Nations Conference on Trade and Development (UNCTAD).
Examples:

E.69.II.D.7	Export Credits and Development Financing, 1969
A/E/F/S.85.II.D.7	Handbook of State Trading Organizations of Developing Countries, 1985
E.87.II.D.7	Trade and Development Report, 1987

II.E. European economy: publications of the Economic Commission for Europe (ECE).
Examples:

E.87.II.E.1	Economic Survey of Europe, 1986/1987
E/F/R.86.II.E.2	Annual Bulletin of Housing and Building Statistics for Europe, 1985
E.79.II.E.16	Study on East-West European Traffic Flows
E.86.II.E.29	Digital Imaging in Health Care

II.F Asian economy: publications of the Economic and Social Commission for Asia and the Pacific (ESCAP).
Examples:

E.87.II.F.2	Economic Bulletin for Asia and the Pacific, June 1986
E.84.II.F.14	Updated Guidebook on Biogas Development
E.79.II.F.13	Mineral Distribution Maps of Asia

II.G. Latin American economy: publications of the Economic Commission for Latin America and the Caribbean (ECLAC).
Examples:

E.84.II.G.5	CEPAL Review, December 1984
E.82.II.G.10	Five Studies on the Situation of Women in Latin America
E.82.II.G.15	Economic Relations of Latin America with Europe
S.85.II.G.18	La pobreza en América Latina: dimensiones y políticas (Estudios e informes de la CEPAL, No. 54)

II.H. Public administration: publications of the DIESA in the fields of accounting, finance, planning and public administration.
Examples:

E/F/S.81.II.H.1	United Nations Directory of Agencies and Institutions in Public Administration and Finance, rev. ed., 1981

E.85.II.H.4	Economic Performance of Public Enterprises: Major Issues and Strategies for Action
E.87.II.H.2	Guidelines for Development Planning: Procedures, Methods and Techniques

II.K African economy: publications of the Economic Commission for Africa (ECA).
Examples:

E/F.84.II.K.2	Directory of African Experts, Vol. 1, Supplement 4 (1984)
E.74.II.K.8	Development Education: Rural Development through Mass Media
E.87.II.K.3	Survey of Economic and Social Conditions in Africa, 1984–1985

III.A Publications of the United Nations University (UNU).
Examples:

E.85.III.A.10	Food as a Human Right
E.85.III.A.12	Arid Zone Settlement in Australia: A Focus on Alice Springs

III.B. Publications of the United Nations Development Programme (UNDP).
Examples:

E.86.III.B.3	Annual Report of the Administrator, 1985
E.85.III.B.2	Generation: Portrait of the United Nations Development Programme, 1950–1985

III.C. Publications of the United Nations International Research and Training Institute for the Advancement of Women.
Examples:

E.85.III.C.2	Development Co-operation with Women: The Experience and Future Directions of the Fund
E.87.III.C.1	The Incorporation of Women into Development Planning

III.D. Publications of the United Nations Environment Programme (UNEP).
Examples:

E.85.III.D.1	Environmental Refugees
E.86.III.D.4	Radiation: Doses, Effects, Risks

III.E. This is used for publications of the United Nations Industrial Development Organization (UNIDO), as of January 1, 1987 (*Catalogue of United Nations Publications*, 1988). See Category II.B. for earlier UNIDO publications.

III.F. Publications of the Latin American and Caribbean Institute for Economic and Social Planning (ILPES).
Examples:

E.85.III.F.16	Notes on Integration, Welfare and Project Evaluation
E.85.III.F.65	Planning a System of Regions
S.85.III.F.4	Control de la ejecución de projectos por el método del camino crítico

III.G. This is used for publications of the Latin American and Caribbean Demographic Centre (CELADE) as of late 1987 (*Catalogue of United Nations Publications*, 1988).
Examples:

E.87.III.H.1	Guide to Sources of International Population Assistance (1988)
E.87.III.H.2	Inventory of Population Projects in Developing Countries around the World, 1985/1986

III.K. Publications of the United Nations Institute for Training and Research (UNITAR), 1987–. (Category XV was used for UNITAR publications prior to 1987.)

IV   Social questions: publications of DIESA's Centre for Social Development and Humanitarian Affairs (CSDHA).
Examples:
E.85.IV.2	Report on the World Social Situation, 1985
E.86.IV.4	Economic Recession and Specific Population Groups
E.87.IV.1	Consolidated List of Products whose Consumption and/or Sale Have Been Banned, Withdrawn, Severely Restricted or Not Approved by Governments

V   International law: publications of the International Law Commission, the Secretariat's Office of Legal Affairs, and other serials and monographs concerned with conferences, treaties, legislation and trade law.
Examples:
E.86.V.4	Yearbook of the International Law Commission, 1985, Vol. 1
E.83.V.5	United Nations Convention on the Law of the Sea
E/F.83.V.8	Review of the Multilateral Treaty-Making Process

VII   Political and Security Council affairs (series prepared by the Secretariat's Department of Political and Security Council Affairs).
Example:
E.86.VII.1	Repertoire of the Practice of the Security Council, Supplement, 1975–1980

VIII   Transport and communications: publications concerning the carriage of goods.
Example:
E.85.VIII.3	Transport of Dangerous Goods: Recommendations, 4th, rev. ed.

IX   Disarmament and atomic energy: publications produced by the Secretariat's Department of Disarmament Affairs.
Examples:
E.86.IX.3	The Naval Arms Race (Disarmament Study Series, No. 16)
E.87.IX.1	United Nations Disarmament Yearbook, 1986
E.82.IX.8	Ionizing Radiation: Sources and Biological Effects

X   International administration.
Examples:
E.83.X.1	Judgements of the United Nations Administrative Tribunal, 1978–1982
C/E/F/R/S.75.X.2	Convention on the Privileges and Immunities of the Specialized Agencies

BIBLIOGRAPHIC ACCESS

Access to documents and publications of IGOs is essential for the primary users of this material (delegations of member states, IGO staff, and others), for intermediate users (notably libraries), and for end users (members of the research community and other interested members of the public). Access would hardly be possible without reasonable bibliographic control. Bibliographic control over IGO material, however, remains uneven and at times inadequate.

The bibliographic apparatus covering IGO documents and publications is varied. It includes bibliographies, indexes, sales catalogs, and abstracts. Some of these bibliographic tools, those produced by the IGOs themselves, cover their own documents and/or publications, while other tools include the output of more than one agency. Still others are produced by national governments (e.g., *International Organisations Publications* issued by Her Majesty's Stationery Office in London as a supplement to its *Government Publications*); nongovernmental entities, such as scholarly institutions or commercial firms (an example of the latter is *International Bibliography: Publications of Intergovernmental Organizations*, published by UNIPUB); and individuals (e.g., Dimitrov's *World Bibliography of International Documentation*). Some bibliographic tools are intended by the producing agency for wide public use, while others (e.g., the *Index of OECD Documents and Publications*) are essentially for internal use. Some (e.g., the *Unesco List of Documents and Publications*) cover both documents and publications, while others include publications only (e.g., the World Bank's *Index of Publications*) or documents only (e.g., the *Catalogue, Part B: Documents* issued by the Commission of the European Communities).

As IGOs increase their production and availability of electronic information, their bibliographic tools keep pace and identify such data. For example, the *Catalogue of United Nations Publications* includes a brief section entitled "Machine Readable Products Available from the United Nations Statistical Office;" the International Monetary Fund's *Publications Catalog* carries information about magnetic tape subscriptions; and the OECD *Catalogue of Publications* has a page on data available on magnetic tape and microcomputer diskette.

The scope of some bibliographic tools is general, while others confine their coverage to a special type or form of material. For example, the *Catálogo de Informes y Documentos Tcnicos de la OEA* covers only OAS technical reports, and the *Price Catalogue for Statistical Information from Databanks* (issued by the Statistical Office of the European Communities) lists data on tape, on diskette, and on computer printouts. Prominent among special compilations devoted largely to describing IGO electronic information is the *Directory of United Nations Databases and Information Systems, 1985*, issued by the Advisory Committee for the Co-ordination of Information Systems of the UN system of organizations (ACCIS). ACCIS has also published the *ACCIS Guide to United Nations Information Sources on Food and Agriculture*, the first of several planned compilations on subjects of interest to the UN system. Less voluminous, but equally informative, is Hardt's (1987) "On Line to Europe: A Guide to E.C. Databases," which describes the bibliographic, statistical, and factual databases of the European Communities.

Some bibliographic aids have chronological, geographic, or language limitations, while others do not. Some aids are produced manually, but more are now computer-produced. Computerized bibliographic information systems include FAO's AGRIS, IAEA's INIS, ILO's ISIS, the UN's UNBIS, the Computerized Documentation System (CDS/ISIS) of Unesco, and SCAD, a database covering official and nonofficial publications of the European Communities.

The corpus of finding aids, complex as it is, does not provide complete bibliographic coverage of IGO documents and publications. In recent years, the UN and Unesco have been among the organizations providing very good, though still not quite complete, bibliographic control over both their documents and publications. The OECD and the World Bank are examples of IGOs that give good, publicly available bibliographic coverage of their publications, but not their documents, in their respective sales catalogs, the OECD *Catalogue of Publications on Sale* and the World Bank's *New Publications*. The European Communities, for many years, supplied fragmented and incomplete coverage of their huge output of documents and publications. However, lately, the European Communities have improved their performance through the annual publication of *Catalogue, Part A: Publications* (kept up- to-date by the quarterly *Publications of the European Communities*) and *Catalogue, Part B: Documents* (kept up-to-date by the monthly *Documents*.)

IFLA has long advocated the ideal of Universal Bibliographic Control (UBC) which, if ever realized, should include bibliographic control over IGO material. IFLA's Official Publications Section and Section of Bibliography are currently sponsoring research into bibliographic control and distribution by IGOs. The purpose of the research is to study new developments in IGO bibliographic tools and to survey depository libraries of IGOs. According to Jacque (1986, p. 11), the research

> project will comprise three main sections: . . . an updated inventory of all the bibliographic sources of a selected number of organizations . . . a worldwide user survey of depository libraries [receiving IGO material, and] . . . a synopsis of the results of the survey and . . . inventory [with recommendations].

The final report on the project should be presented at IFLA's 1988 General Conference in Melbourne, Australia.

Marulli (1979) and Clews (1981), among others, have studied the state of bibliographic control over the document and publication output of the UN system of organizations and have advanced a number of excellent recommendations.[3] Marulli's recommendations include:

---

[3] In addition, the proceedings of the two major symposia on international documentation (Geneva, 1972, and Brussels, 1980) contain much valuable information on all aspects of international documentation, including bibliographic control. See *Sources, Organization, Utilization of International Documentation* (1974); and Dimitrov and Marulli-Koenig (1982).

- Consistent and appropriate bibliographic coverage of material issued by the UN system in languages other than English
- Cataloging-in-publication for publications and important documents
- Better coordination between organizational units producing sales catalogs and those producing bibliographies and indexes; this would ensure that different types of bibliographic tools complement rather than overlap each other
- Better channels of communication between the UN system and the library and information community at large
- The formulation of rigorous and consistent bibliographic standards.

Marulli-Koenig (1988, pp. 51–68) also recommends the utilization of commercial online services by UN organizations, the use of microcomputers by organizations without substantial data processing capacity, setting priorities for covering various types of documentation in bibliographic databases, and identifying the essential elements of bibliographic description.

Some of these recommendations would improve access to the material of UN organizations. Similar improvements could result from Clews's recommendations that aim at the development of an integrated bibliographic information system whose major product would be the generation of a current bibliography of the documents and publications of the entire UN system. Unfortunately, many of these and other recommendations have not been implemented, for lack of will and for reasons of organizational, political, and budgetary constraints on the part of the UN system and other IGOs. On the positive side, the above-mentioned, valuable contributions of ACCIS and the European Communities are steps in the right direction.

COLLECTION DEVELOPMENT

Policy Statements

Libraries collect material, including IGO publications and documents, to meet the needs of their present and future users. Libraries of educational institutions support their teaching and research mandates, while public libraries have to satisfy the educational, informational, and recreational needs of the communities they serve. Special libraries must meet the informational needs of their particular clientele. All libraries should have written policies that guide their collection development and that meet administrative, resource-sharing or network, political, and other requirements. Collection development policies "unify or focus expression . . . [on] the current state and future direction of that collection" (Atkinson, 1986, p. 140). The ideal collection policy should address current collection strength, current collect-ing intensity, and desired collecting intensity (Ibid., pp. 142–148).

Collection policies vary in detail and structure. Nonetheless, they should include the following elements: definitions of the clientele of the library and of the purpose of the collections; scope and level of the collec-tions; geographic, chronological, language, and physical-form inclusions and exclusions; collecting priorities; collecting methods; and administrative as-pects such as the assignment of responsibility for selection, the role of faculty (in academic institutions), and the allocation of funds. Collection develop-ment should be based on regular evaluation and modifications as needed.[4] In addition to general characteristics of collection development, the following special problems of IGO collections must also be considered:

- *Suitability for different audiences.* IGOs produce many public-in-formation brochures and press releases. These sources are intended for non-specialists or the general public, but they can still be useful, at times, for more sophisticated users. In fact, press releases often supply current information about meetings and other events as well as bibliographic notices about new publications and documents. Statistical and other yearbooks, collections of texts, and various special reports are useful to academic researchers, business people, government officials, and other professionals. Summaries of IGO meetings and other official records are intended primarily for the member states of IGOs but are frequently a useful source of infor-mation for non-governmental specialists as well. Documents con-cerned with the internal administration of an IGO (e.g., budgetary and personnel matters) are intended chiefly for the staff of IGOs and for governments of member states, but are also essential for special-ists who study IGOs
- *Physical form.* IGOs issue material in a variety of physical forms: printed, mimeographed, photo-offset, wordprocessed, microform, film and video, sound recordings, and electronic databases and their products. Each form imposes its own requirements in hand-ling, storage, equipment, expertise, and cost. Costs, of course, are associated not only with the acquisition of material; a library may, for example, acquire microform documents free of charge but will have to supply storage cabinets, readers, and reader-printers that must be purchased and serviced regularly. Staff costs, too, apply to the handling of free and priced material in any physical form

---

[4] Several important sources of information on collection development have appeared in recent years, notably: *Guidelines for Collection Development* (1979); Association of Research Libraries. Systems and Pro-cedures Exchange Center (1977); Stueart and Miller (1980); Hernon and Purcell (1982); Futas (1984); Carpen-ter (1984); Robinson (1981; 1982); and Atkinson (1986).

- *Publisher.* There has been an increasing tendency in many IGOs to issue publications jointly with another publisher or to have items published externally (although this may change somewhat as the UN, for one, plans to reduce contracting-out costs). For example, Johns Hopkins University Press is the publisher of many World Bank publications; Pergamon Press now publishes the UN's *Economic Bulletin for Europe*; and Unesco has co-published many items with publishers around the world. An interesting example of a publication of two IGOs is the third edition of the *Macrothesaurus for Information Processing in the Field of Economic and Social Development*, issued jointly by the UN and the OECD. Another example of an external publication is *Mission to South Africa: The Commonwealth Report*, published in 1986 by Penguin Books for the Commonwealth Secretariat. "Significant OAS cultural publications are being contracted out to Latin American publishers who do not advertise widely in North American markets"[5]

- *Secondary material.* A well-rounded collection of IGO documents and publications should be complemented by relevant secondary material: reference works and selection tools as well as interpretative works about IGOs. Hopkins (1985, pp. 214–218) draws attention to characteristics of scholarly literature on the European Communities and European integration, including bibliographies and guides, theses, scholarly monographs, and journal articles. O'Brien and Topolski (1968, pp. 290–291) categorize interpretative writing about the UN into comprehensive studies by academic specialists; writings concerned with improving the Organization, designed to elicit favorable feelings about the UN, or designed to disparage the UN; attacks on the UN, mostly from the far right; ostensibly analytic or descriptive writings designed to serve the interests of a particular state; writings about power politics, leaving the UN almost entirely out of account; writings preoccupied with measurement; specialized studies dealing, for example, with an issue before the United Nations from the standpoint of some particular nation; reflections of people with UN experience (contributions to theory and memoirs including reflections on experience); semi-official writings by officials of the UN Secretariat; and commentaries by journalists accredited to the UN.

  IGOs, understandably, are interested in literature about themselves, and collect it for their own libraries. In addition to collecting such material, Unesco has issued a *Bibliography of Pub-*

---

[5] Thomas L. Welch, Director of the Columbus Memorial Library of the OAS, quoted in *Documents to the People*, 12 (September 1984): 109.

lications on Unesco. Norton's *NATO: A Bibliography and Resource Guide* is a recent example of a commercially-published source of information on secondary material about an IGO.

Part of the written collection policy should address the intensity of collecting, and the strengths of the existing collections. This intensity may be expressed in levels, although some libraries may prefer to use specific policy statements about areas of study and research instead of specifying levels. The American Library Association's *Guidelines for Collection Development* (1979) distinguishes five levels: minimal, basic, study, research, and comprehensive.* The *Guidelines* "are fast becoming the standard means to describe collections" (Atkinson, 1986).

The *minimal* level, which comprises an "area in which few selections are made beyond very basic works," may be appropriate for small public and high school libraries as well as libraries specializing in fields outside the subject scope of the material issued by particular IGOs. IGO material collected at this level would be limited to a few relatively popular, monographic publications and periodical subscriptions (e.g., *Everyman's United Nations, Everyone's United Nations,* and *The Unesco Courier*), supplemented by a few secondary works and reference works about IGOs (e.g., Claude's *Swords into Plowshares,* and the *United Nations Handbook* issued annually by the New Zealand Ministry of Foreign Affairs).

The *basic* level comprises "a highly selective collection which serves to introduce and define the subject and to indicate the varieties of information available elsewhere." Most larger public or small college libraries might find this level suitable for collecting IGO material. In addition to the types of literature indicated under "minimal" level, a basic-level collection would include major IGO yearbooks and periodicals, and selected reports issued by IGOs (e.g., the *Yearbook of the United Nations,* the World Bank's *World Development Report,* and the *OECD Economic Outlook*), as well as additional secondary works and a few bibliographies and other reference works (e.g., Hovet's *A Chronology and Fact Book of the United Nations,* Osmanczyk's *The Encyclopedia of the United Nations and International Agreements,* and Hajnal's *Guide to United Nations Organization, Documentation and Publishing*).

The *study* level is characterized by the *Guidelines* as "a collection which supports undergraduate or graduate course work, or sustained independent study . . . of less than research intensity." University, large college, and special libraries—including governmental libraries and information centers—as well as selected large public libraries would collect IGO material at

---

* Definitions of levels are taken from *Guidelines for Collection Development* (1979).

this level. Such an IGO collection would include a generous selection of sales publications, specialized yearbooks, legal material issued by IGOs, important reports and studies, and current and retrospective bibliographies, indexes, and other reference works published by IGOs (e.g., WHO's *World Health Statistics Annual*, UNCTAD's *Yearbook of International Commodity Statistics*, ILO's *Legislative Series*, and the UN's *UNDOC: Current Index*). Secondary material collected at the study level would include a selection of political, economic, legal, technical, and other studies; other interpretative works dealing with one or more IGOs or with IGOs in general; scholarly journals; works dealing with the role of specific countries in IGOs; and reference works supplementing those issued by IGOs (e.g., Sewell's *UNESCO and World Politics*, Barros's *Office without Power*, Williams's *The Specialized Agencies and the United Nations*, the journal *International Organization*, the annual *Issues before the United Nations*, and the *Index to International Statistics* issued by the Congressional Information Service.

The *research* level consists of "a collection which includes the major published source materials required for dissertations and independent research, including materials containing research reporting, new findings . . . [and] all important reference works." This level is appropriate for large university and other research libraries, including those specializing in subject fields of particular IGOs. A collection maintained at the research level would have as complete a set as possible of current and retrospective IGO sales publications, and all available documents. Some libraries at this collecting level would be depositories for those IGOs that have established depository systems. Collections at this level should also include publications issued by commercial publishers for IGOs and publications issued jointly by particular IGOs and other publishers. Highly specialized reference tools should also form part of a research-level collection (e.g., the *Repertory of Practice of United Nations Organs*, the *Macrothesaurus for Information Processing in the Field of Economic and Social Development*, and *Euro Abstracts*). Complementary, secondary material would include not only trade and governmental publications but also theses, conference papers, and other scholarly material.

The *comprehensive* level consists of "a collection in which the library endeavors, so far as is reasonably possible, to include all significant works of recorded knowledge for a necessarily defined field." Some very large university, research, and governmental libraries might aspire to— if not succeed in—collecting IGO literature at this level. Such a collection might include "limited" distribution documents, other IGO material outside regular distribution channels—newsletters, press releases, and administrative instructions, as well as IGO documents in microform (e.g., Research Publications' edition of League of Nations *Documents and Serial Publications, 1919–1946*), and computerized IGO data files that are available to outside users online, on magnetic tape or other computer media (e.g., DEIN—the DESI Electronic Information Network, a project of the Division of Economic and Social Information of the UN's Department of Public Information).[6] Secondary material collected at this level would include not only as much published material related to IGOs as possible but also manuscripts and other nonprint items.

For a more detailed description of how these levels may be applied to collecting UN documents and publications and related secondary material, with specific illustrative titles, see "Collection Development: United Nations Material" (Hajnal, 1981).

Distribution Policies and Practices of IGOs

Many IGOs designate their publications and documents for various categories of distribution. The UN, for example, classifies its material in the following, major categories:

- "General" distribution documents (basic documents, final meeting records, resolutions, and other decisions of main organs, or studies and reports) receive the widest circulation
- "Limited" distribution documents (e.g., draft reports, draft resolutions, and papers relating to agenda items of meetings) are intended for governments and other recipients whom the UN considers to be interested in the work of the organ concerned. Actual interest in these documents is often wider. Collection development for university or other research libraries as well as some special libraries should take into account ways in which this type of material can be obtained. The contents of some "limited" distribution material eventually find their way into "general" distribution documents such as the final report of the body in which they were discussed. Another way of obtaining "limited" distribution documents is to subscribe to the Readex microfiche (from 1946 to 1981, microprint) edition of *United Nations Documents and Publications*, which includes the "limited" category. (It should be noted, however, that Secretariat documents of all distribution categories were excluded from the microprint edition, *Mimeographed and Printed Documents*.) "Limited" distribution documents bear the letter "L" before the serial number in the document series symbol, as in "E/1984/C.4/L.1"
- "Restricted" distribution is a designation usually given to docu-

---

[6] For more information about DEIN, see Advisory Committee for the Co-ordination of Information Systems (1987a).

ments and meeting records on the basis of confidentiality. The distribution of such documents and records is determined by the originating body. Having met certain conditions, such as the passage of time, many "restricted" distribution documents are subsequently declassified. Declassification is done routinely in the case of "restricted" documents of the UN Economic Commission for Europe. Derestricted project reports of the UN Development Programme (UNDP) were formerly listed regularly, but such lists are no longer issued. For other organs of the UN, declassification is less systematic and inadequately documented. The UN Library has a mandate to prepare an annual list of "restricted" series symbols of documents issued at least five years previously and held by the Library. These lists are then reviewed by the Executive Office of the Secretary-General, circulated to the originating office, and "in the absence of other instructions . . . declassified by a specific date" (United Nations. Department of Conference Services, 1983, p. 494). Derestricted documents are difficult to obtain because of small stocks, except for the declassified project reports of UNDP, which are marketed by University Microfilms. "Restricted" distribution documents bear the letter "R" before the serial number in the document series symbol

- In addition to the "general," "limited," and "restricted" distribution categories, the UN employs some other designations. For example, "provisional" applies to meeting records issued first to participants of the meetings. For the past several years, the UN has offered for sale "provisional" meeting records of the General Assembly and the Security Council—a useful step, because some meeting records may take several years to appear in final form
- Conference room and working papers "are not official documents but informal papers . . . of concern primarily to the members of [a UN] organ." They bear the identifying letters "CRP" or "WP" before the serial number of the symbol (Ibid., p. 488)
- The UN, like many other organizations, holds some highly confidential material, often in its Archives. There is a general restriction period of twenty years for access to records in the Archives. Some records, though, are subject to special rules and require approval by the office of the Secretary-General before access can be given (Unesco, 1984, p. 187; United Nations. Secretariat. *Administrative Instruction*, 1984).

The UN maintains official distribution lists for its documents, meeting records, *Official Records*, and publications distributed free of charge. External distribution lists cover ministries, embassies, and other governmental bodies; NGOs that enjoy consultative status with the UN; specialized agencies and other IGOs; offices of the UN outside New York City; UN information centers; and depository libraries (these libraries are discussed below). Internal lists—for distribution of material at UN headquarters in New York—cover permanent missions of member states to the UN, permanent observers, the press, the UN Secretariat, meetings-service and conference offices, and the UN Sales Section (United Nations. Department of Conference Services, 1983, p. 489).

Other IGOs employ somewhat similar, but often less clearly defined, distribution categories. Many IGOs are more restrictive than the UN in making their source material available to outsiders. Unesco, for example, for many years, made its publications, but not its documents, widely available. In 1983, it began making certain types of documents more easily available on request, free of charge, while other documents may be purchased on microfiche. The World Bank makes a sharp distinction between its documents and publications for distribution purposes; its free and priced publications are easy to obtain, but its documents, as a rule, are inaccessible to most outsiders. The European Communities' attitude to confidentiality of documents has been characterized as falling "between . . . [the] two extremes . . . [of] the bureaucratic paranoia for secrecy of the British . . . [and] the neurotic frankness of the Americans" (Jeffries, 1982, p. 11). Many Community documents are considered internal, but some are released to the public in their original form, and some others reappear as publications. OECD documents, when first issued, are considered confidential, but many are subsequently released for publication. Documents (but not publications) of NATO, to take a different example, are secret, and inaccessible to public or university libraries on a current basis.

Several IGOs offer direct or indirect access to their databases for the public. The recent *Final Report of the Technical Panel on Database Access* (Advisory Committee for the Co-ordination of Information Systems, 1987b) states that five organizations in the UN system "offer online services from their own computers to external users." The report estimates that twenty-five databases of the UN system "are available via public data networks on external online services, such as DIALOG, ECHO, ESA-IRS, and I. P. Sharp." The report includes, in tabular form, a compendium of database access policies for the UN system, indicating:

- Whether each organization has policies or guidelines on the dissemination of its databases
- Whether the database is accessible to users who do not belong to the organization or to the unit that has developed the database
- On what online host (if any) the database is available
- Whether the database producer has a pricing policy

- The type of each database (bibliographic, directory, full text, referral, statistical or numerical, or thesaurus or terminological)
- Whether the entire content of the database is available
- Whether copies or subsets of the database are available on magnetic tape, diskette, or CD-ROM
- Whether the database has a print or microform equivalent
- Whether there are restrictions on access to and use of the database
- Whether the database producer has an active marketing and user-training program
- Whether an original document covered in the database can be obtained from the database producer.

Hardt (1987) gives a brief description of twenty-two databases of the European Communities, indicating language, type (bibliographical, factual, or statistical), chronological coverage, the number of records each one contains, annual growth rate, updating frequency, availability of offline print, costs, and hosts servicing and marketing the database.

Acquisition Methods

Purchase and subscription are important methods of acquiring IGO material. For many libraries, these are the only means of doing so. The UN and a number of other IGOs offer individual items for sale, as well as standing orders and subscriptions (Figure 19–2 lists and illustrates the UN sales categories). In addition, IGO material is available from an extensive, international network of sales outlets comprising commercial and academic booksellers or agents—such as UNIPUB, UNIFO, and Taylor & Francis in the United States—as well as governmental sales outlets—for example, Her Majesty's Stationery Office (HMSO) in Great Britain. Such agents usually handle documents and publications for a number of IGOs. In the late 1970s, Unesco had the widest network of sales agents: 275, in 112 countries. FAO was represented in eighty-three countries; the UN and WHO in sixty-nine each; OECD in thirty-five; and the European Communities in thirteen countries (Cherns, 1982, p. 29). In some countries, more than one bookseller markets publications of a given agency. For example, in the United States, UN material is handled by UNIPUB, Taylor & Francis, UNIFO, and Readex, among others. Readex has been reproducing a major retrospective and current collection of UN documents and publications in microform. Some dealers are exclusive agents authorized to market the publications of a given IGO in a particular country. For example, Le Diffuseur G. Vermette, in Canada, handles World Bank publications.

The Second World Symposium on International Documentation, held in Brussels in 1980, recommended that (Casadio, 1982, p. xxxi):

more effective means should be employed in the marketing of publications. Improvements in the distribution and marketing of international documents are urgently needed. Marketing implies the development of image, good publicity and an active sales force, since the public rarely sees IGO publications in bookshop windows or in advertisements. This could be overcome by more systematic marketing of publications through the book trade or through co-publishing with commercial firms [emphasis removed].

Co-published or externally-published items are generally obtainable from the external or joint publisher as well as from the originating IGO. The World Bank, for example, has mutual distribution agreements with Johns Hopkins University Press and Oxford University Press. The United Nations sells some of its co-published and externally-published items in its bookshops in New York and Geneva, but such items may also be obtained from the joint or external publisher.

A number of IGOs distribute many of their documents and publications free of charge, but, while gifts are a useful means of collection development, especially at times of budgetary restraint, it must be remembered that libraries acquiring "free" material still incur processing, staffing, and other hidden costs. The UN maintains an extensive system of exchange agreements—a method of acquisition that should be considered, even though many institutions find exchanges difficult to administer. Marulli-Koenig (1982, pp. 85–102) has detailed the nature of exchanges, along with other methods and characteristics of building collections of UN material.

Depository Libraries

A number of IGOs maintain a system of depository libraries. The UN has designated some 300 depositories worldwide.[7] These depositories (often national, university, or other large research libraries) receive publications and "general" distribution documents in the official language of their choice. Deposit may be partial or full; the latter includes mimeographed documents. Depository libraries "are expected to place the material received in the care of qualified library staff, to keep it in good order and to make it accessible to the public, free of charge, at ..reasonable hours" (United Nations. Dag Hammarskjöld Library, 1981, Annex I, p. 2). In addition to serving users on library premises, many depositories lend material, and some provide interlibrary loan service. Since January 1, 1975, most UN depositories have been required to pay an annual contribution, now amounting to $960 (U.S.) for full depositories and $600 for partial depositories in developed countries, and $300 for full depositories and $200 for partial depositories in developing

---

[7] These, along with parliamentary libraries and UN information centers or services receiving UN material, are listed in (United Nations. Secretariat, 1987).

countries. This expenditure is worthwhile in monetary terms alone, because the cost of all sales items, including official records, would otherwise be $5,922 (U.S.), as of 1985.[8] Several categories of material are not included in the deposit: most publications of the International Court of Justice, UNICEF, the United Nations Institute for Training and Research, the United Nations Fund for Population Activities, the United Nations Environment Programme, the United Nations Institute of Disarmament Research, the United Nations International Training and Research Institute for Women, the United Nations University, and certain other types of documents and publications (Ibid., pp. 3–4; United Nations. Dag Hammarskjöld Library, Corrigendum 2, 1986). The International Court of Justice and the United Nations University have their own depository networks. The United Nations Industrial Development Organization, formerly a special body within the UN but since 1986 an autonomous specialized agency, still includes its documents and publications, at this writing, in the UN depository package.

Several other IGOs maintain worldwide systems of depository libraries. Unesco, for example, had 379 depositories in 1983. These fell into one of three categories (Hajnal, 1983, p. 206):

> those that receive one or more copies of all publications (including periodicals) and certain types of documents; those that receive publications (including periodicals) but no documents; and those that receive periodicals only but have the right to select other free publications as announced by Unesco.

Among other IGOs that have worldwide systems of depositories are the Food and Agriculture Organization of the United Nations (which asks its depositories to maintain a permanent display of FAO publications), GATT, ICAO, WHO, WIPO, and the South Pacific Commission.

Some IGOs have a more limited system of depository libraries. The World Bank maintained for many years a depository system in developing countries only (Zlatich, 1982, microfiche 3, p. 75). Recently, the Bank began extending the network by allowing one library in each member state to apply for depository status. The Bank requires each depository library to have a public reading room and adequate space to shelve and maintain some 300 new publications a year; have on staff at least one trained librarian responsible for the collection of World Bank publications; place and maintain these publications under bibliographic control (including accessioning, cataloging, classifying, and shelving to ensure retrieval for library users); be open to the public during normal business hours and allow use of the collection without charge; show evidence of the types and number of clients served; and circu-

---

[8] Unpublished information from the United Nations Sales Section, May 1986.

late accession or current acquisition lists regularly to clients.[9] Another IGO, the Organization of American States, has depository libraries in 114 countries (Welch, 1982, pp. 204–205). Still other IGOs (e.g., the IMF and the OECD) have not established depository systems.

The European Communities maintain a worldwide system of depository libraries and European Documentation Centres (EDCs), both of which categories receive free of charge a large amount of material that they are not only expected to service adequately but also to augment with non-Community material bearing on the subject of European integration. A third category of libraries, European Reference Centres, receives from the Communities some basic material free of charge. What is now the depository library system of the European Communities began in the days of the European Coal and Steel Community. (The European Coal and Steel Community was established in 1951, followed by the other two Communities, the European Economic Community and Euratom—European Atomic Energy Community—in 1957.) Most depositories in the United States were established in the 1960s and 1970s. The original idea of European Documentation Centres, initiated by the Commission of the European Communities in the 1970s, called for small, rather limited collections, but, over the years, the entitlements of depository libraries and EDCs have become virtually identical. The estimated value of depository/EDC shipments in 1985 was 320,000 Belgian francs (about US$5,330) for the documents and publications—plus 62,000 Belgian francs (approximately US$1,030) for postage—per library. The two types of recipient libraries are likely to diverge again: a new formula proposed by the Communities would allow specialized EDCs to receive basic documentation "consisting of publications of general interest," optional documentation on request, and a choice of publications under ten of the twenty headings of the *Catalogue, Part A: Publications* of the European Communities. The former concept of full-entitlement EDCs "will be retained for those universities with multi-disciplinary teaching and postgraduate studies in European affairs" (Lastenouse, 1987).

Depository libraries constitute an important means whereby IGOs make their documents and publications available to a wide public. These depositories have improved access to IGO literature, in direct proportion to available staff and other resources, efficient organization of the material, and competent reference service in each particular depository.

Selection Tools

Bibliographic tools covering IGO material have a selection as well as a reference function. Sales catalogs, issued by most IGOs to cover their own

---

[9] Unpublished information and memorandum of depository agreement from the World Bank.

publications, are major sources of selection and acquisition. Varying in scope, completeness, frequency, and timeliness, they generally supply sufficient information for acquisition purposes; in some cases, they are also a good source of brief information about the structure and major activities of IGOs. The *Catalogue of United Nations Publications*, the OECD *Catalogue of Publications on Sale*, the World Bank's *Index of Publications* and *New Publications*, the *ILO Catalogue of Publications in Print*, and the Unesco *Publications Catalogue* are examples of this type of source (see chapter Appendix 2 for a selective listing of IGO sales catalogs). These mostly annual or biennial catalogs are in many cases kept up-to-date by monthly, quarterly, or occasional current-awareness bulletins or leaflets. Somewhat similar in nature are general and specialized listings issued by sales outlets of IGOs (e.g., UNIPUB in the United States and Renouf in Canada).

Bibliographies, indexes, and abstracting services—whether or not produced by the IGOs themselves—may also serve as selection tools, although their primary function is to facilitate bibliographic control and research rather than acquisition. The timeliness of these tools is crucial for acquisition purposes, as IGO documents go out of print quickly. UN mimeographed documents, for example, generally have remained in print for two years, while the average in-print time for UN sales publications has been five to seven years (Hajnal, 1978, p. 206). (In-print time for UN documents and publications is likely to become shorter because of the recent economy measures taken by the UN.) Certain types of Unesco documents are kept in stock for only one year, while others remain available for four or more years (Hajnal, 1983, pp. 199–200).

Several professional and technical journals list or review IGO documents and publications. UNIPUB's quarterly *International Bibliography: Publications of Intergovernmental Organizations* is a useful, though necessarily selective, current-awareness service. *Government Publications Review* had, for a few years, included a regular acquisition guide to significant IGO and other government publications. This feature has been replaced by an annual listing of notable documents; although still interesting and informative, it is no longer sufficiently timely as a selection tool. On the other hand, *Government Publications Review* now carries an excellent current-awareness column, "International Organization News," by Robert W. Schaaf. *Documents to the People*, the quarterly newsletter of the Government Documents Round Table of the American Library Association, has a regular column, "International Documents Roundup," contributed formerly by Luciana Marulli-Koenig and now alternately by Maureen Ratynski and Nellie Moffitt. *United Nations Documentation News*, issued by the Dag Hammarskjöld Library, is an informative source of current news and bibliographic notices about UN material. *EDC/Dep Bulletin* was a similarly helpful source of information about European Community documents and publications; unfortunately, it is no longer published. Journals such as *Government Information Quarterly* and *Serials Review* carry occasional articles, reviews and bibliographic notices about IGO literature.

Periodicals published by IGOs, such as the *UN Chronicle*, ILO's *International Labour Review*, the *OECD Observer*, and the *WHO Chronicle*, regularly publish lists of recent material issued by the respective agencies. Many specialized journals, published by professional associations or academic or commercial publishers, also carry notices of important IGO publications in their subject fields. Informal, direct contact with IGOs themselves, or with professional organizations concerned with IGO activities, is another useful source of information and acquisition; so too are formal and informal networks of documents librarians specializing in IGO material.

All possible sources, whether or not primarily bibliographic in nature, should be considered as aids to bibliographic and physical access to IGO material. Ideally, IGOs themselves should "recognize that easy access, both physical and intellectual, to the information content of their documentation is as important as their original conception, preparation and publication" (Hopkins, 1980, p. 381). It often remains, however, for the readers and researchers themselves, assisted by competent reference librarians, to gain the most important, intellectual access to IGO documents and publications.

FUTURE CHALLENGES

The complexity of IGOs is reflected in their documents, publications, and information systems. The types, quantity, and physical forms of IGO material pose a challenge to librarians, a challenge that is compounded by varying levels and adequacy of bibliographic control over this material, and by the special difficulties involved in developing IGO collections.

IGO material comprises an important source of research data and practical information. Notwithstanding the complexity of IGO material, libraries should select it to satisfy the present and future needs of their clientele. They should assess the merits of available documents, publications, and electronic information, and decide what types of material and what level of collecting would be appropriate for their own institutions.

This chapter has analyzed various aspects of collection development (general and special characteristics, levels of collecting, distribution policies and practices of IGOs, acquisition methods, and selection tools) as a means of access to IGO material. Other writings, some cited in this chapter, also aim to help librarians gain more knowledge on which to base collection development. Library schools, too, have an important role to play in teaching students and librarians to become more proficient in handling IGO material. Courses specifically devoted to IGO documents and publications are one way of achieving this goal; inclusion of information about IGO source material in general reference, literature, and documents courses is another.

It is equally important to be aware of journals that are regular sources of information about IGO material. This chapter cites examples of journals and cautions that some may no longer be as useful as they once were. Fortunately, as this chapter also indicates, new sources of information tend to emerge, testifying to a continuing need. Librarians should, therefore, be aware of the dynamic nature of journal literature.

Knowledge of sources of information will enable librarians to make informed decisions to promote access to IGO material. Equally essential for access are more responsive distribution policies and practices on the part of IGOs themselves. IGOs, quite legitimately, give preferential service to the primary users of their documents and publications—the governments of their member states, officials of their own agencies and other IGOs, and a few other select groups. This is natural, for "the current records of an [international governmental] agency were created, received and maintained by the agency not primarily to facilitate research by non-staff members, but rather to conduct the business of the agency" (Evans, 1982, microfiche 2, p. 69). External constituencies are less well served, especially when it comes to access to documents as contrasted with publications. Part of the problem lies in the nature of accountability; even national governments seem, at times, far removed from the people to whom they are accountable. Because IGOs are accountable only to the governments of their member states, they are still further removed from the public that is the end-user of their source material (Hajnal, 1982, p. 124).

Some promising recent developments show increased IGO responsiveness to the needs of the public. One example of this is the fact that the UN has published, since September 1981, a current-awareness bulletin, *United Nations Documentation News*. Another is the availability, since 1983, of Unesco's non-restricted documents and publications on microfiche from Unesco Microfiche Service through the Unesco Press. A further example is the emergence and gradually increasing public availability of electronic information online, and on magnetic tape, diskette, and CD-ROM.

The worldwide network of depositories has been extremely valuable for access to IGO literature, but some of its limitations must also be kept in mind:

- Each IGO is responsible for the production and distribution of its own documents and publications, and decides autonomously whether or not to have a system of depositories. Some IGOs have established worldwide systems, while others have more limited systems. Still others have no depository system at all. It would be desirable if, at least, all major IGOs had a worldwide system of depositories

- IGOs that have depository programs do not designate all their non-restricted material for depository distribution; in fact, a good deal of the output is not sent to depositories. Thus, depositories must obtain needed non-depository IGO items by purchase, gift, or exchange
- Most IGOs that have depository programs do not specify clearly the extent of the deposit. It would be useful if all such IGOs made clear to depositories the exact nature and extent of their entitlement
- Because even the largest depository networks consist of no more than 300–400 libraries worldwide, many non-depository libraries should acquire appropriate IGO material for the use of their clientele. This would complement the resources of depositories that are available to, and should be utilized by, a wider constituency than the institutions where the depositories are located
- IGOs have not yet made electronic information available to their depository libraries. It would be of great benefit to add such information to the depository entitlement whenever possible.

Bibliographic control is an essential corollary of access to IGO material. It is indispensable both for the selection process and for the purposes of servicing the documents and publications acquired. The scope, quality, and types of bibliographic tools vary greatly. They range from the general to the specific, from the inclusive to the limited, from sales catalogs to bibliographies and indexes, and from the IGOs' own products to items published commercially or academically. The fact that bibliographic control over IGO literature is uneven and often inadequate affects access to such material adversely.

In conclusion, a few recent trends of IGO publishing and documentation should be noted:

- External publishing and co-publishing have been increasing, but may now be cut back, at least by the UN, due to budgetary pressures. Unesco and the World Bank are among the IGOs that use commercial publishers to a great extent. Jointly or externally published material is not always included in the IGOs' normal distribution packages or depository shipments; in such cases, material must be acquired separately
- IGOs increasingly produce their documents and publications in microform; other IGO material is produced and marketed in microform by commercial publishers. Consequently, many libraries that do not have the resources to acquire large IGO collections in paper copy, or do not have the space to accommodate such collections, may be able to obtain microform sets
- Electronic information from IGOs is on the rise. Most databases are not yet available to the public, but an increasing number are be-

coming accessible online, or on magnetic tape, diskette, or CD-ROM.

The challenges posed by the complexities of IGO documents, publications, and electronic information will be met more successfully by librarians and other users of such material if they are aware of the context in which source material originates, and the issues involved in the distribution and acquisition of that material. More than ever, libraries need to obtain administrative integration over all their collections and bring together diverse resources that meet their clientele's information needs. Clearly, issues related to bibliographic control, collection development, reference and referral services, and the management of information resouces, regardless of level of government, become critical. Libraries must manage their resources and ensure linkage to other information providers as well as print and nonprint resources.

APPENDIX 1. CHECKLIST OF EXAMPLES CITED IN THE CHAPTER

Advisory Committee for the Co-ordination of Information Systems [of the United Nations System of Organizations]. *ACCIS Guide to United Nations Information Sources on Food and Agriculture.* Rome: FAO, 1987.

Advisory Committee for the Co-ordination of Information Systems [of the United Nations System of Organizations]. *Directory of United Nations Databases and Information Systems, 1985.* New York: UN, 1984. Sales No. GV.E.84.0.5.

Advisory Committee for the Co-ordination of Information Systems [of the United Nations System of Organizations]. *Final Report of the Technical Panel on Database Access.* Geneva: ACCIS, 16 September 1987. ACCIS 87/009.

Barros, James. *Office without Power: Secretary-General Sir Eric Drummond, 1919–1933.* Oxford: Clarendon Press, 1979.

Claude, Inis L. *Swords into Plowshares: The Problem and Progress of International Organization.* 4th ed. New York: Random House, 1971.

Commonwealth Secretariat. *Mission to South Africa: The Commonwealth Report.* Harmondsworth, England: Penguin Books, for the Commonwealth Secretariat, 1986.

Dimitrov, Theodore D. *World Bibliography of International Documentation.* 2 vols. Pleasantville, N.Y.: UNIFO Publishers, 1981.

Documents to the People. Vol. 1–, 1972–. Chicago, IL: American Library Association, Government Documents Round Table.

European Communities. Commission. *State of the Environment.* 1st- Report, 1977–. Luxembourg.

European Communities. Commission. *Catalogue, Part B: Documents.* 1985[?]-. Luxembourg.

European Communities. Office for Official Publications. *Euro Abstracts.* Vol. 1–, 1963–. Luxembourg (former title: *Euratom Information*).

European Communities. Office for Official Publications. *EDC/Dep Bulletin.* 1981, No. 1–1982, No. 2. Luxembourg.

European Communities. Statistical Office. *Price Catalogue for Statistical Information from Databanks, 1986–87.* Luxembourg.

Food and Agriculture Organization of the United Nations. *Food and Nutrition.* Vol. 1–, 1975–. Rome.

Government Information Quarterly. Vol. 1–, 1984–. Greenwich, CT: JAI Press.

Government Publications Review. Vol. 1–, Fall 1973–. New York: Pergamon.

Guidelines for Collection Development. Chicago: American Library Association, 1979.

Hajnal, Peter I. *Guide to United Nations Organization, Documentation and Publishing for Students, Researchers, Librarians.* Dobbs Ferry, N.Y.: Oceana, 1978.

Hardt, Elisabeth. "On Line to Europe: A Guide to E.C. Databases." *Europe: Magazine of the European Community* (Washington, DC), no. 270 (October 1987): 21–27.

Hovet, Thomas Jr. *A Chronology and Fact Book of the United Nations, 1941–1985.* 7th ed. Dobbs Ferry, N.Y.: Oceana, 1986.

Index to International Statistics. Vol. 1–, 1983–. Washington, D.C.: Congressional Information Service.

International Atomic Energy Agency. *Atomic Energy Review.* Vol. 1–, 1963–. Vienna.

International Bibliography: Publications of Intergovernmental Organizations. Vol. 1–, March 1973–. Lanham, Md. [etc.]: UNIPUB.

International Civil Aviation Organization. *ICAO Bulletin.* Vol. 1–, 1946–. Montreal.

International Labour Office. *ILO Catalogue of Publications in Print.* 1944–. Geneva.

International Labour Office. *International Labour Review.* Vol. 1–, 1921–. Geneva.

International Labour Office. *Legislative Series.* 1919–. Geneva.

International Monetary Fund. *Direction of Trade Statistics.* 1–, 1958/1962–. Washington, D.C.

International Organization. Vol. 1– . Feb. 1947–. Madison: University of Wisconsin Press.

International Organisations Publications. 1955–. London: H.M. Stationery Office (supplement to its *Government Publications*).

International Telecommunication Union. *Telecommunication Journal.* Vol. 29–, 1962–. Geneva (continues *Journal UIT*).

Issues before the United Nations. 19??–. [New York:] United Nations Association of the United States of America.

Joint Inspection Unit [of the United Nations System of Organizations]. *Publications Policy and Practice in the United Nations System.* Geneva: JIU, 1984. JIU/REP/84/5. Transmitted in United Nations. General Assembly. 39th sess. *Questions Relating to Information.* New York: UN, May 14, 1984. A/39/239.

League of Nations. *Documents and Serial Publications, 1919–1946.* Woodbridge, CT: Research Publications.

New Zealand. Ministry of Foreign Affairs. *United Nations Handbook.* 1961–. Wellington.

Norton, Augustus Richard *et al. NATO: A Bibliography and Resource Guide.* New York/London: Garland, 1985 (Garland Reference Library of Social Science, 92).

Organisation for Economic Co-operation and Development. *Catalogue of Publications on Sale.* 19??–. Paris: OECD. Organisation for Economic Co-operation and Development. *Index of OECD Documents and Publications.* 1977–. Paris: OECD.

Organisation for Economic Co-operation and Development. *OECD Economic Outlook.* No. 1–, July 1967–. Paris: OECD.

Organisation for Economic Co-operation and Development. *OECD Observer.* No. 1–, 15 November 1962–. Paris: OECD.

Organization of American States. *Catálogo de Informes y Documentos Tcnicos de la OEA.* 1974/1976–. Washington, D.C.: OAS.

Organization of American States. *Revista Interamericana de Bibliografía.* Vol. 11–, 1951–. Washington, D.C.

Osmanczyk, Edmund Jan. *The Encyclopedia of the United Nations and International Agreements.* Philadelphia/London: Taylor and Francis, 1985.

Serials Review. Vol. 1–, 1975–. Ann Arbor, MI: Pierian Press.

Sewell, James Patrick. *UNESCO and World Politics: Engaging in International Relations.* Princeton: Princeton University Press, 1975.

Tayacan. "Psychological Operations in Guerilla Warfare," transmitted as a United Nations document with *Letter Dated 20 October 1984 from the Permanent Representative of Nicaragua to the United Nations Addressed to the Secretary-General* (New York: United Nations, General Assembly/Security Council, October 22, 1984; A/39/596; S/16789).

Unesco. *Cultures: Dialogue between the Peoples of the World.* No. 1–36, 1973–1985; Special Number, 1986. Paris.

Unesco. *International Social Science Journal.* Vol. 1–, 1949–. Paris.

Unesco. *Publications Catalogue.* 1947–. Paris.

Unesco. *The Unesco Courier.* Vol. 1–, 1948–. Paris.

Unesco. Computerized Documentation System. *Unesco List of Documents and Publications.* 1972–. Paris.

Unesco. Division of the Unesco Library, Archives and Documentation Services. *Bibliography of Publications on Unesco.* Paris, April 1984 (LAD-84/WS/3).

United Nations. *Disarmament: A Periodic Review.* Vol. 1–, May 1978–. New York

United Nations. *Mimeographed and Printed Documents* [on microprint]. 1946–1981. New York: Readex Microprint Corp.

United Nations. *Repertory of Practice of United Nations Organs.* New York, 1955–.

United Nations. *Treaty Series; Treaties and International Agreements Registered or Filed and Recorded with the Secretariat of the United Nations.* Vol. 1–, 1946/1947–. New York.

United Nations. *United Nations Documents and Publications* [on microfiche]. 1982–. New York: Readex Microprint Corp.

United Nations. Dag Hammarskjöld Library. *UNDOC: Current Index; United Nations Documents Index.* Vol. 1–; 1979–. New York (ST/LIB/SER.M/-).

United Nations. Dag Hammarskjöld Library. *United Nations Documentation News.* No. 1–, September 1981–. New York.

United Nations. Department of International Economic and Social Affairs. *Macrothesaurus for Information Processing in the Field of Economic and Social Development*, prepared by Jean Viet. 3d ed. New York: United Nations/Organisation for Economic Co-operation and Development, 1985 (Sales No. E.85.I.15).

United Nations. Department of International Economic and Social Affairs. *Report on the World Social Situation.* 1961–. New York.

United Nations. Department of Public Information. *Everyone's United Nations.* 9th ed. New York, 1979. (Sales Number E.79.I.5).

United Nations. Department of Public Information. *Everyone's United Nations.* 10th ed. New York, 1986. (Sales Number E.85.I.16).

United Nations. Department of Public Information. *UN Chronicle.* 1965–. New York.

United Nations. Department of Public Information. *United Nations News Digest.* 19??- September 11, 1987. New York (Press Release WS/-).

United Nations. Department of Public Information. *Yearbook of the United Nations.* 1946/1947–. New York.

United Nations. Department of Technical Co-operation for Development. *World Cartography.* Vol. 1–, 1951–. New York (ST/ESA/SER.L/-).

United Nations. Division of Narcotic Drugs. *Bulletin on Narcotics.* Vol. 1–, October 1949–. New York.

United Nations. Economic and Social Commission for Asia and the Pacific. *Economic and Social Survey of Asia and the Pacific.* 1947–. Bangkok [etc.] (former title: *Economic Survey of Asia and the Far East*).

United Nations. Economic and Social Council. *Official Records.* 1st- sess., 1946–. New York.

United Nations. Economic Commission for Europe. *Economic Bulletin for Europe*. Vol. 1–, 1949–. Geneva/Oxford: United Nations/Pergamon.

United Nations. General Assembly. *Official Records*. 1st-sess., 1946–. New York.

United Nations. General Assembly. 39th sess. *Publications Policy and Practice in the United Nations System: Comments of the Administrative Committee on Co-ordination*. New York: UN, October 2, 1984 (A/39/239/Add.2).

United Nations. General Assembly. 39th sess. *Publications Policy and Practice in the United Nations System: Comments of the Secretary-General*. New York: UN, August 7, 1984. (A/39/239/Add.1).

United Nations. General Assembly. 39th sess. *Publications Policy and Practice in the United Nations System: Comments of the Secretary-General; Corrigendum*. New York: UN, October 10, 1984 (A/39/239/Add.1/Corr.1).

United Nations. Office of Public Information. *Charter of the United Nations and Statute of the International Court of Justice*. New York, 1984 (DPI/511).

United Nations. Office of Public Information. *Everyman's United Nations: A Complete Handbook of the Activities and Evolution of the United Nations During Its First Twenty Years, 1965*. 8th ed. New York, 1968 (Sales No. E.67.I.5).

United Nations. Sales Section. *Catalogue of United Nations Publications*. 19??–. New York.

United Nations. Security Council. *Official Records*. 1st-yr., 1946–. New York.

United Nations. Trusteeship Council. *Official Records*. 1st-sess., 1947–. New York.

United Nations Children's Fund. *Assignment Children*. No. 1–, 1963–. Geneva.

United Nations Conference on Trade and Development. *Yearbook of International Commodity Statistics*. 1984–. New York: United Nations.

Williams, Douglas. *The Specialized Agencies and the United Nations: The System in Crisis*. London: C. Hurst, in association with the David Davies Memorial Institute of International Studies, 1987.

World Bank. *Finance and Development*. Vol. 1–, June 1964–. Washington, DC: World Bank/International Monetary Fund.

World Bank. *Index of Publications*. 1986–. Washington, D.C.

World Bank. *New Publications*. 1985–. Washington, D.C.

World Bank. *World Development Report*. 1978–. Washington, D.C.

World Health Organization. *International Digest of Health Legislation*. Vol. 1–, 1948–. Geneva.

World Health Organization. *WHO Chronicle*. Vol. 1–, 1947–. Geneva.

World Health Organization. *World Health Statistics Annual*. 1962–. Geneva.

World Intellectual Property Organization. *Copyright: Monthly Review*. Vol. 1–, 1965–. Geneva.

World Meteorological Organization. *Weather Reporting*. 1948–. Geneva.

APPENDIX 2. SELECTED LIST OF IGO SALES CATALOGS

Birchfield, Mary E., and Jacqueline Coolman, eds. *The Complete Reference Guide to United Nations Sales Publications, 1946–1978*. Pleasantville, N.Y.: UNIFO, 1982.

*Commonwealth Secretariat. *Publications Catalogue*. London. Latest: August 1985. Available from: Commonwealth Secretariat, Marlborough House, Pall Mall, London SW1Y 5HX, United Kingdom.

*Council of Europe. *Catalogue of Publications*. Strasbourg. Latest: 1988. Available from: Council of Europe, Publications Section, F-67006 Strasbourg, France.

NOTE: * indicates current catalogs. Many of the titles listed in this appendix are also available from authorized sales agents.

European Communities. Office for Official Publications. *Catalogue des Publications, 1952–1971.* Vol. 1. Bruxelles/Luxembourg.

*European Communities. Office for Official Publications. *Catalogue, Part A: Publications.* Luxembourg. Latest: 1986. Kept up-to-date by the quarterly *Publications of the European Communities.* Available from: Office for Official Publications of the European Communities, 2, rue Mercier, L-2985 Luxembourg.

*European Communities. Office for Official Publications. *Catalogue, Part B: Documents.* Luxembourg. Latest: 1986. Kept up-to-date by the monthly *Documents.* Available from: Office for Official Publications of the European Communities.

*European Communities. Office for Official Publications. *The European Community as a Publisher.* Luxembourg. Latest: 1986/1987. Available from: Office for Official Publications of the European Communities.

European Communities. Office for Official Publications. *Tarif des Publications des Communauts Europennes.* Luxembourg, 1972.

Food and Agriculture Organization of the United Nations. *Catalogue of FAO Publications, 1945–1968.* Rome, 1969.

*Food and Agriculture Organization of the United Nations. *FAO Books in Print.* Rome. Latest: 1986. Available from: Food and Agriculture Organization of the United Nations, Distribution and Sales Section, Via delle Terme di Caracalla, 00100 Rome, Italy.

*Food and Agriculture Organization of the United Nations. *List of Documents.* Rome. Latest: September 1986. Available from: Food and Agriculture Organization of the United Nations.

*General Agreement on Tariffs and Trade. *Publications of the General Agreement on Tariffs and Trade.* Geneva. Latest: 1987. Available from: GATT Secretariat, Centre William Rappard, 154, rue de Lausanne, CH-1211 Geneva 21, Switzerland.

*International Atomic Energy Agency. *International Atomic Energy Agency Publications: Catalogue.* Vienna. Latest: 1988. Kept up-to-date by supplements. Available from: International Atomic Energy Agency, Division of Publications, Wagramerstrasse 5, P.O. Box 100, A-1400 Vienna, Austria.

*International Civil Aviation Organization. *Catalogue of ICAO Publications.* Montreal. Latest: 1988. Kept up-to-date by supplements. Available from: International Civil Aviation Organization, Document Sales Unit, 1000 Sherbrooke Street West, Suite 400, Montreal, Quebec, Canada H3A 2R2.

*International Labour Office. *ILO Catalogue of Publications in Print.* Geneva. Latest: 1987–88. Kept up-to-date by *ILO Publications,* issued three times a year. Available from: ILO Publications, International Labour Office, CH-1211 Geneva, Switzerland.

*International Maritime Organization. *Publications Catalogue.* London. Latest: 1987. Available from: International Maritime Organization, Publications Section, 4 Albert Embankment, London SE1 7SR, United Kingdom.

International Monetary Fund. *Catalogue of Publications, 1946– 1971.* Washington, D.C.

*International Monetary Fund. *Publications Catalog.* Washington, D.C. Latest: September 1986. Available from: International Monetary Fund, Publications Unit, 700 19th Street NW, Washington, D.C. 20431.

*International Telecommunication Union. *List of Publications.* Geneva. Latest: September 1987. Available from: International Telecommunication Union, General Secretariat, Sales Section, Place des Nations, CH-1211 Geneva 20, Switzerland.

*Organisation for Economic Co-operation and Development. *Catalogue of Publications on Sale.* Paris: OECD. Latest: January 1, 1987. Kept up-to-date by *OECD Publications: Supplement.* Available from: OECD Publications Service, Sales and Distribution Division, 2, rue Andr-Pascal, 75775 Paris, France.

*Organization of American States. *OAS Catalog of Publications.* Washington, D.C. Latest:

1986–1987. Available from: Organization of American States, Sales and Promotion Unit, Washington, D.C. 20006.

*Unesco. *Publications Catalogue.* Paris. Latest: 1987. Kept up-to-date by *Just Published.* Available from: Office of the Unesco Press, Unesco, 7, place de Fontenoy, 75700 Paris, France.

United Nations. Dag Hammarskjöld Library. *United Nations Sales Publications, 1972–1977: Cumulative List with Indexes.* New York, 1978 (ST/LIB/SER.B/27; Sales No. E.78.I.10).

*United Nations. International Court of Justice. *Publications of the International Court of Justice: Catalogue.* The Hague. Latest: 1981. (Latest French edition: *Publications de la Cour de Justice: Catalogue,* 1984). Available from: International Court of Justice, Peace Palace, 2517 KJ The Hague, Netherlands.

United Nations. Office of Conference Services. *Catalogue [of] United Nations Publications.* New York, 1967 (ST/CS/SER J/9).

United Nations. Office of Conference Services. *Catalogue [of] United Nations Publications, 1968–1969.* New York, 1969.

*United Nations. Sales Section. *Catalogue of United Nations Publications.* New York. Latest: 1988 (published 1987). Kept up-to-date by the monthly *United Nations Publications: New Publications.* Available from: United Nations Publications, Room DC2–0853, United Nations, New York, NY 10017; or United Nations Publications, Palais des Nations, CH-1211 Geneva 10, Switzerland.

*United Nations. Sales Section. *United Nations Documentation in Microfiche.* New York. Latest: 1988 (published in 1987). Available from: United Nations Publications.

United Nations. Sales Section. *United Nations Publications in Print; Checklist.* 1960–1985. New York.

*United Nations Fund for Population Activities. *UNFPA Publications and Audiovisual Guide.* New York. Latest: 1987. Available from: United Nations Fund for Population Activities, 220 East 42d Street, New York, NY 10017.

*United Nations Research Institute for Social Development. *Available Publications.* Geneva. Latest: May 1987. Available from: United Nations Research Institute for Social Development, Palais des Nations, 1211 Geneva 10, Switzerland.

*United Nations University. *UNU Publications.* Tokyo. Latest: 1987–1988. Available from: United Nations University, Publications Section, Toho Seimei Building, 15–1 Shibuya 2–chome, Shibuya-ku, Tokyo 150, Japan.

*Universal Postal Union. *List of Publications.* Berne. Latest: 1983. Available from: Universal Postal Union, Weltpoststrasse 4, case postale, 3000 Berne 15, Switzerland.

*Western European Union. *Assembly of Western European Union Publications.* Paris. Latest: 1984. Available from: Publications Department, Office of the Clerk of the Assembly, Western European Union, 43, avenue du Prsident Wilson, 75775 Paris, France.

World Bank. *Catalog of Publications.* 1976–1984. Washington, D.C.

World Bank. *Catalog of Staff Working Papers.* Washington, D.C., 1985.

*World Bank. *Index of Publications.* Washington, D.C. Latest: January 1, 1987. Available from: World Bank Publications, 1818 H Street NW, Washington, D.C. 20433.

*World Bank. *New Publications.* Washington, D.C. Latest: Fall/Winter 1987. Kept up-to-date by the bimonthly *Publications Update.* Available from: World Bank Publications.

*World Health Organization. *World Health Organization Catalogue: New Books.* Geneva. Latest: Spring/Summer 1987. Available from: World Health Organization, Distribution and Sales, 1211 Geneva 27, Switzerland.

World Health Organization. *World Health Organization Publications: Catalogue, 1947–1979;* and *Supplement, 1980– 1984.* Geneva.

*World Intellectual Property Organization. *Publications of the World Intellectual Property

Organization: Catalogue. Geneva. Latest: 1982. Available from: World Intellectual
    Property Organization, 34, chemin des Colombettes, CH-1211 Geneva 20, Switzerland.
World Meteorological Organization. *Catalogue of Publications, 1951–1977.* Geneva, 1977.
*World Meteorological Organization. *Catalogue of Publications.* Geneva. Latest: 1986; and
    Supplement (October 1987). Available from: World Meteorological Organization, Pub-
    lications Sales Unit, P.O. Box 5, 1211 Geneva 20, Switzerland.

20

Education of the Government Information Professional

There is a serious crisis in the education of government information professionals. A significant number of depository libraries are managed by staff who lack professional training in government information or documents librarianship. There is limited incentive for depository staff to obtain additional formal education. The range and quality of government information courses available in many library schools are limited. The number of graduates from doctoral programs who can conduct research in government information and who specialize in that area is inadequate. And, the GPO offers little direct support or encouragement to improve the educational basis of depository librarians. But, perhaps, of most concern is the apparent lack of interest on the part of many practitioners about educating the government information professional.

Practicing librarians have various expectations about graduate professional education, especially as it relates to the master's degree for library and information science. Houle (1967, p. 263) provides a succinct summarization of these expectations:

> The voice of the aggrieved alumnus is always loud in the land and, no matter what the profession, the burden of complaint is the same. In the first years after graduation, alumni say that they should have been taught more practical techniques. In the next five years, they say they should have had more basic theory. In the tenth to fifteenth years, they inform the faculty that they should have been taught more about administration or about their relations with their co-workers and subordinates. In the subsequent five years, they condemn the failure of their professors to put the profession in its larger

449

historical, social and economic contexts. After the twentieth year, they insist that they should have been given a broader orientation to all knowledge, scientific and humane. Sometime after that, they stop giving advice; the university has deteriorated so badly since they left that it is beyond hope.

Most library schools want their programs and course offering to prepare students for future leadership roles, to provide a balance between theory and practice, to look toward career patterns for professional mobility, and to provide a foundation from which students can later build. In the process, students gain new knowledge, skills, attitudes, and values so that they can embrace change, start to develop their philosophy of library and information science, recognize the place of libraries as an information provider, and identify issues confronting library and information science. As practicing librarians, they should not be consumed by minute details and problems and lose sight of the institutional mission, goals, objectives, and professional issues.

Those of us associated with library and information science education should identify areas requiring change and act as change agents "by providing the intellectual environment and stimulus for the analysis of that change and the application which will occur" (Stueart, 1981, p. 1990). Library educators should not only transmit knowledge but also create new knowledge. Along with students and practitioners, they must accept lifelong learning as an integral part of professionalism, recognize that research is essential for professional growth, and work together to resolve major problems confronting the profession. Too often, practitioners fail to recognize the importance of research as a basis for planning and implementing information services. The danger is that the position of libraries as information providers may erode, that libraries will be perceived merely as keepers of the book, and that their function as conveyers of information will be superseded by other information providers.

Library schools are responding to these challenges by developing programs with extended time frames, re-examining course content and curriculum offerings, seeking to recruit high quality faculty, reintroducing a practicum or internship program, developing joint degree programs, and so forth. Practicing librarians can serve as a partner in responding to educational challenges. First, they must be concerned about the perception of librarianship that they project to the public, and help to identify people with potential and counsel them into the profession. Second, they must provide encouragement and support for beginning professionals so that they will not become disillusioned with the profession or placed in "non-challenging, quasi-professional positions." Finally, it should be recognized that:

> schools of library and information science are not single- product organizations and probably never have been. Graduates are serving in a variety of informa-

tion-related organizations, in publishing houses, with data base vendors, as information entrepreneurs, or as consultants and information managers (Stueart, 1981, p. 1992).

Clearly, practitioners and library educators must cooperate if they are to meet the challenges and make librarianship an important component of the communication and information fields.

A discussion of education for documents librarianship must occur in the broad context briefly sketched. In addition to a solid foundation in library and information management, documents librarians need to be knowledgeable about history, political science, public administration, public policy, and sociology. They should also have an understanding of legal structures and information handling technologies.

Complicating the situation even more is the fact that they frequently must manage the collection and supervise staff. Consequently, they function as administrators interacting with subordinates and other library staff. Because of the diversity of knowledge and skills required for the position, they must constantly monitor the emergence of new issues, trends, and practices, while improving their problem solving abilities. Perhaps more so than many other areas of librarianship, documents librarianship represents an area of constant flux. Governments reorganize, create new policies or modify existing ones, and change or refine past practices. Further, the private sector is constantly creating new reference aids and microform sets.

Obviously, documents librarians cannot be expected to master knowledge related to all levels of government and the complex issues and problems unique to each level. In many cases, documents librarians in the United States are generalists, with perhaps the greatest awareness of the Government Printing Office (GPO) and its printing and documents distribution services. Yet they experience problems in resolving requests for source material distributed by even this Federal agency (McClure and Hernon, 1983; Hernon and McClure, 1987b). Clearly, the times demand a greater commitment on the part of libraries in assigning full-time professional librarians to depository collections, and in ensuring that government publications/information receive adequate attention and visibility in the organization. At the same time, a number of documents librarians need to develop their referral capabilities and expand the breadth and depth of their knowledge about government publications/information, for various levels of government.

Given the wide assortment of activities performed by documents librarians on a regular basis (e.g., managing human and material resources; engaging in reference and referral services, collection development, and bibliographic instruction; and interacting with staff in other areas of the library) documents staff should identify the range of tasks and responsibilities they perform and prioritize them according to their importance.

The purpose of this process is to re-evaluate activities according to library goals and objectives and to seek ways to accomplish these activities in a more efficient manner.

Formal library school course work and prior training in government information, perhaps through an internship program, should be a basic prerequisite for documents librarians. The notion that brief "on-the-job" experience can replace formal coursework is questionable, and ignores the complexities of government publishing programs and the amount of source material to negotiate. Further, that notion overlooks the quality of service that novices provide to the information-gathering public.

Many institutions no longer subsidize the participation of staff at workshops and conferences held outside the immediate area. Two related problems are that, due to budget constraints, government agencies (e.g., the Bureau of the Census) have curtailed the number of seminars and workshops offered, and that the range of workshop options offered by library schools and special groups (e.g., DIALOG) may be small and intended to attract large numbers of people from various backgrounds. For these reasons, documents librarians may have to seek educational opportunities outside documents librarianship and to transfer such knowledge gained. For example, documents librarians seeking to master online bibliographic database searching may not find a workshop devoted exclusively to government databases. Rather, they might have to take a general workshop covering online searching, and use their newly acquired skills to explore government databases upon their return to the work environment.

If anything, the limited number of workshops and other programs available increases the expectations that practicing librarians have of library schools and their graduates. Unfortunately, many of these expectations are unrealistically high; they assume that much more can be accomplished during a master's program, that students have narrowly defined career interests, and that sufficient positions are available at an acceptable salary, for those willing to specialize.

Reported literature on the topic of documents education is not current. On the whole, it was written before the present decade, and in many cases described selected survey findings about the extent and emphasis of library school course coverage. The literature, therefore, does not suggest current options within and outside the classroom. It also does not analyze contemporary teaching practices, objectives, and methods. Further, the literature does not indicate the number of library schools currently offering separate courses on government publications/information, the levels of government covered, and the amount of time spent in the coverage of various course components. This point will be amplified later in the chapter.

Given the weaknesses of the existing literature, the views expressed in this chapter are based primarily on the experiences of the authors as instructors of government publications and information courses, as well as our discussions with practicing documents librarians, library administrators, and students. Still, we advocate research into the current state of the art of education for documents information professionals. All of us involved in documents librarianship need to know not only what is occurring but also the extent to which program objectives are met. Documents librarians need ample opportunity for self-improvement and participation in high quality programs that further their awareness of key issues, trends, and problems, while at the same time improving their problem solving abilities.

The purpose of this chapter is to highlight formal (continuing education, course work, and internship programs in depository collections) and informal (staff training and self-assessment) methods that documents librarians can use to improve their skills and knowledge so that they can better meet stated objectives and integrate government publications with other information resources. At the same time, they should better be able to evaluate collections, services, and their own ability to meet the goals and objectives of the depository library program. The chapter also examines the role of library schools, the GPO, and professional organizations in the education of information professionals.[1] The concluding section provides an overview of the prospects for employment and career advancement in documents librarianship.

FORMAL OPTIONS

Course Work

Documents librarians can enroll in courses, either for credit or on an audit basis, at colleges and universities in the immediate area. If carefully selected, these courses could provide useful information and insights that can be applied to their work situation. Instruction from a broad range of disciplines, including library/information science, will be valuable for increasing skills, competencies, and knowledge.

Library schools have a role to play in improving the quality of documents librarianship. However, the role is often confined to formal degree programs (the master's and doctorate) or the provision of continuing education programs that will have the broadest appeal. Most of the concentrated attention of many accredited library schools falls on the master's program and preparation of students to begin their chosen careers. In this regard,

---

[1] McClure and Hernon (1983) and Hernon and McClure (1987b) amplify on the role of library schools, the GPO, and librarians on improving the depository library program and the quality of staff servicing depository collections. McClure, Hernon, and Purcell (1986) portrays the role of NTIS in the educational environment.

librarians hold diverse views concerning what library schools should try to accomplish. In some cases, they prefer additional course offerings devoted entirely to government publications (e.g., one for state and local publications), more coverage of source material in existing courses, more opportunities for a practicum, and practical understanding of the assorted routines and duties performed by documents librarians.

Professionals must demand that library education prepare students for the future and not the past or even the present. The ability to think critically and to engage in problem solving should be more highly prized than technical competence. Professionals should also expect that those who teach documents librarianship, be they library educators or practitioners, be at the forefront of the field, actively participating in professional organizations, publication, and research. Nonetheless, the following points should be remembered when practitioners critique formal course offerings related to government publications:

- Teaching load of the faculty member teaching the course
- Importance of the documents course in the curriculum (assuming there is such a course)
- Frequency with which the course is taught
- Variations in quality of the teaching
- Student and instructor expectations—course goals and objectives
- Variations in teaching approach and the nature of class assignments
- Number of course contact hours and length of class period
- Number of documents courses offered (enrollment potential for more than one course may not justify assignment of a full-time faculty member)
- Extent of students' familiarity with governmental structure and operations, as well as publishing programs
- What one course can accomplish (how much information can students absorb and reasonably be taught)
- Relationship of documents course to entire curriculum (e.g., pertinent insights might be derived from courses dealing with evaluation of library services, online database searching, collection development, administration of libraries, research methods, legal bibliography, and literature of the sciences or social sciences
- Extent to which students want to (and should) specialize
- Extent to which students know the type of library and work situation they want; and the extent to which such knowledge matches actually career decisions
- Role of library schools in providing *graduate-level* education
- Characteristics of the job market and willingness of students to be mobile in job seeking.

Discussion of the role of education for documents librarians in library schools must address the full range of factors, and not isolate on a few. Obviously, master's level, professional education may not adequately prepare one for the first professional position. Although it provides a foundation, one documents course in a master's degree program in library and information science should not be regarded as the only education and training necessary for documents librarianship.

Undoubtedly government publications/information receive low priority and visibility in the curriculum of many library schools, where the emphasis is on more tradition forms of publication (periodicals and monographs) and corresponding technologies to improve user access to these forms. Frequently, government publications are introduced in a reference course, but toward the end of the course, and then briefly and superficially. Only a small part of the student body takes a separate documents course. Those who do, then, are subject to the above mentioned constraints.

Ideally, an introductory, graduate level documents course should examine the nature, value, types, and formats of government information, bibliographic control, the reference and research value of this source material, the role of the public and private sectors in the distribution and dissemination of government information, the role of a depository library as one provider of government information, the application of collection management principles to documents collections, and the role of various information handling technologies in documents librarianship. Figure 20-1 identifies areas meriting coverage in such a course. One or more semesters could be spent on these components and meeting the following objectives:

- To provide a working acquaintance with various types of U.S. government information resources and to enhance the student's potential as an information resources manager or information access professional
- To provide an awareness of techniques for implementing search strategies for government information
- To understand the public policy making process and the impact of Federal information policies on access to and the provision of government information
- To introduce trends, issues, and problems associated with existing government information policies and practices, and public access to government information
- To provide an understanding of government information resources as they relate to other library departments and collections. Also as they relate to the information needs of a library's clientele
- To provide an awareness of major sources and where to locate

these, and new sources that are now being published and how to locate these

- To provide an awareness of library collection development, reference services, and bibliographic control issues for government information resources
- To introduce students to the GPO depository library program, its strengths, weaknesses, and potential as an effective and efficient "safety net"
- To introduce students to ways that might increase the use of government publications held in libraries.

The purpose of such a course is not to be comprehensive in scope but to provide students with a foundation from which they can build upon in other courses and apply the information later in their professional careers.

Students obtain a framework and philosophical base that librarians not having taken such a course miss. Further, the students should be able to see similarities in bibliographic control, collection development, and other issues across levels of government. Librarians who have not had a similar course must pursue a patchwork of opportunities to gain a basic background on key issues and problems, knowledge of relevant source material, and a philosophical overview of librarianship. That philosophy should consist of more than a catchy or superficial phrase like "documents to the people." These librarians may also not know how to implement sophisticated documents search strategies and to resolve an array of information needs. It takes an abundance of time and effort to overcome such shortcomings.

Students already working in reference positions may have ample opportunity to apply the insights gained in a documents course; they can see the relationship between theory and practice. They observe the utility of the information presented in the classroom environment. Another advantage of a formal documents course is that students can be exposed to the weaknesses of the basic documentation underlying the GPO depository library program (see Hernon, McClure, and Purcell, 1985) and the significance of these weaknesses to effective decision making. It is hoped that these insights will be useful to them if they assume documents positions and interact with fellow documents librarians, the general public, and representatives of the GPO and the Joint Committee on Printing. They may be more effective advocates of change—change that might lead to the improvement of the depository library program and public access to government information.

After students have received their master's degree, it is hoped that they will be assigned to positions that are stimulating and offer opportunities for professional growth. A definite danger to documents librarianship is the possible consumption of one's time by procedures and routine duties. Clearly, studies must examine the career patterns of documents librarians

Figure 20-1.
Outline of a Course "United States Government Information Policies, Resources, and Services"

Description: Public access to Federal information is presented within the context of the policy framework set by the government. The course examines "safety nets" that protect rights of access. Students are alerted to policy issues and assorted Federal information providers, resources, and services.

Syllabus:
I. Introduction
    A. Definition of Government Publication
    B. Political Climate Affecting Publishing Programs
    C. Information Policy Environment and Concept of Safety Nets
    D. Government Publications As An Information Resource
    E. Federal Government As A Publisher/Producer of Information
II. GPO Depository Library Program
    A. Its Historical Development
    B. Strengths and Weaknesses
    C. Its Basic Documentation
        1. Guidelines and Minimum Standards
        2. Inspection Report
        3. Biennial Survey
        4. Instructions to Depository Libraries
    D. Restructuring the System
    E. State Plans
III. Cataloging and Classification (Sudocs Classification Scheme)
IV. U.S. Government Printing/Information Production
    A. Historical Development
    B. Agencies Engaged in Printing and Distribution
        1. Government Printing Office
        2. National Technical Information Service
        3. ERIC Clearinghouses
        4. Other
    C. Microforms
    D. Pricing of Documents
    E. Copyright
    F. Role of Private Sector
    G. Privatization of Public Information—Good or Bad?
V. Catalogs and Indexes
    A. Overview of Bibliographic Control
    B. General Catalogs, Indexes, Abstracts, and Bibliographies
        1. Governmentally Produced
        2. Commercially Produced
VI. Documents and Other Information Resources of the Federal Government
    A. Freedom of Information Act and Other Key Statutes and Directives
    B. Executive:
        President and presidential publications, executive orders, public papers, presidential libraries, treaties and foreign policy, executive agencies and departments, and administrative rules and regulations
    C. Legislative
    D. Judiciary

      E.   Independent and Regulatory Agencies; Advisory Committees
      F.   Government and the Support of Research
      G. Statistical Publications including the Bureau of the Census and the Bureau of Labor Statistics
      H. Grant and Funding Resources

VII.   Role of Technology
      A. Role of Public and Private Sectors—Types of Products
      B. Types of Databases—Bibliographic, Numeric, and Full-Text
      C. Electronic Availability and Dissemination
      D. Bibliographic Utilities (e.g., OCLC)
      E. Classification/Coding Schemes (e.g., CODOC)
      F. In-House and Local Uses (e.g., Management Information Systems and Concept of Expert Systems)
      G. State-of-the-Art in Library Applications

VIII. Collection Development
      A. The Concept and Process
      B. Aids to Selection
      C. Acquisition of Federal Documents
         1. Depository System
         2. Non-Depository
         3. Other Methods and Techniques
      D. Retention Decisions
      E. Evaluation
      F. The Policy Statement

IX.   Reference and Referral Services
      A. Needs Assessment and Use Patterns
      B. Improving User Access to Collections
      C. Marketing of the Documents Collection
      D. The 55% Reference Rule and Its Implications
      E. Evaluation of Local Services (Planning Process)

X.   Organization of Documents Collections
      A. Patterns of Organization and Their Historical Development
         1. Integration with General Collection
         2. Organization As Special Collection
         3. Mixed Organization
      B. Critical Assessment of Each Organization Pattern

XI.   Management of a Government Documents Department/Collection
      A. Management Issues
      B. Cost-Benefit and Cost-Effectiveness
      C. Planning for the Future

XII.   Future Trends in the Provision of Government Information

---

and the type of person who becomes a documents librarian. Documents librarians must be political—constantly promoting and seeking to upgrade the status of the documents collection in the organization and to the community at large. It would be interesting to administer tests to documents librarians, thereby constructing psychological profiles. Studies might also determine the extent to which documents librarians use their position as a stepping stone to other positions (e.g., those of an administrative nature). Such studies would be especially useful for teaching purposes and counseling students about appropriate career paths.

Three final observations are in order. First, "appropriate" content for a curriculum in documents librarianship appears to be expanding. For example, public policy issues regarding the Federal government's provision of public information continues to undergo increased scrutiny. It is no longer enough for documents librarians to be knowledgeable about reference sources, processing procedures, etc. As professionals, they must be conversant with key policy issues and when called upon to offer a perspective on current information policy issues (such as those identified in Chapter 2), be able to do so.[2] Additional curriculum attention to information policy issues and knowledge of the policy making process can increase the range of job opportunities for documents librarians.

Second, documents librarians should monitor the curriculum of nearby library schools and interact with library school faculty to ensure that the school recognizes the importance of government publications/information, offers a separate course(s) on the topic, and assigns top rate faculty to do the teaching. The purpose is to see that students are introduced to government information resources and the ever changing field of documents librarianship.

Third, some library schools have experienced internal problems that led to their demise. These schools tended to be weak and isolated within the university environment (Paris, 1986). Clearly, faculty should be engaged in research that is broadly recognized, and they should be involved on committees, other than those in the school. In addition, library schools might develop courses that could be cross-listed with other departments and have broad appeal to graduate students in journalism, public policy, public administration, etc. A course such as that proposed in Figure 20–1 might be an excellent beginning point in expanding the visibility of a library school's curriculum within the university setting.

Continuing Education

When continuing education programs encompass government publications, they often confine themselves to an introduction to basic sources and current developments within the GPO or larger information environment. Continu-

---

[2] For example, the American Library Association established the Commission on Freedom and Equality of Access to Information in 1983. In 1986, the Commission issued its report *Freedom and Equality of Access to Information* (Commission on Freedom and Equality of Access to Information, 1986). This report is a good example of the range of information policy issues on which documents librarians must be knowledgeable.

ing education needs of depository librarians must stress additional exposure to nondocument subject areas such as:

- Administration and management
- Automation of library services
- Collection development and management
- Evaluation of services
- Information handling technologies
- Information transfer (how people gather and use information, and the role of libraries in a competitive information environment)
- Interpersonal skills
- Planning
- Reference and referral services and methods
- Research methods
- Systems analysis.

Many staff members may also require "training" in the documents field for topics such as:

- Cataloging, processing, and record keeping (e.g., the use of OCLC and the development of a decision support system)
- Collection organization
- Gaining access to nondepository publications
- Microcomputer hardware and software
- Microforms and related equipment
- Online bibliographic and numeric database searching for government publications/information
- Use of unique reference sources and basic government publications.

Formats, types of workshops, and the vast array of possible occasions for obtaining continuing education opportunities have been covered elsewhere.[3]

Figure 20–2 is a contingency table that assists the planning of continuing education related to government publications for specific constituencies. The column on the left suggests some types of constituencies likely to be found in a library, while the row across the top identifies typical skills or competencies that are important for developing documents collections and the reference services. The cells of the matrix can be completed by developing learning objectives appropriate for a specific constituency in a particular skill area. For example, learning objectives related to the category "government document online database searching" might be appropriate for contin-

---

[3] For example, see Davis (1974) and Conroy (1978).

Figure 20-2.
Contingencies for Government Documents Continuing Education

	KNOWL-EDGE OF DOCU-MENTS SOURCES	REFER-ENCE IN-TERVIEW AND SEARCH SKILLS	INTER-PERSONAL SKILLS AND ATTITUDES	DOCUMENTS COLLECTION DEVELOP-MENT	GOVERNMENT DOCUMENT ON-LINE DATA BASE SEARCHING	DOCUMENTS PLANNING AND DECISION MAKING	USE OF MICRO-FORM AND OTHER EQUIPMENT	OTHER SKILLS/ COMPETENCIES
Constituency								
Documents Staff								
Reference Librarians								
Other Librarians								
Administrative Staff								
Users								

Explanation: In each cell specify learning objectives, level of competency required, and strategies to accomplish those objectives for each constituency.

uing education for the documents staff. Similar objectives, at a different level, might be appropriate for the reference staff; these skills may not be appropriate for "administrative" continuing education. On the other hand, such skills, from a different perspective, may be appropriate for users of the collection. In each instance, the learning objective is likely to be different for each group.

In short, continuing education related to government publications/information must consider the following contingencies:

- The constituencies appropriate for a library to be involved in such learning
- The appropriate skills or competencies, given the nature of the collection, its organization, and relationship with the library
- The level of learning that needs to be accomplished for each constituency.

The learning objectives can be accomplished in both formal and informal learning environments, internal or external to the library. In some instances, librarians can convey their knowledge and skills to other staff members and the user community. In other instances, they will want to be recipients of knowledge and to develop their own skills and competencies. Documents librarians can orchestrate much of the "learning" by using in-house training sessions for other library staff members and library users. But to stay up-to-date on topics such as online database searching, applications of microcomputers to depository collections, the development of decision support systems, the treatment of collection development as information science, and how to conduct research and evaluation, the documents staff will need to attend outside workshops and seminars, as well as receive formal classroom instruction beyond the first professional (master's) degree.

Continuing education should not be regarded as a "one-shot" attempt to improve one's skills (Hernon and McClure, 1987b); rather, it is an ongoing program of setting and accomplishing learning objectives by both the documents staff and other constituencies associated with the depository library program (e.g., the GPO). By using Figure 20–2 as a guide, appropriate skills and constitutencies can be identified as a basis for developing specific learning objectives in order to achieve appropriate levels of understanding.

Internships

Internships provide one means by which students can supplement formal course work and gain practical work experience in return for academic credit or a small financial compensation. Internship programs require prior agreement between library staff and library educators, as well as regular monitoring and refinement. The purpose is to ensure that students receive experience and "hands-on" instruction that will enable them to assume a professional role, one looking to the future. Internships should not supply the documents department with "cheap labor" for the completion of routine tasks (e.g., shelving, shelf reading, and processing newly received publications).

Ideally, students should be exposed to collection development as information science, bibliographic control, reference and referral services, and information handling technologies. They should assist the library in planning for better space and staff utilization, while determining that the collection meets the information needs of the present and future generations. Therefore, they could participate in the conducting of user/use studies and in the formulation of a collection development policy statement, assuming that one has not yet been developed.

INFORMAL OPTIONS

Related to continuing education is the need for formally developed training sessions for all personnel who begin work in a depository collection. Boss and Raikes (1982) have reprinted an excellent general outline for staff training, geared toward paraprofessionals. New depository staff members should not be "dumped" into the collection without considerable training in the sources, manner in which that collection is organized, places and persons for referral, knowledge of how to operate the various viewing and reproductory equipment, and a host of other topics. Included in such training sessions for new employees is coverage of interpersonal skills and attitudes toward public service. Programs of staff training and continuing education for all library employees will greatly contribute to the achievement of stated library objectives.

Documents staff members can also invite members of other library departments to tour the documents collection and to see new source material that they might find beneficial. In addition, documents librarians can share typical questions asked with members of their own staff and the reference department. Role playing and videotaping of reference transactions serve as a means for self-assessment of one's own communication skills, problem solving abilities, and search strategies.

Numerous other forms of informal techniques are possible and include working directly with a mentor, developing a program of self-directed education, promoting in house training and discussion sessions, using videotaping and simulations, and so forth.[4] The specific techniques employed are of less importance than the development of a professional commitment and concern for maintaining and increasing one's competencies and skills related to government publications/information.

A constraint to the effectiveness of these informal options relates to the extent to which staff are willing to engage in introspection, and to change when necessary. Without proper incentive, the informal options may not result in significant improvement. Those in administrative positions, as well as the GPO and other concerned government agencies, must provide the necessary stimulus to change and ensure that documents personnel are committed to the fulfillment of goals and objectives set by the depository library program and the member library.

If the impetus for improvement of one's ability and knowledge is not self-directed, then the library administration or an outside agent (e.g., the GPO) should intervene and require that staff members receive the necessary training or be reassigned to other departments. The GPO should review the educational criteria that presumably result in effective performance as depository librarians. The GPO should also greatly expand the number of inspectors so that each can be assigned a certain number of depositories to work with on a regular basis and to guarantee that depository librarians obtain appropriate continuing education when necessary and appropriate. However, as long as financial conditions are tight, such recommendations will be widely perceived as unrealistic. Change requires an influx of additional monies or an extensive reassignment of staff and the tasks performed. Information handling technologies offer excellent opportunities for libraries to conduct systems analyses and engage in a restructuring of departments and operations. However, such is generally not done with the depository collection/department.

---

[4] *Academic Library Use of NTIS* (1986, pp. 1–17) offers additional strategies.

PROSPECTS FOR EMPLOYMENT AND CAREER ADVANCEMENT

A discussion of education for documents professionals would be incomplete without mention of current prospects for employment and career advancement. A majority of the nearly 1,400 depository libraries employ no more than one-full time documents librarian (Hernon, McClure, and Purcell, 1985). When libraries add staff, it is most often for nondocuments related responsibilities. Granted that, in some cases, documents departments are creating a new position, in many other instances, the job prospects are based upon the retirement, reassignment (e.g., career advancement), or resignation of present documents professionals.[5]

But job prospects for documents librarians can be increased by taking an expanded view of possible situations needing the type of skills that documents librarians possess. For example, law school libraries and private law practices could profit from the employment of documents librarians. In the corporate setting, it is often essential for the information centers to have trained professional staff knowledgeable about how to gain access to government information, current regulations and legislation, etc. Similar arguments can be made for a number of positions in local, state, and Federal government. The point being that there may be a larger market for documents librarians than currently exists—but that market has first to be educated as to the benefits resulting from hiring documents librarians.

Generally, the number of new documents positions will come from a relatively small population—typically comprising existing depositories. The number of GPO depository libraries is ever changing; however, the individuals assuming documents positions do not always have professional status, and may be already employed by the library but reassigned on a part or full-time basis to oversee the depository collection. As this suggests, there is a need for formal education opportunities for documents staff, and encouragement to obtain such education—perhaps through certification, and an ongoing commitment to education and training.

The need for formal education on the part of individuals interested in documents librarianship is evident from a monitoring of the job advertisements for documents librarians appearing in *American Libraries*, the

---

[5] Support for these generalizations can be extrapolated from *Library Human Resources: A Study of Supply and Demand*, sponsored by the National Center for Education Statistics and the Office of Libraries and Learning Technologies, Department of Education, and available from the American Library Association. According to the report, the number of librarians and available positions "will be approximately balanced" during the 1980s, with more jobs in public and special, than in school and academic libraries. "Most library jobs for new graduates will come from the need to replace people who leave the profession, not from the creation of new positions." The report also notes that people with library related education will continue to find nonlibrary-related information positions. See Van House et al (1983).

Chronicle of Higher Education, Documents to the People, and *Library Journal* since 1980. Most typically, the documents positions advertised are calling for knowledge about (and interest in):

- Collection development
- Collection management (e.g., staff supervision)
- Communication and reference interviewing skills
- Experience in OCLC cataloging
- Online searching
- Administration, planning, and budgeting
- Reference service for government publications
- Bibliographic instruction.

Individuals filling the positions should be able to engage in problem solving and be able to work with fellow staff and client groups effectively and agreeably. They should also be familiar with technology and perhaps assist the library in planning for the inclusion of government publications in an online catalog. They might also be expected to work with source material from different levels of government and become the map specialist on the staff. As a substitute for work experience, some libraries will accept course work or an internship in documents librarianship.[6]

Due to retirement or advancement in the library administrative structure, positions open for heads of noted documents departments. Professionals known and active in documents librarianship frequently fill such positions. An advantage to active participation in professional organizations at the local, state, regional, and national levels is that one becomes known and may learn about positions before they become widely advertised. This active participation (or dialogue) should extend beyond interaction with fellow librarians and encompass commercial publishers and government agencies administering depository library programs, as well as other government agencies. Opportunities for employment may result from these contacts.

It is unclear if the number of people interested in documents librarianship exceeds the number of available positions. However, formal course work or knowledge of government publications/information is a prerequisite for almost anyone seeking reference positions in academic, public, or special libraries. These people may become the documents "expert" because nobody else on the staff has similar knowledge or skills. Knowledge of government publications is also beneficial for someone interested in technical services and the cataloging and processing of government publications, or in the acquisition function, as well as in library administration.

---

[6] Additional knowledge areas will apply to individuals who assume positions as head of the department or collection.

Someone in an administrative position should have knowledge of government publications and see that these publications are administratively integrated with other library sources. Knowledge of government publications should also be useful to someone interested in information brokerage and the selling of reference services to businesses, organizations, law firms, etc. Documents librarianship can be more than becoming a depository documents librarian; public and technical service librarians, as well as administrators, would benefit from documents related education, so that more integration and understanding of documents throughout the library will result. After all, one can still practice documents librarianship without being a depository documents librarian. The prospects for becoming a documents librarian might be finite, but the possibilities for using government publications/information in various job setting is infinite.

ENCOURAGING EDUCATIONAL CHANGE

Educational change can come internal to the organization (the individual or administration) or external (professional organizations, the agency governing the depository library program, etc.). Professional organizations support continuing education activities and alert members to the importance of their participation. They can also serve as a bridge between library educators and practicing librarians, to maintain a continual dialogue between the two groups and to guarantee that library educators impact on those who have already completed formal course work and degree programs.

At present, the GPO provides input to depository librarians through methods such as: (1) the inspection program, (2) information published in *Administrative Notes*, (3) meetings of the Depository Library Council to the Public Printer, and (4) a willingness to answer questions by telephone and letter. However, such methods do not go far enough to upgrade the competencies of depository librarians.[7]

There needs to be a regular program whereby depository librarians assess and improve their skills, competencies, and knowledge base. No depository library serving the public interest should be exempt from this program, and the master's in library and information science cannot be regarded as a terminal degree; it provides a foundation from which recipients should be required to build.

---

[7] It is regrettable, but revealing, that the key verb in discussing the role of the GPO as a change agent is "should;" the agency "should" do this or that. Interestingly, it has not experimented with ways to affect change, but is more passive in its approach. Apparently, it does not believe that it can force change. Clearly, we disagree. For depository libraries to provide high quality reference service, to improve document delivery capabilities, and to better meet the information needs of the public for government information, the GPO, with the full support of the JCP, must actICELY and aggressively serve as a change agent and sponsor wideranging educational programs intended to meet specific learning objectives.

The GPO, operating through either the Depository Library Council to the Public Printer or an independent task force, should review the basic documentation governing the depository library program and revise these documents so that they provide trend data and clearer direction for the depository library program. There should also be an analysis of educational opportunities for documents professionals and an exploration of ways to assign high quality staff to depository collections and services.

Although certification has been an ongoing issue for information professions, some form of certification process for the depository program might be developed. Documents librarians might be required to maintain a certain number of continuing education credits, for the receipt of approved instruction during specific time periods, to be "accredited" as depository librarians.[8]

Certification comprises one method of encouraging librarians to improve existing conditions and services. Given the impotence of the depository inspection program to promote meaningful change, ongoing certification and renewal would provide a means by which continuing education, the improvement of interpersonal skills and search strategies, and greater control over the depository program by some certification agency could be obtained.

But certification, in itself, will not address the need to produce more library/information science doctorates with specializations in government information and documents librarianship. Increasing the number of doctoral graduates in this area is essential if the profession is to conduct high quality research on topics related to government information, if the quality of instruction in government information is to be improved, and if members in the profession are to provide leadership in resolving difficult issues related to the provision of and access to government information. Currently, there is a serious shortage of doctoral trained educators and practitioners knowledgeable about government information.

Regardless of the impetus for change—internal and self-directed by librarians or externally directed by the GPO, agencies, or institutions, a certification agency or a professional association—the future of depository librarians to provide high quality reference service, to engage in cost-effective collection development, and keep abreast of new information handling technologies is unclear. These concerns identify fundamental weaknesses in a depository library that raises expectations of a system of interlocking libraries taking advantage of the latest technologies to identify and provide the public with access to current and reliable government information.

A revitalized and restructured depository library system requires high quality educators and practitioners to train high quality staff who are infor-

---

[8] Hernon and McClure (1987b, pp. 152–157) discusses certification and recertification.

mation access professionals. The staff must be able to negotiate different technologies and the information environment to extract and manage those information resources needed by clientele. Application of the 55% Rule to depository reference service (see Hernon and McClure, 1987b) suggests that we have a long way to go in the development of a "new" depository library system and professional, government information specialists. Massive staff retraining and certification of libraries and their depository services may be necessary.

21

Mainstreaming Government Publications/ Information

Increasing public access to government publications/information calls for a carefully developed strategy on the part of documents librarians, library administrators, government officials, and others. Increased access will not occur by accident or by serendipity; only with direct involvement, commitment, and planning can government publications/information be "mainstreamed" with other library/information services. The challenge to government documents librarians, and others concerned about public access to government information, is to (1) identify appropriate strategies that will increase access to government information, and (2) implement those strategies in order to develop more effective information services.

Mainstreaming government information resources implies increased awareness, improved services, greater publicity, tighter bibliographic control, improved institutional status for government publications, and better collections. In short, mainstreaming suggests integration—bibliographically, administratively, and service-wise. Mainstreaming is beginning to receive the national attention it deserves, and a number of practicing documents librarians are consciously attempting to "mainstream" government information resources in their specific library setting.

Cleaning up the GPO's *Monthly Catalog* tapes represents an attempt to include government publications in online catalogs on a large scale. The problem is that only GPO depository publications are being considered for inclusion. Mainstreaming other holdings of government information resources requires additional planning and innovation.

The term "documents to the people" implies that the average citizen, the student, the research in a college or university, the business person, the housewife, and so forth all can successfully resolve their information needs, when appropriate, through government publications/information. Having a large and well-organized collection of government publications, but one that is inaccessible and under-utilized, is of little value in meeting a diverse range of everyday information needs. Further, documents librarians and other information professionals have responsibility to ensure that the public's constitutional right to gain access to government information is exercised. As James Madison so eloquently commented over a century and a half ago ("Letter to W.T. Barry," 1910),

> A popular Government without popular information, or the means of acquiring it, is but a Prologue to a Farce or a Tragedy; or perhaps both. Knowledge will forever govern ignorance: And a people who mean to be their own Governors, must arm themselves with the power which knowledge gives.

The twin themes of mainstreaming government publications/information and "documents to the people" provide cornerstones for a professional philosophy and commitment to excellence. The philosophy of government documents librarians and others who must provide access to government information requires careful consideration—especially in these times when the Reagan administration, some government agencies, and certain members of Congress are drastically reducing the amount of government information to which the public has ready access. In the process, government policy and procedures increase the difficulty of mainstreaming documents.

Another cornerstone for excellence relates to information activities of the United States government in general, and the Government Printing Office (GPO) and Federal clearinghouses in particular. Despite the criticisms leveled against these agencies and U.S. information policy, the United States provides the greatest amount of public access to government information of any country in the world. It distributes more government publications to depository libraries for public access than another other country, and the breadth and overall quality of information made available is far superior to that produced elsewhere.

Further, public laws have been enacted that guarantee the public with access to government information, the free and regular distribution of selected materials throughout the nation, and the public's right to demand access to certain types of publications/information.[1] One should not lose sight of these factors, despite our constant efforts to improve the effective-

---

[1] It might be noted that the data gathering activities of the U.S. Bureau of the Census provide a model for other nations to emulate. In fact, the Bureau advises other countries on procedures for collecting and analyzing census data. See Bair and Torrey (1985) and Hartz, Ray, and Schlueter (1987).

ness of the GPO and the depository library program, and to evaluate the effectiveness with which the information needs of the public benefiting from access to government information are successfully satisfied through government publications and information (see Hernon and McClure, 1988).

The final cornerstone that must be identified as a basis for excellence, as well as for the development of a professional philosophy for increased access to government publications/information, is the knowledge, commitment, and idealism of many government documents librarians and information specialists. A number of individuals in this profession have given unselfishly of their time, knowledge, and personal resources, striving for many of the objectives and activities that have been suggested throughout this book. In the final analysis, *people* make the difference; mainstreaming documents and encouraging "documents to the people" will come about as a result of those dedicated and highly competent leaders in documents librarianship who have committed themselves to excellence.

The purpose of this chapter is to draw upon these cornerstones for excellence and the development of a philosophy that suggests strategies by which change can be accomplished, and by which access to government information can be increased and documents collections/services can better meet the information needs of current and potential users. Second, the chapter will summarize and briefly review the key themes that have been presented in the book. The chapter offers recommendations that may assist documents collections/services to better provide "documents to the people" and to mainstream government publications throughout the information environment. Finally, the chapter concludes with one possible approach by which both the GPO and documents librarians can resolve some of the issues raised here.

ENCOURAGING THE CHANGE PROCESS

Encouraging change is a necessary prerequisite for professional development, organizational effectiveness in the library, and improvement in access to government information through the depository library program. For purposes of this discussion, change is defined as any alteration in the status quo that affects an organization's structure, technology, or allocation of resources. Further, it is assumed that:

- Change is a normal pattern of growth and development for individuals as well as organizations
- Change is neither inherently "good" nor "bad"
- Certain types of management styles and interpersonal techniques best facilitate the change process.

Thus, documents librarians must develop specific strategies to encourage change if they are to be successful in increasing public access to government publications/information.

Most importantly, individuals interested in encouraging the change process must be knowledgeable about the areas and topics related to change. They must know what specifically to change. In short, they must have clearly defined objectives for what changes to accomplish and how to implement such changes. They must also obtain adequate time necessary to accomplish change. Successful change especially at an organizational level, takes time and a receptive managerial climate.

Internal Change in the Organization

In general, the various suggestions that have been made in this book require internal change (e.g., modifying the actions, services, and assumptions under which the library operates) or external change (e.g., modifying the environment and the characteristics of the environment that impact on the provision of government information services). For documents librarians to initiate successful change in the library, they must be politically knowledgeable about the management of the library, have a high degree of interaction with other library staff, and assume a leadership role. In some instances, documents librarians can implement strategies appropriate for producing both internal and external change. The following five strategies are intended primarily for use within the organization (Zaltman and Duncan, 1977).

Demonstration. Demonstration is the process by which the target individual or group of individuals observe, first-hand, the actual innovation or change that is desired. This strategy assumes that people can better understand the nature of the change if they actually witness how it works or is accomplished, and that the change, in fact, can be demonstrated. For this strategy to be effective, the demonstration must be carefully planned in advance, the equipment (if any) must be pretested to make certain it works correctly, and the demonstrator must be competent.

Demonstration is especially effective when dealing with technology. Demonstration tends to be more effective when the demonstrator is someone who is already known by the target group and has established credibility with them. Further, follow-up sessions typically can reinforce learning as well as strategies in which the target group receives "hands-on" experience or personal contact with aspects of the change. If the target individual or group can see that "I could do this . . ." then change may be easier to accomplish.

Re-education. Re-education is the unbiased presentation of facts, in a rational and logical manner, that provides justification for the change. Two assumptions underlying this strategy are that (1) the target individuals are rational human beings capable of discerning facts and adjusting their behavior accordingly when facts are presented to them, and (2) adequate time is available for the target individuals to "learn" or perhaps "unlearn" previous beliefs.

Re-education as a change strategy is best used in conjunction with other strategies suggested in this section. It is especially feasible when there is little direct control over others who are to be changed. And, it is essential when change requires the target individuals to use new skills or competencies. Re-education is best used, all other things being equal, when the change does not have to be immediate. Further, it is most effective when dealing with educated and knowledgeable individuals.

Power. Power is the use of coercion, direct threats, withholding of "rewards," or other action to obtain the compliance of individuals involved in the change process. For this strategy to be successful, however, there must be an obligatory relationship between the change agent and the target individual. An assumption is that the change agent can respond with acceptable rewards and punishment as a result of the target individual's action.

The use of power, as a strategy to encourage change, is likely to be dysfunctional at a later date. Although power strategies may be desirable when commitment from target individuals is low, they are unlikely to increase commitment, even though behavior, in fact, is modified. Further, the less desirable it is to have the change strategy modified, or to change the outcomes desired by the change, the more likely a strategy based on power is necessary. And, finally, power strategies may be useful when the change has to be immediate.

Persuasion. Here, change is encouraged by presenting information to target individuals through bias and careful structuring of the message. Typically, the change agent attempts to create change by reasoning, urging, and inducement. Such strategies can be based on rational or emotional appeal, or unsubstantiated arguments.

The greater the time constraints and the lower the ability to use power, the more necessary it may be to use persuasive strategies. Such strategies often are necessary when the change agent has no direct control over the resources or values of others involved in the change. Finally, persuasive strategies tend to be more effective when the change agent has already established an atmosphere of trust between him/herself and the target individuals.

Facilitative. These change strategies make easier the implementation of changes among target individuals by accommodating the accomplishment of objectives and value preferences, as well as by supplying resources that reinforce intended change. Target individuals, however, must recognize that change is necessary, be in agreement that some change is desirable, and be open to assistance and self-help.

The purpose of a facilitative strategy is to make change easy and to compensate low motivation with appropriate situations and resources. For example, target individuals may be supplied with a personal microcomputer when use of microcomputers throughout the organization is the desired change. Further, individual facilitative strategies based upon the allocation of resources will be necessary with certain individuals. Finally, the larger the magnitude of the intended change, the more important it is to utilize facilitative strategies.

Although the previously mentioned general strategies are presented in isolation, they are most likely to be used in combination. For example, a change objective that advocates the physical renovation of the documents department may require aspects of each of the above described strategies to be successful. In addition, if change is to be successful, a common understanding of the problems posed by that change, agreement and participation in the change process, and establishment of a supportive administrative climate are also necessary (Samuels, 1982). Further, many of these strategies are also appropriate when attempting to affect change external to the library organization.

Affecting External Change

If making changes within the organization call for careful planning, development of specific resources, staff development, and significant time, affecting change outside the organization (especially in the policy environment) requires even greater skills on the part of the change agent. The reasons for this increased difficulty include: (1) the change agent usually has minimal direct control or authority over the external environmental factors, (2) a number of competing views or other individuals are also attempting to make changes related to that specific concern, and (3) greater quantities of resources are necessary. Thus, librarians and other information access professionals wishing to make changes related to a depository library program, government information policy, or networking, for example, must carefully consider political activities and their ability to conduct policy related research. Policy research examines the legal framework, explores all possible options, and makes recommendations about the most feasible option to pursue.

Librarians and other information access professionals can make a greater impact as a group than they can individually. Indeed, because they speak for a broad base of individuals who may use and require government information, they can demonstrate that their "constituency" is broad based—all information gathering segments of society. A number of group strategies to increase political activism are possible. Some specific strategies that can be used include the following (Hoduski, 1983):

- Become a policy maker, run for political office, or obtain an appointed position in an agency or on a committee that makes decisions related to government information
- Write your legislators (local, state, and national), organize letter writing campaigns, and make certain that elected officials know and understand your position
- Work with professional associations to make governments aware of your concerns
- Get out of your library or information center and talk directly to government officials, professional association leaders, and others who influence policy making.

These and other strategies require librarians to be knowledgeable, well-acquainted with influential people or desirous of becoming acquainted with them, and able to express themselves succinctly and effectively. Political activism is essential for any change strategy that advocates action on the part of a government agency.

Environmental change calls for the change agent to have an extremely good understanding of the change situation, its impact on the environment, and the factors that tend to support versus discourage change to occur. For change agents to have such information requires empirical evidence to support their position and excellent knowledge about the relationships affecting and affected by the proposed change. Since environmental change typically results in large impacts, those responsible for such change will want detailed, reliable, and valid data supporting the proposed changes.

In short, documents librarians must be able to convince decision and policy makers that a proposed change has merit. The ability to define a specific problem, obtain or collect data related to that problem, analyze the data, and produce results and conclusions based on that data is essential. Indeed, the research process and the ability to rely on accurate and timely data in support of a specific position is essential for the strategies of re-education, persuasion, and facilitating. Documents librarians and other information access professionals attempting to change broader environmental factors that affect access to government information must be able to conduct research, write succinct and clear summaries of that research, and disseminate those findings to appropriate individuals.

Skills for Change Agents

Some practical suggestions for documents librarians wanting to increase their skills as change agents (those people who attempt to affect change) can be suggested. First, the change agent should learn how to analyze the change situation. Figure 21–1 summarizes these factors. Each of the items in this figure requires careful attention before library staff develop an overall and effective strategy for change. That strategy should overcome resistance and obtain the necessary resources and time for implementation.

Second, the change agent should have certain interpersonal skills and address planning considerations. Figure 21–2 summarizes some of these skills and characteristics. Recognition of these factors, and planning to guarantee that these characteristics are indeed met during a change process, will greatly assist documents librarians in better accomplishing the intended changes. In short, personal skills in areas of learning how to analyze the change situation, and developing characteristics that facilitate change, are likely to increase the probability that the desired change, in fact, will occur (Zaltman and Duncan, 1977).

ISSUES FOR NATIONAL CHANGE

Knowing strategies to facilitate the change process is important, but equally important is having an agenda of areas to apply those change strategies. This book has suggested a number of themes that require specific attention for increasing access to government information resources. The following areas and themes should be considered as top candidates for development of a national agenda that improves access to government information resources.

Importance of Documents

The frequently mentioned stereotype of government information resources as ephemera that have limited value is both incorrect and dangerous. Such an attitude is incorrect because of the broad range of unique and significant information resources that simply are not available elsewhere. Further, for the average person to participate in the governmental process with a certain level of sophistication, knowledge, and understanding, awareness and use of government information resources is essential. Thus, librarians and other information access specialists who provide access to this information have a special responsibility to make certain that such information is both recognized as important and made available when required.

Numerous reasons undoubtedly explain the erroneous stereotype; however, government documents librarians must take a positive stance, develop marketing strategies that publicize useful and important publications, and constantly demonstrate the value of government publications to other librarians, administrators, the public, and government officials. Provision of information services that do not include government information resources may be inadequate and misleading. The importance of government information resources lies with their breadth and uniqueness.

Figure 21-1.
Analyzing the Change Situation

A. Awareness of the change target
   1. Identify specific people/situations to be changed
   2. Describe desirable behaviors/results for change to be "successful"
B. What is the degree of commitment among target individuals for accepting this change?
C. What is the magnitude of the proposed change?
   1. Possible effects on involved individuals
   2. Possible effects on the organization
   3. Possible effects on the environment
D. How much time is available to accomplish the change?
E. What are the motives and justification for the change?
   1. Individual
   2. Organizational
   3. Environmental
F. Anticipated types of resistance to the change
   1. Ignorance
   2. Suspended judgment
   3. Situational
   4. Personal
   5. Experimental
G. Resources available to the change agent
   1. Personal
   2. Money
   3. Equipment
H. Amount of technology needed to accomplish change?
I. Capacity of the target individuals to accept and sustain change once it has been accomplished?
J. Relationship between change agent and target individual(s)
   1. Formal: Superior-Peer-Subordinate-None
   2. Information: Friendly-Acquaintance-None
   3. Value Compatibility: High-Low

There is a genuine and present threat that the public's right to know, and its right to gain access to a broad range of government information resources, might be severely restricted given the present application of Federal information resources management. Currently, there is a:

- Dearth of government-wide information policies that guarantee both equal opportunity and equal access to government information
- Need to ensure an active government information dissemination stance.

The existing structure of piece-meal, decentralized, and uncoordinated laws, guidelines, and procedures should not continue to serve as a framework for Federal information policy. An overhaul of splintered and uncoordinated Federal information policies, including OMB's Circular A-130 on the man-

Figure 21-2.
Characteristics of an Effective Change Agent

1. The change agent should strive to create as broad a power base (legitimate, expertise, and friendship) as possible
2. The change agent should work through opinion leaders when initating the change strategy
3. The change agent should have the self-confidence and positive self-image to accept setbacks with poise and not project anger or frustration to the target individuals
4. The change agent should strive to maximize his/her credibility in the eyes of the target individuals in terms of motives, competence, and truthfulness
5. The change agent should take care that target individuals are accurately informed about the entire change process
6. The change agent should build capabilities within the new system so that a vacuum is not created when the change agent leaves the system
7. The change agent should strive to involve the target individuals as much as possible in the change process
8. The change agent should strive to be sensitive to the needs and perspectives of the target individuals when designing change strategies
9. The change agent must be knowledgeable and competent regarding
   a. Interpersonal skill
   b. The nature of the change itself
   c. Administrative skills
10. The change agent always seeks the simplest solution when designing a change strategy
11. To maximize cooperation between the change agent and the target individual(s) specific benefits for the individuals are clarified and explained.

agement of government information resources, is desperately needed and long overdue. Broad segments of the public cannot afford to be "information poor or deprived." But in the absence of carefully crafted government-wide information policies, and with increased demands for cost curtailment, there may be an erosion in the extent to which the public can gain access to government information, in an effective and efficient manner. Such an erosion could have a negative impact on the public's right to know and gain access to information that their government collects, produces, and retains. Government officials, private sector business people, individual citizens, and other stakeholders in the information sector must recognize the importance of ensuring broadly based and effective access to government information. The public's interests will be better served and its right to government information preserved and improved by the development and implementation of information policies that guarantee effective access to, and dissemination of, government information.

Planning and Evaluation

Ongoing planning and evaluation can greatly facilitate increased access and improved services for depository and other government publications. The development of goals and objectives is critical for the maintenance of an effective documents collections. A frequently heard lament of government documents and other librarians is, "I don't have enough time;" such a statement is indicative of the large amount of work to be done as well as the lack of stated priorities. Government documents collections cannot be all things to all people. Thus, carefully determined goals, priorities, objectives, and activities must be selected. In short, a regular process of planning is essential for the documents collections to be integrated and mainstreamed into "regular" information services.

Evaluation should incorporate planning, research, and change. Ongoing evaluation is integral to a dynamic, effective, and efficient organization. Too often, documents librarians do not know how well they are operating a service, the specific costs associated with that service, the degree to which the collections meet specific user information needs, or the effectiveness with which a specific activity is being accomplished. Further, the process of empirical data collection to provide a valid evaluation of services and collections must be better understood and utilized. And, finally, "evaluation" techniques such as the GPO depository inspection program must be completely revamped and based on measurable objectives and valid methods of data collection. Until meaningful planning and evaluation are incorporated within both the depository program and documents collections, successful change will be difficult to accomplish.[2]

Developing Effective Collections

As part of the evaluation process, the effectiveness of government publications collections must be determined. Realistic collection development must be initiated for these collections rather than reliance on item number selection or no selection process at all. The concept of comprehensiveness for government documents collections must be reconsidered; much of the material included in the depository program simply is neither necessary nor collected by many of the depositories. Selection of specific information resources that meet the information needs of the library's clients should be stressed.

Collection development for government publications must be broadened and consider the vast range of nondepository U.S. government publications/information; international publications, documents, and information; and regional, state, and local information resources. Simply because a library is a depository does not mean that adequate coverage of government publications/information resources of value to the library clientele is guaranteed. For libraries without depository status, much greater effort is needed

---

[2] Librarians engaged in planning should consult McClure et al (1987). For a discussion of evaluation see Rossi and Freeman (1985).

to identify, obtain, and make accessible the vast range of important government information resources. The services and collections of public, school, academic, and special libraries can benefit from the inclusion of government publications/information and the development of collection policy statements that recognize the role and importance of this information resource.

Minimize Attention Given to Bibliographic Access

Although bibliographic access, bibliographic listings, and clarifying techniques for bibliographic control over government publications/information are important, broader attention must be given to physical access and the servicing of government publications/information. Having complete bibliographic access to government resources is of little value if the public cannot locate and obtain the information contained in them. Further, bigger is not always better—more materials, more bibliographic listings, and more bibliographic records do not, in themselves, ensure better access to government publications/information.

Greater attention to the organization, physical facilities, staffing, and servicing of these materials is clearly needed. The difficulties associated with various bibliographic control techniques, when applied to government publications/information, have focused attention primarily on the records themselves, effective control of over publishing output, and the form of entries rather than access and services. Perhaps the difficulty lies with the archival approach frequently encountered in some depository collections. Government publications can no longer be considered as merely "archival" in nature and documenting the historical development and implementation of policies and decision making. Government publications, as well as electronic and machine-readable files, must be integrated into library collections and services as part of the regular information services provided.

More attention should focus on identifying and breaking down the barriers to use of government publications. To repeat, these resources do not deserve second-class residence in library collections. Here are official sources that complement other library holdings. The goal should be to bring the entire resources of a library to bear on meeting the public's information needs.

Exploiting Technology

One of the greatest opportunities and challenges for government documents librarians is to obtain the necessary technological support to provide increased access and services to depository collections—in fact, to all document and nondocument holdings. If librarians are five years behind the business sector in the application of technology, government documents collections are probably another three to five years behind other parts of the library in the application of technology for increased access and improved services.[3] Although technology certainly is not a panacea for government publications collections, its increased use for record keeping, access to materials, control of bibliographic records, decision support, and other functions has yet to be fully realized.

Technological support is essential. Technological applications will benefit the documents collection as well as the larger institution. Clearly, increased skills and education to support and direct these technologies must be acquired.

Continuing Education

Enough cannot be said about the importance of staying abreast of current developments, increasing the level and quality of one's skills and competencies, and adopting an attitude of commitment to ongoing self-improvement. One might speculate that the current rate of obsolescence for graduates in library/information science is three to four years. By this it is meant that, within that time period, half of the knowledge gained for the master's degree has changed, been replaced, or become erroneous. Thus, the burden to stay current is indeed a heavy one for government documents librarians.

Further, simply being a "good" cataloger or reference librarian is no longer adequate for a professional position. The successful candidate must be able to demonstrate skills in systems analysis, computer science, administration, interpersonal relations, research and evaluation, and a host of other areas. But perhaps most importantly, the successful candidate must know how to learn—that is, how to teach oneself and how to think critically. There always are skills and competencies that professional documents librarians can learn or improve upon. If the profession as a whole is unable or unwilling to take on this responsibility for continuing education, outside certification agencies may be (and perhaps should be) established to encourage such activities.

Individual Commitment and Dedication

Related to increased attention to continuing education is a need for further commitment and dedication to high quality services and collections. There always will be constraints that hinder an individual's ability to accomplish

---

[3] *Microcomputers for Library Decision Making* (Hernon and McClure, 1986) discusses different uses of microcomputers in academic, public, and school libraries. The literature on technological applications to depository collections and services does not yet reflect a broad range of uses. The writings tend to concentrate on bibliographic control, particularly the cataloging and indexing aspect, and the benefits of developing an automated collection development or decision support system.

specific objectives. But one's ability to rise above those constraints, to develop strategies that circumvent the problems and result in improved services and collections, is based primarily on individual commitment and dedication. Individuals who become librarians know in advance that the profession will never make them wealthy; the primary component of the profession is one of service.

Dedication to service goals implies a commitment to providing the best possible services, to keeping oneself current and knowledgeable about new developments, and to persevering constantly through the various constraints encountered. If documents librarians do not advocate and strive for improved services and access to government information, who will? Enthusiasm and dedication for increasing public access and improving services and collections often times can compensate significantly for inadequate institutional resources. Indeed, frequently, enthusiasm and commitment contribute to obtaining those necessary resources.

Need for Leadership

The lack of effective leadership in the area of government publications is evident at a number of different levels. At the United States national level, there has been an inability to revise Chapter 19, title 44, of the *United States Code*, or to articulate a viable alternative to the present depository library program. Complicating matters, few spokespersons or associations have emerged to counteract the attack of the Reagan administration and Congress on public access to government information. And no coherent and adequate plan to coordinate U.S. government printing and information distribution/dissemination has emerged. With an extension of OMB Circular A-130, electronic files become part of information resources management and OMB further exerts its control over the life-cycle of an information product or service (see Hernon and McClure, 1987a).

At a more local level, many government documents librarians have neither affected organizational decision making nor effectively promoted the integration of government publications into library services and collections. Nondepository libraries frequently exclude government publications from their collections and provide minimal or no services related to government information. Clearly, government documents librarians must assume a more assertive and public role in their promotion of government information, their justification and exploitation government information, and their integration government information into the mainstream of library services and collections.

However, more than individual action is needed if these and other issues discussed in this book are to be addressed and resolved. A national strategy, a national agenda for increasing access to government information resources, is necessary. The time has come for immediate steps to be taken to establish such a national strategy.

FUTURE PROSPECTS FOR CHANGE

If government publications services and collections are to become more accessible, to be mainstreamed with other information services and collections, and to be made publicly available, significant changes and improvements will be necessary in the near future. Not only do documents librarians have to understand and respond to changes that have been made in our society since World War II, they also have to consider strategies to deal with the changes that are likely to occur in the next decade. They must ensure that the depository program becomes an interlocking network of librarians meeting specific goals and the information needs of both the information advantaged and poor. It must also be remembered that the depository program is but one "safety net" for access to government information. The function of a safety net is to provide a minimal or certain level of access to information. It remains to be determined what that "minimal or certain level" is or should be.

What are the broad trends that can be expected in the future? Naisbitt (1982) has suggested that the following "mega-trends" will change everyone's life and business:

- Restructuring of America from an industrial society to one based on information and knowledge
- Unprecedented diversity among people, groups, and institutions; an incredibly market-segmented, decentralized society
- Return to old-fashioned self-reliance
- Greater direct involvement of employees in organizational decision making
- Home computers will be a liberator; they can provide quick access to information previously available only to other companies and individuals
- Increased demand for personal contacts and expanding human interrelationships, as people are exposed to more high technology
- Decentralization of all our institutions—business, governmental, social, and political—largely due to the proliferation of home computers and information systems.

These are especially important for librarians and other information access professionals as the impact of such trends may increase the gulf between the information advantaged and disadvantaged. If Naisbitt is even partially correct about these trends, significant and prompt changes in library collections, services, and philosophies are needed.

In short, the traditional services and collections associated with government publications merit careful review and analysis if they are to be effective in the immediate future. Of special concern is a frequently encountered belief on the part of some documents librarians that they are the "only government information show in town." This is simply untrue. The information advantaged, for example, may gain access to government information through home computers. They may invoke the Freedom of Information Act and pay high user fees, when these are imposed. They may also order documents online or on microfiche, and conduct a search for government information without aid of a documents librarian. Since current information resolves a large percentage of information needs, clients, in the future, may tend to use print depository collections primarily for access to retrospective or out of print materials. In such instances, the depository collection will become even more of an archival operation than it is today. The combination of Naisbitt's forecasts for decentralization, increased self-reliance, and the home computer as liberator calls for a new philosophical approach to government information services and collection. A sampling of questions and issues to be considered include:

- How can depository librarians publicize their collections to the specific target markets within the community that require specific information sources?
- Can depository collections successfully provide documents delivery services?
- How can the home computer market be exploited by the library in general, and the government documents area in particular. For example, libraries might put catalogs online and searchable through home computers, and provide direct reference services through electronic mail
- How can collections and services be coordinated and marketed to meet the information demands of an expanding list of special interest groups?
- How can the library community successfully affect the development and implementation of Federal information policies?
- How will the GPO support changes in the depository library program, and to what extent should the GPO exercise direct control over participants in the program
- How can the public be assured that professional staff servicing government documents collections are knowledgeable and technologically competent?

These, of course, are just a sampling of the issues and questions to be resolved. Additional questions must be asked and new alternatives considered in the context of the changing nature of our society.[4]

The depository library program must keep abreast of change. Yet, except for the 1962 Depository Library Act, the program has changed little since the 1895 Printing Act. Basic assumptions, many operating procedures, the supporting philosophies, and services have changed little over the years. The field of government publications continues to go on much as it has in the past; there is little planning and evaluation, and minimal integration and mainstreaming of documents with other services and collections. In addition, collections rather than services are emphasized.

New information technologies may well change some of this. However, at this time, depository staff make minimal use of technology. With proper planning, staff training, and an influx of money change could rapidly descend on the depository program. The Association of Research Libraries (ARL) has developed (*Technology & U.S. Government Information Policies*, 1987, p. v):

> a framework for understanding—philosophically, functionally, and fiscally—the patterns that exist for government information today, and the shifts in those patterns resulting from the introduction of government information in electronic formats. Two elements of such a framework are presented: a taxonomy to acknowledge distinctions and categorize the characteristics of government information in electronic format, and a model that identifies potential value-added processes for an information system. What is urgently needed in addition are studies on the budgetary mechanisms that support government information creation, delivery, and usage, and the impact of different electronic formats on these mechanisms. The results of such analysis should contribute to a clearer picture of present and prospective public and private financing of government information programs.

The report of the ARL Task Force on Government Information in Electronic Format:

> focuses on the implications for the library, education, and research communities that have heretofore assumed some responsibility for providing government information to the general public. Five issues are addressed: challenges

---

[4] An example of an alternative is "Maggie's Place" at the Pikes Peak Library District in Colorado Springs, Colorado. An integrated computer system (Maggie) benefits both the staff and the community. Examples of the services and activities include: direct access to the library's catalog by home microcomputer users, bus schedules online, local events calendar, resource management of library materials, wordprocessing, electronic mail, access to DIALOG, and a complete decision support system for increased management of personnel and the budget (Dowlin, 1980, 1984).

to U.S. Government information policies; the roles of the private sector and Government responsibilities in making information available; models for analysis of the distinctive characteristics of information in electronic formats; a changing framework for library services; and the consequent influence of these four sets of issues on the Depository Library Program, a Congressional program designed to provide equitable public availability of government information (Ibid.).[5]

This report is significant because it indicates that the ARL is engaged in planning and laying a foundation for incorporation of information resources. A similar analysis should be initiated by the GPO and place ARL planning in proper perspective—one component of the depository library program.

The time is ripe for an open and extensive discussion of the role and use of, as well as access to, government information resources for the immediate future. Specifically, a national agenda for access to government information is one approach by which everyone interested in government information services could identify issues and areas for discussion. As of now, there are no agreed upon set of questions to address, no set of issues to encourage creative thinking, and no attempt to bring together a diverse and knowledgeable body of individuals regarding the development of such an agenda.[6]

A national agenda for access to government information could be a key discussion area in the forthcoming White House Conference on Library and Information Services II. Direct participation and planning from the state and national library associations, the broad range of other information-related associations, lay people, publishers, library educators, and government officials could provide open discussion, identification of issues, and exploratory remedies for the depository library program and government publications to meet the challenges of the future.

The depository library program, the provision of government information resources and services through library structures in the United States, and the ability of these institutions and their staff to meet the challenges of the information society, require immediate attention. Change, in and of itself, without an underlying change in the philosophy and attitude of those

---

[5] Based on Chapter 1 of this book, the report's conclusion that the depository program is "designed to provide equitable public availability of government information" is questionable. Both "equitable" and "information" are new concepts. The depository program is based on legislation that intended the distribution of print publications.

[6] It might be noted that at the time that this book was written, the Office of Technology Assessment (OTA), United States Congress, is engaged in a study of "Technology, Public Policy, and the Changing Nature of Federal Information." As part of that study, OTA is reviewing future roles for the GPO and the depository library program. Once the study is completed and the report released (presumably in fall 1988), there will probably be an extensive discussion of the report and its recommendations. However, the study should not be regarded as an effective substitute for the development of a national agenda.

who organize, disseminate, and service government information, will not be useful. Without significant and necessary change, as outlined in this book, the role of depository collections and government publications may become increasingly circumscribed in tomorrow's information society.

If government publications are to be mainstreamed with other information services and collections, and to be made accessible to the public at large, if change is to occur and a re-examination of our underlying philosophies is to occur, and if government information services as provided by librarians are to survive and prosper, then much remains to be accomplished. Addressing the issues and questions posed in this book is a first step. But individual dedication, commitment, and leadership on the part of professional documents librarians is essential if depository library collections are to be relevant and integral to the information society and resolve the public's information needs. By addressing these issues the future can be met, new challenges and innovations realized, and documents librarians can have an important and positive role in the information society of the future.

Bibliography

Academic Library Use of NTIS: Suggestions for Services and Core Collections. Prepared by
  Charles R. McClure and Peter Hernon. Springfield, VA: NTIS, 1986 (PB86–228871).
Advisory Committee for the Co-ordination of Information Systems [of the United Nations
  System of Organizations]. "DESI Electronic Information Network," *ACCIS Newsletter,*
  5 (May 1987a): 3.
―――. *Final Report of the Technical Panel on Database Access.* Geneva, Switzerland: ACCIS,
  September 16, 1987b, ACCIS 87/009 (Distribution: Limited).
Akoka, J. "A Framework for Decision Support Systems Evaluation," *Information and Manage-
  ment,* 4 (1981): 133–141.
Allen, T.J. and P.G. Gerstberger. "Criteria for Selection of an Information Source," *Journal of
  Applied Psychology,* 52 (1968): 272–279.
Aluri, Rao and Judith S. Robinson. *A Guide to U.S. Government Scientific and Technical
  Resources.* Littleton, CO: Libraries Unlimited, 1983.
American Library Association. Collection Development Committee. *Guidelines for Collection
  Development.* Chicago, IL: American Library Association, 1979.
―――. "Less Access to Less Information by and about the U.S. Government." Washington,
  D.C.: American Library Association, 1988.
―――. Commission on Freedom and Equality of Access to Information. *Freedom and Equality
  of Access to Information: A Report to the American Library Association* [The Lacy
  Report]. Chicago, IL: American Library Association, 1986.
Amodeo, Anthony J. "Helpful Hints for Moving or Shifting Collections," *College & Research
  Libraries News,* 44 (March 1983): 82–83.
Archer, Clive. *International Organizations.* London: Allen & Unwin, 1983.
Argyris, Chris. "Some Limits of Rational Man Organizational Theory," *Public Administration
  Review,* 33 (1973): 257–269.
Armstrong, Ann and Judith C. Russell. "Public Access," *Information World,* 1 (October 1979):
  1, 11.
Association of Research Libraries. *Performance Evaluation in Reference Sources.* SPEC Kit No.
  139. Washington, D.C., 1987.
―――. Systems and Procedures Exchange Center. "Collection Development Policies." *SPEC
  Flyer,* no. 38. *Collection Development Policies.* Washington, D.C., 1977.

Atkinson, Ross. "The Language of the Levels: Reflections on the Communication of Collection Development Policy," *College & Research Libraries*, 47 (March 1986): 140–149.

Auger, Charles P. *The Use of Reports Literature*. Hamden, CT: Archon, 1975.

"Automatic Bibliographic Control of Government Documents: Current Developments," *Documents to the People*, 15 (December 1987): 224–246.

Bair, Robert R. and Barbara Boyle Torrey. "The Challenge of Census Taking in Developing Countries," *Government Information Quarterly*, 2 (1985): 433–452.

Ballard, Steve. "Federal Science and Technology Information Policies: An Overview," in *Federal Information Policies in the 1980's: Conflicts and Issues*, edited by Peter Hernon and Charles R. McClure. Norwood, NJ: Ablex Publishing Corp., 1987, pp. 195–225.

Basefsky, Stuart Mark. "Bibliographic Citations and U.S. Government Publications: A Conceptual Analysis and Comparison of Style Manuals," MSLS thesis, University of North Carolina, 1979.

Baughman, James C. "Toward a Structural Approach to Collection Development," *College & Research Libraries*, 38 (May 1977): 241–248.

———, Andrea Hoffman, Linda Rambler, Donald Ungarelli, and Harvey Varnet. "A Survey of Attitudes toward Collection Development in College Libraries," in *Collection Development in Libraries: A Treatise*, edited by Robert D. Stueart and George B. Miller. Greenwich, CT: JAI Press, 1980, pp. 89–138.

Becker, Joseph. "U.S. Information Policy," *Bulletin of the American Society for Information Science*, 4 (August 1978): 14–15.

"Biennial Survey Results," *Administrative Notes* [Library Programs Service, Superintendent of Documents], 6 (October 1985): 2–8.

Birdsall, Douglas. "Government Publications in the Arts," *The Idaho Librarian*, 28 (October 1976): 176–178.

Bommer, M.R. and Ronald W. Chorba. *Decision Making for Library Management*. White Plains, NY: Knowledge Industry Publications, 1982.

Boss, Richard W. *Information Technologies and Space Planning for Libraries and Information Centers*. Boston, MA: G.K. Hall & Co., 1987.

——— and Deborah Raikes. *Developing Microform Reading Facilities*. Westport, CT: Microform Review, 1982.

Bower, Cynthia. "OCLC Records for Federal Depository Documents: A Preliminary Investigation," *Government Information Quarterly*, 1 (1984); 379–400.

Bowerman, Roseann and Susan A. Cady. "Government Publications in an Online Catalog: A Feasibility Study," *Information Technology and Libraries*, 3 (December 1984): 331–342.

Boyd, Anne. *United States Government Publications: As Sources of Information for Libraries*. New York: H.W. Wilson, 1941.

——— and Rae E. Rips. *United States Government Publications*. 3rd ed., revised. New York: H.W. Wilson, 1949.

Boylan, Nancy. "Identifying Technical Reports through U.S. Government Research Reports and Its Published Indexes," *College & Research Libraries*, 28 (May 1967): 177–183.

Bradford, Samuel C. *Documentation*. London: Crosby Lockwood, 1948.

Bregent, Ann. "Cost of Regional Depository Library Services in the State of Washington." Olympia, WA: Washington State Library, 1979; Washington, D.C.: GPO, 1979.

Brown, Eulalie W. "Patent Basics: History, Background, and Searching Fundamentals," *Government Information Quarterly*, 3 (1986): 381–405.

Brown, Jeanne Owen and Fred A. Schlipf. "The Use of Microfiche and COM Indexes to Improve Municipal Document Control," *Government Publications Review*, 9 (1982): 289–310.

Buckland, Michael K. *Book Availability and the Library User*. New York: Pergamon Press, 1975.

"But I Want Everybody to Have a Copy!," *Marketing Moves*, 11 (July 1987): 2–3.

Butler, Pierce. *An Introduction to Library Science*. Chicago, IL: University of Chicago Press, 1933.

Caponio, Joseph F. and D. Bracken. "The Role of the Technical Report in Technological Innovation." Fifth International Conference of Scientific Editors. Hamburg, June 14– 19, 1987 (unpublished).

Caponio, Joseph F. and Janet Geffner. "Does Privatization Affect Access to Government Information?," *Government Information Quarterly*, 5 (1988): 147–154.

Carpenter, Eric J. "Collection Development Policies: The Case for," *Library Acquisitions: Practice and Theory*, 8 (1984): 44.

Carroll, Bonnie and Betty F. Maskewitz. "Information Analysis Centers," in *Annual Review of Information Science and Technology*. White Plains, NY: Knowledge Industry, 1980, pp. 147–189.

Case, Donald. *Stanford Evaluation of the Green Thumb Box Experiment Videotext Project . . . .*" Springfield, VA: NTIS, 1981 (PB82–190281).

Casadio, Franco A. "Final Report," in *International Documents for the 80's: Their Role and Use*, edited by Theodore D. Dimitrov and Luciana Marulli-Koenig. Pleasantville, NY: UNIFO Publishers, 1982, pp. xxi–xxxvi.

Castonguay, Russell. *A Comparative Guide to Classification Schemes for Local Government Documents Collections*. Westport, CT: Greenwood Press, 1984.

———. "Maintenance and Management of Local Government Documents Collections: Survey Findings," *Government Information Quarterly*, 4 (1987): 167–188.

"Channel 2000 Viewdata Test Shows Promise for Libraries," *American Libraries*, 12 (June 1981): 204.

"Charter of the Public Printer's Council on Micropublishing," *Public Documents Highlights*, 30 (October 1978): 1.

Chartrand, Robert L. "Information Policy and Technology Issues: Public Laws of the 95th through 99th Congresses." Washington D.C.: Congressional Research Service, February 1987.

Chen, Ching-chih and Peter Hernon. *Information Seeking*. New York: Neal-Schuman, 1982.

———. *Numeric Databases*. Norwood, NJ: Ablex Publishing Corp., 1984.

Cherns, J.J. "Intergovernmental Organisations as Publishers," in *International Information: Documents, Publications and Information Systems of International Government Organizations*, edited by Peter I. Hajnal. Littleton, CO: Libraries Unlimited, 1988, pp. 29–50.

———. "Intergovernmental Organisations as Publishers: A Critical Look," in *International Documents for the 80's: Their Role and Use*, edited by Theodore D. Dimitrov and Luciana Marulli-Koenig. Pleasantville, NY: UNIFO Publishers, 1982, pp. 22–31.

———. *Official Publishing*. Oxford, England: Pergamon Press, 1979.

Childers, Thomas. "Trends in Public I & R Services," *Library Journal*, 104 (October 1, 1979): 2035–2039.

Churchman, C. West. *The Systems Approach and Its Enemies*. New York: Basic Books, 1979.

A Citizen's Guide on Using the Freedom of Information Act and the Privacy Act of 1974 to Request Government Records. Prepared for the House Committee on Government Operations. Washington, DC: GPO, 1987.

Clews, John. *Documentation of the UN System: A Survey of Bibliographic Control and a Suggested Methodology for an Integrated UN Bibliography*. Occasional Papers, No. 8. London: IFLA International Office for UBC, 1981.

Cline, Nancy M. "The GPO and Micropublishing: An Update," *Microform Review*, 9 (Winter 1980): 21–27.

———. "A Librarian's Perspective of the GPO and Micropublishing," *Microform Review*, 8 (Winter 1979): 23–28.

Cohen, Aaron and Elaine Cohen. *Designing and Space Planning for Libraries*. New York: Bowker, 1979.

Cohen, Elaine. "Designing Libraries to Sell Services," *Wilson Library Bulletin*, 55 (November 1980): 190–195.

―――― and Aaron Cohen. *Automation, Space Management, and Productivity*. New York: Bowker, 1981.

Commerce Business Daily (December 22, 1987); (January 6, 1988), p. 4.

Commission on Federal Paperwork. *Information Resources Management*. Washington, D.C., September 9, 1977.

Commission on Freedom and Equality of Access to Information. *Freedom and Equality of Access to Information: A Report to the American Library Association*. Chicago, IL: American Library Association, 1986.

The Complete Guide to Citing Government Documents: A Manual for Writers and Librarians. Bethesda, MD: Congressional Information Service, 1984.

Congress. House. Committee on Government Operations. *Electronic Collection and Dissemination of Information by Federal Agencies: A Policy Overview*. Washington, D.C.: GPO, 1986.

――――. ――――. Committee on Science, Space, and Technology. *Scientific and Technical Information: Policy and Organization in the Federal Government* (H.R. 2159 and H.R. 1615), Hearings, July 141–5, 1987. Washington, D.C.: GPO, 1987.

――――. ――――. ――――. *Review of Intergovernmental Dissemination of Federal Research and Development Results*. Washington, D.C.: GPO, 1976.

――――. Joint Committee on Printing. *Analysis and Evaluation of Selected Government Printing Office Operations*. Prepared by Coopers and Lybrand. Committee Print. Washington, D.C.: GPO, 1979.

――――. ――――. *An Open Forum on the Provision of Electronic Federal Information to Depository Libraries*. Washington, D.C.: GPO, 1985.

――――. ――――. *Provision of Federal Government Publications in Electronic Format to Depository Libraries*. Washington, D.C.: GPO, 1984.

――――. Office of Technology Assessment. *Electronic Record Systems and Individual Privacy*. Washington, D.C.: GPO, 1986.

――――. Senate. Judiciary Committee. Subcommittee on Library. *Depository Libraries*, Hearings . . . 87th Cong., 2nd sess., 1962.

Conroy, Barbara. *Library Staff Development and Continuing Education: Principles and Practices*. Littleton, CO: Libraries Unlimited, 1978.

Cook, Kevin L. "Varying Levels of Support Given to Government Documents Departments in Academic Libraries," *College & Research Libraries*, 43 (November 1982): 459–471.

Copeland, Susan. "Three Technical Report Printed Indexes: A Comparative Study," *Science and Technology Libraries*, 1 (Summer 1981): 48–53.

Corbin, John. *Developing Computer Based Library Systems*. Phoenix, AZ: Oryx Press, 1981.

――――. *Managing the Library Automation Project*. Phoenix, AZ: Oryx Press, 1985.

Coyne, Joseph G., Thomas E. Hughes, and Bonnie C. Winsbro. "Sharing Results of Federal R&D: A Look at the Department of Energy's System for Managing Scientific and Technical Information," *Government Information Quarterly*, 3 (1986): 363–380.

Daehn, Ralph M. "The Measurement and Projection of Shelf Space," *Collection Management*, 4 (Winter 1982): 25–39.

Davis, Larry Nolan. *Planning, Conducting & Evaluating Workshops*. Austin, TX: Learning Concepts, 1974.

DeGennaro, Richard. "Library Automation & Networking Perspectives on Three Decades," *Library Journal*, 108 (April 1, 1983): 629–635.

D'Elia, George. "A Procedure for Identifying and Surveying Potential Users of Public Libraries," *Library Research*, 21 (1980–1981): 239–249.

Department of Defense. *Glossary of Information Handling*. Washington, DC: GPO, 1964.

Depository Library Council. *First Report to the Public Printer 1972–1976*. Washington, D.C.: 1978.

————. "Summary of Meeting," St. Paul, Minnesota, April 28–30, 1980 (mimeograph).

Dictionary of Report Series Codes. New York: Special Libraries Association, 1962; 2nd ed., edited by Lois E. Godfrey and Helen F. Redman. New York: Special Libraries Association, 1973.

Dimitrov, Theodore D. and Luciana Marulli-Koenig, eds. *International Documents for the 80's: Their Role and Use*. Pleasantville, NY: UNIFO Publishers, 1982.

Dizard, Wilson P. *The Coming Information Age: An Overview of Technology, Economics and Politics*. 2nd edition. New York: Longman, 1985.

Dougherty, Richard M., Fred J. Heinritz, and Neal Kaske. *Scientific Management of Library Operations*. 2nd edition. Metuchen, NJ: Scarecrow Press, 1982.

Dowlin, K.E. *The Electronic Library: The Promise and the Process*. New York: Neal-Schuman, 1984.

————. "The Electronic Eclectic Library," *Library Journal*, 105 (November 1, 1980): 2265–2270.

Draper, James and James Brooks. *Interior Design for Libraries*. Chicago, IL: American Library Association, 1979.

"Dual Format Issue," *Documents to the People*, 15 (September 1987): 131.

Durrance, Joan. "Providing Access to Local Government Information: The Nature of Public Library Activity," *Government Information Quarterly*, 5 (1988): 155–167.

————. "Spanning the Local Government Information Gap," *RQ*, 25 (Fall 1985): 101–109.

Edsall, Mariam S. *Library Promotion Handbook*. Phoenix, AZ: Oryx Press, 1980.

Eisenberg, Michael and Keith Williams. "Microcomputer-Based Telecommunications for Management and Decision Making," in *Microcomputers for Library Decision Making*, edited by Peter Hernon and Charles R. McClure. Norwood, NJ: Ablex Pub. Corp., 1986, pp. 130–141.

European Communities. Court of Auditors. "Special Report concerning Publishing, Printing and Reproduction Practices of the Institutions of the European Communities," *Official Journal of the European Communities: Information and Notices*, 24 (June 19, 1981): C150.

Evans, F.B. "Access to Archives of United Nations Organizations," in *International Documents for the 80's: Their Role and Use*, edited by Theodore D. Dimitrov and Luciana Marulli-Koenig. Pleasantville, NY: UNIFO Publishers, 1982, pp. 65– 72.

Evans, G. Edward. *Developing Library and Information Center Collections*, 2nd edition. Littleton, CO: Libraries Unlimited, 1987.

Faull, Sandra K. "Cost and Benefits of Federal Depository Status for Academic Research Libraries," *Documents to the People*, 8 (January 1980): 33–39.

————. "'State Plans': Their Development and Potential for Regional Depository Libraries Participating in the GPO Depository Program," *Government Information Quarterly*, 2 (1985): 157–167.

"FBI Visits to Libraries," *ALA Washington Newsletter* (October 28, 1987), p. 4.

The Federal Data Base Finder. Washington, D.C.: Information USA, 1987.

Federal Depository Library Manual. Depository Library Systems Committee of the Depository Library Council to the Public Printer. Washington, D.C.: GPO, 1985.

Fine, Sarah. "Human Factors and Human Consequences," in *Information Technology: Critical Choices for Library Decision-Makers*, edited by Allen Kent and Thomas J. Galvin. New York: Marcel Dekker, 1982, pp. 209–224.

Folcarelli, Ralph J., Arthur C. Tannenbaum, and Ralph C. Ferragamo. *The Microform Connection.* New York: Bowker, 1982.

Ford, Barbara and Yuri Nakata. "Reference Use of State Government Information in Academic Libraries," *Government Publications Review,* 10 (1983): 189–199.

"Format of Publications Distributed to Depository Libraries," *Administrative Notes* [Superintendent of Documents], 8 (December 1987): 21–23.

Fry, Bernard M. "Government Publications and the Library: Implications for Change," *Government Publications Review,* 4 (1977): 111–117.

————. *Government Publications: Their Role in the National Program for Library and Information Services.* Prepared for the National Commission on Libraries and Information Science. Washington, D.C.: GPO, 1978.

————. "The Need for a Theoretical Base," in *Collection Development and Public Access of Government Documents,* edited by Peter Hernon. Westport, CT: Meckler Publishing, 1982, pp. 1–6.

Futas, Elizabeth, ed. *Library Acquisition Policies and Procedures.* Phoenix, AZ: Oryx Press, 1977, 1984.

"Fugitive Publications," *Administrative Notes,* 6, number 11 (1985): 3–4.

Galitz, Wilbert O. *Humanizing Office Automation: The Impact of Ergonomics on Productivity.* Wellesley, MA: QED Information Sciences, Inc., 1984.

Garay, Ronald. *Congressional Television.* Westport, CT: Greenwood Press, 1984.

Gillham, Virginia. "CODOC as a Consortia Tool," *Government Publications Review,* 9 (1982): 45–53.

————. "The CODOC System: An Update for the Mid-1980s," *Government Publications Review,* 14 (1987): 465–469.

Gilligan, Judith and Susan Hajdas. "A Checklist of Indexed Federal Periodicals," *Government Publications Review,* 13 (1986): 507–518.

Godden, Irene P. *Library Technical Services: Operations and Management.* Orlando, FL: Academic Press, 1984.

"Godort Program," *Documents to the People,* 10 (September 1982): 206–208.

Goodell, John S. *Libraries and Work Sampling.* Littleton, CO: Libraries Unlimited, 1975.

Government Depository Libraries. Joint Committee Print. Washington, D.C.: GPO, 1983.

"Government Information Technology and Information Dissemination: A Discussion Paper." Submitted to the ALA Government Documents Roundtable by the Government Information Technology Committee, December 1987 (unpublished).

"GPO Gives Testing Electronic Formats to Private Sector," *Coalition on Government Information Newsletter,* 2 (January 1988): 1.

"GPO Tape Clean-Up," *Documents to the People,* 15 (December 1987): 205.

Gray, Dwight E. "Organizing and Servicing Unpublished Reports," *American Documentation,* 4 (1953): 103–115.

Guidelines for Collection Development. Chicago, IL: American Library Association, 1979.

Guidelines for the Depository Library System. Washington, D.C.: GPO, 1977.

"Guidelines for the Depository Library System," *Administrative Notes* (a publication of the GPO), 8, number 15 (1987): 3.

Hahn, Ellen Z. "Optical Disk Pilot Program," *Library of Congress Information Bulletin,* 42 (October 31, 1983): 374–376.

Hahn, Harvey. *Technical Services in the Small Library.* Chicago, IL: American Library Association, 1987.

Hajnal, Peter I. "Collection Development," in *International Information: Dcouments, Publications and Information Systems of International Governmental Organizations,* edited by Peter I. Hajanl. Littleton, CO: Libraries Unlimited, 1988, pp. 79–118.

————. "Collection Development: United Nations Material," *Government Publications Review,* 8A (1981): 89– 109.

———. *Guide to Unesco.* New York: Oceana, 1983.

———. *Guide to United Nations Organization, Documentation and Publishing for Students, Researchers, Librarians.* Dobbs Ferry, NY: Oceana, 1978.

———. "IGO Documents and Publications: Volume, Distribution, Recent Developments, and Sources of Information," *Government Publications Review,* 9 (March/April 1982): 121–130.

Hall, Hal W. "Selection Decisions for Choosing Appropriate Hardware and Software," in *Microcomputers for Library Decision Making,* edited by Peter Hernon and Charles R. McClure. Norwood, NJ: Ablex Pub. Corp., 1986, pp. 18–38.

Hall, Richard B. "The Library Space Utilization Methodology," *Library Journal,* 103 (December 1, 1978): 2379–2382.

Hardt, Elisabeth. "On Line to Europe: A Guide to E.C. Databases," *Europe: Magazine of the European Community* (Washington, D.C.), 270 (October 1987): 21–27.

Harleston, Rebekah M. and Carla J. Stoffle. *Administration of Government Documents Collections.* Littleton, CO: Libraries Unlimited, 1974.

Hartz, Michael J., James M. Ray, and Linda A. Schlueter. "Economic Censuses around the World," *Government Information Quarterly,* 4 (1987): 325–339.

Hearings on Electronic Collection and Dissemination of Information by Federal Agencies. Prepared by the House Committee on Government Operations. Washington, D.C.: GPO, 1986.

Heim, Kathleen M. "Government Produced Machine-Readable Statistical Data as a Component of the Social Science Information System: An Examination of Federal Policy and Strategies for Access," in *Communicating Public Access of Government Information,* edited by Peter Hernon. Westport, CT: Meckler Publishing, 1983, pp. 33–74.

Heindel, A.J. and H.A. Napier. "Decision Support Systems in Libraries," *Special Libraries,* 72 (1981): 319–327.

Henderson, Madeline M. "Source Aspects of Technical Report Processing by Federal Agencies," *Science and Technology Libraries,* 1 (Summer 1981): 19–26.

Hernon, Peter. "Academic Library Reference Service for the Publications of Municipal, State, and Federal Government: A Historical Perspective Spanning the Years up to 1962," *Government Publications Review,* 5 (1978): 31–50.

———. *Microforms and Government Information.* Westport, CT: Microform Review Inc., 1981.

———. *Use of Government Publications by Social Scientists.* Norwood, NJ: Ablex Publishing Corp., 1979.

———. "Use of Microformatted Government Publications," *Microform Review,* 11 (Fall 1982): 237–252.

———. "Utility Measures, Not Performance Measures, for Library Reference Service?," *RQ,* 26 (Summer 1987): 449–459.

——— and Charles R. McClure. *Federal Information Policies in the 1980s.* Norwood, NJ: Ablex Publishing Corp., 1987a.

——— and Charles R. McClure. "GPO's Depository Library Program: Building for the Future," *Library Journal,* 113 (1988): 52–56.

——— and Charles R. McClure, ed. *Microcomputers for Library Decision Making.* Norwood, NJ: Ablex Publishing Corp., 1986.

——— and Charles R. McClure. *Unobtrusive Testing and Library Reference Service.* Norwood, NJ: Ablex Publishing Corp., 1987b.

——— , Charles R. McClure, and Gary R. Purcell. *GPO's Depository Library Program: A Descriptive Analysis.* Norwood, NJ: Ablex Publishing Corp., 1985.

——— and Clayton A. Shepherd. "Government Publications Represented in the Social Sciences Citation Index: An Exploratory Study,: *Government Publications Review,* 10 (1983): 227–244.

_____ and Gary R. Purcell. *Developing Collections of U.S. Government Publications*. Greenwich, CT: JAI Press, 1982.

_____ and John V. Richardson. *Statistical Analysis Software for Microcomputers: A Handbook Guiding Library Decision Making*. Norwood, NJ: Ablex Pub. Corp., 1988.

Hitt, Michael A., R. Dennis Middlemist, and Robert L. Mathis. *Management: Concepts and Effective Practice*. St. Paul, MN: West Publishing Co., 1983.

Hoduski, Bernadine E. Abbott. "Political Activism for Documents Librarians," in *Communicating Public Access to Government Information*, edited by Peter Hernon. Westport, CT: Meckler Publishing, 1983, pp. 1–11.

Holmes, Donald C. "Determination of Environmental Conditions Required in a Library," 1970 (ERIC ED 046 403).

Hopkins, Michael. "The Documentation of Intergovernmental Organizations: A Critical Survey of Supply-and-Demand Situations in the United Kingdom," *International Social Science Journal*, 32 (1980): 371–382.

_____. "European Communities Information and Its Use in British Universities and Polytechnics," in *European Communities Information: Its Use and Users*, edited by Michael Hopkins. New York: Mansell, 1985, pp. 195–226.

Horton, Forest Woody, Jr. "Information Policy: The National Information Policy Chameleon," *Information Management Review*, 3 (1987): 79–84.

Houle, Cyril O. "The Role of Continuing Education in Professional Development," *ALA Bulletin*, 61 (March 1967): 259–267.

Huls, Mary Ellen. "Access to Federal Audiovisual Productions," *RQ*, 27 (Winter 1987): 184–189.

"Information Technology Program Update," *Administrative Notes* [Superintendent of Documents], 9 (February 1988): 13–14.

INS v. Chadha, 102 S. Ct. 2764 (1983).

International Federation of Library Associations and Institutions. Official Publications Section. *Proceedings of International Conference of Government Publishers, Printers, Librarians and Users*, Saratoga Springs, New York. August 29–September 1, 1982, edited by Bernadine E. Abbott Hoduski and Maryellen Trautman. Washington, D.C., 1983.

Jacque, Sylvie. "Bibliographic Control of Intergovernmental Publications: User Survey," *International Cataloguing*, 15 (January/March 1986): 10–12.

Jackson, Ellen. *A Notation for a Public Documents Classification*. Library Bulletin no. 8. Stillwater, OK: Oklahoma Agriculture and Mechanical College, 1946.

Janis, Irving L. and L. Mann. *Decision Making*. New York: The Free Press, 1977.

Jeffries, John. "The Public Availability of European Community Documentary Sources," in *International Documents for the 80's: Their Role and Use*, edited by Theodore D. Dimitrov and Luciana Marulli-Koenig. Pleasantville, NY: UNIFO Publishers, 1982, pp. 10–20.

Johansson, Eve. "The Definition of Official Publications," *IFLA Journal*, 8 (1982): 393–395.

Johnson, Edward R. "Financial Planning Needs of Publicly- Supported Academic Libraries in the 1980s: Politics as Usual," *Journal of Library Administration*, 3 (Fall-Winter 1982): 23–26.

Joint Inspection Unit [of the United Nations System of Organizations]. *Control and Limitation of Documentation in the United Nations System*. Geneva, Switzerland, December 1980 (JIU/REP/80/12).

_____. *Publications Policy and Practice in the United Nations System*. Geneva, Switzerland, 1984 (JIU/REP/84/5). Transmitted in United Nations. General Assembly. 39th sess. *Questions Relating to Information*. New York: UN, May 14, 1984 (A/39/239).

Kadec, Sarah T. "Future Dimensions: Where Do We Go from Here," *Government Publications Review*, 11 (1984): 413–420.

———. "The U.S. Government Printing Office's Library Programs Services and Automation: An Insider's Commentary," *Government Publications Review*, 12 (1985): 283–288.

Karp, Walter. "Liberty under Siege: The Reagan Administration's Taste for Autocracy," *Harper's Magazine*, 271 (November 1985): 53–67.

Kaser, David. "Advances in Library History," in *Advances in Librarianship*, Volume 8. New York: Academic Press, 1978, pp. 181–199.

———, Fay Blake, Mary K. Chelton, E.J. Josey, S.M. Malinconcio, Peggy Sullivan, and Roderick Swartz. "Toward a Conceptual Foundation for a National Information Policy," *Wilson Library Bulletin*, 52 (March 1978): 545– 549.

Kast, Fremont E. and James E. Rosenzweig. "General Systems Theory: Applications for Organization and Management," *Academy of Management Journal*, 15 (December 1972): 447– 465.

———. *Organization and Management: A Systems and Contingency Approach*. 4th. ed. New York: McGraw-Hill, 1985.

Kesner, Richard M. and Clifton H. Jones. *Microcomputer Applications in Libraries: A Management Tool for the 1980s and Beyond*. Westport, CT: Greenwood Press, 1984.

Knenlein, Donald R., Director, Federal Information Center Program Division, General Services Administration, sent a letter to Peter Hernon, dated October 7, 1983.

Koontz, Harold and Cyril O'Donnell. *Management: A Systems and Contingency Analysis of Managerial Functions*. New York: McGraw-Hill, 1979.

Kotler, Philip. *Marketing for Nonprofit Organizations*. Englewood Cliffs, NJ: Prentice-Hall, 1975, 1982.

——— and Karen F.A. Fox. *Strategic Marketing for Educational Institutions*. Englewood Cliffs, NJ: Prentice-Hall, 1985.

Kresslein, John C. and Donald A. Marchand. "A Comparative View of Information Resources Management Practices in State Government," in *Government Infostructures: A Guide to the Networks of Information Resources and Technologies at Federal, State, and Local Levels*, edited by Karen B. Levitan. Westport, CT: Greenwood Press, 1987, pp. 105– 122.

Kroll, Rebecca H. "Beyond Evaluation: Performance Appraisal as a Planning and Motivational Tool in Libraries," *Journal of Academic Librarianship*, 9 (March 1983): 27–32.

Krueger, Karen. *Coordinated Cooperative Collection Development for Illinois Libraries*. Springfield, IL: Illinois State Library, 1983.

———. "Resource Sharing: The Invisible Service," in *State Library Services and Issues: Facing Future Challenges*, edited by Charles R. McClure. Norwood, NJ: Ablex Publishing Corp., 1986, pp. 146–173.

Lancaster, F.W. *Libraries and Librarians in an Age of Electronics*. Arlington, VA: Information Resources Press, 1982.

———. *The Measurement and Evaluation of Library Services*. Washington, D.C.: Information Resources Press, 1977.

Lane, Margaret T. *Selecting and Organizing State Government Publications*. Chicago, IL: American Library Association, 1987.

———. *State Publications and Depository Libraries: A Reference Handbook*. Westport, CT: Greenwood Press, 1981.

Larson, Donna Rae. *Guide to U.S. Government Directories*. Phoenix, AZ: Oryx Press, 1981, 1985.

Lastenouse, J. Letter "for the Attention of the Heads of the European Documentation Centres." (Commission of the European Communities, University Information). Brussels, July 23, 1987 (Unpublished).

Lawler III, Edward, David N. Nadler, and Cortlandt Cammann. *Organizational Assessment*. New York: Wiley, 1980.

Leavitt, Edward P. "Government Publications in the University Library," *Library Journal*, 86 (May 1, 1961): 1741–1743.

Leighton, P.D. and D.C. Weber, ed. *Planning Academic & Research Library Buildings*. 2nd edition. Chicago, IL: American Library Association, 1986.

"Letter to W. T. Barry, August 4, 1822," in *The Writings of James Madison*, vol. IX, edited by Gaillard Hunt. New York: Putnam, 1910.

Levin, Marc A. "Access and Dissemination Issues concerning Federal Government Information," *Special Libraries*, 74 (April 1983): 127–137.

Levitan, Karen B. "The Collapse of Traditional Distinctions," *Bulletin of the American Society for Information Science*, 8 (April 1981a): 12–13, 16.

———. "The New Information Hybrid," *Bulletin of the American Society for Information Science*, 8 (April 1981b): 25–26.

Lewy, Cheryl W. "Urban Documents as Reference Tools," *Government Publications Review*, 1 (1974): 269–275.

Luguire, Wilson. "Attitudes toward Automation/Innovation in Academic Libraries," *Journal of Academic Librarianship*, 8 (January 1983): 344–351.

Lunin, Lois and Joseph P. Caponio. "Perspectives on the Federal Government and Health Information: Patterns, Impacts, Expectations," *Journal of the American Society for Information Science*, 38 (January 1987): 25–75.

Lushington, Nolan and Willis N. Mills, Jr. *Libraries Designed for Users*. Syracuse, NY: Gaylord Publications, 1979.

Luthans, Fred. *Introduction to Management: A Contingency Approach*. New York: McGraw-Hill, 1976.

MacDonald, Susan H. and Charles F. Sieger, Jr. "GPO Micropublishing: An Historical Review and Critical Analysis," *Library Acquisitions: Practice and Theory*, 2 (1978): 33–44.

Management of the United States Government: Fiscal Year 1986. Washington, D.C.: GPO, 1985.

"Managing Budget Cutbacks," Symposium of Federal Library and Information Center Committee. Washington, D.C.: Library of Congress, November 2, 1987 (unpublished).

Marchant, Maurice P. *Participative Management in Academic Libraries*. Westport, CT: Greenwood Press, 1976.

Martin, Murray S. "Financial Planning: Introductory Thoughts," *Journal of Library Administration*, 3 (Fall-Winter 1982): 3–9.

Marulli, Luciana. *Documentation of the United Nations System*. Metuchen, NJ: Scarecrow Press, 1979.

Marulli-Koenig, Luciana. "Bibliographic Control of Documents and Publications of Organizations of the United Nations Ststem: Tools, Techniques, Products," in *International Information: Documents , Publications and Information Systems of International Governmental Organizations*, edited by Peter I. Hajnal. Littleton, CO: Libraries Unlimited, 1988, pp. 51–68.

———. "Collection Development for United Nations Documents and Publications," in *Collection Development and Public Access of Government Documents*, edited by Peter Hernon. Westport, CT: Meckler Publishing, 1982, pp. 85–102.

Mason, Marilyn Gell. *The Federal Role in Library and Information Services*. White Plains, NY: Knowledge Industry Publications, Inc., 1983.

Matheny, Bill. "DOE Research Results." Oak Ridge, TN: Department of Energy, Office of Scientific and Technological Information, unpublished memorandum dated June 12–13, 1986. Reported in Charles R. McClure. "The Federal Technical Report Literature," *Government Information Quarterly*, 5 (1988): 27–44.

Matthews, Joseph R. *Choosing an Automated Library System: A Planning Guide*. Chicago, IL: American Library Association, 1980.

———. *Public Access to Online Catalogs: A Planning Guide for Managers.* Weston, CT: Online Inc., 1982.

Mathis, Robert L. and John H. Jackson. *Personnel: Contemporary Perspectives and Applications.* 2nd edition. St. Paul, MN: West Publishing Co., 1979.

McClure, Charles R. "The Federal Technical Report Literature," *Government Information Quarterly,* 5 (1988): 27–44.

———. "Improving Access to and Use of Federal Scientific and Technological Information (STI): Perspectives from Recent Research Projects," in *Proceedings of the 50th Annual Meeting of the American Society for Information Science,* edited by Ching-chih Chen. Vol. 24. Medford, NJ: Learned Information 1987, pp. 163–169.

———. "Indexing U.S. Government Periodicals: Analysis and Comments," *Government Publications Review,* 5 (1978a): 409– 421.

———. "Information and an Individual's Power in an Organizational Setting," in *The Power of Information: Collected Papers Presented at the ASIS 9th Mid-year Meeting,* compiled by K.L. Montgomery. Washington, D.C.: American Society for Information Science, 1980 (microfiche).

———. "Management Information for Library Decision Making," in *Advances in Librarianship,* volume 13, edited by Wesley Simonton. New York: Academic Press, 1984a, pp. 1– 47.

———. "Microformatted Government Publications," *Government Publications Review,* 5 (1978b): 383–387.

———. "Planning for Library Services: Lessons and Opportunities," in *Planning for Library Services: A Guide to Utilizing Planning Methods for Library Management,* edited by Charles R. McClure. New York: Haworth Press, 1982c, pp. 7–28.

———. "Proposed Regulations from the Joint Committee on Printing: Patchwork Remedies for Complex Problems," *Government Information Quarterly,* 1 (1984): 309–326.

———. "Provision of Federal Government Publications in Electronic Format to Depository Libraries— Continued," *Government Information Quarterly,* 3 (1986): 113–116.

———. "Structural Analysis of the Depository System: A Preliminary Assessment," in *Collection Development and Public Access of Government Documents,* edited by Peter Hernon. Westport, CT: Meckler Publishing, 1982a, pp. 35– 56.

———. "Technology in Government Document Collections: Current Status, Impacts, and Prospects," *Government Publications Review,* 9 (1982b): 255–276.

———, Amy Owen, Douglas L. Zweizig., Mary Jo Lynch, and Nancy A. Van House. *A Planning and Role Setting for Public Libraries: A Manual of Options and Procedures.* Chicago, IL: American Library Association, 1987.

——— and Peter Hernon. *Improving the Quality of Reference Service for Government Publications.* Chicago, IL: American Library Association, 1983.

——— and Peter Hernon. "Unobtrusive Testing and the Role of Library Management," *The Reference Librarian,* 18 (Summer 1987): 71–85.

———, Peter Hernon, and Gary R. Purcell. *Linking the U.S. National Technical Information Service with Academic and Public Libraries.* Norwood, NJ: Ablex Publishing Corp., 1986.

McC. Mathias, Jr., Charles. "Second Draft of Letter on Pilot Project and OTA Report," for the Ad Hoc Committee on Depository Library Access to Federal Automated Data Bases Members, dated March 28, 1986.

McKean, Joan M. "Facsimile in Libraries," in *Telecommunications and Libraries: A Primer for Librarians and Information Managers.* White Plains, NY: Knowledge Industry Publications, 1981, pp. 91–120.

Merritt, LeRoy C. *The United States Government as Publisher.* Chicago, IL: University of Chicago Press, 1943.

"Micropublishing and the Government Printing Office," *Public Documents Highlights*, 3 (April 1974): 1.

Miller, Sara J. "The Depository Library System: A History of the Distribution of Federal Government Publications to Libraries of the United States from the Early Years of the Nation to 1895," D.L.S. dissertation, Columbia University, 1980.

Molholm, Kurt N., Betty L. Fox, Paul M. Klinefelter, Ellen V. McCauley, and William M. Thompson. "The Defense Technical Information Center: Acquiring Information and Imparting Knowledge," *Government Information Quarterly*, 5 (1988), forthcoming.

Moody, Marilyn. "Government Information: The Privatization of NTIS: What Are the Implications?," *RQ*, 27 (Winter 1986): 157–162.

Mooney, Margaret T. "Automating the U.S. Depository Item Number File," *Administrative Notes*, 7 (November 1986): 2–3.

Morehead, Joe. *Introduction to United States Public Documents*. Littleton, CO: Libraries Unlimited, 1975, 1978, 1983.

Morton, Bruce. "The Depository Library System: A Costly Anachronism," *Library Journal*, 112 (September 15, 1987): 52–54.

––––––. "Implementing an Automated Shelflist for a Selective Depository Collection," *Government Publications Review*, 9 (1982). 323–344.

–––––– and J. Randolph Cox. "Cooperative Collection Development between Selective U.S. Depository Libraries," *Government Publications Review*, 9 (1982): 221–229.

Murphy, Cynthia E. "A Comparison of Manual and Online Searching of Government Document Indexes," *Government Information Quarterly*, 2 (1985): 169–181.

Myers, Judy E. "The Effects of Technology on Access to Federal Government Information," in *New Technology and Documents Librarianship*, edited by Peter Hernon. Westport, CT: Meckler Publishing, 1983, pp. 27–41.

––––––. "The Government Printing Office Cataloging Records: Opportunities and Problems," *Government Information Quarterly*, 2 (1985): 27–56.

–––––– and Helen H. Britton. "Government Documents in the Public Catalog: The Iceberg Surfaces," *Government Publications Review*, 5 (1978): 311–314.

Nadler, David A. and Michael L. Tushman. "A Congruence Model for Organizational Assessment," in *Organizational Assessment*, edited by Edward E. Lawler III, David A. Nadler, and Cortlandt Cammann. New York: Wiley, 1980, pp. 261–278.

Naisbitt, John. *Megatrends: Ten New Directions Transforming Our Lives*. New York: Warner Books, 1982.

Nakata, Yuri and Karen Kopec. "State and Local Government Publications," *Drexel Library Quarterly*, 16 (October 1980): 40–59.

Nakata, Yuri, Susan J. Smith, and William B. Ernest, Jr. *Organizing a Local Government Documents Collection*. Chicago, IL: American Library Association, 1979.

National Commission on Libraries and Information Science. *Aspects of U.S. Information Policy: An Annotated Bibliography of Federal Laws, Policies, Regulations, Congressional Hearings with Related Monographs, Serials and Studies from the Private Sector*. Washington, DC: The Commission, February 1983.

––––––. *Public Sector/Private Sector Interaction in Providing Information Services*. Washington, D.C.: GPO, 1982.

The National Publications Act. Hearings before the Subcommittee on Printing, Committee on House Administration, House of Representatives. Washington, D.C.: GPO, 1979.

National Publications Act of 1980. Report by the Committee on House Administration of the House of Representatives. Washington, D.C.: GPO, 1980.

National Technical Information Service. "Privatization Study Responses to April 28, 1986 *Federal Register* Notice Request for Public Comment." Springfield, VA: NTIS, 1986 (PB86–211240).

BIBLIOGRAPHY   501

—————. *User's Guide to NTIS*. Springfield, VA: NTIS, 1987.
North, Gary W. "Maps for the Nation: The Current Federal Mapping Establishment," *Government Publications Review*, 10 (1983): 345–360.
O'Brien, Conor Cruise and Feliks Topolski. *The United Nations: Sacred Drama*. London: Hutchinson, 1968.
Office of Management and Budget. "Reform '88: Elimination, Consolidation and Cost Reduction of Government Publications," October 1983 (mimeographed).
Organisation for Economic Co-operation and Development. "Less Publications et documents de l'Organisation de cooperation et de developpment economiques," in *International Documents for the 80's: Their Role and Use*, edited by Theodore D. Dimitrov and Luciana Marulli-Koenig. Pleasantville, NY: UNIFO Publishers, 1982, microfiche 3A, pp. 102–103.
Orr, R.H. "Measuring the Goodness of Library Services: A General Framework for Considering Quantitative Measures," *Journal of Documentation*, 29 (September 1973): 315–332.
"Over 900 Federal Publications Halted," *New York Times* (November 16, 1981), p. B17.
Owen, Amy. "Exploiting Information Technologies," in *State Library Services and Issued: Facing Future Challenges*, edited by Charles R. McClure. Norwood, NJ: Ablex Publishing Corp., 1986, pp. 235–253.
Paris, Marion. "Library School Closings: Four Case Studies," Ph. D. dissertation, Indiana University, 1986.
Parish, David W. *A Bibliography of State Bibliographies, 1970– 1982*. Littleton, CO: Libraries Unlimited, 1985.
—————. *State Government Reference Publications*. 2nd edition. Littleton, CO: Libraries Unlimited, 1981.
Plaunt, James R. "Cataloging Options for U.S. Government Printing Office Documents," *Government Publications Review*, 12 (1985): 449–456.
Pope, Nolan F. "Providing Machine-Readable Numeric Information in the University of Florida Libraries: A Case Study," in *Numeric Databases*, edited by Ching-chih Chen and Peter Hernon. Norwood, NJ: Ablex Pub. Corp., 1984, pp. 263–282.
Porat, Marc. *The Information Economy*. 7 vols. Washington, DC: GPO, 1977.
Powell, Benjamin E. and William R. Pullen. "The Depository Library System," Appendix H, in *Revision of Depository Library Laws*, Hearings before a subcommittee of the Committee on House Administration, House of Representatives, 85th Cong., 1st sess., Washington, D.C.: GPO, 1958.
Powell, Henry. "Federal Micropublishing Policy." Unpublished paper presented at the American University, May 1977.
Powell, Margaret S., Deborah Smith Johnston, and Ellen P. Conrad. "The Use of OCLC for Cataloging U.S. Government Publications: A Feasibility Study," *Government Publications Review*, 14 (1987): 62–73.
A Practical Guide to the Superintendent of Documents Classification System. Washington, D.C.: GPO, 1986 (GP3.29:Pr88).
Prentice, Anne E. *Financial Planning for Libraries*. Metuchen, NJ: Scarecrow Press, 1982.
—————. *Public Library Finance*. Chicago, IL: American Library Association, 1977.
Preparing for a Depository Inspection. Washington, D.C.: GPO, Library Programs Service, n.d.
President's Private Sector Survey on Cost Control. Report on Publishing, Printing, and Reproduction and Audiovisual Activities. Washington, D.C.: GPO, 1983.
The President's Science Advisory Committee. *Science, Government and Information: The Responsibilities of the Technical Community and the Government in the Transfer of Information* ("The Weinberg Report"). Washington, DC: The White House, 1963.
"Privatization Commission," *ALA Washington Newsletter* (September 30, 1987), p. 7.

Purcell, Gary R. "The NTIS Micropublishing Program," in *Microforms and Government Information*, edited by Peter Hernon. Westport, CT: Microform Review, Inc., 1981a, pp. 70–91.

――――. "Reference Use of State Government Publications in Public Libraries," *Government Publications Review*, 10 (1983): 173–187.

――――. "U.S. Government Publication Collection Development for Non-depository Libraries," *Government Publications Review*, 8A (1981b): 31–45.

――――. "The Use of Tennessee State Government Publications," *Tennessee Librarian*, 32 (Spring 1980): 20–31.

Randolph, Susan. "Reducing the Federal Deficit: The Impact on Libraries," *Special Libraries*, 78 (Winter 1987): 7–15.

Rawski, Conrad. *Toward a Theory of Librarianship: Papers in Honor of Jesse Hauk Shera*. Metuchen, NJ: Scarecrow Press, 1973.

"Recent Opinions of the GPO General Counsel," *Documents to the People*, 10 (July 1982): 155–156.

Redmond, Mary. "State Data Centers: Improving Access to Census Information," *Government Information Quarterly*, 3 (1986): 291–303.

Reeder, Franklin S. "Federal Information Resources Management," *Bulletin of the American Society for Information Science*, 13 (1986): 11–12.

Reflections of America. Prepared for the Bureau of the Census. Washington, D.C.: GPO, 1980.

Relyea, Harold C. "The Coming of Secret Law," *Government Information Quarterly*, 5 (1988): 97–116.

Report of the First National Conference on Issues concerning Computerized Public Records. 2 vols. Boston, MA: Office of the Massachusetts Secretary of State, Public Records Division, 1987.

Report Series Codes Dictionary, edited by Eleanor J. Aronson. Detroit, MI: Gale Research Co., 1986.

Reynolds, Catharine J. "Discovering the Government Documents Collection in Libraries," *RQ*, 14 (Spring 1975): 228–231.

――――. "How Many Government Publications in a Linear Foot?," *Documents to the People*, 7 (May 1979): 96, 99.

Richardson, John V. Jr. "The United States Government as Publisher since the Roosevelt Administration," *Library Research*, 4 (1982): 211–233.

――――, Dennis C.W. Frisch, and Catherine M. Hall. "Bibliographic Organization of U.S. Federal Depository Collections," *Government Publications Review*, 7A (1980): 463–480.

Riggs, Donald E. *Strategic Planning for Library Managers*. Phoenix, AZ: Oryx Press, 1984.

Rips, Rae E. "The Reference Use of Government Publications," *Drexel Library Quarterly*, 1 (October 1965): 3–18.

Roberts, Leiia-Jane. "Quantative Measurement for Space Utilization in a Medium-Sized Public Library," in *Quantative Measurement and Dynamic Library Service*, edited by Ching-chih Chen. Phoenix, AZ: Oryx Press, 1978, pp. 87–102.

Robinson, William C. "Evaluation of the Government Documents Collection: A Step-by-Step Process," *Government Publications Review*, 9 (March/April 1982): 131–141.

――――. "Evaluation of the Government Documents Collection: An Introduction and Overview," *Government Publications Review*, 8A (1981): 111–125.

―――― and Athena A. Stone. "The Impact of the Reduction in Federal Government Statistical Publications and Services on State Government Statistical Agencies," *Government Publications Review*, 14 (1987): 433–448.

The Role of Science and Technology in Competitiveness. Hearings before the Subcommittee on Science, Research and Technology of the House Committee on Science, Space, and Technology. Washington, DC: GPO, 1987.

Rosenfield, Harry N. "A New Look at the Constitution's Copyright Clause: Copyright by Government Contractors Is Unconstitutional," *Government Information Quarterly*, 3 (1986): 31–48.

Rosselle, William C. "The Microforms Facility at the Golda Meir Library of the University of Wisconsin, Milwaukee," in *Advances in Library Administration and Organization*, volume 1, edited by G.B. McCabe, B. Kreissman, and W. Carl Jackson. Greenwich, CT: JAI Press, 1982, pp. 84–107.

Rossi, Peter H. and Howard E. Freeman. *Evaluation: A Systematic Approach*, 3rd ed. Beverly Hills, CA: Sage, 1985.

Rothschild, M. Cecilia. "Department of Defense Information Analysis Centers," *Special Libraries*, 78 (Summer 1987): 162–169.

Russell, Judith C. "Trends in Information Technology and Private Sector Activities," *Government Information Quarterly*, 5 (1988), forthcoming.

Sachse, Gladys. *U.S. Government Publications for Small and Medium-Sized Public Libraries*. Chicago, IL: American Library Association, 1981.

Saffady, William. *Computer-Output Microfilm: Its Library Applications*. Chicago, IL: American Library Association, 1978.

––––––. *Introduction to Automation for Librarians*. Chicago, IL: American Library Association, 1983.

––––––. *Micrographics*. 2nd edition. Littleton, CO: Libraries Unlimited, 1985.

Samuels, Alan R. "Organizational Climate and Library Change," in *Strategies for Library Administration*, edited by Charles R. McClure and Alan R. Samuels. Littleton, CO: Libraries Unlimited, 1982, pp. 421–431.

–––––– and Charles R. McClure. "Toward a Theory of Library Administration," in *Strategies for Library Administration*, edited by Charles R. McClure and Alan R. Samuels. Littleton, C: Libraries Unlimited, 1982, pp. 12–28.

Sarndal, Ann G. "Zero Based Budgeting," *Special Libraries*, 70 (December 1979): 527–532.

Saville, Mahala. "Government Publications—What Shall We Do with Them?," *Library Journal*, 65 (September 1, 1940): 681– 684.

Schmeckebier, Lawrence F. and Roy B. Eastin. *Government Publications and Their Use*. Washington, D.C.: The Brookings Institute, 1969.

Schnapper. M.B. "Copyright Camouflage—Its Role in Governmental Manipulation of Public Opinion," *Government Information Quarterly*, 2 (1985): 127–130.

Schwarzkopf, LeRoy C. "Depository Libraries and Public Access of Government Documents," in *Collection Development and Public Access of Government Documents*, edited by Peter Hernon. Westport, CT: Meckler Publishing, 1982, pp. 7–33.

––––––. "The GPO Microform Program: Its History and Status," *Documents to the People*, 6 (June 1978): 163–166.

––––––. "Regional Depository Libraries for U.S. Government Publications," *Government Publications Review*, 2 (1975): 91–102.

––––––. "Regional Libraries and the Depository Library Act of 1962." College Park, MD: University of Maryland, 1972 (ED 066 177).

Schweizer, Susanna. "Online Retrieval of Government Documents Using Teletext and Videotext Services," in *New Technology and Documents Librarianship*, edited by Peter Hernon. Westport, CT: Meckler Publishing, 1983, pp. 60–76.

Shannon, Michael O. "Collection Development and Local Documents: History and Present Use in the United States," *Government Publications Review*, 8A (1981): 59–87.

Shaw, Anne. "Godort Microform Survey," *Microform Review*, 6 (November 1977): 337–339.

Simonton, Wesley. "The Bibliographic Control of Microforms," *Library Resources and Technical Services*, 6 (Winter 1962): 29–40.

Smith, Diane H. "GODORT Program: Cost Benefit Analysis," *Documents to the People*, 10 (September 1982): 206–207.

Smith, Karen F. "Robot at the Reference Desk?," *College & Research Libraries*, 47 (September 1986): 486–490.

Smith, Ruth S. "Interactions within the Technical Reports Community," *Science and Technology Libraries*, 1 (Summer 1981): 5–18.

Soper, Mary Ellen. "Characteristics and Use of Personal Collections," *The Library Quarterly*, 46 (October 1976): 397–415.

Sources, Organization, Utilization of International Documentation. Proceedings of the International Symposium on the Documentation of the United Nations and Other Intergovernmental Organizations, Geneva, 1972. FID Publication no. 506. The Hague: International Federation for Documentation, 1974.

Sprehe, J. Timothy. "Developing a Federal Policy on Electronic Collection and Dissemination of Information," *Government Publications Review*, 11 (1984): 353–362.

State Plans for Federal Depository Documents. Issued for the Federal Depository Library Program. Washington, D.C.: GPO, 1984.

Statutes at Large (Washington, D.C.: GPO).

Stephenson, Mary Sue and Gary R. Purcell. "Application of Systems Analysis to Depository Library Decision Making Regarding the Use of New Technology," *Government Information Quarterly*, 1 (1984): 285–307.

———. "The Automation of Government Publications: Functional Requirements and Selected Software Systems for Serials Control," *Government Information Quarterly*, 3 (1985): 57–76.

———. "Current and Future Direction of Automation Activities for U.S. Government Depository Collections," *Government Information Quarterly*, 3 (1986): 191–199.

Strain, Paula M. "Efficiency and Library Space," *Special Libraries*, 70 (December 1979): 542–548.

Struck, Myron. "Old Printery Undergoes a Makeover: Efficiency Goes up and So Do Prices," *The Washington Post* (The Federal Report) (November 8, 1984).

Stueart, Robert D. "Great Expectations: Library and Information Science Education at the Crossroads," *Library Journal*, 106 (October 1981): 1989–1992.

——— and Barbara B. Moran. *Library Management.* 3rd edition. Littleton, CO: Libraries Unlimited, 1987.

——— and George Miller, eds. *Collection Development in Libraries: A Treatise.* Greenwich, CT: JAI Press, 1980.

Subrumanyam, K. "Technical Literature," in *Encyclopedia of Library and Information Science*, volume 30. New York: Marcel Dekker, 1980, pp. 144–209.

Suchman, Edward A. "Action for What? A Critique of Evaluation Research," in *Evaluating Action Programs*, edited by Carol H. Weiss. Boston, MA: Allyn & Bacon, 1972, pp. 52–84.

Swanbeck, Jan. "Federal Documents in the Online Catalog: Problems, Options, and the Future," *Government Information Quarterly*, 2 (1985): 187–192.

Swisher, Robert and Charles R. McClure. *Research for Decision Making: Methods for Librarians.* Chicago, IL: American Library Association, 1984.

Tate, Michael L. "White Man Speaks with Forked Tongue: American Indian Discontent with Government Reports," in *Communicating Public Access to Government Information*, edited by Peter Hernon. Westport, CT: Meckler Publishing, 1983, pp. 93–107.

Taylor, Bernard and John R. Sparkes. *Corporate Strategy and Planning.* New York: Wiley, 1977.

Taylor, Robert S. *Value Added Processes in Information Systems.* Norwood, NJ: Ablex Pub. Corp., 1986.

Technology & U.S. Government Information Policies: Catalysts for New Partnerships. Washington, D.C.: Association of Research Libraries, 1987.

Ternberg, Milton G. "Regional Government Organizations and Their Publications," *Government Publications Review*, 9 (1982): 493–498.

"Transcript of Depository Library Council Meeting." Held at the Library of Congress, October 16, 1986 (unpublished GPO transcript).

Trauth, Ellen M. "Information Resources Management," in *Encyclopedia of Library and Information Science*, edited by Allan Kent, vol. 43. New York: Marcell Dekker, 1988, pp. 93–112.

Turner, Carol and Ann Latta. *Current Approaches to Improving Access to Government Documents.* OMS Occasional Paper. Washington, DC: Association of Research Libraries, Office of Management Studies, 1987.

Tyckoson, David A. "Appropriate Technologies for Government Information," *RQ*, 27 (Fall 1987): 33–38.

Unesco. *Guide to the Archives of International Organizations. Part I: The United Nations System.* Paris: Unesco, 1984.

United Nations. Budget Division. "Internal Memorandum to the Publications Board." New York, April 23, 1986 (Unpublished).

––––––. Dag Hammarskjöld Library. *Instructions for Depository Libraries Receiving United Nations Material.* New York, January 9, 1981 (ST/LIB/13/Rev. 4). *Corrigendum 2.* New York, March 7, 1986 (ST/LIB/13/Rev. 4/Corr.2).

––––––. Department of Conference Services. "United Nations Documentation," in *International Documents for the 80's: Their Role and Use*, edited by Theodore D. Dimitrov and Luciana Marulli-Koenig. Pleasantville, NY: UNIFO Publishers, 1982, microfiche 3, pp. 51–58.

––––––. ––––––. *United Nations Editoral Manual: A Compendium of Rules and Directives on United Nations Editorial Style, Publication Policies, Procedures and Practice.* New York, 1983 (ST/DCS/2; Sales No. E.83.I.16).

––––––. ––––––. *United Nations Editorial Manual, Revised Text of Articles A to D.* New York, March 5, 1985 (ST/DCS/5).

––––––. General Assembly. *Current Financial Crisis of the United Nations: Report of the Secretary-General.* New York, April 12, 1986a (A/40/1102). *Corrigendum.* New York, April 17, 1986a (A/40/1102/Corr. 2).

––––––. ––––––. "Report of the Group of High-level Intergovernmental Experts to Review the Efficiency of the Administrative and Financial Functioning of the United Nations." *Official Records*, 41st sess., Supplement no. 49. New York, 1986b (A/41/49).

––––––. Secretariat. *Administrative Instruction: The United Nations Archives.* New York, December 28, 1984 (ST/AI/326).

––––––. ––––––. *List of Depository Libraries Receiving United Nations Material.* New York, July 7, 1987 (ST/LIB/12/Rev. 7).

United States Code (Washington, D.C.: GPO).

The Urbana Municipal Documents Center Manual. Urbana, IL: Urbana Free Library, 1987.

Urquhart, Brian. *A Life in Peace and War.* New York: Harper & Row, 1987.

The U.S. Depository Library Inspection Visit Form. Washington, D.C.: GPO, n.d.

Van House, Nancy A., Mary Jo Lynch, Charles R. McClure, Douglas L. Zweizig, and Eleanor Jo Rodger. *Output Measures for Public Libraries.* 2nd edition. Chicago, IL: American Library Association, 1987.

––––––, Nancy K. Roderer, and Michael D. Cooper. "Librarians: A Study of the Supply and Demand," *American Libraries*, 14 (June 1983): 361–370.

Vernon, Christie. "Memorandum: Revision of ALA's Federal Legislative Policy," Washington D.C.: American Library Association, Washington Office, March 25, 1987 (unpublished).

Virally, Michel. "Definition and Classification of International Organizations: A Legal Approach," in *The Concept of International Organization*, edited by George Abi-Saab. Paris, Unesco, 1981, pp. 50–66.

Walbridge, Sharon. "OCLC and Government Documents Collections," *Government Publications Review*, 9 (1982): 277–288.

―――. "OCLC and Improved Access to Government Documents," *Illinois Libraries*, 68 (May 1986): 329–332.

Waldo, Michael. "An Historical Look at the Debate over How to Organize Federal Government Documents in Depository Libraries," *Government Publications Review*, 4 (1977): 319–329.

Wang, Amy and Diane M. Alimena. "Managing the Bell Laboratories Technical Report Service," *Science and Technology Libraries*, 1 (Summer 1981): 28–29.

"Washington Hotline," *College & Research Libraries News* (July/August 1987), pp. 409–410.

Watts, Carol. "The Depository Library Inspection Program," *Reference Services review*, 10 (Summer 1982): 55–62.

Weech, Terry L. "The Characteristics of State Government Publications, 1910–1969," *Government Publications Review*, 1 (1973): 29–52.

―――. "Collection Development and State Publications," *Government Publications Review*, 8A (1981): 47–58.

―――. "New Technology and State Government Information Sources," in *New Technology and Documents Librarianship*, edited by Peter Hernon. Westport, CT: Meckler Publishing, 1983a, pp. 77–87.

―――, ed. "State Government Information Sources," *Government Publications Review*, 10 (1983b): 155–219.

Welch, Thomas L. "The Organization of American States and Its Documentation Dissemination," *Revista Interamericana de Bibliografia*, 32 (1982): 200–206.

Westin, Alan F., Heather A. Schweder, Michael A. Baker, and Sheila Lehman. *Changing Workplace: A Guide to Managing the People, Organizational and Regulatory Aspects of Office Automation*. White Plains, NY: Knowledge Industry Publications, 1985.

White, Marilyn D. "The Communications Behavior of Academic Economists in Research Phases," *Library Quarterly*, 45 (1975): 337–354.

Woorster, Harold. "Historical Note: Shining Palaces, Shifting Sands: National Information Systems," *Journal of the American Society for Information Science*, 38 (September 1987): 321–335.

Wren, Daniel A. *The Evolution of Management Thought*. New York: Ronald Press, 1972.

Yearbook of International Organizations. 1st-ed., 1948– . Brussels: Union of International Associations.

Youngren, Ralph P. "Meeting Library Space Needs," 1976 (ERIC, ED 129 210).

Zaltman, Gerald and Robert Duncan. *Strategies for Planned Change*. New York: Wiley, 1977.

Zink, Steven D. *Government Publications Catalogs*. 2nd ed. Washington, DC: Special Libraries Association, 1988.

―――. "'Non-Depository' or Not: An Examination of the Designation of Non-Depository Titles in the *Monthly Catalog of United States Government Publications*," *College & Research Libraries*, 44 (March 1983): 178–181.

Zipf, G.D. *Human Behavior and the Principle of Least Effort*. Cambridge, MA: Addison-Wesley, 1949

Zlatich, Marko. "Publications and Documentation Systems of the World Bank, the International Development Association and the International Finance Corporation," in *International Documents for the 80's: Their Role and Use*, edited by Theodore D. Dimitrov and Luciana Marulli-Koenig. Pleasantville, NY: UNIFO Publishers, 1982, microfiche 3, pp. 73–76.

Zweizig, Douglas and Brenda Dervin. "Public Library Use, Users, Uses," in *Advances in Librarianship*, volume 7, edited by Melvin J. Voigt and Michael H. Harris. New York: Academic Press, 1977, pp. 231–255.

Zwirn, Jerrold. *Congressional Publications: A Research Guide to Legislation, Budgets, and Treaties*. Littleton, CO: Libraries Unlimited, 1983.

Author Index

A

Akoka, J., 246, *489*
Alimena, D.M., 208, *506*
Allen, T.J., 302, *489*
Aluri, R., 92, *489*
Amodeo, A.J., 287, *489*
Archer, C., 412, *489*
Argyris, C., 234, *489*
Armstrong, A., 18, *489*
Atkinson, R., 426, 427, 429, *490*
Auger, C.P., 210, 217, *490*

B

Bair, R.R., 470, *490*
Baker, M.A., 288, *506*
Ballard, S., 225, *490*
Basefsky, S.M., 105, *490*
Baughman, J.C., 3, 117, *490*
Becker, J., 6, *490*
Birdsall, D., 78, *490*
Blair, R.R., *490*
Blake, F., *497*
Bommer, M.R., 246, *490*
Boss, R.W., 245, 268, 276, 288, 292, 295, 296, 462, *490*
Bower, C., 141, 162, *490*
Bowerman, R., 141, 163, *490*
Boyd, A., 211, *490*
Boylan, N., 220, *490*

Bracken, D., 213, 227, *491*
Bradford, S.C., *490*
Bregent, A., 23
Britton, H.H., 307, *500*
Brooks, J., 301, *493*
Brown, E.W., 92, *490*
Brown, J.O., *490*
Buckland, M.K., 3, 120, *490*
Butler, P., *491*

C

Cady, S.A., 141, *490*
Cammann, C., 334, *497*
Caponio, J.F., 380, *491*
Caponio, J.P., 80, 213, 227, *498*
Carpenter, E.J., 427, *491*
Carroll, B., 80, *491*
Casadio, F.A., 434, *491*
Case, D., 147, 163, *491*
Castonguay, R., 393, 395, 400, 402, *491*
Chartrand, R.L., 27, 42, *491*
Chelton, M.K., *497*
Chen, C.C., 55, 181, *491*
Cherns, J.J., 179, 413, 417, 434, *491*
Childers, T., 170, *491*
Chorba, R.W., 246, *490*
Churchman, C.W., 373, *491*
Clews, J., 425, *491*
Cline, N.M., 188, 191, 195, *491*

Cohen, A., 278, 282, 287, 288, *492*
Cohen, E., 276, 278, 282, 287, 288, *492*
Conrad, E.P., 141, 164
Conroy, B., 268, 460, *492*
Cook, K.L., 240, 258, *492*
Cooper, M.D., *506*
Copeland, S., 219, 220, *492*
Corbin, J., 144, *492*
Cox, J.R., 19, 144, 163, 356, 357
Coyne, J.G., 201, 221, 222, *492*

D
Daehn, R.M., 286, *492*
Davis, L.N., 460, *492*
DeGennaro, R., 160, *492*
D'Elia, G., 177, *492*
Dervin, B., 363, 364, 507
Dimitrov, T.D., 425, *493*
Dizard, W.P., 49, *493*
Dougherty, R.M., 236, *493*
Dowlin, K.E., 485, *493*
Draper, J., 301, *493*
Duncan, R., 472, 476, *506*
Durrance, J., 395, 406, *493*

E
Eastin, R.B., 307, *503*
Edsall, M.S., 271, *493*
Eisenberg, M., *493*
Ernest, W.B., Jr., 402, *500*
Evans, F.B., *493*
Evans, G.E., 114, 136, 440, *493*

F
Faull, S.K., 23, 339, 340, 351, *493*
Ferragamo, R.C., 289, 297, *494*
Fine, S., 159, *493*
Folcarelli, R.J., 289, 297, *494*
Ford, B., 406, 407, *494*
Fox, B.L., 222, 270, *500*
Freeman, H.E., 329, 479, *503*
Frisch, C.W., 15, 309, 369, *502*
Fry, B.M., 2, 16, 58, 76, 202, 275, 376, 377, *494*
Futas, E., 132, *494*

G
Galitz, W.O., 289, *494*
Garay, R., 91, *494*
Geffner, J., 380, *491*
Gerstberger, P.G., 302, *489*

Gillham, V., 163, 309, 313, *494*
Gilligan, J., 108, *494*
Godden, I.P., 306, *494*
Goodell, J.S., 285, *494*
Gray, D.E., 223, *494*

H
Hahn, E.Z., 96, *494*
Hahn, H., 306, *494*
Hajdas, S., 108, 416, *494*
Hajnal, P.I., 431, 436, 438, 440, *494*
Hall, C.M., 15, 309, 369, *502*
Hall, H.W., 359, *495*
Hall, R.B., 285, *495*
Hardt, E., 424, 434, *495*
Harleston, R.M., 306, *495*
Hartz, M.J., 470, *495*
Heim, K.M., 103, 148, *495*
Heindel, A.J., 246, *495*
Heinritz, F.J., 236, *493*
Henderson, M.M., 208, *495*
Hernon, P., 4, 9, 10, 11, 13, 14, 17, 18, 19, 23, 25, 28, 30, 55, 61, 68, 71, 73, 76, 77, 78, 81, 86, 94, 96, 101, 107, 109, 112, 114, 117, 120, 121, 122, 131, 135, 139, 140, 142, 143, 154, 159, 163, 165, 166, 168, 169, 170, 171, 175, 178, 179, 181, 182, 191, 199, 202, 208, 219, 220, 222, 224, 229, 250, 257, 258, 273, 286, 288, 301, 307, 312, 316, 331, 335, 338, 339, 341, 357, 358, 360, 362, 367, 377, 379, 387, 393, 400, 402, 406, 427, 451, 453, 456, 462, 464, 467, 468, 471, 481, 482, *491*, *495*, *499*
Hitt, M.A., 231, *496*
Hoduski, B.E.A., 227, 474, *496*
Hoffman, A., 117, *490*
Holmes, D.C., 300, *496*
Hopkins, M., 428, 439, *496*
Horton, F.W., Jr., 56, 68, *496*
Houle, C.O., 449, *496*
Huls, M.E., 90, *496*

J
Jackson, E., *496*
Jackson, J.H., 244, 307, *499*
Jacque, S., 425, *496*
Janis, I.L., 236, *496*
Jeffries, J., 433, *496*
Johansson, E., 415, *496*

Johnson, E.R., 238, *496*
Johnston, D.S., 141, 164
Jones, C.H., 289, *497*
Josey, E.J., *497*

K

Kadec, S.T., 20, 40, 104, 163, *496*
Karp, W., 56, 57, *497*
Kaser, D., 74, *497*
Kaske, N., 236, *493*
Kast, F.E., 229, 231, 234, 255, 264, *497*
Kesner, R.M., 289, *497*
Klinefelter, P.M., 222, *500*
Knenlein, D.R., 57, *497*
Koontz, H., 234, *497*
Kopec, K., 320, 394, 399, 402, *500*
Kotler, P., 175, 176, 270
Kresslein, J.C., 404, *497*
Kroll, R.H., 245, *497*
Krueger, K., 351, 352, 354, *497*

L

Lancaster, F.W., 120, 150, 151, 265, 276, 316, *497*
Lane, M.T., 320, 394, 398, 401, 403, 404, *497*
Larson, D.R., 87, *497*
Lastenouse, J., 437, *497*
Latta, A., 272, 350, *505*
Lawler III, E., 334, *497*
Leavitt, E.P., 18, *498*
Lehman, S., 288, *506*
Leighton, P.D., 282, 292, *498*
Levin, M.A., 75, *498*
Levitan, K.B., *498*
Lewy, C.W., 394, 397, *498*
Luguire, W., 159, *498*
Lunin, L., 80, *498*
Lushington, N., 282, *498*
Luthans, F., 234, 256, *498*
Lynch, M.J., 328, 336, 346, 464, 479, *499*, *505*

M

MacDonald, S.H., 188, *498*
Malinconcio, S.M., *497*
Mann, L., 236, *496*
Marchand, D.A., 404, *497*
Marchant, M.D., 325, *498*
Martin, M.S., 238, *498*
Marulli-Koenig (Marulli), L., 13, 415, 425–426, 435, *493*, *498*

Maskewitz, B.F., 80, *491*
Mason, M.G., 26, *498*
Matheny, B., 215, *498*
Mathias, R.L., *499*
Mathis, R.L., 231, 244, *496*
Matthews, J.R., 144, *498*, *499*
McClure, C.R., 4, 9, 10, 11, 13, 14, 16, 18, 19, 23, 25, 28, 30, 49, 50, 61, 68, 71, 73, 76, 77, 78, 81, 87, 94, 107, 109, 129, 139, 140, 143, 146, 154, 159, 163, 166, 168, 169, 170, 171, 179, 189, 202, 208, 212, 215, 216, 219, 220, 222, 224, 225, 227, 229, 235, 246, 247, 250, 257, 258, 266, 288, 312, 318, 328, 331, 335, 336, 338, 341, 343, 346, 357, 358, 360, 362, 367, 377, 387, 451, 453, 456, 462, 464, 467, 468, 471, 479, 481, 482, *495*, *499*, *504*, *505*
McCauley, E.V., 222, *500*
McC. Mathias, C., Jr., 5, *499*
McKean, J.M., 150, *499*
Merritt, L.C., 82, *499*
Middlemist, R.D., 231, *496*
Miller, G., *504*
Miller, S.J., 9, 427, *500*
Mills, W.N., Jr., 282, *498*
Molholm, K.N., 222, *500*
Moody, M., 226, *500*
Mooney, M.T., 118, 163, *500*
Moran, B.B., 231, *504*
Morehead, J., 73, 308, 376, *500*
Morton, B., 19, 144, 163, 251, 313, 356, 357, *500*
Murphy, C.E., 109, 142, 202, *500*
Myers, J.E., 105, 163, 307, 310, 317, *500*

N

Nadler, D.A., 326, *500*
Nadler, D.N., 334, *497*
Naisbitt, J., 483, *500*
Nakata, Y., 320, 394, 399, 402, 406, 407, *494*, *500*
Napier, H.A., 246, *495*
North, G.W., 89, *501*

O

O'Brien, C.C., 428, *501*
O'Donnell, C., 234, *497*
Orr, R.H., 337, *501*
Owen, A., 328, 347, 404, 479, *499*, *501*

P

Paris, M., 459, 501
Parish, D.W., 501
Plaunt, J.R., 164, 319, 501
Pope, N.F., 148, 164, 359, 501
Porat, M., 32, 501
Powell, B.E., 376, 501
Powell, H., 187, 501
Powell, M.S., 141, 164, 501
Prentice, A.E., 238, 242, 501
Pullen, W.R., 376, 501
Purcell, G.R., 9, 11, 14, 17, 73, 94, 107,
    114, 117, 120, 121, 122, 124, 131,
    135, 140, 143, 145, 146, 154, 164,
    171, 175, 199, 202, 208, 211, 219,
    220, 222, 224, 229, 250, 258, 312,
    319, 338, 339, 341, 362, 367, 387,
    406, 407, 408, 427, 453, 456, 495,
    496, 499, 502, 504

R

Raikes, D., 245, 268, 292, 462, 490
Rambler, L., 117, 490
Randolph, S., 58, 502
Rawski, C., 1, 502
Ray, J.M., 470, 495
Redmond, M., 502
Reeder, R.S., 70, 502
Relyea, H.C., 42, 502
Reynolds, C.J., 172, 271, 286, 302, 502
Richardson, J.V., Jr., 15, 83, 178, 182, 273,
    309, 369, 496, 502
Riggs, D.E., 343, 502
Rips, R.E., 83, 211, 490, 502
Roberts, L.J., 285, 502
Robinson, J.S., 83, 489
Robinson, W.C., 58, 124, 427, 502
Roderer, N.K., 506
Rodger, E.J., 336, 347, 464, 505
Rosenfield, H.N., 102, 503
Rosenzweig, J.E., 229, 231, 234, 255, 264,
    497
Rosselle, W.C., 289, 503
Rossi, P.H., 329, 479, 503
Rothschild, M.C., 80, 503
Russell, J.C., 18, 149, 489, 503

S

Sachse, G., 306, 307, 503
Saffady, W., 144, 187, 295, 308, 503
Samuels, A.R., 235, 474, 503
Sarndal, A.G., 242, 503

Saville, M., 18, 503
Schlipf, F.A., 490
Schlueter, L.A., 470, 495
Schmeckebier, L.F., 307, 503
Schnapper, M.B., 102, 503
Schwarzkopf, L.C., 1, 12, 171, 187, 362,
    368, 503
Schweder, H.A., 288, 506
Schweizer, S., 96, 146, 503
Shannon, M.O., 393, 400, 402, 503
Shaw, A., 190, 504
Shepherd, C.A., 17, 120, 495
Sieger, C.F., Jr., 188, 498
Simonton, W., 14, 504
Smith, D.H., 239, 504
Smith, K.F., 164, 173, 504
Smith, R.S., 208, 504
Smith, S.J., 402, 500
Soper, M.E., 167, 504
Sparkes, J.R., 343, 505
Sprehe, J.T., 34, 69, 75, 504
Stephenson, M.S., 145, 146, 164, 250, 319,
    504
Stoffle, C.J., 306, 495
Stone, A.A., 58, 502
Strain, P.M., 283, 504
Struck, M., 81, 504
Stueart, R.D., 231, 427, 450, 451, 504
Subrumanyam, K., 211, 213, 504
Suchman, E.A., 329, 504
Sullivan, P., 497
Swanbeck, J., 164, 319, 504
Swartz, R., 497
Swisher, R., 504

T

Tannenbaum, A.C., 289, 297, 494
Tate, M.L., 90, 504
Taylor, B., 343, 505
Taylor, R.S., 37, 360, 505
Ternberg, M.G., 396, 398, 505
Thompson, W.M., 222, 500
Topolski, F., 428, 501
Torrey, B.B., 470, 490
Trauth, E.M., 254, 505
Turner, C., 272, 350, 505
Tushman, M.L., 326, 500
Tyckoson, D.A., 76, 164, 505

U

Ungarelli, D., 117, 490
Urquhart, B., 418, 505

V

Van House, N.A., 328, 336, 346, 464, 479, 499, 505, 506
Varnet, H., 117, 490
Vernon, C., 111, 506
Virally, M., 412, 506

W

Walbridge, S., 140, 164, 311, 506
Waldo, M., 316, 506
Wang, A., 208, 506
Watts, C., 9, 23, 331, 506
Weber, D.C., 282, 292, 498
Weech, T.L., 393, 394, 403, 506
Welch, T.L., 428, 437, 506
Westin, A.F., 288, 506

White, M.D., 50, 506
Williams, K., 493
Woorster, H., 48, 506
Wren, D.A., 234, 506

Y

Youngren, R.P., 291, 506

Z

Zaltman, G., 472, 476, 506
Zink, S.D., 106, 506
Zipf, G.D., 276, 506
Zlatich, M., 436, 506
Zweizig, D.L., 328, 336, 346, 363, 364, 464, 479, 499, 505, 507
Zwirn, J., 90, 507

Subject Index

A

Academic Library Use of NTIS, 174, 312, 463

ACCIS Guide to United Nations Information Sources on Food and Agriculture, 424

Acquisitions, see Collection development

Ad Hoc Advisory Committee on Revision of Title 44, 73

Administration of documents collections, 182, 184, 204–206, 229–254, 460; see also Budgeting

Administrative integration, see Collection integration

Administrative Notes (GPO), 466

Advanced Technology/Libraries, 139

Advisory Committee for Aeronautics, 221

Advisory Committee for the Co-ordination of Information Systems, 424, 426

AGRIS, 425

American Libraries, 464

American Library Association, 61, 63, 105, 111–112, 190, 204, 398, 429, 438, 459, 464

American Statistics Index, 86–87, 121, 124, 132, 199, 257, 267, 314

The American University, 88

Anglo-American Cataloging Rules (AACR), 104, 265, 311, 307, 312–313

Annual Review of Information Science and Technology, 139

ANSI Standards, 36, 95, 195, 301

"The Archival Stability of Microfilm," 191

Armed Services Technical Information Agency, 222

Assignment Children, 419

Association of Research Libraries (ARL), 63, 182, 272, 320, 359, 485, 486

Atomic Energy Review, 419

Attorney-General (U.S.), 88

Audiovisual resources, 14, 84–85, 89–90, 93, 95

Auto-Graphics Inc., 16, 110, 143

Automated systems, 139, 143, 146, 237, 258, 308–309, 313, 318–319, 356–357, 460; see also Technology; and Decision support systems

B

Baker and Taylor, 308

Ball State University, 118–119

Bibliographic accessibility, see Bibliographic control; and Documents accessibility

Bibliographic control, 13–16, 21–22, 29, 31, 34–35, 73, 99–113, 138, 160–161, 186, 194–195, 204, 206, 218–219, 225, 229, 231–232, 245, 265, 267, 272–273, 291, 308, 312–313, 322,

514

350–351, 363, 368–369, 373, 392–
394, 397–400, 408–410, 423–426,
436, 438–439, 441–442, 455–456,
462, 480
definition, 13, 99
Bibliographic instruction, *see* Outreach
programs
Bibliographic Retrieval System (BRS), 220–
221, 313
Bibliography of Publications on Unesco,
428–429
*Bibliography of Scientific and Industrial Re-
ports*, 211
A Bibliography of State Bibliographies, 397
Biennial Report of Depository Libraries, 188
Biennial Survey (GPO), 188, 309–310, 338,
341, 362
Boston Athenaeum, 368
Bradford's law of scattering, 120
Branch Office Deposit Report, 149
Brodart Library Automation Division, 16,
143
Browsing, 21, 109, 111, 167, 200, 257, 406–
407
BRS Information Technologies, 313
Budgeting, 229, 231, 237–244, 251, 260,
268
Bureau of Indian Affairs (U.S.), 90
Bureau of Labor Statistics (U.S.), 65, 82,
86, 96
Bureau of the Census (U.S.), 35, 37, 65, 82,
86, 88, 96, 121, 147–149, 186, 199,
201, 366, 452, 470
Business Periodicals Index, 256
Bulletin on Narcotics, 419

C
*Calendars of the United States House of
Representatives and History of Legis-
lation*, 82
California, 400
Card catalog, 123, 167, 265, 306, 315–316
Carleton College, 144–145, 251, 313, 356
Cataloging and classification, 103–106, 223–
224, 305, 307, 315–316, 319–321,
395, 404, 460; *see also* Anglo-Ameri-
can Cataloging Rules; and SuDocs
classification system
Catalogue, Part A . . . , 425, 437
Catalogue, Part B: Documents . . . , 415,
424–425

*Catálogo de Informes y Documentos Tcnicos
de la OEA*, 424
Catalogue of Publications in Print, 438
Catalogue of Publications on Sale, 425, 438
Catalogue of United Nations Publications,
424, 438
CD-ROM, 63, 105, 107, 143, 148–149, 158,
161, 173, 221, 266, 358, 434, 440,
442
CENDATA, 148
CENDI, 222, 225
Center for Research Libraries, 348, 393, 401
Center for the Utilization of Federal Tech-
nology, 220
Central Intelligence Agency (U.S.), 71, 89,
102, 199, 201
Certification, 467–468
Change agent, 466, 471–476
Chemical Abstracts, 8
Chronicle of Higher Education, 465
*A Chronology and Fact Book of the United
Nations*, 429
CIS "Documents on Demand," 199
CIS Index, 199, 257, 314
*A Citizen's Guide on Using the Freedom of
Information Act and the Privacy Act
of 1974 to Request Government Rec-
ords*, 72
Classified information, 31, 41–43, 71–72,
213, 227
Clearinghouse for Federal Scientific and
Technical Information (U.S.), 219
Clearinghouses, 80–81, 96, 99, 102, 214,
216–217, 219, 223, 225–226
CLSI, 308
Code of Federal Regulations, 62, 76, 82, 89,
188
CODOC, 313–314, 320
Collection arrangement, 19, 167, 183, 223–
224
Collection development, 16–17, 73, 101–
136, 161, 186, 196–200, 205–206,
217, 229, 250, 272, 337, 339, 342,
350–352, 354, 357, 380, 392–393,
395, 397, 400–403, 406, 409, 426–
439, 443, 456, 460–461, 465, 467,
479
Collection evaluation, *see* Collection
development
Collection integration, 124–130, 134–136,
160, 202, 204, 240, 245, 255–275

College of Wooster Library, 141
Commerce Business Daily, 62
Commission of the European Communities, 424
Commission on Federal Paperwork (U.S.), 70
Commission on Privatization (U.S.), 71
Committee on Scientific and Technical Information (COSATI), 214–215
Community analysis, *see* Collection development
Compilation of Presidential Documents, 62
The Complete Guide to Citing Government Documents, 105
Computer Output Microform (COM), *see* Microforms
Computerized documentation system, 425
Congress, 5, 27, 31, 39–40, 42–43, 55, 57, 72–73, 75, 78, 81–82, 84–85, 88–91, 199, 205, 222, 388–389, 470
Congressional Directory, 62, 87, 117
Congressional Information Service, 35, 100, 121, 149, 291, 398, 430
Congressional Record, 17, 59–60, 62, 76, 88, 91–92, 197, 199, 201
Congressional Research Service (U.S.), 78
Consumer Information Center, 60, 80–81
Continuing education, 184, 268, 318, 374, 453, 459–462, 481
Control Data Corp., 405
Cooperation, *see* Resource sharing
Coopers and Lybrand, 191
Copyright, 30, 43
Copyright, 419
Cultures, 419
Current Awareness Bibliography, 222
Current Index to Journals in Education, 221

D
Dag Hammerskjöld Library, 377
Daily shipping lists (GPO), 309
DATATRIEVE, 144
dBASE, 118, 250
Decision making, 229–230, 235–237, 244, 251, 253–254, 268–269, 275, 328, 333, 456
Decision support systems, 196, 230–231, 246–251, 313–315, 319, 461; *see also* Management information systems
DEIN, 431
DESI Electronic Information Network, 431
Defense Technical Information Center (U.S.), 92, 222

Deficit Reduction Act (1984), 67, 94
Department of Agriculture (U.S.), 65, 86, 88, 89, 96, 146
Department of Commerce (U.S.), 89, 226
Department of Defense (U.S.), 56–57, 65, 82, 88–89
Department of Education (U.S.), 221
Department of Energy (U.S.), 37, 39, 62, 199, 201, 215, 220–222, 291, 379
Department of Health, Education and Welfare (U.S.), 187
Department of Health and Human Services (U.S.), 65, 79
Department of Housing and Urban Development (U.S.), 89
Department of Interior (U.S.), 8–9, 79, 89
Department of State (U.S.), 8, 96
Department of State Bulletin, 87
Department of Transportation (U.S.), 89
Department of Treasury (U.S.), 65
Depository Library Act (1962), 1, 5, 9–10, 40, 485
Depository Library Council to the Public Printer, 12, 105, 117, 190–192, 205, 325, 339, 341, 374, 466, 476
Depository library inspection program (GPO), 179, 303–304, 341–343, 368, 466
DIALOG, 37, 123, 148, 220–221, 314, 360, 433, 452, 485
Le Diffuseur G. Vermette, 434
Direction of Trade, 419
A Directory of Computer Software, 147
Directory of Computerized Data Files, 147
Directory of Report Series Codes, 218
Directory of United Nations Databases and Information Systems, 424
Disarmament: A Periodic Review, 419
Document delivery systems, 101, 112, 116, 349–350, 356, 362–363, 365, 375, 401, 407, 410
Documents Expediting Project (LC), 106
"The Documents on Documents Collection," 394
Documents Pricing Task Force, 60–61
Documents to the People, 438, 465
DROLS, 222

E
ECHO, 433
Economic Report of the President, 121

Economic and Social Survey of Asia and the Pacific, 419
Economic Bulletin for Europe, 428
Economic Outlook, 429
Economics and Statistics Service (U.S.), 86
EDC/Dep Bulletin, 438
Education for librarianship, 439–440, 449–468; *see also* Continuing education; Library schools; and Personnel development
Education Resources Information Center, 6, 14, 38, 80–81, 85, 92, 107, 158, 186–187, 199, 221–222, 291, 295, 314, 379
Electronic Collection and Dissemination of Information by Federal Agencies, 151
The Encyclopedia of the United Nations and International Agreements, 429
Energy Abstracts for Policy Analysis, 222
Energy Research Abstracts, 220–221
Energy Research and Development Administration (U.S.), 221
ESA-IRS, 433
Euratom, 437
European Atomic Energy Community, 437
European Coal and Steel Community, 437
European Economic Community, 437
European Communities, 415, 417, 425–426, 428, 433–434, 437–438
Evaluation, 23–24, 124, 128, 178, 185, 230–231, 245, 266–267, 274, 303–304, 323–347, 362, 366–367, 379, 460, 478–479; *see also* Depository library inspection program (GPO)
Everyman's United Nations, 429
Everyone's United Nations, 429
Executive Order 13414, "Facilitating Access to Science and Technology," 39

F
Facsimile transmission, 150
Family Educational Rights and Privacy Act (1974), 75
The Federal Advisory Committee Act (1972), 75
Federal Bureau of Investigation (U.S.), 56
The Federal Data Base Finder, 148
Federal Depository Library Manual, 115, 118, 306
Federal Employee Direct Corporate Stock Option Plan (FED CO-OP), 226

Federal Energy Administration (U.S.), 221
Federal Information Centers (U.S.), 57, 81, 170, 385
Federal Information Policies in the 1980s, 76
The Federal Home Loan Bank Board (U.S.), 149
Federal Information Processing Standards, 36
Federal Power Commission (U.S.), 221
Federal Probation, 120
Federal Register, 59, 60, 72, 76, 82, 87, 89, 120, 199, 201, 301
"Federal Research in Progress," 220
Federal Software Center, 220
The Federal Software Exchange Catalog, 148
Federal Technology Transfer Act (1986), 39
Fifty-Five Percent Rule, 169–171, 257, 468
Final Report of the Technical Panel on Database Access, 433
Finance and Development, 419
Finding the Law, 79
Food and Agriculture Organization, 413, 416, 436
Food and Nutrition, 419
Food Stamp Program (U.S.), 88
Freedom and Equality of Access to Information, 459
Freedom of Information Act (1966), 7–8, 27, 40–44, 47, 57, 71–72, 75, 484
Freedom of Information Reform Act (1986), 72

G
GATT, 436
Gene Essman and Associates, 149
General Accounting Office (U.S.), 61, 88, 190, 199, 290–291
General Services Administration (U.S.), 57, 80–82
Geological Survey (U.S.), 39, 96, 210, 366
Glimpse Corp., 148
Glossary of Information Handling, 210
Goals, 1–2, 12–13, 178, 229, 232, 235–236, 240, 242, 252, 254, 266, 273, 278, 325, 328–329, 336, 340, 343, 365–367, 373, 382, 384, 390, 453, 479
Government Depository Libraries, 1
Government Documents Round Table, *see* American Library Association
The Government in the Sunshine Act (1976), 75

Government information, *see* Government publications/information
Government Information Agency Act (H.R. 1615), 39, 73, 380, 382
Government Information Quarterly, 43, 86, 226, 439
Government Printing Office (U.S.), 7, 9–10, 12, 17, 20, 24–27, 29, 33, 35, 37–40, 55, 58–63, 67, 72–74, 79, 83, 85, 87–88, 93–97, 100, 102–107, 110, 115, 117–118, 120, 124, 140–141, 149–150, 166–168, 170–181, 184, 186–206, 208, 219, 222–223, 249, 272, 290–291, 295, 301, 303, 308–309, 311, 314–322, 325, 330–333, 335, 338–343, 346, 349–350, 352, 356, 365–390, 398, 402, 449, 451, 453, 456, 459, 462–463, 466, 467, 470–471, 485–486
Government Publications, 424
Government publications/information
    definition, 3–5
    formats, 93–97, 100; *see also* Microforms; Audiovisual resources; and Machine-readable data files and magnetic tapes
    functions, 82–83
    mainstreaming, 469–487
    types, 83–93
Government Publications Review, 394, 438
Government Reports Announcements & Index, 88, 105, 107, 143, 168, 202, 220, 222, 257, 312
GPO tapes, *see* MARC tapes
Gramm-Rudman-Hollings Act (1985), 58
Green Thumb, 147
"Group of 18" (UN), 416
Guelph Document System, 309, 313; *see also* CODOC
Guide to United Nations Organization, Documentation and Publishing, 429
Guidelines for Collection Development, 429
Guidelines for the Depository Library System (GPO), 1, 12–13, 154, 303, 331–333, 339–340, 352, 354
Guidelines for Minimizing State Servicing of State Documents, 398
Guidelines for State Documents Checklists, 398
Guidelines for Inputting State Documents into Data Bases, 398

Guidelines for State Publications Depository Legislation, 398
Guidelines for State Distribution Center Activities, 398

H
Half-Life, 120
Her Majesty's Stationery Office, 179
Historical Statistics of the United States, 86

I
ICAO Bulletin, 419
Illinois, 351, 406
Index of OECD Documents and Publications, 424
Index of Publications, 424, 438
Index to Current Urban Documents, 399–400, 402, 405
Index to International Statistics, 430
Index to U.S. Government Periodicals, 87, 257
Indexing, 104–109, 112, 201–202, 209, 405; *see also* Bibliographic control
Information Access Co., 16, 143
Information analysis centers, 80–81
Information dissemination, 22, 26, 29, 31, 39, 56, 68, 70–71, 97, 184, 410
Information gathering patterns, *see* Information needs
Information handling technologies, *see* Technology
Information Industry Association, 34, 189, 205
Information life-cycle, 68, 75, 250, 361
Information needs, 11, 20, 24, 28–29, 40, 98, 100, 107, 123, 132, 166–168, 176, 180, 200, 229, 366, 385–386, 403, 408–409, 455–456, 460, 462, 471, 487
Information policy, 25–77, 184, 207, 225–228, 361, 455, 457, 459, 470, 477, 486; *see also* National information policy
    definition, 26
    STI, 29, 48, 52; *see also* Technical report literature
    typology, 28–43
Information producers and distributors, 79–82, 93–95; *see also* Technical report literature

Information resources management, 27, 52, 56, 63–64, 70–71, 254, 404; see also OMB Circular A-130
Information Technology and Libraries, 139
INIS, 425
INIS Atomindex, 222
INMAGIC, 250, 319
INS v. Chadha (1983), 40, 81–82
Instructions to Depository Libraries, 341
Integration, see Collection integration
Interlibrary loan, see Resource sharing
Internal Revenue Service (U.S.), 7–8, 67, 96, 146
International Atomic Energy Agency, 222
International Bibliography: Publications of Intergovernmental Organizations, 424, 438
International Court of Justice, 436
International Digest of Health Legislation, 419
International Exchange Program, 350–351
International Federation of Library Associations and Institutions (IFLA), 415, 425
International Government Organizations, 411–448
    characteristics, 412
    depository libraries, 425, 435–437, 440–441
    documents and publications, 412–423
    electronic distribution, 441
International Labour Organisation, 413, 416
International Labour Review, 419, 439
International Monetary Fund, 416, 437
International Organisations Publications, 424
International Social Science Journal, 419
Internship, 462
Interstate Commerce Commission (U.S.), 88
I.P. Sharp, 433
Item numbers, 14, 18, 117–118, 134, 141, 192, 195, 273

J
Johns Hopkins University Press, 428, 435
Joint Committee on Printing (U.S. Congress), 4–5, 20, 26, 29, 33, 58, 61,–63, 68, 73, 81–82, 102, 166, 187–189, 204, 303, 332, 356, 369, 380, 387–388, 456

Journal of Academic Librarianship, 168
Judiciary, 84–85

L
Lacey Report, 137
League of Nations, 430
League of Women Voters, 406
"Le Pac," 143, 168
"Less Access to Less Information by and about the U.S. Government," 61
Libraries
    budget, 10
    depositories for international government organizations, 425, 435–437, 440–441
    depositories for local government, 393, 395, 400, 402
    depositories for state government, 394, 397, 399, 401, 404, 409
    depository designation (law and congressional), 10
    depository program goals, 1–2, 12–13
    depository program history, 8–9
    electronic collection and dissemination of government information, 2, 5, 19–20, 23, 26, 29, 40–41, 43–48, 62–63, 76, 152–154, 194, 359–361, 387–388, 441
    general, 28, 30–31, 55, 73–74, 76–77, 90–91, 94–95, 106, 108, 111–112, 114, 117, 122–123, 137, 143, 150–152, 155, 162, 167, 169–175, 177, 181, 184–206, 226, 230, 258, 267, 303, 305–390, 392, 395, 404–409, 450, 452, 455–456, 462, 464–466
Library Human Resources, 464
Library Journal, 465
Library of Congress, 6, 9, 78, 91, 96, 103–104, 140–141, 186, 308, 310–311, 317, 350–351, 367, 376, 382, 393–394
Library Program Services (GPO), 40, 104, 107, 191
Library schools, 439–440, 450, 452–459
Library Services and Construction Act, 349
Library Technology Reports, 139, 296
Local government, 391–406, 409–410, 454
    types of publications, 397
Local Government Information Network (LOGIN), 405
Lousiana State University, 105
LSSI, 16, 143

M

Machine-readable databases and magnetic tapes, 61–62, 68, 76, 93, 95, 103, 105, 147–149, 150, 267, 303, 358–360, 424–425, 427, 431, 433–434, 441–442, 460; *see also* Technology

Macrothesaurus for Information Processing in the Field of Economic and Social Development, 428, 430

Maggie's Place, 485

Management information systems, 19, 145, 231, 247

MARC tapes, 103, 108, 139–140, 272, 310–311, 313, 315, 317, 321, 350, 469

Marcive, Inc., 105–106, 141, 315

Marketing, 23–24, 30, 35, 59–60, 155, 167, 175–183, 269–271, 274, 380, 435

Marketing Moves, 80, 180

Mead Data Central, 221

MEDLARS, 35

Michigan, 340

Microcomputers, 81, 96, 118, 139, 140, 145–147, 150–151, 251, 273, 287–289, 314–315, 358–359, 403, 427, 460–461, 485

Microcomputers for Information Management, 139

Microcomputers for Library Decision Making, 481

Microforms, 2, 10–11, 15–17, 21, 57, 59, 65, 90, 93, 95, 103, 105–107, 111, 121, 131, 141, 149–150, 162, 186–206, 213, 217, 223, 242, 244, 257, 265, 277, 282, 286, 289–303, 308, 310, 314, 316, 318–319, 349, 383, 386, 393–394, 401, 403, 405, 427, 434, 440–441, 460

Micropublishing Advisory Committee, 187

Micropublishing Council (GPO), 190–191

Mimeographed and Printed Documents, 431

Minimum Standards for the Depository Library System, 12–13; *see also* Standards

Mission to South Africa, 428

Monthly Catalog, 14–16, 21, 35, 59, 62, 82–83, 87–88, 101–111, 117, 122, 124, 140, 143, 168, 173, 179, 188, 200–201, 222, 257, 266, 306, 308, 310, 312, 314, 316–317, 320–321, 352, 357–358, 383

Monthly Checklist of State Publications, 393, 398

Monthly Labor Review, 17, 87, 120, 265

Municipal reference libraries, 393, 400

N

Name Authority Cooperative Project, 311

National Aeronautics and Space Administration (U.S.), 82, 92, 220–221, 291, 367

National Archives and Records Administration (U.S.), 9, 81, 90, 186, 191, 352, 377

National Archives and Records Service, *see* National Archives and Records Administration (U.S.)

National Audiovisual Center (U.S.), 90

National Center for Health Statistics (U.S.), 86

National Commission on Libraries and Information Science (U.S.), 27

National information policy, 27, 29, 72–77, 379, 389; *see also* Information policy

National League of Cities, 405

National Library of Medicine (U.S.), 35, 222

National Micrographics Association, 204

National Oceanic and Atmospheric Administration (U.S.), 39, 96, 146

National Publications Act, 73, 377–378

National Science Foundation (U.S.), 49

National Security Agency (U.S.), 56

National Security Decision Directives, 42

National Technical Information Corporation (H.R. 2159), 39

National Technical Information Service (U.S.), 14, 36, 38, 50, 59, 72, 80–81, 85, 88, 92–93, 96, 102–103, 107, 147, 149, 168, 171, 186, 199, 202, 208–210, 217, 219 223, 225–226, 249, 291, 295, 312, 314, 369, 379–380, 383

National Union Catalog, 306

National Weather Service (U.S.), 147

NATO, 429

Needs assessment, *see* Collection development

Networking, 161, 183, 318, 320, 349, 356–360, 362, 364, 369–390, 404

Nevada, 400

New Books, 179, 180

New Publications, 425, 438

New Serial Titles, 306
New York, 340
New York Public Library, 393
New York Times, 65
A Notation for a Public Documents Classification, 307
"NTIS Privatization Study Responses . . . ,"
    226
Nuclear Regulatory Agency (U.S.), 88
Numeric databases, *see* Machine-readable databases and magnetic tapes

O

Objectives, 128, 136, 178, 229, 235–237,
    240, 242–243, 252, 254, 266–267,
    273, 278, 325, 328–329, 336, 339–
    341, 343, 365–366, 372, 384, 389–
    390, 453, 479
OCLC, 103, 106–107, 139–143, 145, 159,
    221, 310–313, 315–318, 321–322,
    350, 359, 374–375, 404–405, 408,
    460, 465
OECD Economic Outlook, 420
OECD Observer, 439
Office of Management and Budget (U.S.),
    25–26, 31–32, 34–35, 38, 49, 63–71,
    75, 80, 94, 482
Office of Personnel Management (U.S.), 71
Office of Science and Technology Policy
    (U.S.), 48
Office of Scientific and Technical Informa-
    tion (U.S.), 92, 201, 221–222
Office of Scientific Research and Develop-
    ment, 210, 222
Office of Technology Assessment (U.S.),
    390, 486
Office of Technical Services (U.S.), 211, 219
Office of the Federal Register (U.S.), 199
Office without Power, 430
OMB directives and guidelines, 65–70, 189;
    see also OMB Circulars A-76 and
    A-130
OMB Circular A-76, 189, 380
OMB Circular A-130, 34, 68–70, 192, 477–
    478, 482
Omnibus Defense Authorization Act (1984),
    57
Online catalogs, 105, 141, 250, 358, 465
Online database searching, 19, 109, 123,
    139, 141–143, 145, 149, 258, 266–
    267, 272, 314, 318, 452, 460–461
"OnLine to Europe: A Guide to E.C.
    Databases," 424
Optical Disk, 76, 93, 150
ORBIT (Systems Development Corp.), 220–
    221
Organization for Economic Co-operation and
    Development (OECD), 416–417,
    425, 428, 433, 437
Organization of American States, 417, 424,
    437
Output Measures for Public Libraries, 346
Outreach programs, 172–175, 178, 183,
    229–230, 272, 465
Oxford University Press, 435

P

Paperwork Reduction Act (1980), 27, 34, 43,
    63, 69–70, 94
Patent and Trademark Office (U.S.), 39, 92,
    96, 366
Penguin Books, 428
Performance measures, 243, 331–333, 335–
    339, 346, 371–373, 389–390
Pergamon Press, 428
Personnel development, 204, 229, 244–246,
    251, 318, 453, 462–463
Photo-Optical Instrumentation Engineers,
    56
Physical facilities, *see* Space management
Physical integration, *see* Collection
    integration
Physical location, *see* Collection integration
Planning, 203, 229–231, 237, 242, 244, 251,
    253–254, 266–267, 269, 274, 303–
    304, 323–347, 390, 460, 462, 465,
    478–479; *see also* Collection develop-
    ment; Space management; and State
    plans
*Planning and Role Setting for Public Librar-
    ies*, 343
*A Practical Guide to the Superintendent of
    Documents Classification System*, 104
Preparing for a Depository Inspection, 341–
    342
*Price Catalogue for Statistical Information
    from Databanks*, 424
Pricing policy for government publications,
    25, 27, 29, 31, 38, 59–62, 181, 225

Printing Act (1895), 9, 39–40, 369, 485
Privacy, 30–31
Privacy Act (1974), 8, 27, 40–41, 43, 71, 75
Private information sector, 57, 63, 71, 75–
77, 85, 100, 102–103, 147, 189, 194,
198, 201–202, 205, 207, 209, 238,
265, 291, 308, 315, 321, 360, 374,
380, 478; *see also* Information Indus-
try Association
Privatization, 27, 50, 57, 71, 209, 225–226
Problems in Communism, 17
Prologue, 87
*Professional Papers of the United States
Geological Survey,* 210
*Provision of Federal Government Publica-
tions in Electronic Format to Depos-
itory Libraries,* 139
Public access, 1–26, 31–32, 38–39, 44, 55–
59, 75, 113, 186, 201, 206–209, 224–
256, 361, 364–365, 370, 380, 382,
399, 403–404, 469–487
Public Affairs Information Service Bulletin,
143
Public Access to Government Information,
83, 394
Public Bills, Resolutions and Amendments,
61
Public Health Service (U.S.), 79
Public information, *see* Government
publications/information
Publications Catalogue, 424, 438
Publications Board (U.S.), 211, 219
Publications of the European Communities,
425
*Publications Policy and Practice in the Unit-
ed Nations System,* 413
Publications Reference File, 88, 107, 111,
115, 124, 199, 257, 314
Published Searches Master Catalog, 221

Q
Quarterly Semiannual Financial Report, 149

R
Readers Guide to Periodical Literature, 108,
256
Readex, 106, 291, 308, 431, 434
Reagan administration, 2, 28, 55–57, 63–70,
72, 75, 83, 101, 205, 226, 229, 257,
266, 272, 470
Reagan, Ronald, 42, 64, 71, 90

Reference service, 13, 17–19, 23, 73, 165–
185, 224, 231, 344–345, 349, 354,
357, 365, 368–369, 375, 385, 395–
396, 409, 433, 451, 460, 462, 465–
466, 484
Referral service, 18, 73, 117, 165, 170–172,
179, 181–185, 267, 272, 365, 368,
375, 403, 433, 451, 460, 462
Reflections of America, 86
Reform 88, 65, 75
Regional government, 396–398
types of publications, 397–398
*Report of the First National Conference on
Issues concerning Computerized Pub-
lic Records,* 403–404
*Report of the President's Special Review
Board* (the "Tower Report"), 54
Report on the World Social Situation, 419
*Repertory of Practice of United Nations
Organs,* 430
Research Libraries Information Network
(RLIN), 140, 310, 350
Resource allocations, *see* Budgeting
Resource sharing, 112, 116, 123, 150, 161,
197, 200, 318, 322, 339, 348–364,
393, 401, 409
Resources in Education, 107, 221
Retention policy, *see* Collection
development
Report Series Codes Dictionary, 218, 225
Revista Interamericana de Bibliografla, 420
Rice University, 105

S
SAS, 273
SCAD, 425
Scientific and Technical Aerospace Reports,
220–221
Scientific and Technical Facility, 221
Scientific and Technical Information Office,
222
Second World Symposium on International
Documentation, 434
Secrecy, 31, 41–43; *see also* Classified
information
Secret Service (U.S.), 42
Securities and Exchange Commission (U.S.),
8, 96, 187
"Selected Research in Microfiche" (SRIM),
217

Serial Set, 78, 84, 110, 120, 199, 201, 301, 362
Serials Review, 439
Skills inventory, 244–245
Slater Hall information products, 148
Smithsonian Institution (U.S.), 78
Sources, Organization, Utilization of International Documentation, 425
South Pacific Commission, 436
Space management, 276–304
Staff development, see Personnel development
Staffing of depository collections, 245, 266–268, 275; see also Personnel development; and Education for librarianship
Stakeholders in the information sector, 29–31, 33–35, 38, 52, 53, 79
Standards, 112, 195, 331–332, 342–343
State and Metropolitan Data Book, 149
State government, 391–394, 396–410, 454
types of publications, 396
State Government Reference Publications, 397
State of the Environment, 420
State plans, 339–341, 351
State Plans for Federal Depository Documents, 340
State Publications and Depository Libraries, 397
Statistical Abstract of the United States, 62, 86, 117, 132, 149, 265, 317
Statistical Package for the Social Sciences (SPSS), 273
Statistical Reporting Service (U.S.), 86
StatPac, 273
Statutory law, 91
StatView 512+, 273
Strategic Planning for Library Managers, 343
St. Olaf College, 251, 356
Sudocs classification scheme, 105, 109–110, 307, 309, 311–313, 316, 322, 333, 335
Superintendent of Documents, see Government Printing Office
Swords into Plowshares, 429
SYSTAT, 273

T
Taylor and Francis, 434
Technical processing, 305–322; see also Collection development; and Cataloging and classification
Technical report literature, 49, 92–104, 106, 168, 207–228
attributes, 211–216
definition, 210
types and formats, 215–216
Technologic Papers of the National Bureau of Standards, 210
Technology, 19–20, 27, 29, 31–32, 35–37, 40, 44, 56, 71, 73, 76, 96–97, 137–164, 167, 195, 203, 206, 276, 303, 315, 320, 322, 356–361, 364, 368, 373, 375, 392, 410, 451, 463, 465, 480; see also Microcomputers
Technology & U.S. Government Information Policies, 357–361, 363, 485
Telecommunication Journal, 420
Tennessee, 406
Tennessee Valley Authority (U.S.) (TVA), 89
Texas, 400
Texas A&M University, 105, 359
Thrift Financial Report, 149
Treaty Series (UN), 416, 419
Turn-key system, 144

U
UNBIS, 425
UN Charter, 411
UN Chronicle, 439
UNDOC, 413, 430
Unesco, 416, 425, 428, 433, 440–441
UNESCO and World Politics, 430
Unesco Courier, 429
Unesco List of Documents and Publications, 413, 424
UNICEF, 436
UNIFO, 434
UNIPUB, 434, 438
United Nations, 366, 411–448
United Nations Documentation News, 438, 440
United Nations Documents and Publications, 431
United Nations Documents Index, 413
United Nations Handbook, 429
United Nations News Digest, 418
United States Code, 4, 12, 26, 28–29, 31, 33, 39, 59–60, 63, 66–67, 72–74, 91, 102, 192, 341, 354, 366, 375, 378, 382, 482

United States Information Agency (U.S.), 102
University of California, Los Angeles, 394
University Microfilms, 432
University of California, Riverside, 118, 250
University of Florida Libraries, 148, 359
University of Guelph, 309, 313
Unobtrusive testing, 168–170, 395–396
Urbana Municipal Documents Center, 405
The Urbana Municipal Documents Center Manual, 405
U.S. Depository Library Inspection Visit Form (GPO), 303–304, 335, 341–345, 354–355, 388
U.S. Government Books, 179–180
U.S. Government Manual, 62, 87
U.S. Reports, 79
Use of government publications, 120–123, 173, 199–201, 205, 224, 397, 400, 405–408
Use of Government Publications by Social Scientists, 131

V
Viewdata, 146
Videotex, 96, 146–147

W
Washington Library Network, 140, 310, 404
Weather Reporting, 420
West Publishing Co., 396
White House Conference on Library and Information Services, 486
WHO Chronicle, 439
World Bank, 413, 416, 425, 433–437, 441
World Bibliography of International Documentation, 424
World Cartography, 419
World Development Report, 429
World Health Organization, 416, 436
World Health Statistics Annual, 430

Y
Yearbook of International Commodity Statistics, 430
Yearbook of International Organizations, 411–412
Yearbook of the United Nations, 429